Old Age
In English History

OLD AGE
In English History

Past Experiences, Present Issues

PAT THANE

OXFORD
UNIVERSITY PRESS

OXFORD
UNIVERSITY PRESS

Great Clarendon Street, Oxford OX2 6DP
Oxford University Press is a department of the University of Oxford.
It furthers the University's objective of excellence in research, scholarship,
and education by publishing worldwide in

Oxford New York

Athens Auckland Bangkok Bogotá Buenos Aires Calcutta
Cape Town Chennai Dar es Salaam Delhi Florence Hong Kong Istanbul
Karachi Kuala Lumpur Madrid Melbourne Mexico City Mumbai
Nairobi Paris São Paulo Singapore Taipei Tokyo Toronto Warsaw

and associated companies in Berlin Ibadan

Oxford is a registered trade mark of Oxford University Press
in the UK and certain other countries

Published in the United States
by Oxford University Press Inc., New York

British Library Cataloguing in Publication Data

Data available

Library of Congress Cataloging in Publication Data
Thane, Pat.
Old age in English history: past experiences, present issues / Pat Thane.
p. cm.
Includes bibliographical references and index.
1. Aged—Great Britain—History. 2. Old age—Great Britain—History. I. Title.
HQ1064.G7 T44 2000 305.26′0941—dc21 99–054442
ISBN 0–19–820382–9

1 3 5 7 9 10 8 6 4 2

Typeset by Graphicraft Limited, Hong Kong
Printed in Great Britain
on acid-free paper by
Biddles Ltd,
Guildford and King's Lynn

For
LUCY
and in memory of
MY GRANDPARENTS

Acknowledgements

I owe an immeasurable debt to many teachers, friends, and students who have contributed to the making of this book over all too many years. The late Brian Abel-Smith and Richard Titmuss first encouraged me to study the history of old age as a research student at the London School of Economics. The late Margot Jeffreys drew me back to the subject. Before that Jenifer Hart was a source of encouragement at Oxford and now is living testimony to one of the themes of the book, about how well people, especially women, can age; as is Eileen Daffern in Brighton. I owe a particular debt of gratitude, over many years, to José Harris and for encouragement and intellectual stimulus at crucial moments, Paul Johnson, Billie Melman, Peter Baldwin, Christoph Conrad, Lincoln and Alice Day, Henry and Annis Pratt, Peter Laslett, Richard Smith, Thomas Sokoll, Richard Wall, Jacky Fogerty, Lynn Botelho, Marguerite Dupree, Anne Crowther, Simon Szreter, Alastair Reid, Sarah Harper, and to all my colleagues at Sussex.

I also wish to thank Tony Morris, who as history editor at OUP commissioned this book and gave it much encouragement; and also his successor Ruth Parr, for her enthusiasm, support, and wise advice.

I am grateful to Mrs Anne Olivier Bell and the Sussex University Library for permission to quote from the Charleston Papers, University of Sussex Library; and to the Trustees of the Mass Observation Archive, University of Sussex (of whom I am privileged to be one), for permission to quote extracts from the archive. Also to Alistair G. Tough, archivist of the Greater Glasgow Health Board, for permission to use the archives of the Board and to quote from the unpublished memoirs of the late Bernard Isaacs.

Contents

List of Figures

List of Tables

Introduction

Throughout the world at the end of the twentieth century societies are age-ing. A growing proportion of their populations are living into their sixties and seventies and often well beyond. The process may continue, and even accelerate, in the next millennium, due to a combination of declining birth-rates and declining death-rates. In 1900 about 7 per cent of the population of the United Kingdom was aged 65 or above; in 2000 about 18 per cent; from 2020 the percentage is projected to rise still further. The proportion of these who were very old, 75 or over, rose from 21 per cent in 1901, to 26 per cent in 1951 to 38 per cent in 1991. An average of 74 people a year reached the age of 100 in England and Wales between 1911 and 1920; in 1997, 3,000 people did so.

The twentieth century has achieved what earlier centuries only dreamed of: in developed countries, and increasingly in many less developed ones, the great majority of people who are born live to old age. They mostly do so in reasonably good health, in conditions which bear no comparison with the miserable destitution of the aged poor in most past times and places. Yet, sur-prisingly, this change is greeted, not with relief and pleasure, but with appre-hension, even panic. Above all, the fears are about the economic outcomes: that increasing numbers of older people will be dependent upon a shrink-ing population of working age, imposing upon younger generations new and intolerable costs of pensions, health care, and personal care. The inevitability of such a 'burden' seems intuitively obvious. One purpose of this book is to ask whether what is happening is so new or such a burden.

The experience of old age and its impact is widely seen as dramatically different in the late twentieth century compared with the past. Most surprisingly, the present of almost universal survival into healthy old age is compared *unfavourably* with a past of very high birth- and death-rates in which, it is often thought, few survived past middle age. It is believed that in 'the past'—an indefinite, unchanging terrain, sometimes vaguely 'pre-industrial' or 'tradi-tional', sometimes more recent, but decidedly 'other'—few people lived to old age. In consequence, old people had a rarity value which meant that not only were they financially less costly, they were culturally more valued and respected than in the present. Families took for granted that they cared for older relatives and so they imposed little or no charge on public welfare. And in societies which changed more slowly than the dizzily accelerating 'runaway world' of the later twentieth century, it is believed that older people had skills and knowledge which were still useful to and valued by the young, which ensured that they were included within their communities.

An influential social science narrative has reinforced this belief in profound difference between then and now. This asserts that not only the growth of numbers and the increasing redundancy of their skills, but also institutional changes, have degraded and marginalized older people in modern British society. As state pensions were introduced and expanded through the twentieth century, their effect was not simply to provide a secure income for older people, also they had the negative cultural effect of constructing them as a distinctive problem group, newly and increasingly excluded from the lives of younger age groups. This process, it is said, has been reinforced by the coming of mass retirement as a normal phase of life for most people, as a new experience in the mid-twentieth century, building a further barrier between the lives of older retired and younger working people, depriving older people of the status and dignity which, it is thought, they previously retained by remaining in paid labour. Among other difficulties, this narrative overlooks the fact that the transition from a lifetime of full-time paid work to full-time retirement has been an experience mainly of men, whereas the majority of survivors to old age, in the twentieth century as before, have been women.

Another twentieth-century innovation, the emergence of geriatric medicine is also said not so much to have improved the medical care of older people, as to have placed another barrier of exclusion between the generations, by 'medicalizing' and in consequence marginalizing old age. Altogether, it is argued, as the numbers of older people have grown, their social position has deteriorated, placing them in a condition of 'structured dependency' in contrast with an assumed greater independence and social inclusion in 'the past'. Popular and social science discourses have united in representing the history of old age, up to the present, as a narrative of relentless decline.

This book explores whether this is so, whether or to what extent these changes have indeed taken place, in order to try to understand the experience of old age in the present and the past. In the past, because, despite the growth of work in recent years, still relatively little is known about the history of old age. As interest has developed in the cultural history of everyday life, the self, identity and interpersonal relations, more attention has been paid to the histories of childhood, youth, adolescence, marriage, sickness, even madness and death, than to old age, despite the importance of age as an aspect of identity. Exploration of the history of old age, of its change and continuity over time, may help us to identify what is indeed new and in need of new responses in the present. It aims to clarify what we do and do not know, to distinguish fact from fantasy, about the history of old age in England.

The focus is upon England because a single country provides a manageable framework for a study of a long time period. England, not Britain, because Scotland (and to some degree Wales) was culturally, economically, and institutionally distinct from England over many centuries, though Scotland is increasingly drawn into the story in the twentieth century, in particular in respect of its pioneering role in geriatric medicine. My starting point, however, is far away in place and time, in ancient Greece and Rome. This is partly to highlight unexpected similarities between what is known about old age in the distant past and in more recent times, to stress that human experience and responses to it, even in the remote past, were less dramatically different than is sometimes thought. The experience of old age in the ancient world is interesting and important in itself; it also profoundly influenced English culture at least until the early twentieth century, through the medium of the influence of classical texts on elite culture and the dissemination of ideas through the wider culture. Aspects of continuity and change are examined over long time periods, drawing together a variety of approaches which are generally kept separate, from demographic and economic history, cultural history, and the histories of the family and of social welfare. It is risky for an historian to stray outside her period and area of specialism, but in a field in which comparisons over long periods of time are made both by academic and popular commentators, often derived from knowledge of just one time period or one methodological approach, we need to bring different approaches and time periods into dialogue.

So, does the conventional narrative of the declining status and increasing numbers and public costs of old people over time survive scrutiny? The popular belief that in 'the past' most people died in middle life, around the ages of 35 to 40, arises from confusion between life expectancy at birth, in the centuries of high infant and child mortality which preceded the twentieth century, and the survival chances of those who survived the hazardous early years of life. Those who made it to 20 had, over many centuries, a good chance of living to their later fifties, or sixties, especially if they were female. Old age has long been predominantly a female experience. The percentage of the population of pre-industrial England and Wales aged 60 and over was not small by modern standards: 9 per cent in the late seventeenth century, 10 per cent in the early eighteenth century. They were supported by a society much poorer than that of the twentieth century, though rich compared with other countries at the time, such as Scotland. The proportion of older people was historically unusually low in the nineteenth century, at around 7 per cent, due to the high birth-rate, which balanced the numbers of older people with larger numbers of young ones. In pre-industrial England life may often have been 'nasty and brutish', but it was not unduly 'short' or indeed, as we shall see, 'solitary'.

But did old age in the distant past begin at the same age as is assumed now, around 60 or 65, or did social conditions cause people to age faster, earlier in life? This is where study over long time periods is instructive: 60 or 70 have long been the officially sanctioned ages at which individuals could withdraw from public duties. In ancient Greece the obligation to perform military service did not end until age 60. In medieval England men and women remained liable for compulsory work under the labour laws and men to attend court or to perform military service, until age 60. The upper age for jury service was 70. Such regulations imply that people were expected to know their ages, which they appear to have done, closely enough. It is improbable that these ages could have been prescribed if they were widely thought to be quite inappropriate for such activities, and certainly men and women in their sixties and seventies filled prominent positions in medieval and early modern England. Ela, Countess of Salisbury (*c.*1191–1261) founded a nunnery after she had been widowed and became its abbess. She retired at the age of 68, two years before her death. Lanfranc was appointed Archbishop of Canterbury by William the Conqueror when he was 65 and died in office in 1089, aged 84. The average age at death of the nine seventeenth-century Archbishops of Canterbury was 73 and the average age of appointment was 60. This suggests that, at least among the elite, people were not regarded as worn out or useless by these ages. It was assumed in medieval towns that male manual workers could not remain fully active at their trades long past 50; still in the twentieth century the fifties are widely seen as the decade of the onset of ageing. Such continuities over time are perhaps not surprising, since those who reached their sixties and seventies in medieval and early modern England were a minority of survivors of larger birth cohorts and perhaps exceptionally fit.

But it has long been recognized—and commented upon by classical and early modern writers, as well as by British observers in the nineteenth century and in the 1980s and 1990s—that old age is not simply definable by birthdate and there is great individual variety in the pace and timing of human ageing. It has also long been conventionally accepted that old age spans a long period of life, from the fifties or sixties to past one hundred, and it is questionable whether people over such a vast age range can be said to have common characteristics. In consequence, old age has long been divided into stages, some of them elaborate, such as the medieval 'ages of man' schema, which divide life into three, four, seven, or twelve ages, often by capacity rather than by chronological age. Commonly, old age has been divided into what in early modern England was called 'green' old age, a time of fitness and activity with some failing powers, and the last phase of sad decrepitude; a division which in the late twentieth century is less imaginatively labelled 'young' and 'old' old age, or, originating in France, the Third and Fourth Ages. Texts describing the decrepit final age cannot be taken to express attitudes to old age in general. Some mistaken comparisons over time arise from comparing accounts of different phases of life. The sad decline with which some, but not all, older lives end has never been represented positively, in any age or culture (as many anthropological studies make clear), with good reason. Disputes about the definition, representation, and experience of old age in the past mainly concern 'young' or 'green' old age.

More important in practical terms than chronological age at most times was 'functional' age, the degree of capacity to carry out essential tasks. A perception of old age as beginning not at a fixed age, but when a man or woman could no longer work for a living (or in the case of a woman look after herself and her home), or, in the case of the better off, control their own property or perform any other expected function, is prominent in early modern English Poor Law and legal records and in earlier sources. In early modern England, people might not be deemed 'old' enough to merit poor relief due to inability to work, or to cede control of their property, until their seventies or eighties, though to some this might come in their forties. Only in the twentieth century have physical capacity and retirement from paid work on grounds of old age become separated for the mass of the population (as it has always been for a privileged minority able to control their own lives) and conventionally tied to a fixed age since the relatively recent spread of the practice of retirement from paid work at the ages of 65 or 60 or below has coincided with rising levels of fitness at these ages and above.

Then visual, cultural, definitions of old age at all times might conflict, and coexist, with both chronological and functional definitions. People might 'look old' but remain vigorous; or they might be old in years, but 'not look their age'; and, subjectively, they might 'not feel old' however they appear to others. Poor women in many different times and places were said to look old at earlier ages than men, following the physical strains of childbirth and menopause, though they generally outlived them. Richer women, even in the seventeenth and eighteenth centuries, who benefited from better diet, cosmetics, and other techniques to disguise ageing, might not be perceived by others to 'look old' until their sixties. In the twentieth century the capacity to disguise ageing has been democratized in developed countries with the increased availability of cosmetics, hair-dyes, cosmetic surgery further separating visual from chronological age. The use of such aids is sometimes interpreted as a further symptom of the degradation of old age in modern society, as evidence that people are ashamed to 'look old' and seek a youthful appearance, rejecting 'natural ageing' and 'growing old gracefully', which is assumed to have been taken for granted in past societies. But those who could afford to do so have always sought to enhance their appearances, at all ages. It is not obvious why they should cease to do so on reaching a certain chronological barrier. Nor was 'natural' ageing for the impoverished majority through most of English history in any way 'graceful'.

Old age cannot simply be a social construct, an artifice of perception, or fashioned through discourse—unquestionably bodies age, change, decay—but the images, expectations, and experiences of older men and women have been constructed in different ways at different times and for different people at any one time. The meaning of old age is not fixed and it has different meanings in different contexts, which this book seeks to explore. Possibly more people 'looked old' in earlier centuries than were chronologically old by modern definitions, hence 'old people' may have been more visible in most communities than the demographic statistics suggest. Certainly old age and old people were deeply embedded in English culture and consciousness from very early times, as is evident in their prominence in literature, in medical, philosophical, and theological texts and in folklore and proverbs. Whether or not individuals lived to be old, they were always conscious of it as a possibility.

If older people were numerous and visible in 'the past' were they also more respected? The belief that people do not respect their elders as they did in 'the past' has itself a very ancient history. It is seriously debated in the opening pages of Plato's *Republic*. There an old man concludes that there has been no general decline in respect, though his ageing friends complain of this; rather 'in the lack of respect their families show [some old men] there is only one thing to blame and that is not their old age, Socrates, but their character'. A similar anxiety, often expressing a similar scepticism about declining respect, resonates through English history, in medieval folktales and in seventeenth-century pamphlets and sermons. The Report of the Royal Commission on the Poor Laws of 1834 thundered dramatically, and in conflict with much of the evidence it received:

The duty of supporting parents . . . in old age and infirmity, is so strongly enforced by our natural feelings that it is often well-performed, even among savages, and almost always so in a nation deserving the name of civilized. We believe that England is the only European country in which it is neglected.

Such commentary could serve the didactic purpose of reminding people of their family duty. Much of the difficulty in interpreting past discourse about old age is that it often served polemical or metaphorical rather than descriptive purposes. In philosophical, theological, and, often, medical texts, from the ancient world at least to the eighteenth century, representations of old age are as often metaphorical as literal: a good, or bad, old age is represented as the reward or punishment for conduct through the life course. Such texts or visual images aimed to teach good conduct and/or temperate living, rather than to represent old age 'as it was'. In all times there have been competing, optimistic and pessimistic, paradigms of old age and we cannot readily determine whether one or the other was culturally dominant. All cultures have a variety of images of ageing available to them from which individuals and groups shape their expectations. These images shift and compete and if any one of them gains hegemony it does not necessarily do so for long. It is tempting, for example, to conclude that Shakespeare's dismal climax to the 'Seven Ages of Man' described by Jaques in *As You Like It*—'Sans teeth, sans eyes, sans taste, sans everything'—is representative of sixteenth-century English perceptions of old age. If, that is, you fail to note that Jaques is a relatively young man, but is given the conventional literary attributes of an old man, such as melancholy; and that the speech describing the decrepitude of very old men is followed immediately by the entrance on stage of an octogenarian, Adam, who has earlier described himself as 'strong and lusty' and has come to the forest to serve his much younger master. The pervasiveness in popular drama and literature (for example in the work of Chaucer and Jonson) of such dialogue between conflicting representations of old age, and its evident familiarity to medieval and early modern audiences, suggests its deep roots in English culture.

It is difficult to find in historical or anthropological studies of any place or time unambiguous respect for old age as such. In ancient and medieval Europe, as in the present, old people in general were not respected or despised by reason of the simple fact of their advanced age: those who continued to wield power at later ages could command respect by virtue of continuing mental or physical powers, or by possession of property or high position, as could others due to past achievements. The very poor of all ages have always lived on the margins. Social, and also gender, difference is as salient in old age as at earlier ages; though the examples of many powerful older women through time should serve as caution against assumptions that old women have automatically been more despised than old men. Rich old women generally carried more clout than poor old men. Older people were, and generally are, respected, or not, for their social position or for their personal qualities rather than on account of their age. Nor in pre-industrial England did skill and knowledge possessed by older people necessarily confer social value or guarantee cultural inclusion. The fact that in medieval and early modern England the memories of a minority of old people (normally men) were employed as legal evidence of ancient custom, for example in property disputes, is not necessarily evidence of a general societal respect for the wisdom of the aged, though it is sometimes taken to be so. Other kinds of traditional knowledge, such as of medicine or midwifery, could lead to old people (normally women) being ostracized, stoned, or burned as witches in the same communities at the same time.

The belief of some contemporary social scientists in the progressive exclusion of older people from mainstream society in contemporary Britain is called in question by many older persons' own representations of their lives as active, involved, and happy. This is not just self-deception. To interpret the spread of retirement as degrading the lives of older people by depriving them of the status associated with paid work is to romanticize often bitter hardship in the past. Far from being a source of status and self-respect, the paid work to which many people for many centuries clung for survival as they aged—as street-sellers, sweepers-up, skivvies, or other shifts to earn pitiful pay—was itself marginalized and degraded and thankfully abandoned for the security of even a small pension. It is also to assume that retired people in the late twentieth century have no status, and to overlook the pleasure retirement can bring to the generations who have been able to expect and plan for it. The first generation of men who were unexpectedly retired from manual work in the 1940s and 1950s had it thrust upon them, bewildered, after adult lifetimes dominated by work, unemployment, and war; they felt the shock of sudden exclusion the more acutely because it was often retirement into poverty without a cushion of accumulated savings. The shock of unplanned retirement was less evident in later generations, but the capacity to enjoy retirement is conditioned by income as well as by expectations. Status and inclusion in any society is acquired by consumption as well as by production. An adequate pension may permit greater independence than the controlled routines of paid work. Rich older people have always retired, sometimes relatively early in life. Poverty rather than retirement in itself can, as it long has, cause exclusion and demoralization among older people and still in the later twentieth century blights the lives of many older people, most of the poorest being very old women, many of whom have never 'retired' because they were not in full-time paid work. But over the century the range of incomes and assets, and of cultural capital, owned by older people has grown. In consequence many have become independent consumers making a variety of contributions, not all of them involving giving or receiving cash, to the economy and to society, rather than being excluded dependants. 'Old people' have never been a homogeneous group of the poor and dependent, though many at all times have been either or both. A lesser proportion are so at the end of the millennium than ever before. Old age is the phase of life in which the range of experience is greatest; that range has expanded in the course of the twentieth century.

If the invention and spread of geriatic medicine in the twentieth century, like the growth of paediatrics, has contributed to the separate medical treatment of different age groups, this has not necessarily disadvantaged older people. As scientific medicine advanced in the nineteenth and twentieth centuries, it paid little attention to the unheroic ailments associated with older people. But this neglect led directly to the invention of modern geriatric medicine, precisely to ensure that older people did not continue to be excluded from treatment, 'always at the end of the queue' as a pioneering Scottish geriatrician put it. Geriatrics has not succeeded in preventing 'rationing' in the health service from excluding older people from treatment, but at least by the end of the twentieth century this has faced open public criticism, in contrast to a past in which it was so taken for granted that even William Beveridge, the architect of the post-war welfare state could write in his famous Plan of 1942: 'It is *dangerous* to be in any way lavish to old age until adequate provision has been assured for all other vital needs, such as the prevention of disease and the adequate nutrition of the young' (my emphasis). Older people have gained most conspicuously in the twentieth century not directly from geriatrics, but from medical procedures not initially directed at their needs, such as hip replacement, heart bypass and transplant surgery. Nevertheless, the existence of geriatics as a specialism with dedicated hospital space has ensured that many older people have received treatment who otherwise would not.

Similarly, to see the growth of pensions as a process of constructing a new form of dependency for older people is both to romanticize their independence in the past and to underrate it in the present. It is true that maintaining independence, providing for one's own needs in one's own home, not being dependent upon others, whether relatives or not, has been the explicit goal of older people as far back in history as it can be traced. They have sought different ways to achieve it at different times but have rarely been able to do so without structured support from the community. Ageing small landholders in medieval England could survive independently in old age by trading their rights to their land for the assurance of lifetime support from younger people, who might or might not be relatives. For example, in 1352 Henry, son of Stephen, transferred a piece of land to a man who was not his relative on condition that thereafter he should give him annually: twenty shillings in cash, forty bushels of grain, eight of rye, twenty-four of barley, eight of wheat, two pairs of sheets, three shillings for various types of clothing, one pair of shoes and two pairs of stockings; quite a good return for a small piece of land. Such transactions were possible and provided real security for older people because manorial courts recorded and upheld the contracts, defining older people as a group with particular needs and providing a structure within which these needs could be met. For many centuries in pre-industrial England, structures were provided which could support older people through the transition from full independence to deepening dependence, if they required it. The Poor Law throughout its history, from its foundation in 1597, often, though not invariably, provided such structures for the support of impoverished older people who lacked other resources. There has been no simple, one-way, transition from independence as the normal condition of older people in the past to a state of dependence in the present.

This suggests that the dependence of some older people on publicly funded welfare also is not a twentieth-century invention. At its best, the Poor Law in the seventeenth and eighteenth centuries could be generous to needy old people, providing an impressive range of benefits, including medical care, nursing, clothing, and subsidized or free housing as well as cash and food. In consequence, some historians have been tempted to describe the Old Poor Law as a 'welfare state in miniature', or to argue that the relief given regularly to some older people, even in the early years of the New Poor Law in the nineteenth century, amounted to 'pensions' at least as good as those provided by the modern British welfare state. This is a useful corrective to the belief that the Poor Law was uniformly repressive or that modern institutions are always better than those of the past, that history always moves in the direction of progress. Rather, there were phases of deterioration over time, since there seems to be no pre-nineteenth-century equivalent to the horror expressed by older (and younger) people for the workhouse and the Relieving Officer instituted by the New Poor Law in 1834. But, whatever the deficiencies of the modern welfare state, there is a difference between a system which provides a secure, predictable, if small, pension, free health care, and other services at a fixed, foreseeable, and relatively early age, and the Old Poor Law system which was regionally highly variable, and, even at its best, gave relief only when older people could show that they could not themselves gather adequate resources for survival through paid work, the help of family, friends, or charity, or by any other means. Very old people, in their seventies and eighties, could be expected to work for their livings for as long as they were able, kept at work by the poor relief system which itself might supplement inadequate earnings. The Poor Law served to support rather than to replace the 'economy of expedients', the patching together of a shifting variety of resources for survival which characterized the lives of very many old (and young) people through many centuries and into the twentieth century. Often local communities, who financed the relief system, could afford nothing better.

Long-run studies can enable us to make comparisons over time on the nature and effectiveness of welfare payments and services, and to assess the legacies of long-established institutions and cultural practices. There was discontinuity between the relative unpredictability of the Poor Law and the relative predictability of modern welfare benefits and services. At least as important was another discontinuity of immense symbolic as well as practical importance: recipients of poor relief were automatically excluded from full citizenship by the loss of rights, in particular the right to vote. No modern British pension system has incorporated such explicit rules of exclusion. On the other hand, there is an important element of continuity in the fact that an important reason for the low level of state pensions in Britain in the second half of the twentieth century, in comparison with other developed countries especially elsewhere in Europe, is the continuing legacy of the long-lived Poor Law (which was not formally abolished until 1948). On the one hand, the Poor Law represents a very long-established English practice of collective provision for the destitute. On the other, it embedded in English culture the conviction that such provision should be no more than a basic, residual minimum for the 'essentials of civilized life', to be supplemented by personal effort. The modern British State pensions system was based upon a restatement of precisely these ideals by William Beveridge in 1942, and it looks set to continue on this track as a 'New Labour' government heads into the new millennium.

The long-run importance of the Poor Law in assisting the aged poor, however minimally, suggests that the popular image of the pre-industrial family as the mainstay of older people may also be mistaken. Some historians have argued, indeed, that such support was not at all a feature of pre-industrial English custom. Certainly throughout English history, wherever the voices of older people can be captured, they have insisted that they do not expect, or want to share their adult children's homes, at least until they are unable to care for themselves. The dangers of giving yourself and your property wholly into the care of offspring recur in the folklore of England and other north European countries from an early date, reaching their most sublime expression in *King Lear*, which was itself a reworking of medieval English folktales.

Clearly, it was never the unquestioned custom in England, as in some other cultures, for families to be the main source of support to older people, and certainly not for the generations to share a home. In part, this was unavoidable: about one-third of people in pre-industrial England had no surviving children when they reached old age, whereas almost all older persons had at least one surviving child in the late twentieth century. Certainly it was unusual in pre-industrial England for older people to live in the households of their children except in circumstances of extreme need on the part of one or other generation. It seems to have been common for a short period before the death of the older person. But family reciprocity was at no time unimportant to old or young. This book explores the long continuity of a particular cultural tradition in intergenerational relations in English families. Adult children felt an obligation to give emotional support to ageing parents and what material support they could. But they were not expected to impoverish themselves and their families to do so. The families of the aged poor were themselves very likely to be very poor, the more so since, given the shorter lifespans in pre-industrial England, parents were likely to become needy at the very time that their own growing families were most costly. Despite a formal clause which survived in the Poor Law legislation throughout its history, which obliged close relatives of 'every poor, old, blind, lame and impotent person' to support them, and which was invoked when poor relief authorities thought it appropriate, rather than expecting the impossible of very poor families, the poor relief authorities might supplement such assistance as families could afford, often subsidizing them to give shelter to declining parents. Poor relief and family support for older people were complementary. Old people without relatives at all times were those most likely to receive poor relief, which further suggests the importance of family support for those who had families. The great majority of older people at all times received occasional, minimal, or no relief.

Family support might take the form of services rather than of cash, since these were more readily affordable: a daughter living near by cleaning the house or providing meals or nursing care, a son negotiating with poor relief authorities, gardening, or doing repairs. Such services were of considerable value, in the past and the present. The cost of such informal care in late twentieth-century Britain has been estimated at up to £24 billion per year, compared with less than £4 billion spent annually on care by the public sector. Such support need not, and usually did not, depend upon co-residence. The extent of intergenerational exchange can be underestimated if we pay attention only to families who lived together. 'Kinship did not stop at the front door', as Michael Anderson commented of family relationships in nineteenth-century

Preston. A succession of research studies shows this also to be true in the seventeenth century and in the twentieth. Relatives living near by could and did at all times provide strong emotional, material, and physical support for older people. But support has never been all one way, from young to old. Older people at all times, far from routinely being dependants, have been givers as well as receivers often on a significant scale: of care for grandchildren, shelter and often financial support for adult children down on their luck, as well as services to the wider community, including formal and informal voluntary care for others.

Intergenerational relations are best characterized as relationships of reciprocity, differently balanced on both sides at different stages of life according to need. The emotional content of such relationships is hard to penetrate and must always have varied widely: from affection, to calculation, to acceptance of custom. They should not be idealized. And at all times, some older people, with or without relatives, have been lonely and neglected, though most were not. The typical older person in pre-industrial England was not a solitary old woman in an isolated cottage; nor do late twentieth-century statistics of the increasing numbers of older people living alone tell a transparent tale of isolation and neglect. Often this means that more older people are at last achieving the ambition their predecessors expressed over centuries, to hold on to an independent home, whilst retaining close contact with relatives and friends.

The tenacity of the belief that in the past families were the mainstay of older people is matched only by the conviction that in the late twentieth century such support is dwindling and vanishing, propelled by greater ease of movement, by the demands of paid work on sons and, especially, daughters, and growing divorce rates. Again, this is partly because a half-understood present is contrasted with an idealized past. The evidence is clear that everywhere in the late twentieth century older people give and receive emotional, practical, and material support to and from relatives when needed, as they have always done. But needs themselves have changed. Older people more often lead generally independent lives, less dependent upon families for sociability or care, if at all, until later in life, than in earlier generations. In consequence their children may be themselves retired when their parents become dependent. Older persons may have to, and often do, give shelter and support to divorced children, as previous generations gave to the widowed; some may do this simultaneously with caring for their own ageing parents. Where caring is required, the responsibility is likely to fall disproportionately upon women, as it has always done. Personal crises may strengthen rather than weaken intergenerational ties. Though ease of global travel can put long distances between the generations, it can also bring them together quickly, as other modern forms of communication, such as the telephone and the internet, can keep them in touch to a degree undreamed of in 'the past'. Though most older people may live at a distance from most of their children, they are highly likely to live close to at least one of them; if not they move closer as they age, and more older people have surviving children than ever before. Wherever it is investigated in the later twentieth century, an enduring feature of the family is its resilience and flexibility; and its emotional importance as a source of security and identity is perhaps increased in a world that seems increasingly insecure in other respects. The commitment to reciprocity between generations has been continuous over time, though the forms and the needs which give rise to it have changed.

If so many features of the experience of older people are less novel than has been thought, do they by reason of their undoubtedly unprecedented numbers, and projections that these will rise higher still, constitute a wholly new and troubling burden on the later twentieth century and, in prospect, on the twenty-first? British society has coped without undue strain with a rise in the proportion of older people of about 10 per cent over the twentieth century, during which time national income has increased much more substantially. The future population structure is, in fact, uncertain in many respects. Population projections which estimate that 27 per cent of the UK population will be over 60 in 2031 assume otherwise unchanged demographic patterns. The future could be different if there were a rise in the birth-rate, and/or changed patterns of international migration in an age of globalization: of young workers moving to Britain, or of more older British people following the growing trend to permanent retirement in sunnier climates, in their Caribbean birthplaces, or on the Spanish coasts, or close to children who have migrated to Australia.

There are few direct lessons to be learned from history, but some have been forgotten from the last time politicians, economists, and demographers were panicked by the 'menace'of an ageing population, in the 1930s and 1940s. Then, gloomy projections produced by the then novel techniques of demography suggested that by 1980 the population of Britain might fall as low as 29 million, about 30 per cent of them above age 65, with severe economic and social consequences. In fact in 1981 the UK population was about 60 million. The birth-rate rose again while the panic was in progress, and from the 1950s wholly unforeseen numbers of young migrants arrived from the Commonwealth. Also, larger numbers of women were in paid work than had previously been known or predicted, further undermining prophecies of a perilous inbalance between workers and dependants in the economy. The fears disappeared, as did the lessons of this episode, which had been wholly forgotten when the 'menace of the ageing population' re-emerged in public discourse in the 1980s.

Even if the age structure of the population and of the active workforce does not change in the twenty-first century, the future, though it is not predictable, is not inexorably and solely driven by demography. At the end of the twentieth century unemployment among younger people in Britain is a larger and more expensive source of welfare dependency than old age. Its elimination would increase the numbers of younger workers available to support those older people who need it. The falling birth-rate is reducing the very considerable public and private costs of childrearing, which are greater than the costs of supporting older people. The future relative costs of ageing can be influenced by government policy, which already by the 1990s had safeguarded against an excessive financial burden by progressively eroding the real value of the basic state pension.

Also, the definition and characteristics of 'old age' are no more fixed in the present and the future than they were in the past. It is statistically convenient to describe the proportions of people aged 65 and over through the twentieth century and projected for the twenty-first, but it is questionable whether 65, which was an accurate enough marker of the onset of old age for most people in 1925, when it became the state pensionable age, remains so in 2000 or will be in 2050. At the end of the twentieth century most people who are physically fit as they enter their sixties remain so at least to their late seventies. A more accurate marker for the onset of old age in 2000 is closer to 75 than 65. Evidence is accumulating that people can work effectively and learn new skills to late ages. It is possible to master a computer in your eighties. If 'life-long learning' in the supposedly rapidly changing new millennium becomes an accepted part of life, workers will retrain many times in a working lifetime and it is not obvious that the capacity to do so stops at age 60 or 65. Some countries are raising pension and retirement ages; though in others, including Britain, the actual retirement age for many people in the late twentieth century has actually been falling, into their fifties, largely as a function of unemployment and recession, at the same time as their physical fitness for work at such ages has generally been rising. Not everyone would wish to delay retirement, as is evident from the US, where the raising of the minimum fixed retirement age has been followed by a fall in actual retirement ages. Postmodern society may bring greater flexibility to the lives of older people who can afford it, in terms of consumption and lifestyle as well, enabling choice as to whether or not to work to later ages. In consequence the gap may widen between those who can afford to make choices and benefit from change and those who cannot, among the old as well as the young.

The meaning and experience of old age has changed in the twentieth century faster and more comprehensively than at any time in history, despite many long-run continuities with the distant past. People in their eighties in 2000 were born around the time of the First World War, when severe primary poverty and high infant mortality rates still prevailed. They grew up amid serious unemployment and were young adults during a second world war. They are survivors of a succession of hazards and traumas. Those who will be in their eighties in 2030 will have grown up with the greater prosperity, improved health services and health awareness of the post-Second-World-War period. But some of them will have experienced the effects of unemployment and increasing poverty in the 1980s and 1990s, though these may not be the survivors to the oldest ages. By contrast, others of the same age have experienced great prosperity—which is not necessarily good for health. Furthermore, we cannot easily assess the long-term effects of environmental degeneration in the twentieth century. Future health experience in old age, or at any age, is hard to predict.

Different age cohorts experience old age in different ways, influenced by different life experiences. By the end of the twentieth century, although people are living longer, they are not making greater demands on medical care. A longer life does not mean a longer period of illness before death; rather, as people live longer, the onset of serious ill-health occurs later in life, if at all, since most older people, including those who live to be very old, do not experience a period of protracted, serious ill-health before death. We cannot foretell the future length of an average healthy, or an unhealthy, lifetime. All too little is known about the actual health and health potential of older people because it has been marginalized by medical research, though their growing numbers were enforcing greater not less attention to the health conditions of older people and forms of treatment in the 1990s. We cannot foretell the future, but if history tells us anything, it is that it will not replicate the present, as much current discourse assumes. The condition of old people in 2000 was unknowable in 1950, but it has certainly improved over the intervening half-century for most people; that in 2050 or 2000 cannot be taken for granted.

It will not be a uniform future for an undifferentiated mass of 'old people'. The age group which is most generalized about in fact incorporates a greater variety of ages, of social, economic, and physical conditions than any other age group and that variety has increased over the twentieth century. It includes people from their early sixties to past one hundred, some of the richest and the very poorest, the very fit and the extremely frail. I have sought to examine that variety over time. This book gives much emphasis to the poor and their means of survival, because most old people for most of recorded history have been more or less poor; but the history of the engagement of the aged poor with poor relief systems and pensions is not the whole history of old age, indeed in most times and places it was the experience of a minority even of the very poor. Such a focus can too easily convey an undifferentiated, dismal picture of old age, and fail to explore the variety of experience at older ages at all times and across time: the 'economy of makeshifts' in which poor old people struggled to avoid the Poor Law; the experiences of rich old people, who generally outlived the poor; the power and status of certain older people at various times; the different experiences of old men and old women; questions of how old people perceived themselves and were perceived by others; and of the meaning of old age in different times and places.

The history and the present of the material life of old people—how they made their living, what they consumed—is not wholly distinct from that of their cultural roles. Representation is not wholly distinct from experience, nor cultural history from economic, social, and political history. Rich old people have generally been represented more positively and often experienced old age more positively than very poor old people. Reciprocally, cultural representations of old age, whether drawn from classical texts, literature, paintings, film, recorded expressions of everyday opinion, or any other source, shape individual imaginings of the life course, and also individual and collective experience. If individuals are culturally conditioned to expect to be helpless and dependent past a certain age, they are more likely to become so, with consequences for their own lives and those of others, which may include dependence upon and provision of formal or informal welfare services. How old age is experienced and how it is perceived by others is influenced by expectations, one's own and those of others. What takes place in the economic and political spheres—for example, the provision of pensions—helps shape private experiences and public and private perceptions.

The prevailing pessimism in public discourse about the ageing of society may appear to be an expression of wholly rational economic fear. At least as probably it may be less transparently rational, as societies at the end of the millennium perceive themselves as ageing and declining, failing to renew themselves, just as ageing bodies decline. Similar fears of 'degeneration' gripped European societies at the end of the nineteenth century, as birth-rates fell and high rates of 'physical deterioration' were perceived especially in developed urban societies. The population panic of the 1930s resonated with fear of international conflict and loss of Empire. Such fundamental fears, at least as much as informed investigation and rational evaluation of the social and economic consequences of demographic change, have shaped the popular and the political discourses about population ageing throughout the century.

It is important to try to capture difference in old age, between men and women and among different social groups, and differing influences on the discourse of old age and ageing, as well as comparisons and contrasts over time. Much cultural history and social science representation of old age has generalized from single groups (astoundingly often male, given the predominance of females among older people) or from a single time period which is assumed to be radically different from any other, so that the status of old people, like that of so many social groups visited by academics is continually either rising or falling. Important social processes have never been so universal or so simple. Such interpretations smooth out the much more complex interplay of continuity and change. This book aims to examine these complexities and to help us think in less stereotyped ways about the most stereotyped of age groups.

Old Age in Pre-Modern England

Did People in the Past Grow Old?

It is widely believed that in the pre-industrial past it was rare to grow old. This is generally because life expectancy at *birth* is taken as evidence of survival to old age. Life expectancy at birth averaged around 35 years between the 1540s and 1800[1] and is unlikely to have been higher at any earlier time, but high infant and child mortality rates drastically pulled down such averages. Those who survived the hazardous earlier years of life in medieval and early modern England had a respectable chance of living at least into what would now be defined as middle age—that is, their late forties or fifties—and often for longer still, though the risk of adult mortality fluctuated in different periods.[2] Even in medieval times the death of someone in their later thirties was not regarded as 'timely' or normal.[3]

HOW MANY OLD PEOPLE?

Establishing that this was so and estimating how large a presence older people were in past communities is difficult. Accurate, large-scale, systematic recording of births and deaths began in England only in 1837, though such information is patchily available in surviving parish records from the late sixteenth century.[4] The practice of recording precise ages in other public documents also developed slowly. Individuals were only gradually required to know their own exact ages as society became bureaucratized and official records increasingly required such information. Before the nineteenth century precise age was rarely required of people of any age, because physical condition did not necessarily correspond with chronological age, and physical fitness was the more important of the two for a worker, soldier, taxpayer, or pauper, the reasons for which most people encountered officialdom. When people were described as 'old' in public or private documents it was normally a description of their apparent physical condition and could be a very imprecise indicator of actual age. But few people at any time would have doubted at what

---

[1] E. A. Wrigley and R. S. Schofield, *The Population History of England 1541–1871: A Reconstruction* (Cambridge, 1989), 528.
[2] E. A. Wrigley, R. S. Davies, J. E. Oeppen, and R. S. Schofield, *English Population History from Family Reconstitution, 1580–1837* (Cambridge, 1997), 281–93.
[3] Shulamith Shahar, *Growing Old in the Middle Ages* (London, 1997), 22.
[4] Wrigley and Schofield, *Population History*.

point they were in the life cycle and most could certainly offer an age when required, sometimes quite precisely, though some would 'round up' their possible age to a plausible round number or add years as they reached later ages.[5]

The further back in time, the harder it is to estimate the age structure or life expectation of any society, despite much ingenious study of tombstones[6] and bones from excavated cemeteries, partly because we have no clue how representative such surviving remnants are of wider populations. Firm knowledge of the age structure of the ancient world is probably lost to us, though no doubt some people *could* live to as late ages as today, very probably in a similar state of health.[7]

For England, fairly reliable estimates of life expectancy exist only from the later sixteenth century.[8] Around 1581 about 7 per cent of the population was aged 60 or over; by 1671 it had risen to about 9 per cent. The percentage of over-sixties rose to 10 in the early decades of the eighteenth century, then fell to about 7 per cent by 1811. It was exceptionally low for much of the nineteenth century, when the statistics become firmer, at under 7 per cent,[9] rising to 7.4 per cent in the 1880s.[10] Then the percentage of older people in the British population began a steady climb to 17 per cent in the 1980s, 18 per cent in the mid-1990s. We cannot doubt that, throughout many centuries, older people were a substantial presence in English society.

But in medieval and early modern England the age structure of populations could vary dramatically from place to place and from time to time due to the effects of migration, famine or disease, or to changes in the birth-rate.[11] If the birth-rate of any community rose or fell whilst the death-rate remained unchanged, the *proportion* of older people in the community would rise or fall accordingly. To give some examples: only 0.7 per cent of the population of the small (population 427) but prosperous community of Ealing, close to London, in 1599 were age 70 or above; this was true of 6.9 per cent of the population of the smaller (188 people) village of Ringmer (Sussex) in 1698, where the rural economy was depressed and younger people moved away in search of work. As Manchester grew rapidly with the expansion of commerce and industrialization, in 1773 only 1.9 per cent of its population was aged 70 or

---

[5] J. Bedell, 'Memory and Proof of Age in England, 1272–1327', *Past and Present*, 162 (1999), 3–27.

[6] Tim G. Parkin, *Demography and Roman Society* (Baltimore, 1992); A. R. Burn, '*Hic Breve Vivitur*: A Study in the Expectation of Life in the Roman Empire', *Past and Present*, 4 (1953), 3–31.

[7] Tim G. Parkin, 'Age and the Aged in Roman Society', D.Phil. thesis (Oxford, 1992), 24, 31–4, 37, K. Hopkins, 'On the Probable Age Structure of the Roman Population', *Population Studies*, 20 (1966–7), 245–64.   [8] Wrigley and Schofield, *Population History*.

[9] Wrigley, Davies, *et al.*, *English Population History*, 614–15.

[10] Wrigley and Schofield, *Population History*, 528–9.

[11] J. Hatcher, *Plague, Population and the English Economy, 1348–1530* (London, 1994); Hatcher, 'Mortality in the Fifteenth Century: Some New Evidence', *Economic History Review*, 2nd ser. 39/1 (1982), 19–36. Zvi Razi, *Life, Marriage and Death in a Medieval Parish: Economy, Society and Demography in Halesowen, 1270–1400* (Cambridge, 1980). P. J. P. Goldberg, 'Mortality and Economic Change in the Diocese of York, 1390–1514', *Northern History*, 24 (1988), 38–55.

over. At the same time this was true of 4.3 per cent of the population of the more settled county town of Chester.[12] The scattered evidence for medieval and early modern England suggests that people at all social levels, other than the very poorest, who survived early childhood had a good chance of living at least into their later forties or fifties and often beyond.[13]

Hence for many centuries before industrialization life in England was often, as Thomas Hobbes claimed, 'poor', 'nasty', and 'brutish', but for very many who survived childhood it was not unduly short; nor, as we shall see, 'solitary'. In most communities there were numbers of visible and active older people.

WHEN DID WOMEN START TO OUTLIVE MEN?

Most historical age statistics refer to men. Men's lives were more public and more likely to be recorded. Even in ancient Rome men were far more likely than women to be commemorated by tombstones or statues which preserved their age at death.[14] In late twentieth-century Britain, when infant mortality is minimal, women have a life expectancy at birth of age 77, men of 71. Since compulsory registration began in England in 1837 females have clearly had the longer life expectancy. In the late twentieth century this is true in very many societies. It has come to be accepted as a human norm, biologically based.[15] Some have argued that female longevity is a characteristic feature of 'modern' society, greater male longevity of 'traditional' and 'developing' societies.[16] This has also been the view of some historians. Historians of the ancient world have argued that it was the norm for men to outlive women. Hence a problem has arisen for some: at what point in history did women start to outlive men? Medieval and early modern historians have dated the transition variously, for example among the thirteenth-century peasantry[17] or in the sixteenth century.[18]

Ancient historians derive their interpretation from the great classical writers. Aristotle believed, in keeping with contemporary humoral theory, that it was natural for men to outlive women because the male 'is a warmer creature than the female', hence women were thought to dry and wither

---

[12] P. Laslett, *Family Life and Illicit Love in Earlier Generations* (Cambridge, 1977), 188.

[13] Razi, *Life, Marriage and Death*, 130. C. Dyer, *Standards of Living in the Later Middle Ages* (Cambridge, 1989), 182.   [14] Parkin, 'Age and the Aged'; Hopkins, 'Probable Age Structure'.

[15] Ann Oakley, *Sex, Gender and Society* (London, 1972), 30–42; David W. E. Smith, *Human Longevity* (Oxford, 1993), 81.

[16] S. R. Johansson, 'Excess Female Mortality: Constructing Survival during Development in Meiji Japan and Victorian England', in A. Digby and J. Stewart (eds.), *Gender, Health and Welfare* (London, 1996), 32–66.

[17] V. Bullough and C. Campbell, 'Female Longevity and Diet in the Middle Ages', *Speculum*, 55 (1980), 317–55.

[18] G. Minois, *History of Old Age*, trans. S. Hanbury-Tenison (Oxford, 1989), 290.

earlier in life than men. The elder Pliny and Galen agreed.[19] The ancient commentaries were immensely influential among the learned of medieval Europe. In the thirteenth century, however, Albertus Magnus, while agreeing with Aristotle that men by nature live longer, noted that women, *per accidens*, in fact lived longer.[20] He explained that menstruation purified women of harmful humours, that sexual intercourse took away fewer of their bodily fluids, and they suffered less from the hazards of work. By the fourteenth century commentators were taking for granted that women lived longer and were a majority of the population.[21] In sixteenth-century Europe Galenic physicians believed that women became more like men as they passed the menopause, becoming leaner, drier, warmer, stronger and healthier than in earlier life and likely to live longer than men.[22] Yet physicians in eighteenth-century France still asserted this male advantage, though they were puzzled by the consistency with which females 'went against nature' and outlived men.

We need to ask whether such statements represent real changes in the relative longevity of men and women; or changes visible in some places, for example, in towns, due to the fact that females were more likely than males to migrate to towns; or represent no demographic change at all but rather shifts in discourse about relations between men and women. Ancient commentaries on the superior life expectancy of men rested upon assumptions about the inferior nature of women and the belief that males more nearly approached the perfection of the species; hence references to superior male longevity may be as often metaphorical as empirical observations.

If there was indeed a shift at some early date in the relative life expectancies of men and women, no convincing dating or explanation has been found. An attempt to date the change in the thirteenth century due to dietary changes is not well supported.[23] With equal lack of convincing evidence, Minois believes that the 'established fact . . . that . . . women died earlier than men from antiquity until the fifteenth century' began to change in the sixteenth century among aristocratic women due to more hygienic conditions of childbirth.[24] The original 'fact' is not established, nor is there evidence that childbirth was a mass killer of aristocratic (or any) women or a greater hazard in medieval or early modern England than death due to accidents at work or to violence to adult men. Information about death in childbirth in the distant

---

[19] Quoted in Bullough and Campbell, 'Female Longevity', 317.

[20] But this often cited statement may have been distorted by mistranslation. Shahar, *Growing Old*, 34.

[21] D. Herlihy, 'Life Expectancies for Women in Medieval Society', in R. T. Morwedge (ed.), *The Role of Women in the Middle Ages* (London, 1975), 1–22.

[22] Margaret Pelling, 'Thoroughly Resented? Older Women and the Medical Role in Early Modern London', in L. Hunter and S. Hutton (eds.), *Women, Science and Medicine, 1500–1700: Mothers and Sisters of the Royal Society* (Stroud, 1997), 63–88.

[23] Bullough and Campbell, 'Female Longevity'. M. Pelling and R. M. Smith, *Life, Death and the Elderly: Historical Perspectives* (London, 1991), 10.   [24] Minois, *History*, 79, 292.

past is difficult to collect and to interpret. Where it has been studied the incidence has generally been found to be relatively low.[25] Schofield has calculated that in a large pre-industrial English village of *c*.1,000 inhabitants (a representative enough place to live) on average one villager would die in childbed in every three years throughout the period from the later sixteenth century to the early nineteenth. Women of childbearing age were more likely to die of other causes, and pregnancy may have increased their vulnerability, in particular to tuberculosis, to which women in all classes from their early teens to middle age were especially vulnerable until the late nineteenth century.[26] But it is not established that their death-rates were regularly significantly higher than those of men of comparable ages.

There is no firm evidence for consistently greater male *or* female longevity in medieval England. Nor is there great value in searching for general national, still less international, trends at a time when patterns of survival were so variable between places and social groups and over time.[27] The sex differential was one of many shifting variables in the demography of medieval England. There is also no obvious reason why the pattern of sex differentials should be radically different in medieval compared with early modern England, where the picture becomes rather clearer.

A study of twelve parishes between 1550 and 1799 concluded that there was very little difference between male and female expectations of life. Mortality levels varied greatly among these parishes which suggests that 'the national trends conceal important differences in the mortality levels of different communities'.[28] John Graunt in 1662 was the first social statistician systematically to compare mortality differences between adults and children, between urban and rural parishes, and between the sexes. He found that women lived on average two to three years longer than men. For the next hundred years his successors, using a variety of sources, repeatedly found a small but consistent advantage for women; though the conviction survived that this female advantage was 'strange'. Among historians, Michael Anderson has calculated that of the English birth cohort of 1681, 18 per cent of men and 21 per cent of women were still alive at age 53.[29] Since official registration began, the greater longevity of females has been undoubted, even whilst tuberculosis remained

[25] But see B. M. Wilmott Dobbie, 'An Attempt to Estimate the True Rate of Maternal Mortality, 16th–18th Centuries', *Medical History*, 26 (1982), 79–90, though the numbers investigated were small.

[26] S. R. Johansson, 'Sex and Death in Victorian England', in M. Vicinus (ed.), *Suffer and Be Still* (Bloomington, Ind., 1971), 163–81.

[27] Goldberg, 'Mortality and Economic Change'.

[28] Wrigley and Schofield, *Population History*, 250–3. The quality of the data for these parishes is imperfect, and there is no reason to believe that they were nationally representative, as the authors point out.

[29] M. Anderson, 'The Social Implications of Demographic Change', in F. M. L. Thompson (ed.), *The Cambridge Social History of Britain, 1750–1850* ii (Cambridge, 1990), 27; Pelling and Smith, *Life, Death*, 10–11.

a scourge of women. There is no clear evidence that the pattern was ever consistently different in 'traditional' English society.[30]

HOW OLD WAS 'OLD'?

But can we in all times and for all men and women define 60 as the age at which 'old age' began? A definition of the onset of old age is a necessary device for comparing the age structures of communities at different times, but did it correspond with reality at all times? Did people age faster in the past? What do we mean by old age? Scholars use a variety of ways of defining old age, all of which are useful in different, if sometimes overlapping, contexts. 'Old age' may be defined chronologically, by birth-date; functionally, in terms of fitness to perform certain tasks; biologically, in terms of physical fitness and other physical characteristics; or culturally, in terms of everyday perceptions and definitions of old age. All of these uses have histories.

The ages of 60 and 70 have been used in official discourse in England to signify the onset of old age at least since medieval times. Sixty was long the age at which law or custom permitted withdrawal from public activities on grounds of old age, though old age as such was not legally defined. Minority and majority were the only age statuses recognized in law.[31] Even in ancient Greece the formal obligation to military service did not end until age 60 and men in their fifties were indeed called up.[32] In ancient Roman writings people were defined as old at ages varying from the early forties to 70,[33] though 60 stands out as 'some sort of *annus climactarius*'.[34]

In medieval England in a succession of enactments from the Ordinance of Labourers of 1349 onwards men and women ceased at 60 to be liable for compulsory service under the labour laws or to prosecution for vagrancy, and men to attend the court leet or to perform military service. From the thirteenth century, 70 was the upper limit for jury service, though there was persistent pressure to excuse the over-sixties. In fifteenth-century London many were so excused on grounds of disability.[35] In general, such official age limits were likely to have been at the higher end of the range of ages at which these activities could be performed. Governments and officials had every incentive to keep as high a proportion of the population as possible in a state of obligation to perform essential services or, as might sometimes be the case,

---

[30] Pelling and Smith, *Life, Death*, 10.

[31] L. Bonfield, 'Was there a "Third Age" in the Pre-Industrial English Past? Some Evidence from the Law', in J. Eekelaar and D. Pearl (eds.), *An Ageing World: Dilemmas and Challenges for Law and Social Policy* (Oxford, 1989), 37–53.

[32] Moses Finley, 'The Elderly in Classical Antiquity', *Ageing and Society*, 4/4 (1984), 391–408.

[33] Parkin, 'Age and the Aged', 9.   [34] Ibid. 14 n. 21.

[35] J. Rosenthal, 'Retirement and the Life Cycle in Fifteenth Century England', in M. M. Sheehan (ed.), *Aging and the Aged in Medieval Europe* (Toronto, 1990), 179. Shahar, *Growing Old*, 24–7.

to pay tax in lieu of service; or to reduce the numbers to whom they might be obliged to pay a pension on retirement.[36] But it is improbable that ages could have been set which were beyond the bounds of credibility in their times. Such rules assumed that people knew their ages, if only approximately; this was all that was required, since fitness for the task was their essential purpose.

There were a number of age-demarcated obligations, but few rights specific to 'old age', other than the customary right to glean which was shared with other needy groups and which survived into the nineteenth century.[37] Charity very rarely and Poor Law relief never were paid as of right on reaching a certain age; 'impotence', i.e. incapacity to work for a living, was the normal test,[38] as it was also for relinquishing public office. 'Too sick and aged' was the reason most often given for the retirement of coroners, with pension, or for retirement from active participation in the House of Lords, or from the senior clergy in fifteenth-century England.[39] Aldermen, the significantly titled governing elders of urban communities, were chosen supposedly for their wise maturity. In fifteenth-century York they were elected probably in their mid-forties and were expected to remain in office until death. About 50 per cent probably lived past age 60. Some resigned, citing age and ill health, but their colleagues granted this with reluctance.[40] In fifteenth-century Coventry 'the stylized age of decrepitude' was placed around age 60 and was the age at which men would become trusted repositories of local custom,[41] those whose memories of unrecorded customary rights had legal status.

The age of 60 was from an early date so taken for granted in official discourse as the gateway to old age that it was seldom discussed or justified. It was assumed that those who survived to that age were normally capable of carrying out their duties. Those who declined at an earlier age were excused, and those who chose and were able could often carry on to later ages. The average age at death of the nine seventeenth-century Archbishops of Canterbury was 73 and the average age of appointment was 60. This suggests that, at least among the seventeenth-century elite, people were not necessarily regarded as worn out or useless by this age.[42]

It was long assumed that most male manual workers could not remain fully active at their trades much past age 50, especially when performance depended upon such physical attributes as good eyesight. In early sixteenth-century

---

[36] L. Botelho, 'Old Age and Menopause in Rural Women of Early Modern Suffolk', in L. Botelho and P. Thane (eds.), *Women and Ageing in British Society since 1500* (London, 2000).

[37] P. King, 'Customary Rights and Women's Earnings: The Importance of Gleaning to the Rural Labouring Poor, 1750–1850', *Economic History Review*, 44/3 (1991), 461–76.

[38] See below, pp. 180–1.   [39] Rosenthal, 'Retirement', 175–7.

[40] Jennifer I. Kermode, 'Urban Decline? The Flight from Office in Late Medieval York', *Economic History Review*, 2nd ser. 35/2 (1982), 192.

[41] C. Phythian-Adams, *Desolation of a City: Coventry and the Urban Crisis of the Late Middle Ages* (Cambridge, 1979), 93.

[42] Steven R. Smith, 'Growing Old in Early Stuart England', *Albion*, 8/2 (1976), 125–41.

Coventry it was believed that the average man's life of regular work at his trade was over by age 45 or 50 and similar assumptions are commonplace in the later medieval and early modern periods—as they continued to be in the nineteenth and early twentieth centuries. Such men did not give up all paid work at these ages; survival required that many of them carried on, working progressively fewer hours at lighter tasks, often in different, less skilled occupations, often for very many years.[43] The Norwich census of the poor of 1570 defined elderly households as those containing one or more persons past age 50. However, it also described as only 'almost' past work three widows aged 74, 79, and 82.[44]

On a cultural level, 'contemporaries seem to have regarded the age of 50 as a milestone, the end of adult maturity and the start of old age, though not necessarily the start of decrepitude and certainly not . . . the end of work', though poorer people 'might legitimately be regarded as old in real terms, prematurely worn out'.[45] Such social and economic differences in the pace of ageing were probably more important than gender differences. Among the poor, in particular, the visible physical changes associated with the menopause may well have meant that in early modern England women were perceived as 'old' at around age 50.[46] But this did not mean that even poorer women were necessarily regarded as being functionally older or more marginalized than men of the same age or than younger women. There are indications that they were less likely to be wholly unemployed than older men and that they could be seen as having a positive value in the community especially as providers of skilled care to the sick or destitute, both paid and unpaid. [47]

Old age pensions, payable at age 50, on the assumption that from this age most people were unable to support themselves regularly by work, were proposed by Defoe in the 1690s and by Dowdeswell in 1772. Thomas Paine in *The Rights of Man* (1791/2) divided old age into two classes:

First the approach of age beginning at fifty. Second old age beginning at 60. At fifty though the mental faculties of man are in full vigour, and his judgement better than at any preceding date, the bodily powers for laborious life are on the decline. He cannot bear the same quantity of fatigue as at an earlier period. He begins to earn less and is less capable of enduring wind and weather; and in those more retired employments where sight is required, he fails apace and sees himself like an old horse, beginning to be turned adrift.[48] At sixty his labour ought to be over, at least from direct necessity. It is painful to see old age working itself to death, in what are called civilized countries, for daily bread.

---

[43] See pp. 90–5.

[44] M. Pelling, 'Old Age, Poverty and Disability in Early Modern Norwich: Work, Remarriage and Other Expedients', in Pelling and Smith, *Life, Death*, 74–101.

[45] Pelling, *Common Lot*, 137–8.   [46] Botelho, 'Menopause'.

[47] M. Pelling, *The Common Lot* (London, 1998), 142.

[48] Thomas Paine, *Rights of Man*, ed. Henry Collins (Harmondsworth, 1969), 264.

Respondents to the Royal Commission on the Poor Laws, 1832, described male labourers as 'old' at 50. Over several centuries poor men and women seem to have been culturally defined as 'old' at around age 50, better-off people at age 60 or above, though among both groups functional and biological age might vary considerably. Popular and official definitions, and subjective experiences of the onset of old age, have changed over time, but to a lesser extent than might be expected, perhaps because those who could survive the hazards of early and middle life in medieval and early modern England were exceptionally robust.

Certainly there were significant numbers of visibly 'old' people in most 'past' communities, whatever their chronological ages, and they had a strong presence in public consciousness.

Representations

2

Representations of Old Age in Ancient Greece and Rome

Human beings seek to explore and to express the meanings of existence through a range of symbolic as well as material forms. Symbols and images—visual and linguistic—express shared meanings and ingrained beliefs and also influence actions and attitudes. Such beliefs assist individuals to construct their own paths through life. 'Old age' is a symbol into which multiple, often conflicting, meanings have been poured over time and at any one time. The aged body has been employed as a 'metaphor for the transience and vanity of this world'.[1] In any time narratives of ageing and old age may as readily express personal fears and hopes as observations of lived experience. Meanings are as often expressed in myth and metaphor and in other forms of symbolic representation as in straightforward descriptive or prescriptive language. Changing representations of old age have not taken the form of simple trajectories of rise or decline in honour or fear of old age, despite commonly held beliefs, which themselves have a long history, that we honour older people less in the present than in 'the past'. Rather there have been striking continuities over very long time periods in representations of, attitudes to and experiences of old age, in the tensions they express between positive and negative representations and in awareness of the variety of experiences of later life. This continuity is one reason for opening a book on old age in England in ancient Greece and Rome; another is that representations of old age in philosophical tracts, medical treatises, literature, and the visual arts produced in the ancient world were highly influential in medieval and early modern England. Sometimes these were attempts to present old age literally as it appeared to the producer of the image; but frequently ageing stood as a metaphor for human existence and as a focus for meditation upon it.

ANCIENT GREECE

There is no doubt that in the ancient world old people were a well-defined presence and that old age was recognized as a phase of life with distinctive characteristics. For Minois these could be schematized simply: for the Greeks

[1] Shulamith Shahar, *Growing Old in the Middle Ages* (London, 1997), 45.

old age was 'sad'. He argued that this world which admired physical beauty marginalized the old. The Roman world is summed up with the heading 'Greatness and decadence of the old man'. Minois describes the power of the old man in the family and the state, and its waning through the history of the Roman Empire. Early Christianity he describes as venerating the wisdom of some old men, whilst recognizing that not all did so. Old women play little part in his story, partly because he is convinced (wrongly) that few survived the rigours of childbirth. Overall, although he admits that:

Western history from antiquity to the Renaissance is marked by fluctuations in the social and political role of the old. What we are seeing is not so much a continuous decline as a switchback evolution

he concludes that 'the general tendency however is towards degradation'.[2]

Literature

For classical scholars the story is less simple and less pessimistic. The ancient Greek language possesses a range of both pejorative and complimentary terms for old people. Greek literature presents a wide range of possible representations of old people, as of other age groups, from caricature to idealization. Age paradigms were widely used and put to multiple uses. A number of Greek poets and playwrights themselves appear to have lived to an advanced age, though exact ages are rarely certain for anyone at this time. Sophocles wrote his last play *Oedipus at Colonus* around the age of 90. He proved by quoting from the play in court that he retained his full faculties and he thus defeated an attempt by his son to take control of his property on grounds of senility. Euripides wrote his *Bacchae* and *Iphigenia in Aulis* at about 80. Plato completed his last and largest work *The Laws* around age 81.[3]

The belief that veneration for physical beauty led the Greeks to shun old age derives from a focus on the lyric and elegiac poets. But these took love and love-making as their theme and regret at the effects of the ravages of time upon sexual attractiveness was a natural corollary. It would be unwise to generalize Greek attitudes to old age from these sources.[4] Representations of old age elsewhere in literature were more varied. In the *Iliad* Achilles' rejection of an old age devoid of fame in favour of an early death bringing eternal glory, suggests an heroic contempt for longevity. Homer also was working within the literary conventions of heroic literature. Yet his more peaceable *Odyssey* suggests how the experience of old age can vary with personal circumstances. Odysseus' father Laertes is presented as a destitute and broken-hearted recluse living in squalor and pining for his lost son, but he is rejuvenated by

[2] Georges Minois, *History of Old Age: From Antiquity to the Renaissance*, trans. Sarah Hanbury-Tenison (Oxford, 1989), 7.

[3] Moses Finley, 'The Elderly in Classical Antiquity', *Ageing and Society*, 4/4 (1984) 391–408.

[4] R. Garland, *The Greek Way of Life: From Conception to Old Age* (London, 1990), 252–3.

Odysseus' return. Nestor, one of the most active old men in the whole of literature, still successful in battle in old age, is presented as 'growing old sleekly' in his palace, in comfort with his family around him. As senior adviser to Agamemnon in the *Iliad* when he appears to be in his sixties or early seventies, he is long-winded, opinionated, and sometimes vain. He is highly critical of the younger generation whom he regards as inferior. Yet his judgements are wise and he is treated with respect and affection. Odysseus himself prayed that he too would reach 'sleek old age', which suggests that this was believed, at least by some, to be a desirable fate, but also that not all attained it, even if they were successful in life. Old men as givers of wise advice in the conduct of war and the ratification of important agreements appear elsewhere in the *Iliad* and the *Odyssey*.[5]

Implicit in such representations was recognition that the wealthy and powerful had the best chance of reaching a comfortable old age. Plato's dialogue *Hippias Major* claimed that the belief of the majority was that the highest condition attainable by a human being was: 'to be rich, healthy, honoured throughout Greece, live to old age and, after burying one's parent decently, to be decently laid out by one's children and buried in magnificent style'.

Myths that the human lifespan had originally been much longer, up to a thousand years, or that the inhabitants of certain remote places had exceptionally long lives were prevalent in Greek writing and for centuries to follow.[6] Finley may be right to suggest that 'Utopian visions of an age of Methuselahs were a protest against the inevitable brevity of life, not a goal to be sought'.[7] Mythology warned also of the perils of seeking immortality. Ageing was one characteristic in which the gods differed from humans. For humans eternal life did not bring eternal youth. In myth the goddess Eos obtained the gift of immortality for her mortal husband Tithonus but forgot to request eternal youth. Tithonus eventually aged, shrivelled, and became so senile that his wife locked him away in a cupboard, to babble away for the rest of time, or, in a more merciful version, she transformed him into a cicada. Such allegories may serve less as an insight into Greek perceptions of old age than as warnings against ill-thought-out desires.

The rejuvenation of old people was a persistent theme of Greek literature. In *Children of Herakles* Euripides rejuvenates old Iolaus for a last heroic stand in battle. But Euripides like many of his successors may have been deliberately holding up to scrutiny a popular fantasy, exposing its absurdity by taking it to extremes. Rejuvenation was a theme of nine of the surviving eleven plays of Aristophanes and was always treated satirically. Another of his plays, *Old Age*, is lost. It apparently featured old men regaining their youth and behaving outrageously, as does the superannuated delinquent Philokleon in *The Wasps*.[8]

---

[5] Ibid. 251–2.   [6] Ibid. 247.   [7] Finley, 'The Elderly', 394.
[8] Garland, *Greek Way*, 269; Bessie Ellen Richardson, *Old Age Among the Ancient Greeks* (Baltimore, 1933), 67.

This cautionary tale lies within a long tradition: the son has become master of the house; Philokleon has been reduced to childlike dependency and behaves appropriately.[9] Whatever their intention, such images challenged any notion of old age as necessarily a time of wisdom and respectability. Aristophanes' old men complain that their finer deeds are forgotten and that the public does not care for them in old age; they say they are jeered in the streets and persecuted by the young. His representation of the lives of old women was no more optimistic; they were portrayed as frustrated, over-sexed, ludicrously pursuing younger men. Aristophanes' *Women in Assembly* portrays a state ruled by women which passes a law that any young man who desires a young woman must first have sex with an old one.

But younger people did not necessarily fare better in satiric comedy.[10] Such representations of old people should not necessarily be read as a statement about old age itself, but may rather be a comment on human behaviour more generally. Classical Greek comedy, like satire in later centuries, presented human nature in terms of archetypes, stock characters and their inversions. It is unwise to read off generalized cultural perceptions from them.

In *Children of Herakles* Euripides presents a different image of an older woman in Alcemene, wife of Iolaus. Compared with other characters, including Iolaus himself, she is defined by her strength and wrath, in contrast to the deference of the younger women. She is active, wielding power and authority in contrast to her husband's weak dependence. Equally assertive older women appear elsewhere in Greek literature; for example Hecuba, towards the end of the *Iliad*. And the old women of Aristophanes were certainly assertive, if also figures of fun.[11]

The old nurse, deeply attached to master or mistress, plays an important and often positive role in Greek literature of all periods, as, for example, the old Sicilian servant of Laertes in the *Odyssey*, who also comfortably cares for her husband and sons. The old nurse in *Medea* is a woman of understanding: she philosophizes on kingship and democracy, and on the respective merits of moderate means and great wealth.[12] These may be examples of dramatic inversion, or they may be representations of the reality in Greek society that women past menopause, at least at higher social levels, acquired new freedoms. For the first time in their lives they were able to appear, and to be active, in public unattended. This may have signified not so much increased status as their reduced value to their husbands, which may also have lessened the wife's need to show deference. Nevertheless older women acquired certain dignified and useful roles, such as certain religious duties of high prestige, for

[9] Tim G. Parkin, 'Age and the Aged in Roman Society', D. Phil. thesis (Oxford, 1992), 182; and 'Ageing in Antiquity: Status and Participation', in Paul Johnson and Pat Thane (eds.), *Old Age from Antiquity to Post-Modernity* (London, 1998), 19–42.   [10] Richardson, *Old Age*, 50–2.

[11] T. M. Falkner and J. de Luce, *Old Age in Greek and Latin Literature* (Albany, NY, 1989), 114–31.

[12] Richardson, *Old Age*, 44–6.

instance as priestesses. Poor older women might take on the socially valued role of midwife.

In the fifth century AD Stobaus collected ninety-five references to old age in the work of forty-two Greek authors in a range of genres between the seventh century BC and the fourth century AD. He found thirty-one passages praising old age, fifty-five disparaging it, whilst nine suggested that 'good sense makes old age unburdensome and worthy of much respect'. References in comedy and satire were most consistently negative.[13] There are indeed few examples of dishonour to the aged in Greek literature outside comedy and satire, nor was it always 'sad'. When the aged were represented as suffering indignities it was often mentioned as exceptional or because they have behaved badly.[14]

Few visual representations of old people survive from the Greek world. Some dignified old men, but few women, survive in sculpture. Lecherous old satyrs with erect penises pursuing young women on vase paintings from the fifth century are the visual equivalents of Aristophanes' frustrated old women; though vase paintings also show old men and women in a variety of situations. Lacking the artistic status of sculpture this form could be freer and more varied in its choice of representation.[15]

Philosophy

Greek philosophical writings provide more consistently optimistic views of old people (though they generally discuss only higher status males) often insisting that older people could remain alert, active, and fit to govern. They also raised questions about the status and experience of old age which have been endlessly repeated through later centuries. In the opening pages of Plato's *Republic* Socrates meets the elderly Cephalus and questions him:

I enjoy talking to very old men, for they have gone before us, as it were, on a road that we too may have to tread, and it seems to me that we should find out from them what it is like and whether it is rough and difficult or broad and easy. You are now at an age when you are, as the poets say, about to cross the threshold, and I would like to find out how it strikes you and what you have to tell us. Is it a difficult time of life or not?

Cephalus replies:

I'll certainly tell you how it strikes me, Socrates. For some of us old men often meet together, like the proverbial birds of a feather. And when we do meet, most of them are full of woes; they hanker for the pleasures of their youth, remembering how they used to make love and drink and go to parties and the like, and thinking it a great deprivation that they can't do so any more. Life was good then, they think, whereas

---

[13] Parkin, 'Age and the Aged', 39–40.   [14] Ibid. 54.   [15] Richardson, *Old Age*, 81–176.

now they can hardly be said to live at all. And some of them grumble that their families show no respect for their age, and proceed to harp on the miseries old age brings. But in my opinion, Socrates, they are putting the blame in the wrong place. For if old age were to blame, my experience would be the same as theirs, and so would that of all, other old men. But in fact I have met many whose feelings are quite different. For example, I was once present when someone was asking the poet Sophocles about sex and whether he was still able to make love to a woman; to which he replied, 'Don't talk about that; I am glad to have left it behind me and escaped from a fierce and frenzied master'. A good reply I thought then and still do. For, in old age you become quite free of feelings of this sort and they leave you in peace; and when your desires lose their intensity and relax, you get what Sophocles was talking about, a release from a lot of mad masters. In all this, and in the lack of respect their families show them, there is only one thing to blame; and that is not their old age, Socrates, but their character. For if men are sensible and good-temperered, old age is easy enough to bear: if not, youth as well as age is a burden.

Socrates was 'delighted by what he said'.[16]

Plato here set a stereotype of deteriorating relations between generations, which was itself to have long life, against a more complex reality. Elsewhere he expressed respect for the moral and intellectual superiority of old men. In his view, virtue and reason increased with age. He compared the reverence that was due to older men with that which was paid to the gods.[17] In part, for him, the authority of old people was a guarantee of social and political stability. *The Laws*, written when he was himself much older, takes the form of a discussion among three old men which echoes the opening of *The Republic*. They stress the need for reciprocity between old and young: old people should show good example to the young and in return they would win respect, if it was merited.[18] What Plato regarded as the desirable condition in old age provided the model for an ideal philosophical type which influenced the Stoics and very many generations thereafter.

Aristotle's *Art of Rhetoric* has been described as opposed to Plato's positive images of old age and as delivering a devastating assault on the capacities of the elderly. It describes the influences upon human emotion on which the rhetorician must learn to play. One such is age:

From having lived for many years and been frequently deceived or in error, and from most of their affairs having been bad, they do not have confidence in anything and are less vigorous in all things than they should be. They have many opinions but no knowledge . . . They are sour-tempered . . . nourish suspicions.

They are small-minded from their humiliations in life and they are illiberal; for money is one of the necessities. Also they know from experience that acquisition is hard and throwing away is easy . . . and they are cowards and fear everything in advance.

---

[16] Plato, *The Republic*, trans. Desmond Lee, 2nd edn. revised (London, 1987), 61–3.
[17] Garland, *Greek Way*, 273.
[18] Plato, *The Laws*, trans. T. J. Saunders (Harmondsworth, 1970), 192–3.

And they are more self-loving than is right.

And they are pessimistic . . . and they live in memory rather than hope . . . garrulous, for they are always talking about the past.

And they live by calculation rather than by character . . .[19]

Yet Aristotle's description of the emotions of 'Youth' (aged up to 35) is equally negative and each is juxtaposed to 'Prime' (ages 30–49) the age he most admired. Conventionally the Greeks divided life into these three stages. As employed here, all three were stylized archetypes, devices to enable the speaker to construct rhetoric designed to persuade his audience. Yet this representation cannot have been wholly divorced from Aristotle's perception of the reality of old age. Elsewhere he commented, somewhat less pessimistically:

Beauty differs for each stage of life . . . that of an old man is sufficiency against inevitable troubles and freedom from pain through lack of any of those things that plague old age. . . .

A good old age is slowness to age and freedom from pain . . . It is a product both of the excellences of the body and of luck . . . and none persists to old age without luck.[20]

Since Aristotle's influential medical writings discussed the possibility of prolongation of life in a positive manner he cannot have been wholly negative about old age. His body of philosophical writing on the subject can be seen as blending the normative, the ideal, and the realistic; suggesting how a good life could, and ideally should, be lived at younger and older ages, and relating it to the less than ideal fashion in which people lived in reality.

Medical writing

Medical ideas about old age contributed to the notion that a happy old age could be achieved, as well as seeking to describe its progress. There was considerable medical interest in old age in the Greek world. Lukian in the *Macroboi* cites climate, diet, occupation, physical fitness, and mental alertness as factors in the promotion of long life. Aristotle's contributions to Greek medical ideas about old people were influential for many centuries. In *Length and Shortness of Life* he described ageing as due to the combined loss of body heat and moisture. Hence people who lived in hot climates lived longer because they cooled more slowly. To live longer moisture, such as semen, and heat should be conserved. Book Three of his *Parva Naturalia* was devoted to *De Longitudine*:

Sexual abstinence, abundance of flesh, being a woman, a moist, warm, maritime climate all contribute to a long life.

In Plato's *Republic*, Socrates and Glaucon describe the ideal diet for citizens of their state—plain but with some luxuries: salt, olive oil, cheese, vegetables,

[19] Aristotle, *The Art of Rhetoric*, trans. H. C. Lawson-Tancred (Harmondsworth, 1991), 174–6.
[20] Ibid. 90.

figs, etc. 'So they will lead a peaceful and healthy life and probably die at a ripe old age.'[21] Such recommendations encouraged an approach which was long to endure: that careful regulation of diet and activity could ease and delay ageing.

Hippocrates believed that from their early sixties most people were susceptible to a number of ailments: difficulty in breathing, catarrh, difficult micturation, arthritis, nephritis, dizziness, apoplexy, itching, sleeplessness, watery discharge from bowels and eyes and nostrils, dullness of vision, glaucoma, and hardness of hearing. His medical theory was fundamentally humoral; that is, that all life processes could be explained in terms of the the interaction of the four humours: warmth, cold, moisture, and dryness, and the changing chemistry of the 'secondary humours': phlegm, blood, choler, and bile. Illness in old age was associated with the progressive drying and cooling of the body. For Hippocrates old age was unavoidably associated with disease.

The other medical theorist of the Greek world who was to be of lasting influence, Galen, shared the humoral interpretation of the ageing process but regarded this as a natural process of weakening rather than pathological or necessarily having pathological effects. In consequence he was sceptical about the possibility of slowing or easing the ageing process. It was a 'natural' process with a 'natural' end; it was unnatural to seek means to prolong life. He put in place an approach which was long to conflict with that of optimists who believed that the worst effects of ageing could be prevented and its progress delayed.

Greek medical writings about old age are mainly descriptive with prescription going little beyond preventive regimens of exercise and diet. In truth, at this time and for very many centuries to follow, little else could be done.

The law

Certain of the Greeks' cultural expectations about old age can be understood from study of the law, though legal like fictional and medical representations refer mainly to the elite and do not transparently express everyday values and practices even at this level. Slaves may have been cared for in the household, or have taken on new roles as they grew older, for example, as teachers, but many may have been left to die of neglect. For the poor who survived to old age it is reasonable to assume that the experience was often grim though probably brief.

The law varied from state to state. In the constitution of conservative Sparta the chief decision-making body consisted of two kings plus twenty-eight men aged over 59 'who were judged to be outstanding in virtue'. They were in power for life and accountable to no one. Old men seem to have been accorded less power in classical Athens. Sparta was a largely illiterate society with few

---

[21] Plato, *The Republic*, book 2, 372 b–d.

written records; the aged served as repositories of knowledge. Athens was more progressive and highly literate. In Athens, in life as distinct from drama or poetry, a man would rarely be called for military service beyond the age of 60, which seems to have been conventionally accepted as the dividing line between maturity and old age, though such evidence as there is does not suggest that there was a fixed upper age limit for public, even military, office.[22]

The care of the elderly was the legal responsibility of male members of the family, though the Athenian state supported parents whose sons died in war. Men of property who lacked male heirs could adopt them, the heir foregoing all kinship with his natural father. One of the questions an elected magistrate was required to answer before being allowed to assume public office was whether he treated his parents well. Athenian law placed sons under a legal obligation not to beat their parents and to provide them with food, accommodation, and all due rites of burial. This obligation extended to grandparents, great-grandparents, and to adoptive parents. The need for such a law may suggest that such obligations were not always willingly observed. The only parents not so protected were those who had neglected or abused their sons. The penalty for neglect or ill-treatment of parents was heavy: total loss of civil rights. Reciprocally, in law, fathers had to leave the bulk of their property to their sons unless they were convicted of neglect or mistreatment. As in all other times, some were convinced that filial care for parents was in decline. In Hesiod's characterization of history as a succession of stages of decline from a perfect Golden Age, he decribed his own, the fifth, as an Age of Iron, so degenerate that 'men will not pay their parents the due reward for their rearing'.

There were competing representations of old age in the Greek world, whose origins and meanings are often obscure. But old age was not universally conceived of as 'sad' and rich old men, at least, were not routinely marginalized. A more accurate interpretation is that: 'throughout the ancient and classical periods the commonplace recurs that happiness is to live moderately and long enough to see one's children survive to have children'.[23] Running through Greek literature is a wholly realistic distaste for the disabilities of advanced old age, combined with recognition that most people would aim to live as long and as full a life as they were able and some at least could achieve this.[24]

ANCIENT ROME

Roman culture was much influenced by the Greeks and consciousness of age appears to have been as widespread, its symbolic uses as commonplace and similar in type, and its meanings as contested. Again, most evidence survives

---

[22] Garland, *Greek Way*, 281.
[23] Laura Nash, 'Greek Origins of Generational Thought', *Daedalus* (Fall 1978), 13.
[24] Garland, *Greek Way*, 253–5.

about powerful old men.[25] Men appear to have been described as *senex* (old) at variable ages, from their later forties, dependent upon their physical condition.[26] Sixty was conventionally accepted as the threshold of old age for high status men. There seem to have been few responsibilities or prohibitions defined by precise ages, and people had little reason to be aware of their exact age. Rome, like Athens, was not a gerontocracy. Senators might be aged 25, or even younger, though judges were expected to retire at 60 under the Republic; in 4 BC the age became 70, in AD 1 it was 65. The relatively healthy food and lifestyles of higher status Romans may have kept those who were not carried off by infectious disease or accident looking and acting youthful to later ages than in the more recent past.[27]

Philosophy

Among philosophers, Cicero had lasting influence. His *De Senectute*, written around 44 BC, when he was about 62, was widely read in Europe from the twelfth century to at least the nineteenth. It was translated by Caxton in 1481 and had a secure place in the classical canon in England thereafter. It influenced Luther, Erasmus, and Protestant theologians whilst also acquiring a prominent place in the curricula of Jesuit colleges. It was admired by Montaigne, who commented 'He gives one an appetite for growing old',[28] by Locke, Hume, Johnson, Gibbon.[29] In turn, it drew on a number of Greek treatises, above all Plato, with whom its continuity is clear. For centuries it was the classic positive statement about old age. Cicero wrote the essay while he was temporarily exiled from public affairs. It has been dismissed by de Beauvoir, in her relentlessly gloomy, tendentious survey of the 'history' of old age, as no more than a plea for his own reinstatement despite his age.[30] Finley dismisses it as having received excessive attention despite conveying nothing useful about the reality of old age in ancient Rome, including Cicero's own.[31] Both may be right. The importance of the text lies in its own long life which suggests that it expresses, as it may have helped to shape, widely held hopes and feelings about old age from the ancient world onwards for many centuries.

It takes the form of a conversation staged in Rome around 150 BC. The main speaker is Cato the Elder, aged 84. It stresses the wisdom of old age; that old age was not wearisome to those who knew how to live a good and happy life. Cato comments that 'Everyone hopes to attain an advanced age;

---

[25] This section is much indebted to Parkin, 'Age and the Aged'.
[26] Ibid. 13–14.   [27] Ibid. 14, 82.
[28] Michel de Montaigne, *Essays*, trans. J. M. Cohen (Harmondsworth, 1958), 211.
[29] Cicero, *Selected Works*, trans. M. Grant (Harmondsworth, 1960), 24–31.
[30] Simone de Beauvoir, *Old Age*, trans. Patrick O'Brian (Harmondsworth, 1977), 133–5.
[31] Finley, 'The Elderly', 404–5.

yet when it comes they all complain'; that his contemporaries grumbled that
they had no pleasures left, that those who used to respect them no longer did
so. But he points out, like Cephalus, that this is not the universal experience
of old age, at least among the prosperous and cultivated. He admits that for
those who are poor and without intellectual resources old age is miserable.
Among the privileged: 'When you hear protests of this kind the trouble is due
to character not age. Since . . . (nature) . . . has planned all the other divisions
of our lives excellently she is not likely to make a bad playwright's mistake
of skimping the last act.'

He insists that if the old remain intellectually and physically active they
can remain sound of mind and active until late ages. But not active in all
things. Like Sophocles in Cephalus' account, Cato asserts that release from
the distractions of sensuality and the channelling of energy into intellectual
pursuits, was another of the pleasures of láter years. Moderation was essential to a contented and productive old age and not just in later years, for 'old
age must have its foundations well laid in early life'. Age should be fought
against, combated like disease, by following a fixed regime and taking exercise in moderation. By such means old people could continue to acquire knowledge and maintain much of their mental and physical strength. Cato
emphasized that respect for the aged was not automatic, but had to be earned,
and that the foundations of respect were laid by responsible behaviour in early
life. But even such a benign old age must come to an end. Cato envisaged the
gradual, peaceful, ideal death, preceded by a process of what is recogniz-
ably, in modern terms, 'disengagement' from everyday life. He commented
that people's interests changed through their lifetimes; finally the interests peculiar to old age fall away 'and when that happens a man has had enough of
life and it is time for him to die'.

One hundred and fifty years later, Plutarch, in his own old age, wrote the
treatise *Whether an old man should engage in public affairs*, arguing that old men,
with what he regarded as their wide experience, wisdom, good judgement,
and preference for moderation, could and should play an important role in
the management of the state and the education of the young. For him, the
pleasures of politics rather than of philosophy compensated for the declining
aptitude and inclination for sex. Mental powers were maintained by constant
practice. The young should perform menial duties until they attained the wisdom of old age; it was laziness for old men to retire from public life.[32] Plutarch
advised his ageing contemporaries: 'Keep your head cool and your feet
warm; instead of employing medicines for every indisposition, rather fast a
day and while you attend to the body never neglect the mind.' The fact that
Cicero and Plutarch felt the need to argue that old men should have a strong
role in the state suggests that in their times perhaps they did not.

[32] Parkin, 'Age and the Aged', 46–7.

There is much of classic Stoicism in Cicero's approach. Seneca's *Letters from a Stoic* written around 62–65 BC when Seneca himself was in his early sixties express more briefly a similar positive view of an old age carefully prepared for. He too was to have enduring influence in the high culture of medieval and early modern Europe.[33] Much later Pliny the Younger (*c.* AD 61–112) expressed similar views.[34] The ideal of an old age in which the pleasures of the mind, poetry, music, friendship replace those of the body appears to have been widespread among powerful Roman men.

Literature

Philosophers offered no such map of life to women, who are more visible in literature. Horace's three odes to ageing women, often quoted as typical of Roman attitudes, are about women who have devoted their lives to love and pleasure rather than to the cultural ideal of *pietas* and family. The odes describe, with varying degrees of revulsion and pity, how these pleasures are no longer available to them and imply that unlike men they have no alternative.[35] The women are toothless, haggard, sex-crazed, disgusting. The respectable woman could no doubt look forward to continuing a life surrounded by her family, perhaps with a wider social role since in Roman as in Greek society certain honorific roles were open to post-menopausal women.

Horace wrote in a similar negative vein about old men. His *Ars Poetica*, advice to prospective dramatists, written *c.* 20 BC, suggested, as Aristotle had done, that the artist adapt his writing to the nature and ages of his audience. He catalogued the characteristics of the several ages of man, most of them quite negatively. Old men he described (probably consciously) in terms similar to Aristotle's as miserly, lacking energy, greedy for longer life, quarrelsome, praising the good old days when they were young, condemning the younger generation.[36] Virgil expresses the variety of old age experience as vividly as Homer.

As in other times comic and satiric writing was nastier about old age. Juvenal's *Satires* were 'one of the most powerful and bitter attacks on *senectus* in the history of the ancient world, if not of all time'.[37] As Hamlet described it to old Polonius, demonstrating for how many centuries these classical texts were familiar to theatre audiences:

the satirical rogue says here that old men have grey beards; that their faces are wrinkled; their eyes purging thick amber and plumtree gum; and that they have a plentiful lack of wit, together with most weak hams.[38]

[33] Seneca, *Letters from a Stoic*, trans. R. Campbell (Harmondsworth, 1969).
[34] Parkin, 'Age and the Aged', 50.
[35] Carol C. Esler, 'Horace's Old Girls: Evolution of a Topos', in Falkner and de Luce, *Greek and Latin Literature*, 172–82.
[36] George R. Coffman, 'Old Age from Horace to Chaucer: Some Literary Affinities and Adventures of an Idea', *Speculum*, 9 (1934), 249–77.   [37] Parkin, 'Age and the Aged', 56–7.
[38] William Shakespeare, *Hamlet*, Act 2, Scene 2, lines 195–215.

Juvenal dwelled upon the physical manifestations of advanced old age, when all capacity for pleasure was gone and old men (to whom he exclusively refers) were repulsive to their families.

Popular Roman drama and literature throughout Rome's heyday tended generally though not universally to depict old age negatively. Philosophical writing highlighted similar fears of ageing, but was more likely to offer consolation.[39]

The law and the welfare of old people

As in Greece, children were expected to honour and care for their parents in return for the care they had received and the obligation was enforced at law, though how consistently is unknown. So far as is known, the co-residing extended family was not the Roman norm. Old people were warned through a variety of channels of the danger of placing themselves at the mercy of the younger generation, though this did not preclude co-residence of the old with the young if only for a short time before death. By law the *paterfamilias* retained control of his property until his death or proven incapacity. Certainly by the second century AD a son was expected to support his father if he could afford it, though not otherwise.[40] When people could not provide for themselves or receive support from their families there were few known alternatives. Army veterans might receive blocks of land on retirement, or a sum of cash. Impoverished old people might share free distributions of corn or other largesse from the rich.[41] Parkin concludes that:

The prestige enjoyed, the part played, the actual status of an old person in the Roman world depended more on the person him or herself than on the general fact that he or she was old. Roman society's view of an elderly person was dictated by the extent to which that individual continued to find a niche in that society.[42]

What survives of the discourse on old age in the ancient world suggests a subtle understanding of its contradictory character and of the variety of experiences of older people and that there were no simple patterns peculiar to each era. Such understandings were carried into medieval Europe by means of the translation of classical texts.

---

[39] Parkin, 'Age and the Aged', 61–2. [40] Ibid. 157–9.
[41] Ibid. 148–67. [42] Ibid. 179.

3

Medieval Images of Old Age

The translation of surviving classical texts was most active in Europe, including England, from the twelfth century and reached its peak in the thirteenth. Classical ideas about the life cycle were disseminated through Latin dictionaries containing citations from the classics, selected by topic. On old age Seneca and Cicero were most often cited.[1] The classical sources provided a language in which old age could be and was discussed and described, though its social meanings and the purposes of such discourse changed in the context of Christianity. Old age had a particular place in theological narratives.

THEOLOGY

Biblical references to old age were contradictory. Whilst stressing that survival to great age and the wisdom of the Patriarchs was the reward for righteous living, the gloomy twelfth chapter of Ecclesiastes had a lasting influence. It begins:

Remember now thy creator in the days of thy youth, while the evil days come not, nor the years draw nigh wherein thou shalt say, I have no pleasure in them.

The ninetieth psalm fixed the lifespan at three score years and ten. Medieval theology concerned itself in detail with the significance of old age and was certainly strongly aware of it as an important phase of life. In Christian belief old age and death were man's punishment for sin, experienced only since the Fall. The *memento mori* theme, the injunction to approach death free of sin for fear of the fires of hell, and hence to live a blameless old age was dominant, though it was not wholly distant from the classical belief that a life of wrongdoing produced an unhappy old age. The popular resonance of this belief is evident from medieval English proverbs:

> He that in youth no virtue uses, in age all honour he refuses.
> What youth does, age shows.[2]

As in classical texts, a 'good old age' was presented in much medieval Christian thought, normatively, as one of closely complementary spiritual and

---

[1] M. E. Goodich, *From Birth to Death: The Human Life Cycle in Medieval Thought, 1250–1350* (Lanham, Md., 1989), 4.

[2] *The Oxford Dictionary of English Proverbs*, 3rd edn., revised by F. P. Wilson (Oxford, 1970).

physical ease, the outcome of correct moral and spiritual choices made earlier in life. On the other hand, both St Augustine and Thomas Aquinas left influential legacies of belief that spiritual development was independent of physical development, for spiritual perfection could be attained at any age other than extreme youth, including extreme old age.

In addition to translations of old texts, new texts on old age were produced, though often in language strongly reminiscent of the classics. The *De Contemptu Mundi sive de Miseria Humanae Conditionis* by the future Pope Innocent III, written in the late twelfth century, described old age (as it did most aspects of human existence) in gloomy terms: the old were easily provoked, mean and avaricious, sullen and quarrelsome, quick to talk, slow to hear, but not slow in wrath, praising former times, despising the moderns, censuring the present, praising the past. In conclusion the author reminded the young not to despise the old because they would one day be old themselves. This treatise became influential and popular in England as elsewhere in Europe.

Throughout Europe between *c.*1250 and 1350 there appears to have been heightened interest in the life cycle and in the possibility of prolonging and improving the span of life. This was partly because translation of the rich ancient texts extended the range of what was imaginatively possible; and improvements in living standards may have increased optimism for further possibilities. There was increased stress upon human potential and the dynamic development of the whole human being from birth to death. This was commonly presented metaphorically in terms of life as a series of stages, in which the foibles and weaknesses of each stage were balanced by virtues and opportunities; or of life as a journey presenting recurrent choices between good or evil. This was a conventional trope of spiritual autobiographies or hagiographies.[3] There was, however, dispute among theologians as to whether old age was to be desired, or early death welcomed as longed-for relief from the inevitable miseries of life. Such conundrums gave old age a secure place in learned medieval thinking.

The thirteenth century saw the spread of treatises designed both to advise princes on how to experience a long and successful reign and to advise a wider, though still limited, learned population how to achieve physical and spiritual health. There was an increase in the number of encyclopaedias, some in the vernacular, aimed at this audience. Speculation of the learned about ageing reached a more popular audience through poetry and sermons. In fourteenth-century England the popular anonymous vernacular religious and didactic poem the *Pricke of Conscience* was written as a guide to the avoidance of hell and attainment of heaven. Its chief concern was with the practical consequences of right and wrong living. It describes old age in dismal detail primarily as a warning to sinners, a reminder that active life is short and beset by temptation.

---

[3] Thomas R. Cole, *The Journey of Life: A Cultural History of Aging in America* (Cambridge, 1992), 3–31.

In the later fourteenth century the Dominican John Bromyard's *Summa Praedicantium* was a manual for preachers, presenting sermon topics alphabetically with examples drawn from a range of scholarly and popular sources. Under the heading *Senectus* it pointed out both the usefulness to the spirit and the great misery to the body of old age; the quality and condition of good old men and the reverence due to them; the perils to those who were evil in old age. It closed with a description of the physical decay of the old using descriptive language evidently drawn directly from Innocent III's treatise. Linguistic conventions had been established for the description of old age which were available for use in many sermons in fourteenth- and fifteenth-century England.[4]

By these means a portrait of the human life cycle achieved widespread currency by the later thirteenth century. Complex schemes of the structure of knowledge linked human ageing to the unifying laws which governed the universe. Fundamental to a way of thinking about religion and the natural world in which the physical and the spiritual were inseparably fused was the belief that God had made humankind the focal point of an ordered world, in harmony with all of nature. Men and women were at the centre of a complex set of correspondences within and beyond the terrestrial world. Hence to discover the pattern of human development and ageing was to learn something about the universe of which man was the microcosm. These cosmic associations appeared in elaborate visual representations.

What was not evident in medieval England or elsewhere in Europe was any simple veneration of old people as such.When they were credited with especial insight it was as often attributed to the innocent wisdom sometimes associated with children—the 'second childhood' to which the very old regressed—as to any special quality of old age.[5]

THE AGES OF MAN

Much discussion of medieval thinking about old age has concentrated upon the stylized divisions of age into three, four, seven, twelve, or occasionally other numbers of stages which were widely employed. Aristotle's three-age division was influential. It expressed the simple prime divisions of life which were widely represented in visual and literary forms. In Christian cultures, though not in Scripture, the Three Magi personified Youth, Prime, Old Age, though in giving homage to a baby they implied a fourth age. A four-age structure was preferred by physiological theorists. This was an influential attempt to explain in terms of medieval science the changes through which human beings

---

[4] George R. Coffman, 'Old Age from Horace to Chaucer: Some Literary Affinities and Adventures of an Idea', *Speculum*, 9 (1934), 249–77.

[5] Shulamith Shahar, *Growing Old in the Middle Ages* (London, 1997), 64.

went in the course of their lives. Its first expression produced in England was the Venerable Bede's *De Tempore Ratione*, composed in 725. In this scheme the four ages were governed by the four humours and harmonized with the macrocosmic order of the seasons and the elements. It was recognized that since all people had different 'complexions' of humours, each related to the elements in different ways; hence all people are different and live for varying lengths of time. To maintain health such differences should be analysed and taken into account. Both Hippocrates and Galen, whose work was translated in the twelfth century, suggested a regimen of diet and conduct of life suited to each phase of life. Within a formal framework which divided life into ages, issues of biological development, the acquisition of virtue, the path to salvation, and the process of learning and the interrelationships of these themes could be expounded.

Such four-age divisions spread widely in the vernacular in the thirteenth century. They became increasingly common in England in the fourteenth and fifteenth centuries, for example, in the proliferating vernacular medical texts. Their popularity was perhaps rooted in a human need to impose a knowable shape upon what might otherwise be experienced as frightening, unexpected, and directionless physical and mental changes. They must have influenced contemporary perceptions of the life course and the language in which it was described. The ages which marked the stages varied, often due to mistranslation, but broadly they were: infancy, youth, maturity, old age.

This scheme vied in popularity with the seven-age scheme, which was especially prominent in classical Arabic astrology and came to England through translation, though it was never so dominant culturally as is sometimes thought. It allowed for a finer differentiation of ages, importantly between 'old age' when powers were diminished but not lost, and the final stage of decrepitude; between 'young' and 'old' old age in modern terms.

Both four- and seven-age schemata coexisted within the conventional vocabulary of an educated person of the early and later Middle Ages, without apparent incompatibility. Consideration of both occasionally included the characteristics of women, though there were disputations among medieval scholars as to whether women did indeed experience equivalent life-stages to men. At a popular level, a late medieval German poem of 1578 divided a woman's life into eight phases: at age 10 she was a child, at 20 a maid, at 30 a wife, at 40 a matron, at 50 a grandmother, at 60 'age-worn', at 70 'deformed', at 80 'confused and grown cold'.[6] All such schemata assumed that people could live to advanced ages.

The Ages of Man were schematized attempts to represent both spiritual and physiological change. They do not necessarily imply, as is sometimes

---

[6] Olwen Hufton, *The Prospect Before Her: A History of Women in Western Europe, 1500–1800* (London, 1995), 251.

suggested, that medieval people had no conception of transition from one stage to another even though stylized leaps from one age to another can be found in literature; for example, Beowulf shifts from youth to old age with no evident intervening transition. The distinction between ageing portrayed as 'stages', or as a continuous 'journey', another popular metaphor, was less stark than has been suggested.[7] The supposed attributes of age stages were employed normatively, often expressing both the desirable moral qualities at each stage of life and the potential for deviation. They represented ideal types not necessarily to be found in everyday life, and were generally drawn from classical sources.[8] Wisdom, for example, was said to be acceptable at any age but was most natural in old age, as love was most natural in youth. But it was recognized that the respect in which humans were distinctive was in not being bound to follow a pre-marked course of life. Since they possessed reason they might choose, for good or ill, to depart from the norm.

The Ages of Man were prominently represented in art and literature. They formed popular themes of late medieval wall paintings and tapestries. From the sixteenth century they were often depicted as a pyramid or bridge of steps often (until the eighteenth century) with representations of death or the devil or love and other hazards of life lurking beneath, lying in wait to ambush one at any age. Such images remained popular long after they had lost the resonance of the richness and complexity of medieval thinking about the human relationship to the universe. In general they represent conventionally the ageing and decline of men and women, generally distinguishing two or more stages of old age.[9]

But this was not the only form in which old age was represented. In medieval as in classical times themes of rejuvenation expressed human regret about the effects of ageing. The notion that a 'fountain of youth' existed in some place or time that could not merely prolong strength but turn age back into youth became absorbed into medieval Western imagery. In literature the theme recurs that there had once existed, or existed still in some remote place, the Golden Age or Place where youth is eternal and could be repossessed if only it or its secret could be discovered. Medieval alchemists sought the elixir of life, the universal means to restore health and prolong life. As in ancient times, such longings were so regularly objects of satire that they must have been widely recognized as hopeless dreams. Yet representations of the Judgement Day generally assumed that bodies would be resurrected as young people, in their early thirties according to St Augustine of Hippo.[10] However benign the images of old age, the longing for eternal youth survived.

---

[7] e.g. in Cole, *Journey of Life*, though in general this is a valuable book.

[8] Goodich, *Birth to Death*, 146.

[9] These representations are most fully discussed in E. Sears, *Ages of Man: Medieval Interpretations of the Life-Cycle* (Princeton, 1986).   [10] Shahar, *Growing Old*, 53.

LITERATURE

In fourteenth-century England the theme of ageing was taken up in vernacular literature and directed at a popular audience. Chaucer adopted the
linguistic conventions of the classical negative description of old age in his
most detailed description of an old man in the the Reeve's Prologue:

> My hoary top-knot ties me down for old;
> Same as my hair, my heart is full of mould
>
> .   .   .   .   .   .
>
> Certain when I was born so long ago,
> Death drew the tap of life and let it flow;
> And ever since the tap has done its task,
> And now there's little but an empty cask.
> My stream of life's but drops upon the rim.
> An old fool's tongue will run away with him
> To chime and chatter of monkey tricks that's past;
> There's nothing left but dotage at the last.[11]

Shakespeare, two centuries later, in *As You Like It* put similar negative imagery
into the mouth of Jaques at the conclusion of his wholly negative description
of each of the Seven Ages of Man:

> The sixth age shifts
> Into the lean and slippered pantaloon
> With spectacles on nose and pouch on side
> His youthful hose, well sav'd, a world too wide
> For his shrunk shank; and his big manly voice,
> Turning again toward childish treble, pipes
> And whistles in his sound. Last scene of all,
> That ends this strange eventful history,
> Is second childishness and mere oblivion;
> Sans teeth, sans eyes, sans taste, sans everything.[12]

We might conclude from this as from other stylized representations of the
Ages of Man that in the age from Chaucer to Shakespeare old age was conceptualized in universally negative terms—indeed Minois draws precisely this
conclusion.[13]

And yet, as Jaques concludes his speech, Orlando enters with the faithful
Adam who has followed him into exile. A little earlier when Adam pledges
his support to Orlando he, at 'almost fourscore' years claims:

> Though I look old, yet I am strong and lusty
> For in my youth I never did apply

---

[11] Geoffrey Chaucer, *The Canterbury Tales*, trans. Nevill Coghill (Harmondsworth, 1977), 123–4.
[12] William Shakespeare, *As You Like It*, Act 2, Scene 7, lines 157–66.
[13] Georges Minois, *History of Old Age*, trans. S. Hanbury-Tenison (Oxford, 1989), 281–7.

> Hot and rebellious liquors in my blood.
> Nor did with unbashful forehead woo
> The means of weakness and debility;
> Therefore my age is as a lusty winter,
> Frosty but kindly. Let me go with you;
> I'll do the service of a younger man
> In all your business and necessities.[14]

This is a quite different representation of old age from that of Jaques, though it remains within the convention that it is temperate living that makes such lusty old age possible. As Adam enters the stage immediately following Jaques's speech, though tired and weak, he visually subverts Jaques's description of aged men as dotards. Shakespeare juxtaposes Jaques's representation of the inexorable march of time with Adam's embodiment of human difference in the process of ageing over which individuals have some control.

In other respects Shakespeare subverts and inverts conventional imagery. Jaques himself, who is derided in the play for 'moralizing' the natural world 'into a thousand similes' is described as 'melancholy', in conventional narrative an attribute of the old, though he is quite young. He delivers his Ages of Man speech alone on stage with Duke Senior, who is relatively old, yet affects the life of a young man, hunting in the forest.[15] Again, the visual scene subverts Jaques's verbal message.

A variety of images of old age can be found in Shakespeare. The elderly Falstaff is pathetic. The first sequence of the sonnets warns the loved one of the ill effects of ageing, in the conventional language of romantic poetry, though it is gently expressed. The story of King Lear takes to extremes the ancient theme of the ingratitude of youth to age and the foolishness of the old who put themselves in the power even of their own children. Yet Lear's behaviour is not attributed solely to the effects of his advancing age. His daughter Regan comments revealingly: 'Yet he hath *ever* but slenderly known himself' (my emphasis).[16]

A similar range of representations of old age can be found in Chaucer. Though the Reeve describes himself in miserable terms in his own Prologue, in the General Prologue Chaucer's description of the Reeve opens conventionally enough: He was old and choleric and thin

> his legs were lean
> Like sticks they were, no calf was to be seen.

But later he describes the old man as a sharp businessman:

> He knew their dodges, knew their every trick
> Feared like the plague he was by those beneath.

---

[14] *As You Like It*, Act 2, Scene 3, lines 47–55.
[15] This is pointed out by Mary Dove, *The Perfect Age of Man's Life* (Cambridge, 1986), 36.
[16] William Shakespeare, *King Lear*, Act 1, Scene 1, lines 292–3.

He is wealthy and still active:

> When young he'd learned a useful trade, and still
> He was a carpenter of first-rate skill.

Chaucer was either unaware of or untroubled by these conflicting images of the old age of the same person, or perhaps he was consciously opposing the conventional, self-pitying, poetic image offered by the Reeve, with his own realistic description of a sharp, healthy old man; just as Jaques offers a familiar, conventional, stylized account in contrast to Shakespeare's description of a real old man.

Chaucer portrays foolish old men betrayed by young wives in the Miller's and the Merchant's Tales. Much less dismally, the Wife of Bath, clearly past menopause, had, after some ups and downs with older husbands, assured herself of a contented fifth marriage with a husband twenty years her junior and is in no way made to look foolish for merrily contemplating a sixth. She presents a strong image of an older woman who has controlled her own life. Yet in her own Tale an old woman is unflatteringly portrayed, again in the language of literary convention:

> A fouler-looking creature I suppose
> Could scarcely be imagined.

But this old woman is powerful for she alone can give the Knight the secret knowledge of 'the thing that women most desire' which he needs to save his own life (following his condemnation for rape of a young woman). She agrees to tell him the secret if he will agree to marry her. She seeks to reconcile him with this fate in a lecture which draws—unexpectedly in an old crone—on learned references to Seneca, Juvenal, and Boethius to discuss the importance of respecting age and poverty and of valuing people for their virtues not their appearance. The concluding joke of this Tale unites male and female fantasy: as the new husband forces himself to kiss his ugly old wife she is transformed into a young and lovely woman and they live happily ever after.[17]

Mary Dove argues that the work of Chaucer, Gower, Langland, and their contemporaries gains power from the fact that they assume each life to be distinctive, none following quite the same course. *Piers Plowman* represents human progress through life, but the Dreamer undergoes unpredicted and extreme changes as he moves from youth to old age. Langland like Chaucer and Shakespeare assumes the reader's familiarity with the concept of ages of life and plays with it to represent the actual unpredictable nature of life's course.

---

[17] Chaucer and his contemporaries have been described as treating the aged wholly 'rhetorically as figures of man's spiritual corruption', as 'grotesques, as vehicles of metaphor rather than as characters', accepting conventions which divided life rigidly into stages with fixed attributes and little sense of development. Alicia K. Nitechi, 'Figures of Old Age in Fourteenth Century English Literature', in M. M. Sheehan (ed.), *Aging and the Aged in Medieval Europe* (Toronto, 1990), 107–18.

Like the author of Sir Gawain and the Green Knight he employs ageing as a metaphor for human existence.[18]

We should not assume that contemporaries confused stylized or metaphorical representations whose objective was spiritual didacticism with the reality of human experience. Certainly they had many literary reminders that they should not. Writers presented competing representations of old age with an ease which suggests that they were employing languages and images and a sensitivity to the variety and complexity of the experience of older ages with which their audiences would be familiar.

MEDICINE

Medical theories of ageing, normally based on the theory of the humours, assumed that ageing was a gradual process, rather than one of abrupt transitions. There was, however, a widespread belief that physical strength began to decline at earlier ages (around 30 to 35) than intellectual capacity (from around age 49) and that mental powers could remain alert until extreme old age, which are very similar to the prevailing medical beliefs of the late twentieth century.[19] The translation in around 1240 of Aristotle's *Parva Naturalia*, which contained treatises dealing directly with the vicissitudes of ageing and the conditions necessary for the prolongation of life, led to a lively interest in the care of the aged and the possibility of extending the human lifespan.[20] A succession of regimens for the maintenance of physical and spiritual health flowed through medieval Europe, seeking to reform body and soul, just as other schemata, often produced by the same writers, sought political and religious renewal. Their recommendations were later disseminated by encyclopaedias and medical texts.

The most widely distributed of these was the *Regimen Sanitatis Salternitani*, couched in the form of a letter to an unidentified King of England, which appeared in prose and poetic versions and reached its final form by the mid-thirteenth century. It divided life into seven ages, each with its unique character depending on the condition of the humours. Stress was laid on good temper, moderate diet, rest and exercise as the keys to health. It contained dietary regulations, lists of herbal medicines, and other kinds of advice for temperate living. Thereafter many leading physicians composed a *Regimen Sanitatis* on similar lines, often evidently borrowing from one another, and from classical sources, especially from Aristotle, discussing diet, rest, evacuation, pure air, the care of the senses, the effect of toxins, maintenance of sound spirits, exercise, massage, sexuality. Such regimens 'became the common heritage of the educated classes'.[21]

---

[18] Mary Dove, *Perfect Age.*   [19] Shahar, *Growing Old*, 38–9.
[20] Ibid. 39–42.   [21] Ibid. 39–43. Goodich, *Birth to Death.*

Also widely influential were the treatises of Roger Bacon (*c.*1200–80) such as his *Liber de Conservatione Iuventutis*. He agreed with Aristotle that ageing was a process of declining natural heat. He described the ageing process and believed that this could be retarded by a healthy regime or by use of medicines, attention to diet, digestion, sleep or rest, bowel functions, good air, exercise, control of the passions, pleasurable activity, such as good music, reading, avoidance of unpleasantness, conversation, gazing at handsome persons, or breathing the exhalations of healthy young girls. He emphasized the need to begin a proper regimen, of moral behaviour as well as diet, in youth in order to survive to a good old age. Individuals could age even before the high point of strength and beauty between age 45 and 50 if they showed insufficient concern for health. If they followed his advice he believed that they could preserve all their powers until the age of 100, when signs of ageing would appear. Until then the body would retain its youthful appearance and vigour. He believed that before the Flood people had lived longer, but he attributed the shortened lifespan not only to sin but to pollution resulting from the increase in population and the increased foolishness of the human race. As human beings failed to observe good rules of health and morality, each generation degenerated into poorer health and shorter lifespans than its predecessor.[22]

Largely as a consequence of the interest in Aristotle and in Arabic medical sources, old age ceased to be characterized exclusively as a time of physical decay in anticipation of death, but was tempered by the hope that the human lifespan could be extended. Bacon's work was widely read, translated, and plagiarized for centuries. One treatise was translated into English as the *Cure of Old Age and the Preservation of Youth* in 1683. Spectacles, whose invention is credited to Bacon, was one of medieval medicine's greatest boons to old age.

Before the fifteenth century only a handful of medical works were devoted exclusively to the care of old age. Medieval writings on 'practical medicine' are mostly prescriptive or normative, theoretical rather than descriptive. It is hard to glean clinical observations about the experience or the treatment of the problems of old age. The first printed monograph on old age, the *Gerontocoma*, was written for Pope Innocent VIII by Gabriele Zerbi, who was assassinated in 1489 apparently by the slaves of a Turkish ruler whose life he had failed to prolong as promised. He and his associates made careful observations of the common pathological conditions of old age. Zerbi stressed that 'the gerontocomus should help not only the body of the ageing patient but also his mind and soul as Cicero says'. Depression and lethargy were the dangers most commonly feared for the old. They were thought to be induced by the coldness of the brain. It was often recommended that old men should sleep close to young girls to conserve their warmth. Zerbi emphasized the

[22] Cf. later 19th-cent. ideas of physical degeneration: see p. 276. Shahar, *Growing Old*, 61–2.

value of conversation, entertainment with music and games, wearing bright clothes, living in brightly coloured rooms.

A new age in geriatric medicine began in the fifteenth century with Paracelsus (1493–1541), who experimented with drugs derived from herbs, minerals, and other substances; the pathological anatomy of Vesalius and Antonio Benivieni (1440–1502), and the work of Leonardo (1452–1519), who carried out clinical observations and dissections of elderly bodies. He concluded that the aged who enjoyed good health died through lack of nourishment due to the thickening of the walls of the veins and the closing up of capillaries. This was 'natural' death.[23]

Medical observation and discourse was mainly concerned with higher status men. Females would rarely consult male medical men and the poor could not afford to. This did not prevent assertions that bodily change afflicted women differently from men. Some believed that cessation of menstruation, which was believed to purify the body, was said to cause a poisoning of women's bodies, especially those of poor old women 'who live on nothing but coarse meat' and in consequence were said to give way to fornication and crime. Like later and earlier representations of the sexually voracious older woman, freed of the fear of childbirth, this may say more about male sexual fears than about clinical observation of female ageing.[24] Yet, as we have seen, at least by the sixteenth century, some physicians saw the post-menopausal woman as fitter, healthier, and also less threatening than her younger self, indeed as more like a man.[25]

Medieval physicians debated in formal *quaestiones* whether old age was itself a disease. They concluded that it was not. They distinguished the normal concomitants from the abnormal or diseased conditions of old age. Medieval views of old age were as complex and realistic as those of the ancient, and the modern, world.

---

[23] J. O. Leibowitz, 'Early Accounts in Geriatric Pathology (Leonardo, Harvey, Keill)', *Koruth*, 7 (1980), ccliv–cclvi.

[24] Shahar, *Growing Old*, 44.

[25] M. Pelling, 'Thoroughly Resented? Older Women and the Medical Role in Early Modern London', in L. Hunter and S. Hutton (eds.), *Women, Science and Medicine, 1500–1700: Mothers and Sisters of the Royal Society* (Stroud, 1997), 63–88.

4
Old Age in the Seventeenth and Eighteenth Centuries

Minois believes that with the coming of the Renaissance, youth—associated with rebirth and creativity—was celebrated and hostility to old people pervaded European culture, creating a literature of lamentation and invective about old age, directed especially against old women.[1] Keith Thomas has argued, in an English context,[2] that the pace of change in the seventeenth and eighteenth centuries, especially with the invention of printing and the wide dissemination of new religion and new science, led to the scorning of old people with old ideas.

Thomas suggests, however, that old people might retain authority if they commanded material resources. Richard Steele commented that: 'Old people commonly are despised, especially when they are not supported with good estates'. The old man spitting at the fireplace was disregarded, but if he 'hath estate of his own to maintain himself and to pleasure his children, oh, then he is held in estimation, his age is honoured, his person is reverenced, his counsel is sought, his voice is obeyed'.[3] Another survey of some of the literature, drama, tracts and sermons of the early seventeenth century reveals ambiguities: old age might be depicted as a period of wisdom or of folly; death as lying in God's hands and either to be welcomed as release from earthly suffering, or, alternatively, postponable by prudent living. The author believes that these contradictions were new and signs of a transition to a 'modern' conception of old age, but, as we have seen, they were very old, even in the seventeenth century.[4]

Thomas concluded that the 'picture of old age yielded by contemporary literature is pessimistic', and that in England 'between the sixteenth and eighteenth centuries . . . stratification by age increased, and the redundancy of the elderly was increasingly emphasized. Culturally inherited milestones like the two key ages of twenty-one and sixty took on a new importance.'[5] If this is so, however, it may indicate a shift of form rather than of degree, a formalization of age distinctions according to chronological age in certain circumstances

[1] Georges Minois, *History of Old Age: From Antiquity to the Renaissance* (Oxford, 1989), 249–87.
[2] K. Thomas, 'Age and Authority in Early Modern England', *Proceedings of the British Academy*, 62 (1976), 205–48. [3] Richard Steele, *Discourse Concerning Old Age* (1688).
[4] Steven R. Smith, 'Growing Old in Early Stuart England', *Albion*, 8/2 (1976), 125–41.
[5] Thomas, 'Age and Authority', 248.

which had previously been more subjectively determined. And, as the quotation from Steele suggests, cultural definitions of old age continued to be as complex and subjective in the early modern period as before, if not in precisely the same forms.

In particular, in deriving past attitudes to 'old age' from past texts historians have tended to elide active, younger 'green' old age with final decrepitude. Henry Cuffe was one of many seventeenth-century writers who was clear about this distinction. In *The Difference of the Ages of Man's Life* (1607) Cuffe broadly accepted Aristotle's division of life into three ages, his humoralism, and his definition of the characteristics of age groups, but he divided old age itself into two parts:

The first where our strength and heat are evidently impaired, yet not so much, but that there remaineth a will and readiness to bee doing and this lasteth from our fiftieth yeare unto our three score and five.

The second part which they call decrepit old age is when our strength and heat is so far decayed that not only all ability is taken away but even all willingness to the least strength and motion of our bodies.

The more miserable depictions of old age generally refer to the latter state, of which positive representation is extremely rare in all times and cultures.

Like texts of earlier and later ages, sermons and advice books of the seventeenth and eighteenth centuries prescribed notions of the proper behaviour of age groups. The dress of old people should be sober, their manners grave and dignified. 'Curled grey hair' was not comely; old women should not dress like the young. Essentially they were to refrain from sexual competition with the young. Lust in the elderly, male or female, was still an infallible occasion for ridicule and censure. Sexual relations between married couples too old to conceive children were regarded as harmful by some doctors and of doubtful morality by some divines, as indeed all age disparities in marriage were disapproved of, especially when the woman was the older. But prescription should not be confused with description. Prescriptive literature may have influenced the behaviour of older people, as was its purpose, but it was just one among many influences and in all periods such texts have sought to promote certain values because they were being disobeyed rather than because they were the norm of the time.

THE SEVENTEENTH CENTURY

Theological and philosophical writings

In religious discourse old age retained its older normative and metaphorical role. It was widely conceptualized as the final stage of the life course, its characteristics shaped by individual behaviour in earlier life. Yet perceptions of these characteristics continued to vary. Symon Goulart the French Protestant theologian whose *The Wise Veillard* was translated into English in 1621 distinguished three different phases of old age. From 50 to 65 'a man is yet lusty, strong and youthful' and could continue to be of service; from 65 'old men may be fit to be counsellors of estate and directors and governors of families'; but after the, rather late, age of 85 they were 'fit for nothing' except possibly conversation and the enjoyment of their children and grandchildren.[6] Goulart believed that old age brought 'ripeness of judgement', prudence, temperance and continency, and more certain knowledge of God. Old men were useful as statesmen because young men could be impetuous. The old had great wisdom which came from experience. As the body grew weak, the mind could remain strong and active. Old people could take comfort from the knowledge that death did not come only to the old: many children and younger people died; and because they were free from the 'desires and lusts of young men' and the problems these gave rise to. Goulart offered examples of old soldiers who had defeated young ones in battle and blind persons who had been useful to others. He urged old people not to complain about the loss of memory, since they would likely remember the important things and forget only the trivial. He concluded that the ills of old age could be eased by leading a good Christian life; salvation was possible at all ages.

The English divine John Reading in *The Old Man's Staffe. Two Sermons, shewing the onely way to a comfortable old age* (1621) opened with the classic Christian view that:

Man's state was by creation immortal, but the day that sin was born, man began to die; had he not sinned there should have been a comfortable maturity in age; if our lives like some long kindled lamps should have been consumed, it must have been without all pain, sickness, want of strength, sense of fear of death; for without sin there could have been no punishment: so that if we define old age, a certain ripenesse of life and length of time to a blessed translation, then age is natural; but if we describe it according to our present being it is a continual disease, the grounds and lees of life, in which the body languisheth.

And yet it need not be so bad, for 'The foundation of a comfortable old age is laid in youth . . . Remember thy creator in the days of thy youth'. He believed that young men were much tempted to sin. If they gave in, old age would come sooner:

Age is coming and the day shall have enough with his own grief; if thou load it with sin, that leaden talent, with excesses, lusts, wicked habits of youth (which deliver an out-worn strengthless body to old age) it must needs couch down between two burdens, sin and infirmity.

The old age of a good man is full of comfort and honour, it reneweth as it fadeth, as it loseth the blossoming youth, it findeth a crown of dignity . . . This point well

---

[6] Smith, 'Growing Old', 130.

learned would first better nurture those despisers of the aged, who have learned . . . to mock the aged or . . . with unreverent usage to eat up their aged parents whom God commandeth them to honour.

He exhorts calm, dignity, and wisdom in old age, rather than regret for lost capacities; but he claims that 'honor' in old age is earned rather than an automatic right:

Honor is due to the aged, not to all, but to the righteous: to all others their gray haires are the displayed banners of God's judgement, a Crown, but a crown of thorns.

Strength, wealth, 'carefull diet', reason, will not protect in old age: 'Vertue onlly hath an immunity and groweth not lame with age'. He reminded older people that it was never too late for sincere repentance and conversion.

John Milton expressed similar views poetically. In *Paradise Lost* (1667) the Archangel Michael describes to Adam the fate of disease and death awaiting humankind after the Fall. Adam pleads:

> But is there no other way, besides
> These painful passages, how we may come
> To death and mix with our connatural dust?
> There is, said Michael, if thou well observe
> The Rule of *Not too much*, by temperance taught
> In what thou eat'st and drink'st, seeking from thence
> Due nourishment not gluttonous delight
> Till many years over thy head return;
> So may'st thou live, till, like ripe fruit thou drop
> Into thy mother's lap, and be with ease
> Gathered, not harshly plucked, for death matured.
> This is old age; but then thou must outlive
> Thy youth, thy strength, thy beauty which will change
> To withered weak and grey; thy senses then
> Obtuse, all taste of pleasure must forgo
> To what thou hast; and for the air of youth
> Hopeful and cheerful, in thy blood will reign
> A melancholy damp of cold and dry
> To weigh thy spirits down and last consume
> The balm of life.

Adam, understandably depressed, responds:

> Henceforth I fly not death, nor would prolong
> Life much, but rather how I may be quit.
> Fairest and easiest of this cumbrous charge . . .

Michael replies:

> Nor love thy life, nor hate; but what thou liv'st
> Live well; how long or short permit to Heaven.

In another puritan classic, *Pilgrim's Progress* (1678), John Bunyan presents life as a journey of perils and choices between right and wrong, the correct choices leading to heavenly bliss. Explicitly the journey of Christiana, Christian's wife, in Part 2 of *Pilgrim's Progress* (pub. 1684) as she follows the path of her husband's pilgrimage, is represented as a long progress through adult life to a calm old age preceding death provided that the correct choices were made.[7]

Prolongation of life[8]

The question as to whether the individual could influence the length of his or her life, and if so by what means, or whether this was fixed by God alone continued as in medieval times to be a matter of theological dispute, since biblical references could be found to support either proposition. Richard Allestree's *A Discourse Concerning the Period of Human Life: Whether Mutable or Immutable* (1677) argued that whilst it was presumptuous to believe that we can under-stand God's actions, the Scriptures laid down nothing about the conduct of life: 'Even in this fallen state there is a huge difference between the lives of those who live upon wholesome food and observe a moderate diet; and of those who are careless in their diet.' Good physicians, he believed, could help to extend life, just as bad ones could shorten it. He argued that those who observed their religion tended to better health. God showed the right way and left people to choose whether to lengthen or shorten their lives by good or bad actions. Allestree, like many others, was convinced that God had fixed man's possible 'lease of life' at seventy or eighty years; that it had been longer before the Flood, but for hundreds of years it had been limited and this was unlikely to change. The possible lifespan of human beings intrigued theological, philosophical, and medical writers as optimism about the human capacity to control nature grew with the intellectual flowering of the seventeenth century.[9]

Francis Bacon influentially discussed old age and longevity in a number of treatises. His *History Natural and Experimental of Life and Death or Of the Prolongation of Life*, written when he was aged 62, was concerned to establish how long a life was possible for humankind and other living creatures, and how the max-imum could be attained. He shared the common view that before the Flood men had lived to many hundreds of years, though none to a full thousand, as some believed. Since that time it was not uncommon even in English vil-lages for people to live beyond 80, but a significantly longer lifespan was rare. Bacon sought means to ensure that the maximum number of people lived out this natural span comfortably, before reaching a 'natural death' through

[7] Thomas R. Cole, *The Journey of Life: A Cultural History of Aging in America* (Cambridge, 1992), 40–7.
[8] G. R. Gruman, 'The Rise and Fall of Prolongevity Hygiene', *Bulletin of the History of Medicine*, 35 (1961), 221–9; and 'A History of Ideas about the Prolongation of Life', *Transactions of the American Philosophical Society*, 56/9 (1966), 1–97.   [9] C. Webster, *The Great Instauration* (London, 1976), xx, 246–7.

gradual dessication. He believed that people lived longer in cold climates, on islands, in highlands, marshes and fens, and in pure air, which preserved their moisture. The age and state of health of their parents at their conception was important and that of the mother while pregnant. 'Thereafter we suppose all things in moderation to be best.' He advocated research into medicines to prolong life but believed that their effects could only be temporary: 'Lengthening of life requires Observation of Diets and attention to the emotions'; grief, fear, and envy were bad; joy and hope good:

We should lead such a youth and manhood that our old age should find new solaces, whereof the chief is moderate ease.

But it was important

that they surrender not themselves to a sluggish ease, but that they embrace something which may Entertain their thoughts and mind with contentation, in which kind the chief delights are Reading and Contemplation; and then the desires of Building and Planting.

It was desirable to exclude air from the body, to anoint it lightly with oil. Moderate exercise was good, and deep breathing, so was the right frame of mind: 'an inward joy, sparingly vented, doth comfort the heart'. Diet should not be too simple, but varied enough to stimulate the appetite; even large feasts were acceptable if they were not too frequent. Bacon discussed how to preserve the blood, the bowels, and other parts of the body; the signs of impending death and the physical and emotional differences between young and old men. He discussed the virtues and the weakness 'Of Youth and Age' even-handedly: the impetuosity of young men was a problem, their inventiveness valuable. Old men might be too cautious, but they were experienced and judicious. He concluded: 'Certainly it is good to Compound employments of both . . . because the Vertues of either Age may correct the defects of both'. Bacon's utopian writings probably reached a wider public than his scientific and philosophical ones. His utopian fragment *New Atlantis* (1626), went through eight editions between 1626 and 1658. These writings described mines, laboratories, and gardens designed to perfect man's control over the environment and provided advice on diet and medicines to prolong life. Bacon collected systematic medical data to enable physicians to come to a new understanding of the mechanisms of the body and the nature of disease.[10]

Others were optimistic that superlongevity not only could but did exist. This belief was encouraged by the existence of apparently attested cases. That these were generally found among the rural poor was taken as proof that the immoderate life of modern, especially urban, society was the chief cause of 'premature' sickness and death. 'Old Parr', for example, Thomas Parr, who was allegedly 153 when he died in London in 1635 aroused both elite and

[10] Webster, *Great Instauration*, 249.

popular excitement. His death followed being brought as a curiosity to the Court. William Harvey dissected him and attributed his death to the sudden transition to the sulphurous air and rich living of London from the 'perfect purity' of air, meagre diet, and freedom from care which the elite believed characterized the lives of seventeenth-century rural labourers. Harvey did not question Parr's longevity, which was probably attained by his, consciously or not, adopting his father's birth-date. The apparent achievement of fit old age— Parr boasted that he had done penance for adultery at age 105—brought the rewards of curiosity value, so that, as Thomas Fuller remarked, 'many old men . . . set the clock of their age too fast when once past seventy, and, grow-ing ten years in a twelvemonth, are presently fourscore'. Only in the nine-teenth century were seventeenth-century claims of superlongevity thoroughly discredited.[11]

Medicine

Harvey represented the contemporary trend away from the previous domin-ance of theoretical, humoral Galenism in medicine, in the direction of induct-ive experimental natural philosophy. The growing interest in pathology, dissection, and practical anatomy in Europe from the sixteenth century, centred on France but widely disseminated in England and elsewhere, increased descriptive knowledge of the ageing body and to some degree of the ageing neurological system. François Ranchin, Professor at Montpellier, in 1627 published in his *Opuscula Medica* a plea that medicine should take the needs of older people more seriously for:

Not only physicians, but everybody else attending old people, being accustomed to their constant complaints and knowing their ill-tempered and difficult manners, realize how noble and important, how serious and *difficult*, how *useful* and even *indis-pensable* is that part of practical medicine called Gerocomica, which deals with the conservation of old people and the healing of their diseases . . . this science has been neglected by our forefathers and even by modern authors too. What has been writ-ten about the conservation of old people and the healing of the diseases of old age, is so bad and so unproductive that we get the impression not only that this noblest part of medicine was not cultivated but even that, yes, it has been flatly suppressed and buried.

Ranchin described what were seen as the specific disorders of older people, both physical and neurological. He related particular types of diet and medical remedies to particular ailments, insisting that even diseased older people were capable of cure. Through the seventeenth and eighteenth centuries in Europe, knowledge about bodily changes associated with ageing grew much faster than effective therapies. This included knowledge about strokes and their effects

[11] W. Thoms, *Longevity in Man: Its Facts and Fiction* (London, 1873).

and about arteriosclerotic changes. Medical men sought to distinguish normal from pathological ageing. It became clearer that many diseases experienced in old age, especially lung infections, ran chronic almost symptomless courses and might be more easily overlooked than in younger people; apparently disease-free 'natural' ageing might mask undetected disease.

Nevertheless Ranchin was correct that this branch of medicine aroused little interest in medical circles and that, still, little could be done for the health of older people other than to advise on a regimen of temperance. The flow of such regimens continued, such as that of Christian Wilhelm Hufeland (1762–1836), friend of Goethe, translated in 1797 as *The Art of Prolonging Life* and widely read throughout Europe. Older rules were popular throughout the eighteenth century. In 1711 Joseph Addison in the *Spectator* enthusiastically endorsed the Italian Cornaro's system of the sixteenth century. In translation it went through fifty editions in English in the eighteenth and nineteenth centuries, expressing as it did the principles of Cicero and the long tradition of observing moderation in all things for preservation of the health of body and soul.[12] In similar vein in England George Cheyne in 1724 published *An Essay of Health and Long Life* and in 1781 Samuel Tissot produced *Advice to the People of England with Regard to their Health*.[13]

Among English medical writers, Dr John Smith whose *Portrait of Old Age* (1666) went through several editions in the seventeenth century, defined three phases of old age, but did not specify their chronological boundaries. During the first which he describes as 'crude, green and while it is yet at the beginning' men could still perform useful work. The second phase 'full, mature or ripe', usually brought retirement from active life, but not physical ruin; this he thought was the 'good old age'. The final phase he described as 'extreme, sickly, decrepit, evergrowing old age', miserable partly because its illnesses could not be cured like those of earlier ages. John Pechey and Robert Burton also described the illnesses attendant upon old age for those who did not take due care.[14]

Literary representations of old people

At the beginning of the seventeenth century Ben Jonson satirized pedlars of elixirs of life and other nostrums for delaying old age both in *The Alchemist* and, in passing, in *Volpone*. Volpone himself is an old man who laments

> So many cares, so many maladies,
> So many fears attending on old age,
> Yea, death so often called on, as we wish
> Can be more frequent with 'em. Their limbs faint.

[12] Shulamith Shahar, *Growing Old in the Middle Ages* (London, 1997), 41.
[13] Cole, *Journey of Life*, 96.   [14] Smith, 'Growing Old', 131.

> Their senses dull, their seeing, hearing going
> All dead before them; yea their very teeth
> Their instruments of eating, failing them—
> Yet this is reckoned life![15]

Jonson employs the classic language of lamentation about old age. Yet the reiteration of the word 'their' distances this old man from such experience. His sobriquet, after all, is the Fox and the theme of the play is his pleasure in tormenting people who seek to inherit his fortune. And, as he goes on, he rejects stereotypical old age for himself:

> Nay here was one
> Is now gone home, that wishes to live longer!
> Feels not his gout, nor palsy, feigns himself
> Younger, by scores of years, flatters his age
> With confident belying it, hopes he may
> With Chains, like Season have his youth restored.

Elsewhere Volpone asserts, as he woos a young woman:

> I am now as fresh
> As hot, as high and in as jovial plight
> As when . . .
> I acted yon Antinous; and attracted
> the eyes and ears of all the ladies present.

Then he tries to rape her. Like Chaucer and Shakespeare, Jonson subverts conventional representations of old age.

In a different genre and tone, at a similar time, John Donne in *The Autumnal* worshipped, beautifully, his 50-year-old mistress, while contrasting her mellow maturity with real old age to come:

> No spring, nor summer beauty hath such grace
> As I have seen in one autumnal face.
> Call not these wrinkles graves; if graves they were
> They were Love's graves; for else he is no where
> Here, where still evening is; not noon, nor night;
> Where no voluptuousness, yet all delight.
> .　.　.　.　.　.　.　.
>
> If we love things long sought, age is a thing
> Which we are fifty years in compassing.
> If transitory things, which soon decay
> Age must be loveliest at the latest day.
> .　.　.　.　.　.　.
>
> But name not winter-faces, whose skin's slack;
> Lank as an unthrift's purse; but a soul's sack;

[15] Ben Jonson, *Volpone*, Act 1, Scene 4.

> Whose eyes seek light within, for all here's shade;
> Whose mouths are holes, rather worn out than made.

Older people were among the butts of satirical drama in early modern England, as in ancient Greece, but so were all other age groups. Restoration drama pilloried older people. For example, 55-year-old Lady Wishfort in Congreve's *Way of the World is* portrayed, as her name suggests, as lusting ludicrously after young men. This has been interpreted as symptomatic of a particular hostility to older women at this time,[16] but Congreve also satirizes old men, such as Foresight in *Love for Love* (1695), an 'illiterate old fellow, peevish and positive, superstitious and pretending to understand astrology, palmistry, physiognomy, omens, dreams etc.', in fact one of the stock figures of seventeenth-century comedy. He is teased for his inability to use his occult knowledge to rejuvenate himself.[17] Congreve also satirized more conventional representations of old age. The central character of his first play *The Old Batchelour* (1693),[18] Heartwell, declares, as he confesses his love for a younger woman:

O dotage, dotage! That ever that noble passion, Lust, should ebb to this degree. No reflux of vigorous Blood, but milky Love supplies the empty channels and prompts me to the softness of a Child.[19]

He complains:

S'death how the young fellows will hoot me! I shall be the Jest of the Town. Nay in two days, I expect to be chronicled in Ditty and sung in woeful Ballad, to the tune of the Superannuated Maiden's Comfort, or the Batchelour's Fall; and upon the third I shall be hanged in effigie, pasted up for the exemplary ornament of necessary Houses and Cobblers Stalls—Death, I can't think on it.[20]

Yet he is fit enough to escape being made a fool by his duplicitous beloved, and in other respects is represented as distinctly sharp and active.

A computer analysis of images and impressions of old age in two hundred and eighty seven 'great works of Western literature' by about eighty-seven authors (the Bible included) 'found no clear patterns over time or in any other dimension'. It identified 15 cases in which old people were presented as abused; 20 were avaricious, 12 were calm, 21 clever or shrewd, 28 irritable, 39 good and compassionate, 22 lustful, 24 austere, 15 ridiculed, 13 respected, 14 noble or honourable, 43 wise, 30 unhappy or melancholic. Whatever the limitations of such an analysis, it confirms the impression from a highly selective sampling that early modern literature, like that of other periods, presents not a

[16] Charles Carlton, 'The Widow's Tale: Male Myths and Female Reality in 16th and 17th Century England', *Albion*, 20 (1978), 118–29.

[17] Congreve, *Love for Love*, Act 4, Scene 1, lines 555 ff.

[18] Very popular in its early years and through the 18th cent. but almost never performed in recent years.

[19] Congreve, *The Old Batchelour*, Act 3, Scene 2.   [20] Ibid.

uniform representation of old age as gloomy or otherwise, nor clear shifts in dominant perceptions over time, but rather a generally realistic representation of the variety of experience of old age, combined with an intriguing vein of satire of the gloomier representations of old age.[21] Analyses of Western art reach similar conclusions.[22]

Popular proverbs first recorded in early modern times but often much older display a similar variety of perceptions:

Old and tough, young and tender.
An old fox is not easily snared.
An old fox need learn no craft.
An old man's bed is full of bones.
Better to be an old man's darling than a young man's warling (i.e. despised, disliked).
Kindness is lost that's bestowed on children and old folks.
He wrongs not an old man that steals his supper from him.
If the young man would and the old man could there would be nothing left undone.
Young men think old men fools and old men know young men to be so.
An old ox makes a straight furrow.
Use an old physician but a young surgeon.
Old Physicians best and young lawyers.
The older the better.
The older the worse.[23]

EIGHTEENTH-CENTURY DISCOURSES ON OLD AGE

The search for control over nature, including over the length of life, continued through the eighteenth century, and its crazier manifestations remained irresistible butts of satirists. Fiercest of all in English was Swift. When Gulliver's travels brought him to Luggnagg he was entranced to discover that a small minority of children of that country were born to experience eternal life. The Luggnaggians politely pointed out that an encounter with the living examples, the Strudbuggs, would disabuse him. Like Tithonus, they had eternal life but not eternal youth.[24] Unlike Tithonus they did not wither into insensibility (or become cicadas) but froze at extreme old age, and indeed were so cast down by the knowledge of their fate that they achieved little after age 30:

---

[21] L. Berman and I. Sobkowska-Ashcroft, *Images and Impressions of Old Age in the Great Works of Western Literature (700 BC–1900 AD): An Analytical Compendium* (Lewiston, NY, 1987). R. E. Yahnke and R. M. Eastman, *Aging in Literature: A Reader's Guide* (Chicago and London, 1990). P. von Dorotka Baguell and P. S. Soper, *Perceptions of Aging in Literature: A Cross-Cultural Study* (Westport, Conn., 1989).

[22] P. McKee and H. Kauppinen, *Art of Aging: A Celebration of Old Age in Western Art* (New York, 1987).

[23] *The Oxford Dictionary of English Proverbs*, 3rd edn., revised by F. P. Wilson (Oxford, 1970).

[24] See p. 33.

When they came to fourscore years, which is reckoned the extremity of living in this country, they had not only the follies and infirmities of old men, but many more which arose from the dreadful prospect of never dying. They were not only opinionative, peevish, covetous, morose, vain, talkative, but uncapable of friendship and dead to all natural affection, which never descended below their grandchildren. Envy and impotent desires are their prevailing passions . . . They have no remembrance of anything but what they learned and observed in their youth and middle age and even that is very imperfect. And for the truth or particulars of any fact, it is safer to depend on common traditions than upon their best recollections.

. . . They are despised and hated by all sorts of people . . . They were the most mortifying sight I ever beheld, and the women more horrible than the men. Besides the usual deformities in extreme old age, they acquired an additional ghastliness in proportion to their number of years . . .[25]

It is a revolting description, though no more so than the normal conventions of describing extreme old age.

Eighteenth-century writing about old age was more secular in tone than before though no less moralistic. Swift's contemporary Defoe also took a gloomy view. 'Young people', he wrote in 1727 'look upon their elders as a different species . . . they . . . ascribe no merit to the virtue and experience of old age, but assume to themselves the preference in all things.' This was perhaps influenced by his personal experience of rejection by his own son. This age-old complaint was challenged in the same year by Edward Hyde, Earl of Clarendon, in *A Dialogue between A an old courtier; B an old lawyer; C an old soldier; D an old country gentleman; E an old alderman, on the want of respect due to age*. These old men, all aged over 70, engaged in conversation, reminiscent, perhaps consciously, of those decribed by Cephalus in Plato's *Republic*.[26] The courtier, the country gentleman, and the lawyer agree that:

Youth is heady and proud and age hath lost all the Reverence that is due to it . . . there is a great difference between the respect we paid when we were young and that which we receive now we are old.

Reverence 'which from the Beginning of the World to the Time in which our fathers died, was never made a question'.

The old soldier and the old alderman vigorously disagree. The alderman proclaims:

From the time I was a boy to this hour, old men have complained how much the Times are worse than they were and how much old age was despised . . . I say grave and wise old men have the same or greater reverence paid to them than they had in former times; and weak and willful and impertinent old men were as little respected then as they are now.

. . . You talk as if old age had such an attractive Beauty, that all Men must fall down at the Feet of everyone that is Old . . . men must have somewhat else than Wrinkles to find Reverence.

---

[25] Jonathan Swift, *Gulliver's Travels* (Harmondsworth, 1967), 256–9.   [26] See pp. 35–6.

The three cannot be persuaded. B asserts that he 'would have no man under Fifty preferred to any place or office of authority, if there be an elder man than he fit for the office'.

C supports E:

My friend Seneca who is my best conversation and indeed keeps me in my right wits when I am ready to fall into your lamentations, complains of the old men of his time, who then complained as we do, of those who were young.

He argues that if elders acted kindly to their children they would be repaid in kind. Princes, he claims, are best advised by people of varied ages and old men should not covet such positions, but should gracefully retire as their faculties diminish, then:

those parts which after the first Decay are in a short time worn out in Action, will by a timely recess remain long with their old lustre and keep their age very venerable to those who shall be admitted to their conversation . . . what monuments of reverence would be raised to such men.

B and D are convinced, but A obstinately is not.

Alexander Pope expressed a popular contemporary theme when he claimed in his own version of the Ages of Man, *An Essay on Man* (1733–4), that the human capacity for hope blinded people to the miseries of each stage of life:

No-one will change his neighbour with himself
See some strange comfort every state attend
And Pride bestowed on all, a common friend,
See some fit Passion ev'ry age supply
Hope travels through nor quits us when we die.
Behold the child, by nature's kindly law,
Pleas'd with a rattle, tickled with a straw:
Some livelier play-thing gives his youth delight,
A little louder but as empty quite: Scarfs, garters, gold amuse his riper stage:
And beads and pray'r-books are the toys of age:
Pleas'd with this bauble still as that before;
'Till tir'd he weeps, and Life's poor play is o'er.

A negative view of old age, before the onset of senility, was by no means dominant in eighteenth-century learned discourse. Hume's *Enquiry Concerning Human Understanding* (1748) describes old people (implicitly old men; as in earlier times, old women rarely figure) as experienced skilful, learned, knowledgeable:

There are changes in sentiments and inclinations in the different ages of a human being, but his character remains fundamentally the same. Experience makes the aged more skilful and knowledgeable.

Adam Smith in *Wealth of Nations* (1776) commented that 'an old man provided his age is not so far advanced as to give suspicion of dotage, is everywhere more respected than a young man of equal rank, fortune and abilities'.[27]

Samuel Johnson wrote frequently about the variety of experience and expectations of old age, for example in *Rasselas* and *The Vanity of Human Wishes*. His own old age (he died aged 74 in 1784) is described in detail by Boswell and in his own letters.[28] Despite increasing illness, (asthma, gout, dropsy, a stroke), he is represented as remaining socially highly active, until his final year dining out almost daily, and mentally alert 'and his mind happier than perhaps it had ever been'.[29]

From the seventeenth century we can reconstruct how some people at least —the literate and generally the relatively powerful—represented their own old age, and how they were seen by others, in letters, diaries, biographies and autobiographies. Many such sources describe old ages of varying degrees of discomfort but of continuing lively engagement with the world, and little sign of disrespect from others. The exceptionally powerful Sarah, Duchess of Marlborough, died in 1744 aged 84. She was a friend of Queen Anne, wife of and profound influence upon the Queen's most powerful subject, John, Duke of Marlborough. She was highly intelligent and had wide interests though little formal education. At 63 she was still described as beautiful, with 'the most expressive eyes and the finest hair imaginable'; she rejected a proposal of remarriage from the wealthy and proud Duke of Somerset because she preferred her independence.[30] From her later sixties her mobility was inhibited by 'gout' (probably a form of inflammatory arthritis or rheumatism) and she was more often ill in winter but she remained a major creditor of the government and was still politically active. Even when she walked uneasily on a stick at George II's coronation in 1727 she was described as making 'a better figure than many of her juniors'.

In her seventies she was ill more often than not, unable to walk and able to write only with difficulty. She grieved for the deaths of children and grandchildren and unashamedly used her control of the family wealth to dominate those who survived. Her immobility frustrated her but she was still able to place her grandsons in positions of influence, wishing that she were a man so that she could exert power overtly. She joined the king and queen at their gaming table and, in the eyes of a court observer, 'she really look'd as well and young as she has done these ten years and much better than most people there'. She travelled unsuccessfully in search of a cure. She did not give in to old age as a period of dependency and passivity or even as one of well-earned rest. Instead at 75, unable to walk and itching from a skin condition, she chose to be active and influential at the centre of opposition to the government.

[27] Adam Smith, *The Wealth of Nations* (3rd edn., 1784), book ii, p. 233.
[28] *Boswell's Life of Johnson*, vol. iv, ed. G. Birkbeck Hill (Oxford, 1934).   [29] Ibid. i. n. i.
[30] Frances Harris, *The Life of Sarah, Duchess of Marlborough* (Oxford, 1991), 252.

She wrote at the time: 'At my age I cannot expect to continue long, nor have I anything now left to make me desirous of it'. But she had been writing thus for twelve years and more and more her actions continued to belie her words. She spent more time in the country, reading, accompanied by her dogs—and buying yet more land, extensively and profitably. She complained of constant pain, but was fully mentally agile and could use her wealth to compensate for her disabilities. Servants cared for her, carried her about, wrote at her dictation, obeyed her every wish.

In her eighty-first year she bought and furnished a town house for her daughter. Like many old people, poor as well as rich, in all times she gave to younger people at least as much as she received. Singing ballads as she worked, she congratulated herself on being still 'the best upholsterer in England'. She held regular musical supper parties which lasted until two or three in the morning and went out with friends to eat cheese-cake and to 'hear fine Musick'. She was always alert to the fear that she was being overlooked in politics because, as she said, 'an old woman is a very insignificant thing'. There is little sign that anyone regarded her as insignificant even at such an advanced age, but it is notable that she employed the negative stereotype, presumably conscious of fighting against it. In her final year she was weaker. Her final illness lasted only four days.

Sarah's old age is unusually fully documented. She was an unusually powerful woman and a well-known public figure. Her positive image of old age was highly visible. Her experience, and that of other elite women,[31] calls in question notions that women were normally treated and represented negatively in early modern England. She was by no means the only powerful old widow of her time.[32]

Old women and men of the middling sort could also represent themselves and be represented positively.[33] The Quaker merchant William Stout recorded in 1736, when he was 71, that he had just travelled to a meeting of Friends in Whitehaven

which I performed with as much ease as when I was about 20 years of age . . . And I had hitherto had my health very well and have not been at 1s expence to doctor, apothecary or physik or surgery for therty years last past. And I have hitherto accustomed my selfe to rise at the sunrise in summer and walke a round of two miles in the morning . . . and in my garden an hower or more in the evening. I began to use spectakles at 50 years of age and could not see to read or write without them till I was 70 years old; but since then my eyesight had recovered gradualy, so that I can now see to write and read without them.[34]

[31] e.g. Anne Kugler ' "I Feel Myself Decay Apace": Old Age in the Diary of Lady Sarah Cowper (1644–1720)', in L. Botelho and P. Thane (eds.), *Women and Ageing in British Society since 1500* (London, 2000).   [32] Harris, *Sarah*.

[33] Amy M. Froide, 'Old Maids: The Life-Cycle of Single Women in Early Modern England', in Botelho and Thane, *Women and Ageing*.

[34] J. D. Marshall (ed.), *The autobiography of William Stout of Lancaster, 1665–1752* (Manchester, 1967), 219.

Stout's life changed little until 1743, when he was seriously injured by a run-away horse and his diary ceases. He died in 1752.

Old people who were a visible presence in society influenced perceptions of old age in early modern England, as did drama, sermons, medical texts, and the range of media of representation. All expressed the variety of the experience of old age, the difference between 'green' old age and later decrepitude and the positive potential of the earlier phase of old age. Not evident in such English representations and self-representations of old age are the shifts discerned in eighteenth-century France, where, it seems, older people came to be more honoured and less derided than before.[35] Rather, as for long before, and after, honour and dishonour were simultaneously experienced by, and attributed to older people, contingent upon their personal and social situations. As in all times 'old people' were not a homogeneous category.

---

[35] David G. Troyansky, *Old Age in the Old Regime: Image and Experience in Eighteenth-Century France* (Ithaca, NY, 1989); and 'Balancing Social and Cultural Approaches to the History of Old Age and Ageing in Europe', in Paul Johnson and Pat Thane (eds.), *Old Age from Antiquity to Post-Modernity* (London, 1998), 96–109.

Experiences

5

Independent Old People: Making a Living in Medieval England

Old people were a substantial presence in past societies and they had an unmistakable presence also in the self-images of those societies, as expressed in a variety of forms of representation. But how did they perceive themselves and how did they live through the experience of ageing?

Material resources were obviously crucial. In medieval Europe to have sufficient personal resources for a comfortable life required ownership or secure tenure of real property, though cash resources became increasingly important over time. Such material security enabled older people to be agents in the management of their own lives and extended the range of options available to them.[1] Those who could afford it might extend their landholdings as their families grew and might adjust to ageing by gradual disposal, beginning when they were in their fifties, though the possibility of making such transactions depended upon local custom and upon the state of the property market.[2] Property might be transferred to offspring, as a means of discharging the strong social obligation upon parents in England to assist their children to acquire independence.[3] If children were already provided for, or there were none, property might be leased or sold to others, the ageing tenant living on the income, retaining such property as he or she could manage; or ageing people could pay others to work the land.

A substantial and persistent body of folklore, sermons, and proverbs warned old people not to give away complete control of their property to others, even to close kin, an ancient message which achieved its most sublime expression in William Shakespeare's *King Lear*, a story which itself existed in many variants in medieval Europe.[4] Much earlier, and international, is the cautionary tale of the man who, tired of caring for his old father, started to carve a trough from which the old man was to eat (or in another version took up a piece of sacking for his father's only bedding).[5] As he did so his own son passed by and remarked that he would make a similar trough when

[1] C. Dyer, *Standards of Living in the Later Middle Ages* (Cambridge, 1989), 244.
[2] C. Dyer, 'Changes in the Size of Peasant Holdings in some West Midland Villages, 1400–1500', in R. M. Smith (ed.), *Land, Kinship, and Life Cycle* (Cambridge, 1984), 287–319. Elaine Clark, 'Some Aspects of Social Security in Medieval England', *Journal of Family History*, 7/4 (1982), 307–20.
[3] Below, p. 120.   [4] Shulamith Shahar, *Growing Old in the Middle Ages* (London, 1997), 94.
[5] B. Hanawalt, *The Ties that Bind: Peasant Families in Medieval England* (Oxford, 1986), 227.

his father aged (or the son tears the sacking in half and says that he will save half for his own father's old age). The father is duly chastened. In a simpler and more brutal version the old man is gradually demoted from a place of honour at the top of the table to a bench behind the door, where he dies in misery.[6] Another popular tale grants the old person canny agency: an old man cures his son and daughter-in-law of neglecting him by claiming that he had not, after all, given them the whole of his fortune. The remainder was locked in a chest and would be theirs on his death, if they treated him well. When he dies they rush to open the chest. It contains a large club inscribed: 'He who gives so that he must beg ought to be clubbed until he lies out flat'.[7]

Dives and Pauper, 'perhaps the most comprehensive and popular late medieval English exposition of the ten commandments',[8] stated that it was more seemly for parents to put themselves in their children's keeping than in that of strangers; but however much they trusted them they should always retain ultimate control of their estates and thus 'kepyn her [their] chilryn in her daunger (power)'. Such warnings reverberate through the centuries and through Europe. They prevailed in the peasant cultures of poorer parts of Europe, including Scandinavia, north Germany, Scotland, France, and Italy at least into the eighteenth century.[9] In the later eighteenth century on the town gates of some cities of Brandenburg hung large clubs with the inscription:

He who has made himself dependent on his children for bread and suffers from want, he shall be knocked dead by this club.

The Scots expressed similar sentiments in a poem:

> Here is the fair mall
> To give a knock on the skull
> To the man who keeps no gear for himself
> But gives all to his bairns.[10]

Peasant proverbs conveyed similar warnings: 'To hand over is no longer to live.' 'To sit on the children's bench is hard for the old.' 'Do not take your clothes off before you go to sleep.'[11] Anthropologists find similiar injunctions not to bequeath property in one's lifetime to be almost universal.[12]

---

[6] R. Houlbrooke, *The English Family, 1450–1700* (London, 1984), 190; Shahar, *Growing Old*, 93.

[7] Houlbrooke, *English Family*, 190.   [8] Ibid.

[9] David Gaunt, 'The Property and Kin Relationships of Retired Families in Northern and Central Europe', in R. Wall, J. Robin, P. Laslett (eds.), *Family Forms in Historic Europe* (Cambridge, 1983), 249–80; O. Hufton, *The Poor of Eighteenth-Century France, 1750–1799* (Oxford, 1974), 112–13; Shahar, *Growing Old*, 93.

[10] Gaunt, 'Property and Kin', 259.

[11] M. Mitterauer and R. Sieder, *The European Family* (Oxford, 1982), 167.

[12] P. Amos and S. Harrell (eds.), *Other Ways of Growing Old: Anthropological Perspectives* (Stanford, Calif., 1981), 12.

RETIREMENT CONTRACTS

Against this background it is not surprising that in most European countries strategies emerged whereby individuals ensured that they and/or their surviving spouses would be provided for in old age. The most formalized of these was the retirement contract. This was common in various forms in most peasant societies.[13] They survive in significant numbers in England from the thirteenth century and continued everywhere for as long as a substantial small landholding class survived.[14] They were agreements whereby the tenant or owner of property transferred control to another on condition that he or she received care and/or an effective 'pension' for the remainder of his or her life. In medieval England such contracts involving tenants could not be made without the agreement of the lord who controlled the land and they had always to be recorded in the manorial court. Lords seem rarely to have interfered in such transactions if their own interests were not disadvantaged. Such arrangements enabled them to solve the problem of finding a successor if the tenant died without an heir. The lord gained from the fees levied for such contracts. It was in his interest to have the land worked by fit and able tenants and to keep a stable, and contented, tenant population. Furthermore, the prevention of pauperism on the manor was his responsibility. Land transfers designed to provide for the upkeep of a widow or of ageing people, sanctioned by the lord, provided effectively for the welfare of needy people at a time when no formal welfare system existed.

The conditions agreed in the contracts could include provision of shelter, food and drink, clothing and much else. The details of contracts varied with the needs and whims of the person who was retiring, the value of the holding, and the extent of his or her bargaining power, which was in part determined by the scarcity of land and the enthusiasm of takers for such an encumbered holding. In periods of land shortage, such as the early fourteenth century, older people could drive particularly hard bargains. We have no idea how widespread such contracts were in England, or in what circumstances individuals did or did not make them, or whether there were systematic changes over time and from place to place in the terms and conditions. Their value lies in the glimpses they provide into the otherwise hidden lives of older people in the distant past, in particular the picture they convey of ageing people

---

[13] Smith, *Land, Kinship*; Gaunt, 'Property and Kin'; Thomas Held, 'Rural Retirement Arrangements in 17th and 18th century Austria: A Cross-Community Analysis', *Journal of Family History* 7/3 (1982), 227–50, among others.

[14] As in Canada and Ireland well into the 20th cent. Liam Kennedy, 'Farm Succession in Modern Ireland: Elements of a Theory of Inheritance', *Economic History Review*, 2nd ser. 44 (1991), 477–99. J. G. Snell, 'Maintenance Agreements for the Elderly: Canada 1900–50', *Journal of the Canadian Historical Association*, NS, 3 (1992), 197–216.

directing their own lives and striving to preserve their independence, contrary to the stereotype of passive dependency of older people. They display old people carefully planning the maximum use of resources available to them.[15]

The surviving English contracts rarely specify the ages of the people concerned. Peasants in northern Europe are found entering into such contracts in the eighteenth and nineteenth centuries at ages ranging from 37 to 81.[16] Contracts were entered into, generally, because older people could no longer manage independently on the land or no longer wished to. They might be prompted by illness, the death of a spouse, or marriage of an heir. Details of surviving medieval English contracts varied but certain characteristics were common to many of them. The 'pensioner' generally preferred, at least in the first instance, not to move house. Since only the well-to-do could afford to retain a separate dwelling, this often entailed sharing accommodation with the new tenants, whether or not they were kin. When there was room the elderly person, or couple, might specify their entitlement to space in order to avoid one of the fates prevalent in folklore: relegation to some unregarded corner of the dwelling. Most surviving agreements specify that the old person(s) concerned should occupy a separate apartment. The less fortunate could claim only a 'small space for a bed' and a 'place by the fire', though it should be remembered that neither they nor their successors at this time would be accustomed to much space or privacy. Ageing people ensured their own freedom of movement by demanding access to kitchens, pantries, latrines, wells for drawing water, barns for stocking wood. Sometimes they remodelled a house to include a 'parlour', a 'bedchambre', or a room called the 'spense' for their own use.[17]

In 1286 William de Toneville entered the manorial court at Heacham in Norfolk and spoke of his 'old age, his physical disability and poverty', which prevented his cultivating his land without help from 'friends' or his son. The bailiff and steward took counsel with their lord, the Prior of Lewes. It was decided to approve the surrender of the father's house and lands to his son, along with the father's obligations for rent, service, and the maintenance of a daughter. The son agreed to feed, clothe, and 'honestly support' both his father and his sister. To confirm the arrangement he paid the Prior one mark.[18]

It was not uncommon for contracts to include such obligations to landless dependants of the 'pensioner' nor for the obligation to maintain to be put in such general terms, relying upon trust rather than exact specification. More specific details may have been inserted when trust was uncertain, or the pensioner cautious. In 1305, at Gressenhale, Henry the son of Leste transferred seventeen acres to a man apparently unrelated to him, on condition of 'honest and competent' care for the remainder of his life. But it was specified

[15] Clark, 'Some Aspects', 315. See also Elaine Clark, 'The Quest for Social Security in Medieval England', in M. M. Sheehan (ed.), *Aging and the Aged in Medieval Europe* (Toronto, 1990), 189–200.
[16] Gaunt, 'Property and Kin'.   [17] Clark, 'Some Aspects', 314.   [18] Ibid.

that if discord arose the new tenant must provide yearly eight bushels of wheat, eight bushels of rye, and thirty-two bushels of barley; if the old tenant predeceased the new, the latter must pay twenty shillings to cover burial and funeral expenses.[19]

More specific was the contract whereby Henry son of Stephen transferred five acres plus a meadow to another man who was not his relative, his wife and their heirs at Gressenhale in 1352, on condition that they pay him twenty shillings at the next feast day of St Martin, forty bushels of grain annually on 20 September, twenty-four of barley each Christmas, eight of wheat at Easter, eight of rye annually and also annually two pairs of sheets, three shillings for various types of clothing, one pair of shoes, and two pairs of stockings. On the basis of a small piece of land Henry drove a hard bargain even at a time when there was no land shortage. When such large amounts of goods were specified it is likely that he intended to enhance his income by selling some of them.

At Wymondham in 1412 William Hardyng and Agnes his wife assigned to Richard Hardyng and Margaret his wife two specified pieces of land. In return the older couple were to be supplied with food and drink, clothing, footwear, and all other necessities. The new tenants were to discharge all the old tenants' debts, to cover all funeral expenses, and arrange for the celebration of masses for their souls. Also at Wymondham, Norfolk, in 1419 William Notte transferred to his son one messuage [a dwelling plus outbuildings and adjacent land], plus a fairly substantial amount of land, the conditions being the reservation for his use of one room at the northern end of the hall. Also he was to receive food and clothing, to be allowed to warm himself at the fire, and to have a horse and saddle in order to ride whenever he wished; also annually the son was to plough and seed three acres of his land and maintain twenty-four ewes.

Contracts could be based on quite modest holdings. In East Anglia between the mid-thirteenth and the mid-fifteenth centuries only 25 per cent (about thirty-eight) of known contracts concerned the surrender of ten acres or more. Many pensioners:

stipulated how their land was to be cropped, what portion of the yield they expected . . . whether comprised solely of wheat or barley, a combination of both or a mixture that also included oats, rye and beans . . . Pensioners also planted gardens, kept bees for honey and tended little orchards for apples and pears. When the farmstead included animals, pensioners ordered them kept at the new tenant's expense and in this way ensured for themselves a supply of meat, milk, eggs, and wool. On tenements with ponds old men claimed the right to go fishing whenever they wished. All assigned the upkeep of buildings, along with the repair of fences and boundaries, to new tenants.[20]

---

[19] Ibid. 317–18.   [20] Ibid.

Contracts could be made by men or women or by a married couple jointly. At Horsham St Faith in 1429 Margaret, widow of Clement Chapelyn, transferred to John Chapelyn and his heirs four acres plus one rod. The widow was to keep for life one hall called 'la newhalle', a storeroom at the east end of the hall, access to a kitchen under the roof of the new hall, easement in (access to) the bakehouse for malting, thirty-two bushels of barley with use of John's kiln, a stable at the west end of the messuage except during the fair of St Faith when its use was reserved to John; easement to a well for drawing water; free ingress and egress in the garden for 'visiting' bees; one cow, one pig, one cock, six hens kept in the messuage. If John were to predecease the (evidently very active) widow, whose age is unknown, his heirs or assigns were to pay her six shillings and eight pence each year for life. John was to have free entry and exit to the widow's upper room in order to enter his own upper room and easement in the kitchen. This suggests not only a widow with a clear idea of what she wanted in later life but also how an active older country woman spent her time.

Since, strictly, contracts concerned the property rather than the individual, it was not unusual for obligations to be placed upon successive tenants, as in the above example. In 1290 a widow exploited particular circumstances to drive a still harder bargain. Matilda Saleman entered into a covenant whereby Henry Cosin married her pregnant daughter. In return they were to serve her well and faithfully for the remainder of her life. For as long as they did so, Matilda would provide them with food and clothing and allow them an unsown acre each year which they were to sow and crop at their own expense. Matilda had turned the young couple's misfortune to her own good, ensuring that she was cared for for life, without even committing herself to pass the land to them or ruling out the possibility of her own remarriage.

The sanction of the manorial court added to the security of the deal for the older person, since the authority of the court could be invoked should the new tenant renege. The 'pensioner' could, and some did, reclaim the tenancy in such circumstances. In the manor of Great Waltham in Essex in 1327 a widow, Estrilda Nenour, claimed in court that in 1322 she had made a contract with her daughter Agnes, transferring her holding of one messuage and fifteen acres of land and specifying in return that Agnes should maintain her by providing accommodation in the messuage plus food and clothing of unspecified amount. It was specified that if Agnes defaulted Estrilda should regain possession of her property and chattels. Estrilda claimed such a default against the now married Agnes. A jury reported that Estrilda's claim was just. Her rightful property and goods were seized by the court and she received six shillings and eight pence compensation. In the next court Estrilda registered a new agreement with Robert Levekyn and his wife, who appear to have been unrelated to her. They agreed to provide her with the same benefits that Agnes had promised, but this time a clause was entered stating that if Estrilda was unhappy with the working of that arrangement Robert and Alice were to provide her with an annual cash payment of twenty shillings and eight pence.[21]

If an aged person became incapable without making arrangements the lord could reclaim the property and make alternative arrangements for his or her care. At Hindolveston, Norfolk, in 1382 lived a 'poor little woman', a widow holding some eighteen acres of arable. She was 'feeble of body and simple of mind', unable to care for herself and without the means to render service to the lord. He therefore granted the land to her 'nearest heir', ordering him to support her for life and feed and clothe her as befitted a widow. In case of default the lord could enforce the order.[22] In another Norfolk case of the later fourteenth century, in which a woman judged mentally incompetent and worn out by age had no relatives living near by, the lord assigned her holding of three acres to two local men on condition that they seed, plough, and harvest the land, using its crops to provide the widow with 'all her necessities'.[23]

Increasingly after 1380 arrangements for an ageing partner could be made on the death-bed, a practice which preceded will-making.[24] A representative of the manor court could record the wishes of the dying person which would later be formally agreed in court. At Wymondham in 1426 the court roles record that when dying Richard Sothereye transferred to Nicholas Blithe and Alice his wife two acres, a half-rod of customary land, and one built-up property with appurtenances. In return they were to pay to his wife Alice a cash sum in yearly instalments and reserve to her one room at the south end of the hall; she was to warm herself at their fire as often as she wished. They were to build for her a 'chimne' of clay. If the new tenants predeceased the widow or the husband died and the wife remarried a room must still be reserved for the widow.[25]

Contracts had the advantage for an ageing person that they enabled him or her to specify their successor. For the other party to the contract, it could be a means for the landless to obtain land or of the landed to extend their holdings. They were also made by holders of urban tenements; or an urban business might be traded for care or a pension in old age. The existence of contracts has been interpreted as evidence of intergenerational tension[26] on the grounds that where trust existed there would be no need for such

---

[21] R. M. Smith, 'The Manorial Court and the Elderly Tenant in Late Medieval England', in M. Pelling and Richard M. Smith, *Life, Death and the Elderly: Historical Perspectives* (London, 1991), 54. Evelyn Searle, 'Seigneurial Control of Women's Marriage: the Antecedents and Function of *Merchet* in England', *Past and Present*, 82 (1979), 37.

[22] Clark, 'Some Aspects', 311.   [23] Ibid. 310.

[24] L. Bonfield and L. R. Poos, 'The Development of the Deathbed Transfer in Medieval English Manor Courts', *Cambridge Law Journal*, 47 (1988), 403–27. Smith, 'Manorial Court', 50.

[25] Similar examples have been found in 16th-cent. Cambridgeshire, Margaret Spufford, *Contrasting Communities* (Cambridge, 1974), 164, 168.

[26] Alan MacFarlane, *The Origins of English Individualism* (Oxford, 1978), 141–3.

formality. Tension there may well have been, and as we have seen, medieval people had no illusions about it. But this is not the only possible explanation. At no time before the twentieth century could an older person confidently expect to die before his or her children. The early death of an heir would leave the older person vulnerable had the property already been passed on without a formal agreement. The formal contract transferred the obligations to the next successor or enabled the retired person to resume control and to make a new contract with another. It was a means for older people to maintain control over their own lives.

It is impossible to tell whether such contracts were just the formal expression of a much more widespread, unrecorded, customary practice of intergenerational support, though this is highly likely.[27] Since only the formal terminology of the contracts survives we know nothing of the informal, unwritten assumptions and expectations that may have shaped transactions between generations, the sensitive negotiations and relationships which lay behind the formal agreements. Given the strong 'moral obligation to use the family land to provide for all its members',[28] it may have been taken for granted that those children who, if they survived, lived near by in what even in the fourteenth century was a highly mobile society, and had sustained good relations with parents, would make all provision they could, and that formal agreements were made only in exceptional circumstances. In Halesowen between 1270 and 1348 forty-one ageing villagers handed their holdings over to their sons; only eight found it necessary to make maintenance agreements. As Razi comments, if they proceeded without an unrecorded understanding that their children should provide for them, 'the retiring landholder of Halesowen must have been really stupid'.[29] By the sixteenth century uncontracted surrenders were not uncommon in Cambridgeshire.[30] When after *c.*1430 more wills survive there are frequent references to informal agreements similar to those in surviving contracts.[31]

Intergenerational transactions varied also with economic circumstances. Where cash transactions were relatively rare and land was the mainstay of the whole family, and relatively scarce, as in the early fourteenth century, ageing landholders could, so long as they retained their faculties, exert considerable power over the younger generation. Willingly or not, the heirs were trapped in the parental household awaiting their inheritance. Such arrangements could, but need not, be tense and normally involved a gradual shift of responsibilities between the generations as the elders declined.[32] The long-run

[27] Dyer, 'Peasant Holdings'.

[28] Zvi Razi, 'Family, Land and the Village Community in Later Medieval England', *Past and Present*, 93 (1981), 7.

[29] Ibid. 8.   [30] Spufford, *Contrasting Communities*, 162–3.

[31] I am grateful to Christopher Dyer for this information.

[32] Ian Blanchard, 'Industrial Employment and the Rural Labour Market, 1380–1520', in Smith, *Land, Kinship*, 228–66.

tendency through the later Middle Ages was towards the greater importance of cash transactions. Richard Smith found that contracts after 1350 specified cash annuities more frequently than before and that co-residence was more rarely specified.[33] But it was not a simple one-way trend; in the inflation of the early sixteenth century, in some districts at least, the patriarchal family dominated by the elder male took on renewed salience.[34] As social polarization increased in the later Middle Ages, however, an increasing proportion of the population had no property with which to set themselves up in old age.

Use of their property in various ways enabled an unknown proportion of older people to achieve a comfortable old age by controlling not only their own lives but those of others. Their influence and prestige derived at least as much from power derived from control of property actively exercised by the ageing person as from any abstract customary esteem for older people.

CORRODIES

Another means whereby people in medieval times, mostly those with means, acquired security in old age, was by negotiating a corrody. When these became more prevalent in the twelfth century the corrody normally involved residence in a religious house, monastery, or hospital on fixed terms similar to those specified in retirement contracts, in return for a gift or a promised inheritance. By the later Middle Ages they were often bought for cash and might consist of food, drink, clothing, or other goods provided for ageing people who rarely or never set foot in the religious house. Not all corrodians were old, but they were one, not necessarily very commonplace,[35] means of providing for one's old age or that of a spouse, servant, or other dependant.[36]

By the thirteenth century there were four main means to obtain a corrody:

1. At royal request. Edward III sent his retired servants north to Durham Priory to be sustained until they died. The peak of royal demands came around 1300 and were becoming an expensive burden on religious foundations, until they learned to evade them by pleading poverty.[37]

2. In return for service to the house. Most religious houses provided corrodies for faithful servants. Archbishop Simon Islip (1349–66) gave to Philip de Milton, as a reward, and because he was 'declining into the feebleness of old age', tenpence halfpenny each week while he remained in the archbishop's service. After his full retirement he was to be received into the hospital of SS Peter and Paul at Maidstone, Kent, and there to be given a room and

---

[33] Smith, 'Manorial Court'.   [34] Blanchard, 'Industrial Employment'.

[35] Joel T. Rosenthal, 'Retirement and the Life Cycle in 15th Century England', in Sheehan, *Aging and the Aged*, 175.

[36] Ibid. 173–88. Barbara Harvey, *Living and Dying in England, 1100–1540: The Monastic Experience* (Oxford, 1993), 179–209.   [37] Ibid. 186.

provided with the same amount of food and drink (or the money to purchase them) that was the ration of one of the brothers of the hospital. This was to last until his death.[38]

A corrody could be a means to ease out an abbot who was too old, incompetent, or otherwise unsuitable. Townsmen who were patrons or business associates of a house might end their days as corrodians within it, as could their servants. At the Carmelite Friary of Lynn (Norfolk) in 1367 a corrody was granted to John Baker, formerly servant of John Pentney, who was prominent in the civic affairs of Lynn, in return for a payment of five marks. Baker was to have for life food and drink, like one of the brethren, a seat in the refectory next to the porter and a bedchamber in the precincts for his own use. He was to serve the friary in the bakery and brewery except in extreme old age and in time of bodily infirmity and to have all emoluments of these offices except wages. Any goods or chattels belonging to him should pass to the friary at his death.[39]

3. As part of a property transaction with a religious house. This was mutually convenient: the house deferred payment for the permanent acquisition of property and the agreement provided security for the old age of the vendor. In the 1230s Alfred of Penhull gave all his lands to Winchester Cathedral Priory. The lands were already deeply in debt, so the prior must have paid the debts. He also gave Alfred a house and a croft to live on and a life pension in grain and cash for himself, his wife, and mother.[40] In 1278 Elias of Foxcote, the steward of Sherborne Abbey, made over all his Sherborne land to the abbey and in addition made a cash payment of one hundred marks (£66.70) in return for a life pension from the abbey of food, clothing, and shelter—an investment in a comfortable old age. Bolton Priory in 1308 started to pay a corrody worth £7.38 per year to William Desert in return for land, and an apartment was constructed for him within the priory. The corrody was still being paid in 1325. However, the land yielded more in rent than the 'pension' and Desert gave the priory good service as administrator and representative in various business dealings.[41] Such transactions were not invariably expressions of monastic charity. The monks could drive hard bargains especially with landholders driven by debt or by some other source of desperation. Sometimes houses put quite unscrupulous pressure on their own tenants to give up their land in exchange for a corrody.[42]

4. Payment of a lump sum in cash for residence and/or provisions for life or for a fixed number of years. Such payments became more common over the course of the Middle Ages but some occurred even amongst the earliest

---

[38] Richard A. Harper, 'A Note on Corrodies in the 14th Century', *Albion*, 15 (1983), 97–101.

[39] Ibid.

[40] R. H. Hilton, *A Medieval Society: The West Midlands at the End of the 13th Century* (London, 1966), 51.

[41] Ian Kershaw, *Bolton Priory: The Economy of a Northern Monastery, 1286–1325* (Oxford, 1973), 135.

[42] Harvey, *Living and Dying*, 192–4.

known arrangements. A woman bought herself a lavish corrody from Winchcome Abbey in 1317 for the considerable sum of 140 marks (£93.38). She received a daily ration of two monk's loaves, a small white loaf, and two gallons of ale. Every year, in addition, she received six pigs, two oxen, twelve cheeses, one hundred stock fish, one thousand herrings, and twenty-four shillings worth of clothing. Presumably she had servants to provide for.[43] A poorer man, also in 1317, John of Staunton, paid Winchcombe Abbey ten marks and all of his worldly goods and declared his willingness to accept any employment the abbot should choose for him. His rations were six bushels of grain every eight weeks; two mutton carcases and two pigs a year; pottage with the other abbey servants and two acres of grain.[44]

Such transactions could be hazardous for the monks. It was reported from Humberstone Abbey in 1440 that the abbot had sold a corrody to John Herdene, harper, for ten marks, granting him in return forty shillings a year 'and so it has been for eight years'.[45] The original investment would have been exhausted in a little over three years. The outcome of such investments was always uncertain because the length of life of the corrodian was unpredictable; it was a form of gambling in life insurance without any of the security underpinning land transactions. Increasingly corrodies were sold for shorter periods for cash, for periods of months or even by the week. The gamble was tempting for houses in financial trouble, but by the fifteenth century monks were increasingly criticized by bishops for indulging in such transactions.[46] Monks were also increasingly criticized for diverting food and care from the poor to normally comfortably off corrodians. Initially corrodians came from backgrounds ranging from the lesser gentry to the landholding peasantry; increasingly over time they came also from the middling sort of townspeople.[47] They received food which might have been given to the poor and were often lodged in the infirmary, where they might also displace needier people.

It is hard to know how many corrodians there were or how many of them were aged. Recorded numbers seem to have reached a peak around 1300, declining to more modest levels by the time of the dissolution of the monasteries in 1530. About one in ten of the residents in dissolved houses were corrodians. Most of the hundreds of monastic institutions in medieval England cared for some old people.

WIDOWS

As we have seen, women might be agents in or beneficiaries of any of these transactions. Given their often longer lives and normally inferior access to

---

[43] Hilton, *A Medieval Society*, 111.   [44] Ibid.   [45] Harper, 'Note', 98.
[46] Harvey, *Living and Dying*, 186.   [47] Ibid.

property rights compared with those of men, it was especially imperative to safeguard their old age. After the Norman Conquest widows were often put under strong pressure by their lords to remarry; in the course of the thirteenth century they acquired greater freedom and choice in the matter.[48] Since Anglo-Saxon times widows had had a legal right to one-third of the husband's property for their lifetimes. In the fourteenth and fifteenth centuries most marriage contracts granted the wife a joint share in part of the husband's lands. This in addition to the one-third dower right could often be kept for life, even if the widow remarried. Widows could fight tenaciously for such rights.

Widows were not necessarily old, but older women were always less likely to remarry than older men. Husbands routinely made careful provision for them, in contracts, on their death-beds, or in later generations in their wills. The details of the arrangement depended upon the fitness of the widow and the age of children.[49] In Orwell (Cambridgeshire) in the fifteenth and sixteenth centuries it was normal to leave the holding to the widow until the heir reached the age of 21 and carefully to specify house room for her thereafter. Similar provision was made at all social levels. William Sam(?)pfield, a labourer who died in 1536, had acquired a cottage with a garden and an orchard by the time of his death. According to his will his wife was to have the whole tenement until her son was aged 22 and then have the right to the 'chamber that I lie in' with the right of entrance and egress both to it and to the fire in the hall. She was also to have one white apple tree and one 'sweting' tree in the orchard and 'roome upon the said ground to harbour one bullock'.[50]

Active widows of some means could support themselves. The most prominent economic function of the widow of moderate property in rural society was money-lending.[51] The extent to which urban widows could succeed to the control of their husband's businesses and hence to a source of support in old age appears to have varied from place to place and over time.[52] For the poorer widow brewing was a common source of income at least until the seventeenth century.

Others managed far more substantial resources to late ages. Some very wealthy dowagers in medieval England exhibited power and independence. One of the wealthiest was Elizabeth de Burgh, Lady of Clare. She was born in 1295. Her first husband died in 1313 and her third in 1321 when she was

<hr />

[48] Jennifer C. Ward, *English Noblewomen in the Later Middle Ages* (London, 1992), 39–40.

[49] Spufford, *Contrasting Communities*, 88 ff. B. Holderness, 'Widows in Pre-Industrial Society', in Smith, *Land, Kinship*, 457.

[50] Spufford, *Contrasting Communities*.   [51] Holderness, 'Widows'.

[52] C. Phythian-Adams, *Desolation of a City: Coventry and the Urban Crisis of the Late Middle Ages* (Cambridge, 1979), 93; Barbara Todd, 'The re-marrying widow: a stereotype reconsidered', in Mary Prior (ed.), *Women in English Society, 1500–1800* (London, 1985), 54–92. V. Brodsky, 'Widows in Late Elizabethan London: Remarriage, Economic Opportunity and Family Orientation', in L. Bonfield, R. M. Smith, K. Wrightson (eds.), *The World We Have Gained: Histories of Population and Social Structure* (Oxford, 1986),122–54. J. Boulton, 'London Widowhood Revisited: The Decline of Female Remarriage in the 17th and Early 18th Century', *Continuity and Change*, 5/3 (1990), 323–55.

aged 26. All three left her with the control of substantial amounts of land. Thereafter she was almost forty years a widow, until her death in 1360 actively managing an estate which produced *c.* £3,000 per year in the 1320s, part of which she gave to endow a Cambridge college. Most wealthy Englishwomen remarried at least once. They were less likely to retire to a nunnery than their European counterparts.[53] The Nevill family produced a remarkable succession of long-lived women. The two daughters of Ralph Nevill (d.1367) were, respectively, twenty and forty-eight years dowagers. In the next generation the two older daughters of the first Earl of Westmorland were dowagers for twenty-four and forty-three years respectively. The third, Katherine Nevill, married John Mowbray Duke of Norfolk in 1412. He died in 1432 having directed that Katherine in addition to her dower and jointure should have a life interest in all his estates. She lived for a further fifty-one years, remarrying three times, on the third occasion, when probably in her sixties to a teenager, Sir John Woodville, to the chagrin of the heirs awaiting reversion of the estate; or, at least, of those who survived, since she outlived her son, grandson, and great-granddaughter. Woodville was assumed to be at least partly in pursuit of her fortune. If so he was unlucky because she outlived him by fourteen years. She died in 1483, in her eighties, having deprived a succession of male heirs of the full enjoyment they expected of the Mowbray estates. Her three younger sisters were dowagers for fifty, thirty-five, and twenty years. There is every sign that many of these women enjoyed their wealth, independence, and power.

On occasion a widow or a subsequent husband might waste the estate left to her, but so also did some male heirs. Many rich widows certainly acted with considerable independence of mind to ensure their own security in old age, including risking social opprobrium and substantial royal fines to marry men of their choice below them in rank or age—marriages perhaps too readily interpreted as based solely on male fortune-hunting and the gullibility of ageing women.

PENSIONS

A number of public and religious offices carried with them a good chance of an effective pension in old age. 'Pensions' were paid under a variety of arrangements in return for faithful service to the royal family, the great aristocratic houses, or indeed to any grateful employer able to afford it. People with religious callings or those working for them made up a significant portion of the population of medieval England. By the fifteenth century, parish clergy could

---

[53] Ward, *Noblewomen*. Rowena E. Archer, 'Rich Old Women: The Problem of Late Medieval Dowagers', in Tony Pollard (ed.), *Property and Politics: Essays in Later Medieval English History* (Gloucester, 1984), 15–35.

commonly expect a pension, though it was not certain. It had become a matter for negotiation between an ageing incumbent and his successor, the latter effectively buying the living with a cash sum and sometimes also allowing
his predecessor continuing residence in part of the rectory. As some safeguard
against corruption, such transactions required an episcopal licence. They also
ensured that the incomer or his patron had means, or that the living was well
enough endowed to provide for both the pension and a living for the new
incumbent.

Some clergymen were unable to make such arrangements or did not wish
to leave a familiar role or environment in old age. In consequence their parishioners suffered, unless the bishop intervened. An aged cleric could seek permission to employ a curate to carry out his duties though this also required
means. Ageing clergymen might seek tranfer to the lighter duties of a
chantry (saying mass for specified souls but without parish duties).[54] They might
become chaplains in a private household, though such posts must have been
relatively rare; or they might seek a corrody, though these were also becoming rare and expensive in the fifteenth century; or they might seek a private
retirement arrangement, paying a parishioner to care for them. Another possibility was resort to one of the numerous hospitals of medieval England which
provided care of variable quality.[55]

GUILDS AND FRATERNITIES

Another method whereby those with some means safeguarded themselves against
poverty in old age or at other times was through membership of guilds or
fraternities. These were lay organizations, sometimes based on a specific craft
but with close links with the Church. They were 'the characteristic institution of late medieval popular religion in England as in the rest of Catholic
Europe',[56] rooted in an ethic of spiritual brotherhood. They were usually formed
within a parish and dedicated to a particular saint, and clergy could be members, though they were under lay control. Their origins are obscure but ancient,
possibly pre-Christian.[57] The fourteenth and fifteenth centuries were their period
of maximum growth.[58] Of varying size and strongly socially stratified they
existed in large and small towns and villages. In many towns by 1350 there
were several, finely socially graded, at their apex the exclusive fraternities of

[54] K. W. Wood-Legh, *Perpetual Chantries in Britain* (Cambridge, 1965), 212–33.

[55] N. Orme, 'Sufferings of the Clergy: Illness and Old Age in Exeter Diocese, 1300–1540', in Pelling and Smith, *Life, Death*, 62–73.

[56] Susan Brigden, 'Religion and Social Obligation in Early 16th Century London', *Past and Present*, 103 (1984), 67–112; B. Pullen, 'Support and Redeem: Charity and Poor Relief in Italian Cities from the 14th to the 17th Century', *Continuity and Change*, 3/2 (1988), 177–208.

[57] Gervase Rosser, 'Communities of Parish and Guild in the Late Middle Ages', in S. J. Wright, *Parish, Church and People: Local Studies in Lay Religion, 1350–1750* (London, 1988), 29–55.   [58] Ibid.

the town elite.[59] In rural communities all adults, male and female, who could afford the entrance fee would be members. In England, unlike much of continental Europe, most guilds were open to women.[60] Generally the fee was low enough to admit all but the labouring poor,[61] though sometimes the deserving poor were admitted at a reduced fee.[62] Whole families and communities might be members, though those judged disreputable by the community might be excluded.[63]

In England there were no large fraternities devoted primarily to charitable works comparable with those of the great Italian cities.[64] They existed mainly for mutual aid among their own members funded by their contributions and bequests. Such provision was a vital mechanism of mutual welfare for all but the very rich in a time when all knew life to be insecure. An analysis of the charters of 507 guilds which were functioning in 1389 showed that about one-third (154) provided benefits to members in periods of personal distress including old age. One-fifth of these mandated a weekly allowance of about sevenpence (enough to buy a loaf of bread a day) and perhaps clothing or hospitality in the home of another member, though the statutes normally limited such payments to a few months or at most a couple of years.[65] They were intended to cover a temporary crisis or a terminal illness rather than prolonged retirement. Some historians have questioned whether the statutes were actually followed,[66] but clearly they were, at least in some places.[67] At their best, the guilds operated flexibly according to the needs and means of their members. They offered comradeship and psychological support to the aged by providing company at regular meetings, hearty sustenance at feasts, visitors to the sickbed, the services of a chaplain, or, at the very least, prayers and guaranteed remembrance after death. They must have provided for a considerable amount of life-cycle or accidental poverty especially in the more prosperous towns. The richer guilds of London by the early sixteenth century gave enough to sustain sick members until recovery and perpetual alms to the permanently disabled, provided that they had been members for

---

[59] M. Rubin, *Charity and Community in Medieval Cambridge, 1200–1500* (Cambridge, 1987), 251–8.

[60] B. Hanawalt and B. R. McRee, 'The Guilds of *Homo Prudens* in Late Medieval England', *Continuity and Change*, 7/2 (1992), 163–79.   [61] Brigden, 'Religion and Social Obligation'.

[62] B. Hanawalt, 'Keepers of the Lights: Late Medieval English Guilds', *Journal of Medieval and Renaissance Studies*, 14/1 (1984), 21–37.

[63] Rosser, 'Communities'.   [64] Dyer, *Standards of Living*, 246.

[65] H. F. Westlake, *The Parishes of Medieval England* (London, 1919), 137–238. Hanawalt and McRee, 'The Guilds of *Homo Prudens*'.

[66] Caroline Barron, 'The Parish Fraternities of Medieval London', in Caroline Barron and Christopher Bill (eds.), *The Church in Pre-Reformation Society: Essays in Honour of F. R. H. Du Boulay* (Woodbridge, 1985), 27. Barry McRee, 'Charity and Guild Solidarity in Late Medieval England', *Journal of British Studies*, 32 (1993), 195–225.

[67] Claire R. Schen, 'Strategies of Poor Aged Women and Widows in Sixteenth Century London', in L. Botelho and P. Thane (eds.), *Women and Ageing in British Society since 1500* (London, 2000), and 'Charity in London, 1500–1620: From the "Wealth of Souls" to "Most Need"', Ph.D. thesis (Brandeis, 1995).

at least four years. For the larger, richer, higher status associations the foundation and maintenance of almshouses was an important feature of their activities. These became important sources of support for the favoured and respectable poor, and for guildsmen or their widows down on their luck in old age. Such large fraternities also performed acts of charity towards those outside their ranks. Smaller rural fraternities and urban craft guilds confined themselves to making modest grants to members down on their luck, where possible helping them to start again in trade, paying for their funerals, or supporting their widows. These associations helped to reinforce the status hierarchy of the community, but they also encouraged neighbourliness, mutual aid, and sense of community.[68]

By such means older people with some property and connections survived in medieval England. They assertively safeguarded their own well-being, assisted by family and the community.

[68] Dyer, *Standards of Living*, 246–7.

6

The Aged Landless Poor:
Work and Welfare in Medieval and
Early Modern England

Possession of land enabled older people to try to control and plan their later lives in medieval and early modern England. The landless poor in all age groups and at all times found it much harder to patch together a living. Their numbers grew in the century of population increase and land shortage which preceded the Black Death in the mid-fourteenth century; the steady rise was resumed in the mid-sixteenth century.[1] Since the poor leave fewest records behind, we know even less about them than about the better off in medieval England. But their strategies for survival, driven by necessity, appear to have changed little over the centuries and information about them becomes less scanty over time. The poor of medieval and early modern England, and indeed in the nineteenth century and into the twentieth, struggled in an 'economy of makeshifts',[2] that is, they patched together whatever resources they could gather, in ever-shifting combinations: paid work when possible, growing food, use of common rights, help from family, friends, charity, poor relief, debt and begging. The struggle grew harder with advancing age and the components of the economy of each individual shifted gradually from dependence upon work to reliance on the help of others. Some lost the battle. Old people died of neglect and starvation, such as the 'old stranger' found dead of cold and exposure in a cowshed in 1362.[3]

WORK

Men and women without other means were normally obliged to work for their own support to the maximum of their ability to the latest age possible.

[1] C. Dyer, *Standards of Living in the later Middle Ages* (Cambridge, 1989), 4.

[2] O. Hufton, *The Poor of Eighteenth-Century France* (Oxford, 1974), esp. 69–130. Claire S. Schen, 'Strategies of Poor Aged Women and Widows in Sixteenth Century London' in L. Botelho and P. Thane (eds.), *Women and Ageing in British Society since 1500* (London, 2000).

[3] Barbara A. Hanawalt, *The Ties that Bind: Peasant Families in Medieval England* (Oxford, 1986), 237. P. Horden, 'A Discipline of Relevance: The Historiography of the Later Medieval Hospital', *Social History of Medicine*, 1/3 (1988), 371–2.

This is vividly conveyed by the Norwich census of the poor of 1570 which described as only '*almost* past work' three widows aged 74, 79, and 82. All were spinning white warp, the normal work of the poor of Norwich, which was the centre of the cloth trade and the wealthiest city in provincial England at this time. Their earnings were supplemented with poor relief.[4] The role of public funds was to fill the gap, for the reputable poor, between survival and what they could gain from work and other sources. Poor relief and charity will be discussed later but they cannot wholly be separated from the world of work, for they were not so separated in the lives of the aged poor. When, for example, in the late sixteenth century, Norwich established an impressive civic health care system, the primary object was to keep the poor fit enough to be self-supporting. The fact that it was available for anyone aged from 4 years old to 80, again indicates contemporary expectations of the ages at which productive work was possible.[5]

Workers did not necessarily remain in the same occupation throughout life, but moved through a succession of occupations as they aged. Craftsmen kept up their skills as long as they could. If sight failed or hands became less flexible they had to move on, not necessarily to physically lighter tasks. The Norwich census recorded a goldsmith and a worsted weaver who had become labourers. In eighteenth-century Ludlow two shoemakers and an innholder were described as labourers by the time they came to enter the almshouse.[6] The search for work might necessitate migration even in later life. The Norwich census of its settled poor in 1570 found that almost one-quarter of the over-fifties on the list had migrated to the town after the age of 50. Most local economies provided occupations, mainly casual and low-paid, which were conventionally reserved for older people and for others who were less than fully fit. These were most varied and numerous in towns. They included caretaking, sweeping, portering, watching prisoners, 'keeping kitchen' and turning spits, among other activities in sixteenth-century Norwich.[7] In inner London John Clove, who was described as a cook in 1601, petitioned the vestry in the 1630s stating that by becoming 'a common watchman He lived without being chargeable to the parish as long as he was able'.[8]

Among the poor of sixteenth-century Norwich older women were more likely than old men or women of childbearing age to be in paid employment outside the home, though some became housekeepers and childminders for younger families. Sometimes this was because the younger generation was as much in need of material support from the older as vice versa. The Norwich

---

[4] M. Pelling, 'Old Age, Poverty and Disability in Early Modern Norwich', in M. Pelling and R. M. Smith, *Life, Death and the Elderly: Historical Perspectives* (London, 1991), 82.
[5] Pelling, 'Healing the Sick Poor: Social Policy and Disability in Norwich, 1550–1640', *Medical History*, 29 (1985), 115–37.
[6] S. J. Wright, 'The Elderly and the Bereaved in Eighteenth Century Ludlow', in Pelling and Smith, *Life, Death*, 102–33.   [7] Pelling, 'Old Age, Poverty', 82–4.
[8] Jeremy Boulton, *Neighbourhood and Society: A London Suburb in the Seventeenth Century* (Cambridge, 1987).

census found John Tittle 'very sick and unable'. His mother lived with him adding her income as a spinster to that of his wife and helping to look after the children.[9] Commonly old women, like many poor people, combined casual occupations as they came available. They washed, cleaned, helped sick or otherwise needy neighbours, dressed meat and drink, laid out corpses, and much more. From medieval times older people ran alehouses, which were often small and poor, when no longer capable of other employment, though opportunities diminished with the growing scale and commercialization of the brewing and sale of ale in the seventeenth and eighteenth centuries.[10]

Still, in eighteenth-century Maidstone, then the fastest growing town in Kent, the aged worked on market days in the market itself and in the numerous inns on the quayside. They held horses, swept up, carried goods.[11] In any prosperous town such as Tunbridge Wells or Ludlow in the eighteenth century, casual work for capable old people was widely available.[12] In the eighteenth century, the countryside was still within easy reach of most town centres and closely integrated with urban economies. Old people were part of the large band of occasional day workers needed during the busy agricultural seasons at planting, hoeing, and harvesting. In Kent villages old people were paid for bark stripping, hop-picking, haymaking, fruit-picking. They collected and sold herbs for medical use; sold posies of flowers at street corners and weekly markets. Old men cut hazels for beanpoles, osiers for basket-making. Men and women collected and sold rushes for rush lighting.[13] On the Lancashire coast or that of the Wash they could gather and sell cockles and mussels. In many of these tasks they were in competition with the younger poor, especially women and children; indeed aged people were mostly continuing the habits of lifetimes of precarious survival. Casual carrying was another fragile standby. A man who died in Ludlow in the 1730s lamented in his final days that he was 'very poor haveing three children to maintaine and nothing comeing to support himselfe and his family but what [he] gets by carrying Raggs and being fourscore yeares of age and very infirme'.[14]

The surviving local censuses of the poor suggest how the aged poor combined work and poor relief. That of Salisbury in 1635 aimed to list those who might be employed or trained for work. The 'wholly impotent', who could not be expected to earn any portion of their living, included people aged from 62 to 100; those only 'impotent in part', who could be expected to earn something, include one 85-year-old man, an 80-year-old woman, a man of 74, a woman of 70, and three others of 60 and above. It included a 90-year-old

[9] Paul Slack, *Poverty and Policy in Tudor and Stuart England* (London, 1988), 85.
[10] Peter Clark, *The English Alehouse: A Social History, 1200–1830* (London, 1983).
[11] Mary Barker-Read, 'The Treatment of the Aged Poor in Five Selected West Kent Parishes from Settlement to Speenhamland, 1662–1797'. Ph.D. thesis (Open University, 1988). This is the most thorough study of the aged poor in a specific context yet available. [12] Wright, 'Ludlow'.
[13] Barker-Read, 'West Kent', 263–73. [14] Wright, 'Ludlow', 120.

woman described as 'lame in arm' who was earning sixpence per week supplemented by twelve pence poor relief. 75-year-old widow Bagges, 'lame in her hands', earned eightpence weekly and also received twelve pence relief. Walter Danyell at age 81 earned one shilling per week supplemented by fourpence relief, his wife earned sixpence. Widow Harty earned sixpence at age 80 and received twopence relief. Presumably she had other resources, perhaps from her family since she could not have lived on eightpence a week.[15]

The poor relief authorities in sixteenth-century Norwich as elsewhere gave relief sufficient for an individual to live on only to those plainly 'past work', 'wholly impotent', or 'labour done and had no other resources'. Residents of almshouses in early seventeenth-century London were expected 'to labour daily on the working days according to their ability of body and former manner of honest life' on pain of fine or expulsion,[16] as they were also in poor law institutions in sixteenth-century Norwich and in eighteenth-century Kentish villages. Where the local labour market did not provide sufficient paid work for old people, the poor relief system itself sought to do so. In 1623 the Justices of east Norfolk bought, as the Poor Law enjoined, stock:

that for such as are so oulde and weake as they are not able or fitt for any other worke, there be provided a stock of hemp in the pillinge whereof they may be imployed and for that purpose every man who is an occupier of land shall sowe hempe.[17]

Employment in minor parish or manorial office was a recognized means whereby aged, poor, and infirm men and women could support themselves. Before the Reformation testators might leave legacies to aged poor people of the neighbourhood, asking in return that they mourn and pray for the dead donor. Such practices were banned at the Reformation, removing one small source of income from the aged poor, but parishes continued the practice of supporting them by providing paid employment. In Southwark in inner London Oliver Lee, described as an ostler in 1593 and a shoemaker in 1595, was appointed one of four 'bearers' by the vestry in 1621. Duties included 'looking to the gutters of the church'. He was described as a 'bearer' at his death two years later. Such posts were valuable since they included subsidized accommodation and a regular income.[18] St Botolph's in London in the late sixteenth century hired older women to oversee the maids' gallery in the church and to maintain order by regulating the social interaction of unmarried men and women.[19] Some of the paid tasks reserved for older women by public authorities were particularly honoured. In Elizabethan London the Orders for the Plague stipulated that two 'sober ancient women' should serve as

[15] Paul Slack (ed.), *Poverty in Early Stuart Salisbury* (Devizes, 1975). For similar examples from the Ipswich census of the poor of 1597 see Tim Wales, 'Poverty, Poor Relief and the Life-Cycle: Some Evidence from Seventeenth Century Norfolk', in R. M. Smith (ed.), *Land, Kinship and Life Cycle* (Cambridge, 1984), 351–405.   [16] Boulton, *London Suburb*, 93.
[17] Wales, 'Norwich', 368.   [18] Boulton, *London Suburb*, 88.
[19] Schen, 'Strategies of Poor Aged Women and Widows in Sixteenth Century London'.

viewers in each parish to inspect the sick for signs of plague. Likewise 'two honest and discreet matrons' known as searchers, generally also older women, were to inspect bodies to determine the causes of death. In sixteenth-century Norwich they were employed at 'keeping sick persons' and 'tending almspeople' and older women were selected by the town authorities to run schools in which they instructed poor children to knit and spin.[20] There and in many other towns and villages, before and for long after, they were employed to nurse the sick and at a range of other tasks. In Kent throughout the eighteenth century parishes employed older women to keep lodgers—often people still older than themselves who were unable to manage alone—and to wash, nurse, and attend to the sick and disabled. Some could make a reasonable living giving paid short-term foster-care to children of the parish whose mothers were sick or deceased. Tonbridge in the eighteenth century regularly employed women pensioners to wash and mend surplices and other church linen, to clean the plate, weed the paths, or clean the church. In 1756 several old people in Cranbrook, Kent, both male and female, were occupied in knitting stockings and making clothes for parish orphans and workhouse inmates. They could earn sixpence for a day's washing for the workhouse. Tending the roads and verges of the parish was a regular employment of old men.

Where the Poor Law could sustain people in more profitable work it might seek to do so. Old Launcelot Watson and his second wife were both over 70 and apparently destitute in 1674 when Tonbridge parish bought them a new bed, reclothed them, and restocked their butcher's shop. How successfully their independence was re-established we do not know. In eighteenth-century Kent overseers of the poor commonly provided tools such as spades, sickles, hoes, or more specialized tools and materials for craft work. Such investments could reduce claims for poor relief. Edmund Missingham of eighteenth-century Cranbrook received a pension of only sixpence per week for thirteen years before he died aged 81, though the overseers occasionally gave him clothing, a new spade, and paid his rent in later years. He presumably partially supported himself with his spade.[21] John Taylor, shoemaker, was also the town scavenger of Maidstone until he became too old in 1770. The parish then set him up to mend shoes for workhouse inmates. He managed for three years until he was himself admitted to the workhouse. There he continued to repair shoes until he died aged 80 in 1782. James Carr, parish coffin maker and carpenter of Cowden parish, took his carpentery tools into the workhouse in 1800, where he made coffins as needed and carried out minor repairs. John Wells of Tonbridge, said to be old and infirm in 1768, was provided with seeds to plant his garden in 1772. The cost of 1s. 6d. suggests a large plot. Since Wells never became a regular pensioner it is likely that he, like other old people, kept himself at least partly by the sale of his produce. 1772 was a year of scarcity

[20] M. Pelling, *The Common Lot* (London, 1998), 142.   [21] Barker-Read, 'West Kent', 208.

and high prices in which he may have needed extra support. Other old men regularly sold produce to the workhouse. Cornelius Pollard grew quickset, which was much in demand by parish officers and presumably others for hedging. The joint poor relief payment paid to him and his wife never went above 1*s*. per week, though he was 85 when he died in 1705.

Growing and selling produce or living off the profits of livestock kept on common land assisted survival. In eighteenth-century Kent two-thirds of male paupers kept pigs; the women kept poultry. Traditionally a cow kept on the common had been the support of the ageing widow. Poor people in the late eighteenth century were said to value their cows at five to six shillings per week, at a time when agricultural labourers might earn only seven or eight shillings. A pig, cow, or goose could be fed cheaply. In the later 1790s a pig bought for twenty shillings (sometimes with assistance from the parish)[22] at Michaelmas would be worth three pounds by Christmas.[23] The profits could be invested in more piglets. Customarily the vendor kept the offal and part of the carcase, providing meat for some months.

The resources of the aged poor might include customary rights. The right to glean after the harvest was retained by the respectable poor (primarily widowed mothers and old people) into the nineteenth century. It was a worthwhile addition to income. A family of four could make gleanings worth about fifty shillings a year.[24] But it was back-breaking work, particularly hard for old people, and it is difficult to imagine that they made substantial gleanings unaided, though they may have worked with younger relatives. Old people might use common land for growing food for use or sale and for keeping livestock. This was gradually eroded by the process of enclosure. Its particular importance for the economy of the elderly is suggested by Arthur Young's unsympathetic comment on opposition to enclosure in Northamptonshire:[25] 'The advantages of inclosing to every class of the people are now so well understood and *combated at present but by a few old women*.'[26] Other common rights lost by enclosure included the cutting of turves for fuel, wood for fuel, housing, fences, implements; fishing, killing wild fowl, or cutting hay in a common meadow.[27] The increased poor relief expenditure which followed enclosure suggests the importance of common rights in the economy of the poor. Even after enclosure, fuel could still be gathered, free, from wastes: wood, peat, sticks from hedgerows, cow and horse-dung, seaweed, heather, broom or gorse. The ashes could be sold to farmers. So also could useful food supplements. Those

[22] Barker-Read, 'West Kent', 267.

[23] Jane Humphries, 'Enclosures, Common Rights and Women: The Proletarianization of Families in Late 18th Century and Early 19th Century Britain', *Journal of Economic History*, 50/1 (1990), 17–42.

[24] P. King, 'Customary Rights and Women's Earnings: the Importance of Gleaning to the Rural Labouring Poor, 1750–1850', *Economic History Review*, 44/3 (1991), 461–76.

[25] Quoted Humphries, 'Enclosures', 38–9.

[26] K. D. M. Snell, *Annals of the Labouring Poor: Social Change and Agrarian England, 1660–1900* (Cambridge, 1985), 177.   [27] Ibid. 180.

too old or too wary to poach could collect crab apples, cobnuts, brambles, whortles, juniper berries, mint, thyme, balm, and other wild herbs or water-cress from running streams.[28]

We get the most frequent glimpses of the lives of those old people who appear regularly in poor relief records. The huge numbers who just survived, without more than occasional recourse to relief are more elusive. Old people —many of them very old—were a significant presence among the poor in all times and places. The fact that so many survived to late ages despite lives of poverty was not cause for comment in their communities. Nevertheless, mostly their lives were hard-earned and became harder the longer they lived. More positively, old people, for as long as they retained some capabilities, very often retained a certain dignity and a role in the community.

CHARITY AND POOR RELIEF BEFORE THE POOR LAW

Poor relief, from various sources, made an important contribution to the sur-vival to late ages of many very poor people. Its precise contribution is imposs-ible to quantify, though there is a danger that its relative significance may be exaggerated because both its theory and practice are so much better documented than other resources for survival available to the aged poor. Nevertheless, its theory and practice, its early emergence and long history in England, can tell us much both about how poor old people were represented and about their own experiences.

Throughout the medieval period it was acknowledged that the rich had an obligation to help the desperately destitute and the deserving poor. There was an intensive, ongoing debate, as there has been throughout history, as to who was 'deserving'.[29] In general, 'the old and the sick who could not seek food by their own labour'[30] were defined as deserving, though incapacity for work and absence of other resources were always more important signifiers of need than old age in itself. The poor, including the aged, were assisted in a variety of ways, including casual giving to beggars in the street, royal bene-volence, or the endowment of institutions by rich men or women.[31] Monasteries supported them, to variable degrees, not always with great generosity.[32] From

[28] Humphries, 'Enclosures'.

[29] B. Tierney, *Medieval Poor Law: A Sketch of Canonical Theory and its Application to England* (Berkeley and Los Angeles, 1959); and 'The Decretists and the "Deserving Poor" ', *Comparative Studies in Society and History*, 1 (1958–9), 360.   [30] Tierney, *Poor Law*, 57.

[31] Dyer, *Standards of Living*, 235–6. Shulamith Shahar, *Growing Old in the Middle Ages* (London, 1997), 165 ff. M. Rubin, *Charity and Community in Medieval Cambridge* (Cambridge, 1987). Edward J. Keeley, 'Anglo-Norman Policy: The Public Welfare', *Albion*, 104 (1978).

[32] Barbara Harvey, *Living and Dying*, in England, 1100–1540 (Oxford, 1993), 7 ff. Dyer, *Standards of Living*, 240. M. McIntosh, 'Local Responses to the Poor in Late Medieval and Tudor England', *Continuity and Change*, 3 (1988), 209–45.

the eleventh to the thirteenth centuries, there was a wave of foundations of hospitals and almshouses, of varying sizes and endowments, providing free care and accommodation for the aged and sick.[33] The numbers of almshouses increased further, especially in the fifteenth century. Both hospitals and almshouses were often founded and managed by gilds or fraternities. For example, at Sherborne, Dorset, in 1437–8, poorly endowed almshouses for twelve elderly paupers stood next to the church in the centre of the town.The leaders of the town decided to increase the endowment sufficiently to give each of twelve male and four female residents food worth $7\frac{1}{2}d$. per week, clothing costing 6*s*. 8*d*. per annum, and a bed. The scheme was designed to bring both worldly credit and God's indulgence to the town. Twenty leading townsmen formed a fraternity to serve as governors of the scheme, to which townspeople generously subscribed. The beneficiaries were to be 'poor, feeble and impotent', deserving of charity and, preferably, local residents. They were to swear to obey the rules and could be ejected for misbehaviour. They were forbidden to beg and required to wear a badge.They were selected by the twenty governors, who investigated their character and circumstances. Not all were desperately poor, to judge by the gift of 66*s*. 8*d*. by one inmate to the fund. Some inmates had the same surnames as wealthy townsmen. The rules of the fraternity allowed that if any of the twenty governors fell on hard times he was entitled to receive 20*d*. per week, well above the allowance to the paupers, but in keeping with the tradition that those fallen from comfort to hardship deserved more than those accustomed to poverty. As Dyer comments, the poor labourer with a reputation for drinking might never gain access to such an institution, whereas the widow of a leading tradesman well might.[34] This is not to suggest that the widow was not in need, for 'need' described a very wide range of conditions upwards from the edge of starvation.

The clergy had an obligation to devote a proportion of parish revenue to the poor.[35] A custom of parish responsibility for the local poor was established from a very early date and was to be of lasting importance. This was increasingly reinforced by government. Early labour laws forbade begging and wandering without a licence. That of 1388 implied that those incapable of working should be allowed to beg, but only within their accustomed community. They must not wander as vagrants but must settle. That legislators were able to take this local responsibility for the poor for granted, apparently evoking no protest, suggests that they were building upon existing customs of neighbourly hospitality and reciprocity; that local communities, essentially defined on a parish basis, in the later fourteenth century expected to be responsible at least for their local, settled poor. Parochial charity could be

---

[33] Dyer, *Standards of Living*, 242, Rubin, *Cambridge*, 291. Felicity Heal, *Hospitality in Early Modern England* (Oxford, 1990). Tierney, *Poor Law*. C. Rawcliffe, 'The Hospitals of Late Medieval London', *Medical History*, 27 (1984), 1–21. McIntosh, 'Local Responses'.

[34] Dyer, *Standards of Living*, 265–6.   [35] Ibid. 241–8.

administered by lay people as well as clergy. By the mid-fifteenth century, and in some places possibly much earlier, churchwardens kept a parish 'common box' for donations (occasionally compulsorily levied in hard times), from which alms were distributed at the churchwardens' discretion. This was another feature of the reciprocity which bound communities together, facilitating survival in a subsistence economy.[36] Parishioners also participated in less formal and more social forms of charity such as 'church ales', convivial gatherings at which neighbours paid a little over the odds for food, drink, and fun so that the surplus could be given to those in need, including the elderly.[37] Urban neighbourhood feasts could serve a similar purpose.[38]

Such care for the settled poor might sit alongside harshness towards strangers. Communities, by definition, exclude as well as include. Also, community support should not be romanticized nor its effectiveness exaggerated even for the settled poor; the communities concerned were often themselves too poor to spare much for those who were poorer still; but nor were strangers invariably rejected. The motives for community action were, of course, mixed. Along with real compassion and a sense of Christian duty went fear of disorder, of the parish overrun with destitute beggars, and also awareness even among the comfortably off that they too might some time—most probably in old age—fall into need and be grateful for neighbourly and parochial charity. Also, the dispensing of charity was one of the ways in which status was established and affirmed, as well as being a public expression of moral worth.

In total, formal lay alms-giving, though not insubstantial, fell short of clerical expectations, just as clerical charity fell short of ideals of canon law, and both fell short of the immense need of the poor. It is impossible to measure the value of informal personal gifts of food, clothing, cash, or housing, which must have made a substantial contribution to the relief of the poor throughout the medieval period. 'Offering hospitality and distributing excess food were social obligations incumbent upon the wealthy and the ethic of informal assistance seems to have been shared by people of limited means.'[39] Such practices contributed to the strikingly lower levels of mortality directly attributable to starvation in later medieval England compared with Scotland or much of continental Europe.[40]

'ALL THE DECAYED POORE CYTTEZENS': CHARITY AND POOR RELIEF AFTER THE REFORMATION

The monasteries were dissolved between 1536 and 1539. This was followed by closure of chantries, religious fraternities, and some hospitals and almshouses.

[36] Ibid. Z. Razi, 'Family, Land and Village Community in Later Medieval England', *Past and Present*, 93 (1981), 7. Paul Slack, *The English Poor Law, 1531–1782* (Cambridge, 1990).
[37] Judith M. Bennett 'Conviviality and Charity in Medieval and Early Modern England', *Past and Present*, 134 (1992), 19–41. [38] C. Phythian-Adams, *Desolation of a City* (Cambridge, 1979), 140.
[39] McIntosh, 'Local Responses', 214. Heal, *Hospitality*. [40] Dyer, *Standards of Living*, 277.

Charitable provision must have fallen, but it reasserted itself, finding new out-
lets alongside the increasingly organized provision of relief by local and central authorities. After the dissolution the number and value of individual bequests
and gifts to the poor increased sharply. There was an increase in the number of almshouse foundations throughout the country, which suggests that older
people were seen to be suffering from the loss of long-established forms of relief.

CIVIC POOR RELIEF

London

There was serious poverty in late sixteenth-century London. In 1582 the City
authorities:

devysed to be taken oute of the streates all the lame and aged people such as had
not any place to go into. And they should all be conveyed to the Hospital of St. Thomas
in Southwarke where they should have meate, drincke and lodging, Chirurgians, other
officres to attend upon them . . . they also devysed yet more that all the decayed poore
Cyttezens shoulde have wekelye a pencion according to his necessite.

The authorities also ordered every alderman and the wardens of every city
company to search:

what number of poore fatherlesse children, what number of aged, lame, impotent
persons, and what numbers of ydell roges as well woemen as men. As also what nomber
of decayed householders were in everiye companie and ward within the Cyuttie of
London and lyberties of the same.[41]

They discovered 2,160 impoverished people, four hundred of them aged. Two
hundred and sixty old and lame people were sent to St Thomas's. Once admitted they were unwilling to leave when it was felt that their needs had been
met.[42]

   This is one example of the vigorous civic action which was evident in the
towns of the later sixteenth century. Between 1544 and 1557 the rulers of London
founded or re-established hospitals to cater for each of the different categories
of pauper in the capital. Of the five great institutions (St Bartholomew's, St
Thomas's, Christ's Hospital, Bethehem, Bridewell) St Thomas's had primary
responsibility for old people. The poor were taken from the streets and wherever possible it was sought to improve their condition within the appropriate
institution by means of medical treatment, training, work, or discipline. The
network of institutions was to be centrally controlled by a board of governors, to be funded initially by a temporary tax on citizens, later to be taken

---

[41] R. H. Tawney and Eileen Power, *Tudor Economic Documents* (London, 1924), iii. 416.
[42] Slack, *Poverty and Policy*, 114–15.

over by charity.[43] Funding flagged and in the hard days at the end of the six-teenth century the hospitals were caring for fewer of the poor. The civic organ-ization was undercut by the growth of the parish as the administrative unit for poor relief under the statutory Poor Law. None the less the hospitals survived.

Both city leaders and the clergy continued to remind rich and poor of their duty to care for the poorest. Most civic relief went to older and 'impotent' people, who were still defined as the most deserving and were the most likely to receive relief on a regular basis. No recipient of regular relief (or 'pensioner' as they were called) in St Bartholomew Exchange in 1599 was aged under 66 and the rules for recipients were strict.

Priority for relief went to respectable members of the neighbourhood. There was a residential qualification of three to six years for regular relief or a place in an almshouse. In some communities at least, publicly expressed gratitude was the price to be paid. 'Pensioners' in St Bartholomew Exchange were expected to give thanks at each Sunday service. Vestries removed disorderly pensioners from almshouses or temporarily deprived them of relief with the aim of improving their behaviour. The aged poor could not regard relief as a right; it was conditional, at least in theory, on observing strict norms of behaviour. Their dependence was signified in their mode of dress and in the roles they played in public ceremonies, but they were not always simply defer-ential objects of control. The language of reciprocal rights and obligations:

was no empty rhetoric and ritual because it provided a set of values to which the dis-advantaged could appeal and because it shaped popular expectations of their roles. Humble citizens appear to have enjoyed relatively easy access to the mayor.[44] . . . The less advantaged could manipulate the obligations of the wealthier that mem-bership of a community entailed, to mobilize elite support for the redress of their grievances.[45]

Members of the local elite were sensitive to criticism for harsh treatment of the disadvantaged. Some actions aroused more disapproval than others: dis-ciplining marginal groups less than disregard for the needs of widows, orphans, and old people. The relationship between rich and poor was reciprocal and dynamic, though of course unevenly balanced. It is possible to overstate both the 'social control' and the 'community' perspectives on poor relief; they were complementary, and both integral to the stable functioning of society.[46]

Even regular 'pensions' were, more often than not, inadequate for subsist-ence and presumed that the pensioner had some other income from charity, earnings, family or friends. The fact that begging continued, though licensed,

---

[43] Slack, *Poor Law*, 15–16.

[44] Ian Archer, *The Pursuit of Stability: Social Relations in Elizabethan London* (Cambridge, 1991), 54.

[45] Ibid. 259.

[46] Jeremy Boulton, 'Going on the Parish: The Parish Pension and its Meaning in the London Suburbs, 1640–1724', in T. Hitchcock, P. King, P. Sharpe (eds.), *Chronicling Poverty: The Voices and Strategies of the English Poor, 1640–1840* (Basingstoke, 1997), 19–46.

suggests that official relief did not eliminate poverty even among the deserving.[47] Begging was a resource of the aged poor in town and country. In rural Norfolk in the 1590s the settled poor were allowed to beg within the parish. They included one couple aged 86 and 84 whose house had been burned down, and a man who had

Very honestly lived in his vocation, taking great pains for his living, until by reason of his age and sore diseases, which are fallen to his legs and other parts of his body, he was enforced to leave his former labour and painstaking, which have been the only cause of his extreme poverty.[48]

Informal giving remained an essential component of the incomes of the very poor. The poor probably received more from formal charity and informal giving than from the poor-rate even by the 1590s, but still far from enough to meet need. Charity was unevenly spread and was often most available in the parishes where there was less need because those with means tended to make bequests to their own parishes, which were unlikely to be the poorest. In Elizabethan London,

In practice the limits of the formal relief system meant that the poor kept their heads above water by selling off what few comforts they had left and by mobilizing the support of their kin and exploiting the informal charity of their neighbours.[49]

Norwich

Civic vigour was equally evident in Norwich, the second richest city of sixteenth-century England. In particular it developed effective publicly funded provision of medical services based on a well-developed awareness of the social and economic impact of ill health.[50] A high proportion of the practitioners in the town were called upon to treat the poor. The city reopened institutions closed at the Dissolution and founded others for the care of the sick poor. The system was funded primarily by voluntary donations.

Norwich gave especial attention to the health care of those who 'myght well labour if they were hoole'. Those incapable of labour were supported separately, by the comprehensive poor-rate which Norwich introduced in 1549, apparently the first provincial town to do so. Old people often came into the secondary 'incapable of labour', category, but medical relief designed to rehabilitate individuals into fitness for work was made available to people of any age from 4 to 80, if the individual was judged capable of some work. In the provision of medical relief there appears to have been minimal discrimination between deserving and undeserving. The refusal of treatment to a wastrel would leave him or her a festering danger in the streets. The authorities were

---

[47] Boulton, 'Going on the Parish', 149.   [48] Slack, *Poverty and Policy*, 63.
[49] Ibid. 197.   [50] Pelling, 'Healing the Sick Poor'.

as concerned with the health of women as of men, old as well as young, since all could work and also spread disease. Old people were certainly a substantial proportion of the poor of Norwich. The Census of the Poor of 1570 found that 14.83 per cent of the settled poor (who made up 25 per cent of the population of the town) were aged over 60 compared with 7.6 per cent of the total population of England and Wales.[51] The aim in Norwich was to limit poverty through prevention of disease, though it was unclear which of these came first. Begging and indiscriminate charity were said to cause ill health by encouraging beggars alternately to gorge and to neglect themselves, with the result that:

So cared they not for apparell though the cold strooke so deepe into them that what with diseases and wante of shyftenge their Fleshe was eaton with vermyne and currupte diseases grewe upon them so faste and so grevouslye that they were paste remedye . . . both the olde and the yonge falle (by extreme povertye) into suche incurable diseases and filthines of bodye as one so corrupteth another that the charge to heale them is verye greate.[52]

Not least this gives a glimpse of how the very poor appeared to contemporaries. If few seem to have starved to death, such vignettes suggest the squalour in which they might survive. It also indicates the inadequacies of charity and relief that such conditions prevailed. It is unlikely that they were eradicated even in Norwich and the other provincial towns (at least three) which appointed town physicians around this time. Once serious diseases were established, care was expensive and cure sometimes impossible.

The Norwich scheme was implemented in the 1570s and was probably most fully developed three decades later. It then apparently declined in the 1630s perhaps due to the increased costs caused by the plague from 1625. However, it did not disappear and seems to have survived into the eighteenth century, funded by the town and largely independent of the poor-rate, adapting to changing circumstances. By that time St Augustine's, a lazar house in the sixteenth century, had become an infirmary for aged poor people past work. It was still in use for this purpose in 1814 supported by the poor-rate.[53]

The poor relief activities of the two leading urban centres, London and Norwich, in the later sixteenth century were shaped by their specific problems and customs as much as by government policy. Similar innovations emerged in smaller towns which shared their developing prosperity and communal institutions.[54]

---

[51] E. A. Wrigley, R. S. Davies, J. E. Oeppen, and R. S. Schofield, *English Population History from Family Reconstitution, 1580–1837* (Cambridge, 1997), 815.

[52] Tawney and Power, *Economic Documents*, ii. 317–18.

[53] The account of Norwich is drawn wholly from Pelling, 'Healing the Sick Poor'.

[54] e.g. the woollen cloth manufacturing centre of Hadleigh, Suffolk, in the later 16th cent. Marjorie McIntosh, *A Community Transformed: The Manor and Liberty of Havering* (Cambridge, 1991).

THE ROLE OF GOVERNMENT—THE EMERGENCE OF THE POOR LAW

On this foundation of parochial and charitable initiative, through the sixteenth century, the state gradually built formal statutory structures. In 1552 parishes were ordered, rather than as before permitted, to appoint collectors of charitable contributions for the relief of the poor. Parishes were to compile lists of the poor, to ask all parishioners what they were willing to contribute and to collect it. Those who did not pay could be ordered to do so by the bishop. Public begging was (unsuccessfully) forbidden. From 1563 parishes possessed powers to compel parishioners to contribute to the common poor fund, enforceable by a magistrate although the contributions were still called charitable alms. This legislation, very gradually, influenced local practice. Generally the chief beneficiaries were the aged and mostly female. In some rural Essex and Suffolk parishes regular collections were introduced, and both regular and emergency provision in cash, kind, or care for old people as well as to widows and children in need.[55]

In 1572 further legislation enabled 'overseers' of the poor to be appointed in association with the collectors, to investigate and supervise clients. Houses of correction could be established to provide accommodation for the deserving, work for the able-bodied, and punishment, as well as work, for vagrants. In 1576 JPs were directed to 'appoint and order stocks of wool, hemp, flax, iron or other stuff' for the employment of the poor, old or young, 'able to do any work'. There were only minor statutory changes thereafter until 1594–8, when there was a great scarcity of corn, leading to price rises, disturbances, and distress. The Act of 1597 consolidated the poor relief legislation of the earlier part of the century. It contained little that was new, but aimed at enforcement throughout the country. An Act of 1598 set out to facilitate the foundation of almshouses and hospitals. The Poor Law Act of 1601 was practically a re-enactment of that of 1597 with minor variations.[56] Thereafter a national poor relief system was permanently in place.

Again, however, the impact of the legislation upon day-to-day practice especially in the rural parishes is obscure and was probably slow. We can catch occasional glimpses. Throughout the years 1591–8 a Bedfordshire village, Eaton Socon, provided poor relief to the full extent intended by parliament. The parish made regular money payments to the aged and impotent, the sick were cared for and a few old people and children were found 'house room' at parish expense. People were supported in their own homes for as long as possible and only the 'impotent' were boarded out with a pension. In 1595 twenty-five shillings was paid 'to Robert Bonfield, 15s for kepinge iii quarters of a yeare his mother at Wildene'. Occasionally the parish also paid for

---

[55] F. G. Emmison, 'The Care of the Poor in Elizabethan Essex', *Essex Review*, 62–3 (1953), 7–28. McIntosh, 'Local Responses', 229.   [56] Slack, *Poor Law*, 17–21.

burials.[57] In the crisis at the end of the sixteenth century many rural parishes were forced into local experiments to support their poor; most had to raise compulsory rates at least in the worst years.

After as before 1601 charity and poor relief were complementary rather than distinct or competing sources of support for the very poor. Private gifts and bequests continued to be administered by parish officials. It was widely agreed that voluntary assistance was the ideal method of relieving the deserving poor. Parish and town officials encouraged gifts and bequests and invoked compulsory giving when voluntary action failed. Though wandering beggars were prohibited, the poor continued to seek alms within their own parish with impunity.[58] Voluntary charity still provided the bulk of relief though it could not meet all need. But by the early seventeenth century parishes could impose local taxes for the aid of the poor, made possible by the exceptional prosperity of England compared with other European countries. By 1600 most larger towns levied a regular poor-rate. By 1700 it was universal in England.[59]

THE POOR LAW IN THE ECONOMY OF POOR OLD PEOPLE IN THE SEVENTEENTH CENTURY

As the Poor Law developed it becomes clearer how it fitted into the personal economies and lives of the aged poor. People aged over 60 made up almost 10 per cent of the poor of Norwich in 1570, 20 per cent of those of Warwick in 1587, almost 10 per cent in Ipswich in 1597, more than 30 per cent in two parishes of Salisbury in 1635.[60] Poor old women outnumbered poor old men by almost two to one. Such extensive poverty in old age was no less true in rural parishes. Manorial support for the tenant weakened during the sixteenth century to 'relative insignificance' in some places at least[61] whilst landlessness increased. The poor relief system became an increasingly important source of support for the aged poor.[62]

Over the course of the seventeenth century the sums given in regular poor relief increased as did the numbers relieved, though with some irregularities during the civil war and interregnum.[63] The administration of the Poor Law was integrated with or complementary to that of charity whenever possible. In some places by the end of the seventeenth century parish paupers may

---

[57] F. G. Emmison, 'Poor-Relief Accounts of Two Rural Parishes in Bedfordshire, 1563–98', *Economic History Review*, 3, (1931), 102–16.   [58] McIntosh, 'Local Responses', 230.

[59] Slack, *Poor Law*, 36.   [60] Smith (ed.), *Land, Kinship*, 75–7.

[61] K. Wrightson and D. Levine, *Poverty and Piety in an English Village: Terling 1525–1700* (Cambridge, 1979), 344.

[62] Slack, *Poverty and Policy*, 188–9. T. Arkell, 'The Incidence of Poverty in England in the Later Seventeenth Century', *Social History*, 12/1 (1997), 23–47.

[63] A. L. Beier, 'Poor Relief in Warwickshire, 1630–60', *Past and Present*, 35 (1966), 77–100. R. Herlan, 'Poor Relief in London during the English Revolution', *Journal of British Studies*, 18 (1979), 30–49.

have had a comparable standard of living with a day-labourer.[64] This is not a startling claim since below the level of the poor day-labourer lay starvation. An old man or woman living with and wholly supported by their labouring children might well have been less well off than on regular parish relief. It remained a central principle of the poor relief system that its role was to supplement the incomes of people who could not find any other means to put together sufficient resources for survival, due to no fault of their own. Most older paupers were only partially dependent upon poor relief and very many poor old people received no relief at all. It was only one component of the economy of the poor and it only rarely provided for full support.

The number and proportion of aged paupers, and the generosity with which they were treated, varied from place to place in relation to local resources, to the structure of the local economy and local custom, as well as to need. Some parishes paid regular weekly or monthly 'pensions', sometimes over several years, in addition to the much larger number of payments of occasional relief. Most 'pensioners' (or 'collectioners' as they were sometimes known) were elderly or widowed, or both; most were female. The percentage of old people who were pensioners varied from place to place and time to time, but everywhere they were a minority of the aged poor. Once on the pension it was normal to receive it until death: widows might be pensioners for forty years and more; though most people went on the pension in their fifties or sixties, women generally did so at earlier ages. The pension might increase over time as the pensioner's capacity to supplement it with earnings declined.[65]

The experience of a very old and poor pensioner is conveyed in a petition to the quarter sessions at Walsingham (Norfolk) in the hard winter of 1647/8:

yor said poore petitioner being aged fourescore years, almost blinde and very lame of his ancles, by wch infirmityes he is made unable by labour to sustaine himselfe any longer or to travell abroad to gather reliefe from charitable people, and is allowed but six pence by the weeke from the towne wherein he inhabiteth, which in these hard times of dearth and scarcitye will not buy any considerable or competent maintenance for his reliefe; also the house wherein he dwelleth for lack of repaire (wch he is utterly unable to bestow upon it) will not shelter and defend him from wind and raine. Soe that he perceiveth such distresse comeinge upon him in his decrepete old age that he is likely to perish by hunger and cold, and sees noe meanes left to him whereby to escape that imminent misery which otherwise will inevitably come

---

[64] Wrightson and Levine, *Terling*, 41. Wales, 'Norfolk', 357. D. Marshall, *Poor Law in the Eighteenth Century.* (London, 1928), 100–1. Boulton, 'Going on the Parish'. S. King, 'Reconstructing Lives and Social Structures in Britain: The Poor, the Poor Law and Welfare in Calverley, 1650–1820', *Social History*, 22/3 (1997), 318–38.

[65] Wales, 'Norfolk', W. Newman-Brown, 'The Receipt of Poor Relief and Family Situation: Aldenham, Herts, 1630–90', in Smith (ed.), *Land, Kinship*, 406–20. Stephen King, 'The Nature and Causes of Demographic Change in an Industrializing Township: Calverley, 1681–1820', Ph.D. thesis (Liverpool, 1993); and 'Reconstructing Lives'.

upon him, but onely by makeing knowne this his pitifull distressed condition to yor Worships the Justices . . .[66]

This 80-year-old had exhausted the possibilities of both working and begging but his parish still did not give him enough to sustain an even barely tolerable existence.

As this example suggests, disappointed claimants could appeal against a decision of the parish authorities to the magistrates in quarter sessions. Many older people did so. As Slack points out, 'We should not think of the poor as passive recipients of doles or charity. They were well able to manipulate the system for their own purposes . . . putting pressure on overseers and if necessary justices.'[67] Petitions by disappointed claimants bring to light the reality of the lives and expectations of the aged poor. Their very existence suggests that communal obligations were not always observed spontaneously. In south Lancashire in 1627 Thomas Twiss sought weekly relief because he was over 80 and 'not able to work nor go abroad to receive alms of well-disposed people'. In 1628 John Scath also in south Lancashire petitioned that he was aged 72 and could still work but could not earn enough to keep himself and his wife. She was 80 and 'not able to work nor go abroad to receive alms of well-disposed people'. They were granted twenty shillings per year. In the same year Ann Read, a poor, blind, lame 97-year-old widow, claimed that she had been accustomed 'to seek relief among her neighbours', but now she petitioned instead to receive it from Ormskirk parish, where she had lived all her life. Gerald Walsh, an Ormskirk carpenter, in 1633 reported that he had earned his living and brought up nine children but could no longer practise his craft being 'dim of sight' and 74 years old, his wife bedridden for three and a half years, and his 'former gotten goods' now spent. William Gill, also of Ormskirk, petitioned that he had been independent all his life and had brought up seven children, but in 1631 he had been injured in a fall. For over a year he had been dependent upon his neighbours, but now, at age 90, he sought, and obtained parochial relief.

All of these petitions indicate the late ages to which poor people survived without regular relief, and also that infirmity disabling them from self-help, even from begging, rather than age alone was seen as an essential qualification for relief. Begging by known members of the community was evidently, as in the case above from Norfolk, tolerated, despite the letter of the law. Indeed the implication of these statements is that it was expected whilst old people were still able to leave their houses. Beggars most often received donations of leftover food from neighbours.[68] This could be seen as an efficient use of

[66] Wales, 'Norfolk', in 388.

[67] Slack, *Poverty and Policy*. P. Dunkley, *The Crisis of the Old Poor Law in England, 1795–1834: An Interpretive Essay* (New York, 1982). J. S. Taylor, *Poverty, Migration and Settlement in the Industrial Revolution: Sojourners' Narratives* (San Francisco, 1989).　　　　　　　　　　　　　　　　　　　[68] Wales, 'Norfolk', 357.

local resources, serving to keep poor-rates to a minimum. Expectations of the means by which the aged poor should support themselves may have depended upon the pauper's former status, and may partly explain the larger sums of relief paid to those who had once been above the begging classes. Longevity could outwit the almost successful attempts of some poor people at lifelong self-sufficiency. William Glover 'laboured all his life at his calling as a husbandman' until he requested and obtained relief in 1631 because he was unable to work 'by reason of his old age or otherwise by the Judgement of God', at the age of 97. Most such petitioners were awarded regular pensions.[69]

Charities imposed similar conditions. Almshouses continued to grow in number. In Aldenham in 1600 a London brewer endowed almshouses which gave each almsman and woman (mostly old people) a home, an income of two pounds per year, and a gown worth twelve shillings. Admission to almshouses was often closely integrated with the poor relief system and operated on similar principles. In the parish of St Saviour, Southwark, in the 1660s sixteen inmates were nominated to the almshouses by churchwardens and other parish officers. Most were aged and those who petitioned for admission also stressed their infirmity: Susan Coleman, 'near upon 80 years of age . . . is now past labour being full of aches and dim of sight'. Nicholas Purchase was '76 years of age and upwards . . . did so long as he was able truly labour for his living, but his sight now failing him, he is altogether inable to get anything towards the same, being a very poor man destitute both of friends and means and his wife also blind'.[70] Most were long resident in the parish. Each received a regular pension plus free fuel, bread, and accommodation and extra payments at Easter, Christmas, in cold weather, and when sick. They were also expected 'to labour daily in the working days according to their ability of body and former manner of honest life on pain of fines and expulsion'. They were subject to 'rigorous godly discipline'. Poverty was not the only criterion for admission; the elected pauper was to be 'honest and godly . . . none but such as can say the Lord's prayer, the articles of the Christian faith and belief and the ten commandments of God in English'. These were tested regularly by the parish clerk. Prayers composed by the founder were to be recited daily immediately after the shutting of the gates and each morning immediately after the opening 'upon their knees with loud and audible voices' on pain of a fine of four pence for non-attendance. There was a chapel in the college but those able to do so were expected to attend church every Wednesday, Friday, and Saturday. Tippling, begging, swearing, and 'railing' were prohibited. The doors were locked at night and unauthorized absences were prohibited and fined; licensed absences were restricted to four a year and the inmates were obliged to wear a badge so that they could be easily identified.

[69] G. W. Oxley, 'The Permanent Poor in South Lancashire under the Old Poor Law', in J. R. Harris (ed.), *Liverpool and Merseyside* (London, 1969), 21–4. Wales, 'Norfolk', 351.

[70] Boulton, *London Suburb*, 162.

There was a scale of punishments for misdemeanours: 'for the first time lose eighteen pence, for the second time a whole month's pension . . . and for the third time shall be deemed expulsed out of the said college forever'. At least one man was expelled 'for his misdemeanours' in 1621. The strictness of the regime caused a number of people to refuse a place after election or to leave voluntarily, despite the regularity and amount of the pension.[71] Normally almsmen and women were chosen from among the parish pensioners, thus reducing the cost of poor relief; most were female.

The seventeenth and eighteenth centuries saw a succession of experiments with methods of poor relief. The Puritan governors of Salisbury from 1623 to the civil war ran an ambitious scheme, financed both by charity and poor-rates, for providing employment and essential goods for the needy of three parishes. The scheme was relatively generous to the 'deserving', who, in return, were expected to attend church regularly. Public begging was forbidden, but collecting boxes were installed in each inn, attended by two 'aged, impotent poore people' who should 'stande by the boxe in a quiete and stille manner and . . . use noe clamour or other words of begging but to say this . . . in a quiet voyse "We pray you for God's sake to remember the Poore".'[72] There were similar experiments elsewhere.

The introduction of the Law of Settlement in 1662 lessened the burden on parishes of in-migration by confining the responsibility of the parish to those who acquired a local settlement by right of birth, marriage, or by a substantial period of productive and trouble-free local residence.[73] Ejection of the non-settled poor had been practised by the cities for some time.[74] It operated in a variety of ways, from great harshness to 'the care extended by St Luke Chelsea to an ex-mental patient, to an aged and thievish alcoholic, to an attempted suicide'.[75] Old people were rarely removed from a place where they were long established, rather a mutually convenient agreement for transfer of relief payments would be reached between the parishes concerned; though there are signs that old people were less generously treated by some parishes in the hard times of the later eighteenth century.[76] The law in practice, some complained, encouraged the poor to believe that statute and custom gave them a right to relief.[77]

Such beliefs and practices arose in part from the fact that poor relief had grown out of and was embedded in long-established traditions of communal reciprocity. In the seventeenth century the 'community' was no romantic abstraction. It was a tangible mesh of support and exchange made up of complex interactions and reciprocities, rights and obligations, created out of need and

---

[71] Ibid. 129.   [72] Slack, *Salisbury*.

[73] Taylor, *Poverty, Migration and Settlement*; and 'The Impact of Pauper Settlement, 1691–1834', *Past and Present*, 73 (1976), 42–74.

[74] Boulton, *London Suburb*, 95.   [75] Taylor, 'Pauper Settlement', 61.

[76] Barker-Read, 'West Kent'.   [77] Slack, *Poverty and Policy*, 192.

fear of need, and the customary obligations of hospitality and neighbourliness. Care for the poor was among its essential features. The neighbourhood was 'a reference group and a moral community . . . within a context of personal familiarity, individual standing and reputation were constantly assessed and reassessed . . . the neighbourhood was inclusive. It was intimate and supportive. It could also be narrow, restrictive and highly demanding.'[78] If in any sense poor people believed that they had a 'right' to poor relief, it was a right strictly circumscribed and subject to withdrawal on suspicion of misdemeanour or concealed resources, and conditional on loss of a more firmly established right, to the ownership of property; paupers forfeited their property to the parish, if not immediately, then at death.[79]

In rural communities convivial traditions continued. Still in the eighteenth century there were regular parish feasts celebrating saints' days, the seasons of the year, or special events such as the King's birthday in which old people shared. Farmers gave lavish harvest suppers in which they would include aged people who were past helping with the harvest. There were still small distributions of money, bread, or clothing in the church porch, on Sundays, on saints' days, and at Christmas. Door-to-door collections were held in response to particular crises such as flooding. Communal reciprocity survived in the city, even in London, as in the countryside. In Southwark in the early seventeenth century 'such evidence as there is suggests that for householders their neighbours rather than outsiders were the single most important source of financial and social support'. Pensioners were paid weekly, in a regular face-to-face transaction, by whichever of their wealthier neighbours held the appropriate local office at the time.[80] But neighbourliness, especially in communities where few were well off, had strict limits. Neighbours could be watchful of the administration of relief for which they were taxed. In 1631 inhabitants of Terrington St John (Norfolk) petitioned quarter sessions against their overseer, charging, among other things:

That the said Jo: Waters hath given by waye of Colleccon (as by his accounte maye further appeare) fortye or fiftye shillings or there abouts to the said Widdow Addeson in money and coles, and hath payd and allowed to him self for her house rent xs., yett he knew that John Rawlinge senior and Robert Borthesby did offer the said Widdowe her dwellinge and dyett with them for her worke and shee should not bee chargeable to the towne, yf shee would leave her sonne in lawe (John Game) who lived idle and refused to labour although able of body.[81]

Poor relief authorities made every attempt to keep aged paupers living as active members within the community. This was cheaper than the expensive

[78] Wrightson and Levine, *Terling*, 279–94.   [79] Boulton, 'Going on the Parish'.
[80] Boulton, *London Suburb*, 273.   [81] Wales, 'Norfolk', 368.

upkeep of institutions, more practicable in rural parishes, well adapted to custom, and was what older people preferred. Commonly parish officers paid neighbours, or even needy close relatives, to care for the mentally or physically sick, disabled, and aged poor, thus often keeping the carers themselves off relief. Or relatives might pay the authorities to look after people in need. Carers were normally female, but men might for example look after heavy or bedridden old men.[82] In 1661 the vestry of St Margaret Lothbury in London agreed:

for as much as Edwin Bush a poore Old Pentioner of this parish is at Michaelmas like to be destitute for a place for his lodging and the said widow Twine hath a roome to let and is willing to intertaine him it is agreed that shee be allowed and paid three pounds a yeere for rent of the said roome for the said Bush from Michaelmas by quarterly instalments and shee undertaking to make his bed and to assist at otherwyse unto him, it is agreed that shee be paid after tenn shillings per annum for the same to be paid as aforesaid.[83]

Poor old people were not necessarily dependants. Active old people might be paid to foster parish orphans, who could in turn help them about the house, whilst keeping them company. These might be their own grandchildren, as when John Lane of Tonbridge was paid six shillings per month from April 1678 to keep his grandchild Rose Conchman. When he died in 1679 she was fostered by a widow until she was apprenticed in 1684.[84] Commonly old people would be paid to foster children in the short term whilst their mothers were ill or giving birth.[85]

Parishes could provide a wide range of services. It became increasingly common to provide medical care, to prevent illness from prolonging pauperism. In the mid-seventeenth century, for example, Newcastle employed a town physician for the benefit of the poor and also a plumber to deal with the sewerage system—equally important for the prevention of ill-health. Rent, clothing, and fuel might be provided. Provision of housing was especially important in rural parishes. Agricultural workers lived in tied cottages and moved with every job. When their working life ended the parish might effectively inherit the farmer's responsibility to house them, to which he contributed through the poor-rate. The elderly labourer or his widow might be evicted by the farmer and rehoused by the parish, or allowed to stay in the cottage while the parish paid the rent.[86] Many parishes had a stock of rent-free housing acquired from bequests or from owners unable or unwilling to carry out repairs or to pay rent, but demand always outstripped supply, hence the frequency with which parishes paid rent for paupers. They might be moved as

---

[82] Barker-Read, 'West Kent', 106. P. Rushton, 'Lunatics and Idiots: Mental Disability, the Community and the Poor Law in North-East England, 1600–1800', *Medical History*, 32 (1988), 34–50.
[83] Boulton, *London suborb*, 138.   [84] Barker-Read, 'West Kent', 204.
[85] Marshall, *Poor Law*, 111.   [86] Barker-Read, 'West Kent', 44.

circumstances changed. Someone living in an outlying spot but requiring frequent assistance might be moved to a more central location. Pensioners might be moved to share with someone who could support them or with whom they could exchange support; in a cottage with a garden, for example, one resident could grow food for two. Such moves were not necessarily imposed coercively but with attention to the needs and personalities of those involved. Barker-Read rightly comments that:

The view that in pre-industrial England the old were left to live and die alone is as much in need of qualification as that which places them in the centre of a loving, caring family.[87]

One old woman who does seem to have lived alone, but with a great deal of parish support was widow Jane Cooksey of Aldenham. She was supported by the parish for almost twelve years before her death in 1661. Throughout this time her monthly collection rose and fell between three and five shillings, stabilizing at five shillings for the last eight years of her life. This was supplemented on seven occasions by supplies of wood from a substantial ratepayer. The need for wood suggests that she had her own hearth; that is, that she lived independently. She also received rent subsidies. Relief payments increased with the years as she evidently found it more difficult to gather fuel or to cultivate her garden. In the last four years of her life her annual income from the parish was £4. 15*s*. (£3. 5*s*. collection, 16*s*. rent, 14*s*. fuel).[88]

The system was not benevolent and effective everywhere. A handful of old, lame, and blind men and women 'like to perish or die in the streets with cold' were found among vagrants in early seventeenth-century Salisbury.[89] In 1678 people were forced into begging on the streets of London by inadequate weekly doles. In St Martin-in-the-Fields in central London the real value of the pension changed little over the seventeenth century, despite price changes. Boulton calculates that the average pension would have met between 58 and 61 per cent of minimum subsistence needs throughout the century; and that its value fluctuated between 27 and 30 per cent of the money wages of building labourers. The amount each individual received in St Martin's depended upon a wide range of circumstances: physical condition and family circumstances were not always more important than the behaviour of the applicant and the prejudices of officials. A pension might be reduced for drunkenness or other bad behaviour, or because the parish ran short of funds. Most pensioners in St Martins-in-the-Fields were women and most received a regular pension only for a relatively short time, in a third of cases for just one year, often the last year of life. The average stay on the pension was five and a half

[87] Barker-Read, 'West Kent', 79.   [88] Newman-Brown, 'Aldenham', 414.

[89] P. Slack, 'Vagrants and Vagrancy in England, 1598–1664', *Economic History Review*, 27/3 (1974), 366.

years.[90] Only one-third of pensioners received additional payments (e.g. for rent) and most of these were small.[91]

There was striking variety of treatment of the aged poor, as of all paupers, among the fifteen thousand or so parishes of early modern England and little is known about most of them. Parts of West Yorkshire in the late seventeenth and eighteenth centuries were decidedly ungenerous. The township of Calverley cum Farsley depended chiefly upon the production of woollen cloth, manufactured on an artisan basis. Many small clothiers rented small landholdings, though over the course of the eighteenth century fewer could do so. There was little waged labour. Like many other northern parishes,[92] Calverley was much less generous than the southern parishes on which we have most information, relieving fewer people and giving fewer and lower regular pensions. Long-term pensions were extremely rare and it is unlikely that they provided subsistence. There was no year between 1743 and 1804 when most pensioners received more than one shilling per week. At no point between 1650 and 1820 were more than 15 per cent of all old and widowed people receiving any poor relief and very few received it on a regular basis. Nor are there signs of their being assisted in other ways, such as work around the parish or free accommodation. Poor relief does not appear to have had an important place in the culture of Calverley or of many other northern parishes; and it was severely stigmatized. The cost of living was not lower in the north than in much of the south; Calverley was not exceptionally poor. Support from family and other networks and the advantages of landholding were more salient than poor relief in the survival strategies of older people.[93]

Wide variations in the willingness of parishes to pay relief and in the amounts paid have been found in rural Lancashire between 1700 and 1830.[94] In west Kent by the later seventeenth and eighteenth centuries, pensions were more commonplace and were fixed at a level just sufficent to enable the aged poor to buy barely adequate supplies of food. Other needs were met by additional payments for rent, food, clothing, or medical care as required. Prices fluctuated seasonally and could vary from place to place. Such changes could put great strain on a pensioner's budget.[95] Between 1697 and 1800 doles of wheat, flour, sometimes rice and potatoes, were made regularly during the winter months. Whenever possible Kentish parishes, like those elsewhere, assisted old

---

[90] Shorter than found by Wales, 'Norfolk', comparable to Barker-Read's findings for west Kent, longer than King, 'Reconstructing Lives', finds in west Yorks.

[91] Boulton, 'Going on the Parish'.

[92] E. Midwinter, *Social Administration in Lancashire 1830–1860* (Manchester, 1969). King, 'Reconstructing Lives'. S. King, *Poverty and Welfare, 1700–1870* (Manchester, forthcoming).

[93] King, 'Reconstructing Lives'.

[94] Margaret Hanley, 'Poverty and Welfare in Rural Lancashire, 1700–1830', unpublished paper to annual conference of the Economic History Society, St Catherine's College, Oxford, 26 March 1999. [95] Barker-Read, 'West Kent', 133.

people to find paid work rather than providing relief.[96] The definition of capacity for work was very broad. Katherine Sheaf of Cranbrook in Kent was evidently a frail ageing lady in 1678 when she was widowed, aged about 55. Until 1682 she received relief from the parish for frequent periods of 'sickness'. From 1682 she received a regular pension, but it was only 2s. 6d. per month plus her rent, not enough to live on. The parish also bought her 'cards', suggesting that she supplemented her pension by carding wool, a common form of employment for married women in the town. This continued until at least 1690, when the overseers for the first time described her as 'old' and she must have been in her late sixties. She may have been so defined because she could no longer work for pay. She had at least one son living in Cranbrook who might also have helped her, though since he himself became a parish pensioner in 1722 he may have been as poor as she. In 1691 her pension was increased to three shillings a month and the parish began to supply her with winter fuel, suggesting that she was now too weak to gather it. In June 1691 she was allowed eleven shillings for sickness and removed from her own home to be lodged with a younger widow who was paid sixpence per week for her house room. The pension was increased to one shilling and sixpence, a subsistence sum. The parish thus met all her basic needs until her death in 1692, but it did so only when the remnants of her capacity for self-sufficiency were gone.[97]

Cranbrook was a poor parish. A richer one might have given more relief at an earlier stage. Alice Hall of Tonbridge, a wealthier Kentish parish, was widowed at around age 70 in 1689. She had no children and was entirely dependent upon the community. Within a week of her widowhood she was granted three shillings per month pension, rent of one pound per annum, and one hundred faggots each winter. The cash payment was small but there is no evidence that she had other resources. Records of additional grants are as patchy in this case as always, but they indicate that she received loaves from time to time and was given new clothing annually. Old people might be granted furniture and kitchen utensils when necessary, though in poor parishes these would be second hand—either gifts or items left by deceased paupers. In 1695 Alice Hall's pension was increased to 1s. 3d. per week and she was moved to an almshouse which she shared with Widow Green, who earned an occasional threepence or sixpence for 'attending' her.[98]

These must have been relatively common experiences. Full subsistence relief was still the last resort of the parish. Parishes were not necessarily ungenerous; most did their best with limited resources. They saw their role as that of

---

[96] King, 'Reconstructing Lives'. Lynn Botelho, 'Provision for the Elderly in Two Early Modern Suffolk Communities', Ph.D. thesis (Cambridge, 1996); and 'Aged and Impotent: Parish Relief of the Aged Poor in Early Modern Suffolk', in M. Daunton (ed.), *Charity, Self-Interest and Welfare in the English Past* (London, 1996), 91–112.

[97] Barker-Read, 'West Kent', 66–7.   [98] Ibid. 69.

safety-net when other resources were lacking, rather than the first line of defence for the poor, and very many poor old people could marshall a range of alternative resources to support the low living standard to which they were accustomed.

The complex role of poor relief in the economy of a poor family over its life cycle is indicated by the story of John Platt, apparently a shoemaker (1598–1669) of Aldenham. He had nine children, of whom four survived to adulthood. In its early years the precarious Platt family economy was supported by parish payments for attendance on others in need. In 1628 his wife received between sixpence and one shilling weekly for caring for an aged bachelor. When he died in 1629 the account books record a final payment to 'Goodwife Platt for watching with him the night he did depart and bread and beere as she had others that were with her'. John himself in 1631, soon after the birth of his first child, was paid six shillings per month for six months for 'keeping Eldridge's boy'. The second child Alice first received payments in 1665 for 'looking to visited people'. From 1636–7 until the late 1650s the Platts received relief in some form on at least one occasion in each year some-times for months on end. In 1648 the overseers paid one shilling and sixpence for the burial of a son, in 1650–1 they paid twenty shillings 'for redeeming Platt's house from Timson', paid his rent of fifteen shillings and gave him three shillings and sixpence, though some payments to Platt continued to take the form of relief for caring for the impotent or for fostering children. Between the late 1650s and 1667–8 the Platts appear to have achieved unusual self-sufficiency, perhaps because their children were able to assist their ageing parents. By 1667–8 John was aged 68 and ailing. He was granted payments for medical treatment. His regular monthly pension rose to five shillings in the months preceding his death in August 1669. The parish paid his burial expenses. His widow, who is unlikely to have been less than 63 at the time of his death, received a monthly pension for the next twenty-four years until her death.[99]

Poor relief, like charity, was not given on morally neutral terms but medi-ated through social relationships and customary norms of behaviour. None the less, censorious judgements were not automatic. Ann Wright of Cratfield in Suffolk was consistently given relief into old age, though she was one of the parish's 'most notorious idlers, whose life is well documented through a sequence of bastard-bearing, communication and visits to the parish stocks'.[100] Most parishes were not large or rich enough for officers to treat the poor as a distinct social group or as objects of manipulation. They were not a distinct 'underclass', but, apart from the small core of regular pensioners, were a shift-ing population among whom almost any member of the community might fall, due to sickness, accident, or old age. There was no stark distinction between

---

[99] Newman-Brown, 'Aldenham', 216–17.
[100] Botelho, 'Provision for the Elderly', 240; and 'Aged and Impotent'.

paupers and wage-earners, since many paupers were also partial wage-earners and many wage-earners potential paupers. The Old Poor Law formalized and supplemented customary neighbourly charity but did not transform it into a wholesale disciplinery machine. It was one of many formal and informal mechanisms in society for stating and policing the bounds of respectable behaviour, but the bounds had a certain flexibility and policing was not always aggressive. Respectable pauperism was not in most places stigmatized as it was to become in the nineteenth century, though the ungenerous inhabitants of seventeenth-century Calverley were known to stone their paupers on their way to church on Sundays.

Most recipients of relief did not require discipline. Poor old folk and widows were rarely a source of danger to society unless they became sources of contagious disease. Even those who trangressed the accepted code of behaviour—such as Ann Wright of Cratfield—would be allowed at least the minimum necesary for survival. The officials continued to treat the poor as individuals and the settled poor were often well known to them.[101] The aged poor were usually privileged. Rather than routinely functioning as an impersonal machine designed to deter applicants, the system had the capacity to seek out the truly needy even when they did not request relief. Each annual rate assessment was based upon a survey of local need. In conscientious parishes this necessitated searching out the poor. When the overseers of Maidstone conducted their annual search of the parish in 1692 they found Edward Black dressed in rags with literally no possessions except a bundle of straw on which he slept. He was aged 82. For the past year he had been unable to work and had been selling off his possessions to survive. In all that time his serious plight had not reached the attention of the poor relief authorities. His story suggests the weakness as well as the strength of the system.[102]

THE EIGHTEENTH CENTURY

In the later eighteenth century the pattern of poor relief was destabilized by the pressure of rising rural unemployment. Over the century expenditure grew. Even so, Barker-Read's uniquely detailed reconstruction of the relief of the elderly poor in west Kent in the eighteenth century shows that most old people even among the labouring poor did not receive regular relief or payments at subsistence level, though they were often the largest single group on relief. Pensioners comprised between 0.8 and 2 per cent of the population of the west Kent parishes at a time when the percentage of people aged over 60 in the national population was between 10 and 8.[103]

---

[101] Slack, *Poverty and Policy*, 205–6.   [102] Barker-Read, 'West Kent'.
[103] Ibid. Built up from 1,500 biographies reconstructed from the Poor Law records.

A significant minority of aged paupers in west Kent were downwardly mobile from relative prosperity. They shared two-room cottages, flimsy and rarely in good condition, but warm enough and perhaps with a small garden. They lived on a staple diet of bread and cheese. They rarely are meat, though it might be supplied to the sick by the parish.[104] Pensioners could not normally afford tea but drank ale or infusions made from sloe or whitethorn leaves. Like the younger poor they had minimal possessions. When widow King removed from Headcorn parish to Maidstone in Kent in 1724 the overseers found her a cottage and furnished it with a bed, a cooking pot, and a skillet; this was considered adequate furnishing. When 80-year-old James Carr of Cowden entered the workhouse in 1801, after several years as a pensioner, his goods were listed as: a bed, two bedsteads, two blankets, one pair of sheets, a table, a case of shelves, a knife box, a salt-box, a flat-iron, a case of earthernware.

Parish medical services improved from the later seventeenth century.[105] Parishes might pay lay or trained healers for medical or surgical treatment according to need and custom. In 1686 Wrotham parish in Kent paid thirty shillings for a surgeon to come from Tonbridge to treat an old man's broken leg.[106] Serious cases were sent to hospital sometimes at a distance. Wrotham spent £14. 15s. 9d. on a year's treatment for arthritis in St Luke's hospital in London for old Judith Hills. Both philanthropic and Poor Law expenditure on the medical care of the poor increased in the eighteenth century.

More generally, the eighteenth century saw a series of experiments designed to cut Poor Law costs. One of these was the establishment of work-houses, most actively in the 1720s, though still in only a fraction of all parishes. They were intended not as the punitive institutions they were to become in the nineteenth century but as one more attempt to provide work for the workless. They did little to help the able-bodied unemployed, but they pro-vided a little work for the 'impotent' as well as extending the resources of accommodation of the parish. In Kent aged pensioners were swept into the workhouses when they first opened. There was a sharp drop in the number of pensioners in all west Kent parishes as workhouses spread between 1700 and 1750; parishes also became more reluctant to pay rent. Old people in very serious want were not receiving pensions in west Kent in the first three decades of the century.[107]

Some old people saw the workhouses as punitive. When Martha Pyle was widowed in 1692 she earned a living for many years boarding orphans. When Cranbrook parish considered her too old to work she was sent to the work-house, following three years in which the parish obtained a succession of orders from quarter sessions seeking unsuccessfully to force her son John to support her. She fled from the workhouse and lived in near destitution in the parish

---

[104] Ibid. 123.   [105] Rushton, 'Lunatics and Idiots', 44–6. Boulton, *London Suburb*, 131.
[106] Barker-Read, 'West Kent', 102.   [107] Ibid. 153.

for two years with only occasional parish relief. By late 1733 her condition was so poor that the parish applied to quarter sessions for a warrant compelling her to enter the workhouse, where she died in 1734.

Ann Welsh, a widow of Cranbrook, for fifteen years from 1699 to 1714 was paid and housed by the parish to care for a crippled spinster. When her charge died she was given free lodging, a pension, and allowances in kind and until 1723 received periodic assignments to tend the sick. When the workhouse opened in 1723 there were fewer opportunities for work of this kind. She, now aged 62, refused an order to enter the workhouse. Her work and her pension ceased. For seven years she survived, appearing periodically in the overseers' records as 'in want' and receiving small sums of casual relief. In 1730 the parish arranged for her to live with and care for her very aged father who had been discharged from the workhouse. She did so until his death in 1736. Thereafter she vanishes from the records, evidently not dying in the parish, perhaps moving elsewhere to live with her son. Her long service had brought her no favours from the parish. This was not so everywhere. In richer Maidstone similar service was recognized by a slightly higher than standard pension. In Tonbridge such women were not sent to the workhouse but lodged with a householder.[108]

Thomas Malthus, an advocate of the workhouse for the control of younger poor people, agreed with the old people who fled from the workhouse. He wrote in 1796:

it is the duty of society to maintain such of its members as are absolutely unable to maintain themselves, it is certainly desirable that the assistance in this case should be given in the way that is most agreeable to the persons who are to receive it . . . it seems peculiarly hard upon old people, who perhaps have been useful and respectable members of society and in their day 'have done the state some service' that as soon as they are past their work, they should be obliged to quit the village where they have always lived, the cottage to which time has attached them, the circle of their friends, their children and their grandchildren, and be forced to spend the evening of their days in noise and unquietness among strangers and wait their last moments forlorn and separated from all they hold dear.

Workhouse conditions may not have been materially more austere than the life of the poor outside, though they were often overcrowded and life was highly disciplined. Inmates might work outside the workhouse but they were subject to regulations which those in rented or parish accommodation were not, though they were comparable with those of the stricter almshouses; regulations included regular attendance at church and at prayers; good behaviour and restrictions on the use of tobacco, snuff, and tea. Some workhouse rules however emphasized that aged inmates should always be spoken to kindly and always approached quietly and calmly.[109] At Strood and Farnborough there were rules that the aged should be treated with tenderness and not expected

---

[108] Barker-Read, 'West Kent', 109–10.   [109] Ibid. 239.

to work beyond their capacity. Diets may well have been better than those of the poor outside, especially when supplemented by produce tended by inmates in the workhouse garden. Maidstone in 1720 provided beer for five men over 70 and two old widows, and soft rolls from a local baker for a toothless old man. In the three years before her death Widow Brumstead received beer each week and sometimes extra milk, sherry, fish, and fancy cakes.

Sir Frederick Eden described the large (one-thousand-inmate) Liverpool workhouse in 1795:

The old people in particular are provided with lodging, in a most judicious manner: each apartment consists of three small rooms, in which are one fireplace and four beds and is inhabited by eight or ten persons. These apartments are furnished with beds, chairs and other little articles of domestic use that the inmates may possess, who being thus detached from the rest of the poor, may consider themselves as comfortably lodged as in a secluded cottage; and thus enjoy in some degree (even in a workhouse) the comforts of a private fireside. The most infirm live on the ground floors; others are distributed through two upper stories.

A large workhouse could provide specialized accommodation in this fashion[110] as smaller rural ones could not.

Workhouses brought to some parishes improved professional medical care. They provided in-patient care to the elderly sick and were the base for outdoor services from the parish doctor. Yet once the initial enthusiasm subsided, it became clear that they were expensive to maintain and that inmates earned very little. They facilitated the spread of contagious diseases, to which old people were especially vulnerable. Before the end of the eighteenth century, west Kent parishes ceased to send old people to workhouses until their circumstances had been carefully assessed and other options tried and exhausted. Canterbury incorporated into its private Act of Parliament a statement that no ancient person should be compelled to go into the workhouse against his or her will.

Parishes sought to do their best for the aged poor in the old ways, but it became more difficult under the pressures of the later eighteenth century, in particular the growing need to support younger people with families. In a sample of parishes the value of 'pensions' given to old people did not rise though living costs rose sharply. The proportion of old people, especially of old women, among recipients of regular relief fell faster than their share of the total population.[111] Older women may also have lost out as impoverished younger women took over some of their accustomed parish occupations.[112]

---

[110] Oxley, 'Permanent Poor', 37.

[111] Richard Smith, 'Charity, Self-Interest and Welfare: Reflections from Demographic and Family History', in Daunton (ed.), *Charity*, 39 ff. The sample consists of 110,000 pension payments to persons of all ages in twenty English parishes, 1660–1740.

[112] P. Sharpe, 'Literally Spinsters: A New Interpretation of Local Economy and Demography in Colyton in the 17th and 18th Centuries', *Economic History Review*, 44/1 (1991), 61.

Maidstone, Tonbridge, and Wrotham, all relatively prosperous parishes, abandoned payment of regular pensions by the 1790s. Instead money doles were given at irregular intervals of two to three days. Wheat, flour, rice, or potatoes were distributed regularly. The very high price of food, especially bread, at this time undermined the pension system. In west Kent at least poor old people do not appear to have been receiving less in total—parishes made strenuous efforts to relieve distress and prevent starvation—but what they received and when and how was less regular and more insecure than before. The picture was similar in the hard year of 1796 in the large, wholly rural and poor parish of Ardleigh in Essex, where little charity was available and families could do little to help older members.

Barker-Read sums up the situation in west Kent at the end of the eighteenth century:

The aged had a moral and legal right to relief under the old Poor law but in most parishes this was a minimal maintenance, sufficient to sustain life when bread was cheap, but requiring something more to avoid malnutrition and disease and also to provide them with a small modicum of treatment.

CONCLUSION

Charity and poor relief in early modern England were complementary and deeply rooted. There was a strong sense of communal obligation to help at least the deserving local poor, at a minimal level. Both were essential components of the complex economy of makeshifts of the very poor. There are no national statistics of the provision for old people under the Old Poor Law, just a scatter of localized studies. These suggest that for poor relief purposes old age was defined functionally, as the point at which people could no longer support themselves by any means. The great majority of old people were poor, as most had been throughout their lives, and they carried on to the end, juggling resources for survival. But most continued to have active lives, giving to their communities as well as receiving. There is no obvious sign that they were despised or degraded because they were old, any more than were poor people of any age. Older people appear to have been treated as people, and as 'old' only when they became dependent, which could occur at a variety of ages.

7

Old People and their Families

It is a mystery how so many poor people survived so far into old age on the resources described so far. It is improbable that paid work, charity, and poor relief on the scale known to be available, however 'packaged', could have provided for the survival of most poor old people. Some historians have suggested that support from the family might have filled the gap. Non-historians often take for granted that the family must have been the mainstay of older people in pre-industrial England. On the other hand, historians of the family have created conflicting images of the relationships of old people with their families, and historians of household structure have asserted that younger people had little obligation to support their elders.

Lawrence Stone asserted as 'demographic facts' that in the sixteenth and seventeenth centuries:

There were relatively few aged parents to be looked after, even among the landed classes . . . among the will-making part of the population, bereaved parents were obligatorily looked after by the children. So long as they did not remarry, most widows had a legal right to a room and board, and access to the communal fire in the house of their eldest child.

However in the later eighteenth century, Stone believes:

Another victim of change was the aged . . . the old did not merely lose power as the patriarchs of the lineage, they also lost respect. The rise of alms-houses and of institutionalized poor-relief to look after them, suggests that their children were increasingly shedding responsibility for their support and transferring it to the community at large. The fate of King Lear at the hands of his daughters foreshadowed a century of change and uncertainty in family and societal attitudes to old people.[1]

Almost simultaneously, Stone suggested the opposite: that there were no fundamental changes in attitudes to and treatment of old people in the eighteenth century, or at any subsequent time, for they had always been grim, though with movement possibly in the direction of greater generosity towards them in the twentieth century compared with 'the past'.[2]

Keith Thomas emphasized the solitary state of poor elderly women and their vulnerability to charges of witchcraft in the later sixteenth and seventeenth

---

[1] Lawrence Stone, *The Family, Sex and Marriage in England 1500–1800* (London, 1977), 59–60, 403–4. *Lear* was written *c.*1599.

[2] Lawrence Stone, 'Walking over Grandma', *New York Review of Books*, 24/8 (May 1977).

centuries.[3] Slack comments for the same period that 'a lonely old age was . . . the lot of most of the labouring poor',[4] whilst Alan Macfarlane asked: 'At what date in England did the major support in time of risk . . . shift from children to other wider units?' He answered that, at least since Chaucer's time, such support from children had never been certain, whilst the wider community had long acknowledged a responsibility for the aged poor.[5]

THE PRE-INDUSTRIAL PATTERN OF FAMILY SUPPORT

The most systematic work on this theme is that of Peter Laslett and his colleagues. Their reconstructions of the demographic past[6] have clarified the structure of households in pre-industrial England, from the late sixteenth century, establishing that most were not large and composed of extended kin, as was once thought to be the classic case in pre-industrial society. Rather, a distinctive household pattern characterized much of pre-industrial north-western Europe, consisting normally of small 'nuclear' units of parents, two or three surviving children, and/or one or more servants and sometimes 'lodgers'.

An important related characteristic was that servanthood was a normal phase of the life cycle for young people between their early teens and marriage, not only among the poorest. 'Servants' were not always the socially inferior drudges familiar in more recent history. Males and females left their parental homes to live and work often in the homes of social equals, whose lives they shared, acquiring skills, experience, and sometimes capital. Laslett has argued that once they had left the parental home as servants and certainly after marriage offspring rarely returned to it to live for any extended period, and there was no obligation upon them to contribute from their earnings to the support of their parents. Migration in search of work, which long characterized pre-industrial Britain, might permanently separate the generations. Parents who could afford to do so would continue to give support to their offspring when needed, and, when possible, would set them up with property on marriage. The line of material obligation was downward not upward through the generations. The timing of marriage was not as in some other cultures determined by paternal death and inheritance.[7]

---

    [3] Keith Thomas, *Religion and the Decline of Magic* (Harmondsworth, 1973), 660–73.
    [4] P. Slack, *Poverty and Policy in Tudor and Stuart England* (London, 1988), 85. See also Peter Laslett, *The World We Have Lost* (London, 1965), 11.
    [5] A. Macfarlane, *Marriage and Love in England* (Oxford, 1986), 105–16.
    [6] P. Laslett and R. Wall (eds.), *Household and Family in Past Time* (Cambridge, 1972). J. Hajnal, 'European Marriage Patterns in Perspective', in D. V. Glass and D. Eversley (eds.), *Population in History* (London, 1965), 101–43; and 'Two Kinds of Pre-Industrial Household Formation System', *Population and Development Review*, 8 (1982), 449–94.
    [7] P. Laslett, *Family Life and Illicit Love in Earlier Generations* (Cambridge, 1977).

The relationship of the household nucleus with older generations and others living outside it is said to have varied with a range of circumstances, according to no evident customary rules. The advantage was flexibility. The disadvantage was the hardship that could result. This is thought to have been frequent and systematic enough to have acquired a label: 'nuclear hardship'; that because there was no strong sense of mutual obligation within families, casualties (the widowed or deserted wife or the failing old person) had no automatic right to support from relatives and in consequence they might suffer isolation and hardship. However, it is believed that the Poor Law provided what the family did not; it was both a product and a reinforcement of this prevailing family structure and its accompanying value system, and was closely integrated with it.[8] This interpretation focuses upon material support between generations; it relies upon sources which can tell us little about emotional relationships. Sources for the study of pre-industrial household and family structures are primarily census-type listings of households in certain communities. These can tell us, up to a point, who lived with whom, but little more about relationships among kin. 'Households' for purposes of such study have been defined as consisting of people living under the same roof on a regular basis. These excluded:

kin and affines who live close by, even if they collaborate so closely in the productive work of the family that for economic purposes they form part of it and may frequently or usually take their meals at the family table,

such as:

retired members of a former generation . . . even if supported by it and still working with it, provided that they would not be regarded by the family, or by an enquirer, as resident in the family home . . . a retired couple occupying a cottage in the yard, or 'doing for themselves' in rooms set aside for them in a farmhouse, are not members.[9]

By this definition it was found to be rare for elderly parents and married offspring to live together. The focus of such studies has been on households and not families. If households, or anything else, are to be studied over long periods of time, formal rules have to be established which make comparison over time possible. Problems only arise if we try to draw conclusions from such measurements about things they were not designed to measure. This definition of a household is not well suited to measuring important aspects of relationships between generations, as the above quotation suggests, since it describes physical closeness and potential emotional closeness, as well as sharing of material resources, among family members who were not, according to the formal definition, sharing a household.

---

[8] P. Laslett, 'Family, Kinship and Collectivity as Systems of Support in Pre-Industrial Europe: A Consideration of the "Nuclear-Hardship" Hypothesis', *Continuity and Change*, 3 (1988), 153–76.

[9] Laslett and Wall, *Household and Family*, 27.

Nevertheless studies of the household using this strict definition can tell us much about relationships of older people to their younger relatives. In 1977 Peter Laslett pointed out that:

The fragmentary though suggestive evidence . . . indicates that the aged in pre-industrial England were more frequently to be found surrounded by their immediate family than is the case in the England of today.[10]

This did not contradict statements about the rarity of the extended family because Laslett was not suggesting that married offspring lived with their parents, but that elders were more likely to have unmarried children living with them than in modern times. This was due to the combination of the relatively high marriage age (normally around the mid-twenties for men and women) with the longer period of childbearing compared with the twentieth century. If a woman bore her last child in her forties that child might still be at home when the mother was defined as 'old' in her late fifties or sixties. Also higher rates of widowhood and the relatively high remarriage rates especially of widowers, often to women of childbearing age, meant that ageing people would have sometimes very young children around them, and, more problematically, dependent upon them.

Laslett concluded that there was:

no clear pattern of failing fathers and mothers joining households of married offspring or requesting it and parents did not strive to keep children at home. Where the elderly shared households with the young it was because they were useful or were head of the household.

Such co-residence, he argued, was based on sentiments of affection, duty, or charity rather than on:

any socially sanctioned expectation that such an action should take place . . . the legal duty [under the Poor Law] of a child to assist his parents never seems to have been construed as an obligation to receive or to maintain him or her in the household. . . . It would certainly not be justifiable, however, to suppose that the story of welfare relationships between the young and the old, between children and their ageing and infirm parents in traditional English society was one of indifference or neglect.[11]

This was to draw inferences about emotional relationships within families from sources which primarily provide information about household structure, but Laslett is clearly correct to infer that there has been no tradition in English culture as in others, such as in those of East Asia, automatically to assume that the older generation shares house-room with their offspring as they grow older. The question for England is how often did the generations live together and in what circumstances and the nature of their relationships when they did not.

---

[10] Laslett, *Illicit Love*, 176.   [11] Ibid. 177.

Laslett pointed out that 'the wisps of evidence we have suggest that in some families elderly persons and children did live in close proximity and others not'.[12] He and his colleagues found that it was rare for widowed old people to live alone or in institutions, though the latter was more probable for widowers, as was 'lodging' with people apparently unrelated to them. Widows were more likely to live with married children. But both elderly men and women were most likely to remain in and head the households in which they had lived when younger, accompanied by unmarried children, servants, or lodgers, related or unrelated.[13] Old people retained their independence until as late an age as possible rather than entering a taken-for-granted state of dependence upon younger relatives, at least until this became physically inescapable.

There were social class differences. The gentry were more likely to have relatives living with them in extended households. But in all classes old people kept their residential independence for as long as they were able. Those who could afford to do so lived with servants in their own households.[14] Even at lower social levels people when possible lived independently of married children. Laslett concluded:

Those who could afford to do just what they wanted about their aged parents did not have them at home. They seem to have set them up with their own servants in their own households, or was it rather that the old gentlemen and old ladies themselves amongst the rich and powerful saw to it that they did not have to live with their married sons and daughters but maintained their own establishments with their own staffs?[15]

He emphasized the importance of not abandoning belief in the support provided by the extended kin network to the individual since there was no strong evidence against it. In particular, he suggested, kin connections might be important in certain life course transitions, such as widowhood, in all social groups, though how important in relation to other sources of support remains debatable.[16]

This description of relations between generations as often close, emotionally and materially, but variable and based upon individual needs and choices rather than upon rules or custom, voluntaristic rather than rule-bound, opens the possibility of a range of possible relationships, co-residential and otherwise. Over time Laslett and his colleagues have shifted to an increasing emphasis upon the variability of family forms around the nuclear norm, to emphasizing that the 'nuclear rules were not rigid'. Especially in times of need the generations might live together for mutual support: deserted wives did

[12] Ibid. 180.

[13] R. Wall, 'The Residence Patterns of Elderly English Women in Comparative Perspective', in L. Botelho and P. Thane (eds.), *Women and Ageing in British Society since 1500* (London, 2000).

[14] Laslett, *Illicit Love*, 212.   [15] Ibid. 212–13.

[16] See also Zvi Razi, 'The Myth of the Immutable English Family', *Past and Present*, 140 (1993), 3–44.

rejoin their parents' households; the elderly did live with married children. But in neither case was it the invariable pattern.[17] Emotional relationships are harder to detect, but there is every sign that they also were highly variable.

As Laslett described it, evoking perfectly the family 'economy of makeshifts', when families lived together, everyone contributed as they could:

> The earnings of all household members were pooled as a family fund and included the moities paid in by the old and the very old who could earn, beg, scrounge or even pilfer little bits until very late in life as could children from an early age.[18]

Laslett later concluded that in pre-industrial England only a small proportion of old people needed to be completely dependent upon poor relief and charity for any extended period of time and that 'it may be that too strong an insistence has been laid on the claim that in earlier times English people invariably preferred independent nuclear families'.[19] The family, it seems, made a definite contribution to the range of resources available to old people. The problem is to estimate how great a contribution, partly due to its variability, and also to the limitations of historical sources.

DESCRIBING ENGLISH FAMILIES AND HOUSEHOLDS

For the period from 1599 to 1800 for the whole of England and Wales, only eight listings have been found of a parish or township which record the ages of inhabitants and provide adequate detail of the family relationships of household members. These are all one-off, 'snapshot' listings, which give no indication of change over time. They come from different parts of the country and from a variety of time periods. No one has tried to claim that they are representative of the whole population over two centuries but, limited though they are, they have formed the basis of calculations about whether the generations lived together in pre-industrial England.

For all their limitations these local censuses give glimpses of living arrangements of older people in particular places and times. That of rural Ealing, near London, in 1599 described eighty-six households, composed of 427 people. Twenty-seven of these included people past their mid-fifties, twenty of them over 60. Only three people over 60, all male, lived alone. The vicar, aged 54, had no wife and shared his household with a daughter and son-in-law, two teenage sons, and one servant. A 78-year-old merchant, Peter Hayward, shared a home with his schoolmaster son, eighteen scholars, and two servants. Richard Phillips, gentleman, aged 61, lived with his wife, two teenage children, and servants. John Maynard, yeoman of the guard, aged

---

[17] Laslett, 'Family, Kinship', 154–5.   [18] Ibid. 164.
[19] P. Laslett, *A Fresh Map of Life: The Emergence of the Third Age* (London, 1989), 122–35.

60, lived with his wife of the same age and four servants. 60-year-old yeoman Symon Barringer lived with his younger wife, daughters aged 12 and 3, and four husbandmen. 60-year-old Elizabeth Sherborne lived with her 55-year-old yeoman husband, two adult daughters, two younger sons, a 4-year-old daughter, described as hers, and farm servants. The wife of 30-year-old William Lawrence was recorded as aged 67 and they lived with 'their' children aged 1 and 4. 60-year-old Rachel Smalewood lived with her 32-year-old husband and 'their' son aged 7; 60-year-old Elizabeth Fote, with her 40-year-old husband and their teenage daughter. In some of these cases either the ages or the precise parenthood of the children must be misrecorded; widowers with children may have married older women willing to care for them and their children. Only three older people in Ealing lived in households headed by their children. 60-year-old widow Ate's 24-year-old daughter lived with her. 67-year-old William Williams's 25-year-old son lived with him. 60-year-old Richard Hall, yeoman, lived with his 50-year-old wife; John Wilkin with his of 72. Three husbandmen in their early sixties lived with wives ten years or more younger and their children, several of them very young. This suggests both the variety of living arrangements of older people even of similar status in a small community, and the difficulty of deducing the nature of some relationships from such lists.

The Norwich census of the poor of 1570 suggests how often grandchildren, or sometimes unrelated young children, lived with old people. Trace was aged 80 and his wife 60. He was past work and deaf; she spun white warp and they had a secure tenancy of their house. They received no alms and were very poor. With them lived a grandchild, aged 10, who also spun. He could learn skills from his grandmother whilst helping the old people around the home and in negotiating the outside world. Alice Coles, a widow of 92 and unable to work, had living with her a 'childe's daughter' of 18 who knitted hose. The children of poor widows might live with others because their mothers could not afford to keep them. Richard Sandlying, a blind man of 54 unable to work, lived with his wife of the same age who spun white warp and a 'child' of 21 who also spun. The household also included a fatherless child of 12 who led Richard about. The Hales, a couple both in their eighties and 'not hable to worke' had with them a 'mayd' of 18 who spun and 'loke to them'. They received the high rate of 12*d.* per week alms, but were still in extreme poverty. Young people might be placed with needy old people by the poor relief authorities as a means of providing for the needs of both generations, though it is also highly likely that the poor made their own arrangements of mutual convenience. The mobility and alertness of a child could greatly enhance the viability of an ageing household.[20]

---

[20] M. Pelling, 'Old Age, Poverty and Disability in Early Modern Norwich: Work, Remarriage and Other Expedients', in M. Pelling and R. M. Smith, *Life, Death and the Elderly: Historical Perspectives* (London, 1991), 86–90.

In other places in the late sixteenth and seventeenth centuries old people took in their deserted or widowed daughters and/or their grandchildren, often at some personal cost. When widow Manning's daughter and grandchildren were deserted by her son-in-law in Salisbury in 1634 she offered to take them in. She asked help from the Salisbury overseers, claiming that 'motherly love' prompted her to 'suffer in her old age and bear some part of her daughter's misery and poverty, though she suffer herself'.[21] Similarly, a Northumberland widow petitioned the Poor Law authorities in 1711 that she cared for two girls,

that's my grandchildren and the youngest is about thirty years of age and neither of them can tell to twenty . . . I am burthened something with them because they are not capable of service.[22]

The conventions adopted by Laslett and his colleagues for analysing household listings may lead to underestimation of co-residence between the generations. Their definition of a household excludes lodgers, yet aged relatives could be described in the censuses as 'lodgers', 'sojourners', or boarders. This convention may therefore overlook some three-generation families where surname or other evidence does not make relationships clear, as when a parent lived with a married daughter. For example, William King, a yeoman of Little Gransden, Cambridgeshire, was reckoned to be about 92 in 1646–9 when his evidence was taken in a lawsuit as the oldest inhabitant. He had been a bailiff and rent-collector and had lived in the parish for sixty years. He had been a farmer of four different farms but, his wife being dead and his children grown up, he now 'liveth as a sojourner with one of his sonnes'.[23] Such language long continued. Married children living with parents were listed as lodgers in Corfe Castle in 1790 and in a description of Sandwich, Kent, in 1776.[24] In the census of 1851 the household of John Allton, a labourer at Chilvers Coton in Warwickshire, was described as consisting of himself, his wife, Richard Coton, son-in-law married, lodger; Millicent Coton (John's daughter) married, lodger; another daughter Harriet Evans, married, lodger.[25]

Thomas Sokoll included lodgers in his definition of the household in his study of the Essex parishes of Ardleigh in 1796 and Braintree in 1821–30. Of the pauper households in Ardleigh eight (15 per cent) consisted of more than one generation. Five consisted of a young couple, two without and three with children, all sharing homes with the wife's mother; two of a young family plus

---

[21] P. Slack, *Poverty and Policy*, 86.

[22] Peter Rushton, 'Lunatics and Idiots: Mental Disability, the Community and the Poor Law in North-East England, 1600–1800', *Medical History*, 32 (1988), 34–50.

[23] Margaret Spufford, 'Peasant Inheritance Customs and Land Distribution in Cambridgeshire from 16th–18th Centuries', in J. Goody, J. Thirsk, E. P. Thompson (eds.), *Family and Inheritance: Rural Society in Western Europe, 1200–1800* (Cambridge, 1976), 174.

[24] M. Barker-Read, 'The Treatment of the Aged Poor in Five Selected West Kent Parishes from Settlement to Speenhamland, 1662–1797', Ph.D. thesis (Open University, 1988), 166.

[25] Laslett and Wall, *Household and Family*, 35 n. 50.

the husband's mother. One was made up of a young shoemaker and his wife, four children and two journeymen, plus the wife's father and her grandfather, aged 86, the only four-generation household in the community. In all eight households the young man was the head, suggesting that the widowed parent was taken into the home of the younger couple.[26]

Six households (12 per cent) which were not dependent on poor relief contained more than two generations. In four of these, the father of one of the spouses was the head. Two of these household heads were blacksmiths, one a brickmaker, one an innkeeper. Perhaps the younger people worked for, and hoped to inherit, the business. Two families, both of large farmers, included the mother of the head of the household. Thirteen of thirty-seven paupers aged over 50 at the time of the census lived with their children; and twenty of seventy-seven non-paupers aged over 50. In late eighteenth-century Ardleigh, 'the taking in of elderly people into the households of their married children might have been a distinctive behavioural pattern among the poor'[27] though it was also observable among the non-poor.[28]

It is widely assumed by historians that the very poor were more likely than the better off to live alone or in very small households.[29] However, Sokoll suggests that this is based on misreading the early censuses of the poor. All of these list as living alone individuals who cannot have formed independent households. For example, that of Salisbury included children as separate entries, including one 4-year-old bastard, who is most unlikely to have been living alone. The pauper censuses were not concerned with listing households as such but with people receiving or claiming poor relief, who may have shared households with non-paupers. Sokoll concludes that many apparently isolated poor people in fact lived with non-paupers.[30]

Ardleigh in 1796 was 'economically and socially a fairly representative rural community' and in consequence suffering deteriorating conditions. More than half of its households were on regular poor relief at this time. On the other hand, in Braintree in 1821, also a poor community suffering from the decline in handweaving, with few well-off ratepayers and, in consequence, below-average relief payments, relatively few elderly people lived with their adult children: not above 14 per cent of all over 50. The difference between the two communities is hard to account for and illustrates the variability of local practice.[31]

---

[26] Thomas Sokoll, 'Household and Family among the Poor: The case of Two Essex Communities in the Late 18th and Early 19th Centuries', Ph.D. thesis (Cambridge, 1988), 195; and *Household and Family among the Poor: The Case of Two Essex Communities in the Late 18th and Early 19th Centuries* (Bochum, 1993); and 'Old Age in Poverty: The Record of Essex Pauper Letters, 1780–1834', in T. Hitchcock, P. King, P. Sharpe (eds.), *Chronicling Poverty: The Voices and Strategies of the English Poor, 1640–1840* (Basingstoke, 1997), 127–54.
[27] Sokoll, thesis, 205.   [28] Ibid. 220.
[29] e.g. P. Laslett, *The World We Have Lost—Further Explored* (London, 1983), 46, 64. Slack *Poverty and Policy*, 85.
[30] Sokoll, 'Household and Family', 72–5.   [31] Ibid.

TABLE 7.1. *Percentage of all wills including house-room bequests to widows*

Kings Langley	1489–1659	15
Salisbury	1540–1639	4
Kibworth Harcourt	1550–*c.*1750	*c.*15
Abingdon	1540–1720	3
Orwell	*c.*1550–*c.*1700	*c.*100
Sussex	1579–1682	3
Lincs.	1591–1682	0
Yorks.	1640–90	3

Source: A.-L. Erickson, *Women and Property in Early Modern England* (London, 1993).

Barker-Read estimates that at least 6.9 per cent of the 1,053 'pensioners' she can trace in poor law records in west Kent in the late seventeenth and eighteenth centuries at some time lived with close kin. All were female. Since this is calculated from evidence of shared surnames alone it must be an underestimate.[32]

The limited statistical evidence does not suggest a clearly established customary right of the elderly to share a home even with very close relatives, but it equally clearly shows that it occurred with some frequency—though how frequently and in what circumstances is elusive.[33]

WILLS, DIARIES, AND OTHER SOURCES

Census statistics can be supported by other forms of evidence. Examples survive in wills from the fifteenth, sixteenth, and seventeenth centuries of 'old folk being provided with bed, board and access to the fire', 'sleeping in the little low chamber off the hall'. Wills specifying that widows should be provided with house-room by the heir have been found widely in place and time between the fifteenth and eighteenth centuries, though their incidence varies widely for reasons which are quite unclear. See Table 7.1.

Not only the prosperous made such stipulations. Wills can suggest change in family arrangements over time as one-off parish listings cannot and can convey something of the reality of family relationships, including their tensions. John Adam junior, according to the will of his father made in Orwell, Cambridgeshire, in 1592, was to support and give house-room to both his mother and his grandmother if need be, one in the chamber and one in the

[32] Barker-Read, 'West Kent', 283, 281.
[33] See also S. King, 'The Nature and Causes of Demographic Change in an Industrializing Township: Calverley, 1681–1820', Ph.D. thesis (Liverpool, 1993).

kitchen.[34] Robert Salmon, a landless man with a cottage, willed at Willingham, Cambridgeshire, at the end of the sixteenth century that his unmarried adult daughter was to inherit the cottage, but he left

Rose, my wife, a bedroom in my kitchen with the easement of the fire there . . . and if my said wife Rose and Agnes Salmon my daughter cannot agree for the kitchen then I will my said daughter . . . at (her) costs and charges shall build her a little house at the backside of the kitchen with a Chimney in it. And if so my said wife shall depart from the kitchen into the little house before mentioned.

William Brasier, who left a half-yardland in 1589, specified that his widow be given space in the house bequeathed to his son, but provided that if they 'cannot agree together in the house, she is to be paid £3 a year for life'.[35]

At a higher social level, some decades later, Ralph Josselin left his wife sufficient land and moveable property to protect her and

her dwelling in three or four rooms of the mansion house wherein I now dwell together with free ingress, egress and regress out of the same into the yard . . . with all the wood, logs, broom, coal and whatsoever in the yard is laid in for firing during her natural life.[36]

Spufford concluded from her study of fifteenth- and sixteenth-century wills from rural communities in Cambridgeshire that 'living with in-laws, or rather, having a widowed parent to live with one, when one was of age to inherit the farm was very much the ordinary expected thing to do'.[37] It is less clear that this was so 'ordinary' elsewhere. Wills from rural Kibworth Harcourt, Leicestershire, from the sixteenth to the eighteenth centuries, indicate that in that district when an heir married he was given house-space, if his parents survived, but the father remained head of the household and farm. When the father died the widow either remained head or retired and was given, usually, a room, with a hearth, and storage in the yard. When John Carter died in 1690 he had been occupying seven rooms. His widow continued in three of them until she died in 1711. Her son occupied the remaining four while she remained head of the household.[38]

In two Suffolk villages in the sixteenth and seventeenth centuries wills regularly provided for the care, though not necessarily the house-room, of widows into old age, whatever their age of widowhood, sometimes (and less frequently over time) on condition that they did not remarry. The widow might inherit her husband's entire estate, receive an annual pension or a fixed lump-sum legacy or household goods and tools, or children might be required to provide food, care, and housing. By the seventeenth century wills in these

---

[34] Margaret Spufford, *Contrasting Communities: English Villagers in the Sixteenth and Seventeenth Centuries* (Cambridge, 1974), 117.   [35] Ibid. 163, 164.

[36] MacFarlane, *Marriage and Love*, 114.   [37] Spufford, 'Peasant Inheritance Customs'.

[38] Cicely Howell, 'Peasant Inheritance Customs in the Midlands, 1280–1700', in Goody *et al. Family and Inheritance*, 113–50.

villages were less likely to specify that the widow be given house-room.[39] In an increasingly cash-based economy, money settlements became more common, especially in more prosperous communities. Such devices were apparently successful in protecting widows against destitution; no widow provided for by any of these means went onto poor relief or local charity. Wills may overrepresent co-residence. Whilst will-making was relatively rare, as it was before the eighteenth century, they were disproportionately made by fathers of children under age and with property to dispose.[40] They might be expected to make provision for the widow when she had brought the children to maturity.

Discoveries that widowed old people sometimes lived with their children do not necessarily conflict with the conclusion that co-residence was uncommon in most communities at most times in pre-industrial England. It is estimated that only 5.8 per cent of all households in England between the late sixteenth and the early nineteenth centuries contained more than two generations. On average at any one time only 6.2 per cent of the population was widowed. It is quite possible that a very high proportion of widowed people (very many of whom would not have been aged) lived with their married children, yet that multi-generation households were a small proportion of all households; and clearly there were important local and regional variations.

Diaries, memoirs, autobiographies, biographies, and historical studies of communities provide further insights into family relationships. Such evidence is patchy and perhaps unrepresentative, but no more so than the statistical data. Such sources were produced mainly by the literate and comfortably off. As such they can complement the evidence from Poor Law records which mainly concern poorer families, and contribute to a picture of relations between the generations at all levels of society. These sources overwhelmingly suggest that the generations lived together in certain circumstances, not as a matter of routine (though in some agricultural areas this may have been so) but often in response to need on the part of one or other of the generations, not always the older: the ageing landholders experiencing difficulty in working their land or the younger generation needing help with children. They also demonstrate that considerable support could be exchanged between the generations when they lived not in the same household but close by.

In early sixteenth-century Coventry at all social levels, though least among the poorest, relatives provided support for needy elders. Elderly parents lived close to such offspring as they had, though the 1523 census suggests that 'only in a tiny minority of cases (invariably mothers) can elderly parents have survived long enough to become so enfeebled that they had to be taken into a

---

[39] L. Botelho, 'Provisions for the Elderly in Two Early Modern Suffolk Communities', Ph.D. thesis (Cambridge, 1996), 165–78; and ' "The Old Woman's Wish": Widows by the Family Fire? Widows' Old Age Provisions in Rural England, 1500–1700', R. Wall, ed., *The History of the Family* (forthcoming).

[40] Botelho, 'Provisions for the Elderly', 51.

filial home'.[41] In Coventry old people kept their residential independence for as long as they were able, sharing with married children only in the last phase of life. Similarly in Southwark in 1618 Roger Cotten's son-in-law moved next door to him, possibly in part of Cotten's house divided for the purpose. Cotten was then in process of social decline. Following Cotten's move to an almshouse the son-in-law Willis seems to have left the district but to have lived close enough by to provide financial support to Cotten in his last illness, as a petition from his daughter to the churchwardens suggests:

whereas Roger Cotten your petitioners late father lived in one of the almshouses of your parish and now by the will of god is deceased. And whereas your petitioner hath been at great charges and expenses with him by reason of providing things necessary for him in time of his sickness and likewise for the burying of him, which he desired might be by her mother in the churchyard . . . which was accordingly performed. Therefore your petitioner in consideration of her great expenses and charges desires your worships favour to grant unto her such small things of household stuff which are remaining in the said almshouses as her said late father left behind.[42]

Support from offspring was important even for the relatively favoured inhabitants of almshouses.

A number of Southwark householders moved to live near or with relatives who were undergoing a period of hardship. In 1619 Richard Ashton, shoemaker and parish pensioner, lived in Counter Alley and Henry Ashton shoemaker in Goat Yard. In 1622 both were sharing a household in Counter Alley. Richard was not then receiving a parish pension, perhaps because he was being supported by his family. Richard was elected to the College of the Poor, an almshouse, where he died in 1625.[43]

Later in the seventeenth century the diary of Ralph Josselin records that he housed his father-in-law who 'delighted to be with us until his death'. Josselin himself lived to age 68 but to the end retained control of his wealth and of his estate, never fully retiring or handing over his property to his children, though he distributed much of it among them as they married. He received much affection from them but no obvious material support, though nor is there much sign that he needed it more than they did. Josselin felt both a duty and a desire to support his father even though he expected to inherit nothing and they did not share a home:

In reference to my father I bless god to give me a spirit careful to please him so that I had his blessing being a joy and not a grief of heart unto him [He was] grieved that he should leave me no estate and I told him if he had enough for himself I hoped god would so bless me as that I should if need were to be helpful to him; it is a continual comfort to think of my tender love to him.[44]

[41] C. Phythian-Adams, *Desolation of a City: Coventry and the Urban Crisis of the Late Middle Ages* (Cambridge, 1979), 150.

[42] J. Boulton, *Neighbourhood and Society: A London Suburb in the Seventeenth Century* (Cambridge, 1987), 260.

[43] Ibid. 258.   [44] MacFarlane, *Marriage and Love*, 113.

Richard Gough's gossip about his neighbours in the parish of Myddle (Shropshire) in the later seventeenth century provides many examples of relatives giving shelter, and other forms of support, to elders down on their luck. Thomas Hoskins was one of many residents of Myddle whose poverty in old age was due to 'his practice to go to the alehouse dayly'. He

was well-educated-hee was a good father and a good farmer and a good Clarke and a good companion and that marred all. He spent his Estate faster than his ancestors gott itt and tooke noe care to leave somewhat to maintain him in his old age. After the death of his first wife he married a rich widow, but spent all she had.

Then 'Hee went to his son-in-law' Edward Tong, by whom he had also been 'kept on charity' before his re-marriage, whilst his ruined wife 'poore woman went to live in the Lodge on Haremeare Heath and had nothing to maintain herself butt what her neighbours sent' and 'dyed in a poore cottage in great poverty and want'.[45]

This was not the only case of separation of an older couple in Myddle. Rowland Mucklestone married three times, in no case happily. Whilst Gough was writing in 1700, 'he and his third wife are both liveing, but live not together for hee lives with his son att Meriton, and shee with her son at Astley'.[46] Samuell Downton, another son of 'a person well to pass in the world', made a second marriage to the servant girl who looked after his children. He fell into debt and gradually sold off his land. He and his wife stole away one night leaving their children to the parish, 'into Staffordshire and there hee went a begging like an old decrepite person and shee carryed a box with pinnes . . . and laces'. Until she ran off with another man, 'and then this Samuell came again to Alderton to his son Thomas who maintained him during his life'.

This Thomas

by his parsimonious liveing had spared soe much out of his rent . . . as had paid all the money he borrowed to pay his father and had gott a good stocke of catell and was in a condition to live well.

But then,

unexpectedly hee marryed a wife with nothing . . . and she proved such a drunken woman as hath never beene heard of; shee spent her husband's estate soe fast that it seemed incredible . . . This Thomas Downton was a sickly aged man when he marryed and had noe childe.

When all his property had been spent he too 'returned to his son John, who maintained him untill he dyed, which happened soone after his return'.[47] It is impossible to estimate what proportion of the old people of Myddle lived with adult children, but it is notable that Gough does not seem to regard offering them house-room or other forms of support by children for even

---

[45] R. Gough, *History of Myddle* (London, 1993), 121.   [46] Ibid. 118.   [47] Ibid. 138.

thoroughly disreputable parents as in any way unusual. The families he described were not poor. Most, apart from their phases of dissipated decline, were middling comfortable rural families, living in a prosperous, settled agricultural community.

Other diaries and memoirs convey a similar picture. In 1632 when Adam Martindale's mother died, his married sister hurried from London and offered her father a home with her family. She and her husband decided instead to move to the country to be close to her father 'so that' as Martindale puts it 'my father and she might be comforts and assistants to one another'. But shortly after she died of smallpox. The father was then in his early fifties. When he reached 60 he decided to retire and to share his tenement with his elder son. However, the son managed the land so incompetently that the father had constantly to support him. He died aged 80 still supporting himself, and intermittently his son also, apparently on income from his land.[48]

Later in the century, the squire Ralph Thoresby recalled how his father-in-law decided to 'live upon his children', moving from house to house, apparently assuming it as his right. Thoresby found it expensive. He could,

By no means quit my father-in-law who gave over house-keeping and came with his wife, daughter and servant to live upon his children and though he sometimes went to brother Ws and Rs yet I think he was half if not two-thirds of his time at my house, and being of a generous spirit was too liberal of my liquor to visitants that I saw it absolutely necessary to give over wine.[49]

It is striking how many of these references concern fathers and in-laws, for whom Laslett and his colleagues suggest the younger generations felt least responsibility.

The diary of William Stout, the Quaker merchant of Lancaster (1665–1752), gives a full picture of the relationships with close relatives first of his mother then of himself as they aged. Both lived into their eighties. Stout's mother was widowed in middle age, with teenage children to raise. She brought them up, then ran her house for the youngest son, Josias, who neither moved away nor married. At age 65 she began to find this too much. Josias was inclined neither to marry nor to have servants manage the house, so he let the estate to a tenant and moved to live with his second brother, Leonard; the mother shared her time between Leonard's and William's houses. The tenant turned out disappointingly. Josias and his mother moved back and managed with the help of servants. When the mother reached the age of 76, in 1709, she could no longer cope with this arrangement and had become 'very infirme and uneasy with the care of the house and was urgent on [Josias] to marry, he not being willing to keepe house with a servant'. Obediently Josias, aged 48, married.

[48] R. Parkinson (ed.), *The Life of Adam Martindale* (Manchester, 1895).
[49] MacFarlane, *Marriage and Love*, 112.

But there were frictions between Mrs Stout and her daughter-in-law, who had been accustomed to keeping her father's house and did not like interference. After a year Josias asked William to 'entertain' his mother. She remained in William's household 'in much content and unity till the time of her death, which was about eight years, without any consideration except what my said brother Josias would freely offer'. She died aged 84 and was still spinning within four months of her death.

Stout himself lived through a variety of living arrangements as he aged. He never married and for much of his life his house was kept by his sister, who was discouraged by their mother from marrying 'considering her infermetys and ill state of health . . . knowing the care and exercises that always attended a marryed life and the hazard of hapiness in it'. She died when he was about 60. A niece then kept house for him for three years until she married. Another niece took over, until she started seeing a young man whom Stout regarded as unsuitable, and was returned home to her parents. Stout engaged a housekeeper and another niece lodged with him until she met the same fate as her sister (Stout had little sympathy with young people). Fourteen months later he let his house to Mary Dillworth and 'lodged' in it with her and her sister for four years. By then he was aged 69. This arrangement came to an end and he gave over the house to the nephew to whom he had passed his business, having decided to retire, though he was still very active. He went to live in the rooms over the shop near by, with his two youngest nieces as housekeepers. One of these, however, also had an unfortunate taste in men and the other was sickly,

so I gave over housekeeping and borded with my nephew William Stout and allowed him £20 a year for the same, but kept the roomes to lodge in. But it was not easy there seeing they were going to ruine.

He ate with William's family but kept separate rooms and 'only came to my victuals in the house, being no way easy with their way of living'.

Before long William jun. was bankrupt. Stout sent him and his family to live elsewhere, though he continued to support them, while continually threatening not to. He kept house with a servant, but took in his young great-niece 'free, in order to improve herself in learning'. This arrangement continued satisfactorily to 1741 when he was aged 76. A year later the servant married. His great-niece was now aged 20, so 'I resolved to be served by her and to get a woman each weeke or two to wash, brew and clean the house as there was occasion'. The niece kept house 'more to my satisfaction than I could have expected'. Stout remained fit and active. He supported his surviving brother and his wife and gave frequent gifts to his nieces and nephews, despite his distaste for their behaviour. His great-nieces's housekeeping satisfied him until 1743 when at age 78 he had a serious accident. Immediately his brother, he and his wife being old and infirm, sent one of their sons and a servant to care for him. There his diary ended, though Stout lived another eight years. This diary documents both the closeness of family relationships within this Quaker branch of the merchant/small landowner class of eighteenth-century Lancaster, even when family members did not share a household, and the power and control over his life that a fit and prosperous old man could exert; and also the shifts and experiments necessary to achieve satisfactory living conditions, which were in the end highly contingent upon personalities.[50]

Unmarried children—or as in Stout's case other unmarried relatives—might stay in the home, willingly or not, or return to it, to care for ageing parents. This was part of a long tradition. In later medieval England Dyer has commented that: 'at home, young people were pressurized to stay and become the "son and servant" or "daughter and servant" of their parents',[51] as they were still in nineteenth-century and late twentieth-century England.[52] Stout describes how in 1702 Thomas Greene, a 74-year-old grocer and draper of Lancaster sent for his two daughters, then living with relatives in London, 'in hopes and expectations that they might be assistant to him and their mother in his trade and other ways in their old age'. The need was occasioned by the fact that their son, whom they had expected to assist them in their old age, had drunk himself to death at the age of 35. The arrangement with the daughters did not work out happily.[53] In 1695 the minister Henry Newcombe expressed in his will his confidence that his daughter Rose would stay with his wife after his death. Ultimately he wished 60 per cent of his goods to go to her 'in consideration that she hath denied herself and spent her time and strength in painful, tender attendance upon us both in our old age and great infirmities'.[54] In Braintree in 1821 older widows, both paupers and non-paupers, were most likely to live with unmarried daughters and to retain the household headship, for example, Rebecca Thompson, aged 95, the oldest person on record in Braintree in 1821, lived with her daughter Mary aged 70.[55] Unmarried children may indeed have been the most important sources of assistance to the old.[56] Again, however, we must not assume that assistance always flowed upwards through the generations. As we have seen, the reverse might be the case, or the support mutual, though the balance was likely to shift as the older person aged and declined.

A striking feature of all these past accounts is their taken-for-granted assumption that mutual support between older and younger generations and, where necessary, sharing a household, was normal at all social levels, when circumstances required it.

[50] J. D. Marshall (ed.), *The Autobiography of William Stout of Lancaster, 1665–1752* (Manchester, 1967).
[51] C. Dyer, *Standards of Living in the Later Middle Ages* (Cambridge, 1989), 231.
[52] See pp. 299–301.   [53] Marshall, *Stout*, 140–1.
[54] R. Parkinson (ed.), *The Autobiography of Henry Newcombe MA* (Manchester, 1852).
[55] Sokoll, thesis, 311.   [56] Laslett, *Illicit Love*, 119–202.

DID OLD PEOPLE HAVE FAMILIES?

Families could provide close support and comfort for ageing people whether or not they shared a household. But they did not always do so. Some old people were neglected by their adult children and many others outlived their surviving children in times of high mortality, such as generally prevailed in pre-industrial England. How often they did so surviving sources cannot tell. Computer simulation exercises suggest that about one-third of women living to age 65 in the sixteenth and seventeenth centuries would have had no surviving child, a proportion which fell to below 20 per cent by the late eighteenth century. These measures are imperfect, but they plausibly suggest that many old people would have no surviving children to support them.[57]

If children did survive, in the highly mobile society of pre-industrial England they might migrate beyond reach. It is estimated that up to 50 per cent of old people would have had no children close at hand, a far higher proportion than in late twentieth-century surveys.[58] And the children of old people too poor to be self-supporting were highly likely themselves to be too poor to give much help even if they lived near by. The typically late age of marriage further limited the potential for support between generations; the younger generation's own children were likely to be at their peak dependency at the time when parents declined into need. A final reason why old people might not have been supported by their children was conflict and estrangement; as we have seen, awareness of this possibility was deeply embedded in English and more generally in North European culture, sometimes with good reason, as the fate of Daniel Defoe suggested. To avoid attempts by his enemies to destroy his estate he legally conveyed his property to his son Daniel for the remainder of his life, for the benefit of his wife and two unmarried daughters. The son proceeded to convert the property to his own use. Defoe wrote in his last letter in 1730:

I depended on him, I trusted him, I gave up my two dear unprovided children into his hands; but he has no compassion and suffers them and their poor dying mother to beg their bread at his door and to crave as if it were an alms what he is bound under hand and seal besides the most sacred promises to supply them with: himself at the same time living in a profusion of plenty.[59]

Very many old people in early modern England would not have had children able to shelter and support them even if they had wanted and needed them to. Equally, quite a high proportion of those who could have lived with

---

[57] E. A. Wrigley, 'Fertility Strategy for the Individual and the Group', in C. Tilly (ed.), *Historical Studies in Changing Fertility* (Princeton, 1979), 255–6. J. Smith, 'The Computer Simulation of Kin Sets and Kin Counts', in J. Bongaarts, T. Birch, K. J. Wachter (eds.), *Family Demography, Methods and their Applications* (Oxford, 1987), 261–5.
[58] Ibid. See pp. 430–3.   [59] MacFarlane, *Marriage and Love*, 111.

their children may well have done so. Ruggles cautiously estimates that this might have been true of two-thirds to three-quarters between the late sixteenth and late eighteenth centuries.[60] Still more would have received essential support without living with their adult children and would never have experienced full dependency. When old people did share homes with their children they were not necessarily happy or well cared for. Equally, absence of children able to give support did not necessarily leave old people bereft of care. In societies where the family is the only socially recognized form of support for old people the childless, where possible, adopt parentless or propertyless heirs, who in return care for them in old age.[61] We have seen examples from medieval times onwards of people living in mutually supportive relationships who were not parent and child or in any way related. Old people without families have in all times been active in seeking to plan their own lives and have created alternative networks of support.

MARRIAGE AND OTHER STRATAGEMS

A variety of expedients were available to old people who wanted to avoid solitude. One was marriage. This might be designed to solve multiple family difficulties. In a petition to the Poor Law authorities a Northumberland woman claimed in 1699 that she had been persuaded to marry a 'simple man', the son of the house where she was a servant, because his parents had grown too old to 'manage their concerns as they had formerly done'. This would have brought her both security and upward social mobility, care for the parents and long term for their 'simple' son. But these plans were destroyed when she suffered a crippling accident. She was ejected from the house and forced to return to her pauper mother.[62]

Remarriage of poorer widowed people as they aged was more common for men than for women and was often to someone younger and capable of providing some support. Only ten (5 per cent) of the poor, aged men in the Norwich census of 1570 were without wives. Of these, three lived with children under 16; one, a cobbler aged 78, with another male cobbler, his 'servant' whom he had taken in four years previously. Of the three who lived alone, 'one was described as beside himself a little, that is mentally ill and another as an evil husband'.[63] Among 526 old people identified in Norwich there were 130 marriages in which one spouse was at least ten years the older. In 71 per cent of these the male was the older and the age discrepancies were

---

[60] S. Ruggles, *Prolonged Connections: The Rise of the Extended Family in Nineteenth-Century England and America* (Madison, 1987).

[61] Mead Cain, 'Welfare Institutions in Comparative Perspective: The Fate of the Elderly in Contemporary South Asia and Pre-Industrial Western Europe', in Pelling and Smith, *Life, Death*, 251.

[62] Rushton, 'Lunatics and Idiots', 39.

[63] Pelling, 'Old Age . . . in Norwich', in Pelling and Smith, *Life, Death*, 88.

greater than where the woman was the older. The incentive may sometimes have been that the older partner owned his or her house. More important, however, was probably the ability to work and/or to provide care. Where the younger partner was male he might have young children from a previous partnership in need of care. Disability or sickness characterized one in three such marriages in Norwich, a higher rate of disability than among the elderly poor in general. For example, John Wytherley was 80 but 'in worke'; his wife Elizabeth was 40, 'a lame woman'. They had three children aged between 3 months and 7 years. They had income of 3*d*. per week and were 'veri pore'.[64]

In west Kent in the late seventeenth and eighteenth centuries a number of male pensioners had wives who were considerably younger and several had small children.[65] Above the level of pauperism, in seventeenth- and eighteenth-century Colyton, 'many men entered their second or third marriages with a young wife when they were themselves in their fifties or sixties and found themselves raising families when their ability to labour was diminishing'.[66] At higher social levels, marriage to a propertied old man could bring security to a poorer woman and provide the old man with care, especially if she was an experienced servant—though in two such cases in Myddle the wives drank away the elderly husband's property and a third disgraced and made a laughing-stock of her rich, 'weake and old', husband by murdering the wife of her lover.[67] It might be less risky for those who could afford it to employ a servant as carer, as William Stout did when necessary. Marriages between elderly spouses of similar age, successful or otherwise, for support and companionship of course occurred. The first marriage performed by Parson Woodforde in 1764 was between 'an old farmer widower of 80 and a widow of 70'.[68]

Also, voluntarily or not, old people might share a household with others in need who were apparently unrelated to them. As we have seen,[69] this was often arranged by the poor relief authorities. The household listing for Puddletown in Dorset in 1724 includes:

Elizabeth Lovelace, born 1659 [i.e. age 65]. Maiden. In moderate circumstances. May Daug. [hter] of Lawrence Boyce, lives with her, born in 1701. 2 in fam[ily] Sarah Clutter, a maiden born 1654. Sarah Whitten a poor, lame widow. In ye same house on ye left hand have two sisters, Jane born in 1659 and Elizabeth George, 1665. All poor and maintained by ye Parish. 4 in fam. David [?] widower and John Wellstream a widower, both maintained by ye Parish. 2 in fam.

In Ardleigh in 1796 one pauper household contained an elderly widow, Abigail Johnson, aged 64, who received a regular pension of 2*s*. per week from the

[64] Pelling, 'Old Age . . . in Norwich', in Pelling and Smith, *Life, Death*, 87–90.

[65] Barker-Read, 'West Kent', 282.

[66] P. Sharpe, 'Gender-Specific Demographic Adjustment to Changing Economic Circumstances: Colyton, 1538–1837', Ph.D. thesis (Cambridge, 1988).   [67] Gough, *Myddle*, 120–1.

[68] J. Beresford (ed.), *James Woodforde: The Diary of a Country Parson, 1758–1802* (Oxford, 1978), 28.

[69] pp. 109–10.

parish. With her were Martha Loft aged 26 and her daughter Charlotte, aged one, who were also on relief.[70] In eighteenth-century Colyton in November 1752 the overseer of the poor 'Pd Old Widow Venn, Widow Denning and Susannah Anton more than their usual pay when Mr Panice turned them out of the house in the open street'. All were certainly over 50 and frequently sick. All had close relatives in the town. Susannah Anton moved in with two other women of similar age. The parish decided to patch up the house, so they 'Pd John Sweetland for reed and thatching Agnes Wishlade's house where Grace Long and Susannah Anton now lives'. Widow Denning's house rent was shared with different single women for each year after the eviction until she died in 1766. She was also paid for helping Jane Ford's (illegitimate) child who was 4 years old.[71]

In Braintree most very poor widows lived with other poor widows or single women. There were eleven such in 1821 aged between 50 and 81 in five households consisting of women who were not evidently related to each other:

1. Widows, aged 57, 50.
2. Elizabeth Cooper, 71; Mary Livermore, 61.
3. Widow Hudson, 70; Priscilla Cannon, 59.
4. Ann Pearson, widow, 70; Sarah Cowel, 81; Mary Clerk, 72.
5. Mary Sly, widow; Jane Willsher, widow.

There were five non-pauper households of this type, occupied by six unmarried and seven widowed women, also mainly aged.[72] Such arrangements might occur by choice at other social levels. Samuel Johnson shared his house in his declining years with three other ageing people, Mr Levett and Mrs Williams, both of whom died a year or so before him, and Mrs Desmoulins who outlived him but in a feeble state.[73]

Old people received support from others and supported one another in a variety of ways. They established networks of support for themselves when they could and they might be assisted to do so by the poor relief system when they could not. The image of the solitary, impoverished, marginalized old person, usually a woman, as a relatively common feature of early modern society, should be treated with caution.

FAMILY RESPONSIBILITY AND THE POOR LAW

Assertions that relatives especially children took little responsibility for old people have been based not only upon statistics of household structure but

[70] Sokoll, *Household and Family*, 160.

[71] P. Sharpe, 'Literally Spinsters: A New Interpretation of Local Economy and Demography in Colyton in the 17th and 18th Centuries', *Economic History Review*, 44/1 (1991), 59.

[72] Sokoll, *Household and Family*, 248–51.

[73] J. Boswell, *Life of Samuel Johnson*, 6 vols. (Oxford, 1964).

also upon records of Poor Law practice, in particular examples of poor relief being paid to those who had children living near by, or even living with them. For example, in Clayworth in 1688 Nicholas Bacon had succeeded to his father's trade of cooper and to the family house, so is unlikely to have been impoverished, yet his mother and sister were housed in 'the common houses on alms' he being unwilling or unable to support them after his marriage. There were old people in seventeenth-century Aldenham supported by charity or poor relief who certainly had surviving children. Agnes Hall (Hoyle) a widow had eight children baptized between 1570 and 1586. In 1603 she was over 60 and on relief while her eldest son lived in the parish with his own family of six children.[74] Old Launcelot Watson and his second wife were both over 70 and apparently destitute in 1674 when Tonbridge parish bought them a new bed, reclothed them, and restocked their butcher's shop. There is no evidence of any approach to his son Launcelot, who had a thriving business a few hundred yards away. The younger Launcelot died in 1688 and his inventory shows him to have been well able to support his father both financially and with house-room. In west Kent in the eighteenth century it was apparently common for parishes not to insist that locally resident children support their parents even when they were well able to do so. Old Thomas Broomfield, aged 83, became a pensioner of Maidstone in April 1728 and remained so until his death four years later. A son Thomas lived near by, rented property worth £5 per year, and was an overseer in 1731.[75]

The sums granted in such cases were rarely adequate for subsistence and may have been supplements to support known to be provided by relatives. Furthermore the law gave parishes the right to acquire the entire property of the pensioner at death and to recover charges from next of kin. Such arrangements may have been preferred by pensioners, who were enabled to retain their independence, by relatives, and by the parish, which escaped the costs of pursuing relatives through the courts, perhaps fruitlessly, and whose outlay on relief might eventually be repaid. After his father's death Thomas Broomfield, for one, repaid all expenses incurred by the parish for his father.[76]

Old people might receive poor relief whilst living with their children or children might be paid to care for their parents. In 1643 Henry Gill of Tottenhill (Norfolk), labourer, petitioned quarter sessions, being

a pore man and dwelling in part of A house belonging to the Towne and doeth mayntayne itt in Repayre and have contynewed in itt with his mother, ffirst being a poore widow and had ffower small Children he the said Henry Gill being the eldest of them and did worke for his mother and the other Three Children Twelve or Thirteene

[74] W. Newman-Brown, 'The Receipt of Poor Relief and Family Situation: Aldenham, Herts, 1630–90', in R. M. Smith (ed.), *Land, Kinship and Life Cycle* (Cambridge, 1984), 414.

[75] Barker-Read, 'West Kent', 60.

[76] J. Boulton, 'Going on the Parish: The Parish Pension and its Meaning in the London Suburbs, 1640–1724', in Hitchcock *et al.*, *Chronicling Poverty*, 19–46.

yeares and did helpe to Repayre sum part of those houses and since I was marrid I did helpe to maynetayne my mother according as I was able she being of Three score and tenne yeares of age before she died and I did maynetayne her Aleaven weakes in her sicknes when she was not able to helpe her selfe, the Towne then did allo her but six pence the weake, and after I was marrid I hired a house for my selfe and my wife, my mother Contynewing in that house with another widow, tell part of the house fell down they not being able to Repayre itt and about Two yeares ago Thomas Marison being one of the Church wardens of the said Towne did wish me to Repayre itt agayne and dwell in itt with my mother and so I did.[77]

Nurse Chambers of Tonbridge lodged with her daughter and son-in-law for twenty-three years. Between 1771 and 1781 from the ages of 52 to 62 she followed her profession and the parish paid 6*d*. per week for her house-room. Then the payments slowly increased until her pension reached 1*s*. 6*d*. and her daughter received occasional extra sums for nursing her. This went on until her death in 1794 aged 75. Similarly, widow Hollands of Cowden lodged with her son-in-law for seven years before her death in 1736 aged 72. The parish paid between 1*s*. and 2*s*. per week depending on her state of health and she continued to earn small sums preparing herbal medicines as she had earlier in her widowhood.[78]

Such episodes may seem strange in view of the clear provision in the Poor Law statute of 1597 that:

It is expounded that the great grandfather, grandfather, Father and Sonne upward and downward in lyneall descent or degree shall relieve one another as occasion shall require.

This indicated that kin responsibilities were vertical rather than lateral and apparently confined to the male line. However, the statute of 1601 stated that:

The father and grandfather, mother and grandmother and children of every poor, old, blind, lame and impotent person, or other poor person not able to work, being of sufficient ability, shall at their own charges relieve and maintain every such poor person, in that manner, and according to that rate, as by the justices . . . in their sessions shall be assessed.

The vertical obligation had been reduced from four to three generations, grandchildren were absolved from responsibility, but it was broadened to include female relatives. The new 'liable relatives' clause, as it became known, also included the important qualification 'being of sufficient ability' to provide support.

It has been argued that this clause was of little significance, was rarely activated, that under the Poor Law there were minimal expectations that families cared for old people and they were minimally fulfilled, rather responsibility for the aged poor fell mainly upon the poor relief system. This was certainly the view of some lawyers. In the later eighteenth century Blackstone's *Commentaries* thundered:

---

[77] T. Wales, 'Poverty, Poor Relief and the Life Cycle: Some Evidence from Seventeenth Century Norfolk', in Smith, *Land, Kinship*, 386.   [78] Barker-Read, 'West Kent', 59–70.

The abuse of the poor laws and of charitable institutions in general have tended much to the dissolution of family obligation. The patriarchal roof is unknown in England. Children able to maintain their parents seldom redden to see them become suppliants for parish and other mendicant relief. Perhaps the laws which render the maintenance of an indigent parent imperative upon his more able offspring are too seldom enforced.[79]

From such observations of Poor Law practice, conclusions have been drawn about norms of family obligations towards the elderly in English society at large, that it was, as Thomson has asserted, 'unEnglish behaviour to expect children to support parents'.[80] Thomson's argument is supported mainly by limited research into Poor Law practice in the rural south of England in the mid-nineteenth century, generalized to a wider history of the Poor Law. He also asserts, quite inaccurately as we have seen, that 'a reading of eighteenth and nineteenth century literature produces few mentions of any monetary or other exchange transactions between elderly and more youthful households'.[81]

There were indeed occasions when Poor Law officials positively discouraged family obligations. In 1606 the vestry of St Botolph's, in London, decreed that 'no poor of the parish receiving pension or alms weekly shall have any pension or alms paid by the churchwardens or overseers of the poor if they be found to entertain inmates, lodgers or keep their children sons or daughters either married or marriageable within their own houses and dwellings'. Other London parishes around the same time refused pensions to older women who took younger relatives into their households. Occasionally such households were condoned, on strict condition that the younger people did not also apply for poor relief.[82] The chief concern of the parish authorities was to avoid additional demands for poor relief from the relatives of the aged poor, who were likely to be very poor themselves. Following the Salisbury survey of the poor in 1625 it was reported that, 'Mistress Talbot hath received her son's wife great with child, likely to charge the parish. We desire she may be removed.'[83] In the mid-seventeenth century a poor husbandman in Wiltshire who lodged his father and mother-in-law 'out of charity' was persuaded to 'quietly put them away'; having no local settlement the old people threatened to become a burden on the rates. An effect of the establishment of the Law of Settlement from 1691 'was to reinforce constraints on movement arising from illness, having a family or growing old'.[84] These examples suggest that such support for relatives was normal behaviour which would not have been constrained by any outside authority, and hence would not enter the official

[79] MacFarlane, *Marriage and Love*, 111.

[80] D. Thomson, 'The Welfare of the Elderly in the Past: A Community or Family Responsibility', in Pelling and Smith, *Life, Death*, 199.   [81] Ibid.

[82] Claire Schen, 'Strategies of Poor Aged Women and Widows in Sixteenth Century London', in L. Botelho and P. Thane, *Women and Ageing in British Society since 1500* (London, 2000).

[83] Slack, *Poverty and Policy*, 73.

[84] J. S. Taylor, 'The Impact of Pauper Settlement, 1691–1834', *Past and Present*, 73 (1976), 57.

record, when practised among the better off or when the needy relative had a settlement in the parish.

There are more frequent examples of the Poor Law reinforcing family obligations, including enforcement of the 'liable relatives clause'. A century after the introduction of the Poor Law the parish of Myddle took up the case of Andrew Weston, who 'beeing aged, and his wife dead, went to Merington to Thomas Williams, who had marryed his dayghter and gave him all his goods and cattle on condition hee would maintaine him dureing his life'. Not long after, Thomas Williams's wife had died, and Weston became blind and helpless. Thereupon:

Thomas Williams prevailed with the Parish officers of Preston Gubballs to procure an order, and to send his father-in-law, Weston, into the Parish of Myddle, beeing the place of his last settlement, which was done accordingly. . . . Wee (the ratepayers of Myddle) fetched witnesses from Wrexham to prove the bargaine beetweene Andrew Weston and his son-in-law Williams; butt Mr Berkley [counsel for Myddle] insisted upon the Statute of the 43rd of the Queene, cap. 2, whereby it is enacted that the grandfathers, grandmothers, fathers, mothers and children of any poore, lame, blind etc. beeing of sufficient ability, shall make such allowance for the maintenance of such poore etc. as the Justices att theire Quarter Sessions shall allow . . . and soe it had been resolved in that Court and in severall other cases which hee shewed. Mr Atkis [for Williams] did not gainesay any of this, butt hee insisted upon these words in the Statute, beeing of sufficient ability, and that Thomas Williams was a poore man and not able to doe it. To which Mr Berkeley answeared that Thomas Williams did hold a tenement of about £16 or £18 per annum and had a stocke upon it, that hee had lands in fee simple of about £8 to £10 per annum, and that was worth but £6; that he had lately married a second wife with £100 portion. Upon this the Court resolved that Weston's settlement was in Myddle parish and that Thomas Williams ought to maintaine him. (Williams) tooke the blinde man home with him.[85]

This suggests that retirement contracts still occurred in the seventeenth century, and could still fail; that the 'liable relatives' clause was taken seriously in this and other courts; and that the phrase 'being of sufficient ability' carried considerable weight in the courts.

Though the subject has not been systematically researched, attempts to enforce the clause were clearly not uncommon. In 1727 Cranbrook parish in west Kent obtained an order from a magistrate compelling Daniel Gyles, living in Frittenden, to support his father who was 'in want'. Further warrants were required in 1730 and 1731. In 1734 a similar warrant against John Pyle for support of his mother Martha who had refused to stay in the workhouse on three occasions appears to have been ignored. Defaulting following a court order to pay maintenance appears to have been common and is another likely reason for parishes to avoid the costly legal process. Nicolas Jackson, husbandman of Maidstone, was ordered at the Easter Session of 1688 to provide

---

[85] Gough, *Myddle*, 167.

2s. per week to support his mother, living in Bexley, 'he being well able to provide and she being old and poor'. Humphrey and William Baldwin, sons of Thomas Baldwin of Wrotham, were the subject of an order in 1712 to support their father at 2s. per week 'turn and turn about by the year'.[86]

But it does not seem likely that such cases were frequent. Thomson takes this as evidence of the absence of a cultural norm of supporting elders in the family. Other interpretations are possible. Where an aged poor person possessed traceable liable relatives, it was pointless for a parish to prosecute unless the relative was indeed 'of sufficient ability' to provide support. The relatives of the very poor were likely to be poor themselves. There was nothing to be gained from a parish pauperizing one parishioner to depauperize another, though they might feel differently about someone who would fall a charge to another parish.

Where locally resident relatives were judged not to be giving as much help as they could afford parish officers might put them under strong moral pressure in place of formal legal action—action likely to appear rarely in the sources. Where relatives could not afford full assistance the parish might encourage them by reducing or overlooking rate payments in return for the support they gave. In Maidstone John Osborne and John Burwash were both exempted between 1726 and 1731 for keeping their mothers.[87] Parishes would pay children to take in parents as lodgers or supplement the family income where the old person lived with them. If children failed to respond to such pressure or inducements to care for ageing parents, parishes seem to have given up. There is no means of knowing how frequent any of these occurrences were and practice varied from place to place and time to time. Studies of Lancashire parishes in the seventeenth and eighteenth centuries, among the very few studies of the Old Poor Law in the North of England, indicate their extreme reluctance to give regular or adequate relief in any circumstances to old or young; there was a strong presumption of family responsiblity.[88]

The Poor Law evidence may suggest not that families felt no obligation to support elders, rather that families generally did their best to maintain themselves and their elderly relatives, but often could not afford to do so or could do so only with help, which many parishes were willing to give. Poor Law practice may not have been symptomatic of customary disinclination for family support, but rather offered practical reinforcement of a customary assumption that such support was normal.

In any case it is unwise to derive general societal norms from a series of highly technical legal decisions arising from a statute designed for the problems

---

[86] Barker-Read, 'West Kent', 61.   [87] Ibid.

[88] King, 'Calverley'. A. J. Gritt, ' "I ham old, broken down and ready to die": Approaches to the Poor, Experiences of Poverty and the Life-Cycle in South-West Lancashire during the Eighteenth and Early Nineteenth Centuries', BA diss. (University of Central Lancashire, 1995).

of the very poor. Especially when it is very firmly stated in one of the widely used digests of parish law, published in 1830, that:

The poor laws were never intended to supercede the obligation which the ties of kindred impose upon all mankind to support the helpless and destitute members of their family. Although . . . it must appear that all who stand in that relation are either incapable or unwilling to discharge this duty, yet the statute which forms the groundwork of the whole system expressly recognizes the primary right of the indigent to claim support and assistance from their relatives and affords its sanction to this moral duty.[89]

A reference to this 'moral duty': 'By the law of nature a man was bound to take care of his own father and mother' appears also in a widely used eighteenth-century digest.[90] The importance of family support is further suggested by the finding that in two parishes near Bristol between 1764 and 1803 people without relatives near by drew far more heavily than others on parish resources.[91] The Poor Law was vitally important for the support of the aged poor, but it worked in a close, complex, and shifting relationship with such support as families were able and willing to give.

CONCLUSION

It is possible to suggest that there were some generally observed social rules about family support for old people in early modern England. First, there was no obligation to shelter an elderly relative, though this clearly occurred where the generations felt that they could live together amicably or where there was need on one side or the other which could not otherwise be satisfied. But there was deep awareness of the dangers of such a course. It was most likely to occur at the very end of the older person's life and might extend for just a brief period before death. When older people lived independently of kin it was not necessarily because they were neglected but, then as now, because they preferred to do so.

Secondly, there was a strong obligation on individuals to give what material and emotional support they could to elderly relatives, even if they did not live in the same household; but only within reason, and not if by doing so they would impoverish themselves or their families. The obligations of married sons and daughters were first to their spouses and their children and only secondarily, if they had resources to spare, for their parents. When old people were not physically dependent—as most were not—and did not need wholesale care,

---

[89] J. Steer, *Parish Law: Being a Digest of the Law* (London, 1830), 455.

[90] E. Bott (ed.), *A Collection of Decisions of the Court of King's Bench Upon the Poor Laws Down to the Present Time* (London, 1773), 87.

[91] Mary Fissell, '"The sick and drooping poor" in Eighteenth-Century Bristol and its Region', *Social History of Medicine*, 2/1 (1989), 35–58.

such needs as they had could be met by a relative living in a separate household. And old people gave as well as received from family and community.

Thirdly, when relatives could not help or were non-existent and an old person could find no substitute and was rendered destitute, the poor relief system would provide as much support as local resources and custom allowed, though rarely above a minimal level. Family support and poor relief were not alternatives but both were shifting and variable components in the 'economy of makeshifts' in which poor old people long struggled.

8

'Lives of Expedients': Old People and the Old Poor Law

It has been suggested that, especially in its treatment of older people, the Old Poor Law, far from being as harsh as was once thought, was a 'welfare state in miniature',[1] even that the Poor Law could be more generous to old people than the British welfare state of the late twentieth century.[2] Whatever the inadequacies of the modern welfare state, there is an important difference between the certainty of basic income support and health care at a certain age which it ensures and the extreme uncertainty which continued to characterize access to poor relief into the nineteenth century.

THE POOR LAW IN THE 1790S

This uncertainty and the variety of experiences of old people under the Old Poor Law were investigated by Sir Frederick Eden in the mid-1790s, when it was under particular pressure due to high levels of poverty especially in the countryside. Eden sought information from all the parishes in England and Wales, though not all responded, and those who did so were uneven in the details they provided. He and his respondents were less concerned with old people than with the new problem of large numbers of pauperized younger families. Eden commented: 'a *bare subsistence* for the aged poor is no more than the fair right of those who have spent their best days and exhausted their strength in the service of the public'[3] (my emphasis). The evidence he published indicates that this view was widely but not universally shared.

The twenty-eight parishes which provided particularly detailed information about their treatment of the aged were conveniently spread geographically and in terms of social and economical structure. In none of them did people described as 'old' and receiving regular 'pensions' amount to more than 2.7 per cent of the estimated local population at a time when about

[1] Thomas Sokoll, *Household and Family among the Poor: The Case of Two Essex Communities in the Late 18th and Early 19th Centuries* (Bochum, 1993), 293. T. Hitchcock, P. King, P. Sharpe (eds.), *Chronicling Poverty: The Voices and Strategies of the English Poor, 1640–1840* (Basingstoke, 1997), 'introduction', 10.

[2] D. Thomson, 'The Decline of Social Security: Falling State Support for the Elderly since Early Victorian Times', *Ageing and Society*, 4 (1984), 451–82.

[3] Sir Frederick Morton Eden, *The State of the Poor*, 3 vols. (London, 1797), i. 411.

7.7 per cent of the total population of England and Wales is estimated to have been aged 60 and above.[4] Most aged paupers received one shilling or one shilling and sixpence a week, in exceptional circumstances two shillings or more. This was so in a prosperous parish where average male wages were high, such as Ealing, Middlesex (where a garden labourer could hope to earn ten shillings per week all through the year), in poor rural parishes such as some of those in Cumberland in the north, or in Somerset in the south, and in large towns such as Birmingham. Some parishes sent claimants to the workhouse, rather than give out-relief, as at Harrington, Cumberland (which had a mixed economy of mining, manufacture, and agriculture), on the grounds that 'the poor have such a dislike to this mode of provision that it is expected that this new system will lower the rates very considerably'. In consequence, Harrington had only eight regular pensioners over age 60 (0.56 per cent of the estimated parish population). Most of the older residents had received a weekly allowance in the previous year (1792) but now received only house-rent. For example, 'J.J. a baker, lame aged sixty, his wife nearly of the same age: last year they were allowed five shillings a week from the parish but now prefer receiving thirty shillings annually for house-rent to going to Workington poorhouse.' 'J.H. a widow, paralytic, receives twenty-one shillings a year for house-rent.' 'J.S. aged sixty a miner: last year he received one shilling and sixpence a week, but now rather than go to the poor-house he declines receiving anything from the parish.'[5]

Eden commented on the 'comfort' of some workhouses, for example in Liverpool.[6] By contrast, in Alford, Lincolnshire, the poorhouse was governed by 'an old woman who is almost a pauper . . . and is scarcely able to retain the reins of government much less to enforce good order and industry'.[7] In Hampshire, Petersfield, Portsea, and Portsmouth kept their old people mainly in workhouses, as did rural Ellesmere and urban Shrewsbury in Shropshire. Ellesmere gave no out-relief to those under the age of 70 and no more than one shilling a week thereafter. In Bishops Castle, also in Shropshire, 'eleven or twelve' old people (about 2 per cent of its population) received sixpence to one shilling a week. The administration of poor relief was contracted out and the contractor refused to pay more. For the same reason in Farnham, Surrey, just a few old people received 'very trifling' weekly payments. In rural Alcester, Warwickshire, 'the poor are relieved at their own houses so long as they can be satisfied with one shilling and six pence'. The parish of All Saints, Colchester (Essex), gave more generously. Most elderly pensioners received two shillings and sixpence, but an 80-year-old blacksmith's widow received five shillings as did another widow of 70 and a 76-year-old single woman 'rather disordered in her understanding' received three shillings and sixpence; but

[4] E. A. Wrigley, R. S. Davies, J. E. Oeppen, and R. S. Schofield, *English Population History from Family Reconstitution, 1580–1837* (Cambridge, 1997), 615.

[5] Eden, *The Poor*, ii. 78–80.   [6] Ibid. 328.   [7] Ibid. 390.

there were only fourteen regular pensioners in an estimated population of eight thousand.[8]

With extremely rare exceptions the levels of relief were inadequate for subsistence and were clearly expected to supplement other resources. Even very old women were expected to contribute to their own support through their labour whenever possible. Cumwhitton, a Cumberland community of eighty-six families, mostly low-paid agricultural workers, supported ten elderly pensioners. Among these, J.L. aged 80 and his wife, 82, had received parish aid for more than twenty years. They were formerly engaged in agriculture but a fall had incapacitated him, throwing him on the parish. The wife 'occasionally spins a little lint and earns about three farthings a day besides doing her other necessary household work. They receive at present two shillings regularly each week and £1. 6s. annually for house-rent, for digging and carting peat and turves for fuel etc.'. This unusually forthcoming parish provided other examples of the circumstances in which old people qualified for regular relief. A mother aged 80 and her son aged 45 were both formerly employed in agriculture. 'The cause of the mother's having recourse to the parish was old age and natural infirmities which, though industrious, she could not provide against; that of the son was a lameness which could never be accounted for. He earns a little money by making baskets, bee-hives etc. They receive one shilling and sixpence.' Another pensioner M.R. was 100 years old. 'Besides house-rent fuel etc. receives ninepence a week from the parish. Her son allows her threepence a week more. She is the widow of a very noted beggar who would never follow any other occupation.' The parish had 'no charities' to supplement poor relief.[9]

Such sums of relief, supplemented by further allowances for fuel and house-rent, support Barker-Read's conclusion that the cash 'pension' was normally fixed at a level which ensured that together with other known resources the pensioner had sufficient income for a diet that just barely met their needs for survival.[10] Other needs, such as clothing and rent, were expected to be met from other sources; the parish provided only when these could not be found. Unless the geographically scattered parishes surveyed by Eden were very unusual, overwhelmingly old people did not receive regular parish 'pensions' in the mid-1790s and most of those who did so were assumed, as at Minehead 'to be partly maintained by their friends'.

Even these minimal and variable levels of relief were impressive achievements for many poor parishes. Equally impressively the great majority of the aged poor themselves 'managed to keep themselves independent of the Old Poor Law'.[11] Neither in the stringent period of the late eighteenth century

---

[8] Ibid., vol. ii *passim*.   [9] Ibid. 72.

[10] M. Barker-Read, 'The Treatment of the Aged Poor in Five Selected West Kent Parishes from Settlement to Speenhamland, 1662–1797', Ph.D. thesis (Open University, 1988), 122.

[11] Ibid. 40.

nor earlier did the Poor Law provide a 'system of old age pensions'[12] in any recognizable sense, or indeed 'a generous and widely encompassing' system of relief[13] which 'English men and women could count on'.[14] Indeed the proportions of old people on relief at this time were comparable with the numbers reported in a sample of parishes in 1900, when the Poor Law is generally acknowledged to have been highly restrictive and stigmatizing.[15]

THE PICTURE IN 1802

This picture is supported by official statistics. An ad hoc *Abstract of . . . Returns Relative to the Expense and Maintenance of the Poor* in 1802–3 asked parish officials to report the total number of old and infirm paupers. Unfortunately, it did not distinguish between the old and the infirm or between those receiving institutional or outdoor relief. Only about one thousand of the fifteen thousand parishes in England and Wales failed to respond. 166,400 (16 per cent of all paupers) were described as 'persons above sixty years of age or disabled from labour by permanent illness or other infirmity'. This amounted to 1.8 per cent of the total population at a time when about 8 per cent of the population were aged 60 or above; and to 26 per cent of the estimated over-60 population (though the category must have included a number of younger people).[16] Many more older people must have been 'poor' by any reasonable definition. The return was made at a time of high prices, food shortages, and especial hardship.[17] The statistics reinforce the view that the Poor Law at the beginning of the nineteenth century was a long way from providing a regular pension for the aged poor. Locally based improvisation and experimentation, reform of the Poor Law and lack of it, continued into the nineteenth century, though there was an increasing tendency towards a more restrictive and uniform administration from 1815 onwards.[18]

---

[12] D. Thomson, 'Provision for the Elderly in England, 1830–1908', Ph.D. thesis (Cambridge University, 1981), 40.

[13] K. D. M. Snell, *Annals of the Labouring Poor: Social Change and Agrarian England, 1660–1900* (Cambridge, 1985), 105.

[14] Peter M. Solar, 'Poor Relief and English Economic Development before the Industrial Revolution', *Economic History Review*, 48/1 (1995), 1.

[15] *Report of the Departmental Committee on the Financial Aspects of the Proposals made by the Select Committee of the House of Commons of 1899 about the Aged Deserving Poor*, Parliamentary Papers (1900), vol. x. See Ch. 10 below.

[16] Wrigley *et al.*, *English Population History*, 615.

[17] J. D. Marshall, *The Old Poor Law, 1795–1834* (London, 1985), 32–6. Karel Williams, *From Pauperism to Poverty* (London, 1981), 147–55.

[18] J. Innes, 'The "Mixed Economy of Welfare" in Early Modern England: Assessments of the Options from Hale to Malthus (*c.*1763–1803)', in M. Daunton (ed.), *Charity, Self-Interest and Welfare in the English Past* (London, 1996), 139–80. P. Mandler, 'The Making of the New Poor Law *Redivivus*', *Past and Present*, 117 (1987), 131–57. D. Eastwood, response, *Past and Present*, 127 (1990), 183–94.

THE ROYAL COMMISSION ON THE POOR LAWS, 1832

Between 1832 and 1834 the first national investigation of the Poor Law in its history was carried out, in the form of a Royal Commission, which led to the major reform of the Poor Law in 1834. The recommendations of the Commission and the Poor Law Amendment Act, 1834, were based on investigations which were scarcely more systematic or comprehensive than those of Eden, and the Report took little account of them when the findings did not suit the inclinations of the Commissioners.[19] Like Eden's survey this investigation gives tantalizing, incomplete, glimpses into the variety of experiences of the aged under the Old Poor Law. Parishes received a detailed questionnaire and Assistant Commissioners made reports on local practice, though they varied immensely in their method, their thoroughness, and their preoccupations. The treatment of the aged was not a priority for any of them or for the Commission. They were, rather, concerned with the 'demoralization' of the able-bodied poor due to their increased dependence on poor relief. The Report asserted that relief to the able-bodied was more subject to abuse than that to the 'impotent':

The great source of Poor Law mal-administration is the desire of many of those who regulate the distribution of the parochial fund to extract from it a profit to themselves . . . but no use can be made of the labour of the aged and the sick and there is little room for jobbing if their pensions are paid in money. Accordingly we find that even in places distinguished in general by the most wanton parochial profusion, the allowances to the aged and infirm are moderate.[20]

Nevertheless the Assistant Commissioners elicited much information about the treatment of the aged. The most widespread response was expressed by the Master of St Pancras workhouse in central London:

The only proper objects for parochial relief appear to me to be the aged and impotent . . . this class which I would call the deserving poor, I should say that too much could not be done to make them comfortable.[21]

But there were differences of opinion as to the most appropriate means to ensure this 'comfort' and frequent references to the danger that too secure a certainty of public provision in old age would undermine the need to 'induce labouring people when able to work to make provision against the infirmities of age as well as the casualties of life'.[22]

A small minority of parishes had fixed scales of allowance varying from one to four shillings per week, most commonly two shillings or two shillings

---

[19] Marshall, *Old Poor Law*, 18–23; George R. Boyer, *An Economic History of the English Poor Law, 1750–1850* (Cambridge, 1990), 61.

[20] *Report from His Majesty's Commissioners for Inquiry into the Administration and Practical Operation of the Poor Laws, Parliamentary Papers*, xxvii (1834), 24.

[21] Ibid., app. A, *Parliamentary Papers*, xxviii. 74.   [22] Ibid. xxvii. 241–2.

and sixpence. At this time agricultural labourers could expect to earn an average of ten shillings and sixpence per week, other male manual workers sixteen shillings and twopence.[23] Allowances might still be supplemented, to highly variable degrees, by medical care, payment of rent, or provision of housing and the other extras. The majority of parishes had no relief scale and claimed to make grants on the basis of need. The Commission were anxious to stamp out payment of rent or the provision of housing in the belief that it caused rents to rise overall, though they received little evidence of any such effect and a number of denials that it was so. Those who could not afford their own housing were to be placed in the workhouse.

If any practice can be called typical it was that described by the Assistant Commissioner for Suffolk and Norfolk:

The relief of the diseased, the aged and the orphan who are not taken care of in the workhouse is in general regulated according to the peculiar circumstances of each case and may generally be said to be judiciously and humanely administered.[24]

Relief was commonly paid to old people who lived with family or friends. In Somerset, Cornwall, and south Devon, 'In general such of the aged as have friends to take care of them received weekly allowances, varying from three shillings to one shilling and sixpence.'[25] This suggests that the guiding principle behind cash relief continued to be to ensure that old people could provide themselves with adequate food, to encourage relatives to give what support they could and old people to earn what they could, continuing what one Assistant Commissioner described as their 'life of expedients'.[26] Some districts preferred to offer the workhouse rather than regular allowances, as in much of Shropshire. Assistant Commissioner Lewis was satisfied that elderly residents there were well fed and cared for; their time was completely at their own disposal.

The Commissioner for the West Riding of Yorkshire found that the weekly allowance to the aged and infirm varied according to the circumstances of each case and the amount differed in almost every town. As little as one shilling per week was given in some places to those 'who can do a little for themselves'. As much as seven shillings was given occasionally in cases of age combined with sickness, when the pauper required a nurse. The average payment was about two shillings and sixpence. In general, rent was refused where the workhouse was available.[27] In Wiltshire generally old people received two shillings and sixpence per week 'and feed themselves' in addition to receiving medical relief and rent. London parishes reported little about older people, appearing overwhelmed by the poverty of the young. The parish clerk of Streatham, south of London, reported that no one was on regular outdoor

---

[23] E. H. Hunt, 'Paupers and Pensioners, Past and Present', *Ageing and Society*, 9 (1989), 420.
[24] *Report on Poor Laws*, xxvii. 337.   [25] Ibid. 338.   [26] Ibid., app. A, xxviii. 4.
[27] Ibid. 726–836.

relief, about ten currently received casual relief and the numbers would rise in winter to between thirty and forty.

East Sussex, according to its investigator was the 'greatest place of abuse of the Poor Law', not least because payment of rent was especially common. Ardingley he believed was the 'worst parish in the worst county', where 'the workhouse is of a piece with the management of other particulars . . . the sick and aged . . . are neglected, they are clothed in tattered garments and have no comforts allowed them'. In one of the better administered, prosperous parishes, Rottingdean, 'some of the aged receive small pensions at their own houses'. In Eastbourne, which had been 'alarmingly ill-administered, especially since the riots of 1830', a widow of 76 was paid two shillings and six-pence a week, another aged 90, two shillings, and another aged 75, one shilling and sixpence.[28]

Where the proportion of old people on relief in a community can be estimated it was highly variable. About 6.7 per cent of the population of England and Wales were aged 60 or over in 1834.[29] At Dunstew in Oxfordshire 7 per cent of the population were on relief because they were 'aged sick and infirm'. In Eastbourne eighty-six men and women above their later fifties, 3 per cent of the population, were on regular pensions. 2.66 per cent of the population of Southampton were regular pensioners, though it is unknown how many of these were older people; as were 1.3 per cent in Carlisle, 7 per cent in the rural parish of Wimborne Minster (Dorset), 2.5 per cent in Grantham. In Kidderminster, reported to be an 'extreme case of apathy and neglect in the management of the poor' two hundred old people 'who can-not earn enough to maintain themselves' were on relief (1.3 per cent of the population).

The Report provides glimpses into 'the lives of expedients' of the aged poor. A list of 'some labourers', all aged but not all paupers, in the parish of Thurgarton, Nottinghamshire, included:

William Hearson, who was blind and had four children, all living. He received two shillings from the parish, two shillings from his club. He rented a garden at three shillings, paid no cottage rent.

John Greasley had seventeen children born, six living, and was the parish clerk earning £2. 12s. a year (one shilling a week) plus about one pound in surplice fees. The rent of his cottage and garden was £3. 10s. and he 'labours a little'. 'Would have been very comfortable in his old age as his late master left him an annuity of ten pounds, but keeping a shop and letting people run into debt he is now in bad circumstances.'

John Thornton, formerly a shepherd, had had eight children of whom seven survived and had 'about £45 among them in Savings Bank'. He had about £36 per year in wages and about twelve acres of land. He paid about £25

---

[28] Ibid. xxvii. 174–99.   [29] Wrigley *et al.*, *English Population History*, 615.

per year in rent for cottage, garden, and land. 'Had an annuity of £10 p.a. left him by his late master; lives on this, on the profits of his land and on the interest of money saved in service.'

Anne Kirkham had had seven children, of whom five were living. She was nearly blind and a grown-up daughter kept her house. She rented a cottage and five acres of land for £13 per year. 'Their cottage maintains them, i.e. their cows—they keep two.'

Mrs Spencer had five surviving children, of eight born: 'Lodges with John Harvey, parish pays seven pence weekly for lodging . . . has been very trouble-some to the parish, keeping a disorderly house; but is mastered at last.'[30]

Uley in Gloucestershire, a poor, declining weaving community provided an unusually detailed list of the changes in the treatment of regular paupers between the adoption of stricter regulation in August 1830 and November 1832. In 1830 three hundred and thirty-six families were listed, containing 977 paupers, seventy of whom were described as, or appear to be, old. By 1832 the total had fallen to one hundred and twenty-five. Most who remained on the list had their relief reduced unless they were very infirm; a few received an increased allowance due to deteriorating circumstances. Many were re-ported to be supported by their children. Ann Hale, 'an old woman', had her allowance lowered from one shilling and sixpence to one shilling 'and is assisted by her daughter'. Constance Martin, 'old woman, occasionally washes', received one shilling in place of two shillings. John Powell, 'old and infirm', received two shillings and threepence as he had in 1830; whereas Mary Powell, who had previously received one shilling and sixpence, 'a widow, now gets washing and assistance from her daughter, receives nothing'. Lionel Smith, 'eighty-five years old, receives one shilling and sixpence, carries a basket with fruit', had received six shillings a week in 1830. Sarah Tilley who had re-ceived two shillings a week in 1830 was an 'old woman; receives one shilling and sixpence; is assisted by her daughter'. Hester Tilley had received one shilling previously, now she was 'an old woman, carries matches, receives nothing'. Daniel Tilley was 'in the poor-house; old and infirm with son an idiot and children subject to fits'.[31]

Possession of even small amounts of land, a garden or an allotment, was crucial to the survival of many older people. The Assistant Commissioner for Huntingdon, the Isle of Ely, and the town of Cambridge commented that allotments kept many people off relief except in winter, 'several of them are quite old men'. All the tenants he met 'appeared to be highly pleased with the possession of the land and stated that it had been a great assistance to them'. At Waterbeach near Cambridge (as in many Dorset parishes) land was let to the labourers in half-acre allotments. Tenants grew potatoes and wheat alternately:

[30] *Report on Poor Laws*, app. A, xxviii. 604–5.   [31] Ibid. 624–33.

One of the occupiers, an old man above 70 told me that after payment of his rent and poor rates and allowing for labour at the farmer's rate of wages, his clear profit yearly from his half acre was about £3. 10s. p.a. and he thought that the clear profit of the other occupiers was as great. Another half acre is occupied by a widow, who cultivates the land herself with no other assistance than that of a little girl, her child. She receives 2s. per week from the parish for her child, but nothing for herself; and is unable to do other work in consequence of having to attend upon a sick mother.

In this district widows or aged persons 'usually received two shillings and six-pence, their own lodging . . . a widow, whether old or young, seems to be fixed almost as a matter of course as a pensioner upon the parish from the moment of her husband's death'.[32]

Overall, most striking is the variety of experiences within a strong frame-work of stringency. The general picture was of poor relief as residual and com-plementary to income from work and to support from family, friends, and charity. It provided a safety net when all else failed. This was best described by the Commissioner for West Sussex:

The practice of relieving aged and infirm persons in money is so uniform and gen-eral in every parish I have visited, that it will be unnecessary to do more under this head than to state the practice.

Those who from their infirmities or age are incapable of contributing anything towards their own support, or have outlived others on whose protection or assistance they had a natural claim to rely; or who from the absence of all friends or near relations, would be neglected or considered as a burden, are generally inmates of the work-house. At the same time it is usual for parishes to grant a weekly allowance to those who have friends or relations willing to assist in maintaining them but who from their own circumstances have not the ability to support them entirely. This allowance varies according to the respective capability and opportunities of the individual to earn any-thing from 1s. 6d. to 3s. a week; but in no case except Brighton did I find it reach-ing to the amount which it would cost the parish to maintain the individual in the poorhouse. The degree of relationship and size of the family of the person with whom the applicant is to reside are generally and justly taken into consideration; perhaps also the previous character and situation in life of the applicant in regulating the amount of allowance.[33]

Other evidence from the period suggests that poor relief could be suddenly and arbitrarily reduced or withdrawn. Though some complained that the poor regarded relief as a right, 'it was one paupers had constantly to plead for'.[34]

---

[32] Ibid. 676–8.   [33] Ibid. xxvii. 538.
[34] Pamela Sharpe, ' "The bowels of compation": A Labouring Family and the Law, *c.*1790–1834', in Hitchcock *et al. Chronicling Poverty*, 87–109. See also Thomas Sokoll, 'Old Age in Poverty: The Record of Essex Pauper Letters, 1780–1834', 127–54.

THE 'LIABLE RELATIVES CLAUSE'

The Assistant Commissioners were instructed to assess how extensively the 'liable relatives clause' of the Poor Law was enforced. As we have seen,[35] it has been argued that this was rarely enforced, mainly because it was contrary to English custom to expect the younger generation to care for the older.[36] Some Commissioners carried out this instruction with more enthusiasm than others. Most Commissioners were as concerned with the application of the clause to absent fathers for the support of children as to adult children for the support of aged parents. The Report of the Royal Commission concluded that:

It appears from the whole evidence that the clause of the 43rd Elizabeth which directs the parents and children of the impotent to be assessed for their support is very seldom enforced. In any ordinary state of society, we much doubt the wisdom of such an enactment. The duty of supporting parents and children, in old age and infirmity, is so strongly enforced by our natural feelings, that it is often well performed even among savages and almost always so in a nation deserving the name civilized. We believe that England is the only European nation where it is neglected.[37]

The conclusions of those commissioners who investigated the question were less clear-cut. The Commissioner for Suffolk and Norfolk commented:

Where the whole of the lower orders are reduced to a state of pauperism, it does not frequently happen that relations are found in circumstances to support those who, from age or impotency, are unable to maintain themselves. When opportunities do occur, the Act is put into force and in many parishes to some extent. It is however rarely that such cases do offer.[38]

The Commissioner for Huntingdon, Ely, etc. commented without reservation:

I met with no instances of aged persons being supported by their relatives. Inability in the relatives to support the increased charge of such maintenance is the chief bar to the enforcement of the statutory provision upon the subject.[39]

In the West Riding of Yorkshire it was found that:

There are instances in most of the large townships in which the relatives of paupers have been compelled to maintain them; but these cases do not frequently occur, owing to the difficulty of proving the ability of the relation.[40]

In Settle, also in Yorkshire, the Commissioner found:

no instance in the past eleven years of the 43rd Elizabeth put in force, as to the obligation of the relatives of paupers to maintain them, but we have found the knowledge of it useful as a threat.[41]

[35] See pp. 139–45.
[36] D. Thomson, 'The Welfare of the Elderly in the Past: A Family or a Community Responsibility?', in M. Pelling and R. Smith (eds.), *Life, Death and the Elderly: Historical Perspectives* (London, 1991), 194–221.　　　　　　　　　　　　　　　　[37] *Report on the Poor Laws*, xxvii. 25.
[38] Ibid. 338.　　　[39] Ibid. 677.　　　[40] Ibid. 729.　　　[41] Ibid. 750.

This was also the case in Dewsbury and Doncaster. In Leeds:

> There are two cases in which sons on notice being given by the Board have allowed
> 5s. to their parents and generally it is done rather by recommending paupers to apply
> to their relations than by enforcing the law against them.[42] And it has been enforced
> by order of the magistrates in some neighbouring townships.

In Wiltshire the Commissioner commented that the clause 'is not so much put in force as it ought to be'. And in Dorset, it 'is almost entirely disused. I can see no obstacle whatever to its enforcement.'[43] However, in Wimborne Minster in Dorset outdoor paupers 'are frequently visited by the overseers and great pains are taken to ascertain whether the paupers have children and relatives able to sustain them and when it is the case orders are made on them if they refuse to perform their duty'. In Totnes (Devon) it was noted that 'relatives are disposed to assist one another if capable of doing so. Applications to enforce the 43rd of Elizabeth are rarely made.' In strictly reformed Southwell (Bedfordshire) it 'is regularly carried into effect . . . without any obstacles to its enforcement'.[44]

The 'liable relatives clause' clearly was not overlooked by Poor Law officials. The overwhelming reason for not enforcing it was the poverty of close relatives rather than customary assumptions about the nature of obligation between generations.

WORKHOUSES

The Commissioners presented a generally benign picture of the treatment of old people in the workhouses of the Old Poor Law. Old people were a high proportion of inmates. That at Tickhill, Yorkshire, was typical enough of smaller workhouses. Of forty-nine inmates, twenty-six were aged. Old women who were fit enough were engaged in the domestic duties of the house. One old man worked on the roads; mending or cleaning the streets was a common employment of elderly paupers. Those who worked received as much food as they could eat, the remainder a sufficiency. The policy of local Poor Law officials was, 'to make the old and infirm as comfortable as they can and the able-bodied, if dissolute characters, as uncomfortable as they can'.[45] Inside as outside the house people were expected to work as long as they were able. In the large (capacity 1,750 paupers) and comfortable Liverpool workhouse no one was exempted from work by reason of age below the age of 80. Below that age people were expected to work in proportion to their ability and strength: 'Those who from age or infirmity have a limited task are allowed to choose their own time for performing it'.[46]

---

[42] Ibid. 783.   [43] Ibid. xxix. 12.   [44] Ibid. 105a.
[45] Ibid., app. A, xxviii. 844.   [46] Ibid. 918.

Workhouses were not universal. In Wiltshire and much of Dorset they had almost been abandoned by the 1830s and effectively converted into almshouses for the aged and infirm together with a few bastards and orphans; they were well-fed, clothed, and lodged. By contrast in Darlington, 'no inmate is allowed to leave the house without special permission, except for two old men, each of them past eighty years of age, who have liberty to crawl about as they please'.[47] Some workhouse authorities segregated different categories of pauper, as at Canterbury, where the sexes were separated and there were separate wards for the aged and for children: 'Some indulgences of tea and tobacco are made for the aged, but there is no difference in the diet, as all the labourers are set to hard work.'[48] In some workhouses, such as that in Manchester, married couples were separated.[49]

Elsewhere the aged might routinely be granted their 'indulgences', as in Chester, where all over age 50 'who have been used to tobacco and snuff' were allowed one half-ounce per week, women one half-ounce of tea and one quarter of a pound of sugar. Several old people also had a half-pint of ale a day and, added the commissioner: 'Some are allowed *gin!*'[50] Some Commissioners believed that any indulgence created disincentives to independence. The Commissioner for Surrey commented:

The aged and infirm are fully entitled to every comfort arising from kind treatment, wholesome food, cleanliness, healthy accommodation; but they should not be indulged with luxuries, at all events at the parish expense; nor should too great facilities be afforded them for visiting and receiving visits from their friends because I consider that such a course would materially weaken the inclination which their relatives would have to see them out of the house and also the desire which the paupers would have to obtain support out of it from those relatives.[51]

Whereas the Commissioner for Shropshire approved of the treatment of the impotent poor, which,

as respects not only their 'necessary relief' but also their decent comfort and subsistence is such as the most humane could not impugn. Their weekly food consists generally of porridge, bread and cheese, potatoes, with meat occasionally and in sickness such additional comforts as the medical attendant of the parish might consider necessary are liberally furnished. They are well clad and as regards their time, it is completely at their own disposal. There is much to be said in favour of this treatment of the impotent poor.[52]

CONCLUSION

The Old Poor Law in its last days, as it long had, provided a very basic safety net for the aged who were very poor, but rarely more. As Sokoll has put it:

---

[47] *Report on the Poor Laws*, xxvii. 143.   [48] Ibid. 217.   [49] Ibid. xxviii. 918.
[50] Ibid. 275.   [51] Ibid. 94.   [52] Ibid. 661.

'while support for the elderly *could* be fairly generous under the Old Poor Law, this was by no means the norm'.[53] If this was a 'miniature welfare state', it was ungenerous, even by the uneven standards of modern welfare states. The Poor Law evidence suggests the complementarity of poor relief with the other resources available to older people, and further illustrates how many even of the poorest old people were integrated into their families and communities rather than living alone or as a socially distinct group of 'pensioners'. Evidence from other sources of the period also demonstrates that older people were not always passive recipients of the inconsistencies of poor relief practice. They protested and requested adequate relief. They stood up for themselves independently and also exhibited pride in their capacities to survive their precarious 'lives of expedients'. Most never received poor relief; those who did so requested it only when this capacity failed.

[53] Sokoll, 'Old Age in Poverty', 145.

Old Age in Modern England

Inventing the Old-Age Pensioner

9

The New Poor Law and the Aged Poor

What changed with the coming of the New Poor Law, the reform of the Poor Law which occurred following the Poor Law Amendment Act of 1834? Some historians believe very little,[1] others that it became increasingly severe.[2] Such differences arise mainly because research has been focused upon different geographical areas or different groups of poor people. Able-bodied men were treated more punitively than before; this was a major purpose of the change. The effect upon old people, who were still the largest single group of paupers has been more contested and was probably more mixed. Exploration of the practical implementation of the New Poor Law can tell us much about the lives of poorer old people and about how they were perceived by others.

Thomson argues that immediately following the Poor Law Amendment Act 'the majority of all elderly persons were maintained by the poor law, receiving a weekly pension with a relative value in excess of pensions paid by late twentieth century welfare states . . . in many villages and hamlets this meant that every aged person, except perhaps an elderly vicar or landowner was a poor law pensioner'. He suggests that such 'pensioners' received a 'standard payment' of 2s. 6d. to 3s. per week.[3] Snell, however, argues that the weekly pensions of 2s. 6d. to 3s. which he believes were regularly paid to widows and the elderly before 1834 were generally reduced to one to two shillings and that increasing numbers of old people were forced into workhouses. Snell asserts that the 1837–8 Select Committee on the Poor Law Amendment Act looked 'with hesitant approval' on the fact that elderly people (and others) were selling their furniture to try and avoid the workhouse.[4] This committee in fact saw things quite differently and commented:

---

[1] D. Thomson, 'Provision for the Elderly in England, 1830–1908', Ph.D. thesis (Cambridge University, 1981). Anne Digby, *Pauper Palaces* (London, 1978).

[2] K. D. M. Snell, *Annals of the Labouring Poor: Social Change and Agrarian England, 1600–1900* (Cambridge, 1985). P. Mandler, 'The New Poor Law *Redivivus*', *Past and Present*, 117 (1987), 131–57.

[3] D. Thomson, 'The Welfare of the Elderly in the Past: A Family or a Community Responsibility?', in M. Pelling and R. Smith (eds.), *Life, Death and the Elderly: Historical Perspectives* (London, 1991), 202–4.

[4] Snell, *Annals*, 131–5.

That it appears that relief to the aged and infirm has been generally given out of the workhouse, and that allowances to this class of paupers have been rather increased than diminished since the passing of the existing law; the committee approve of this mode of administering the law.[5]

The Select Committee was set up to investigate widely publicized complaints about the harsh treatment of paupers in certain unions (Petworth and Westhampnett in Sussex; Fareham and Droxford in Hampshire; Ampthill, Bedfordshire, and Basford, Nottinghamshire). They found it hard to reach judgements amidst a mass of contradictory accusations, though they castigated the relieving officer of Plomesgate Union for neglectful treatment of a dying old man of 90. He had refused the workhouse and was left without medical assistance or 'linen necessary to keep him in a decently clean state'. In general, however, they concluded that the law was implemented benignly.[6]

The Poor Law Commissioners, who administered the New Poor Law nationally in its early years did not press for the restriction of relief to old people, though some of the Poor Law Inspectors, who were appointed to oversee the Poor Law locally, were less benign. Sir John Walsham, reporting on South Shields, on the north-east coast, told the Commissioners:

Pauperism in these districts in any shape is inexcusable, although by presenting itself here in the guise of decrepitude and age, it shows a far less revolting front than in the southern counties, it is not the less to be firmly, however gently, resisted.[7]

There were conflicting attitudes to the role of the workhouse in the lives of the aged poor, between those who believed, like Walsham, that it should be a grim deterrent designed to force younger people to save for old age, and others who saw it as a haven where the helpless, friendless, aged could, in the words of the Royal Commission on the Poor Laws of 1834, 'enjoy their indulgences'. The conflict was never resolved.[8] In general, however, there was a far greater stigma attached to entering the workhouse in the minds of older people after 1834 than before, as they became embedded in the consciousness of poor people of all ages as pitiless 'bastilles'.

Local conflict over rates of outdoor relief arose from the grouping of parishes into Unions, under the 1834 Act, for the administration of poor relief, despite sometimes profound differences in their previous policies. It was officially recognized, however, that needs and conditions varied from place to place. The Assistant Poor Law Commissioner for Nottinghamshire and Lincoln commented in 1837 that the amount of relief needed by old people varied considerably within his district. Fuel, for example, could be had for 'almost nothing' in coal-mining districts. He believed that local relief rates were 'sufficient

[5] *Report from the Select Committee of the House of Lords on the Poor Law Amendment Act, Parliamentary Papers* (1837–8), xxviii. 39.   [6] Ibid., p. x.
[7] P. Mawson, 'Poor Law Administration in South Shields, 1830–1930', MA thesis (Newcastle University, 1971).   [8] M. A. Crowther, *The Workhouse System, 1834–1929* (London, 1981).

to enable them to live in decent comfort' and that 'their comforts are greater than they were under the old poor law'. It was a 'complete exception' for an old person to be placed in a workhouse; he or she would have to have a 'bad character' or have nowhere else to go.[9] Neither he nor the Select Committee approved of another trait he identified in the poor:

people like to have the management of their own affairs and they feel a great jealousy of having that management taken out of their hands.[10]

Nevertheless the language of the members of the Select Committee, and of most of those who gave evidence to it, was sympathetic to the aged poor. Questions as to whether 2s. 6d. was an adequate weekly rate of relief were more in evidence than criticism of its profligacy. The curate of a parish in Droxford Union (Hampshire) criticized the reduction of relief to two of his elderly parishioners on the grounds that they had children able to support them, 'because I consider that those men are entitled to a pension from their country in the same way as men in higher ranks of life have pensions for not more important services'.[11] It seems that 60 had become accepted as the lower boundary of old age for purposes of relief administration. When a Commissioner was asked by the Select Committee: 'Where do you draw the line between the aged and those that are not aged?' He replied, 'The commissioners draw the line at 60.' 'The term of 60 years is taken as a general indication of infirmity?' 'It is.' He knew of no case of necessitous people above that age being refused relief, though also 'I can point out a great number of instances of men above 60 working at 12s. a week'.[12]

But the attitude to the aged was benign only in comparison with the treatment of able-bodied men; the old restrictive rules still applied. Poor relief remained a strictly residual safety net for those unable to survive on other resources. The existence of liable relatives suspected of being able to provide support often determined whether outdoor relief was given and how much, though action was rarely taken against relatives through the courts. The threat of the workhouse had emerged as an effective alternative. The evidence taken in 1837–8 showed that Poor Law officials expected families to support older relatives and were prepared both to enforce it when it was not willingly undertaken and to reinforce it when it was. It was taken for granted that any older paupers would live with relatives who could not afford wholly to support them, and rates of relief were fixed with this expectation in mind. The Assistant Commissioner for Lancashire and the West Riding was just one of many who argued that: 'wherever arrangements can be made by the friends of aged people for them to live with them, in those cases those arrangements should be made'. A Nottinghamshire magistrate acknowledged that 2s. 6d. a week

---

[9] *Report* (1837–8), questions 899–904; 7658.   [10] Ibid. 248.
[11] Ibid. 5020.   [12] Ibid. 1182–90.

was adequate only if an old person could supplement it with other resources in cash or in kind: 'If it were not for the assistance that he may receive from his friends and neighbours I should say that he could not live on 3*s*. a week . . . if he has nobody to take care of him he had better live in the house'.[13]

Several well-publicized cases of alleged harshness by the Poor Law authorities revolved around disputed assessments of the capacity of sons to support elderly parents. The disputes were not about whether they had a *duty* to help, which no one denied, but about whether they could afford to do so. A curate from Droxford complained that an old couple aged 72 and 76 had four shillings a week before the Act came into force. This was reduced to two shillings because 'he had a son in service in London who ought to support his father'. The son agreed to pay two shillings a week towards the maintenance of his father, 'but to my knowledge the son had before this time paid his father's rent which was £4. 10*s*. a year. The son now says that he cannot afford to pay the father's rent and consequently they are in a much worse condition than they were before. The old man stated that he never suffered so much as he has done this winter.' In places as diverse as Nottinghamshire mining villages, Colyton in Devon, and the Staffordshire Potteries, from the 1840s to the 1880s, a similar picture appears. Even when children were forced to contribute they could afford very little.[14]

Old people themselves were not passive victims of the poor relief system, but could manipulate it in order to hold onto their independence. In the Potteries in 1872 the mother of John, William, and Ralph Beech preferred to receive one shilling and a loaf weekly from Wolstanton-Burslem Union rather than to live with any of her sons. William was a brewer and owned several houses; John was a printer and beerseller; Ralph was a joiner earning thirty shillings a week. All were willing to support her if she would live with one of them. She refused to do so and the magistrates chose to order the sons to pay an amount each week to cover her support through the Poor Law. The mother seems to have used the Poor Law to enable her to continue living independently for as long as she was able.[15]

Other sources confirm this general picture of the early years of the New Poor Law. Inspector Tufnell investigated the state of the poor, mainly hand-loom weavers, in the township of Castleton in Rochdale (Yorkshire) in September 1841. It had a population of 14,279 in 1841, 328 of whom were on the poor relief list in the last week of September (2.2 per cent of the population). We are not told how many of these were on long-term relief. Tufnell

[13] *Report* (1837–8), 1090–4, 1629–31, 2664.

[14] Jean Robin, 'Family Care of the Elderly in a 19th Century Devonshire Parish', *Ageing and Society*, 4/4 (1984), 505–16. M. Dupree, *Family Structure in the Staffordshire Potteries, 1840–1880* (Oxford, 1995), 309–10. Sonya O. Rose, 'The Varying Household Arrangements of the Elderly in Three English Villages: Nottinghamshire, 1852–1881', *Continuity and Change*, 3/1 (1988), 101–22.

[15] Dupree, *Staffordshire*, 315–16.

listed the first forty paupers alphabetically, with ages. Nineteen were aged 60 or above. The maximum relief normally given to people over 60 was 2s. 6d., with the exception of three shillings to a man of 90 who was 'unable to work'. A man of 75 and his wife, 'both infirm', received five shillings, whilst another 75-year-old and his wife, whose 'son assists a little', received three shillings. Only five old people received 2s. 6d. a week and all were aged 75 or above. If this was a representative sample, forty-one old people might have received relief of up to 2s. 6d. a week in a population of 14,279, only a small minority of whom received the maximum. This can hardly be described as a 'pension' for a majority of all old people comparable with twentieth-century pension systems.

In the township of Wardleworth Tufnell also listed the first forty outdoor paupers in the alphabetical list, but did not give the total for the township. Twenty-two were aged 60 or above. None received more than 2s. The variety of circumstances of the eleven who received this sum suggests that it was not expected to provide full maintenance. They included a 60-year-old man 'not able to work, lives with a daughter and son-in-law'; 75-year-old man 'infirm lives with a daughter'; 65-year-old man 'partly employed in selling sand'; 75-year-old man 'living with son'; 70-year-old man 'works a little, wife sick'; two 64-year-old men and an 80-year-old woman suffering from 'infirmity'; a 60-year-old woman who 'receives something beside from a sick club'; a 60-year-old man 'earns a little by weaving; generally has a lodger'.[16]

Such patterns of packaging together survival from a variety of sources could have been found throughout the history of the Poor Law. They contrast with Thomson's assertion that three shillings was the 'standard' weekly allowance and that it was received by a 'majority of all elderly persons'.[17] According to his own calculations, in rural Ampthill, Bedfordshire, in 1844, the percentage of old people receiving regular relief—paid weekly on a six-monthly basis— varied from 55 per cent in one parish to 18 per cent in another. National statistics showed similar extreme variations.[18] 58 per cent of women in their sixties were on relief in Ampthill, 10 per cent in Stourbridge, 8 per cent at Barton-upon-Irwell on the edge of Manchester. Even after age 70 judgements on eligibility for relief, especially of men, related to assessments of their capability for work. In Ampthill up to around age 74 men were always entered on the relief books as 'out of work', 'past work', 'worn out by work'. There were instances of first application for relief as 'past work' by men aged 80, 85, 79.[19]

---

[16] 'Report by Mr Tufnell on the State of the Poor in the Township of Rochdale', *Parliamentary Papers*, xxxv (1842), 4–6.

[17] Thomson, 'Provision for the Elderly', 17, 21, gives the example of Maldon, Essex, where over one-quarter of male 'pensioners' received only 1s. to 1s. 9d. per week. They could not have survived on such sums. He also calculates that no more than one-third of the over-60 population of Ampthill, Bedfordshire, in 1844 received some outdoor relief, not necessarily regularly.

[18] Ibid. 38–9.   [19] Ibid. 96.

In three Nottinghamshire mining villages from the 1840s to 1880s 'relatively meagre' relief was paid to just a minority of old people. In rural Norfolk, after as before 1834, payments to old people were often grudgingly made and allowances were kept low to encourage recourse to relatives or to charity. The situation was similar in Kirby Lonsdale, Westmorland, in the rural north, in the 1830s.[20] Treatment in the Norfolk workhouses, the famed 'pauper palaces', was generally though not invariably more liberal, though in some respects conditions hardened after 1834; for example, elderly couples were more likely to be separated. At Farehoe workhouse in the mid-nineteenth century the old men were stopped from working in the garden because they were producing a more luxurious diet than was thought suitable.[21] Everywhere poor relief payments to older persons were significantly below the earnings even of lower-paid workers[22] and could not, unsupplemented, have provided an income adequate for survival.

The Out Relief Regulation Order, 1852, attempted to increase stringency, stating that for persons helpless from age 'one-third at least of such relief should be given in kind'. After protests from guardians throughout the country this was withdrawn.[23] The next detailed official investigation of the administration of poor relief was that of the Select Committee on Poor Relief of 1861–2. This was mainly concerned with the condition of the able-bodied poor in urban areas during the recent period of 'distress', but it gave some insights into the treatment of the aged poor, especially in London. The amounts they received in out-relief varied from 2s. 3d. to 9d. a week. The chairman of Bethnal Green guardians said that they gave 1s. 6d. or 2s. to the old and infirm. The amount depended upon whether they had sons or daughters to assist them. This was the pattern throughout east London. The Relieving Officer of the poor parish of St. George the Martyr in Southwark admitted that the sum of 2s. 6d. regularly given to old people was not enough for them to live on. In the small and rich City of London there were few poor old people and out-relief policy must have been the most liberal in the country. It was perhaps the only place which provided subsistence: the highest sum given to an individual was eight shillings, for someone 'perfectly destitute . . . and very aged'. The average given to old people was 5s. 6d. and they had built 'a very magnificent workhouse, quite a palace'.[24]

Witnesses also revealed that Poor Law employees themselves fell into pauperism in old age because they earned too little to save for later life. The

[20] Lynn Hollen Lees, *The Solidarities of Strangers: The English Poor Laws and the People, 1700–1948* (Cambridge, 1998), 172.   [21] Digby, *Pauper Palaces*, 161–5.

[22] Lees, *Solidarities*, 189. Sarah Horrell and Jane Humphries, ' "Old Questions, New Data and Alternative Perspectives": Families' Living Standards in the Industrial Revolution', *Journal of Economic History*, 52/2 (1992), 871.

[23] J. Quadagno, *Aging in Early Industrial Society: Work, Family and Social Policy in 19th Century England* (Cambridge, 1982), 100.

[24] *First Report from the Select Committee on Poor Relief, Parliamentary Papers* (1862), vol. iv.

Clerk to the City of London guardians described an old woman who had been a nurse in another union for sixteen or seventeen years: 'She was an exceedingly clever midwife and had worn herself out in the service with all night and day work'. She was obliged to resign due to physical disability and the guardians did not know what to do with her; she had no money and had earned only £15 a year plus her rations. They gave her five shillings a week from the common fund, though they had no legal power to do so. It was legally possible to pay pensions to officers of lunatic asylums and gaols with the agreement of the magistrates, but not to Poor Law officials.

Throughout the nineteenth century a large minority of old people received poor relief, but they often received very little, very late in life and grudgingly. Outdoor relief was intended to be matched by other resouces if the claimant was to survive outside the workhouse. It was assumed that close relatives would give what support they could afford.

'THE CRUSADE AGAINST OUT-RELIEF'

The statistics

After 1871 the percentage of people receiving poor relief (indoor and out, regular and irregular) fell. This was an intended outcome of central Poor Law policy. Since no age-related statistics were published before 1890 we can only estimate the effects upon older people.

Table 9.1 shows the maximum possible numbers of aged outdoor paupers, as not all 'non-able-bodied' paupers were over 65.

When age-specific statistics were published, at the end of the century, it became clear that, overwhelmingly, non-able-bodied paupers were aged 65

TABLE 9.1. *Non-able-bodied paupers compared with the population aged 65 and over, 1851–1901 in England and Wales*

	Pop. over 65	Non able-bodied paupers
1851	830,800	350,300
1861	931,800	383,500
1871	1,074,900	451,800
1881	1,188,500	357,200
1891	1,372,500	365,200
1901	1,517,800	387,900

Sources: B. R. Mitchell and P. Deane, *Abstract of British Historical Statistics* (Cambridge, 1962), 12. K. Williams, *From Pauperism to Poverty* (London, 1981), 204–5.

TABLE 9.2. *Paupers aged 65 and over, 1890–1900*

	Indoor	Outdoor	As % of pop. 70 and over	As % of pop. 65 and over
1890 (Aug.)	54,800	190,900	22.9	18
1892	63,400	205,000	n.a.	19.5
1900	74,600	212,300	22.8	19.5

n.a. = not available.

Source: Williams, *Pauperism to Poverty*, 206–7.

TABLE 9.3. *Indoor paupers over age 65*

	Non-able-bodied	Total pop. over 65	As % of pop. over 65
1851	34,800	25,100	3
1861	51,000	29,400	3.2
1871	68,500	38,500	3.6
1881	88,300	n.a.	n.a.
1891	98,500	59,600	4.3
1901	109,700	76,100	5

n.a. = not available.

Source: Williams, *Pauperism to Poverty*, 204–5.

and above. The numbers of older people receiving outdoor relief fell after 1871, as did the proportion of outdoor paupers in the 65-and-over age-group. We should be cautious, however, in interpreting these trends as wholly the outcome of the tightening of Poor Law policy. The final quarter of the nineteenth century saw improvements in working-class living standards, due especially to a fall in the prices of essential foodstuffs. These were probably slow to work through to the aged poor but are likely to have had some effect, not least in enabling relatives to provide more support. The trend of indoor relief was different (see Table 9.2).

The increased numbers in institutions was also an intended consequence of the policy change after 1871. Even so, the proportion of older people in institutions was small (see Table 9.3).

The policies

The 'crusade' was essentially an attempt by the central authorities to exert control over the variety of local Poor Law practices, but it was underpinned by a new approach to relief policy. The intention was to give outdoor relief to fewer people, but to target it upon the genuinely helpless, at levels adequate for survival, and to mobilize alternative resources. Claimants were to be carefully assessed. Where possible they were to be referred to charities for help. Liable relatives were to be vigorously pursued. Old people who could not manage in their own communities were to be given shelter in the workhouses, which were to be reorganized to give positive and rehabilitative care in appropriate cases, in addition to their punitive role for the recalcitrant. The aim was maximum mobilization of resources, from all sources, to be targetted upon the needs of the poor as assessed 'scientifically'. The ideas of the Charity Organization Society (founded 1869) were shared in the higher reaches of Poor Law administration. As it turned out, the extent of poverty was too great, its causes and cure too complex for such simple 'scientific' treatment; also charitable and family resources were too few and too unevenly distributed. After a decade or so the policy was an admitted failure.[25]

Indeed the approach was never fully implemented, or indeed fully understood, by some of the inspectorate and local administrators. Some unions were slow to implement it, others never did so. It had more punitive effects on single mothers, including even widowed mothers, than on old people. There was striking continuity over the century in the proportions of the 'aged and infirm' receiving relief: 1.4 per cent of the population in 1802–3; 1.2 per cent in 1901.[26] Thomson believes that after 1871 rates of out-relief payments to old people fell to a new 'standard' of two shillings per week.[27] This is questionable, but even if it was so, this was a time of of falling prices, with the result that the real value of 2s. relief could have been as great as that of higher relief rates in earlier decades.

Poor Law practice continued to be almost as varied as before. An unintended consequence of the harsher treatment of old people in some districts resulting from the crusade was heightened public awareness of poverty in old age as a discrete problem, especially relative to the rising living standards of many working people in the later nineteenth century. The ensuing furore provides an exceptionally clear picture of the condition of the aged poor and of how others perceived them at the end of the nineteenth century.

CHARLES BOOTH: THE AGED POOR IN ENGLAND AND WALES

Charles Booth began his great survey of *The Life and Labour of the People in London* in 1886. One of his first discoveries was the extent of destitution among old

---

[25] S. and B. Webb, *English Poor Law Policy* (London, 1910). Quadagno, *Aging*, 124–35. K. Williams, *From Pauperism to Poverty* (London, 1981), 91–135.   [26] Williams, *Pauperism to Poverty*, 41.
[27] D. Thomson, 'The Decline of Social Security: Falling State Support for the Elderly since Early Victorian Times', *Ageing and Society*, 4 (1984), 451–82.

people. He realized that many people struggled to achieve moderate comfort until they reached old age. The poverty they then suffered was not due to personal failing but to inability any longer to earn a living. He resolved both to expose and to improve the condition of the aged poor. His studies of east London indicated that about 39 per cent of all people over 65 were paupers.[28] He decided, with the encouragement of Canon Samuel Barnett, the founder of Toynbee Hall (who had advocated universal non-contributory state old-age pensions since 1883),[29] that the only solution was a pension to be paid entirely by the Exchequer as a right to all above a certain age. This, he believed, was the only means to ensure support for all who were in need. He believed strongly in the need for a deterrent Poor Law to encourage 'economic virtue', and consequently in the necessity to treat the deserving under a different system. It is, however, a serious oversimplification of Booth's views to argue that he had 'no concern' for the aged poor themselves and proposed pensions above all as a step towards achieving a more restrictive Poor Law.[30] His real concern for the aged poor was clearly evident.

Initially, Booth proposed a pension of five shillings a week for all over 65. He recognized that the cost would be astronomical and substituted 70 as the qualifying age. He estimated the cost at £20m. per year; his critics put it at £26m., a little over one-sixth of total UK public revenue in 1899.[31] The proposal was attacked by the Fellows of the Royal Statistical Society as 'inadequate, impracticable . . . ruinously expensive'.[32] Booth set out to convince his opponents with more statistics. He set researchers to survey aged poverty in two parishes in London and one in the countryside. This confirmed his earlier findings. When the findings were published[33] both in full and as a sixpenny summary, it was again widely condemned, including by the Charity Organization Society as 'the most outrageous and absurd yet promulgated'.[34]

Booth set out to collect more evidence. He recruited more researchers to investigate the condition of the aged poor in all 648 Poor Law Unions in England and Wales.[35] This survey attempted to assess the outcome of the crusade; the results were published in 1894. They confirmed the general fall in out-relief but found that it was geographically uneven. Of the forty-one unions Booth defined as especially enthusiastic supporters of the crusade, most were urban and twenty-four were in London. The others included the big cities of

[28] C. Booth, 'The Enumeration and Classification of Paupers and State Pensions for the Poor', paper to the Royal Statistical Society, Nov. 1891.

[29] B. Webb, *My Apprenticeship* (Harmondsworth, 1938), 218.

[30] John Macnicol, *The Politics of Retirement in Britain, 1878–1948* (Cambridge, 1998), 78–9.

[31] E. P. Hennock, *British Social Reform and German Precedents: The Case of Social Insurance, 1880–1914* (Oxford, 1987), 122–3.

[32] T. S. and M. Simey, *Charles Booth* (Oxford 1960), 162.

[33] C. Booth, *Pauperism—a Picture and Endowment of Old Age, an Argument* (London, 1892).

[34] *Charity Organization Review*, Sept. 1892.

[35] P. M. Williams (Thane), 'The Development of Old Age Pensions in the UK, 1878–1925', Ph.D. thesis (London School of Economics, 1970), 72–6.

Liverpool, Manchester, Salford, and Birmingham. These achieved a 68 per cent reduction in outdoor numbers compared with a national figure of 37 per cent over the period 1871–93. The 1870s saw the most rapid fall. In most of these unions this was accompanied by improved workhouse relief including the introduction of specialized institutions, and improved and professionalized standards of care, for example in nursing.[36] A higher proportion of paupers were in workhouses in London than elsewhere.

Above all, Booth's survey showed how the living conditions of old people and also Poor Law practice still varied from place to place. Questionnaires were sent to the 648 unions in England and Wales, 285 of which returned useful responses. A clear majority (224 with a total population of 9,958,750) claimed not to pursue the 'strictest' policies towards the aged. Twenty-eight, with a total population of 1,282,893, gave out-relief 'subject to good behaviour, not only in cases of actual destitution, but with a view of assisting the old who are in a state of poverty'. Ninety-six unions (pop. 4,564,760) granted it subject to '(1) good character, (2) actual destitution, (3) contributions from relatives legally liable; but without pressure on other relatives, and without entering into the question of adequate maintenance being assured'. Only eight unions (total population 320,000) claimed a policy of 'practical refusal of out relief'. Booth found no correlation between the proportion of old people in a union and relief policies. In general less relief was given in the north, which he believed was 'undoubtedly due to the character of the people'. Booth reported that in 1891, on average, 30 per cent of people aged 65 and over were on relief. But the percentage varied among unions from 5 to 85 per cent. Most of the population lived in districts where not less than 20 per cent or more than 50 per cent were relieved. The highest proportions were in very poor London unions. Levels of pauperism rose with age; the ages 70–5 were 'the most prolific of pauperism'.

Booth sought to assess the extent of poverty, as distinct from pauperism, in old age in each union by seeking the opinions of clergymen, charitable workers, and other interested people. He omitted London from this investigation because it was so large and complex and he received the least satisfactory reports from other large towns. The reports were impressionistic and Booth had difficulty in extracting a 'general consensus' from them, for 'not only are there inherent differences in the circumstances of the old in various parts of the country, but interpretations and opinions differed'. It seemed clear, however, that:

the old are altogether much better off in the country than in town . . . but the condition of many if not most old people even in the rural districts is far from satisfactory. It is abundantly evident that in town and country alike the large majority of the aged when past work are dependent upon someone; either on their children or

---

[36] Crowther, *Workhouse System*, 54–87.

on the guardians or on the charitable or on all three. They very often live very hard lives and one of the most striking features throughout is the extreme smallness of their means even when their condition is said to be satisfactory.

He made a detailed study of 262 rural parishes, surveying in particular the 'sources of maintenance' of old people. It was obvious that most still lived 'lives of expedients', packaging together their living from a variety of sources. Only 5 per cent of people aged 65 and over lived solely on poor relief; 5.3 per cent lived on support from relatives alone, 24.4 per cent on earnings alone. For 22 per cent, the parish provided part of their income, combined, to varying degrees, with earnings, charity, and help from relatives. 18 per cent admitted to some assistance from charity, 22 per cent from relatives; 49 per cent had some earnings. Again, there were local variations. The Poor Law provided the largest part of old people's incomes in eastern districts; in the Midlands relatives and charity shared this role; earnings were most important in the north.

Booth concluded that:

The essential and remarkable feature of these figures is the extraordinary difference that exists, without as it seems any sufficient reason, in the extent of pauperism under apparently similar conditions.[37]

. . . there are a few parishes where out relief is considered a disgrace, but in most places no stigma attaches to its acceptance by the old. It is regarded as a matter of course and often claimed very much as a right. Great variety prevails in the conditions under which out relief is granted. In some cases earnings of any kind are forbidden, in others they are encouraged, while some again allow casual but not regular earnings to be made. It is evident that opposing principles are here at work.

As regards entering the workhouse, it is the one point on which no difference of opinion exists among the poor. The aversion to the 'House' is absolutely universal, and almost any amount of suffering and privation will be endured by the people rather than go into it. Loss of liberty is the most general reason assigned for this aversion, but the dislike of decent people to be compelled to mix with those whose past life and present habits are the reverse of respectable is also strongly felt. There is no doubt too that there is widespread dread of the separation of man and wife . . . but the main explanation is to be found in the fact that the objection to the workhouse is a sentiment. The poor neither know nor want to know anything about it or its regulations.

In most places the aged are said to be comfortable and contented in the workhouse when they once make up their mind to go there, and grow used to the peculiarities of the life it offers, but its comforts have no charms in anticipation.

There is some clash of evidence as to whether those who receive out relief, or those just above them in the social scale, who do not receive it, are the worst off. Even from the same place both are reported. Perhaps there is not much to choose as to deprivations.

As to the causes of poverty, the fact is emphasized that most of the worst destitution is due to intemperance or vicious habits, and in some of the large towns and mining districts thriftlessness and betting go together.

[37]   C. Booth, *The Aged Poor in England and Wales* (1894; repr. New York, 1980), 101.

Half (or rather more) are self-supporting. About one-fourth obtain help from relatives or friends or charity but do not receive parish relief.

The remaining fourth receive out relief. Those in the workhouses (not a very large number) are omitted in this calculation.[38]

Booth worked in parallel with a Royal Commission on the Aged Poor, of which he was a member. This was established in 1893 to investigate a problem about which there was growing public discussion and disquiet. The withdrawal of outdoor relief from old people in some districts had made the destitution of some of them strikingly visible, the more so in comparison with the parallel rise in the living standards of many other working-class people. Among other things the discourse about poverty in old age which emerged gave rise to a sustained campaign for state old-age pensions, to provide for deserving old people separately from the Poor Law. The membership of the Commission included a substantial number of representatives of the Charity Organization Society, led by its secretary, C. S. Loch. The Commission reported in 1895 after interviewing a variety of witnesses. It provided a strikingly similar picture to that which emerged from Booth's investigations.

THE ROYAL COMMISSION ON THE AGED POOR

The Commission's terms of reference were to consider 'whether any alterations in the system of poor relief are desirable in the care of persons whose destitution is occasioned by incapacity for work resulting from old age'. The picture presented unanimously to the Commission, by supporters and critics of the poor relief system, was that in all but the strictest unions necessitous old people, if they were not notorious reprobates—and sometimes even if they were—could normally expect to receive outdoor relief. However, this was almost invariably 'inadequate for the maintenance of the recipients in the belief that all are able to be supported from other sources which often exist even when they are not brought before the guardians'. If they had no such support they were expected to enter the workhouse.[39]

Assessments of the 'other sources' available to old people varied immensely, as no doubt did the reality. For some—still in the 1890s—begging was a regular option. The Clerk to the Carnarvon Guardians in North Wales described scenes that would have been familiar centuries before: 'Every Monday morning crowds of aged people may be seen going from door to door and also on Saturday mornings . . . to the doors of the better class of people.' In the Welsh countryside: 'They call often at the farmers' houses and

---

[38] Ibid. 320–2.

[39] *Report of the Royal Commission on the Aged Poor, Parliamentary Papers*, xiv (1895), pp. viii–xxxvii. Minutes of Evidence. Evidence of: Owen, questions 2455, 2477; Knollys 582; Allen 2042; Davy 1257; about Birmingham 2807, 2834, 2844, 2807; Brighton 3298; in Cranborne 4586; Cardiff 5194; Brixworth 4426, 6069, 7282; Poplar 13775.

they seldom or ever leave without taking with them some little farm produce in the shape of potatoes or milk or oatmeal'. It was a district with few clubs, benefit societies, or formal charity and where 'the guardians are kindly disposed and the paupers generally though not exactly of their own class, often mix with them in their different chapels and other small social communities'.[40]

The socialist and Poor Law guardian George Lansbury described how in the very different community of east London, outdoor paupers,

Have to supplement [relief] by begging, very often in the streets. I have seen women who have been relieved and are being relieved by the committee selling laces and that sort of thing in the streets which is only another form of begging.[41]

It was generally agreed that the workhouse was hated and feared but that no degradation attached to receiving outdoor relief,[42] indeed that many regarded it as a right.[43] The sum of out-relief most commonly given was between two shillings and 3s. 6d. a week.[44] The Permanent Secretary at the Local Government Board (LGB), the department of central government responsible for administration of the Poor Law, commented that 'it is impossible for a man to live upon 3s. a week unless he is helped in some way'.[45] A guardian from St Pancras Union in central London said that their policy was to supplement income up to a total of seven shillings a week, which they estimated provided subsistence in that district; but they never gave more than four shillings and the character of the recipient was taken into account.[46] Grantham (Lincolnshire) gave 5s. 6d. a week to all old men over 75, five shillings to women at 70, and nine shillings to couples, but they had stopped all extras, even medical relief except in cases of severe illness.[47] A guardian from the strict board of guardians in Paddington in central London stated that they offered outdoor relief only if 'they were deserving at the time of application, had shown signs of thrift, had no relations legally or morally bound and able to support them and were unable to obtain sufficient assistance from charitable sources'. He believed that most of the deserving aged received help from charities with which the guardians co-operated.[48] The strict Whitechapel Board was currently giving out relief to only two old people in a very poor district (though about one-third of the population were Jewish immigrants, who had access to Jewish charitable relief agencies); however six hundred old people in Whitechapel received pensions through the COS and the charitable Tower Hamlets Pension Society. The latter fixed six shillings as the minimum for a single old person, nine shillings for a couple; though even on six shillings a week a witness believed that they could not always meet necessities. Some unions still gave relief partly in kind.[49] Treatment in workhouses was equally variable.[50]

[40] *Report of the Royal Commission on the Aged Poor, Parliamentary Papers*, xiv (1895), 7286–7538.
[41] Ibid. 18778.   [42] Ibid. 211, 76715.   [43] Ibid. 7538.   [44] Ibid. 572, 1161, 2799.
[45] Ibid. 247.   [46] Ibid. 2243.   [47] Ibid. 5800.   [48] Ibid. 2277.
[49] Ibid. 2850, 3665, 6588.   [50] Ibid. 973.

The Commission recognized[51] that 'there is no doubt that the cases where pauperism is due clearly to misfortune are very much more frequent among women than among men'.[52] The capacity of the poor for thrift was a central issue for the Commission. Many witnesses stressed that poor people earned too little to save for old age.[53] Others were said to be victims of unsound Friendly Societies and attention was given to ensuring that sound ones were generally accessible.[54] Not all middle-class witnesses were stereotypical advocates of working-class saving. An actuary with much experience of Friendly Societies, Ralph Price Hardy, an advocate of state old-age pensions, argued:

Thrift is quite a relative term, and the mere saving of money, to the neglect of other duties, is not to be held up as the sole virtue of a citizen. To stint the education of children, to continue to overburden a woman with domestic duties, to stand churlishly aside from support of all great humanitarian movements, with the object of saving something for personal old age, would deteriorate the nation far more than even the present pauperism does. The true citizen first performs such duties as will keep his family together, by providing sick and burial allowances, and then last of all, thinks of himself. This elevation of character exists among the poor to a much larger extent than is commonly believed and, this is one of the grounds upon which they object to a diversion of their income to merely pension purposes.[55]

Even the more conventional philanthropist Octavia Hill asserted that 'the thrifty, careful, industrious, and sober people' cared about providing for old age 'enormously', but 'it takes the form of putting themselves and their children in a better position; and in a position of owning something; they do not so much save especially for old age'.[56]

Similarly controversial was the relationship between old people and their close relatives. The Permanent Secretary at the LGB described how some guardians put pressure on relatives to give support by refusing relief outside the workhouse, they believed effectively. Inspector Knollys believed that 'the neglect of parents by their sons and others who are legally liable to support them amongst the poorer classes is one of the crying sins of the day'.[57] He noted, however, that in country districts the 'thoroughly respectable and respected' would be assisted by 'friends' (i.e. including family) and probably not allowed to enter the workhouse. The trade unionists among the Commissioners resisted such assertions, arguing that low-paid workers with families to support could not also support their parents. Poor Law officials insisted that pressure was put only upon those able to pay. Joseph Arch of the Agricultural Workers Union claimed that men earning only eleven shillings a week were made to contribute one shilling for the support of their fathers.[58]

---

[51] Ibid. xliii. [52] George Bartley, MP, 8145. [53] Ibid. 5058.
[54] Ibid. 5367. [55] Ibid. 11706. [56] Ibid. 10473. [57] Ibid. 594.
[58] Ibid. 999–1007 Guardians from such dissimilar districts as Wimborne in rural Dorset and the city of Manchester agreed with this, adding that children gave willingly when they could afford to.

George Edwards, General Secretary of the Norwich Amalgamated Labour Union, agreed. He was not 'opposed to the principle of men being compelled to support their parents where they were able to do so', but assented to a somewhat leading question from Joseph Arch:

You find do you not, generally speaking, that when labourers are called upon to assist their aged parents they would much rather do it in kind than be compelled to pay 1s. into union funds. And invariably you find that those children rendered their parents more help in kind than they would do if they had to pay the money. That the assistance they render in kind as well as many little things and comforts that they take their aged parents would be worth more than the 1s. per week that they pay into the union?

Edwards responded:

I have known cases in which they assist them with reference to garden produce in the way of a few potatoes and suchlike and they are very anxious to assist them in any way they can outside of monetary assistance.

They are enabled to give far more than a shilling a week in kind. For example in the shape of garden food, and the old lady would go and see after the children and they would have their tea and dinner with them, so that they are enabled to and do render a large amount of assistance in kind.

He believed that a majority of old people were helped in these ways by family and friends. Edwards, Arch, and other working-class witnesses vehemently opposed any attempt to convert support for parents from primarily a service to a cash transaction which few working people could afford.

The definition of old age itself caused dissent. Owen, the Permanent Secretary at the LGB, stated that there was no official definition of old age recognized by the Poor Law, but that guardians ordinarily adopted 60 years as the dividing line between the able-bodied and the non-able-bodied. Inspector Hedley agreed but thought this undesirable for 'I know many a man of 60, or 61 or 62 who is much more able-bodied than another man of 55'. The St Pancras Guardians took 65 'as what you would call an old person . . . I should not think that there were very many above 65 able to earn their living; that is to say do regular work. They would be able to do odd jobs; but I think after 65 there would not be many.'[59]

Working men who gave evidence were conscious of the varied demands imposed by different occupations and preferred a flexible age definition geared to the age at which people became incapable of self-support.[60] The experience of the Northumberland and Durham Miners Permanent Relief Fund, founded 1862, which gave relief to men who ceased to be able to work above a minimum age of 60, was that the average age of taking the pension—in this heavy occupation—was 67. One man, however, did not take his pension

---

[59] George Bartley, 2005, 11893.   [60] Ibid. 6621–4.

until age 90, three were 87, four 84, ten 82; about seventy-four altogether first took their pensions past the age of 80.[61] The experience was similar in the lighter trade of printing though 'it is by no means an uncommon thing to find in the London printing trade members working up to 70, 75 and I have known them up to 80 years of age.'[62] The Report concluded that guardians should retain their discretion but that no one 'alleging themselves to be over 60 . . . should be classed as able-bodied except with the approval of the medical officer'.[63]

A number of witnesses commented that one reason why the living stand-ards of the aged were rising more slowly than those of the employed work-ing class was that their chances of employment had diminished, in country as well as town.[64] Some welcomed this as due to the disappearance of degrad-ing tasks, such as the employment of old men to drive children in the gang system once prevalent in Norfolk agriculture.[65] Official policy was never to supplement regular earnings. Knollys, however, distinguished between 'wages' and 'earnings', the latter being 'means of an uncertain character which old people would be able to pick up and would be entirely distinct from continu-ous wages'. Inspector Davy, however, believed that old people should not earn anything because all of their earnings took work away from younger people.[66] The economist Alfred Marshall failed to persuade the Commission that many of the casual tasks for which old people were paid would not necessarily be taken over by younger people, and that expenditure of their earnings created work for others.

There were fundamental differences of opinion about the desirable role of the State in providing for the aged poor. On the one hand, Davy stated

I am, I suppose, by constitution very much against state aid . . . my own judgement is rather in favour of subsidizing private efforts for the simple reason that I do not believe that the State does these things well.[67]

On the other, the trade unionist Henry Broadhurst claimed 'for large classes of workers . . . thrift means, not the saving of any part of their weekly wage but its judicious expenditure'. Hence he believed that the maintenance of the aged poor should be 'a public charge to be borne by the whole commun-ity' for which workers should not have to contribute. The majority of the Commission was anxious to find means of encouraging 'independence' (a key word in its vocabulary of approbation), enabling the mass of people to pro-vide for their own old age with minimal support from the state. They sur-veyed a variety of mutual help and savings schemes and pressed for ways to improve Friendly Society provision, especially for women. They surveyed the range of proposals for state old-age pensions and examined the systems recently introduced in Germany and Denmark, but found them all wanting.

---

[61] Ibid. 9130.   [62] Ibid. 10716, 10869.   [63] Ibid., Report, xii.
[64] Ibid., Minutes of Evidence, 4426, 7159, 10869.   [65] Ibid. 7240.
[66] Ibid. 1718.   [67] Ibid. 1822–3.

The question of the aged poor was one of a range of issues, including unemployment, education, and levels of pay, which at the end of the nineteenth century engaged politicians, administrators, philosophers, and social reformers in a wide-ranging discourse which was as much concerned with political and social philosophy and with ethics as with technical solutions to social problems. Centrally the discourse concerned the role of the state in relation to individual and family responsibility at a time when the steady extension of rights of citizenship, symbolized by the franchise, and the assertion of rights by excluded groups was calling this relationship in question.

THE VIEWS OF EXPERTS

Intellectuals, reformers, and politicians expressed their views on these issues to the Commission, delivering strikingly different accounts of the causes and experience of poverty in old age. They presented no uniform, stereotyped set of 'middle-class' attitudes. Alfred Marshall, the Cambridge economist and supporter of the COS, indeed insisted that it was not enough for the Commission to hear middle-class experts pronouncing upon the working class, rather they should let working people speak for themselves as the Royal Commission on Labour had recently done:

The test of the proposition [that the Poor Law and charity could provide for all the needs of the aged poor] I think, is to be sought in the direct expressions of opinion by working men. I have been led to take this line after frequent conversations with them. I always find that they do not believe that the Charity Organization Society and the Poor Law between them do all that is needful . . . until working men's evidence has been brought forward on this subject, the evidence that has been got by this and previous Commissions seems to me useful, in a way, but, as far as this particular question goes, the least important half.[68]

He warned, however, that 'there are not very many of the working men who are at all ready to submit themselves to the ordeal of examination by a Commission'. The 'higher ranks of artisans' could tell them little for they 'under ordinary circumstances have no more to do with the Poor Law than any well-to-do citizen'.

Marshall was convinced that working men should be integrated into the administration both of charities and poor relief:

I am convinced—for I have made inquiries on this subject from representative working men—that the leaders of the working men would be as firm as anyone in insisting that scamps and lazy people should be put to a severe discipline; that they would be in many ways sharper than people not in the same rank of life in seeing through

---

[68] George Bartley, 10198.

a fallacious story, and would have no sympathy at all with the tramp. . . . in 1834 there was not the trained working class intelligence which could have been utilized for the purpose. The working class intelligence that we want to utilize is almost entirely a creation of the last sixty years, and in a great measure of the last twenty years.[69]

For, 'the one fundamental flaw of the Charity Organization Society . . . [is] . . . that their basis consists exclusively of those people who used to be the governing classes but who are not the governing classes now'.[70] Marshall was very conscious of the growing political assertiveness of working people and of the danger of their being driven into serious opposition to the existing political system.

Marshall believed that the aged had shared less than others in the general improvement in economic conditions, making 'the case of the old harder than it used to be', despite the fact that, in his opinion, there had been an increase in support from relatives. Though improved wages and conditions should enable more working people to provide for themselves in future he could not agree that this would happen equally quickly to all. The causes of low agricultural wages, for example, were 'so firmly rooted in the country that I should not be very hopeful of changing those conditions rapidly'.[71] He sought 'to strengthen the springs of moral action not to impose duties by positive law', but he opposed 'hardships which cause more pain than they are worth for the purposes of education'.[72] He believed that poverty had changed its character since 1834 and that a different response was justified: 'I regard all this problem of poverty as a mere passing evil in the progress of man upwards', for:

While the problem of 1834 was the problem of pauperism, the problem of 1893 is the problem of poverty; that a man ought not to be allowed to live in a bad home, that extreme poverty ought to be regarded not indeed as a crime, but as a thing so detrimental to the State that it should not be endured . . . The people of 1834 argued with perfect truth that the independent labourer often had not nearly enough food. So they could not allow even the most deserving of the dependent poor to have more than the bare food which they were compelled to allow for all. But that is no longer the case . . . the destitution that the framers of the 1834 Report had in their minds does not exist now among the same class of people . . . now you can do a great deal that could not be done then without breaking that canon . . . that one must not make the dependent labourer better off than the independent . . . because the position of the independent labourer is so much better.[73]

Octavia Hill, who followed Marshall as a witness, was also a supporter of the COS. Her very different views were a pure expression of COS orthodoxy at that time. She had observed in London

a very great increase of thrift among the more intelligent . . . on the other hand whereever you get either unwise charity or lax administration of the Poor Law it does seem to

[69] Ibid. 10204. [70] Ibid. 10210. [71] Ibid. 10441.
[72] Ibid. 10444. [73] Ibid. 10379.

me that the less educated people are less thrifty than when I first knew them . . . of course they must be very much sorted into the more intelligent artizan and the person who is hovering on the brink of either independence or pauperism, and it is to the men in that position that any temptation to relax is so fatal.

She was wholly hostile to proposals for state pensions: 'any process of provision for old age should be unassisted by the State and by the locality . . . entirely voluntary and independent' for 'people can provide for themselves or their children can provide for them'.[74] She could only approve of a state scheme, 'if the thing is independent and self-supporting', otherwise

my fears are very great now of the people looking more and more to what can be done for them and less and less to what they can do themselves and in my talk with all the poorer people, that is the great tendency that I find among them. They are always talking about other people's duties, or something they are hoping to come from the skies, whereas if they would just turn round and do the things within their power, they would begin to grow more prosperous and they would be far better, richer, and happier.[75]

. . . if I could stop all charities in any given parish to-morrow I really think I would do it. I think it would be the worst plan to do it quite suddenly, but really I do not think the people would much miss them.[76]

Hill believed that even low-paid labourers could save. When Booth suggested that she find such a person to give evidence to the Commission as to how they managed, she became a little flustered: 'I do not recall any at the moment from whom you could learn much . . . I am afraid that we should find that we see the disadvantages to the poor of outdoor relief more clearly as a rule than they see it themselves'. She was equally doubtful about involving working men in Poor Law administration:

I have been struck by the great want of moral courage among the lower orders of working people in doing anything which is not quite popular. . . . The people who know the poor best are those towards whom the poor have themselves duties . . . I would rather go for information to the employer or to the landlords or to the schoolmistress—even the schoolmistress—though I do not think that they are good authorities.[77] You see the people are always on their best behaviour to the people from whom they expect anything such as missionaries or clergymen.[78]

Though she agreed that 'the habits and character of the poor vary as much as the habits and character of the other classes . . . quite as much, almost more . . . directly they get up a little, not in class, but in character, you find such happy homes and such comfortable ones'.[79] Such sentiments are sometimes regarded as culturally dominant in late nineteenth-century Britain. Octavia Hill was in fact among an extreme minority before the Commission in her

---

[74] George Bartley, 10544.   [75] Ibid.   [76] Ibid. 10556.
[77] Ibid. 10523.   [78] Ibid. 10535.   [79] Ibid. 10540.

assertion that the difficulties of the very poor could be solved wholly by self-help and voluntary action.

Charles Booth, who was altogether more sympathetic to poor people, summed up before the Commission the findings of his investigations. He did not believe that the Poor Law, charity, and self-help could solve the problem of poverty in old age in the foreseeable future and 'too high a proportion of those low-paid during working life received poor relief in old age to make sweeping condemnation of'.[80] Most of these were female: 'the general sweeping condemnations apply far more to the men than to the women in my judgement'. Withdrawing public support and throwing them onto the care of family and friends was not a sure way to make poor old women independent:

These old women are necessarily dependent . . . my impression is that most of the women would feel more independent if they lived in their son's house with a small allowance from the parish and still more with a pension which had no such stigma to it, than they would feel if they were entirely dependent upon the child.[81]

The politician Joseph Chamberlain, who was also a member of the Commission, defended his recent proposals for state old-age pensions:[82]

It is ridiculous to assert that one out of every two, or one out of every two and a half of the working classes and of the poorer classes are either drunken, idle or improvident . . . it is certain, it is a matter of common experience, that as regards the great bulk of the working classes, during their working lives, they are fairly provident, fairly thrifty, fairly industrious and fairly temperate. I do not think that a moderate consumption of drink is in any way wrong on the part of the working man.[83]

He argued that Booth's survey,

shows conclusively that the chief and predisposing cause of pauperism is old age and consequent on old age a man's inability to work . . . I contend that if a working man and a poor man is able to keep himself from the Poor Law up to the age of 60, I am not prepared to attach any blame to him if, after 60, he finds it difficult to provide for himself.[84]

He believed that the 'ordinary working man' had little possibility of saving, and

I would point out that the majority of old age paupers are women and, as is well known, women are very seldom intemperate, and at the same time they are persons who by the very necessity of their lives are in the majority of cases almost precluded from saving. It is the commonest thing in the world for a working man to give a fixed sum to his wife, which is calculated upon the daily necessities of the family, and to keep the rest for himself; and there can be no doubt that in such a case no allowance is made for such a luxury as old age provision.

---

[80] Ibid. 10859.   [81] Ibid. 10865.
[82] P. Thane, 'Contributory vs Non-Contributory Old Age Pensions, 1878–1908', in Thane (ed.), *Origins of British Social Policy* (London, 1978), 84–106.
[83] *Royal Commission on the Aged Poor*, Minutes of Evidence, 12174.   [84] Ibid. 12179.

. . . when we know that a very large proportion are due to women who cannot save, nothing could be more cruel than to say that their position is the result of their own fault. There is no neglect, there is no drunkeness and there is no idleness.[85]

I think that in dealing with the poor some economists expect from them a virtue which we certainly do not find in ourselves. The poor, of course, have less opportunities of thrift than the well-to-do classes, and it is a little too much to expect of them, unless in very exceptional instances, the extremely penurious lives which would be necessary if they were to make by their own efforts, a sufficient provision for old age . . .[86]

Chamberlain firmly defended state funding of pensions:

That is part of our social arrangements, that the rich should contribute out of their superabundance in aid of those who are less fortunate. It is socialism, it is Christian socialism at any rate and is the basis of a great deal of our present taxation. They may say, however, that they get indirectly an advantage: the foundations of property are made more secure when no real grievance is felt by the poor against the rich.[87]

Asked about the causes of pauperism in old age, he insisted:

Very often an old man is improvident or drunken or idle just before he comes into the workhouse . . . it is true that people get so hopeless towards the close of life that they frequently become drunken and idle; and I do not think in those cases that it ought to be said that drunkeness and idleness are the causes of their being in the workhouse.[88]

I do not think there is any more inclination on the part of the upper and middle classes to make sacrifices for the future than there is on the part of the poor . . . if you told a rich man that he was to give up every chief enjoyment of his life, every recreation, in order to make a provision of this kind, I do not think he would make it.[89]

The majority of the influential experts who gave evidence to the Commission expressed sympathy and respect for the aged poor, and appreciation that in general their plight was not of their own making.

THE VIEWS OF WORKING PEOPLE

The Commission took Marshall's advice and interviewed a selection of working men and one women. They conveyed a picture of the reality of working-class life at later ages which confirmed the insights of Marshall, Chamberlain, and Booth rather than those of Octavia Hill.

James Grout, a wireworker of Finsbury Park in London expressed a view put forward by most of them: 'I think a man who has worked in the country for forty or fifty years is entitled to be taken care of for the rest of his life. I should hold that he has paid sufficient as the result of his labour during that time.' He believed that wages were too low to enable many to save or to contribute to a pension. He favoured a non-contributory pension of at least

[85] *Royal Commission on the Aged Poor*, Minutes of Evidence, 12181.   [86] Ibid. 12182.
[87] Ibid. 12258.   [88] Ibid. 12259.   [89] Ibid. 12262.

five shillings a week, payable between the ages of 60 and 65 and earlier to men or women disabled from work.[90] He admitted that people 'aged' at varying ages, 'but I think we must strike the line at some age or other and I do it at 60'. The pension should be payable only to those below a certain income limit, perhaps the income tax limit.[91] In some trade unions, including his own, the 'very small' London Society of Wireworkers, 'there is an implied leniency towards aged men'. They were allowed to work for sixpence an hour rather than the eightpence or ninepence paid down for younger men. He believed that the state of the working classes was 'very much better than in father's day', but that they were under greater pressure. He believed that his own health was in consequence worse than his father's.

Thomas Pitkin, aged 64, lived, by contrast, in the country, at Swanbourne, Bucks. He gave a clear account of how an elderly rural labourer lived. He had given up his regular job of looking after cattle two years before and now worked his acre: in addition, '[I] catch a few odd jobs . . . I have done a little on the bye-road this winter and now . . . I am agent for a seeds merchant and sell a little seed'. He had managed to save £10 in the savings bank while working: 'I put that amount in the land and the land pays me a very good return . . . I am very comfortable.'[92] He earned about thirteen shillings a week and extra in haytime and harvest. He had a cottage and garden for which he paid £3 a year in rent and rates and rented a one-acre allotment and kept a pig or two. He described how allotments helped keep people off the parish until they got too old to work them.[93] He had been a teetotaller for fourteen years. He had received poor relief only once when very ill with influenza forty years before;[94] his wife had been ill for six years before her death and 'I nearly starved'. He knew of no relatives on relief. He believed there was a great dread of the workhouse.

Pitkin had had eleven children, seven of whom survived to adulthood and five were still alive. One son was caretaker of a Board School a long distance away in Oldham (Lancashire), three others were agricultural labourers, living only three or four miles from him. One, a daughter, lived 'near by'. He lived alone. Asked if he had help from his children he replied, 'No. I have had to help them when I can. They have got large families, most of them. I do what I can in that sense. I do not get anything from them in any way.' However, he added: 'The daughter that I have lives about the length of this room, perhaps, from me and she looks after my house.'[95] The very considerable amount of help in kind which his daughter evidently gave him was so taken-for-granted that he did not regard it as 'help'. Two of Pitkin's sons each had seven children; the other four, 'I do not see how they could help me'. Asked whether children should be called upon to help their parents he

[90] Ibid. 13219–30.   [91] Ibid. 13245.   [92] Ibid. 14227.
[93] Ibid. 14123.   [94] Ibid. 14054–90.   [95] Ibid. 14105.

replied, 'Well I think that in some cases it ought to be done and in some cases it is a great hardship on the people.' He claimed to know of cases where children were unfairly compelled to support their parents and cases where they should be but were not.[96] He had belonged to a savings club but it broke up. He did not believe that agricultural labourers could afford to contribute to any of the pension schemes proposed. He had 'no idea' what he would do when he could no longer work his allotment: 'I am in great hopes that it will not come for a year or two; for two to three years'.[97]

Alfred Jephcott was a working engineer from Birmingham. He was an archetypal respectable working man: a member of the Birmingham School Board, elected by the City Council as artisan representative on the Birmingham Municipal Technical committee, a member of the Birmingham Trades Council, representing the Amalgamated Society of Engineers, and for three years a representative on the executive of the Independent Order of Oddfellows Friendly Society. He believed that:

The feeling among the working classes is that the (Poor Law) is too stringent; that more leniency should be shown to aged people; that they should not be called upon to enter the house where it is possible for them to spend their remaining days along with their friends, by having administered to them a better system of outdoor relief.[98]

Three shillings was the amount usually given in out-relief in Birmingham. This was too little. He thought four shillings the very least with which it was possible to buy sufficient food. He believed that those living in squalid conditions—he singled out the Irish—got more than those who strove to be respectable. He did not attribute more than one-third of old age pauperism to 'misconduct', for no man with a wife and family could save adequately for old age on less than twenty-five shillings a week.

Like other witnesses, he believed that work was becoming more stressful for older men and that it was increasingly difficult for them to find employment. In the Birmingham engineering trades, if 'he gets up to fifty, if he shows grey hairs in his head it becomes very difficult for him to obtain a situation in Birmingham factories, unless a man is specially skilled'. He believed that this was the employers' response to the unions' refusal to allow older men to work for reduced wages, 'though in fact local branches will wink at it for a deserving older man'. The union, the Amalgamated Society of Engineers, assisted older men who were dismissed for this reason.

The Birmingham men with whom he had discussed the issue approved of Chamberlain's pension proposals, though they believed that 65 was too late a pensionable age, even for workers in a relatively healthy trade such as engineering. He thought 60 would be preferable. He believed that relief would be better spent in the interests of the poor 'when we have guardians more popularly elected', for:

---

[96] *Royal Commission on the Aged Poor*, Minutes of Evidence, 14128–37.
[97] Ibid. 14269.   [98] Ibid. 14507.

we working men say that while we help to make the wealth of the country, we do not have the opportunity that our more favoured brethren have of making a provision for ourselves like they do, and that consequently we are not so depauperized as some would attempt to make us, because our wealth has been conserved in another direction. We have not received it to the extent, but we have helped to produce it and we are fully entitled to a portion of it without being termed in its broadest sense, paupers, although we may not actually have received the money during our working life.[99]

Working people should receive 'a small amount of money . . . more as a right than a favour'. It was especially necessary to help the large numbers who could not afford to join a Friendly Society.[100]

James Callear of Tipton, Staffordshire, who represented the iron workers of south Staffordshire, said: 'I have never been drunk in my life. I think I have been thrifty.' When young he had saved in a building society and he owned 'small house property . . . notwithstanding I am what is called a skilled workman, and I have been able to earn better wages than the generality of my fellow working men, such has been the condition of work with us, I mean we have lacked it so much, that had I been wholly dependent upon it I should have had nothing to look forward to in my old age but the workhouse on the one hand or to live at the expense of private charity on the other. We are of opinion that only a small proportion of pauperism in the Black Country is due to idleness or lack of thrift. It is mainly due to enforced idleness and low wages.' Some of his fellow workers earned only 4*s.* per day:

I do not wonder that some of them in old age have lost hope and heart and taken to drink and that others unfortunately have preferred suicide after having sought to make ends meet, to live respectably after having worked hard and feeling a repugnance to the workhouse.[101]

He did not belong to a Friendly Society and his union paid benefits only at death and in strikes and lock-outs. He believed that out-relief was always too little but that old people accepted it rather than enter the dreaded workhouse. A state pension would be preferred in his district. Working men had told him that:

England is the workshop of the world and that is so largely, if not mainly, in consequence of her working men. In consequence of their industry, their painstaking application and thoroughness, as the result we are prosperous and as the result of our prosperity we are able to pay, not only a good salary to those who serve us—our Civil servants, those who fight for us and others—but are able to give them a pension, after they have served us a certain number of years. If we are able to do this, and we are, how comes it that our working men, who help to make this possible, are in their old age neglected, pauperized and sent to the workhouse?[102]

---

[99] Ibid. 14647.   [100] Ibid. 14505–694.   [101] Ibid. 14911.   [102] Ibid. 14906.

Engineering work required physical strength and men could rarely continue at it past age 55. Firms kept older workers on at lighter work until about the age of 63. He knew of one still working at 74, 'he has been a stubborn one certainly and he is rather an exception and he seems, well, quite as young as his oldest son . . .'. In private companies in Mr Callear's district, employers did their best to find employment for old men. In larger, more impersonal, limited companies 'the same sympathy is not experienced and the same help is not afforded'.[103] He agreed that it would be better for employers to give adequate wages to enable working men to save for old age, 'but we can hardly see how it can be made possible and guaranteed'; and that it could not be guaranteed that all would be in work and able to benefit.[104]

Edwin Nokes was a 62-year-old working gardener also from Birmingham.[105] His wife was alive; he had ten living children and had buried four. Two still lived at home. The youngest was 12, the oldest 38. He had had a hard life and brought up his children mainly on potatoes, bread, and a little bacon. He had been a nailer and an agricultural labourer simultaneously, working at nailing from 7 to 9 p.m. after a day in the fields. He commented that 'children in the district have been summoned to help support a parent . . . but they are not able really' due to low wages—10–15s. per week for labourers. He did not know whether his own children could help; they were agricultural labourers with children of their own. He belonged to a failing sick club; he favoured Chamberlain's pension scheme which he believed to be popular and practicable. He now had a regular gardening job at seventeen shillings a week and he paid 2s. 6d. a week rent. He had a quarter-acre allotment 'one of the greatest advantages a working man has: it always provides him something for his dinner table the year throughout'. He hoped to work for some years, then 'I have nothing in view but the union that I know of'. He thought out-relief normally too meagre and that people wanted better treatment of those 'who are not drunken, the people who are honest and straightforward and have striven in life to do the best they could'. Many people on out-relief lived with their children. He would be satisfied if respectable old people received a regular four to five shillings outdoor relief.[106] He claimed that all the working men loathed the workhouse, thought outdoor relief inadequate, and supported the idea of a state old-age pension.

Fifty-six-year-old Frank Pickering of Ashby de la Zouch had worked as a miner since the age of 8. A group of old miners had told him to inform the Commission that they wanted an Act of Parliament compelling contributions throughout working life 'if it were only for a small living after they have become

---

[103] *Royal Commission on the Aged Poor*, Minutes of Evidence, 14944.   [104] Ibid. 14907–962.
[105] The West Midlands was so heavily represented among these witnesses that it suggests that Joseph Chamberlain, who was prominent in West Midlands politics, was involved in the selection of many of them.   [106] *Royal Commission on the Aged Poor*, Minutes of Evidence, 14984–15149.

incapacitated through old age'.[107] For, he believed, 'the working classes do not so object to compulsion as people seem to represent they do, if it is a right cause and a right way . . . because the greater part of their life is compulsion . . . they would not object to any scheme that would secure them an equivalent to the workhouse pay or a little more'.

Amy Hurlston of Coventry spoke for women in the various Midlands trades. She had served a short apprenticeship in watchmaking, her father's trade. She had no official position but had studied women in other trades. In the metal trades wages averaged 10s.–12s. a week, but in the biggest, chainmaking, only 4s. 6d.–6s. Most women saved for sickness and burial insurance but not for old-age. Most said they would subscribe to an old-age fund, but could not afford the sums proposed by Chamberlain. Twopence a week had been suggested to her as the sum they could afford. They selected 55 as the desirable pensionable age: 'they are practically worn out at fifty years old for factory work'. The pension should be five shillings. The seasonality of the work would make even a small contribution difficult, but the women were willing to make great efforts. It should be compulsory, and returnable at death, which would enable them to withdraw from burial clubs and better able to afford the contribution. Women would be unable to afford contributions after marriage. Some domestic servants were also too low paid to contribute.

Hurlston believed that a contributory old-age pension scheme was 'practicable but difficult for women'. She agreed with the Chairman's supposition that 'you are hardly satisfied by the provision made under present arrangements for the future of the women?' 'Very far from satisfied; distinctly dissatisfied . . . A very large proportion of the thrift of the men is directed to their own old age.' She also agreed 'that if there is to be an old age pension established for women it must be on lines of its own . . . However thrifty she may be, a woman rarely earns more than sufficient to pay her way honestly and dress respectably and maintain an appearance that will give her a chance of marrying decently'. The women believed that:

A sum corresponding to that paid by each woman worker should be enforced as a contribution from the employer, on the score that wherever it is possible men's labour is supplanted by women at probably less than half the cost. This they would regard somewhat in the light of a law of compensation, while, on the other hand, they fear that such a method of procedure would suggest itself to employers as 'a bit too "high-handed"' and might tend to depress the already too low rate of wages.[108]

Contrary to all the other working-class witnesses, John Stevens, a tinplate worker from Birmingham, secretary of his local branch of the Ancient Order of Foresters Friendly Society, claimed that 'the artisan portion of the working classes in Birmingham are nearly entirely opposed to Mr Chamberlain's old age pension scheme'. Most men who had sufficient wages already had ample

---

[107] Ibid. 16422.   [108] Ibid. 16928.

opportunities to save; 65 was in any case too late for a pension to begin since work could cease at any time after 55. It was 'impossible to fix an age which would suit all conditions of labour'. However, 'I think that the question of aged women is a question deserving the attention of this Commission. Many could find a home among friends if they had some little income.' Also he believed that men who had tried to be thrifty also deserved more liberal administration of the Poor Law.[109]

CONCLUSION

After hearing the evidence the Commission chose to endorse the principles introduced in 1871: that poor relief should discriminate between 'the respectable aged who became destitute and those whose destitution is distinctly the consequence of their own misconduct'. It desired 'to place on record in strong terms our conviction that where outdoor relief is given, the amount should be adequate to meet fully the extent of the destitution and that proper investigation and supervision should be ensured in all cases in which application is made for relief'. The final report stressed the importance of co-operation between charitable agencies and Poor Law authorities and recommended amendment of the Friendly Societies Acts to encourage the establishment of separate funds for saving for old age. The obligations of 'liable' relatives should continue to be enforced. Of the original members of the Commission the Chairman, Lord Aberdare, died before its work was complete, the Prince of Wales resigned and declined to sign the Report because the issue had become political; nine members signed dissenting memoranda and five a separate report recommending more serious investigation of proposals for old-age pensions in place of poor relief for the aged deserving poor. The trade unionist Henry Broadhurst's memorandum, said to have been drafted by the Fabian Sidney Webb, urged a non-contributory state pension of at least five shillings a week, to be paid through the Post Office.[110] No member of the Commission appeared to have changed his views as a result of their inquiries.

The government responded by adopting one recommendation of the majority of the Commission even before publication of the reports. On 29 January 1895 the President of the LGB issued a circular to guardians recommending that outdoor relief should be readily granted to the aged poor. It advised that this change should be made public, in order to overcome the reluctance of the aged to apply, and to reassure the young that respectable poverty brought its ultimate reward. Those who needed institutional care were to be allowed more 'comforts' in the workhouses: to wear their own clothes, to give and receive visits, to smoke and to eat other than the prescribed diet. As always, this advice was followed slowly and unevenly by Poor Law administrators.

[109] *Royal Commission on the Aged Poor*, Minutes of Evidence, 17227–17316.
[110] Williams (Thane), thesis, 89.

The report crystallized the widespread awareness and concern at the end of the nineteenth century about the aged poor as a distinct social group, and a growing sense that they deserved, and that the country could afford, a new, more secure, and less degrading form of public support than in preceding centuries. It also expressed the divided opinions as to the form this should take, above all concerning the role of the state in social provision. The evidence and the report expressed concern and respect for all but the thoroughly disreputable among the aged poor and an especial awareness of the vulnerability of old women. Macnicol, and in the past Thane,[111] have been mistaken to argue that 'the late nineteenth century debate about old age poverty was always a debate about older male workers', and that 'there was a marked reluctance to discuss the poverty of older women'.[112] Rather, awareness of the particular problem of poverty among older women had a profound influence in shaping the discourse about pensions and the problems of the aged poor and the subsequent legislation.

The question as to why old age acquired such prominence as a distinct social problem at this time cannot simply be explained either in terms of the growing proportion of older people in the population,[113] since this, although rising slightly, remained at an historically low level; or in terms of labour market changes which prioritized the need to impose labour discipline on young men; nor is there any convincing evidence that such a strategy on the part of employers, if it existed, increasingly excluded older men from paid employment.[114] Rather, the focus upon poverty in old age was a feature of a wider tendency at this time to differentiate and to define the distinct components of the 'social question'. Unemployment and housing[115] similarly came to be defined as social problems in the last two decades of the nineteenth century. Also important and widely shared was the realization expressed to the Royal Commission by Alfred Marshall, that although many old people shared the general rise in working-class living standards of this period, more did not. The relatively increasing poverty of some older people became the more starkly apparent as their treatment by the Poor Law became more restrictive. The evident incapacity of the Poor Law either to prevent or to cure the major problems of poverty of the later nineteenth century, and the growing and varied pressures for reform,[116] further focused attention on the forms of provision best suited to the needs of the aged poor.

[111] Pat Thane, 'Women and the Poor Law in Victorian and Edwardian Britain', *History Workshop*, 6 (1978), 29–51.   [112] Macnicol, *Politics of Retirement*, 30–2.
[113] P. Laslett, 'Necessary Knowledge: Age and Aging in the Societies of the Past', in D. Kertzer and P. Laslett (eds.), *Aging in the Past: Demography, Society and Old Age* (Berkeley, 1995), 10–14.
[114] As Macnicol argues, *Politics of Retirement*.
[115] J. Harris, *Unemployment and Politics: A Study in English Social Policy, 1886–1914* (Oxford, 1972). M. Daunton, *House and Home in the Victorian City: Working Class Housing, 1850–1914* (London, 1983).
[116] For a summary see Pat Thane, *The Foundations of the Welfare State*, 2nd. edn. (London, 1996), 31–7.

The Campaign for Old-Age Pensions

Not all old people were poor—some were wealthy and powerful—but many were very poor in the later nineteenth century when poverty in old age was defined as a social problem more distinctively than before. Increasingly state pensions were demanded as the solution to this problem. This discourse about aged poverty contributed to the construction of a definition of old age which was to be influential throughout the twentieth century: the 'old-age pensioner' emerged as the archetypical older person.

Underlying the campaign for pensions was the failure of the Poor Law to cope with the most severe poverty in old age; but another theme was the perceived failure of the leading institutions through which working people sought to protect themselves against poverty in old age: the Friendly Societies.

FRIENDLY SOCIETIES

These descendants of the medieval guilds and fraternities existed throughout England by the end of the eighteenth century[1] and their numbers expanded rapidly in the nineteenth century. They varied immensely in size and structure but their principal purpose was to provide mutual insurance against sickness and death, and generally also regular convivial gatherings, often in public houses, or, in the case of the numerous temperance organizations, in more sober settings. Sickness could become almost permanent in old age and many societies provided their older members with regular sickness payments which were in effect pensions.

The total membership of Friendly Societies was estimated at over 600,000 in more than 7,000 societies in 1801. By 1815 they appear to have offered some form of cover to about one-third of all households in England and Wales.[2] By 1851 it was estimated that almost half the adult male population of England and Wales (about two and a half million) belonged to a society: by 1872 the number was over four million in about 30,000 societies (about two-thirds of the adult male population).[3] By the end of the nineteenth century

---

[1] F. Eden, *The State of the Poor*, vols. i and ii (London, 1797). Martin Gorsky, 'The Growth and Distribution of English Friendly Societies in the Early Nineteenth Century', *Economic History Review*, 51/3 (Aug. 1998), 489–511.　　　　[2] Gorsky, 'English Friendly Societies', 507.

[3] B. Supple, 'Legislation and Virtue: An Essay on Working Class Self-Help and the State in the Early Nineteenth Century', in N. McKendrick (ed.), *Historical Perspectives: Studies in English Thought and Society in honour of J. H. Plumb* (London, 1974), 211–54.

the total was put at about five and a half million, a slight fall in percentage terms.[4] The Societies did, however, include an unknown number of women and some men belonged to more than one Society. The figures covered a variety of institutions, from the Societies providing only opportunities to save for burial or for medical care to those offering a wide range of benefits: from the very small, local, and sometimes ephemeral institutions to the large national (indeed international, many had branches in the colonies) 'affiliated orders' which were organized through local branches. These were often romantically or whimsically named—Ancient Order of Foresters (AOF), Manchester Unity of Oddfellows (MUO) were two of the largest—and equipped with regalia and ritual and had a strong ethos of fellowship and mutual support. In the later nineteenth century the affiliated orders were becoming the predominant form of Society. Their size provided security, but their relatively high rates of regular weekly contribution tended to exclude poorer men (for whom irregularity of work was as great an obstacle to regular saving as low pay) and most women. If women were not themselves working for reasonable pay, as few were, households could rarely afford contributions for both husband and wife. Some low-paid men and women would join less formal 'dividing-up' or slate clubs (called 'tontines' in some regions) which provided sickness and burial benefit, but did not accumulate a fund, rather dividing surplus funds among the members at the end of the year. These provided a means of saving and offered some protection to people who could not afford long-term risk.[5] The most successful clubs were organized by and for working people, and possessed a strong ethos of fraternity and mutual aid. Others were philanthropic, subsidized by wealthy patrons, but these seem rarely to have been popular.[6]

By the 1860s much concern was publicly expressed at the apparently high rate of failure especially of smaller Societies. It was believed that respectable savers were let down by clubs which did not ensure that income was sufficient to cover outgoings. In particular it was feared that many clubs founded earlier in the century had ageing memberships and increasing costs of permanent sick relief to older members which had not been taken into account in calculating subscriptions. It is impossible to judge the seriousness of this problem because official statistics do not distinguish between Societies which went into voluntary or involuntary liquidation.[7] Expressions of concern led to increasing inquiry into and closer regulation of the financial operations of Friendly Societies through the nineteenth century.[8]

[4] P. Johnson, *Saving and Spending: The Working-Class Economy in Britain 1870–1939* (Oxford, 1985), 57.
[5] Ibid. 48–74.
[6] P. H. J. H. Gosden, *Self-Help: Voluntary Associations in Great Britain* (London, 1973), 1–114.
[7] Patricia M. Williams (Thane), 'The Development of Old Age Pensions in the UK, 1878–1908', Ph.D. thesis (London School of Economics, 1970), 33. Numbers of Friendly Societies were published annually from 1846 by the Registrar of Friendly Societies.
[8] P. J. H. J. Gosden, *The Friendly Societies in England, 1815–1875* (Manchester, 1961); Gosden, *Self-Help*, 77–114.

CANON BLACKLEY AND OLD-AGE PENSIONS

Little of the concern about, and criticism of, the Societies came from their members, who were mainly working people. It is tempting to wonder how much of the alarm derived from the doubts of the better-off about the capacity of working people to manage financial institutions. Some of the concern, however, was about the many who were not members of Societies, who were described in extreme terms as: 'young labourers by the dozen, without a change of decent clothes, continually and brutally drinking, living almost like savages while earning fully £1 a week'.[9] This was the judgement of Canon William Lewery Blackley, who sought to remedy this situation by promoting the first influential scheme in Britain of 'National Provident Insurance'—compulsory insurance for sickness and old age. He was, quite wrongly, convinced that the great majority of Friendly Societies were insolvent and he played a leading part in promoting this belief. Blackley proposed that every citizen between the ages of 18 and 21—when most working men and women had earnings but had fewer responsibilities than later in life—should contribute to a fund supervised but not subsidized by the state. The fund would accumulate and provide all 'wage-earners'—to be distinguished from 'wage-payers and leisured and salary earners', who would contribute but not benefit—eight shillings a week sick pay until age 70, and four shillings a week pension thereafter.[10]

Blackley was over-optimistic about the amount young people could afford to save, the likely rate of interest, and the yield, but he promoted his scheme tirelessly for ten years and placed old-age pensions on the British political agenda.[11] He was assisted by the interest aroused when, between 1883 and 1885, Bismarck introduced in Germany the first scheme in the world of compulsory national insurance for sickness and accident at work.[12] The *Times* commented that:

the German is accustomed to official control, official delays and police supervision from the cradle to the grave . . . whereas self help and spontaneous growth are better suited to Englishmen.[13]

Nevertheless public interest was sufficient for a Select Committee to be appointed by the government to investigate the possibility of national insurance in Britain. This concluded that no existing proposals, including Blackley's, would solve the problems of poverty in sickness and old age because the lowest paid could not afford adequate contributions. They noted, correctly, that

---

[9] M. J. J. Blackley, *Thrift and National Insurance* (London, 1906), 50.

[10] W. L. Blackley, 'National Provident Insurance', *Nineteenth Century* (Nov. 1878), 834–37.

[11] Williams, 'Old Age Pensions', 38–47.

[12] E. P. Hennock, *British Social Reform and German Precedents: The Case of Social Insurance, 1880–1914* (Oxford, 1987), 109–112.

[13] *The Times* feature, 'State socialism in Germany', by the Berlin correspondent (19 June 1889).

low-paid and casual workers, who were most vulnerable to poverty in old age, were excluded from the German scheme.[14]

Thereafter Blackley faded from the pension campaign. Public interest seemed also to be fading, until in 1889 Bismarck chose once more, as he put it, 'to add a few drops of social oil to the recipe prescribed for the state'. He introduced the first old-age and invalidity pensions law in the world. The pensions were to be payable at age 70, but invalidity pensions for permanent incapacity for work might be claimed at any age on condition of five years' insurance. Once more, the scheme excluded the poorest, including most women. Again the *Times* commented:

Natural as free individual development is to the English, equally necessary is for Germany a rigid, centralized, all pervading state control . . . how exceptionally is Germany fitted to be the scene of this great philanthropic experiment.[15]

National stereotypes and rivalries apart—and rivalry between Britain and Germany was intense at this time—the German situation was very different from the British. Bismarck had explicitly introduced pensions as part of a strategy of undermining the rapidly growing power of the socialist Social Democratic Party. The aim was to demonstrate that the existing political system could benefit workers and merited their support.[16] Hence the scheme was targeted at better-paid male workers, who possessed the vote and were tending to vote socialist, rather than at women and the very poor, who could not vote in either country, but were the main focus of concern of British pensions politics. The German pension incorporated contributions and payments graduated according to income, which ensured that the better-off during working life remained so thereafter. This was not seriously considered in Britain, where the vision of the purpose of state welfare was not maximum income replacement in hard times, but provision of the 'safety net' of a 'national minimum' to enable the poorest to survive. British reformers strove for an extension of traditional Poor Law principles rather than a radical new departure. Nevertheless the real value of the German pension was lower than of that introduced in Britain in 1908.[17] Such differences were long to mark the social policy approaches of the two countries.[18]

In Britain there were increasing demands for clarification of how many old people were desperately poor, in order to assess the extent of need. In 1890 a parliamentary question from Thomas Burt, a trade unionist and Lib–Lab MP for the mining constituency of Morpeth in the North-East led to the first

[14] *Final Report from the Select Committee on National Provident Insurance, Parliamentary Papers*, vol. xi. HC 257 (1887). Williams, 'Old Age Pensions', 49–54.
[15] *The Times* (19 June 1889). [16] Hennock, *British Social Reform*, 109–16.
[17] W. H. Dawson, *Social Insurance in Germany, 1883–1911: Its History, Operation and Results and a Comparison with the National Insurance Act, 1911* (London, 1912).
[18] P. Baldwin, *The Politics of Social Solidarity: Class Bases of the European Welfare States, 1875–1975* (Cambridge, 1990).

'Return of numbers over age sixty-five receiving poor relief on August 1st 1890' (see Table 9.2). This showed that 18 per cent of all people over age 65 were receiving relief in some form, including short-term medical relief, on that day. Even allowing that numbers of paupers were always lower in summer than in winter, and that the total numbers of old people receiving relief at some point in the year would have been higher, this was a lower proportion of paupers among the old than many had thought. Nevertheless, it suggested that a large number of old people were poor, and it was well known that very many old people dragged out lives of desperate misery rather than apply for poor relief.

JOSEPH CHAMBERLAIN AND OLD-AGE PENSIONS

The first major politician to take up the issue was Joseph Chamberlain. In the late 1880s he was in transit to the Conservative Party from Gladstone's Liberal Party, with whose support for Irish Home Rule he disagreed. He was also concerned about the growing political power of the labour movement, though he was convinced that it could be stalled by 'a political leader with genuine sympathy with the working class and a practical programme'[19] of social reform, such as himself. Chamberlain had a background in personal philanthropic work, and as Mayor of Birmingham had sponsored real social improvement. As President of the Local Government Board in 1886 he had both provided a Poor Law subsidy to public work schemes for the unemployed and removed the stigma of disfranchisement from those receiving poor relief for medical needs only. Between 1890 and 1899 he sought to devise a 'practical programme' in which old-age pensions had a major place. He had been impressed by the German scheme. Pensions became a major theme in his campaign speeches. He emphasized, indeed exaggerated, how many working-class people ended their lives on poor relief.[20] When the popularity of the theme became evident Chamberlain settled down to devise a scheme of pensions. He could not contemplate a state-funded scheme, which would be redistributive and 'socialistic' to a degree he found ideologically unacceptable. He recognized that neither the German nor any other contributory scheme could include the underemployed, underpaid poor.[21] He recommended, instead, a state subsidy to the existing voluntary Post Office annuities scheme (introduced by Gladstone in 1864) which would enable contributors to receive 5s. per week at age 65. This scheme also was inaccessible to the very poor.[22] These proposals were prominent in Chamberlain's election manifesto in 1892. For the first time pensions were a major election issue.

---

[19] Joseph Chamberlain MSS, Birmingham University Library, JC 11/30 544: Joseph Chamberlain to Sir Charles Dilke, 21 Apr. 1893.
[20] Williams, 'Old Age Pensions', 55–9.   [21] Ibid. 68–9.   [22] Ibid. 70–2.

At the same time Charles Booth was arousing both interest in and hostility to the idea of state pensions.[23] He won the support of the Fabian Society and of trade unionists for his plan for a costly universal non-contributory pension.[24] In 1893 the President's address at the Trades Union Congress claimed:

It would seem as if times were ripe for an effort to be made by the state to formulate some system of old age pensions whereby the closing years of an honourable life of honest toil should be rendered less grim than at present. The best organized of our trade unions have done much in this direction by their superannuation funds and it is for the state to take up the work in directions which they cannot possibly reach.[25]

The Conference passed a resolution that:

The maladministration of our Poor Law demands the instant attention of parliament and in the opinion of this congress, the best means of dealing with such is by a national state-aided system of old age pensions—the superannuation funds of our trade unions and other associations not to be interfered with.[26]

Chamberlain by contrast sought to provide for poverty in old age at minimal cost to the state. To the Royal Commission on the Aged Poor he advocated, first, personal contributions to be made before the age of 25, supplemented by a contribution from the state: secondly, that the state should double any pension accumulated through a Friendly Society. Neither was costed and neither could solve the problem of the inability of the poorest to save. When this was pointed out, Chamberlain replied, against all the evidence, that the very poor did not survive to 65. Pensions once more had a prominent place in his campaign in the general election of 1895. This was won by the Conservatives and Chamberlain joined the Cabinet as Colonial Secretary.

This was not a government anxious to promote social reform and Chamberlain's new responsibilities were absorbing. There were, however, growing extra-parliamentary pressures for state pensions. The labour movement continued to expand and increasingly supported Booth's proposals. And, contrary to some interpretations,[27] leading Friendly Societies increasingly favoured some form of state pension. This arose partly from concern for those who could not afford to join the Societies. The annual High Court of the Ancient Order of Foresters in 1893 resolved unanimously to:

welcome any equitable system of old age pensions which without interference with the friendly societies or their work, shall provide for the large number of persons who are unable to avail themselves of those institutions.[28]

[23] See pp. 173–7.   [24] B. Webb, *My Apprenticeship* (Harmondsworth, 1938), 255.
[25] *Report of the Annual Conference of the Trades Union Congress* (1893), 30.   [26] Ibid. 50.
[27] B. B. Gilbert, *The Evolution of National Insurance in Great Britain* (London, 1966), 159–232. J. H. Treble, 'The Attitudes of Friendly Societies towards the Movement in Great Britain for State Pensions, 1878–1908', *International Review of Social History*, 15/2 (1970), 266–99.
[28] *Report of the Royal Commission on the Aged Poor, Parliamentary Papers*, xiv (1895), qn. 12422.

Less altruistically, some Societies were becoming alarmed at the potential cost of their own ageing memberships. A state pension would remove their sense of responsibility to provide for older members. Younger members in particular were often more concerned to maintain solvency than to sustain the fraternal tradition which underlay the feeling of obligation to prevent long-term members from dying in poverty. In 1895–6 the Independent Order of Oddfellows, Manchester Unity, was split on the issue between 'state-aiders' and 'anti-state aiders'. After vigorous internal debate, their Annual Moveable Conference in 1896 narrowly resolved that:

any well-considered and suitable scheme propounded by the legislature for the relief of the aged and infirm, benefiting our unfortunate brethren, will receive the cordial support of the Manchester Unity provided that the pension is independent of the Poor Law and does not create any power of government interference in the general management of the Manchester Unity.[29]

Two years later this was reversed by a similarly small margin, but the Society was too divided to oppose state pensions decisively. In 1897 the large, flourishing, and solvent United Ancient Order of Druids became the first Society to support a non-contributory state pension 'of not less than five shillings per week for all persons over 65 applying for the same and considered deserving'. They also recorded their opposition to any form of state interference in the Societies.[30] There were divisions and shifts of opinion within and between most Societies which did not correlate simply with solvency.[31] There was no united Friendly Society front for or against state pensions.

Gilbert has attributed the failure of proposals for insurance pensions and the success of non-contributory pensions primarily to the opposition of the Friendly Societies to state insurance. This is greatly to overestimate the power, the unanimity, and the selfishness of the Societies. In a somewhat teleological analysis of 'the evolution of national insurance' he seriously underestimates the importance of the late nineteenth-century focus upon the needs of the very poor, especially of women, who were outside the Societies: and hence the extent of positive support for non-contributory pensions as a potentially more effective means of provision for these needs than an insurance scheme.[32]

THE ROTHSCHILD COMMITTEE ON OLD-AGE PENSIONS

The continuing climate of support for state pensions must explain the Conservative government's appointment in July 1896 of a departmental committee chaired by Lord Rothschild. Its terms of reference were:

[29] R. W. Moffrey, *A Century of Oddfellowship* (Manchester, 1910), 124–5.
[30] Williams, 'Old Age Pensions', 99.   [31] Ibid. 99–101.
[32] Hennock, *British Social Reform*, 117–25. Gilbert, *National Insurance*, 159 ff. Pat Thane, 'Contributory versus Non-Contributory Old Age Pensions, 1878–1908', in Thane (ed.), *Origins of British Social Policy* (London, 1978), 84–106.

To consider any scheme that may be submitted to them for encouraging the industrial population, by state aid or otherwise to make provision for old age and to report
whether they can recommend the adoption of any proposals of the kind either based
upon or independent of such schemes: with special regard, in the case of any proposals which they may approve of, to their cost and probable financial results to the
Exchequer and to local rates: their effect in promoting thrift and self-reliance: their
influence upon the property of the Friendly Societies: and the probability of securing the co-operation of these institutions in their practical working.[33]

It was a small expert committee which included three Treasury civil servants, the Chief Registrar of Friendly Societies, a leading actuary, and representatives of Friendly Societies. It called few witnesses, believing, with good
reason, that little could be added to the voluminous hearings of the Royal
Commission on the Aged Poor. It concentrated upon collecting the views of
Friendly Societies and undertook a survey of the opinions and provision for
the aged of thirty-eight Friendly Societies and branches. The committee received
over one hundred pension schemes—a measure of popular interest in the question. They interpreted their terms of reference as excluding consideration
of any scheme involving compulsory insurance, or any non-contributory
scheme limited to a portion of the working population; that is, most current
proposals. The committee members especially objected to schemes which
'would involve the accumulation of great funds in the hands of the state
to provide for distant and uncertain liabilities'.
　They assumed:

the duty of every man to exercise reasonable thrift and self-denial in the attempt to
make provision for old age . . . that the industrial classes show an increasing disposition to appreciate and discharge this duty . . . State aid cannot be justified unless it
is limited to aiding the individual when circumstances beyond his control make it
practically impossible for him to save from his own earnings an adequate provision
for old age.[34]

The committee recognized that they had excluded attempts to assist 'the really
destitute who for good and bad reasons can provide nothing for themselves'. They could not envisage that any form of assistance would be free
from the danger of discouraging thrift. They also thought it undesirable to
provide payments at a level which would create a 'compulsorily unoccupied
class', even among the aged. They were more concerned with the encouragement of 'thrift and self-reliance' in the long term than with the immediate problem of poverty in old age.
　The members of the Committee were strikingly more negative about state
pensions and more alarmed about the danger of 'state interference' than most
of the witnesses they interviewed. Working-class representatives were notably

---

[33] *Report of the Committee on Old Age Pensions, Parliamentary Papers*, C. 8911, vol. xlv (1898).
[34] Ibid. 13.

sanguine about the role of the state. Representatives of Friendly Societies displayed a variety of views. Tom Hughes of the Board of Directors of the Manchester Unity was prepared to accept a state supplement to Friendly Society pensions and he resisted the Committee's insistence that this would lead inevitably to interference in the general affairs of the Society. He commented: 'I should imagine it would be a very easy arrangement.[35] I have sufficient confidence in the State that they would not embarrass Friendly Societies in any way.'[36] Sir Alfred Watson, Chief Actuary to the Manchester Unity and a member of the Rothschild Committee, insisted: 'The state is a master more feared than liked may I say with the Societies.'[37] Hughes responded, 'I do not see why they should not have confidence in the State. The State would only insist upon what was right and proper.' Asked, in somewhat leading fashion, why he would prefer 'an irresponsible government official' to an elected council of a Society to control such matters, Hughes replied: 'Would you call him irresponsible to that extent: he would be a government official armed with the authority of government and it would be his duty to see that the lodge and its administration was carried on as it ought to be. . . . I take it that there would be the act of appeal from his ruling or decision to some central authority in London . . . .'[38] Hughes and other witnesses[39] expressed greater faith in the constitutional process than did members of the Committee.

Two leaders of the AOF opposed all state pensions as being unavoidably subversive of self-reliance and family support.[40] State aid, one claimed, 'would hurt the manliness, if I may so speak it, of the members generally';[41] though they thought it 'the state's duty to provide for the destitute when they have done what is right', though, 'outdoor relief does weaken responsibility'.[42] However, an ordinary member of the AOF argued aggrievedly that these were not the views of the membership at large: 'I have never yet met with an individual member that is opposed to state pensions'.[43]

Robert Knight and Thomas Allen of the Boilermakers and Iron and Steel Shipbuilders Union agreed with Rothschild's description of theirs as a 'typical society of working men'. Their executive committee supported 'old age pensions granted by the state to all deserving poor', the same amount to be given to members of Friendly Societies and trade unions to supplement their own savings. They believed that the amount currently expended on poor relief would supply adequate funds for such pensions. Knight was asked to define the 'deserving poor', a term he used quite unselfconsciously. He replied:

They are men such as labourers and other men whose incomes during life, with the expense of their family, have not enabled them to make any provision for old age.[44]

---

[35] *Report of the Committee on Old Age Pensions, Parliamentary Papers*, qn. 83.
[36] Ibid., qn. 92.   [37] Qn. 221.   [38] Qns. 242–52.   [39] e.g. qns. 351–7.
[40] Qns. 1301–3, 1297.   [41] Qn. 1390.   [42] Qn. 1423.
[43] Ibid., app. IIIA.   [44] Qn. 2566.

They included, he believed, both those who had been quite unable to save, and members of Friendly Societies and trade unions who could not afford to save specifically for old age since they had low wages and, often, large families to support. In his view such people deserved a full state pension, of an unspecified amount. Sir Courteney Boyle MP twice asked him: 'where is the deservingness in that: it is a mere question of poverty?' Knight patiently repeated: 'The deservingness would be that the man never had an opportunity of providing for himself . . . I would not consider it deservingness if he had been a lazy, an indolent or a drunken man.'[45] Under pressure from the Committee he insisted, referring to his own experience as a Poor Law guardian in Newcastle, that, although it was difficult to assess people's past lives, 'in almost all towns the deserving poor are generally pretty well known'.[46] The Committee tried to pin him down to a more precise definition of 'deservingness' in keeping with their preconceptions. He replied:

If it had been found that he had had opportunities to better his condition and he had not done so, if he spent his money on intoxicating liquor, I, for one, would condemn him very strongly for it.[47]

He was asked how much drink pushed men over the boundary of respectability: 'If a man had two pints of beer on a Saturday night?' Knight replied, 'It would be a question that I do not think anyone would be able to answer.' The questioner persisted: 'Suppose a man was convicted of drunkenness over ten years ago, took the pledge and broke it?' 'I could not answer', Knight replied, and commented that he thought these questions 'on the face of it a little stretched'.[48]

Courteney Boyle compared Knight's proposals to the evils of the Speenhamland system. With exemplary patience in the face of a hostile Committee Knight denied any similarity: 'We have learned considerably since 1834 in dealing with questions of this kind.[49] My people do not want to encourage laziness: we want to encourage, as much as you do, thrift among all classes of people, and we would not give to anyone an encouragement to be lazy.'[50] Knight believed that a pension would encourage rather than discourage thrift, 'as I do not suppose that anyone anticipates that the government is going to give such relief that will make gentlemen of them when they get old'.[51] He described his own union's scheme, which like most union pensions,[52] had never been valued actuarially and which paid pensions out of the main union fund. The Committee pressed him on the danger of insolvency resulting from a large strike. Knight insisted that this was improbable,[53]

[45] Qns. 2600–1.   [46] Qns. 2568, 2601 ff.   [47] Qn. 2617.   [48] Qns. 2617–24.
[49] Qn. 2640.   [50] Qn. 2647.   [51] Qn. 2569.
[52] Kazuko Fukasawa, 'Voluntary Provision for Old Age by Trade Unions in Britain before the Coming of the Welfare State', Ph.D. thesis (University of London, 1996).
[53] *Royal Commission on the Aged Poor* (1895), Evidence, qn. 2697.

but that he believed that the trade union would be willing to establish a separate superannuation fund, audited by the state, if this became a condition of a state pension scheme.[54]

The Committee issued a questionnaire to 179 Friendly Societies. Thirty-four replied. They varied in size from 68—the Grand Protestant Friendly Society of Loyal Orangewomen, Preston District—to 769,969—the MUO. All but five supported their aged members, mostly in the form of extended sick benefit. This ranged in amount from one shilling per week (the Druids and the Nottingham Oddfellows when running short of funds) to five shillings (several societies). The median amount was three shillings. The Societies were asked: 'Has the society ascertained the opinion of its members on the question of a state-aided old age pension system for the industrial classes?' Nine societies, with a total membership of 1,066,579, clearly indicated their support for a state pension for members of Friendly Societies. Only two opposed it. The replies were moderate in tone and expressed a general willingness to co-operate with the state, though there were some outbursts of hostility: 'There is too much tomfoolery and humbug about all state business. If we cannot manage this better than the state we had better shut up shop altogether' (the Independent Order of Rechabites, a temperance society). More typical was the view of the United Order of Foresters, Ilkeston and Erewash branch: 'We believe a state pension would be an advantage to the Friendly Societies and a universal advantage to the country as it would give greater inducement to young men to swell our ranks and try to make some provision.' By 1896 there was substantial support for state-aided pensions among the Friendly Societies, but there was also opposition and division about the form pensions should take.

After two years' deliberation, in June 1898 the Committee declared itself unable to make any positive recommendation. Chamberlain and a handful of radical Liberals, including David Lloyd George, denounced this 'exhaustive negation'. However, Chamberlain's interest in pensions was flagging: he had failed to develop a popular scheme. But the issue would not go away. In 1899 eight private members' Bills promoting pension schemes came before parliament, eminent churchmen advocated pensions, and there was increasing support from the labour movement. Support for contributory pensions was slipping. The heart of the problem of the aged poor was the desperate plight of the very poor, most of them female, and, if the official investigations so far had shown anything, it was that no contributory scheme could help them. The debate thereafter was between selective or universal non-contributory pensions.[55]

---

[54] *Royal Commission on the Aged Poor* (1895), Evidence, qns. 2711–20.
[55] Williams, 'Old Age Pensions', 112–13.

THE NATIONAL COMMITTEE OF ORGANIZED LABOUR FOR THE
PROMOTION OF OLD AGE PENSIONS

Support for non-contributory pensions was mobilized by Revd F. H. Stead, brother of the campaigning journalist W. H. Stead and warden of the Congregationalist Browning Settlement in Walworth, south-east London. He was concerned about the poverty of old people in his district. In November 1898 he asked the New Zealand High Commissioner, the Fabian W. Pember Reeves, to address a meeting at Browning Hall about the selective non-contributory state pension recently introduced in New Zealand, with which Reeves had been closely involved and which was the work of New Zealand's first Lib–Lab government. Inspired by Reeves, Stead invited Charles Booth to describe his pension proposals to a similar meeting. Stead then began to plan a campaign for state non-contributory pensions.

With George Barnes, secretary of the powerful Amalgamated Society of Engineers (which had pioneered trade union superannuation),[56] Stead organized meetings in seven provincial cities, at which Booth described his proposal 'that all old people should receive an allowance of five shillings a week after sixty-five and that the money should be raised year by year by suitable taxation'.[57] Shortly afterwards, Booth published yet another volume of statistical proof of the extent of poverty in old age, *Old Age Pensions and the Aged Poor—a Proposal*. This did not, and was not intended to, add to his comprehensive earlier findings. It proposed, however, a revised pension plan. Booth now suggested a pension of seven shillings, on the grounds that this was the lowest amount on which an individual could subsist. But, on grounds of cost and for the scheme to have any chance of being politically acceptable, he regretfully proposed the higher pensionable age of 70. The total cost he estimated would amount to a 'socialistic transfer' of £20m. a year. A few days later Stead and Barnes founded the 'National Committee of Organized Labour (trade unions, trade councils, federations of these bodies, Friendly Societies and Co-operative Societies) for promoting old age pensions based on the principle that every old person on attaining a given age should be entitled to a free pension from the state: and charged with the instruction to promote the legal enactment of this principle' (hereafter NCOL). This operated through seven regional committees mainly composed of representatives of Friendly Societies and trade unionists. It was funded largely by Booth and by George Cadbury, the Quaker chocolate manufacturer, with some financial support from trade unions. The London committee included such prominent figures in the labour movement as Will Crooks, J. R. Clynes, Thomas Burt, and John

---

[56] Fukasawa, 'Voluntary Provision for Old Age by Trade Unions'.
[57] Williams, 'Old Age Pensions', 116–17.

Burns. The founding meeting of the NCOL at Browning Hall rejected Booth's revised proposal. The delegates thought 70 too late a pensionable age, for by that age many people had died in poverty. They preferred a five-shilling pension at 65. They adopted the slogan: 'a free state pension of five shillings a week'.

In July 1899 the post of full-time paid secretary went to Frederick Rogers, a considerable figure in the labour movement. A self-educated man, he had been president of the small vellum-binders union and a member of the London County Council. In 1900 he became the first chairman of the Labour Representation Committee, the forerunner of the Labour Party.[58] From its foundation the LRC was committed to a universal non-contributory pension of five shillings per week at age 65, a commitment carried on by the Labour Party at its formation in 1906. Rogers was willing to work with any political group which would support pensions, but he was aware that:

at the back of the pensions agitation was a force as yet unmeasured by the principles of the political world: the new and growing force of labour organized to realize political ideals.[59]

Rogers became a tireless missionary for pensions, travelling throughout the country addressing groups of all kinds, discovering that 'officers of friendly societies or co-operative stores and deacons of dissenting chapels were often more conservative in their ultimate thinking about the aged than were members of the (Conservative) Primrose League'.[60] Rogers, Stead, and others put pressure on prominent groups and individuals to support pensions. Stead was delighted when he persuaded the Congregational Union to pass by a large majority a resolution in favour of a national system of pensions. The NCOL published leaflets and pamphlets: their first publication, by George Barnes, *The Case Briefly Stated* (1899), ran to 100,000 copies.[61]

Meanwhile, the Liberal Opposition tabled an amendment to the Address at the opening of parliament, regretting that it included no reference to pensions. Early in March 1899 one hundred Conservative and Unionist MPs petitioned the government to make a 'definite attempt to fulfil the pledges on pensions given by so many of them'.[62] Shortly after, during the second reading of a Bill proposing a non-contributory, means-tested, pension of five shillings a week at 65, put forward by Lionel Holland, Conservative and Unionist MP for an east London constituency, Chamberlain rose to announce the appointment of another Select Committee 'to examine the subject'. He confessed that he now thought contributory pensions impracticable:

[58] Frederick Rogers, *Labour, Life and Literature* (London, 1913). Williams, 'Old Age Pensions', 122–6.
[59] Rogers, *Labour*, 244.   [60] Ibid. 223.
[61] G. Barnes, *From Workshop to War Cabinet* (London, 1924), 66.
[62] C. A. Whitmore, 'Is the Unionist Party Committed to Old Age Pensions?', *National Review*, 33 (July 1899), 713.

we must try to put aside at once any further attempts to secure compulsory contributions from the working class . . . they are at present either unable or unwilling to purchase deferred annuities.

But Booth's proposal he thought grossly expensive and incapable of discriminating between the provident and the drunkard and spendthrift.[63]

The Select Committee was appointed in April 1899:

To consider and report upon the best means of improving the condition of the aged deserving poor and of providing for those of them who are helpless and infirm: and to examine whether any of the Bills dealing with old age pensions submitted to parliament during the present session can with advantage be adopted, with or without amendment.[64]

These were wider terms of reference than those of previous investigations. The Committee was chaired by Henry Chaplin, President of the Local Government Board, who was favourably inclined towards pensions.

THE SELECT COMMITTEE ON THE AGED DESERVING POOR

The Chaplin Committee agreed with its predecessors on 'the remarkable development of habits of thrift and providence among the working classes in recent times', but:

we are unable to ignore the fact, abundantly supported as it is by the evidence we have had before us, that cases are too often to be found in which poor and aged people, whose conduct and whose whole career has been blameless, industrious and deserving, find themselves from no fault of their own, at the end of a long and meritorious life, with nothing but the workhouse or inadequate outdoor relief as the refuge for their declining years . . . it is also true no doubt that in the great majority of unions, outdoor relief is given in the case of poor and aged people who are known to the Guardians to be deserving.

But this kind of relief . . . is said to be too often wholly inadequate to provide for the reasonable comfort and even for the barest necessities of the poor.[65]

The Committee heard an account of the Danish pension scheme (established in 1891), which was non-contributory and means tested; also about the role of charity in providing for the aged. Sir Henry Longley, Chief Charity Commissioner, reported that endowed charities now devoted £611,664 annually to pensions and almshouses and:

The experience of the commissioners has led them to think it advisable not to fix the pension age and in making schemes they have usually abolished the precise age limits often fixed by the original trusts.

---

[63] *Hansard* (4th seri.), House of Commons, vol. 69 (22 March 1899), cols. 74–5. Williams, 'Old Age Pensions', 119–20.   [64] *Hansard*, vol. 70 (24 April 1899), col. 405.

[65] *Report of the Select Committee on the Aged Deserving Poor, Parliamentary Papers* viii (1899), p. iv.

There were, he believed, 'too many hard cases where the line has been drawn at sixty and a man of fifty-eight was obviously more deserving of pension than all the other candidates'.[66] The commissioners almost never approved a scheme providing a minimum stipend of less than five shillings. Longley pointed out how unevenly charities were distributed over the country. They could not on their own meet the needs of the deserving poor.

The Committee heard a proposal from the Old Age State Pension League. This had been formed in the previous year and was said to have the support of almost every Affiliated Order among the Friendly Societies. It proposed a state-funded pension of five shillings a week at age 65 for all who had been members of friendly societies, trade unions, or Co-operatives for a minimum of twenty years and for 'necessitous women who have lived honest, industrious and thrifty lives and who have been unable to belong to a Friendly Society because non-existing . . . because the government of the country has never done its duty to the old women of the country.' The League argued that very few men could not afford membership of a thrift institution of some kind.[67]

Gertrude Tuckwell of the Women's Trade Union League[68] asked permission to give evidence about the needs of women. She pointed out that there was a particular problem of women in dangerous trades, such as the lead industry. They were not paid more than in other trades but were incapacitated earlier in life: 'in the dangerous trades very often a woman is unable to earn her own living when she is still quite young. We are helping to support girls who are still quite young, well, under thirty.' Such women needed access to invalidity as well as old-age pensions. She stated that there was no age limit to factory work: she thought there were old women working in factories and that 60 would be an acceptable old-age pension age. Tuckwell told the Committee:

When I heard I should be called to give evidence, I consulted the women in the organizations with which we work, because we virtually work with all, and I received letters from them stating their views. They all answered with the most extraordinary promptitude and almost without exception the answers were that they felt very strongly on the subject, that it was impossible for women to subscribe to pension schemes because of their earnings.

This was as true of the relatively well-paid Lancashire cotton operatives as of other female workers. Tuckwell had also consulted Margaret Bondfield, the prominent trade unionist, 'who represents the shop assistants (a somewhat different class) who took exactly the same view, and Miss Llewellyn Davies who represents the Women's Co-operative Guild,[69] and her view very strongly

---

[66] *Report of the Select Committee on the Aged Deserving Poor*, Minutes of Evidence, qn. 337.

[67] Ibid., qns. 1370–1739.

[68] A philanthropic organization, mainly concerned to improve conditions of work for women.

[69] The largest working-class women's organization at the time composed mainly of married housewives.

endorsed mine also . . . a good many of them said that they hoped no pension would begin later than 60'.[70]

Fifteen trade unions sent resolutions to the Committee, all of which supported non-contributory pensions. Strikingly, almost all of these mostly male-dominated unions stressed the particular needs of women and the incapacity of contributory schemes to provide for them. Typical was the view of the Bradford Textile Workers Association:

We are of opinion that old age pensions should be granted to all persons making application for the same and that the only test to be applied should be incapacity by physical disablement to work. The Committee desire most respectfully to protest against the application of what is considered the thrift test constituted by membership of a friendly society, this test virtually destroying the claim of women workers for old age pensions.

Apart from sentiments of altruism, most male trade unionists had wives, who were likely to outlive them. Trade unions generally did not provide widows' pensions.[71] Trade unionists had strong incentives to support state pensions for women.

The Chief Poor Law Inspector put the case for meeting the needs of the aged poor simply by allowing guardians to grant higher levels of poor relief.[72] He described how workhouse accommodation had improved for old people in some unions. His description of life in 'improved' workhouses suggested how grim were those which were not. In Coventry:

applicants and inmates of good character, being 60 years of age and upwards, not having received parish relief, either in Coventry or elsewhere and having resided in Coventry for the last ten years previous to attaining that age are to have day and night rooms for males and females and to be provided with suits of ordinary clothing, to be allowed to attend their own place of worship on Sunday morning and to have three hours liberty each Thursday.[73]

The Committee, however, also received a resolution from the Association of Poor Law Unions of England and Wales: 'That it is desirable that a system of Old Age Pensions should be established'. The Association recommended that this should be administered by pension committees appointed by boards of guardians: 'paid not earlier than age 60 or later than 70: of amount not less than five shillings: means limited and aliens excluded. The cost of administration should be borne locally and the pension funded partly from the National Exchequer, partly from local rates', but 'in no circumstances should the proportion payable out of local rates exceed one-third of the pension fund'.[74] This scheme was recommended by the Chaplin Committee in its final report. At last an official report produced an unequivocal recommendation

[70] *Report . . . Aged Deserving Poor*, Minutes of Evidence, qns. 1760–1807.
[71] Ibid., app. 5.   [72] Ibid., qns. 1964–2062.   [73] Qn. 2065.   [74] Ibid., app. 6.

in favour of a specific scheme of state pensions and one which was likely to have wide appeal. Within a month, in August 1899, the government had appointed a Treasury committee of civil servants to cost the proposals. This was chaired by Sir Edward Hamilton, Joint Permanent Secretary at the Treasury. This was a normal preliminary to legislation, though the Prime Minister, Lord Salisbury, was unenthusiastic.[75]

The NCOL felt encouraged, but was determined to press for universal pensions. The TUC at its annual conference in September 1899 adopted its first unequivocal commitment to universal non-contributory pensions at age 60, as it was to do annually until pensions were introduced in 1908.[76] In the following month the large (500,000 members) and prosperous Hearts of Oak Friendly Society supported a similar scheme, to be administered by the Friendly Societies.

In November 1899 Arthur Balfour, heir apparent to the leadership of the Conservative and Unionist Party, put to the Cabinet a proposal for a modified version of the Chaplin proposals. It differed in proposing a local administrative structure quite separate from the Poor Law.[77] The Chancellor of the Exchequer, Sir Michael Hicks-Beach, responded with a long memorandum rejecting all pensions proposals as 'socialistic' and too costly for taxpayers to accept. He acknowledged that it was politically impossible to do nothing for the aged poor in the existing state of public opinion, but argued that the government should go no further than amendment of the Poor Law 'to make a real difference of treatment in favour of persons of good character and industrious and provident lives'. He judged, probably correctly, that to go further and adopt the Chaplin/Balfour proposals would not satisfy Labour in particular, whilst alienating the Conservatives' tax-paying supporters.[78] Salisbury shared this view.[79]

At the end of 1899 the war in South Africa became serious enough to drive other issues from public debate. The NCOL found it difficult to arouse interest in pensions. Balfour observed that 'Joe's war stopped Joe's pensions'.[80] Balfour's own proposal went no further. In the following year an LGB circular to guardians for the first time advised that 'systematic and adequate' outdoor relief be given to all aged persons who were both destitute and deserving. This marked a significant change of policy. Previously the key term had been the vague word 'necessary'. The destitute and deserving aged were not to be urged to enter the workhouse unless they were incapable of survival

[75] Williams, 'Old Age Pensions', 130, 139.
[76] *Report of the Annual Conference of the TUC*, (1899), 82.
[77] PRO CAB 37/51/57, 15 Nov. 1899, 'Pensions and Poor Law Reforms, Preliminary suggestions for discussion'. Williams, 'Old Age Pensions', 134–5.
[78] PRO CAB 37/51/89. Williams, 'Old Age Pensions', 136–8.
[79] P. Fraser, *Joseph Chamberlain* (London, 1966), 232.
[80] Elizabeth Balfour to Beatrice Webb, 25 Dec. 1910: Passfield MSS, British Library of Political and Economic Science, section II/4/e, fo. 91. Williams, 'Old Age Pensions', 140–1.

outside.[81] C. S. Loch referred to this move, with disgust, as 'a new poor law'. However, it was no more widely observed than previous policies. Four months later the LGB took the unusual step of writing to guardians to inquire what steps they had taken to comply with the circular. The replies showed no greater uniformity of practice than before.[82] Evidence taken in 1903 by a Select Committee investigating the care of old people in workhouses showed little change in official attitudes or practice at all levels of Poor Law administration.[83]

THE HAMILTON COMMITTEE

Meanwhile, the Hamilton Committee worked on and reported in January 1900.[84] On Chaplin's suggestion, in order to estimate the likely demand for a selective pension, it undertook a national sample survey of aged people which provides a snapshot of their material situation at the opening of the twentieth century. The investigators selected representative areas of twenty-eight unions, which were themselves chosen as being representative of metropolitan, urban, mining, and rural districts in England and Wales. The clerk to the guardians of each selected union was invited to nominate individuals who could be trusted to conduct house-to-house inquiries 'carefully and tactfully'. The Committee judged that the work was carried out 'efficiently and intelligently'.

The total population of the selected areas was 285,250. 13,529 (4.7 per cent) of the total were aged 65 or over, equal to the national average. However, the percentages of older people ranged between 3.3 and 3.5 per cent in the metropolitan, large urban, and mining areas, to as high as 7.6 in rural areas. The migration of younger people from the countryside, especially due to the decline in agriculture from the 1880s, together with the normally longer life expectancy in rural areas, accounted for their relatively large older populations. The percentage of over-sixty-fives aged over 75 was 22 in metropolitan and large urban unions, 20 in mining districts, and 32 in rural ones. The majority of very old people everywhere was female. Only 74.3 per cent of respondents were willing to state their income. 2,086 (16.8 per cent) said they were maintained by relatives or friends but did not state the amount of support. 1,818 of these were female. These recipients of family maintenance were 23.6 per cent of all older people in mining districts, 18.7 per cent in the metropolis, 17.2 per cent in large towns, and, contrary to expectations, only 14.2 per cent

---

[81] Circular of 4 August 1900, 30th Annual report of LGB, (1901), app., pp. 18–19.

[82] S. and B. Webb, *English Local Government*, vol. viii. *English Poor Law History*, vol. ii, pt. ii: *The Last Hundred Years*, p. 354.

[83] *Report from the Select Committee on the Cottage Homes Bill, Parliamentary Papers* (1899), vol. ix.

[84] *Report of the Departmental Committee on the Financial Aspects of the Proposals made by the Select Committee of the House of Commons of 1899 about the Aged Deserving Poor, Parliamentary Papers*, Cd. 67, vol. x (1900).

in the countryside, probably due to the very low incomes of rural households. 44.5 per cent of the total sample claimed to have incomes below ten shillings a week. These were most heavily concentrated in rural areas (47.7 per cent).

The gender gap in income was predictably large. 27.3 per cent of males claimed incomes of twenty shillings or above, but only 11.4 per cent of females. Incomes of ten shillings and under were reported by 40.7 and 47.6 per cent respectively. 15.3 per cent of men and 27.3 per cent of women admitted to receiving poor relief at some time past or present. Among women the regional disparity was insignificant, for men it ranged from 11.9 per cent in the metropolis to 16.8 in rural unions. The investigators examined in closer detail old people with incomes of ten shillings or less, to whom they added those who claimed unspecified support from family or friends. The total of these very poor people amounted to 7,624, more than half the total sample, only 2,603 of whom admitted to ever having received poor relief—striking testimony to the failure of the Poor Law to support many of the very poor. Again there was a clear picture of women being in greater poverty than men.

The Committee investigated the sources of these very low incomes. It found it 'noteworthy and . . . not surprising to find, that the earning capacity of elderly men appears to be highest in London', but that 'it is not so easy to explain the fact that the earnings of both men and women aged over 65 years in the mining districts is not only below the average but also below those recorded in the rural districts'. In reality, mining districts provided little paid work for women at any age and there were more light tasks for elderly men in the countryside than in the mines. 16.2 per cent of the men but only 1.7 per cent of women received friendly or trade society benefits. In this very low income group, 27.9 per cent of men and 70.3 per cent of women received 'assistance from children, relations or friends', a higher proportion than received poor relief. Predictably, incomes fell and dependency increased at later ages.

The Hamilton Committee submitted a comprehensive and well-reasoned costing exercise for a set of proposals which were politically defunct by the time of the report.

However, with the ending of the South African war in 1902 pressure for pensions revived, from the NCOL and in parliament. For some time, the government was able to keep it at bay by protesting that the costs of the war wiped out any possibility of social expenditure.[85] By 1905 pressure on behalf of the aged poor and by the unemployed drove the Conservatives to establish another Royal Commission to investigate the whole, massive, contentious question of the Poor Laws and the Relief of Distress. They were aware that a general election was imminent which they were unlikely to win. Meanwhile, another survey of poverty was in progress.

---

[85] Williams, 'Old Age Pensions', 159–61.

ROWNTREE AND POVERTY IN YORK

By 1902 Booth had withdrawn from campaigning for pensions. Significantly largely silent in this debate was the other great poverty researcher of the time, B. Seebohm Rowntree. His survey of York, carried out in 1899 and published in 1901,[86] confirmed the findings of Booth's London survey in many respects. Though smaller than London his survey convinced him that York was a typical English town.[87] Rowntree's descriptions of 'typical' examples of life at the level defined in the survey as Class A (income under, often well under, eighteen shillings a week) included a number of people who were old and impoverished. The survey illustrates how many old people at the beginning of the twentieth century still patched together pitiful incomes, often supplemented by inadequate poor relief. One woman survived by taking in lodgers; another 'goes out to nurse occasionally'; a spinster, 'blind . . . earns a little by knitting', received 'two shillings a week from a former employer, spends a lot of time with relatives'; 'widow, sixty-three, two rooms. Takes in washing . . . will not give up work though suffering from a tumour . . . will not apply to guardians for help while she can work.' Some were described as 'disreputable', 'drinks', 'not clean', others 'sober and industrious'. The descriptions of the conditions of the aged poor were hardly different from those of the poverty surveys of the sixteenth and seventeenth centuries. Of 1,957 people Rowntree identified in this poorest class, 370 were described as 'ill and old' (18.9 per cent of the total).[88]

Rowntree added to the study, 'in response to suggestions made to the writer', a section on 'the probable effect of universal old age pensions on poverty in York'. He calculated that of the estimated 75,812 inhabitants of York in 1899, 20,914 were in poverty: only 759 of these (323 men, 436 women) were aged 65 or above (3.62 per cent). In consequence, universal pensions, he calculated, would reduce the impoverished portion of the population of York only from 27.59 per cent to 26.59 per cent. Rowntree did not offer this as an argument against old-age pensions, but he emphasized how large a problem of poverty would remain if they were introduced. Booth's great study of poverty in London, conducted through the 1890s and published two years after Rowntree's survey of York,[89] also concluded that poverty in old age, however terrible for those who experienced it, was not the greatest source of poverty: low pay, especially for workers with large families, was a greater cause of misery. This perhaps

---

[86] B. Seebohm Rowntree, *Poverty: A Study of Town Life* (London, 1901).

[87] E. P. Hennock, 'The Measurement of Urban Poverty: From the Metropolis to the Nation, 1880–1920', *Economic History Review*, 40 (1987), 208–27. Recent research questions whether levels of poverty in York were as high as in London. I. Gazeley and A. Newall, 'Trying to Make Sense of Poverty in Britain, 1880–1914', *Explorations in Economic History* (forthcoming).

[88] Rowntree, *Poverty*, 59–65.

[89] Charles Booth, *Life and Labour of the People of London*, 17 vols. (London, 1903).

TABLE 10.1. *Poverty in York, 1899, by age group*

Age	% York pop. 1891	% in poverty
Under 1 year	2.47	2.99
1–5	9.47	10.96
5–15	21.89	29.80
15–65	61.53	52.63
65 and over	4.67	3.62

Source: Rowntree, *Poverty: A Study of Town Life*, 442.

TABLE 10.2. *Percentage of each age group in poverty, York, 1899*

Age	% in poverty
Under 1 year	33.3
1–5	31.91
5–15	37.58
15–65	23.60
65 and over	21.39

accounted for his withdrawal from the pensions campaign: the problems of poverty were greater and more complex than he had anticipated.

Rowntree further pointed out that 4.67 per cent of the York population were aged 65 or above, but only 3.6 per cent of the poor, whereas 43.75 per cent of all in poverty were aged 15 or under, but only 33.8 per cent of the total population (see Table 10.1). Rowntree demonstrated that poverty was much more heavily concentrated among the very young than among the old. Investigation of later age cohorts than the undifferentiated 65-and-over category might have produced different results, but the absolute numbers of the very young in poverty were much greater than those of the very old. The demographic distribution of poverty became clearer still when Rowntree calculated the percentage of each age group in poverty in York (see Table 10.2).

Rowntree demonstrated that although poverty was a problem for all age groups in York, it was *least* among older people and greatest among those under 15, a discovery which did not become prominent in public discourse until the 1920s. Rowntree was clear that the chief cause of poverty was low parental wages. He calculated that 'illness or old age of the chief wage-earner' accounted for 5.11 per cent of the population in primary poverty, and 'low wages in regular work' for a more dramatic 51.96 per cent. Acknowledgement of the need to deal with the immense problem of child poverty was potentially far more costly than responding to the limited problem of the aged poor.

It was also ideologically more problematic. Whereas the aged poor were widely seen as objects of pity, whom it was hard entirely to blame for their condition, provision for children raised the highly controversial issue of state intrusion in the family and fears of the consequences of relaxing the obligation of parents to support their children. This was emerging as an issue in the public discourse of the early years of the twentieth century, but was a greater source of conflict than pensions for the aged.

Rowntree's study of York suggested why so many younger people could neither save for old age nor support their elderly parents. Their own survival was too hard-earned.

11

'The First Piece of Socialism Britain has Entered upon'? The Introduction of Old-Age Pensions

In 1906, after a decade of Conservative and Unionist government, the Liberal Party won a clear majority. The election was also notable as the first in which Labour members won a significant number of seats (29) and the Labour Party became firmly established. The new Liberal government was to introduce an impressive succession of social welfare measures. It is often stated that the Liberals came into office uncommitted to any specific social reform including pensions. This is so in the sense that neither they nor the Conservatives published party programmes, hence neither party was formally committed to anything. However, both parties 'more than made up for this by flooding the electorate with propaganda leaflets on all the major topics of the day.'[1] In addition, most candidates issued their own election leaflets, which 'presented a kind of programmatic choice to the electors that was clear enough'.[2] Russell's analysis of the election addresses shows that 59 per cent of Liberal candidates supported pensions. It was less prominent than Free Trade, which was almost universally supported, or amendment of the Education Act and reform of the government of Ireland, but none the less, substantial.[3] 81 per cent of Labour Representation Committee (LRC) candidates pledged themselves to old-age pensions, which came a close fourth in their list of preferences after increased working-class representation, reform of the trade union law, and provision for the unemployed.[4] Among Conservative candidates pensions and Poor Law reform was the most popular social reform, supported by 22 per cent.[5] The difference between the parties on the 'social question' was clear enough.

Once in office the Liberals were under pressure from Labour and from the vocal reforming wing of their own party to introduce pensions[6] among other social measures. Increasingly, the larger Friendly Societies associated themselves with the NCOL campaign.[7] The Prime Minister, Henry Campbell-Bannerman,

---

[1] A. K. Russell, *Liberal Landslide: The General Election of 1906* (Newton Abbot, 1973), 64.
[2] Ibid. 65.   [3] Ibid. 71.   [4] Ibid. 79.   [5] Ibid. 83.
[6] Patricia M. Williams (Thane), 'The Development of Old Age Pensions in the UK, 1878–1908', Ph.D. thesis (London School of Economics, 1970), 170–7.
[7] e.g. by sending representatives to its annual conference in Dec. 1906. Williams, 'Old Age Pensions', 180.

and Chancellor of the Exchequer, H. H. Asquith, received a series of deputations on the issue from NCOL and from Members of Parliament.[8] But the Liberals took few initiatives in social policy during their first two years in office. One reason was the large Conservative majority in the House of Lords, which threatened to reject 'advanced' legislation. At least as important was the problem the Liberals inherited from their predecessors, that government revenue could barely keep pace with growing government expenditure. An urgent task for Asquith was to review the taxation system in order to increase government income. The social legislation of the Liberals' first two years in office was notable for either placing the burden of cost on local ratepayers (such as the introduction of free school meals in 1906) or for costing nothing to the public purse (such as the Miners Eight Hours Act, 1908).

PLANNING FOR OLD-AGE PENSIONS

Nevertheless, within a year of the election Asquith asked a Treasury civil servant, Roderick Meiklejohn, to investigate the practicability of a state pension scheme. This was a significant step. It was highly unusual for an official of the Treasury, which regarded its role as control of the spending departments of state, to be asked to draw up a plan for new expenditure.[9] Meiklejohn surveyed both existing pension proposals and the activities of Friendly Societies. Asquith read and carefully annotated a detailed report on the German scheme.[10] In December 1906 the Cabinet discussed a Treasury memorandum embodying Meiklejohn's research. This focused upon poverty in old age as a major problem and one that might even be growing. It stated:

after forty-five it becomes increasingly difficult for a man to obtain work in most of the skilled trades . . . for those over fifty-five the chances of getting regular work are rare. For the unskilled labourer over fifty-five the opportunity was still less . . . the whole tendency of the age is to pay men better but to retire them earlier.

These were propositions for which there was, in fact, very little supportive evidence.

The memorandum summarized Trade Union and Friendly Society provision, commenting that this could not cover all in need because most low earners were excluded from both institutions. Since state pensions were undoubtedly to the financial advantage of both forms of institution they were not expected to oppose legislation. An insurance scheme was rejected, above all because of the impossibility of including the lower paid. The memorandum acknowledged the attraction of a universal pension, but 'the difficulty is

---

[8] Ibid. 177–80.

[9] George Peden, *The Treasury and British Public Policy, 1900–59* (Oxford, 2000), ch. 2.

[10] Asquith MS, box 74. fo. 14. Williams, 'Old Age Pensions', 178.

one of money; all other objections to the scheme fall into comparative un-importance beside this one'. Hence the only possibility was a limited non-contributory scheme on the lines of Balfour's proposal of 1899. The memorandum emphasized the importance of dissociating pensions from the Poor Law. This evidently genuine desire no longer to stigmatize and punish the poorest was a real change from the discourse which had dominated the nineteenth century. The memorandum recommended that:

a start can be made by putting a fixed sum of reasonable amount at the disposal of specially created bodies throughout the country. They could use information from the Poor Law, Charity Organization Society etc and grant pensions to the truly needy with no stigma of poor relief attached.[11]

A central aim of those immediately responsible for framing pensions legislation was to target pensions on the poorest old people without stigmatizing them.

The Cabinet approved the memorandum and Asquith began to prepare his second Budget. His priority was to find new sources of revenue. The Liberal commitment to Free Trade ruled out the option of raising income from tar-iffs on imports. Asquith's favoured alternative was to move from the estab-lished single rate of income tax on all incomes to a graduated tax, which would increase the tax contribution of higher earners. He succeeded in overcoming Treasury resistance to this, but had to move cautiously to win parliamentary and popular acceptance. He proposed in the Budget of April 1907 to differ-entiate for the first time between earned and unearned income (the latter to be more heavily taxed) and between incomes below and above £2,000 a year. He did not believe that pensions could yet be afforded, but in his Budget speech he promised them for the following year. Also, in the spirit of Gladstone's determination that the costs of state action should lie equally upon all classes, he announced: 'If we are ready to have social reform we must be ready to pay for it . . . I mean the whole nation, the working and consuming classes as well as the wealthier class of direct taxpayers'. He retained the additional taxes upon tea, sugar, and cocoa which had been introduced to pay for the war, of which working people paid a high proportion, and announced that the yield would be used to finance pensions.[12] Contrary to Gilbert's assertion that 'as a way of transferring wealth from one income group to another, tax-supported pensions were of almost unequalled effectiveness',[13] every effort was made to minimize any such transfer, which was indeed insignificant.

Shortly afterwards Booth emerged from his silence on pensions and pub-lished a revised version of *The Aged Poor—a Proposal*. He again advocated a universal pension at age 70, but now proposed a means-tested supplement,

[11] PRO CAB 37/85 1906, no. 96, *Memorandum on Old Age Pensions*, 14 Dec. 1906. Signed R. S. Meiklejohn and M. Sturges. Williams, 'Old Age Pensions', 183–5.
[12] *Hansard* (4th ser.), House of Commons, vol. 172, col. 1195. Williams, 'Old Age Pensions', 90–1.
[13] B. B. Gilbert *The Evolution of National Insurance in Great Britain* (London, 1966), 159.

to be assessed by the Poor Law authorities, for those in need between the ages of 60 and 70. Asquith was sufficiently attracted by this proposal to refer it to Meiklejohn. The latter found it 'unacceptable . . . for the taint of pauperism is glaringly present'; he believed that this would inevitably generalize from the means-tested supplement to the pension.[14] It received no further consideration. The NCOL kept up its public demonstrations and private deputations to Ministers, lest Asquith change his mind.[15] But drafting of a pensions bill was in progress. Asquith delegated the work to Reginald McKenna, President of the Board of Education. He was not the obvious choice, but Asquith trusted him and was determined to keep the Bill out of the hands of the LGB which might seek to associate it too closely with the Poor law.

McKenna confessed to Beatrice Webb the difficulty of devising a scheme within the strict financial limits set by the Treasury.[16] Three months later he dined with the Webbs and discussed his progress. 'The scheme he thrashed out with us', wrote Mrs Webb, 'was a universal, non-contributory pension to all over sixty-five with less than ten shillings a week, with a sliding scale five shillings upwards and income under five shillings not taken into account. No disqualification for pauperism present or future—some contribution from rates on account of potential paupers. To be administered evidently by a stipendiary. He calculated it will cost the Exchequer £7–10 million.'[17] The Webbs approved.

The likelihood that the government was shortly to introduce noncontributory pensions brought a last-minute flurry of support for social insurance. Among others, the Liberal correspondent on social questions for the Conservative *Morning Post*, William Beveridge, took a step on the long road towards his famous Report on Social Insurance of 1942. A visit to Germany early in 1907 to investigate their system of employment exchanges aroused his interest in national insurance. He was convinced that no government would finance an adequate non-contributory pension. Means-tested benefits, he believed, were inefficient for detecting need and administratively wasteful. He added, not entirely seriously, that if the scheme was to be limited there was much to be said for limiting it to women: the grounds for qualification were unmistakable and the need undeniable. An extensive study of trade union retirement pay convinced him that most workers required superannuation around the age of 63, but that the age of physical incapacity for work varied considerably among individuals and occupations. For this reason he was impressed by the German system of invalidity pensions which 'gave not

[14] Asquith MS, Meiklejohn and Sturges to Asquith, box. 74, fo. 76. Williams, 'Old Age Pensions', 189–90. [15] Williams, 'Old Age Pensions', 193–4.
[16] Beatrice Webb's diary, 27 Apr. 1907: Passfield MSS, British Library of Political and Economic Science, vol. 25, p. 68. Williams, 'Old Age Pensions', 196–8.
[17] Beatrice Webb's diary, 18 July 1907: vol. 25, p. 79. Williams, 'Old Age Pensions', 199.

pensions at a fixed age, but pensions whenever invalidity began'.[18] In 1907 most German pensioners qualified under this heading.[19]

Asquith was impressed by Beveridge's criticism of means tests. Meiklejohn dissuaded him from reconsidering social insurance by arguing that the Friendly Societies would not co-operate in a scheme which might divert working-class savings from themselves to the state. Meiklejohn also asserted that to establish a new administrative structure for such a system would be financially impossible.[20] The personal role of this civil servant in formulating the pensions legislation was considerable.

In November 1907 a Cabinet committee was established to draft a Bill based upon McKenna's recommendations. It consisted of Asquith, McKenna, and John Burns, the former trade unionist, now President of the Local Government Board and the first working man to sit in a British Cabinet. The Treasury made it clear that they were prepared to allow no more than £7m. per annum for pensions.[21] The Committee's main task was to fit a pension scheme within that budget. For estimates of cost they used the Hamilton Committee's findings of seven years previously. They decided upon a five-shilling pension to be paid to those with incomes below ten shillings per week. Their chief saving was achieved by raising the pensionable age to 70. They also recommended a reduced pension of 7s. 6d. a week for married couples.[22] The LGB was anxious to include a test of 'character', which McKenna, following Mrs Webb's advice, had omitted. It was decided to exclude all who received poor relief after 1 January 1908, and all those unable to provide proof of thrift during working life. The committee did not suggest how thrift was to be defined. 'Criminals, lunatics and aliens' were also excluded. By 'alien' was meant all residents of the country who did not possess British nationality; the largest group of these at the time were Jewish immigrants.[23] An NCOL circular to MPs in January 1908 had stated: 'there is absolute unanimity of opinion that pensions must not be given to aliens, an opinion which rises into passion in districts where aliens congregate'.[24]

The scheme was to be administered by unpaid local committees assisted by a paid clerk. At the Treasury's insistence the responsibilities of the local inspectors of Customs and Excise were extended to include supervision of the pensions administration. These officials were responsible to the Treasury; hence the Treasury could control the administration at no additional cost. They would make the initial investigation of all claims and report to the local

[18] *Morning Post*, 23 Apr. 1908.
[19] E. P. Hennock, *British Social Reform and German Precedents* (Oxford, 1987), 131 n. 4.
[20] Williams, 'Old Age Pensions', 204–5.   [21] Williams, 'Old Age Pensions', 205–6.
[22] PRO CAB 37/90/115; Williams, 'Old Age Pensions', 208–9.
[23] D. Feldman, *Englishmen and Jews: Social Relations and Political Culture, 1840–1914* (New Haven, 1994), 268–90. Pat Thane, 'The British Imperial State and the Construction of National Identities', in B. Melman (ed.), *Borderlines: Gender and Identities in War and Peace, 1870–1930* (London, 1998), 29–46.
[24] NCOL, *Ninth Annual Report and Balance Sheet*, July 1908.

committees. John Burns was furious about the appointment of Treasury watch-dogs over this unprecedented new form of public expenditure.[25] Claims were to be made and pensions paid through the Post Office, the only government department possessing offices in every district.

Early in 1908 the Cabinet committee decided to solicit the views of the Friendly Societies about the proposals. A circular produced 151 replies, evenly divided for and against. In general, the larger Societies and the less solvent were in favour, though some still believed that state pensions would irretrievably damage the 'savings instinct' of the working man.[26] On 1 April 1908 the proposals were presented to the Cabinet. In the same month Campbell-Bannerman resigned due to ill health and was succeeded as Prime Minister by Asquith. He appointed David Lloyd George to succeed him as Chancellor. Winston Churchill took his first Cabinet post as President of the Board of Trade. Asquith presented the Budget which he had prepared to the House of Commons and took the opportunity to outline the coming Pensions Bill.

The response was predictably mixed. 'Well begun—half done', commented Frederick Rogers. The NCOL pressed on with demands for an age limit of 65 and a higher means limit.[27] The TUC supported them.[28] The *Times* commented:

The promise of a pension at seventy is too remote to create any very lively feelings, and so far where it has been mentioned at public meetings it has been received with ironical cheers.[29]

The Liberal *Nation* and the *Economist* welcomed the announcement. Beveridge, quite correctly, pointed out that there was no sign that the government had planned for the future costs of a potentially expensive system, especially as the proportion of old people in the population was expected to increase.[30] He continued to argue that the establishment of an insurance system, however costly in the short run, would not only be more efficient but more cost-effective in the long run, since it would be self-financing. 'It affords', he claimed, 'the basis of knowledge and organization which is essential if social reform is to be something other than chaotic philanthropy.'[31] Beveridge was especially critical of the ad hoc nature of the Liberal approach to social reform. He was convinced of the need for a grand design of welfare such as, he believed, the Germans had carried out. He conceived of pensions as the first instalment

---

[25] PRO PIN 3/1, Working Papers on Old Age Pensions Act 1908, Cabinet Paper, 30 Mar. 1908. Sir Robert Chalmers, Head of Board of Inland Revenue to Cabinet Committee, PRO CAB 37/92/52. John Burns, 'Confidential Cabinet Paper on Old Age Pensions', 15 Apr. 1908: John Burns MSS, British Library, Add. MSS, diary, 13 Apr. 1908. Williams, 'Old Age Pensions', 212–13.

[26] *Circular from the LGB to Friendly Societies*, Mar. 1908, HC 177, 1908, *Parliamentary Papers*, vol. lxxxviii (1908).   [27] NCOL *Ninth Annual Report*, July 1908.

[28] *The Times*, 16 May 1908.   [29] *The Times*, 12 May 1908.

[30] *Morning Post*, 8 May 1908. Awareness was just beginning that the fall in the birth-rate discernible since the 1870s combined with the fall in infant mortality and the rise in life expectancy at later ages would lead in future to a rising proportion of older people in the population.

[31] *Morning Post*, 29 May 1908.

of a wider ranging programme of remedies for the major causes of need. His preference for social insurance was not only pragmatic but consistent with his wider social vision and political theory. For Beveridge, the state had an important and wholly acceptable role in creating the conditions for the social cohesion which was desirable and necessary in early twentieth-century Britain. He wrote:

A non-contributory scheme sets up the state in the eyes of the individual as a source of free gifts. A contributory scheme sets up the state as a comprehensive organism to which the individual belongs and in which he, under compulsion if need be, plays his part. Each view involves abandonment of traditional laissez-faire. The first, however, represents a change for the worse which it will be hard to remove. The second is a natural recognition of the growing complexity and interdependence of industrial life.[32]

Social insurance, in his view, could facilitate social integration because all sections of society (workers and employers directly through regular contributions, taxpayers indirectly through the state's contribution) contributed, for the good not only of the very poor and of working people but for all of society, which gained in stability and productivity when workers had stable, secure lives and felt that the state supported them. At the same time, he believed, working people, because they were obliged to contribute towards their own social support, retained their sense of obligation to practise self-help, and of obligation towards others, as well as their feelings of independence.[33]

Beveridge dismissed the problems of integrating the poorly and irregularly paid into an insurance system: 'surely they waste more than twopence a week on drink, let them contribute that . . . how can a man better prove that he needs and deserves a pension than by paying for it?'[34] His approach was, however, much influenced by his assumption that 'Their whole working life is one which will not be allowed to continue permanently in a well-organized state.'[35] He was to devote the next decade to the reduction of low-paid casual labour by means of the introduction of labour exchanges and the unemployment insurance scheme, both of which he helped to devise as Churchill's adviser at the Board of Trade.[36] Beveridge's comprehensive approach to social reform was not widely shared and non-contributory pensions continued to be viewed in most public discourse as a solution to a problem of poverty which was not easily preventable. A major weakness of his diagnosis was that he had nothing to say about the poverty of older women who had not necessarily been in paid work throughout their adult lives and even when employed had often been very low paid.

---

[32] Hennock, *British Social Reform*, 136.
[33] José Harris, *William Beveridge: A Biography*, 2nd edn. (Oxford, 1997), 168 ff.
[34] *Morning Post*, 11 May 1908.   [35] Ibid.   [36] Harris, *Beveridge*, 168 ff.

PENSIONS IN PARLIAMENT

The Old Age Pensions Bill received its second reading in the House of Commons on 15 June 1908. It was introduced by Lloyd George, who ever after was to receive credit for the scheme actually devised by Asquith. The pensions even came to be known popularly as 'the Lloyd George'. It became clear that claimants would undergo investigation hardly less rigorous than under the Poor Law. Their income would be assessed. The disqualifying character defects were now defined as 'habitual failure to work according to his ability, opportunity or need, for his own maintenance or that of his legal relatives'. Receipt of poor relief after 1 January 1908 also disqualified, as did imprisonment for crime without option of fine and conviction for drunkenness, in both cases within ten years of the claim. 'Aliens and wives of aliens' were also excluded. This was to prove a shock to many non-Jewish women who had married Jews who had not taken British citizenship. Obtaining citizenship, which had previously been a relatively cheap and simple process was becoming more difficult in this period of rising anti-Semitism.[37] One advance on Poor Law principles in the proposed legislation was that pensioners were not to be deprived 'of any franchise, right or privilege'.

Lloyd George's opening speech on the pensions Bill was described as 'halting in tone and apologetic in manner'.[38] As the debate went on, he became ever more uneasy about the deficiencies of the scheme.[39] He stressed repeatedly that it was 'only a beginning . . . the scheme is necessarily incomplete . . . this is a great experiment . . . we say it is a beginning, but a real beginning'.[40] He made it clear that the five-shilling pension was not intended to provide an income adequate for survival, but to supplement and to encourage saving and the support available from relatives and others. The Conservatives had decided not to oppose the Bill in the Commons,[41] though a small right-wing group, led by Lord Robert Cecil, chose to do so. Cecil warned:

War might be approaching, and if the government had weakened the moral fibre of the country by a system and a policy of which this is only the beginning, then a statesman who had mentioned this miserable backsliding from the fine statesmanship of Empire would have something to answer for.[42]

---

[37] Feldman, *Englishmen and Jews*, 268 ff. Thane, 'British Imperial State'.

[38] *Spectator*, 20 June 1908.

[39] Sir Henry N. Bunbury (ed.), *Lloyd George's Ambulance Wagon: Being the Memoirs of William J. Braithewaite, 1911–1912* (London, 1957), 71. J. S. Sandars to Arthur Balfour, 11 June 1908: Balfour MSS, British Library. Williams, 'Old Age Pensions', 221–2.

[40] *Hansard* (4th ser.), House of Commons, vol. 190, col. 585.

[41] Williams, 'Old Age Pensions', 222.

[42] *Hansard* (4th ser.), House of Commons, vol. 190, col. 624.

Austen Chamberlain, son of Joseph, who led for the Conservatives in these debates, disowned Cecil as 'utterly opposed to old age pensions'.[43] Cecil spoke for a point of view which was dying, though slowly.

The Labour Party approved the Bill 'as a beginning' but pressed for a universal scheme and strongly opposed the disqualification of paupers. In the course of the debates, Labour succeeded in amending the Bill to include a review of this provision after two years (in consequence, it was abolished from 31 December 1910). Lloyd George also agreed not to apply the disqualification to medical relief. Conservative back-benchers achieved a modification of the means test to incorporate a sliding scale. It was finally accepted that old people with incomes of up to £21 a year would receive the full pension. Incomes up to £31. 10s. would qualify for a pension reduced by one shilling a week for each shilling of income above £21. The minimum pension would be one shilling. Those with incomes as low as £26 would receive only three shillings a week. In fact, in the first ten years of the pension the proportion of pensioners receiving less than five shillings never rose above 7 per cent.[44] The government also agreed to an amendment granting the full pension of ten shillings a week to married couples who were otherwise qualified. Friendly Societies won the concession that ten years' membership of a thrift society would be accepted as fulfilment of the 'industry test'.[45] The government imposed a closure to avoid further costly amendments. Lloyd George and the Treasury civil servants became very aware that there would be relentless pressure to extend the scope of this limited scheme. In particular, the closure prevented debate on the contentious issue of the age limit.[46] The Bill completed its progress through the Commons. The *Times* attacked 'the vagueness of the conceptions underlying the Bill and the haphazard way in which its proposals have been flung together with no coherent theory or aim ... the government are taking a leap in the dark with no more real knowledge than the rest of whether they will land on solid ground or quagmire'.[47] The writer was quite correct.

In the House of Lords there was strong opposition. Some Conservative peers were evidently rehearsing the revolt against the Liberal Commons which was to follow the Budget of 1909. In the recent past the Lords had not tampered with financial measures. On this occasion, they suggested some amendments but these were ruled to have contravened Commons privilege and the amendments were deleted when the Bill returned to the lower house. In response, the Lords passed an unprecedented measure of censure against the Commons. The ageing Lord Rosebery, past leader of the Liberal Party, delivered his verdict on the ways that society and Liberalism were changing. He

---

[43] *Hansard* (4th ser.), House of Commons, col. 1745.
[44] Sir Arnold Wilson and G. S. Mackay, *Old Age Pensions: An Historical and Critical Study* (Oxford, 1941), 55.   [45] Williams, 'Old Age Pensions', 228.
[46] Ibid. 220–9.   [47] *The Times*, 8 July 1908.

thought this 'the most important Bill . . . in the forty years I have sat here', more important in its implications even than the parliamentary reform bills, for, he believed, it was a

pauperizing bill, symbolizing the final passing of family pride in caring for their elderly . . . it is, of course, socialism pure and simple . . . but . . . we have advanced to that period of socialism where some such measure as this is required . . . it is part of the almost daily transfer of burdens from the individual to the state . . . it will absorb money which in the past has gone to charity . . . it is the beginning of a long process which will culminate in the handing over of hospitals to the state.[48]

As indeed it was. Rosebery did not, however, advise the Lords to oppose his fellow Liberals.

The Old Age Pensions Act received the royal assent on 1 August 1908. It gave a pension, which was not intended to provide full subsistence, to the very old, the very poor, and the very respectable, provided that they were also British subjects. In effect it was an amendment of the Poor Law and operated on very similar principles. Yet it was not the Poor Law. The government and its administrators were careful to protect pensioners from the language of opprobrium which had characterized the poor relief system since 1834. Successfully it seems, in view of the much larger numbers of impoverished old people who were prepared to apply for the pension than for poor relief, and of their reactions to it.[49] Also, entitlement and administration were uniform throughout the country, which had never characterized the Poor Law. For the first time, the state was to give a cash payment to a group in need as an undoubted right, if they met the criteria, without deterrent penalties. For the first time, also, in the welfare system old age was defined by age rather than by other characteristics. Lord Rosebery recognized the implications of the new system as, in a different spirit, did the Dockers' leader Ben Tillett, who greeted it joyfully as 'the first piece of socialism Britain has entered upon'.[50]

The unstable Tillett soon changed his mind. A resolution to the annual conference of the TUC shortly afterwards, thanking Asquith for the start made on pensions, was fiercely opposed by Tillett and referred for redrafting. The Conference finally agreed that it was 'of opinion that the Act will not be satisfactory until amended so as to provide for a minimum pension of 5*s*. per week, without condition to men and women of sixty; in the case of persons who by reason of their affliction by blindness are rendered incapable of earning their living, the age limit to be entirely removed'.[51] A similar resolution was passed annually for the next sixteen years. The National Conference of Friendly Societies in September 1908 was opened by the President (J. Duncan of the Ancient Order of Foresters) with the statement:

[48] *Hansard* (4th ser.), vol. 192 (20 July 1908), col. 1383.   [49] See below, p. 227.
[50] F. Rogers, *Labour, Life and Literature* (London, 1913), 140.
[51] TUC, *Annual Conference Report* (1908), 57, 194.

it is exceedingly gratifying to some of us who have laboured long and earnestly for such a desired object as a right for aged workers in our country . . . and I consider that the agitation of this conference in past years has had much to do with the now accomplished fact of old age pensions.[52]

Several Societies responded to the Act by ceasing payment of extended sick benefit at age 70 and introducing separate superannuation schemes.

The NCOL spent several months advising the first pension claimants before winding itself up. It left to the Labour Party the task of pressing for improved pensions.[53] The COS prepared, fruitlessly, for 'the popular reaction against the Old Age Pensions Act . . . which is bound to come'[54] and developed proposals for an alternative insurance scheme. Meanwhile they, like the Friendly Societies and trade unions, worked to ensure that they were well represented upon the new local pension committees. These were established in the later months of 1908 by every county borough, urban and county council to serve areas of approximately 20,000 inhabitants. These areas were divided into sub-districts served by sub-committees. Councils tended to appoint from among their own members, though some included representatives of charities, Friendly Societies, and Trade Unions;[55] some made a point of appointing women.[56]

Members of COS, individual Poor Law guardians, and others assisted needy old people to prevent their resorting to poor relief in the year before the first pensions were paid and thus cruelly suffering disqualification at the last minute.[57]

THE FIRST PENSIONS

The first old-age pensions were paid to 490,000 people on 1 January 1909, overwhelmingly at the maximum rate. Most of the pensioners were women. 37.4 per cent were men (30 per cent in London). At the time of the 1911 census men accounted for 41.4 per cent of the over-70 population, but only 36.7 per cent of pensioners. This gender division remained constant for some time: 36.6 per cent of all pensioners were male in 1915, in 1919, 36.2 per cent.[58] The total number of pensioners rose to 650,000 in March 1909 and to 1,070,626 after removal of the pauper disqualification in March 1911. The LGB had estimated 572,000 in the first year. Lloyd George had to request an additional £900,000 to finance the first year of the scheme. On 1 March 1906 about

---

[52] *Grand United Magazine*, June 1909.

[53] *Report of the Proceedings at a Public Presentation made to Mr Frederick Rogers at Browning Hall on Nov. 5th 1909* (privately printed, 1909). Williams, 'Old Age Pensions', 245–6.

[54] *Charity Organization Review*, Apr. 1909.   [55] Williams, 'Old Age Pensions', 251–3.

[56] Margaret Jones, 'The Old Age Pensions Act, 1908: A Break with the Poor Law?', MA diss. (University of Huddersfield, 1996). Work in progress, M. Takada, D.Phil. student, University of Sussex.

[57] C. S. Loch, *The Charity Organization Society* (London, 1961), 115.

[58] Wilson and Mackay, *Old Age Pensions*, 55.

168,100 people age 70 and over were receiving outdoor relief. This fell in 1910 to 138,200. The dramatic fall came with the abolition of pauper disqualification, to 9,500 in 1912. Increasingly, guardians granted five shillings a week to paupers believed to be 'old' whether they were above or below the age of 70.[59] The numbers of people aged 70 or above in workhouses were (not surprisingly) much less affected. The total on 1 March 1906 was 61,400, in 1910, 57,700, in 1912, 49,300.[60] Overall, in the first years of the pension about 40 per cent of the over-70 age group qualified for the stringently means-tested pension, whereas only about 24.5 per cent of the same age group had received poor relief in 1906.[61] This suggests the extent of severe unmet need before the introduction of the pension.

The process of claiming a pension began with completing a form available at the post office. This was sent to the local pensions officer, who investigated the claim. He reported to the local committee, which made a decision and notified both the claimant and the pensions officer. Where the officer and the committee disagreed, there could be further investigation and a hearing which both officer and claimant might attend. If disagreement persisted, each had a right of appeal to the LGB. Where a pension was approved, the pension was payable each Friday at the local post office. Grateful pensioners were said to have offered flowers, apples, even rashers of bacon to the postmasters and mistresses who handed them their first pension. For years they showered their gratitude on the Chancellor who had done no more than to steer it doubtfully through the Commons.[62] For all its inadequacy, the impact of the pension upon the immense poverty of Edwardian Britain should not be underestimated. John Burns reported to Asquith after the first pensions were paid:

I visited the shopping places where most of the poor do congregate. After chats with the butcher, the cheesemonger and the police the general view was that the five shillings to one was a boon, but where a couple received the joint pension it meant a great deal to the honest and provident poor. So far there was no evidence of waste or spending on drink and from many sources there were really grateful thanks for those who had brought this boon to the deserving poor.[63]

Lloyd George commented to Parliament in 1909, in the course of defending the additional cost of pensions:

Pensions officers and pensions committees . . . have all told me the same story of people facing poverty and privation for years with resignation, with fortitude and with uncomplaining patience, they all ask the same question and they ask it in vain—how

[59] *43rd Annual Report of the Local Government Board for England and Wales* (1913–14), 75.

[60] Noel A. Humphreys, 'Old Age Pensions in the UK', *Journal of the Royal Statistical Society*, 74 (Dec. 1910), 71–3. Wilson and Mackay, *Old Age Pensions*, 45. Williams, 'Old Age Pensions', 249.

[61] K. Williams, *From Pauperism to Poverty* (London, 1981), 207.

[62] *The Times*, 2 Jan. 1909. Williams, 'Old Age Pensions', 249.

[63] Burns MSS, British Library, Add. MS 46282, fo. 46: Burns to Asquith, 8 Jan. 1909.

on earth these poor people could have managed to keep body and soul together on such slender resources. It is not that they have understated their resources, on the contrary there are cases where they have overstated them with a sort of pride . . . what strikes you is their horror of the Poor law . . . this pension act has disclosed the presence amongst us of over 600,000 people, the vast majority of whom were living in circumstances of great poverty, yet disclaimed the charity of the public . . . it has cost more than was anticipated, but the greatness of the cost shows the depth of the need.[64]

Claimants seem, on the whole, to have been gently treated, though the administration of the pension has hardly been studied.[65] There was a certain tension, as intended, between the voluntary committees, supervised by the LGB, and the pensions officers appointed by the Treasury. Sometimes the two departments issued conflicting directives. The LGB instructed committees to value income from rented rooms at the cost of rent less that of upkeep. Pensions officers were instructed to take account only of the amount of rent. The exemption of medical relief from the pauper disqualification was interpreted by the LGB at face value. The Treasury introduced the concept of 'chronic' sickness and decreed that a pensioner whose calls upon relief were 'too frequent' might be disqualified. Many of the difficulties arose because the statute had been drafted hastily. They were worsened by the fact that neither branch of the administration had access to the regulations of the other and that claimants might see neither of them. Claimants could appeal against a decision, but the appeal was decided within the LGB. Lloyd George had refused to incorporate into the legislation any appeal to a court of law, contrary to the tradition of the Poor Law.

In practice, however, the system seems to have worked harmoniously, with few appeals and generally good relations between pensions committees and officials. The 'character clause' seems to have proved almost unworkable and hardly to have been applied.[66]

PENSIONS IN IRELAND

Nowhere did the pension make a bigger impact than in poverty-stricken rural Ireland. Here lay the chief source of the underestimate of take-up. The undercount for the UK by 31 March 1909 was 10,000, for Ireland it was 70,000. In the first month the number of pensioners equalled 90 per cent of the population of Ireland recorded as age 70 or over in the (possibly very inaccurate) Irish census of 1901, despite the fact that one-third of this age group were

---

[64] *Hansard* (5th ser.), House of Commons, vol. 1 (1 Mar. 1909), col. 1174.

[65] Jones, 'The Old Age Pensions Act, 1908'.

[66] Williams, *Pauperism to Poverty*, 270–82. Jones's pioneering study, 'The Old Age Pensions Act, 1908', 53, shows that it was applied once in Salisbury (Wilts.) and not at all in Wakefield (Yorks.) before 1914.

known to be receiving poor relief at the time that the pension was introduced. In England and Wales 40.63 per cent of the age group qualified, in Scotland 50 per cent.[67] Lloyd George admitted that 'calculations have broken down entirely'.[68]

Five shillings might bring a little improvement to the life of an impoverished old person in London. It was a fortune in Donegal. £2 million was pumped into the Irish economy. The shopkeepers of Enniskillen were said to have cheered the first payment and thought it 'as good as if the government had opened a small factory in the town'.[69] Forty pounds had been added to the town's weekly income. The farmers and shopkeepers who made up local pension committees had every incentive to maximize this sum, the more so because it was funded by the English Exchequer and not, like poor relief, by local ratepayers; all the more so given the state of tension in Ireland about English rule. There were those, however, who believed, optimistically, that 'pensions have solved the Irish question'—arguing that they provided a new reason for the Irish to preserve the Union.[70]

English newspapers, on the other hand, clamoured against the fraudulent Irish. The Chief Secretary to Ireland, Augustine Birrell, at least in retrospect was more sympathetic:

Poor western peasantry! what a struggle for existence was theirs in their rain sodden cabins, with the shadow of potato failures and other disasters always before them in the years before the pensions act passed! The wonderful, incredible pensions, bringing ten shillings every Friday morning as regularly as the rising sun. It was a stupefying stroke of good fortune . . . that the pension increased enormously the stock of Irish happiness cannot be doubted, and I feel sure it degraded nobody, unless it is degradation to be willing to persuade yourself that you are two years older than you have good reason to believe you are.[71]

Lloyd George agreed:

Especially in Ireland, the pension officers have been appalled at the amount of poverty and that is why I am really not disposed to criticize too harshly the administration of the Act . . . The facts as to poverty in Ireland are perfectly horrifying. It is a disgrace to any civilized country that reasonable human beings should be allowed to live under such conditions.[72]

Treasury officials took a sterner view. In March 1909 they sent a committee of investigation to Ireland. They found that the English administration

[67] *Hansard* (5th ser.), vol. 1, col. 1138. PRO T 170/3, Departmental Committee on Old Age Pensions Statistics, Jan. 1910. *Old Age Pensions and Irish Pauperism*, Cd. 7015 (1913). Noel A. Humphreys, 'Old Age Pensions in the UK'. Williams, 'Old Age Pensions', 264.

[68] *Hansard* (5th ser.), vol. 1, col. 1138.   [69] *The Times*, 4 Jan. 1909.

[70] Austen Chamberlain, *Politics from Inside* (London 1936), 278.

[71] A. Birrell, *Things Past Redress* (London, 1937), 210–11.

[72] *Hansard* (5th ser.), vol. 1, col. 1173.

had overlooked the fact that compulsory registration of births had begun in Ireland only in 1865 and few reliable alternative records survived. Many claimants had no evidence of their birth-date and initially the administration had accepted circumstantial evidence. In the circumstances the 'big wind' of 1839 had done a great service to the aged peasantry of 1909. 'It was', wrote Birrell, 'a wonderful wind. Dickens alone could have done it justice. It ought to have blown itself out in 1839, but there it still was sweeping pensions officers and local government officials off their feet in 1908 . . . though a terrible memory it was still a priceless asset. Question any old man as to his claim and you learned that his age "had gone astray on him", but he was a fine hardy lad on the night of the "big wind". How could anyone doubt Biddy Flaherty's age when she remembered her mother telling her that she was old enough to eat a potato out of her hand on the night of the "big wind".'[73] 'I always thought I was sixty', Mr Tim Joyce explained to Birrell, 'but my friends came to me and told me they were certain sure I was seventy and as there were three or four of them against me, the evidence was too strong for me. I put in for the pension and got it.'[74] It should have been easier to prove disqualification for pauperism, but surprisingly often the records of guardians were 'lost' or 'temporarily unobtainable'. The Irish magistracy became unwilling to sentence without option of fine anyone within ten years of a possible seventieth birthday.

Even assessment of means presented peculiar difficulties in rural Ireland. It was difficult to estimate the income of subsistence farmers. Traditionally, also, they assigned the farm to the eldest son on his marriage or when the father became too old for regular work. Before 1908 such settlements (similar to 'retirement contracts' in medieval England)[75] were generally informal and implied no change in the way of life of the older generation or any fixed arrangement about income. After the passing of the Pensions Act, it became common for assignment to be made close to the possible seventieth birthday of the father, by legal deed of contract. This deed fixed the maintenance of the old people 'at a sum' commented the Irish Local Government Board, 'which will not debar them from receipt of old age pensions . . . these formal transfers which are now taking place all over the country would beyond all question disqualify claimants for pensions under . . . the Act, were it not for the fact that they represent a continuance in valid form of standing custom'.[76]

In the year ending 31 March 1910 12,670 pensions were withdrawn from old people in Ireland on grounds of mistaken assessment of age and 3,875 on grounds of excessive incomes. The old people had to repay the sums received. The pensions committees of Ireland rose in revolt, threatening mass

[73] Birrell, *Things*, 221.   [74] Ibid.

[75] See pp. 75–81. Liam Kennedy, 'Farm Succession in Modern Ireland: Elements of a Theory of Inheritance', *Economic History Review*, 2nd ser. 44 (1991), 477–99.

[76] *37th Annual Report of the Local Government Board for Ireland* (31 Mar. 1909), Cd. 4810.

resignation if the withdrawals continued. They did not resign and there were fewer withdrawals thereafter. Pensions officers were expected to scrutinize claims more carefully.[77] Still, the 1911 census revealed that the number receiving pensions amounted to 90 per cent of the population of Ireland aged 70 or above. The Irish LGB commented: 'Every claim refused on account of means turns up again within a few months claiming altered and reduced circumstances. There seems no good reason why such cases should not come up several times every year.'[78] The extent of conscious deception is difficult to estimate. Irish nationalist sentiment probably did encourage Irish people to extract all they could from the English taxpayer. The government in London, for its part, very probably underestimated the poverty and the longevity of the Irish.

THE INTRODUCTION OF NATIONAL INSURANCE

Lloyd George's experience with old-age pensions made him increasingly aware of the limits of non-contributory, tax-funded social security schemes. He was also aware of other social problems: 'the sick and infirm, and the unemployed with which it is the business of the state to deal; they are problems the state in both cases has neglected too long'.[79] Lloyd George's belief in the need for a wide-ranging, co-ordinated attack upon such problems was shared by Churchill and, as we have seen, by Beveridge, Churchill's adviser at this time. Churchill wrote to Asquith:

we must look ahead and make bold, concerted plans for the next two years . . . I believe there is an impressive social policy to be unfolded which would pass ponderously through both houses and leave an abiding mark on national history . . . the need is urgent and the moment ripe.[80]

In this radical phase of his career, impelled as much by fear of the rise of Labour and by the belief that improved social welfare would enhance national economic and military efficiency as by concern for poverty as such,[81] he urged the necessity for labour exchanges, unemployment insurance, 'national infirmity insurance', industry to be run by the state, a road plan, a modernized Poor Law, amalgamation of the railways under state control, and a new education bill.[82] Lloyd George was sympathetic. So the 'heavenly twins of social reform', as contemporaries ironically named them, came together, despite their

---

[77] *38th Annual Report of the Local Government Board for Ireland* (1910), p. x. Cd. 5319.
[78] Ibid., p. ix.
[79] *Hansard* (5th ser.), House of Commons, vol. 25 (4 May 1911), col. 609.
[80] Churchill to Asquith, 26 Dec. 1908, in Randolph S. Churchill, *Winston S. Churchill*, ii: *Young Statesman, 1901–14* (London, 1967), 307.
[81] Paul Addison, *Churchill on the Home Front 1900–1955* (London, 1993), 51–4, 61.
[82] Churchill to Asquith, 29 Dec. 1908, in *Churchill* (above, n. 80).

fundamental differences of approach, to drive forward an important and innovative social welfare programme.

Lloyd George's first move was to travel to Germany, three weeks after the
Pensions Act received the royal assent. He returned admitting that he had
'never realized on what a gigantic scale the pension system is concocted. Nor
had I any idea how successfully it worked'.[83] He remained convinced that
'the non-contributory pension . . . was the best for old men and women over
seventy years of age'.[84] But he was considering 'whether a contributory scheme
could eventually be grafted onto the non-contributory'.[85] Lloyd George had
in mind an invalidity pension combined with health insurance. The mount-
ing costs of pensions were changing the views of the Treasury about social
insurance and were profoundly to influence the background to the introduction of national health and unemployment insurance in 1911.[86]

THE ROYAL COMMISSION ON THE POOR LAWS AND RELIEF OF DISTRESS, 1909

Before Lloyd George could act further, the Royal Commission on the Poor
Laws, established in 1905, submitted both Majority and Minority Reports.
These differed on practical aspects of reform but rejected the tradition of the
New Poor Law by agreeing that poverty should be recognized as generally
an involuntary state for which contemporary social and economic organization should take most of the responsibility. Both recommended that provision,
even for the residue of irredeemable poor, should be adequate for subsistence
and should not seek to exclude or to stigmatize those in real need. Both
rejected the principle of 'less eligibility' and proposed new and separate but
co-ordinated services for the chief categories of need, including the aged poor.
The main difference between them was the preference of the Majority (among
whom the COS was influential) for voluntary action and of the Minority (dominated by Beatrice Webb and including Charles Booth) for publicly funded social
services.

Both reports advocated improved and separate institutional provision for
the aged. The Minority provided an accurate picture of the relief process as:

in practice a sort of bargain between a good-natured but penurious destitution authority
and each and every infirm person in turn, as to how little that person would consent
to make shift on rather than consent to the abhorred general mixed workhouse.[87]

---

[83] *Daily News*, 27 Aug. 1908. Williams, 'Old Age Pensions', 238–9.
[84] *The Times*, 4 Jan. 1909.   [85] Ibid.
[86] For details see Hennock, *British Social Reform*, Williams, 'Old Age Pensions'. A. McBriar, *An Edwardian Mixed Doubles: The Bosanquets versus the Webbs, a Study in British Social Policy 1890–1929* (Oxford, 1987).
[87] Minority Report, p. 313.

Equally vivid were the descriptions of the lives of paupers reported by the investigators whom Mrs Webb persuaded the Commission to appoint. For example:

We are certain that among many aged out-workers we visited are to be found the most pathetically industrious workers in the community. They may be doing work which machines should do, they may be slow, but they are rarely idle or drunken. The extra 3s. or 4s. from the parish makes the difference between chronic semi-starvation and a low minimum of comfort. They would live on somehow if the relief was withdrawn. Now they are enabled to obtain fresh vegetables and a little fruit in summer and some extra coal and meat in winter. It would otherwise be always bread, margarine and tea. Out-relief varies the diet and warms the single room.[88]

In keeping with Mrs Webb's views, the Minority recommended separate institutional accommodation in order to make 'a very clear distinction between the deserving poor who are harmed by present policy' and the 'dirty, dissolute and vicious old man and woman'.[89] Helen Bosanquet, on the part of the Majority and the COS, took a notably less punitive approach. She was dubious as to whether such distinctions could be made 'without favouritism or injustice' and believed that the needs of the aged in or out of the workhouse should be carefully assessed, adequately provided for, and adjusted as their needs changed.[90]

Both groups hurriedly appended criticisms of the Pensions Act to their Reports. The Majority recommended compulsory invalidity insurance within a wider scheme of compulsory health insurance. Mrs Webb was 'dead against'[91] compulsory insurance, because it was paid as a right and allowed little discretion in the payment of benefits with reference to the character of the claimant. In consequence the Minority recommended a means-tested non-contributory pension payable at age 60, at rates linked to the local cost of living. They expected this gradually to be replaced by voluntary insurance against sickness and old age. Both reports objected to the pauper disqualification and thought the age limit too high.

Lloyd George took little interest in these Reports. One of their few direct results was an LGB circular of May 1910 urging guardians to supervise aged paupers more closely, but with the aim of caring for their needs rather than policing them, ensuring that they had 'adequate' resources and were looked after in good conditions. For the first time it was insisted that:

the guardians should endeavour to acquire a complete knowledge of the circumstances and needs of the applicants and should inform themselves, by every means in their power of the resources of the applicant, so that they may be in a position to form a

---

[88] Royal Commission on the Poor Laws, Interim Report (no. 1) by Miss Williams and Mr Jones: London-General Report.   [89] Minority Report, p. 323.

[90] H. Bosanquet, *The Poor Law Report of 1909* (London, 1909). McBriar, *Mixed Doubles*.

[91] Bunbury, *Ambulance Wagon*, 79.

considered judgement as to the necessities of the case and the right mode of dealing with it.

This approach was also to apply to widowed mothers and their children. It was confirmed in a 1911 Relief Regulation Order. This recommended new administrative procedures such as the use of detailed files of individual cases, an approach introduced by the COS. The aim was to improve knowledge of the claimant's circumstances in order to improve provision. In practice little changed before the outbreak of the First World War, though a significant shift in policy had been signalled.[92]

CONCLUSION

In 1910–11 Lloyd George and his colleagues were preoccupied with the refusal of the House of Lords to accept the 1909 Budget, primarily because it introduced a new tax on the value of land and increased income tax on higher incomes. This precipitated two general elections in 1910, which the Liberals won. In 1911 the Lords' veto on financial legislation was removed. The Liberals were then freer to promote social legislation. They moved quickly to amend some of the outstanding weaknesses of the pensions scheme: aboli-tion of the pauper disqualification was confirmed; they reduced to two years the period of disqualification for imprisonment and to six months the period of conviction for drunkenness. Following much protest, the English-born wife of an 'alien' was to be eligible for the pension, provided that her husband was dead, divorced, or they were legally separated for at least five years.

The introduction of the pension highlighted the problem of old people who could not manage to live independently or with relatives or friends and had no resort but the workhouse. Despite efforts to improve workhouse conditions for old people, which were more effective in some places than others, the stigma of poor relief remained and the plight of these old people was no better than before. A campaign for publicly funded 'cottage homes for aged persons' developed, supported by, among others, F. H. Stead and the labour alliance which had campaigned for pensions. It was interrupted by the declaration of war in August 1914.

Meanwhile National Health Insurance was in preparation in the Treasury. Initially it proposed a benefit of five shillings a week for long-term or per-manent invalidity, up to age 70. Actuaries advised that to provide the com-prehensive pension that Lloyd George aspired to would require a contribution higher than the capacity of the poorest to pay—the familiar problem. Treasury officials advised that eligibility should be narrowed to those 'totally unfit to follow any occupation'; that is, the very severely disabled. This

---

[92] Williams, *Pauperism to Poverty*, 126–34.

destroyed for the time being any hope that National Health Insurance could effectively extend the pension system.[93] So old-age pensions remained in 1914.

Something new—old-age state pensions—had been introduced, which were profoundly to shape the experiences of old people and the ways in which they were perceived by others for the remainder of the twentieth century.

[93] Bunbury, *Ambulance Wagon*, 145, 190, 313. Braithewaite MSS, British Library of Political and Economic Science, section II, box (i), item 46.

12

Pensions for the Middle Classes:
The Growth of Occupational Pensions

As formal pension schemes gradually became a normal feature of the life-courses of most English people, they changed these lives by, for the first time, guaranteeing a right to a secure, if small, income at a fixed age. The fixed pensionable age itself strengthened and universalized a notion long present in English culture: that old age began somewhere between 60 and 65. It made this definition of old age more rigid, with ambiguous effects. On the one hand, it had the beneficial result of rescuing many old people from a desperate struggle for survival until they could at last prove to the poor relief system their incapacity for self-support. On the other hand, the pension paid at a fixed age contributed to the construction of old people as a new and increasingly dominant (though never uncontested) cultural stereotype, the 'old-age pensioner', who was represented as a dependent rather than a contributing member of society once pensionable age was reached, in contrast to older assumptions that people aged and became dependent, if at all, at variable ages. Pensions for better-off workers developed in parallel with pensions for the very poor.

THE ORIGINS OF CIVIL SERVICE PENSIONS

Formalized pensions emerged first in the public sector. The first known were in the Customs and Excise Departments of the British government service in the eighteenth century. There are hints of similar developments in other departments.[1] However, Customs and Excise were by far the largest and fastest growing departments in a state bureaucracy which grew significantly in size and importance from the end of the seventeenth century.[2] The efficiency of these two departments was crucial for the British Crown and then for elected governments, which sought and achieved throughout the eighteenth century the highest tax revenues in Europe, from which they financed successful war, imperial expansion, and domestic stability and prosperity. Notions of the British

[1] The following discussion of Customs pensions is drawn largely from Marios Raphael, *Pensions and Public Servants: A Study of the Origins of the British System* (Paris, 1964).

[2] John Brewer, *The Sinews of Power: War, Money and the English State 1688–1783* (London, 1989), 65–7.

state apparatus as historically 'minimal', or, in political science terminology, 'weak' because its bureaucracy was small are misleading.[3]

As the tax-gathering departments grew they were the first departments of the British state to acquire the classic characteristics of modern bureaucracies: full-time employees, selected on the basis of ability and fitness for the post, paid by salary rather than by fee, on a career ladder of graded appointments, with progressively higher remuneration culminating in a pension. Departmental heads increasingly expected administrative loyalty and sought to encourage an ethos of public duty and private probity. Other departments of state whose adaptation was less immediately vital to the modernizing polity continued to operate in the old ways, composed of sinecurists and plural office holders[4] until reform began to encroach upon them also in the later eighteenth century.

The emergence of civil service pensions was integral to this process of change. Before the 1680s the convention in the Customs and other departments[5] (as among officers of the army and navy and in the fee-paid professions) was that a retiring officer sold his office to his successor either for a lump sum or an annuity, in effect for a pension. Substituting a formal pension scheme for this customary practice gave the administrators of the civil service increased control over appointments. The first such scheme was an adaptation of the previous practice. The first known civil service pension was awarded to an official of the Port of London in 1684. Following a report that 'Mr Horsham (by reason of his very ill-health) is not in a capacity to execute his office', the Treasury issued a warrant that Horsham 'is soe much indisposed by a great melancholye that he is at presens unfitt for business'. G. Scroope was appointed in his place 'with the established allowance of £80 per annum for his sallary, out of which he is to allow £40 per annum to the said Martin Horsham until we give order to the contrary'.[6]

In 1685 J. Jennings replaced Scroope and took over Horsham's £40 pension. In 1686 he petitioned that this burden should be lifted. It was decided that he should take over another pension payment of only £30 per year and Horsham's £40 be transferred to a more recent recruit to the service; also that these and future pensions should regularly be transferred to the most junior officials. This also became established practice. Hence pensions and incremental salaries emerged together. The Commissioners encouraged the practice 'for the encouragement of others to fidelity to the service'. However, it was not intended as a right of all ageing officers nor was it paid at a fixed age. It was to be 'designed principally for persons disabled by age or otherwise

---

[3] Brewer, *Sinews*. Pat Thane, 'Government and Society in England and Wales, 1750–1914', in F. M. L. Thompson (ed.), *The Cambridge Social History of Britain 1750–1850*, vol. iii (Cambridge, 1990); and 'Women in the British Labour Party and the Construction of State Welfare, 1906–39', in S. Koven and S. Michel (eds.), *Mothers of a New World: Maternalist Politics and the Origins of Welfare States* (London and New York, 1993), 343–77.   [4] Brewer, *Sinews*, 69.

[5] K. Ellis, *The Post Office in the Eighteenth Century* (Durham, 1958), 22.

[6] Raphael, *Pensions and Public Servants*, 34–5.

in H. M. Service that are in want and not in a condition to support themselves and their families'.[7] In 1689 one such 'pension' was disallowed because the recipient was considerably better off than the payee.

Such arrangements applied only to senior officers. In 1708 the Customs Commissioners informed the Treasury of a problem with some lower level officials: 'twelve superannuated Tidesmen who had not been able to discharge that duty several months past and being unwilling to put them off without some provision for their maintenance since most of them have been worn out in the Service of the Revenue'. That a situation which could hardly have been new was now seen as a problem indicates a new approach to management at all levels of the department. It was proposed that twelve new men be appointed from whose salaries of £40 per year, £14 each year should be paid to each superannuated officer. It was later decided that these charges also should fall successively upon the most junior officers as they were appointed. In this way pensions of different amount, related to previous income, emerged for different grades.[8] This gave rise, however, to protests from those who paid pensions from their incomes whilst those of identical rank did not. The irregular flow of retirements requiring pensioning obviously created inequities. In 1712 a Superannuation Fund was established for the lower ranks only, such as tidesmen, watermen, weighing porters. All members of these grades had to contribute sixpence per year per pound of their salary, and the pension, of maximum £14 per year, was payable after seven years' service 'except by some extraordinary accident in the service he becomes disabled sooner'. In the following years the scheme was extended to other grades, though not to the highest, or to the lowest (i.e. those paid by the day). The amount of pension was fixed at one-third of final salary. It was payable not at a certain age but on proof of disability for regular employment in the service. It was still paid only in cases of need. It was also payable only on condition of good behaviour in the service. The Commissioners retained discretion as to whom to pay. The scheme operated in part as a system of labour discipline.

At the lowest levels of the service, worthy men ineligible for the superannuation scheme were frequently given informal, ex gratia pensions. In 1717 two shillings and sixpence a week was paid from public funds to a noontender (men who guarded the quays whilst more senior officers were away at their midday meal), 'incapable of his duty by age and not entitled . . . by way of pension'. In 1725 one shilling per week was allowed to messengers who 'become superannuated and not able to attend the service'. Retired watchmen were allowed one shilling per week pension from 1730. Such rewards for long and faithful service had no doubt long been customary at all levels of the civil service, as they were in other occupations, but, of their nature, they have left few traces in the records.

<hr />

[7] Raphael, *Pensions and Public Servants*, 39.   [8] Ibid. 41.

An effect of the formalized pension system for the middle ranks of the civil service was to encourage recruitment of younger, fitter men who would not require superannuation too soon, though not until 1782 was an age limit of 50 established for first appointment, reduced to 45 in 1786. In the 1760s and 1770s the contributory scheme was extended to all officers whose salaries did not exceed sixty pounds a year. The pensions (usually one-third of final salary) were low in relation to real as distinct from formal earnings, since most Customs officials supplemented their earnings, often substantially, from more or less corrupt fees from merchants and others with whom they dealt. As such corruption was cleaned up at the end of the eighteenth century, some compensation was awarded from 1798, in the form of the abolition of the superannuation contribution and the doubling of pensions. The Customs Commissioners recommended that superannuation should be paid as a public responsibility, in the interests of developing an efficient public service of high probity.

At the higher levels of the service pensions were still paid from successors' salaries in cases of need. This itself could breed corruption. In the general course of reform, in 1803 a separate pension system was agreed for senior officers and the system of payment by successors abolished. The pension was non-contributory, providing a pension of a minimum one-third of final salary and was related to age, length, and quality of service, but no longer to lack of means. Pensioners were to have served at least ten years 'with absolute diligence and fidelity', and to be reported by the Customs Commissioners as 'absolutely incapable from infirmity of Mind or Body to execute the Duties of his Office and as a fit object to retire'; that is, the pension was still discretionary, conditional, and disciplinary no matter what the age of retirement; there was no fixed retirement age.

In 1806–7 all fees and gratuities were abolished in the ports and in compensation the non-contributory pension was extended on the same basis to all grades. In 1810 it was extended to the whole civil service as a complement to the abolition of corruption and patronage. Pensions were paid on more favourable terms above the age of 60; a doctor's certification was required only below age 60. A Treasury Minute of 1811 said firmly 'that the Act . . . does not entitle any person to be superannuated as of right after any given period of service', but by 1828 the pension had in effect become a right at age 60. The Customs' superannuation scheme provided the model for the whole civil service and later for the public and private sectors more generally. All the committees which investigated the public service with a view to abolishing corruption, between the 1780s and 1810, recommended generous pensions paid from public funds as an essential component of an efficient, incorrupt service.

The civil service pension system was subject to a number of modifications over the following decades, not least as parliament realized the cost of this generous scheme and sought to cut it back and to introduce contributions from officers in the harsher economic climate which followed the Napoleonic Wars. Such proposals were strenuously and effectively resisted by civil servants. In 1856–7 the civil service, including its superannuation schemes, was subject to a major review by a Royal Commission, with the principal aim of further promoting efficiency especially in the older departments where reform moved slowly. The report represented the civil service as an analogue to a retirement home for the physically enfeebled:

It may be noticed in particular that the comparative lightness of the work, and the certainty of provision in case of retirement owing to bodily incapacity, furnish strong inducements to the parents and friends of sickly youths to endeavour to obtain for them employment in the service of the government; and the extent to which the public are consequently burdened first with the salaries of officers who are obliged to absent themselves from their duties on account of ill-health, and afterwards with their pensions when they retire on the same plea, would hardly be credited by those who have not had opportunities of observing the operation of the system. . . .

We desire to call attention to the importance of establishing a uniform and consistent system of regulating the amounts to be granted to superannuated public servants with reference to the character of their service . . . No grant of superannuation allowance or good service pension should be made by the Treasury without a previous report from the Board of Examiners embodying this information . . . bearing on the services of the officers in each department.[9]

It was argued before the Commission, as it was to be argued against further extensions of public sector pensions and later against state pensions, that civil servants should not be provided with pensions but with salaries adequate to enable them to make their own provision for old age. The Commissioners responded that 'with a view to the due performance of his duty, it is important that a Civil Servant should feel himself in a safe and independent position' and not be worried about the future; and that public opinion would not allow a man who had given long and faithful service to starve, even if he ought to have made provision in advance.[10] They deemed sound service more important that the 'thrift and self-reliance' which, in other circumstances, was so much valued in nineteenth-century England.

The Commission recommended the retention of the non-contributory scheme, with retirement possible at age 60, but not compulsory until 65; even past that age certain exceptions were to be allowed. Sixty was described as 'an age at which bodily and mental vigour often begins to decline'. A compulsory retirement age was explicitly recommended to ease the task of heads of department embarrassed by the presence of officers who stayed past their capability, and by the delicacy of having to persuade them to leave. It was

[9] *The Civil Service*, vol. i. *Report of the Committee* 1966–8, app. B: The Northcote–Trevelyan Report, *Parliamentary Papers* (1967–8), xviii. 117–18.

[10] G. Rhodes, *Public Sector Pensions* (London, 1965), 19.

advocated, above all, as a means to achieve a younger and more efficient service. However, compulsory retirement was much resisted in the service and in parliament and this element was withdrawn on the grounds that it should not be applied to those fit to work to later ages, though in effect 60 became the normal retirement age. The civil service pension was now almost, but not formally, a legal right. The scheme remains more or less unchanged in its principles to the present, with some broadening over time of the scope of benefits.

When the civil service was again investigated by a Royal Commission in 1888, the Commissioners added the further justification that: 'Pensions help to retain in the service men who might otherwise be tempted elsewhere'.[11] This was repeated by another investigation in 1903.[12] The emphasis throughout was upon the advantages of the pensions to the efficiency of the state machine rather than to the individual civil servant. About four thousand men received civil service pensions in each year in the 1850s; most retired between ages 60 and 64.[13] In addition, significant numbers of men, not all of them old, though they had normally served for at least twenty years, received military and naval pensions throughout the eighteenth and nineteenth centuries. These were costly to the state, especially following major wars: 21.6 per cent of total national expenditure 'for effective establishments and other National Expenses Exclusive of the National Debt' in 1828, and a still substantial 14.28 per cent in 1848, thirty-three years after the end of the Napoleonic Wars.

THE SPREAD OF PUBLIC SECTOR PENSIONS

Other public employees, who were not formally civil servants, aspired to pensions on the civil service model but met resistance, often from civil servants. Until the end of the nineteenth century the efficiency and morale of lower level public employees was clearly thought to be less important to the state than that of the central departments.

Schoolteachers fought a long battle for pensions. Their position was ambiguous since, strictly, none of them was directly employed even by local government before the 1870s, though the central state funded much of their pay through voluntary agencies and the state increasingly regulated their employment. In 1846 the Committee of the Privy Council on Education, which administered the first state grant to working-class education minuted that 'Retiring Pensions' might be paid to 'Schoolmasters and Mistresses for long and efficient services', if after at least fifteen years' service they were 'incapable by age or

---

[11] Ibid.

[12] *Report of the Royal Commission on Superannuation in the Civil Service, Parliamentary Papers*, vol. xxxiii (1903), para. 10.

[13] D. Thomson, 'Provision for the Elderly in England, 1830–1908', Ph.D. thesis (University of Cambridge, 1981), 93.

infirmity of continuing to teach a school efficiently'; and conditional on a report on their character and conduct.

Teachers proposed contributory pensions to lessen the element of discretionary payment. Successive governments argued that teachers, unlike civil servants, should practise 'the economy which is incumbent upon them, in common with all other workers, while their strength lasts'; that is, they should save for old age.[14] Elementary school[15] teachers were expected to be among the prime purveyors of this message of self-help to working-class children and it was no doubt thought desirable that they practised what they preached. Discretionary pensions continued to be paid but in very restricted numbers; and it was emphasized that not only the qualities of the teacher but the needs of the school should be taken into account in the exercise of discretion; for instance, whether the school could recruit a well-qualified replacement for the teacher seeking retirement. When, by the 1870s, the state played a bigger role in providing and funding schools and working-class education came to be seen as more vital to the economy, government inspectors of schools also began to urge pensions as a means of attracting and retaining better qualified teachers of higher social status, and of keeping them happier while in post. But the teachers' aspiration for pensions continued to be held back because as employees of local authorities they were caught in a battle between local and central government over who should pay the costs, part of a wider expenditure battle between the two levels of government.

The debate continued for twenty years, until in the 1890s a compulsory contributory scheme was at last introduced for teachers in state elementary schools, amid the general climate of intensified concern about poverty in old age, which highlighted the possibility that this also could be the fate of relatively poorly paid teachers. Again, the pension was justified largely in terms of work efficiency. The scheme was based on a fixed contribution (£3 a year for men; £2 for women, who were lower paid), the pension varying according to numbers of years of contribution rather than with salary. In 1918 this was replaced with a scheme similar to that of the civil service, though it was notionally contributory.[16]

Other public sector employees had to wait as long or longer for a pension, for similar reasons. All had access only to discretionary pensions—a discretion exercised variably by their employers—until, also in the 1890s, many of them succeeded in obtaining formal pension schemes, all to some degree modelled on that of the civil service, though none so generous: the police in 1890, Poor Law officials in 1896, local government officials at varying dates in different local authorities, until they acquired a uniform scheme in 1922.

---

[14] Rhodes, *Public Sector*, 24. 　[15] i.e. state-funded working-class schools.
[16] Rhodes, *Public Sector*, 62.

PRIVATE SECTOR PENSIONS TO 1914

It is more difficult to trace the growth and numbers of occupational pension schemes in the private sector since they were not systematically surveyed before 1936.[17] There are strong indications that ex gratia payments to retiring employees were prevalent and had a long history. Also that they long had an important and well-understood role in management practice, though historians tend to discount their importance due to their apparently casual nature and because we underestimate transactions which do not leave extensive evidence behind. They were intended to, and often did, contribute to good relationships between workers and management and the promotion of efficiency. Their apparent informality made them flexible tools of management which many employers were reluctant to abandon. Whether or not informal payments transmuted into formal pension schemes depended upon a range of calculations on the part of management. As in the civil service, the history of pensions cannot be dissociated from the history of workplace relations.

Apparently informal payments could have formal rules in the private as in the public sector. The rules might simply allow the directors to fix the pension according to their judgement of the merit of the case. An alternative to ex gratia payments at lower status occupational levels was to keep older workers on, either in their old jobs for as long as they could manage some work, or in posts reserved for the elderly, such as sweeping up, keeping watch, making tea, carrying messages. As we have seen, this was long-established practice and it survived long into the twentieth century though tending to decline, especially after the Second World War; nor in the twentieth century could the practice keep pace with the growing absolute numbers of old people.[18] It survived for as long as it did in the face of growing criticism. Seebohm Rowntree commented in 1906 when his family chocolate firm introduced a pension scheme:

Many firms may hesitate to adopt a Pension Scheme . . . but it is probable that these very firms carry heavy costs in 'hidden pensions' without realizing the fact. If a firm establishes a liberal pension scheme it will doubtless at the same time fix a definite retiring age and will thus never find itself with a number of old workers of low working capacity drawing full pay . . . such employees are very costly, not only does the firm lose on them individually but their presence tends to lower the pace and lessen the output of the whole shop . . . But they are kept on because they have worked faithfully for a great number of years and the management does not care to dismiss them.[19]

[17] R. Fitzgerald, *British Labour Management and Industrial Welfare, 1846–1939* (London, 1988) is the most thorough attempt so far to survey this and other aspects of company welfare.

[18] S. Riddle, 'Age, Obsolescence and Unemployment: Older Men in the British Industrial System, 1930–39; a Research Note', *Ageing and Society*, 4/4 (1984), 517–24.

[19] Quoted Alice Russell, *The Growth of Occupational Welfare in Britain* (Aldershot, 1991), 28–9.

The role of pensions in the development of modern management techniques designed to enhance efficiency could not be expressed more clearly.

Until the twentieth century the state had no active involvement in private sector pensions. In the late seventeenth century occupational pensions had been provided by statute in private firms closely linked with government and especially important for national prosperity, including the Bank of England and the East India Company. Occasional early legislative attempts were made to compel manual workers in specific occupations to contribute to funds providing sickness and old-age benefits, but they were generally short-lived, such as schemes in 1757 for coalheavers on the Thames and in 1792 for shippers and keelmen on the River Wear.[20]

Formal pension schemes developed earliest in the largest and most bureaucratized firms. This was most characteristic of large, multi-site firms in which centralized management demanded uniformity across the firm, which was rare in British business even in the nineteenth century. The railways were by far the largest undertakings in Britain for much of the nineteenth century and their workforces were necessarily scattered. Most of the railway companies by the 1860s ran compulsory contributory schemes providing sickness, superannuation, and funeral allowances. They paid pensions of between two shillings and six shillings weekly after a minimum of twenty-five years' service. The better paid, higher status workers enjoyed superior schemes. The elite subscribed from one shilling to one shilling and sixpence a week to the Engineman and Fireman Mutual Assurance, Sick and Superannuation Society. They received superannuation benefit of seven shillings and sixpence to twelve shillings at age 60, or permanent disablement benefit after a minimum ten years' contribution. Clerks and station masters fared better still. Company schemes rarely included senior management, who were generally provided for informally and generously. Such status divisions characterized British occupational pension arrangements as they did other aspects of company organization.

Other large undertakings were early to produce formal pension schemes. The Gas, Light and Coke Co., the largest company supplying this important new source of energy, paid discretionary pensions from the 1830s. They introduced a formal scheme for staff in 1842 and for manual workers in 1870. The management believed that pensions were necessary in an industry 'where only the fittest could be retained in employment', but they retained their discretion in awarding them. Applicants for pensions in 1877 were refused for joining a strike five years previously.[21] Other gas companies followed this lead by the end of the century.

By the end of the nineteenth century, Joint Stock Banks were among the faster growing centralized business institutions. They were under pressure from

[20] Russell, *Occupational Welfare*, 25–6.   [21] Fitzgerald, *Industrial Welfare*, 63–70.

their clerks to turn their tradition of ex gratia payments into formal pension schemes, which reluctantly most did. In most such firms management was wholly internally recruited from those who entered as clerks straight from school. Young male entrants expected to spend some years on a low salary, with the expectation of promotion to management, and to spend their lives with a single firm. As the banks grew, the number of clerical posts grew in relation to the number of higher management posts, lessening promotion prospects and lengthening periods of dull work on low salaries. Clerks became increasingly restive, hence for example the formation of a trade union, the Bank Clerks Association, in 1906. Improved pension schemes were part of the banks' strategy to attract and keep high-quality clerks. The banks were in direct competition for clerical labour with the civil service; and clerks themselves were coming to regard pensions as part of their conditions of service, as conferring status as well as providing personal security. Even financial institutions which clung to ex gratia payments, in practice kept them close to civil service levels. The Bank of England long had a generous scheme providing similar levels of pension to the civil service, but they were careful to insist that pensions were entirely at the discretion of the Bank. Management in general was reluctant to relinquish the control over the workforce which they gained from discretionary payments.

Manufacturing industry was most variable in its pensions provision, not surprisingly given its varied character. The timing and form of pensioning at any time before the First World War was strongly influenced by how management assessed the needs of the firm. Pension schemes were slow to emerge in small firms, which characterized most of British industry in the nineteenth century and into the twentieth; particularly in those which made intensive use of manual labour with high turnover such as engineering, shipbuilding, textiles.

Mining developed a distinctive pattern of workers' mutual aid funds.[22] These were the most extensive pension schemes for manual workers, funded by a combination of employer donations, employee contributions, charitable donations, and investment income. They were normally controlled by the miners themselves, with strong support from the employers, who felt that the security obtained by the workers calmed industrial relations in the industry. Contributions were deducted from wages. The characteristically small mining companies could not provide adequate welfare benefits individually and so combined for this purpose on a regional basis. This was unusual and was presumably influenced by the need to attract and hold workers in sometimes remote locations in the rapidly expanding mining business of the later nineteenth century.

The miners' funds provided for sickness, accident, and old age in one of the most hazardous occupations. The largest, the Northumberland and

---

[22] See pp. 194–5.

Durham Miners Permanent Relief Fund Friendly Society was founded in 1862 and by 1892 had 108,000 members (total membership of such schemes in that year was about 250,000). The superannuation fund was established in 1874, paying pensions to men aged above 60 or, if unfit for work, at an earlier age. Also in the 1890s, the Fund began to provide subsidized housing for retired miners. In 1911 most such schemes were incorporated into the National Insurance system, retaining their separate superannuation funds to supplement the state old-age pension. The benefits they provided could, however, serve to deprive members of a portion of the state pension. Hence the Friendly Societies' and Trade Unions' continual petitioning of government to exempt their benefits from the pension means test.[23]

Formal pension schemes were introduced relatively early into firms which were paternalistic for reasons of humanity and/or because they judged this the best technique for holding a loyal, hard-working labour force. These motives were by no means mutually exclusive.[24] Pensions were generally discretionary and dependent upon a satisfactory work record, and as such they functioned as part of the structure of workplace incentives and deterrents. For example, at the beginning of the nineteenth century, the Crowley ironworks, in the northeast of England, paid pensions as part of a comprehensive scheme including sick benefits and medical care, widows' allowances and children's schooling. Contributions were compulsory for workers and the employer also contributed, but they conferred no right to benefit. Payment of a pension remained at the employer's discretion and was related to good behaviour. Also the scheme could be folded at the wish of the employer, as was that at Crowleys in the depression following 1815.[25]

Pensions were usually confined to skilled workers whom firms most wished to retain or attract, only occasionally extending to 'ordinary hands'. In 1897 Courtaulds textile business was making small weekly allowances to forty-six retired 'hands'. At Kenrick's Hardware Co. foremen could expect a retirement pension; for other workers, payments were at the firm's pleasure. For lower level workers, firms had no great incentive to provide benefits since their labour was not scarce, except in remote locations. Such workers normally could not afford to contribute for adequate benefits for themselves and pensions were costly for firms to provide.

Manufacturing industry was slower than the public sector to grow in scale and to bureaucratize. A distinct, though still slow, movement of firms towards formal pension schemes came in the last years of the nineteenth and the first years of the twentieth century, when some of the larger manufacturing firms, including Wills, the leading tobacco manufacturer, Cadburys, Rowntrees, Boots Drug Co., Kenricks, W. H. Smith the newspaper and book retailer,

[23] Fitzgerald, *Industrial Welfare*, 159–63.   [24] Ibid. 179 ff.
[25] Russell, *Occupational Welfare*, 43.

J. & P. Coats thread manufacturer, Colmans mustard (all beneficiaries of rising living standards and expanding consumer demand), introduced pension schemes.[26] Such firms were growing in size, international competitive pressure was increasing, as was the power of trade unionism and also the political campaign for state pensions. All if these changes heightened awareness of the pensions issue among employers and workers.

After the introduction of state pensions in 1908 employers were motivated partly by desire, partly by pressure from employees, to provide for their staff an equivalent to what poorer workers received from the state. In 1910 Pilkingtons, the glass manufacturer, established a staff scheme, but not for many years one for their manual workers, though they might provide them with light work and discretionary pensions as they aged. On one occasion the management noted that an elderly worker:

has been applying for assistance in the shape of a pension and has written saying that he has been fifty years with the firm etc. Don't think him entitled to anything, been a regular blacksheep.

But they employed him for several years longer on light work instructing younger glass-blowers.[27]

Some schemes, such as that introduced by the South Metropolitan Gas Company in the 1880s, were specifically designed to undermine the appeal of trade unions and their welfare benefits by providing superior security through the firm. They were apparently successful.[28] One major phosphorous producer by 1895 had a non-contributory superannuation scheme for all its work-people (male and female) whose earnings were not above £300 a year, though given the highly toxic nature of the product it is questionable how many survived to claim it, and what motivated the scheme.

Some firms sought to impose compulsory saving for old age. In 1889 Wills tobacco firm in Bristol devised a bonus scheme to enable workers to share the firm's profits. Workers were advised, via a note in their wage packets, to invest 25 per cent of their bonus in the company savings bank at a favourable rate of interest. Few did so and in 1899 the directors condemned their prodigality and revised the scheme: one-third of each worker's bonus was withheld and placed in an account with the company, to be withdrawn only with the firm's permission. It was made clear that it was to be withdrawn only on retirement or on leaving the firm.

Overwhelmingly, private sector occupational pension schemes before 1914 were initiated by management, from above, with an eye to the interests of the firm rather than negotiated with the workers. By 1914 a quite comprehensive system of occupational pensions appears to have existed in Britain,

---

[26] Fitzgerald, *Industrial Welfare*, 179, 202; Leslie Hannah, *Inventing Retirement: The Development of Occupational Pensions in Britain* (Cambridge, 1986), 12, 18.

[27] Hannah, *Retirement*, 43.   [28] Russell, *Occupational Welfare*, 47.

though how comprehensive is difficult to establish, and often pensions were discretionary or apparently informal ex gratia payments. Most people in regular work, especially if they stayed long with a single employer, even if they were not necessarily highly skilled and were low paid (e.g. agricultural labourers) could expect a pension in some form, perhaps provided partially in the form of light work for as long as it could be sustained.

The attitude of employers to state pensions varied as much as their attitudes to company pensions and fitted no tidy pattern, though their perception of their firm's material interest was at least as important as ideological commitment for or against state welfare. Some welcomed state assistance with the invidious problem of encouraging older workers to retire; others feared the loss of an element of control over their workforce. When in 1908 the pension age was fixed as high as 70 and confined to the poorest and most marginal workers, many employers felt that they could gain credit from the mass of their workers by supplementing the state scheme with their own. Others, often in larger firms, believed that this and other features of state welfare would improve industrial efficiency by creating a fitter workforce with a greater feeling of personal security; and/or that by displaying its beneficence the state would undermine the growing political and industrial power of labour. Some supported non-contributory pensions because they feared the costs of an insurance scheme; others preferred insurance pensions because they would place part of the cost on the workers rather than on the employers as taxpayers. From 1906 the official policy of the influential National Association of British Chambers of Commerce was support for a scheme of national insurance against sickness, invalidity, and old age. The prominent manufacturers Edward Cadbury, William Lever, and Alfred Mond, supported the state non-contributory pension scheme. Indeed it was the welfare reform of the 1906–14 period that employers opposed least, because it interfered least with company welfare strategies, and in terms of personal taxation, it cost them little.[29]

PRIVATE SAVING AND MUTUAL AID

For those who could afford it, private saving was an important means of providing for old age. Insurance and life assurance incorporating annuities had grown especially strongly in the eighteenth century and after. Working people who could afford to do so bought property in order to live in old age on rental income. The Amalgamated Society of Engineers (ASE), the most elite of craft unions, invested its superannuation fund in the union's own building society, whose purpose was to enable their members to acquire property for

---

[29] J. R. Hay, 'Employers and Social Policy in Britain: The Evolution of Welfare Legislation, 1905–14', *Social History*, 4 (1977), 435–56. Fitzgerald, *Industrial Welfare*, 220–2.

this purpose.[30] In the nineteenth century much effort was spent by those who could afford to save in persuading those who could not, or who could do so only very inadequately, also to do so. Also of course the incentive to save specifically for old age was small among those for whom demographic reality meant that it was a less probable, and certainly a less immediate, cause of need than a range of other contingencies, in particular sickness and unemployment. The problem was that for those who did survive, old age could be the period of most desperate want in the life cycle and, most problematic of all from the point of view of personal saving, one of unpredictable length.

The government's first positive move into the field of income maintenance in old age, apart from the Poor Law, was Gladstone's introduction in 1853 of tax relief on premiums for insurance policies, including those designed as saving for old age. About one-fifth of taxpayers held such policies and devoted about 5 per cent of their income to them by the end of the century.[31] In 1864 Gladstone also established an annuity scheme through the Post Office Savings Bank, specifically to encourage working-class saving. Both proved more popular with the lower middle than the working classes, especially with unmarried women, though overall the take-up was disappointing. Between 1875 and 1893 only 1,681 annuities were taken out, largely, contemporaries believed, because providing for old age was not a priority for the limited savings working people could manage. Friendly Societies and trade unions could provide more appropriately for their needs.[32]

The fact that a high proportion of more secure workers had access to pensions of some kind focused the attention of the state pensions movement upon the needs of those who had not, in particular women. In countries such as Germany where even the better paid workers had lesser access to benefits in old age, the needs of these superior workers played a larger role in the discourse about state pensions.

An effect of the introduction of state pensions, contrary to one of the most often expressed fears of its opponents, was that working-class savings may well have risen rather than fallen. State-guaranteed security in old age provided an incentive rather than a disincentive to saving, as its proponents had hoped. Individuals could better attempt to save 'because they had been raised above the threshold of economic independence by the pension itself'.[33] Relieved of the more or less hopeless task of saving long term for old age, younger people could make the more rational effort to save short term for relatively expensive necessities, such as boots and shoes.

---

[30] Kazuko Fukasawa, 'Voluntary Provision for Old Age by Trade Unions in Britain before the Coming of the Welfare State', Ph.D. thesis (University of London, 1996), 83–93.
[31] Hannah, *Retirement*, 5.   [32] See pp. 194–5.
[33] P. Johnson, 'Self-Help vs State Help', *Explorations in Economic History* (Oct. 1984), 348.

THE INTER-WAR YEARS

After the First World War it becomes ever harder to discuss state and occupational pensions in isolation from one another. Public sector pensions continued to spread and to improve partly because the public sector itself grew. It employed 6 per cent of the working population in 1900, 10 per cent in the 1930s. By 1931, 80 per cent of all local government officers were in statutory superannuation funds; in 1939 this became compulsory for all such officials. Formal public sector schemes continued to cover more workers than private sector schemes.

In 1936, for the first time, the government surveyed formally constituted occupational schemes. They found that 6,544 employers had schemes in operation in the private sector; 4,944 of these applied only to administrative, professional, or clerical staff. There were 1,600 schemes for manual workers. Of the total membership of occupational schemes 802,635 were non-manual, 814,458 were in the much larger manual labour force. Over a quarter of the non-manual schemes were in banks, insurance companies, or other financial services; another sizeable group included the academic and administrative staff of universities and staff of professional offices such as those of solicitors and stockbrokers. Few female workers had access to occupational pensions.

However, it was in the private sector that pension schemes spread fastest in this period, despite the Depression. White-collar workers still benefited to a greater extent than manual workers, but the latter were increasingly demanding pensions. In part this was due to increased life expectancy; most workers now expected to survive to old age and they were more concerned about their incomes in later life. Pensions played a larger part in industrial bargaining in a labour force which was much more strongly unionized than before the war, though the Depression and the restructuring of the economy made union influence variable over time, in different places, and between sectors.

The need of employers to attract and hold workers at all levels by means of pensions also varied by sector of the economy. Management practices were the chief influence upon the spread and form of pension schemes, but such practices and the role of pensions within them also changed over time and varied with the perceived needs of each firm. Employers showed a strong preference for informal schemes for as long as they could hold onto them, for the greater control over the workforce which they conferred.[34] The State also played an increasing role. The Joint Industrial Councils set up by the government during the First World War to provide negotiating machinery, especially in low-paid occupations, provided one forum in which pensions were negotiated between workers and employers. One result was a scheme introduced in the flour-milling industry in 1931. This owed much to the work of

[34] Hay, 'Employers', 439.

Ernest Bevin, the powerful leader of the Transport and General Workers' Union, and was unusual in being transferable among all firms in the industry, except for one which refused to join. It was the outcome of agreement among the employers to rationalize the whole industry by a process which included buying out superfluous mills and sacking long-serving workers. The scheme was designed initially to compensate these workers.[35]

Both unions and employers overtly used pensions as a tool of industrial relations. Employers were advised in such matters by new specialist bodies such as the Industrial Welfare Society.[36] In the 1930s Johnson's wiremaking firm near Manchester offered pensions as an inducement to co-operation in the introduction of the Bedaux system of production. Workers feared that the system would bring about redundancies and went on strike. The company announced that only those who promptly agreed would benefit from the pensions scheme they were about to introduce. Not all employers were so crass. One employer, Edward Cadbury, argued against more mechanistic fashions in management theory by stressing the gains to industrial harmony from treating workers well.[37]

On the trade union side, the National Union of Railwaymen tried unsuccessfully to negotiate standardization of the myriad railway pension schemes at the level of best practice; many employers insisted that they could not afford this. An attempt by the Nottinghamshire miners to negotiate a scheme foundered over the degree of control expected by the employers.

Unions were divided as to whether they preferred state or occupational pensions. By 1939 they were tending to prefer the former in view of the uses to which some employers put pensions and the difficulty of diminishing employer control once schemes were established. In 1912 Port of London employees had pensions withheld as punishment for participating in strikes; in 1926 Pilkingtons' glass-workers who supported the General Strike of that year forfeited their pension rights. They were reinstated, but with one shilling reduction in benefit.

Employers introduced pensions when it suited them rather than the workers. Formal schemes were fewest for manual workers in occupations in which piece-rates, labour subcontracting, and insecurity were common, as, for example, in engineering and shipbuilding. These were especially insecure occupations in the Depression and their unions were less able to compensate by providing benefits of their own. The engineers suspended all benefit payments in 1922; by January 1923 they had lost 25 per cent of their membership.[38] This diminishing ability to provide for their own members combined with antagonistic labour relations in certain industries led unions to look increasingly to the state.

[35] Hannah, *Retirement*, 43; Fitzgerald, *Industrial Welfare*, 182–3.
[36] Fitzgerald, *Industrial Welfare*, 203 ff.   [37] Ibid. 207–8.
[38] N. Whiteside, 'Social Welfare and Industrial Relations, 1914–1939', in C. Wrigley (ed.), *A History of British Industrial Relations, 1914–1939*, 2nd edn. (London, 1993), 211–42.

In white-collar occupations, workers and unions were content with occupational pensions and sought to extend them, judging them the best pensions they were likely to get. White-collar unions were growing, especially in the public sector. The National Association of Local Government Officers was formed out of the battle to establish local government pension rights. The Union of Distributive and Allied Workers pressed for pensions, and by 1932 62 per cent of Co-operative store employees, where the union was strongest, were covered.[39] Bevin supported occupational pensions as preferable for the individual to dependence upon the state, but this view was resisted by many workers who, quite rationally, were unwilling to pay contributions to occupational schemes whilst the real value of the state non-contributory pension was improving, as it was between the wars. Workers' resistance to dependence upon employers' pension schemes had some justification. In the steel industry, formal pensions did not generally replace ex gratia payments until after 1930. In the firm of Dorman, Long a contributory scheme for staff and foremen was introduced in 1920, principally to prevent their joining a union. It was open only to those who did not do so; those preferring a union to the pension had to submit a written explanation. By 1922 the scheme pension included all workers who were not daily or hourly paid, but each pension claim was individually assessed. With the introduction of contributory state pensions in 1925[40] the firm reduced its contributions to the fund and confined the scheme to those staff who would not qualify for the state pension. In 1934 the pension fund was wound up and all pensions became ex gratia. The firm was performing poorly and required only a small core of permanent workers; it now had no need for pensions.

Other steel firms responded differently to the economic crisis. Through the process of rationalization and increased concentration of capital, the companies supported joint contributory pension and sick-pay schemes which demanded a new level of commitment from and to individual employers. In the large corporate enterprises which were emerging, management sought to safeguard rates of return by planning the numbers and stability of their workforces on whose co-operation the full and efficient use of plant would depend. They required a skilled permanent workforce as they had not before, and pensions enabled them to ease out workers who could not adapt to new techniques. The unions played a large role in negotiating the pensions and successfully bargained for participation in their administration, though the rules could not normally be changed without the agreement of all employers.[41]

Lever Bros. in 1929 introduced a contributory scheme because ex gratia payments were becoming costly. In the brewing industry an ex gratia system had been so successfully established by the mid-nineteenth century, that it 'helped produce a labour force which remained at work even during the General

[39] Hannah, *Retirement*, 26–7.   [40] See pp. 323–7.   [41] Fitzgerald, *Industrial Welfare*, 83–105.

Strike'.[42] The industry had kept old men on at work. Draymen, whose reliability was vital to the trade, were pensioned at age 50 or 55, when the hard job took its toll. Brewing underwent extensive rationalization between the wars and the industry introduced a formal pension scheme to ease the process. A prominent manager in brewing spelled out the purposes of industrial welfare as he saw them in 1926 in a pamphlet, *Industrial Welfare in Practice*. He stressed the importance of industrial welfare for industrial relations. Pensions schemes should be under employer control, to bind employer and worker together with 'not a chain of slavery, but a chain formed of such links as good will and gratitude'. Pensions should be awarded only for 'continuous and faithful service' and so should not be paid to strikers, rather pensions 'will often be the means of staving off a disastrous strike'. Widows' pensions should be paid to ensure that husbands worked hard and regularly.[43]

Firms which remained small increasingly associated together to provide welfare. The Fine Cotton Spinners Association of employers, formed from thirty firms in 1898, in 1919 set aside £100,000 for pensions for its 25,000-strong workforce, mainly in order to encourage 'assiduous and whole-hearted service' and to achieve industrial peace. The Bleachers Association in 1926 replaced ex gratia pensions with non-contributory pensions from a joint fund under the complete control of company directors. In 1925 the Bradford Dyers Association formed a scheme for staff and operatives, as an approved society under the 1925 Pensions Act. There were similar developments in the expanding but very diversified electrical goods industry. The also expanding motor industry began to introduce formal pension schemes in the 1930s.[44] The introduction of redundancy payments and marriage gratuities (for women leaving employment on marriage) for those who would not remain with the firm long enough to gain a pension, emerged from the same approach to management. When Imperial Chemical Industries (ICI) was formed in 1926 from the four largest chemical firms in the country it initiated a new industrial relations and welfare policy designed to integrate all workers into a single structure, on principles much influenced by the tradition of paternalistic welfarism of the Mond Company, one of the components of the merger. ICI was not hostile to trade unions but did not want them to be powerful and wished to enhance loyalty to the firm to counteract loyalty to the union and to ease the process of merger, with apparent success. A share ownership scheme was introduced and also works councils which could discuss matters of welfare and safety, though not of wages, hours, or conditions of employment. Discretionary pensions were paid until contributory schemes were introduced in 1937, separately for 'staff' and 'workers'. These were introduced from above, without negotiation.

---

[42] Ibid. 140.   [43] Ibid. 146.   [44] Ibid. 172–9.

The expansion of occupational pensions in the inter-war years also owed something to the work of insurance companies, some of which adopted aggressive US methods of selling pensions packages to employers, promoting them as a feature of modern business practice. In particular they could provide for small and medium-sized companies financial management services which large companies could provide for themselves. By 1936 about one in eight of the labour force (though only one in ten in the private sector) belonged to an occupational scheme compared with about one in twenty at the beginning of the century.

The state, largely through tax changes and perhaps not always consciously, encouraged private sector pensions. In 1921 lobbying by the newly formed pressure group, the Conference of Superannuation Funds, won exemption from tax for the whole of the investment income of the funds. Workers' and employers' contributions were already tax-exempt. In the inter-war years firms grew in size and more acquired formal bureaucratic structures; there was more experimentation with methods of management, some adopted or adapted from abroad especially from the US. But, private sector pension schemes remained variable and above all not transferable from one employment to another. Transferability went against the employers' objective of using schemes to hold and manage key workers.

STATE PENSIONS AND OCCUPATIONAL PENSIONS

The introduction of state insurance pensions in 1925 enabled some firms to cut back their pensions payments, which some greeted with relief in the Depression. Following pressure from the pensions industry, the state scheme allowed for limited contracting out, provided that occupational pensions provided adequate cover. This was allowed only to employees of the Crown, of local authorities, and private companies whose schemes were governed by statute, such as railways and gas companies. The Great Western Railway reduced allowances from its pension fund by the amount payable under the 1925 Act and wound up its widows and orphans fund, promising help to those who did not qualify for state pensions. The London and North Eastern Railway adjusted its pension payments to ensure that, combined with the state pension, employees received an adequate total pension in the opinion of the company, in the light of past service.[45] Employers had tried to resist the contributory element in the 1925 scheme, without success, hence the adjustment many of them made in their contributions to occupational schemes. In 1949 the Industrial Welfare Society pointed out that when the 1925 Act was introduced:

[45] Fitzgerald, *Industrial Welfare*, 202.

Many employers asked how this position was likely to affect the firm's pensions schemes. Experience has furnished the answer to this question. Pensions and Superannuation schemes grew at a far more rapid rate after 1926 than before . . . the very provision of government pension directed the workers' attention to the need to provide for old age.[46]

CONCLUSION

The certainty of receiving a pension changed the lives of middle-class people as much as those of the poor, gradually creating fixed and predictable retirement ages, a secure if sometimes minimal income after retirement, and a period of later life free from paid work, which could be planned for. Pensions were introduced primarily on the initiative of employers, as a tool of management, though increasingly they were sought by workers, often through their trade unions, as a desirable form of security.

Formal pensions first emerged in the eighteenth century in the public sector. These provided a model which spread though the society over the following two centuries. There is no clear sign in England that the introduction of pensions was associated with enhanced respect for the older people concerned, as is said to have been the case for France.[47] Rather pensioned retirement was intended to signal declining competence at work. Nor can the emergence of formalized pensioning and retirement be said to mark the beginning of a quite new self-consciousness about the life-course and of old age as a distinct stage of life associated with retirement. Such a consciousness had long existed in English culture, though the threshold of old age acquired a more formalized chonological definition. What changed over the centuries was that an old age of pensioned retirement became a real possibility for a widening range of people.

[46] Ibid. 236–7.
[47] D. Troyansky, *Old Age in the Old Regime: Image and Experience in Eighteenth-Century France* (Ithaca, NY, and London, 1989); and 'Balancing Social and Cultural Approaches to the History of Old Age and Ageing in Europe: A Review and an Example from Post-Revolutionary France', in Paul Johnson and Pat Thane (eds.), *Old Age from Antiquity to Post-Modernity* (London, 1998), 96–109.

Living Longer in a Changing World, the 1830s to 1930s

13

'An Unfailing Zest for Life':
Images and Self-Images of Older People in the Nineteenth and Early Twentieth Centuries

How did older people from differing backgrounds see themselves and how were they seen by others in the nineteenth and early twentieth centuries? Diaries, letters, biographies, and autobiographies in particular give some insights into the lives of the many older people who were not poor and whose private lives, in consequence, were unlikely to be exposed in public documents. Some were powerful enough to be regarded by others as individuals worthy of interest, rather than as 'old people' worthy of pity.

ARTICULATE OLD WOMEN

Georgina Burne-Jones (1840–1920) spent most of her adult life supporting her husband, the Pre-Raphaelite painter Edward Burne-Jones. She was a close friend of John Ruskin and William Morris. Only in her fifties did she discover the confidence and energy to enter public life independently, and to ignore the complaints of Edward about this distraction of her attention from his affairs. She had been raised as a Methodist with a strong sense of public duty; onto this had been grafted a commitment to socialism. As she grew older, and as women came to play a larger part in public life towards the end of the nineteenth century, this commitment became more open, at the same time that her husband's politics became more conservative.[1] In 1894 she stood for election to the Parish Council of Rottingdean in Sussex, where she lived, a village community which was not an obvious socialist centre. She took advantage of a new opportunity for women to stand for election to newly created local authorities.[2] Edward was alarmed but supportive, commenting: 'She is so busy—she is rousing the village—she is marching about—she is going like a flame through the village'.[3] She was the only woman to be elected, along with nine

[1] Jan Marsh, *Pre-Raphaelite Sisterhood* (London, 1985), 340–1.
[2] Patricia Hollis, *Ladies Elect: Women in English Local Government 1865–1914* (Oxford 1987), 355–71.
[3] Ina Taylor, *Victorian Sisters* (London, 1987), 157.

men. She was open about her socialism and in no doubt about the necessity for women to be active in public life. She commented: 'Women can think and understand in matters that men would pass over. In private life women are often like the mortar between bricks—they hold the house together—men know this and expect it of them.'[4] As a councillor she worked for the, very necessary, improvement of conditions for rural labourers such as the provision of allotments, improved water-supplies, public baths and wash-houses, and the first paid village nurse, for whom she purchased a cottage. She was a highly practical socialist.

Georgina coped resiliently with her husband's death in 1898 and, convinced that her own life would not last much longer, ably wrote his biography, which was published in 1904. She carried on with her public duties and her political radicalism. When jingoists were celebrating the relief of Mafeking during the Anglo-Boer war, in May 1900 she hung a banner from her house criticizing the war. The crowd threatened to burn the house.[5] In Rottingdean she was seen as a formidable old lady, despite her diminutive size. Her granddaughter, the novelist Angela Thirkell, wrote that 'we children had a nervous feeling that we never knew where our grandmother might break out next'.[6] At 60 she still sought to convert the villagers to socialism. As her granddaughter described:

She would have a worthy carpenter or wheelwright to the house once a week to discuss the socialism in which she so thoroughly believed. All the snobbishness latent in children came to the fore in us as we watched the honoured but unhappy workman sitting stiffly on the edge of his chair in his horrible best clothes while my grandmother's lovely earnest voice preached William Morris to him.[7]

At the same time she was a pioneer motorist. Also, over the next twenty years until her death she looked after ailing and poverty-stricken relatives and friends, travelled, and was cheered by the Labour Party's success in the General Election of 1906. To the end she lived independently, with one maid to assist her, trying to put into practice her belief that 'one of the lessons of old age is to avoid being a nuisance'.[8] She died suddenly and peacefully.

Her contemporary, Octavia Hill (1838–1912) did not marry and certainly never became a socialist. She was active in public life, especially in the world of philanthropic housing, from her twenties. Like Georgina she remained active into her seventies, almost to her death. At 68 she made an active contribution to the work of the Royal Commission on the Poor Laws of 1905–9. In her final years she worked hard to extend the properties supported by the National Trust.[9]

---

[4] Taylor, *Sisters*, 157.   [5] Marsh, *Sisterhood*, 349–50.
[6] Angela Thirkell, *Three Houses* (Oxford, 1932), 80.   [7] Ibid. 78.   [8] Taylor, *Sisters*, 180.
[9] William Thomson Hill, *Octavia Hill* (London, 1958). For an account of the old age of another great philanthropist and near contemporary of Hill, Louisa Twining and of her attempts to help poor old women, see Theresa Deane, 'Old and Incapable? Louisa Twining and Elderly Women in Victorian Britain', in L. Botelho and P. Thane (eds.), *Women and Ageing in British Society since 1500* (London, 2000).

Maria Jackson (1818–1892), in contrast, was ailing in her fifties, due mainly to rheumatism, and had few concerns outside herself and her immediate family and friends, though she had a certain interest in literature and the arts. For the remainder of her life she wrote almost daily to her daughters, most frequently to Julia Stephen, mother of Virginia Woolf. In her letters[10] she chronicled in detail her ill health, ageing, and decline until her death aged 74. In her later fifties she and her husband spent much time at European spas seeking cures for the swollen joints, headaches, and bilious attacks of which she complained in her letters. She complained of the fatigue of travelling. Travel outside Britain seems to have ceased in her sixties. She wrote to her son-in-law Leslie Stephen:

I am dry–not a spark of fire in me–only the dear letters brighten existence. If one could get away upon the hills life would be tolerable enough in its outward form but to sit at a closed window and look into the street is cheerless eno'. I am reading Carlyle's *French Revolution* and it stirs my languid blood—languid for all but my beloved ones.

She grew increasingly anxious about her family's and her own safety in public places, warning Julia in 1883, as on many occasions:

Pray my own, avoid to go in carriages where men are or to be by yourself for at any station a man might get in—my precious one—my fears grow and grow.

By the age of 65 she was largely confined to a wheelchair, despite efforts by her doctor to encourage her to walk. She was also increasingly deaf and dependent upon morphine for the relief of pain and to assist her to sleep. She and her husband (until his death in 1887) regularly now took the waters at English spas such as Bath. She described herself as old and was seen as such by others. Until her death she lived in Brighton, frequently visited by family, who mostly lived in London, and by friends, and well provided with servants.

By the late 1880s Maria Jackson seems to have become accustomed to her ailments, commented upon them less often and showed more concern for the health of her relatives, though she commented often on her sleeping difficulties. She now routinely signed herself 'old mother', or to her granddaughter Stella Duckworth, who frequently stayed with her, 'your most loving old granny'. She remained in her own house in Brighton, despite offers by the Stephens that she live with them. She was cared for by servants and by another granddaughter, Mary Vaughan. Mary sent regular reports on her grandmother's condition to Julia by letter or, in emergency, by telegram. Maria retained control to the end of a life that was limited and private, but not much more so than in her unadventurous earlier years. She aged physically at a relatively early age and resigned herself to this emotionally. Her correspondence with her daughters provided an outlet for her complaints about ageing. The rapid

---

[10] About 400 of which survive. University of Sussex, Charleston Papers, Ad. 1 (i–iv).

postal service of the later nineteenth century and the ease with which the comfortably off could travel, kept her in close and continuous contact with her family, though most of them lived seventy miles away. Her letters provide a clear if uninspiring picture of the ageing of a relatively wealthy woman with few evident public interests.

Her more eminent and longer-lived contemporary, Florence Nightingale (1820–1910) notoriously also was obsessed with her health, was voluntarily bed-ridden from her late thirties and constantly anticipated death, dealing with the world by correspondence; but in her case with a very public world, as she continued, from her bed, to shape modern nursing and associated areas of public policy. She also defined herself as old in her fifties, at the same time that she observed the decline of her very old parents; her previous antagonism to them diminished as they became enfeebled. She wrote to her father, perhaps revealing as much about herself as about her mother:

While my dear mother loses her memory (consciously, alas! to herself) she gains in everything else—in truth of view, in real memory of the phases of the past, in appreciation of her great blessings, in happiness, real content and cheerfulness—and in lovingness.

I am quite sure that, during the nearly half-century in which I have known her, I have never seen her anything like so good, so happy, so wise or so really true as she is now.[11]

When her father died in 1874 Nightingale claimed that she could not look after her mother herself, 'who ought to have someone to take charge of me', but expected her equally reluctant sister to take it on. Their mother was set up to live in her own household with a companion and servants until her death in 1880.[12]

In her seventies Nightingale complained more about her infirmities, but talked less of her impending death, as increasing numbers of her contemporaries died before her. She remained publicly active, while still housebound, taking up district nursing as the chief mission of her later life and she still made younger friends. But in her eighties she went into sad decline. By 1900 she could read and write only with difficulty. In 1902 a companion was engaged to help her. She received visitors for a few years more but was coached beforehand to converse with them. Her sight, hearing, and intellectual capacities gradually failed. In 1907 she was the first woman to receive the Order of Merit, in 1908 the second to gain the Freedom of the City of London, but it is unlikely that she was aware of either honour. In the end she conformed to the age-old image, and reality, of the saddest end to old age.

Beatrice Webb (1858–1943) was another affluent woman, born in the mid-nineteenth century, who was active in public life into very old age. Her diaries show her to have been much more resistant to ageing than Maria Jackson or

[11] M. Vicinus and B. Neegaard (eds.), *Ever Yours Florence Nightingale: Selected Letters* (London, 1989), 311.
[12] Ibid. 353–4.

Florence Nightingale. She came from a prosperous manufacturing family and married a man of lower middle-class origins, Sidney Webb, who became a Labour Party Cabinet minister and a peer. They had no children. Beatrice became a public figure only in her late forties, through her involvement with the Royal Commission on the Poor Laws.[13]

After the traumatic fall of the Labour government in 1931 she and Sidney, aged 73 and 74, retired to their country house. Not, however, to a restful, passive old age. She described their life in 1932. They were preparing to take their first trip to the Soviet Union:

You must not become a monomaniac about Russia, Sidney warned me. 'What does it matter what two "over-seventies" think, say or do, so long as they do not whine about getting old and go merrily on, hand in hand, to the end of the road?' I answer back. In spite of old age Sidney and I have had a delightful time since he left office and studies and thoughts about Russian Communism have added to the zest of our honeymoon companionship.

On their return Beatrice reported that she was tired,

And alas! I lack the self-discipline which I admire so much in the Communist teaching. Old age does not include the capacity for hygienic self-control. One is apt to indulge in another cigarette beyond the regulated number, in the cup of tea too early in the sleepless night.

They wrote a lengthy and successful book in praise of Soviet Communism.[14] In their way, they were still giving more to the community than they were receiving as they had done when they were younger. They asked in their introduction to the volume:

Why did two aged mortals, both nearing their ninth decade, undertake a work of such magnitude? We fear our presumption must be ascribed to the recklessness of old age. In our retirement, with daily bread secured, we had nothing to lose by the venture—not even our reputation, which will naturally stand or fall upon our entire output of the past half-century. On the other hand we had the world to gain—a new subject to investigate; a fresh circle of stimulating acquaintances with whom to discuss entirely new topics, and above all a daily joint occupation, in intimate companionship, to interest, amuse and even excite us in the last stage of life's journey. This world we have gained and enjoyed.[15]

In her diary Beatrice reflected on her own and Sidney's ageing, measuring their real lives against the expectations they and others had of the experience. She had unusual opportunities to discover how her ageing was perceived by others. On her 75th birthday in 1933 she recorded:

[13] What follows is drawn from N. and J. MacKenzie, *The Diary of Beatrice Webb*, vol. iv (London, 1986). The old age of Beatrice and her sisters is also well discussed in Barbara Caine, *Destined to be Wives: The Sisters of Beatrice Webb* (Oxford, 1986).

[14] Sidney and Beatrice Webb, *Soviet Communism: A New Civilization?* (London, 1935).

[15] Ibid. xii.

'Mrs. Webb retains to a remarkable degree her mental vigour and industry' observes the *Evening Standard*. Telegrams, greetings, newspapers ringing me up for interviews which I refuse. I don't feel mentally vigorous and industrious, but relatively to the senility usual at that age I suppose I am so. And Sidney certainly *is* so.

She suffered from an uncomfortable skin condition and from sleeplessness. She asked herself in 1933:

Ought one ever to attempt to cure the 'natural' ailments of old age? Is it not a case of sitting still and slowly curling up, accepting inaction of body and mind? Once the book on Russia is finished, I think I shall curl up into the inevitable senility, leaving Sidney to carry on.

Of course, she did not. Later in 1933 she reported:

Watching the milestones of departing strength. For the first two or three years of our life here—1924–6— the longest walk was eight miles or a little over; for the next five or six years, six to seven remained my limit. Yesterday I dared for the first time in six months the shorter round, which is five miles and was overtired in heart and muscle. Sidney can do more than I, but he claims he is tired at five or six miles.

A few months later she was more optimistic:

Still I have my eyesight and my hearing; I can go for a three or four mile walk; sort material, read and talk, listen to my wireless; above all I have the companionship of my beloved.

She observed her friends as they aged, commenting on Charlotte, wife of George Bernard Shaw in 1934, 'She maintains the rare quality in old age of a zest, an untiring zest for life'. An old friend, Betty Balfour, came to lunch:

As a woman verging on seventy she seems as charming to me as she was as a young one thirty years ago . . . she used to be good to look at—so she is at present as a somewhat withered flower; if the form is crippled and the movements infirm, there is the same charm of expression.

But a visit to an 84-year-old friend was saddening:

Louise is hopelessly crippled and creeps about the house. Her mind is clear and old age and helplessness have softened her outlook on the world . . . but she is desperately lonely and bored with existence . . . The plain truth is that the aged feel what their children and some of their friends are thinking about . . . 'If you are not enjoying life, why don't you die and be done with it.' And the old person may feel that there is no answer, except that he does not want to die or does not see any comfortable way of doing it.

Meanwhile Beatrice's youngest sister, Rosy, who as a young woman had been a highly problematic anorexic, at almost 70 was enjoying greater independence than ever in her life. She visited for a week:

between her voyage to the Arctic regions round about Spitzbergen and returning to Majorca for the winter . . . at seventy Rosy is happier and healthier than I have ever known her during her youth and prime of life . . . she has become a globe-trotter with a purpose—the enjoyment and picturing of nature and architecture . . . Her husband and children are more or less dependent upon her for subsidies and she certainly is generous with her limited income—travelling third-class or cheap tourist, staying at cheap lodgings . . . the secret of her happiness is her art, her freedom to go and do as she likes and make casual friends . . .

Weaker but still active, the Webbs carried on despite Beatrice's operations for kidney problems, and they still travelled abroad occasionally until in 1938 Sidney suffered a stroke from which he did not fully recover although he lived until 1947. Beatrice cared for him with the assistance of servants. She suffered increasing illness but not complete dependency, cared for by servants, as was normal at her social level. In April 1943 she died aged 85.

Beatrice Webb was an unusual woman in her fame and influence. Her diary conveys an explicit sense of struggling against, defining her own and Sidney's life against a stereotype of helpless dependency, triumphantly initially, though with diminishing success as they reached older age.

Her near contemporary, Selina Cooper (1864–1946) was an equally determined if more radical socialist, with a very different life. She worked half-time in a cotton mill at age 11, full-time at 13. Her mother, Jane Coombe, by the age of 55 was too crippled with rheumatism to continue her work as a dressmaker, but she still cared for her widowed 78-year-old mother-in-law, who had recently moved from Cornwall to live with them. By the time Jane Coombe reached 60 she was bedridden, though she continued to work at her sewing machine, which was fixed to her bed. Seventeen-year-old Selina, the youngest daughter, left the mill to care for her mother and grandmother, supported financially by her older brothers and by her earnings from taking in washing. A year later the older Mrs Coombe was dead and Selina and her mother moved to keep house for Selina's three unmarried brothers. Selina ran the household and continued to take in washing, while her mother sewed for the family until her death in 1889.

From her mid-thirties Selina Cooper was active in trade unionism, women's suffrage, and Labour politics. She married a trade unionist. In 1924 at the age of 60 she became a town councillor in Nelson, Lancashire, and one of the first female magistrates. Ten years later she joined a women's delegation to Nazi Germany and on her return was active in publicizing the plight of women prisoners there. She campaigned vigorously for peace and at the age of 77 was expelled from the Labour Party for her willingness to ally with Communists in opposition to fascism. This deeply distressed her, but did not stop her campaigning. By this time she could no longer climb stairs or travel easily, but she remained a figure of authority in the town of Nelson, still active and effective in politics and on the magistrates' bench and a compelling speaker, much in demand. 'When you saw Mrs Cooper coming,' said a member of the local Women's Section of the Labour Party, 'you thought, "Oh, there'll be some good discussion now." '[16] Large and imposing, she could appear formidable: 'Frightened was the wrong word, but', her great nephew admitted, 'you'd to behave yourself in her presence and you knew it.'[17] The local cinema was her chief relaxation. She exerted authority there also. Someone who was then a young boy in the audience later recalled:

She could keep us all in order . . . Anyroads, rough lads [would] shuffle us feet. That were it [She'd just give us one look] and if we didn't behave—'Percy!'—[the] chucker-out—'Percy! Quiet those boys.'[18]

The boys would fall quiet.

At the age of 76 Selina Cooper became chair of the local Board of Poor Law Guardians and was still a magistrate, but on her eightieth birthday she retired from public office. Her eyesight was poor and her health deteriorating; two years later she died. In her later years her unmarried daughter looked after her while working half-time in local government. She made up their income with poor relief; Selina Cooper was never rich.

POWERFUL OLD MEN

The ageing of the Liberal Party leader William Gladstone (1809–98), as with much else about his life, was in no way typical—with good reason he was popularly know as the 'Grand Old Man'. His diaries provide as clear, if not always so frank, an expression of his experience of ageing as those of Beatrice Webb. They give a rare reflection on the process of ageing by an exceptional man.

In 1875, at the age of 65, he retired from the Liberal leadership and announced his intention to give less time to politics. He 'prepared for the great business of unwinding the coil of life and establishing my freedom'. He did not look forward to mere leisure. He had always regarded politics as a secondary activity. He wanted freedom 'for growth, for my work, for the great duty and business of solemn recollection and preparation'.[19] The work was the salvation of the Church of England in part through theological and philosophical writing. Between 1875 and 1880 he wrote almost sixty substantial pamphlets, articles, and reviews, whilst remaining a Member of Parliament.[20] At this age:

He was fit spare and sprightly. A *bon viveur* in the sense of enjoying meal-time conversation, he ate and drank convivially but lightly; he did not smoke. His life-style in London and his regular walking and tree-felling at Hawarden kept him in excellent

---

[16] Jill Liddington, *The Life and Times of a Respectable Rebel: Selina Cooper, 1864–1946* (London, 1984), 427.
[17] Ibid.   [18] Ibid. 426.
[19] H. C. G. Matthew, *Gladstone 1875–1898* (Oxford, 1995), 1.   [20] Ibid. 44.

condition, as was shown by his ability even in his early eighties to undertake with-out preparation the most demanding Scottish mountain walks. . . . His voice retained its remarkable capacity to fill vast halls and to lash or cajole the Commons . . . He was a dapper 65 with the physical resilience of a 30 year old.[21]

His wife Catherine 'at sixty-four had the vigour and freshness of thirty-four'. They had a good relationship, despite William's obsession with 'rescuing' pros-titutes.[22] Their daughter Mary increasingly took over the management of the household as her parents aged, whilst acting as secretary and political assis-tant to her father.[23] Catherine Gladstone engaged in extensive charitable work and in caring for members of their extended families, as well as in manag-ing and supporting her husband's political campaigns. She opposed his retirement from politics and was relieved that it was short-lived. Concern about the 'Bulgarian Atrocities' drew him back. In 1880 at the age of 70 he again became Prime Minister, and also Chancellor of the Exchequer and Leader of the House of Commons—a heavy burden even for a much younger man. He expected this government to be short-lived, but it lasted five years. He set himself a series of deadlines for retirement, all of them deferred by urgent political events. In 1885 was he immersed in the Irish Home Rule crisis. After a brief break in 1885 he was to remain Prime Minister until 1894.

Gladstone remained conscious of the tension between public duty, 'the pro-longation of cares and burdens so much beyond my strength at any age', and 'the great work of penitential recollection'.[24] He reflected in his diary on his seventy-ninth birthday:

Congratulations came and gifts. Never until the great change hoped for in my life occurs can I on this great day have proper recollection or detachment. All I can see is that I am kept in my present life of contention because I have not in the sight of God earned my dismissal.[25]

In consequence, he refused to let politics take over his life, continuing to find time to reflect and to write on non-political matters. He read prolifically—novels as well as theology and politics—and he was a regular theatregoer. He could be a convivial, even boisterous, companion, dancing with his wife and singing at dinner parties—always aware of the impression he was making, per-haps engaged in 'a calculated attempt to keep age at bay'.[26] He managed both the experience and the public presentation of his advancing age with careful deliberation. He regularly reviewed the balance of his activities, dis-cussing it with family and friends. Between 1885 and his death he wrote six books, sixty-eight articles and book reviews, many of them substantial. He was none the less conscious of some failing of his powers, though they remained superior to those of many younger people. In the 1880s he limited his public

[21] Ibid. 2.   [22] Ibid. 69.   [23] See p. 300.   [24] Matthew, *Gladstone*, 78.
[25] H. C. G. Matthew, *The Gladstone Diaries*, xii: *1887–1891* (Oxford, 1991), 174.   [26] Ibid. 279.

appearances, but this had advantages. Like his age itself, distance enhanced his mystique and his status; he could present himself as above party, as a leader recalled to the public stage to settle great moral questions. He recognized that political crusades gave him much of his energy and he carefully marshalled his resources. For all his expressions of ambivalence about participation in politics, he was aware that it did much to keep him active.

Gladstone suffered bouts of illness, often directly related to the strains of office: poor eyesight, diarrhoea, lumbago, neuralgia, spells of insomnia, periods of voice loss. But he had great powers of recovery and even when ill could perform better in the Commons than many younger men. Staying at Balmoral, the Queen's residence in Scotland, in 1884, aged 75, he climbed Ben Macdhui, the highest point in the Grampians, a distance of twenty miles in seven hours and forty minutes 'with some effort'. He compared it with his previous ascent by a longer route in 1836 and noticed a change in his capacities. Nevertheless, he was fit enough when knocked down by a cab at age 79 to pursue it, though badly shaken, to apprehend the driver and stay with him until the arrival of the police, without revealing his identity.[27] He noted on his eightieth birthday;

My physical conservation is indeed noteworthy. In the senses of sight and hearing and in power of locomotion there is decline and memory is not quite consistent. But the trunk of the body is in all its ordinary vital operations, so far as I can see, what it was ten years back; it seems to be sustained and upheld for the accomplishment of a work.[28]

He is last known to have practised his pastime of tree-felling in 1891 at the age of 82.

Gladstone became Prime Minister for the fourth time in 1892. He was still a 'mesmeric' public speaker, not only on political platforms. He spoke on Homer at Eton and on medieval universities at Oxford.[29] But 'his body was failing faster than his mind, his physical system was maintained by will'.[30] Poor eyesight made him increasingly dependent upon secretaries; he suffered neuralgia, colds, flu; deafness brought his theatregoing to an end. He suffered short-term memory loss. He admitted to his diary: 'Frankly for the condition (*now*) of my senses, I am no longer fit for public life, though bidden to walk in it'. The 'bid' he believed was the call of God.[31] He did not accept decline easily. The Liberal politician and Gladstone's future biographer, John Morley, found him one day angry and almost incoherent:

He soon came to what was, I verily believe, the real root of his vehemence, anger and exultation. 'The fact is', he said, 'I'm rapidly travelling the road that leads to total blindness.'

---

[27] Matthew, *The Gladstone Diaries*, xii: *1887–1891*, 310 n.
[28] Ibid. 258.   [29] Ibid. 299.   [30] Ibid. 304–5.   [31] Ibid. 305.

This was perhaps the most painful thing about it—no piety, no noble resignation, but the resistance of a child or an animal to an incomprehensible and incredible torment. I never was more distressed. The scene was pure pain, neither redeemed nor elevated by any sense of majestic meekness before decrees that must be to him divine. Not the right end for a life of such power and long and sweeping triumph.[32]

But Gladstone could still work until the early hours of the morning and perform highly effectively in the Commons and in public. Until very near the end, his party showed no desire to dislodge him as leader. He was not perceived as too decrepit for the highest public office. But by 1894 he was in visible decline and he resigned. The following day he resumed work on his edition of the Works of Bishop Butler (published in 1896). But both he and his wife were failing fast, well cared for by a close family. He died in 1898, she in 1900.

William Beveridge (1879–1963) was another powerful, long-lived old man of a later generation. He was active in public affairs throughout his adult life, but became widely known only in 1942 at the age of 63, with the publication of his great report on Social Insurance.[33] After the war he chaired the development of two New Towns established by the Labour government, and from 1945 to 1950 he chaired an official committee on broadcasting. He was dismissed from his New Towns role in 1952 by the Conservative administration, formally because he was 'too old', in reality because he was an outspoken critic of the Minister of Housing Harold Macmillan, whom he tactlessly but characteristically described as a 'pompous ass' with 'no manners'.[34] Beveridge reflected: 'And he's quite right in one sense. I'm not too old to be Chairman. But I am too old and too distinguished to be subordinate to his third-rate officials.'[35]

He continued to be an active member of the House of Lords and he and his wife travelled extensively, lecturing on social welfare. In 1948 they went on a round-the-world tour. On board ship Beveridge, in his seventieth year, rose every morning before six and took a dip in the ship's pool before putting in two hours' work before breakfast. 'Even in the tropics he thought nothing of playing three or four strenuous games of deck tennis and entered for most of the organized games and sporting events.'[36] He overwhelmed his fellow-passengers with his 'amazing vitality' and relentlessly filled idle moments by organizing debates on world peace. This vitality lasted to his late seventies. Much of his time in old age was absorbed in writing books and making speeches on social policy.[37] Domestically, he and his wife shared household chores, apparently enjoyably in the strange, new, servantless world that followed the Second World War.

---

[32] Quoted ibid. 350.   [33] See pp. 364–8.
[34] José Harris, *William Beveridge: A Biography*, 2nd edn. (Oxford, 1997), 454.
[35] Ibid. 454.   [36] Ibid.   [37] Ibid. 457.

Beveridge became increasingly critical of the inadequacies of the post-war welfare state, which he had done so much to construct, especially, as he grew old himself, of the problems faced by many other older people. He thought the condition in which many of them were still living was 'a disgrace to civilization'.[38] He called for more adequate pensions to free them from the means-tested National Assistance and for more voluntary and state services such as home helps and home visiting. His physical and intellectual vigour began gradually to decline in his late seventies, though he still hungered after new ideas. He urged these on politicians, who took little notice; and worked away on his monumental history of prices over the centuries. Friends and then his wife died, leaving him very lonely. 'I am a busy and rather unhappy old man' he recorded in his diary in 1960. He was cared for by his secretary and spent much time in the homes of his stepchildren. He kept working to the end. His last audible words were: 'I have a thousand things to do'.[39]

These stories of later life suggest what can be retrieved about the experiences of older people between the mid-nineteenth and the mid-twentieth centuries from a variety of sources. They demonstrate the different ways in which people with wealth, status, or power could be recognized as old yet still command, and know themselves to command, authority, within the family and/or in public life. Their status was determined as much by their position of power as by their age, but they provided highly visible models of what old age could be, most of them offering challenges to easy stereotypes of its characteristics. Their lives also suggest how differently people of similar background could age and respond to their own ageing. The experiences of the great majority of older people—the less powerful—survive much more rarely. They are visible more often through the observations of others than in their own words.

POWERLESS OLD PEOPLE

Individual poor old people through the nineteenth and twentieth centuries were shown by social and medical investigators to live through old age as variously as the better off.[40] Henry Mayhew's classic *London Labour and the London Poor* (1861)[41] described older as he described younger people, with an eye to what he perceived of the variety of individual characteristics. His observations were originally written for a newspaper audience. The older people he met were mainly still active and striving to earn a living, though often very inadequately, such as the woman selling bootlaces who told him 'I just drag on, sir, half-starving on a few bootlaces rather than go into the workhouse'.

---

[38] Harris, *Beveridge*, 467.   [39] Ibid. 469–70.   [40] See Chs. 15, 21, 22.
[41] H. Mayhew, *London Labour and the London Poor* (1861–2; repr. New York and London, 1968).

Happier was 'an old woman who with the assistance of her son and daughters continued to live in a most praiseworthy and comfortable manner . . . in a large airy room on the first floor'.

By contrast, in a miserable attic he found:

a poor old woman resembling a bundle of rags and filth stretched on some dirty straw in the corner of the apartment. The place was bare . . . There was nothing in it except a couple of old tin kettles and a basket . . . To my astonishment I found this wretched creature to be, to a certain extent, a 'superior' woman; she could read and write well, spoke correctly, and appeared to have been a person of natural good sense, though broken up with age, want and infirmity.

She told the tragic story of her gradual decline through the illness and death of her husband and her children, until she was alone, struggling and failing to work to survive, refusing to fall to the indignity of poor relief. An 80-year-old was managing a little better, working as a crossing sweeper, 'though almost beyond labour, very deaf and rather feeble in all appearance, yet manages to go out every morning between four and five . . . She bears a strong character.' She also told a story of poverty following the death of her husband. Mayhew told these and other stories in tones of respect for the people he described, unless he believed them to be disreputable. They were certainly poor but they were visibly struggling for independent control of their own lives.

The private diaries of the clergyman Francis Kilvert, written over a decade later in a rural community, similarly convey a sense of widely shared respect for the great majority of the poor older people of his parish whom he frequently visited. Typically:

I went in and sat chatting with (Hannah Whitney) an hour, listening reverently to the words of wisdom which dropped from her. Hannah is a very wise woman, wise with mother wit, matured and broadened by the wisdom of age.[42]

Social observers in the twentieth century convey similar stories of the variety of the lives of poor old people.[43]

Most of these observers described individuals. Stereotyping of old people as a group was perhaps more evident when collective provision for them, such as state pensions, was discussed, when they were being considered as a group with similar needs. The long debate which preceded the introduction of old-age pensions in Britain in 1908 produced, as we have seen in previous chapters, a wide range of representations of old people as individuals and as a group. Though a minority of observers from higher social classes condemned all the aged poor as feckless failures who had not saved for the needs of old

[42] William Plomer (ed.), *Selections from the Diary of Rev. Francis Kilvert* (Harmondsworth, 1969), 20 Oct. 1870.

[43] P. Thompson, C. Itzin, and M. Abendstern, *I Don't Feel Old: Understanding the Experience of Later Life* (Oxford, 1990), 40 ff. P. Townsend and D. Wedderburn, *The Aged in the Welfare State* (London, 1965), 140–3.

age, more frequent was sympathy, especially for old women, who were the majority of the aged poor. It was recognized that greater female longevity left many of them in widowed poverty and that the limited work and low pay available to women made it almost impossible for them to earn a living or to save at any age. As a group they were treated with sympathy and some respect. Poor old women struggled hard for survival, suffering often greater poverty than men through no fault of their own. As one investigation put it:

A woman is more adaptable, more ready to turn her hand to any way of earning which presents itself; she is more useful also in the home of married children . . . she can keep her little home together and do for herself on a small income.[44]

A strikingly similar picture emerges from surveys throughout the early twentieth century: of 'active independent elderly women and passive dependent elderly men'.[45]

The campaign of the 1930s for a lower pensionable age for women[46] was based on the belief that older women were generally held in low regard and hence found it hard to find respectable paid work, in shops, factories, or offices, past around age 50. This episode suggests that in early twentieth-century England there was a certain bias against at least some older women, expressed in negative assessments of their competence and appearance. It is less clear whether this was stronger than before or simply more visible because by the 1930s more women were employed in a wider range of occupations of this type than before, especially in the white-collar sector.

The 'old age' with which the discourse of social welfare was concerned was active old age. The decrepit 'oldest-old' were recognized as a reality but as needing sheltered care, rather than pensions which were intended to assist active older people to lead an independent life, and as deserving care and sympathy rather than anything recognizable as 'respect'. How old age was perceived, represented, and experienced in the nineteenth and early twentieth centuries can be explored further by looking into the experiences and representations of older people of work, retirement, family life, and public welfare through this period of dramatic social change.

---

[44] Quoted in Jane Roebuck and and Jane Slaughter, 'Ladies and Pensioners: Stereotypes and Public Policy Affecting Old Women in England, 1880–1940', *Journal of Social History*, 13/1 (1979), 105–14.
[45] Ibid. 109.   [46] See pp. 284–6, 331–2.

14

Work and Retirement,
the 1830s to 1930s

Pensions enabled some older people, and forced others, to give up paid work earlier in life than might otherwise have been possible. The development of pensions, and of formalized pension ages have been described by some as aspects of a process of marginalizing and degrading older people in the twentieth century, as they were progressively excluded from paid work and the social status assumed to be associated with it.[1] We have seen that the degraded work into which many old people had been forced over many centuries was hardly status-enhancing. More prosperous older people whose paid work did confer status were generally powerful enough to resist encroachment upon that status by involuntary pensioned retirement.

WORK

Over centuries poor old people carried on paid work for as long as they were able, or as Joseph Arch, the agricultural trade unionist put it, they kept on 'toiling and moiling and scratching and contriving'[2] until late in life. Some better-off people chose also to keep working. Among many others, W. E. Gladstone became Prime Minister for the last time in 1892 at the age of 83. Octavia Hill was aged 69 in 1905 when she was appointed to the Royal Commission on the Poor Laws, of which she was an active member. She was among the founders of the National Trust two years later and until her death in 1912 fought as tirelessly to preserve the countryside as to promote her principles of philanthropy.

Old people engaged in an immense variety of paid work in the nineteenth and early twentieth centuries, as before. The Factory Inquiry Commission in 1833 interviewed a number of older female textile workers. They were generally positive about their work. A 62-year-old silk worker told them: 'I have worked in a factory 30 years. I have had my health very well. I get 6s. I am

---

[1] J. Macnicol, *The Politics of Retirement in Britain, 1878–1948* (Cambridge, 1998), 400. Alan Walker (ed.), *The New Generational Contract: Intergenerational Relations, Old Age and Welfare* (London, 1996).

[2] J. R. Fogerty, 'Growing Old in England, 1878–1949', Ph.D. thesis (Australian National University, Canberra, 1992), 55.

in no club. I am a widow. I have two children.'[3] Other factory workers were less sanguine. William Skelton, aged 72, told the Children's Employment Commission of 1843 that he had:

lived in the Potteries all my life and have been a potter sixty years . . . handling and pressing have been my chief employment; I have three children all potters; we work piece-work and do but little every day; I don't feel able at my time of life to do much; I get about eight shillings or nine shillings per week; my sons get different prices; some more, some less, all of them live with me. I have become a teetotaller for the past two years; wish I had now the money I have spent on drinking. I shouldn't be a handler then.[4]

Forty-nine-year-old Mary Walters was younger, but was clearly reaching the point at which she could no longer cope physically with her trade. She had been a lace-runner 'since she was a little bit of a thing' and appeared to be in poor health, but was unable to give up her tiny earnings. She worked generally from five in the morning to between nine and ten at night: 'she can't sit longer, because she is a poor creature now . . . her sight has suffered a great deal, that happens generally to runners . . . her eyes are getting worse'. She earned an average of two shillings and sixpence per week.[5]

As Henry Mayhew wandered about London in the 1850s he met 'an old woman who had . . . seen better days', reduced to keeping an oyster stall. Also an 'old couple' selling dry fruit who 'stand all the year round at the corner of a street running into a great city thoroughfare. They are supplied with their fruit, I am told, through the friendliness of a grocer who charges no profit and sometimes makes a sacrifice for their benefit.' Old men and women of all ages sold oranges at the doors of theatres every evening. Old women sold lavender alongside young girls going from door to door in the suburbs. Among the lowest of street sellers were the sellers of 'greenstuff', watercresses, chickweed, groundsel, plaintain, and turf required for cage birds. Looked down upon by the costers, they were mostly very old or very young; the old 'reduced' as a general rule 'from other avocations'. This trade required only a few halfpence stock money:

old men and women crippled by disease and accident who in their dread of a work-house life, linger on the few pence they earn by street selling . . . the men have been sometimes one thing and sometimes another, porter, seafarer . . . many a one has been a good mechanic in his younger days, only he's got too old for labour. The old women have, many of them been laundresses, only they can't now do the work you see and so they're glad to pick up a crust.[6]

---

[3] Factories Inquiry Commission, *First Report of the Central Board, Parliamentary Papers* (1833), vol. xx, C. 1. 23.

[4] *Children's Employment Commission, Parliamentary Papers* (1843), vol. xiv, appendix to the Second Report of the Commissioners, part 1, C. 15.   [5] Ibid., C. 39–40.

[6] Henry Mayhew, *London Labour and the London Poor* (1861–2; repr. New York and London, 1968), vol. i. 145–50.

Much 'work' provided for old people in mid-nineteenth-century London was a form of charitable giving designed to preserve their self-respect. A street seller of cutlery described how:

It is customary with many trades for the journeymen to buy such articles as they require in their business of those members of their craft who have become incapacitated for work, either by old age or some affliction. Mayhew commented that these sellers for example of needles and 'trimmings' to the tailors, were all either 'decayed' journeymen tailors, or their widows, aged sixty to seventy: these sellers are the most exemplary instances of men *driven* to the streets . . . and they are one and all distinguished by that horror of the workhouse . . . The journeymen treat them very kindly, the needle-sellers tell me and generally give them part of the provisions they have brought with them to the shop. If it was not for them the needle-sellers, I am assured, could hardly live at all.[7]

At the lowest level, street-selling of small articles—bootlaces, tracts, matches, kettle-holders, etc.—was little more than a respectable cover for begging, carried on 'partly to keep clear of the law and partly to evince a disposition to the public that they are willing to do something for their livelihood'.[8]

Old men could work longest in agriculture. As they aged further, this tapered off until it was available only at harvest, the time of peak demand for labour in the countryside. Then they were most likely to be employed unloading wagons or building ricks—a hazardous occupation for an elderly person and sometimes their last. In 1847 at least one aged man dislocated his neck in a fall from a wheat rick, and a 75-year-old in County Durham collapsed and died climbing back to work on a rick. Similar fatalities continued through the century.[9]

Old people might be kept working at a shadow of their previous employment, as a form of pension. A footman in a grand house in the 1870s described how:

The coachman who drove was old and tottering and his chief duty was looking on in the stables. He kept the old family coaches in good order though they were not now in use and filled up his time trout-fishing at which he was still an expert . . . He was too old for London so a town coachman was kept who knew London perfectly.[10]

Technological change might erode the occupations old people could cling on to, as among the ribbon weavers of Chilvers Coton.[11] It was widely believed, but remains unproven, that employers had less use for older workers in the larger scale, more mechanized, industry of the later nineteenth century, and

---

[7] Ibid. 339–42.   [8] Ibid. 363.

[9] David H. Morgan, 'The Place of Harvesters in Nineteenth-Century Village Life', in R. Samuel (ed.), *Village Life and Labour* (London, 1975), 33–4.

[10] John Burnett, *Useful Toil: Autobiographies of Working People from the 1820s to the 1920s* (London, 1974), 189.

[11] See pp. 296–8. J. Quadagno, *Aging in Early Industrial Society* (Cambridge, 1982), 65–93.

that the redundancy of older workers was exacerbated by the Workmen's Compensation Act of 1897 which made employers liable to compensate workers for accidents at work. Some employers at least believed older men to be at particular risk. A notice was posted by the general manager of the Barrow Steel works in 1898:

From this day forward please note that no men are to be engaged who are known to have any defects, such as the loss of a limb, defective sight or hearing. Further, no men to be engaged in any department who are older than 50 years of age. Any man already in the employ of the company in the excess of this age may be retained but in case of their leaving they are not to be re-engaged.[12]

Twentieth-century studies suggest that older workers are, in fact, less likely than younger ones to suffer accidents at work, due to their greater experience and caution.[13] Booth's 1892 survey reported another common view: that men, especially in towns, were physically feebler than in previous generations and found difficulty in obtaining work at earlier ages than before. This was perhaps an expression of the prevailing contemporary discourse of urban physical deterioration as a feature of late nineteenth-century life.[14]

The established pattern of declining pay and opportunities with advancing age may have accelerated in the later nineteenth century. A Fabian pamphlet in 1897 described how:

Wages of men from forty-five years upwards show a gradual and persistent decline. The roughest forms of labour are the first to suffer; but in skilled trades where deftness of handiwork is the first condition of efficiency and of continued employment, the attainment of fifty-five years of age is usually accompanied by a reduction of earnings. The Bradford weaver has to abandon one of his two looms as he advances in years; the Lancashire cotton-spinner and the head-piecer who has never become a spinner, have to seek for work in mills where the machinery is older and does not run so rapidly; the bricklayer is unable to lay as many bricks and the compositor to set as many ems; the seamstress's sight fails; the dock-labourer, rheumatic through exposure to the weather, finds his place occupied by more vigorous competitors from the country villages.[15]

But not all of these were occupations transformed by modern technology. We cannot be sure that such conditions indeed represented deterioration compared with the past; rather, long-established patterns may have been more closely observed in the many social surveys of the increasingly self-conscious culture of the later nineteenth century.

A survey of Married Women's Work undertaken for the Women's Industrial Council in 1909–10 examined change in women's employment as

---

[12] Quadagno, *Aging*, 139.
[13] *First Report of the National Advisory Committee on the Employment of Older Men and Women* (1953), Cmd. 8963.
[14] José Harris, *Private Lives, Public Spirit: A Social History of Britain, 1870–1914* (Oxford, 1993), 241–5.
[15] Quadagno, *Aging*, 154.

they aged. Twelve women were interviewed in a guano works in Newcastle, one of these:

a widow of sixty-six returned to work when her husband died twenty-nine years ago . . . She stayed indoors and mended bags. Her hours are from six in the morning to six at night and her wages were nine shillings a week, but they used to be ten. She had brought up a family of five and then lived with a married daughter in two rooms, which cost 3*s*. a week. She was rather deaf and rheumatic, but maintained herself and paid sixpence a week insurance.[16]

In Yorkshire woollen-weaving many married women worked, overwhelmingly, in order to augment low household earnings. One of these was a widow of 69:

She began work at the age of four selling tea-cakes from house to house; at eight began rag-picking and afterwards became a weaver . . . has worked regularly whenever she could get the work to do, until recently, when her health had broken down . . . [she had] . . . earned good wages, taking home as much as 34*s*. or 40*s*. . . . Her husband always sickly ceased work in 1886 and she had to work for both and meet the expense of a protracted illness. Her savings disappeared and when he died in 1891 she owed £12 for rent. She has paid off every penny of debt, but been unable to save anything. She went back recently to rag-picking at 10*s*. a week, in the hope of keeping off the Poor Law until she can claim her pension . . . In spite of all her troubles and hard work (she) has brought up a large family. She has had fifteen children of whom seven are living and 22 grandchildren.

It is touching to learn that this old lady, having been ill, was fearful she would not live long enough to draw her old age pension. Perhaps many a great soldier's pension has been less hardly earned.[17]

Some old women had less work experience than this, as Clara Collett perceived in east London for Booth's 1889 survey:

The unskilled workwoman at the bottom of the social scale finishes trousers; the unskilled workwoman at the top in the same neighbourhood finishes shirts. She is generally elderly if not aged, infirm, penniless and a widow; she never expected to have to work for a living, and when obliged to do so has recourse to the only work she ever learned to do. She is nervous and timid and takes work at whatever price it may be offered her; the price after all matters little to her; whether she gets five pence a dozen for finishing shirts given her by the first distributor or three pence a dozen from a fellow lodger who has taken home shirts, it is equally impossible for her to live on her earnings. . . . These shirt finishers nearly all receive allowances from relatives friends and charitable societies and many of them receive outdoor relief.[18]

Late nineteenth-century censuses indicated a higher density of older male workers in 'old' occupations, such as agriculture and fishing, than in new and

---

[16] Clementina Black, *Married Women's Work* (1915; repr. London, 1983), 198–9.
[17] Ibid. 149–50.
[18] C. Booth, *Life and Labour of the People* (London, 1889), i: *East Land on*, 410.

expanding ones such as clerical work or electrical engineering.[19] Up to the Second World War, older men continued to be most highly concentrated in the agricultural, clothing, labouring, sales, professional and managerial, and service categories; with the important exception of 'professional and managerial', all occupations characterized by low pay and weak worker organization. The proportion of older workers was relatively low in mining, chemicals, engineering, printing, and transport. These were well organized and highly paid manual working occupations, which also generally required skill and physical fitness.

The diverse category of 'general labourer' was disproportionately composed of old men, who shifted into casual labour later in life. Booth's 1892 survey and many others show old factory hands 'presented with a broom, shovel and wheelbarrow', old farmworkers employed at stone-breaking and roadwork, old artisans in repair work, old miners working at odd jobs at the pithead, old dressmakers on rough sewing work, and old servants at daily work and charring. But it was never an easy transition. An elderly engineer explained in the 1930s that having to turn to unskilled work 'tears you up in here . . . I lay awake nights and its a nightmare'.[20] Such work was not necessarily light. Many old men turned to casual dock labour. Mayhew observed of the heavily casualized London docks:

Those who are unable to live by the occupation to which they have been educated, can obtain a living there, without any previous training. Here we find men of every calling labouring at the docks. There are decayed and bankrupt butchers, master bakers, publicans, grocers, old soldiers, old sailors, Polish refugees, broken down gentlemen, discharged lawyers, clerks, almsmen, servants, thieves—indeed every-one who wants a loaf and is willing to work for it.[21]

In 1894 J. A. Spender reported that the inability of older dockers to carry out a whole day's work was so well known that other men would hang about waiting to take their places: 'knackerhunters' they were called.[22] In Southampton in 1931 dockers had an average age of 47 compared with 38 for all occupied males in the town. Two-thirds of all new applications for registration for the trade were over 40 and half were former seamen. It was hard, danger-ous work: 'there would always be ambulances standing by. Every day some of the casuals would collapse from hunger and exhaustion.'[23]

Agriculture declined as a major employer of labour in Britain, especially from the 1870s. The impact upon the employment of old people might have been greater had not younger people deserted the countryside as employment prospects contracted. The conditions of work for old people were not always enviable, at a time when elsewhere in the labour force hours and conditions

[19] Paul Johnson, 'The Employment and Retirement of Older Men in England and Wales, 1881–1981', *Economic History Review*, 47/1 (1994), 114.

[20] Fogerty, 'Growing Old', 26.　　[21] Quadagno, *Aging*, 155.

[22] J. A. Spender, *The State and Pensions in Old Age*, 2nd edn. (London, 1894), 40.

[23] Fogerty, 'Growing Old', 50.

were improving. A journalist described the life of an 80-year-old farmworker in 1891:

His day's work was eleven hours of hoeing, or nine hours with allowances for meals. And every winter the old man spends in the workhouse. 'And does he find any fault with the workhouse', I asked of the landlord . . . 'No, he don't find no fault. He takes it all quiet enough.'[24]

Old people could be employed well past their competence, as was bitterly recalled by a man who as a child had been dragged into bushes and sexually assaulted close by an aged playground attendant who was too deaf and short-sighted to notice.[25] Much of the paid work performed by people past their mid-sixties was marginal and casualized and its range was gradually shrinking through the late nineteenth and twentieth centuries. In the 1890s the overhaul of rural local government following the formation of county councils in 1888 led to pressure for greater efficiency in such matters as road-mending and the loss of this traditional old man's job.

In highly skilled crafts, in which skill was valued over speed, so long as eyesight remained adequate, workers could continue to late ages, especially where self-employment was the rule, though their incomes declined with age. Others took up new forms of self-employment. It was reported in 1895 that railway engine drivers and other particularly well-paid artisans often set themselves up in small business ventures. Other surveys showed that these almost as often failed.[26]

At the bottom layer of 'employment', at least up to the Second World War, the churches, as they had for centuries, offered small paid tasks such as pew-opening, bell-ringing, church-cleaning, looking after halls and meeting rooms. A mass of social surveys from the 1890s to the 1930s tell tales of old people struggling to earn a living. This had always been so. What changed in the later nineteenth century was the emergence of a widely expressed revulsion that old people should be forced to such straits in an increasingly prosperous society. Their employment was seen as a source of degradation rather than of status. This coexisted with the more gradual spread of technological change and of management demands for efficiency, which eventually replaced many such jobs. It came to be accepted conventionally that old people, like young children, should no longer be expected to toil for survival.

RETIREMENT

The 1881 census was the first to classify the 'retired' as a separate category rather than recording them by their previous occupation. This change may indicate the emergence of the 'retired' as a distinct social group, an expression

---

[24] Ibid.   [25] Ibid. 52.   [26] Ibid. 24–5.

of the growing accessibility of retirement to wider sections of the population. More immediately it was related to the change in the purpose of the census at this time, from a focus upon providing information about the effects of occupation upon health, to describing socio-economic structure as such.[27]

Retirement became a reality for more people, but slowly. Even after 1881 some older men recorded themselves in the census as 'occupied', even though they must have been functionally retired; 'general labourers' in their eighties or nineties were surely expressing aspiration rather than reality. Some were recorded as 'pensioners', for example, from the army, when they probably also held paid work. Others were recorded in occupations which plainly could not have yielded a subsistence income, such as 'pew-opening'; or had disabilities which suggest restricted capacity for the occupation recorded. A blind man aged 78 was recorded as a Thames waterman, an occupation which could be sub-contracted.[28] Fogerty persuasively suggests that 'retirement' was not a familiar concept among the late nineteenth-century working class. Poor people went on, as they had always done, hoping that they could earn, however advanced their ages and however remote the reality. By the 1920s the word and the concept of retirement were more firmly entrenched in the culture, and old men were more often described as 'retired', 'pensioner', or 'superannuated',[29] though still in 1935 the research and pressure group Political and Economic Planning commented that 'the term "gainfully occupied" must be interpreted with caution when applied to elderly persons . . . [many] are loath to admit that they are no longer "gainfully occupied" and continue to record themselves as such on the flimsiest pretext of paid work'.[30]

Changing perceptions of retirement should be located within the process of change in concepts of employment over the first half of the twentieth century. Successive governments, much influenced by Beveridge, guided largely successful attempts to decasualize the labour market in order to eliminate underemployment and low pay. People of working age came to be clearly divided into the fully employed and the wholly unemployed as intermediate, casual categories dwindled; similarly, they were to be demarcated from older people who were expected to 'retire' wholly from paid work. 'Retirement' entered everyday language alongside 'unemployment' and together with a new conception of the labour market.[31]

---

[27] M. Drake, 'The Census, 1801–1891', in E. A. Wrigley (ed.), *Nineteenth-Century Society* (Cambridge, 1972), 7–33. E. Higgs, 'The Tabulation of Occupations in the Nineteenth-Century Census with Special Reference to Domestic Servants', *Local Population Studies*, 28 (1982), 58–66.

[28] Fogerty, 'Growing Old', ch. 1.   [29] Ibid. 15.

[30] PEP Employment Group memorandum, 'A Retirement Policy for Industry', 21 Jan. 1935, quoted in Macnicol, *Politics of Retirement in Britain*, 250.

[31] José Harris, *Unemployment and Politics: A Study in English Social Policy, 1886–1914* (Oxford, 1972); and *William Beveridge: A Biography*, 2nd edn. (Oxford, 1997). G. A. Phillips and N. Whiteside, *Casual Labour: The Unemployment Question in the Port Transport Industry, 1880–1970* (Oxford, 1985). N. Whiteside, *Bad Times: Unemployment in British Social and Political History* (London, 1991).

But, we should be wary of assuming that census statistics give a full picture of change in older people's experience of paid work. Anyone declaring themselves in the census as 'retired' can be assumed not to be in full-time work, but not all part-time workers would declare themselves retired, and we cannot tell how many 'retired' workers in reality continued in how much part-time work. At best the census can indicate trends. In the census of 1891 about 65 per cent of men over age 65 were recorded as being in employment; in 1901, about 61 per cent; by 1911, 56 per cent; by 1931, 47.5 per cent.[32] Rates of women's retirement are still harder to assess. Their paid work, especially the casual work undertaken by many women, was inconsistently recorded in the census. That of 1901 attempted to estimate the numbers of women who declared themselves retired from an occupation, as distinct from those who were no longer working due to marriage. This revealed that at ages 55 to 64, 17 per cent of all females declared themselves to be in the labour force and 8.4 per cent declared themselves retired. At ages 65 to 74, 13.3 per cent were in the labour force and 28.14 per cent retired. Above age 75 the figures were 6.5 and 91.78 per cent respectively. Most older women who had a permanent occupation recorded in the census continued to work past age 65. They admitted to retirement at later ages than men.

Retirement trends were not noticeably affected by the introduction of the old-age pension in 1908. The effects of the reduction in the pensionable age from 70 to 65 in 1925[33] are difficult to assess because it was quickly followed by the high unemployment rates of the 1930s. The numbers reported as 'retired' rose in the 1930s, probably because older unemployed people had particular difficulty in re-entering employment.[34] It is hardly surprising that the small pension introduced in 1908 did not tempt those able to continue in full-time work; their earnings could scarcely have been lower than the five-shilling pension. However, the census statistics may not convey the real impact of the pension on old people, especially women engaged in the types of casual work unrecorded in the census. The pension may have enabled many of them to give up that portion of their 'income package' derived from struggling and sometime degrading casual work. A civil servant described the impact of the introduction of Supplementary Pensions in 1940 on:

two cases with invalid husbands where the pension had been supplemented by the wife's wages as a cleaner; in one of these a rather frail woman with asthma and a severe hernia had worked as a hotel cleaner up to the age of sixty-eight; in a third case a woman with severe heart trouble, once in good employment as a charge hand at Liberty's had struggled along as a cleaner up to the age of sixty-two, when the Doctor ordered her to give up and she obeyed because it did not now mean a resort to Public Assistance or to the charity of grudging relatives.[35]

[32] Johnson, 'Employment and Retirement', 116.   [33] See Ch. 16.
[34] Johnson, 'Employment and Retirement'. Leslie Hannah, *Inventing Retirement: The Development of Occupational Pensions in Britain* (Cambridge, 1986).   [35] Fogerty, 'Growing Old', 58–9.

It is entirely probable that the legislation of 1908 and 1925 had similar effects.

Census statistics do not support suspicions that men in their fifties were increasingly pushed out of the labour force in the later nineteenth century,[36] indeed the employment rates of men in their fifties increased somewhat over the thirty years from 1891. A major reason for the aggregate decline in the employment of men over 65 recorded in the censuses was the continuing decline in agricultural employment. In other sectors, the incidence of recorded male retirement was almost constant in Britain between 1881 and 1921; also non-agricultural sectors to some extent compensated for the decline in agricultural employment for older men by providing alternative job opportunities.[37] Conrad found no significant increase in recorded retirement of older men in industrial or service occupations in England and Wales, Germany, or France before the 1920s.[38]

Trade union evidence points in the same direction. For the skilled elite of the Amalgamated Society of Engineers the average age of superannuation *rose* from 61.5 in 1885 to 63.5 in 1907. Among the highly skilled printers the average age of superannuation was 68 in 1880.[39] However, trade union statistics should be treated with caution. Normally men were unable to claim superannuation benefit until they had paid contributions for a fixed number of years, often thirty; this caused some claims to be delayed. Also, the typographers discovered that some members found casual work more profitable than superannuation and claimed the pension only when this employment also dwindled.[40]

There was increased demand for the labour of older people during both world wars of the twentieth century. In both wars a number of old people sought to return to the labour force only to be forced out by ill health. The employment of older people continued at relatively high levels in the post-war boom of 1918–20.[41] Older men in the Depression which followed were not more likely to become unemployed than younger men in the same occupations, but they were less likely to be re-employed once they lost a job and they were more densely concentrated in the older industries, such as mining, which were hardest hit by unemployment, than in new more flourishing industries, such as motor-car manufacture. It is not clear that the difficulty experienced by older men in re-entering the labour market was new. In 1894 Booth commented that older workers 'may not actually be dismissed, but if any mishap breaks the thread of their employment, it is difficult for a man of fifty to make a fresh start, and even at forty-five it is, in some trades, not easy to do so'.[42]

---

[36] Most recently supported by Macnicol, *Politics of Retirement*, though he offers little convincing evidence.   [37] Johnson, 'Employment and Retirement', 116–17.

[38] Quoted in Elles Bulder, *The Social Economics of Old Age: Strategies to Maintain Income in Later Life in the Netherlands, 1880–1940* (Tinbergen, 1993), 31–2.

[39] Kazuko Fukasawa, 'Voluntary Provision for Old Age by Trade Unions in Britain before the Coming of the Welfare State', Ph.D. thesis (University of London, 1996).

[40] Ibid. 144 ff.   [41] Bulder, *Social Economics*, 88.

[42] Charles Booth, *The Aged Poor in England and Wales* (London, 1894), 321.

J. A. Spender wrote in 1895 of the 'pathetic blundering attempts' of men in their fifties to conceal their age. Older men bought hair dye or used domestic substitutes such as mixed soot and butter.[43]

Official unemployment statistics in the inter-war years excluded agriculture, and much female employment. Older people slipped out of the unemployment insurance records, as their entitlement expired, onto poor relief (renamed Public assistance in 1929) or to no recorded form of relief if they were married women or had working children in the household. In 1929, not an especially bad year for unemployment, over half of all Public Assistance recipients in Stepney (east London) were over 55.[44] The government tried to encourage employment of younger rather than older workers during the inter-war years. This was a reason for the lowering of the pensionable age to 65 in 1925.[45] Also in the 1930s more older people in the middle and lower middle classes could afford retirement, due to the spread of occupational pensions and other assets.[46]

Fogerty concludes convincingly that: 'For English workers, the significant change during this period was not in the age of retirement from substantial employment in a "career" or major lifetime occupation, but in the source of livelihood adopted *after* this event.' Increasingly the state pension substituted for the low-paid casual work at which for centuries old people had struggled to supplement their incomes.

OLDER WOMEN AND WORK

We have already seen that retirement of women from paid employment is even harder to trace than that of men. Retirement from women's unpaid work in the home certainly came late in life and gradually, though the distinction between paid and unpaid domestic work was less clear at the beginning of the twentieth century than it was later to become. Charles Booth explained in 1894:

It is in home-work, or house-work of some kind, either for those with whom they live, or for others who in return give them food or a little money, that the great majority of old women find employment. This employment is, as a source of maintenance, very closely connected with assistance from children, and is in its essence social rather than economic. It can scarcely be said to provide a living.[47]

---

[43] Fogerty, 'Growing Old', 41.

[44] Dudley Baines and Paul Johnson, 'The Labour Force Participation and Economic Well-Being of Older Men in London, 1929–31', *Working Papers in Economic History*, 37/97 (London School of Economics, 1997). For a similar picture in the United States see R. Ransom and R. Sutch, 'The Impact of Ageing on the Employment of Men in American Working-Class Communities at the End of the Nineteenth Century', in D. Kertzner and P. Laslett (eds.), *Ageing in the Past: Demography, Society and Old Age* (Berkeley, 1995), 301–27.

[45] See Ch. 16.   [46] See pp. 250–4.   [47] Booth, *Aged Poor*, 322.

Booth did not understand that he was observing part of the normal family and neighbourhood network of exchange on which the survival of the poor depended. The district nurse Margaret Loane commented in 1911 that very many older people would have been unable to maintain themselves without 'valid and recognized claims on the services of neighbours or relatives earned by former kindness or exertion'.[48]

There were growing signs after the First World War, however, that women in full-time paid work were likely to be dismissed on account of age at earlier ages than men, most notoriously from domestic service and the retail trades. In these occupations the Pilgrim Trust Survey of the unemployed noted in 1936 'a young appearance counts so heavily'. Censuses of the unemployed in Manchester in 1909 showed that women's chances of unemployment increased after age 35, and rose faster after 45 when their representation among the total unemployed was almost double that in the total workforce.[49] In 1937 the Parliamentary Secretary's Committee on the Older Unemployed reported that several London stores dismissed female employees over a certain age: in one store at 35.[50]

The extent of this enforced early retirement from certain occupations is hard to assess because women's unemployment, like women's work, was rarely adequately counted, or the causes analysed. F. Le Gros Clark estimated that of all working single women aged 45–54 in 1921, 18 per cent had left the workforce within ten years for reasons other than death or marriage, compared with 8 per cent of men in this age group.[51] In 1936 the Pilgrim Trust noted that older women in particular were liable to 'nervousness and diffidence' and to underrating their employability.[52] In 1939 the LCC opened an institution for 'able-bodied middle aged women' intended to 'foster their sense of usefulness . . . [and] recreate their self-confidence'.[53]

Women were employed in a wider range of paid occupations in the 1920s and 1930s than before. In 1935 'spinsters', as unmarried women were known, formed the National Spinsters' Pensions Association to demand state pensions at an earlier age than men—at 55—on the grounds that women became unable to earn a living at earlier ages.[54] They claimed that this had various causes: the poorer health of women, discrimination on the part of employers, or the fact that many unmarried women gave up employment in middle life to care for ageing parents. Such women were unable to re-enter paid employment after the parents' death and many 'dutiful daughters' were left destitute.

---

[48] Margaret Loane, *The Common Growth* (London, 1911), 104.

[49] S. J. Chapman and H. M. Hallsworth, *Unemployment: The Results of an Investigation made in Lancashire* (Manchester, 1909).   [50] Fogerty, 'Growing Old', 37.

[51] F. Le Gros Clark, *Women, Work and Age* (London, 1962), 78.

[52] The Pilgrim Trust, *Men Without Work* (Cambridge, 1938), 237.   [53] Ibid. 41, 42.

[54] Dulcie M. Groves, 'Women and Occupational Pensions, 1870–1983: An Exploratory Study', Ph.D. thesis (King's College, University of London, 1986).

The Association was founded in Bradford by Florence White, who operated a small confectionery business. It claimed many textile workers among
its 150,000, largely working- and lower-middle-class, members. It was strongly
supported by textile trade unions, though not by the TUC, which preferred
to aim for higher pensions for all men and women. The textile industry, which
traditionally employed large numbers of women, was hard-hit by unemployment. The campaign gained little support from professional women's organizations, who feared that an earlier pension age would further encourage
discrimination against women, especially in gaining promotion. White argued
that the need was greatest among working-class women, because they started
work earlier in life and were worn out at earlier ages.

The Association's claims were investigated by a Committee appointed by
Parliament which reported in 1938. It contained three women among its six
members. The evidence was mixed, but the committee commented that:

It is impossible to say in a general way that women, married or unmarried, are or
are not unfit for work at fifty-five. The answer must depend on the type of work and
the physical condition of the woman. It is probable that most women who have had
the necessary nourishment and leisure in their lives are still fit for work at fifty-five.
On the other hand we feel sure that many are unfit at that age because the conditions of their life have been too hard. In some occupations women are less fit to continue after the age of fifty-five than in others. Thus fifty-five is the normal retiring
age for nurses in voluntary pension schemes and that pension age has no doubt been
fixed at fifty-five because the work of a nurse makes larger and constant demands
upon all her energies.

If we consider industries in which both men and women are largely employed their
respective rates of unemployment are said by the Ministry of Labour to be usually
similar. They say that chances of getting back into employment after they have lost
it decrease for men and women as they get older. But they state that the rise in unemployment between 45 and 64 is somewhat more rapid amongst spinsters than
amongst men and it is more difficult for spinsters to regain employment.[55]

They concluded that it was more difficult still for widows and for married
women,[56] perhaps because a spinster had a stronger incentive to regain
employment than widows who received state pensions or married women who
had husbands to support them.[57] The Committee expressed greater concern
about the problem of women who were left pensionless and often in poverty
after caring for elderly parents or other relatives. A survey of eight hundred
unmarried women aged above 40 in Bradford, Blackburn, Huddersfield,
Bermondsey, and Manchester found that about 30 per cent in each area wholly
supported or contributed to the maintenance of relatives or other dependants;
40 per cent of these were the sole source of support. Official statistics, in particular the report of the Government Actuary, convinced the committee that

[55] Report of the Committee on Pensions for Unmarried Women (1939), Cmd. 5991, 33–4.
[56] Ibid. 65.   [57] Ibid. 36.

all women showed a marked deterioration in health from age 55,[58] also that age-specific death-rates at ages 45 to 65 showed slightly lower rates for unmarried than for married or widowed women.

The Committee feared that a pension at 55 would be treated as an old-age pension by employers and would increase the number of women forced into retirement.[59] It recognized that the statistics were unsatisfactory but concluded that 'on the whole' the spinsters' case for special treatment was 'not established' and that to concede it would provoke a furore among married women. The pensionable age was reduced to 60 for all women in 1940.[60]

CONCLUSION

Macnicol argues, but does not clearly demonstrate, that 'from the eighteen eighties onwards, workers were more steadily shaken out of a labour force that was becoming more technologically intensive and segmented into an increasingly specialized division of labour'.[61] He claims that this was the driving force behind the introduction of state pensions, and a prime causal agent altering the status of old people, which he assumes to have declined due to the loss of opportunities to work at late ages. There are few clear signs of a significant decline in the, very limited, opportunities of older people to obtain adequately paid, status-conferring labour before the 1920s, and the decline thereafter was due to rising unemployment rather than to any other cause. What may have begun to diminish, especially following the introduction of old-age pensions, were some of the pathetic or degrading ways of making a living, some little short of begging, into which old people had long been forced. They had conferred no status and any change to the social position of older people that might have resulted from their loss was beneficial rather than degrading.

---

[58] And indeed it is hard to believe that the health of unmarried working women could have been worse than that of many women who bore and raised children in the 1930s. See M. Spring-Rice, *Working Class Wives* (London, 1939; repr. 1981).

[59] *Committee on Pensions for Unmarried Women* (1939), Cmd. 5991, 66.

[60] See pp. 331–2.   [61] Macnicol, *Politics of Retirement*, 44–8.

15

'Kinship Does not Stop at the Front Door': Old People and their Families, the 1830s to 1930s

How important were families, alongside poor relief, pensions, and paid work in enabling older people to survive in the nineteenth and twentieth centuries? And what role did the generations play in each other's emotional as well as material lives? The richer variety of sources compared with earlier periods conveys a range of vivid images which merge into a clear if complex picture of family relationships.

LONDON IN THE 1850S

Henry Mayhew described the reciprocity between old people and their families among London labourers and the London poor in the 1850s. Among the costermongers he chose as representative of 'those who by having a regular trade and by prudent economy are enabled to live in comparative ease and plenty', the home of:

an old woman who with the assistance of her son and girls continued to live in a most praiseworthy and comfortable manner . . . the woman lived in a large airy room on the first floor . . . I found her laying out the savoury smelling dinner looking most temptingly clean . . . her sixteen year old daughter was there suffering from a cold and her son working as costermonger. With his help, the woman assured me she could live comfortably.[1]

An example of 'the third class of the very poor' was a 'close, small, smoke-filled room' of about nine square feet, with a hole in the roof letting in rain, which housed three women, 'an old dame about sixty, with long grisley hair spreading over her black shawl' and 'a pale faced girl of about eighteen lying on a straw mattress'. She had just been confined and the child had died. 'But we only pay ninepence a week rent', said the old woman, 'and mustn't grumble.' 'The parish, the old woman told me, allowed her 1s. a week and two

---

[1] Henry Mayhew, *London Labour and the London Poor* (1861–2; repr. New York and London, 1968), i. 47.

loaves . . . the neighbours helped her a good deal and often sent her part of their unsold greens—even if it was only the outer leaves of the cabbages, she was thankful for them. Her other girl—a big-bosomed wench . . . did all she could and so they lived on.' 'As long as she kept out of the big house', the workhouse, she would not complain.[2]

A fish seller 'lived with his mother, his wife and four children in one of the streets near Gray's Inn Lane'. They lived in two rooms, which were 'ragged and littered'. His average earnings were fifteen shillings a week throughout the year with the help of his wife, who would mind his stall sometimes while he went on a sales-round. He had had rheumatism the previous winter and had been unable to work and they had almost exhausted their savings. 'Nothing could tempt him to apply to the parish.'[3]

An old woman, who with her daughter kept a corner fruit stall in Marylebone as she had for thirty-eight years, gave an account of her life. Her married son had lost his job due to ill health. He and his wife had gone to the country to his wife's mother, but she

got her living by wooding and in other ways and couldn't help him and his wife, so he left and he's with me now. He has a job sometimes with a greengrocer at 6*d.* a day and a bit of grub. . . . I must shelter him. I couldn't turn him out. . . . out of 6*d.* a day, my poor son, he's only 27—wants a bit of baccy—a pint of beer.

He worried about his wife and little girl who had stayed with the wife's mother.

A rare complaint that a family did not help came from an 80-year-old female crossing sweeper who made no more than 'a few pence' a day:

At Christmas I get a few things—a gentleman gave me these boots I've got on and a ticket for a half-quartern loaf and a hundred of coals. . . . I've had eleven children. I'm grandmother to fifteen and a great-grandmother too. They won't give me a bit of bread though any of them. I've got four children living as far as I know, two abroad and two home here with families. I never go among them. It is not in my power to assist 'em, so I never go to distress 'em.[4]

RURAL OXFORDSHIRE IN THE 1880s

In the 1930s Flora Thompson published a memoir of her childhood in an Oxfordshire village in the 1880s[5] which is as perceptive as Gough's memoir of Myddle two hundred years earlier.[6] She described the lives of the major-ity of working people who did not receive poor relief:

There were three distinct types of home in the hamlet. Those of the old couples in comfortable circumstances, those of the married people with growing families, and

---

[2] Mayhew, *London Labour*, 47–8.   [3] Ibid. 71–2.   [4] Ibid.
[5] Flora Thompson, *Lark Rise* (Oxford, 1939).   [6] See pp. 132–3.

the few new homes which had recently been established. The old people who were not in comfortable circumstances had no homes at all worth mentioning, for as soon as they got past work, they had either to go to the workhouse or find accommodation in the already overcrowded cottages of their children. A father or mother could usually be squeezed in, but there was never room for both, so one child would take one parent and another the other, and even then, as they used to say, there was always the in-law to be dealt with. It was a common thing to hear ageing people say that they hoped God would be pleased to take them before they got past work and became a trouble to anybody.

But the homes of the more fortunate aged were the most attractive in the hamlet, and one of the most attractive of these was known as 'Old Sally's'. Never as 'Old Dick's' although Sally's husband, Dick, might have been seen at any hour of the day, digging and hoeing and watering and planting his garden. . . . Sally, though still strong and active, was over eighty . . . she was the dominating partner.

'Excepting the inn', theirs 'was the largest house in the village'. Thompson describes its comforts and the large garden:

A continual subject for speculation was as to how Dick and Sally managed to live so comfortably with no visible means of support beyond their garden and beehives and the few shillings their soldier sons might be supposed to send them, and Sally in her black silk on Sundays and Dick never without a few ha'pence for garden seeds or to fill his tobacco pouch.

Dick and Sally did not talk about their affairs. All that was known about them was that the house belonged to Sally, and that it had been built by her grandfather; but they came to confide in young 'Laura', who as she grew into her teens helped them with their business affairs. The old people had had little schooling and could barely read. Laura/Flora discovered that:

After Sally's mother died she became her father's right hand, indoors and out. When the old man became feeble, Dick used to come sometimes to do a bit of hard digging or to farm out the pigsties . . . When at a great age the father died, he left the house and furniture and his seventy-five pounds in the savings bank to Sally, for, by that time, both her brothers were married and needed no share. So Dick and Sally were married and lived there together for nearly sixty years. It had been a hard, frugal but happy life. For most of the time Dick had worked as a farm labourer while Sally saw to things about the home . . . But when Dick retired from wage-earning the seventy-five pounds was not only intact but added to. It had been their rule, Sally said, to save something every week, if only a penny or twopence, and the result of their hard work and self-denial was their present comfortable circumstances. 'But us couldn't've done it if us'd gone havin' a great tribe of childern' Sally would say, 'Took us all our time to bring up our two'.

They had their little capital reckoned up and allotted, they could manage on so much a year in addition to the earnings of their garden, fowls, beehives, and that much and no more was drawn every year from the bank.

'Reckon it'll about last our time', they used to say, and it did, although both lived well on into the eighties. This couple had worked hard and never earned much, but the inheritance and their disciplined frugality made the difference between real comfort in old age and poverty.

Less fortunate was Queenie, who:

lived in a tiny thatched cottage . . . She seemed very old to the children, for she was a little, wrinkled yellow-faced old woman in a sunbonnet; but she cannot have been nearly as old as Sally. Queenie and her husband were not in such comfortable circumstances as Sally and Dick; but . . . they managed to keep their home going. It was a pleasant home, though bare, for Queenie kept it spotless.

She also kept a hive of bees and sold the honey to a dealer once a year. 'Queenie's ideal of happiness was to have a pound a week coming in . . . [her] income fell short of even half that.' Her husband had retired from regular farm labour due to chronic rheumatism but still worked occasionally on the farm, though he had a reputation for idleness and a liking for drink. When he died, 'with parish relief and a little help here and there from her children and friends, Queenie managed to live'.

A bachelor, a retired soldier known as 'the Major', without relatives in the village, or, so far as was known, elsewhere, was better off at first:

All went well until he became old and feeble. Even then, for some years, he struggled on alone in his little home, for he had a small pension. Then he was ill and spent some weeks in Oxford Infirmary. Before he went there Laura's mother nursed him and helped him to get together the few necessities he had to take with him.

When he returned home he brought presents for all her family. Thereafter:

Mother made his bed and tidied his room, and Laura was sent with covered plates whenever there was anything special for dinner. But the Major was too old and ill to be able to live alone much longer, even with such help as the children's mother and other kind neighbours could give. The day came when the doctor called in the relieving officer. The old man was seriously ill; he had no relatives.

He had to go to the workhouse and was taken off without warning. When he realized where he was being taken he 'collapsed and cried like a child'. Six weeks later he died.

'Laura's' grandparents lived near by. Her grandfather had bought and sold eggs around the district until his carthorse died and he was forced to retire because he could not afford another.

He had given up smoking when he retired and they had to live on their tiny savings and the small allowance from a brother who had prospered as a coal-merchant. Perhaps what he felt most keenly of all was that he had to give up giving, for he loved to give.

Until he became bedridden with rheumatism he would bring his daughter's family most days:

a little basket of early raspberries or green peas, or a tight little bunch of sweet williams or moss rosebuds, or a baby rabbit . . . He would come indoors, and if anything in the house was broken he would mend it, or he would take a stocking out of his pocket and sit down and knit, and all the time he would talk in a kind, gentle voice to his daughter.

The couple just managed to survive independently. The old man was a good and popular fiddler, but when his wife was ill he had to sell the fiddle for five pounds. When he died his wife went to live with her eldest son.

Struggle though they did, these were the better-off old people of the village:

Then there were one or two poorer couples, just holding on to their homes, but in daily fear of the workhouse. The Poor Law authorities allowed old people past work a small weekly sum as outdoor relief; but it was not sufficient to live upon, and unless they had more than usually prosperous children to help support them, there came a time when the home had to be broken up. When, twenty years later the Old Age Pensions began, life was transformed for such aged cottagers.

Yet, as Rowntree also described,[7] if life was hard for old people, it was harder still for working people with young children. Thompson commented:

To go from the homes of the older people to those of the besieged generation was to step into another chapter of the hamlet's history. All the graces and luxuries of the older style of living had disappeared. They were poor people's houses, rich only in children, strong, healthy children . . . but in the meantime their parents had to give their all in order to feed and clothe them.[8]

Flora Thompson's account conveys much of the reality of the lives of old people who mostly did not appear in the Poor Law records, and the resources they put together for survival. Exchange with relatives and friends appears in all these stories as a taken-for-granted fact of life. Those without children, such as the Major, for all the help that neighbours gave, lacked the safety net of a family, and were more likely to end their lives in the workhouse.[9]

YORK IN 1899

Rowntree's survey of York in 1899 included among his 'typical' examples of survival on low incomes, a carter with a wife and two children, earning twenty shillings a week driving a lorry but still clearing his debts after a period of unemployment in the previous year. At that time his wife's brother 'was very kind to her and bought shoes for herself and the children, her mother gave her odd things and for the rest they got into debt'.[10] A labourer with five children aged between 2 and 11 lived on an income of about seventeen shillings and

---

[7] See p. 214.   [8] Thompson, *Lark Rise*, 75–102.

[9] Barry Reay, *Microhistories: Demography, Society and Culture in Rural England, 1800–1939* (Cambridge, 1996), gives a good picture of the importance of kin in providing assistance in times of difficulty in one area of rural England.

[10] B. Seebohm Rowntree, *Poverty: A Study of Town Life* (London, 1902), 272–4.

sixpence a week. Their food was 'very inadequate . . . especially so during the last period of nine months when Mrs R's mother was living with her'.[11] Another labourer with three children, aged 2½ to 8, an income of twenty-five shillings and suffering a 25 per cent protein deficiency according to Rowntree's calculations, 'now contributes to support of Mrs S's mother'.[12] Another labourer, earning twenty-one shillings, with four children under 6, in debt following several months' unemployment, survived because 'Mrs T's mother is very kind to her and helps her, and a brother living away from York sends her things now and again.'[13] In this as in other studies, reciprocity between the generations, mutual support in times of need, was as notable as the dependency of aged parents.

THE RURAL POOR IN 1912

A similar picture emerges from Rowntree's survey of the rural poor of 1912 undertaken with May Kendall. They visited an agricultural labourer in Oxfordshire who lived with his wife and four young children on about twelve shillings a week. Their relatives could not help, they 'have all they can do to help the mother . . .'.[14] Another Oxfordshire family with three young children had an income of about thirteen shillings a week:

her father, a hale old man of over seventy, with a fresh colour and a benignant expression, was sitting at the table finishing his meal. . . . the old man generally comes for dinner two or three times a week, as he has no-one at home to look after him and on these occasions he generally 'brings a bit of bacon' with him to replenish the larder—but not more than half a pound or a pound a week at the outside.

The diet of this family was judged to be 26 per cent deficient in protein.

The Knight family, of the North Riding of Yorkshire, were bringing up three young children on an irregular income rarely as high as fifteen shillings a week, 'if his father, himself only a working man with seventeen shillings a week did not give them a meal sometimes when nothing is coming in, they would have been little more than half starved many a time'.[15] Other relatives, 'though badly off themselves help to some extent with clothes and occasionally there is a cast-off coat from someone for whom he has worked'.[16] In many other families desperately poor older and younger people shared the little they had, more often in kind than in cash. Rowntree and Kendall concluded that:

It is difficult to realize the extent to which even families in which the breadwinner is earning a comparatively high wage are only enabled to keep up a respectable appearance by the gifts of richer people or relatives in a slightly better position.[17]

---

[11] Rowntree, *Poverty*, 311–12.   [12] Ibid. 326.   [13] Ibid. 32.
[14] B. Seebohm Rowntree and May Kendall, *How the Labourer Lives. A Study of the Rural Labour Problem* (London, 1912), 48–51.
[15] Ibid. 98.   [16] Ibid. 102–3.   [17] Ibid. 335.

MIDDLESBROUGH, 1907

In the early years of the twentieth century, Lady Florence Bell, the wife of a local manufacturer, explored working-class life in Middlesbrough, a heavy industrial town in north-eastern England[18] and produced a similar picture of the family lives of older people. She observed that old people in Middlesbrough stayed in the labour market for as long as they were able. When they could no longer work 'in nearly every case' they would be 'taken in and cared for by a younger relative'. Those quite alone would go into lodgings, applying for parish relief only as a last resort. But, observed Lady Bell, such occasions were rare, for most people had been married and had 'belongings' to look after them. She commented:

Over and over again one comes upon these joint households among the working homes. One finds a poor old man, whose declining strength is no longer equal to his work, living, if his wife is dead, with his married daughter or married son and looked after by them. Or, what is perhaps more likely to be a subversive element in the household, the mother, if she has been left a widow, and cannot work or make a living by taking in lodgers, is taken in by one of the family. Sometimes even the husband and wife are both taken in if the husband is alive too and cannot work. It is true that the result is not always all that can be desired; in many cases as might be expected there is friction, there are difficulties: the manners of the inmates to one another are often unspeakable . . . But even if their relations to one another may not be ideal, there is, at any rate, no attempt made to shirk these duties, and the younger people usually seem to take it for granted that elder kinsfolk left alone and unprovided for must be taken in and harboured. Indeed this claim of kinship is sometimes stretched to a surprising extent.

She described how an old Irishwoman turned up at the home of a distant younger kinswoman, whom she had not seen since the latter was a child. Finding herself alone, she had decided without warning to travel to live with these relatives. 'They appeared to have taken it as a matter of course and so far the arrangement seemed to be prospering.' The better off, commented Lady Bell, 'can never in their lives hope to approach to the hospitality with which, without hesitation, the poor will give up some of their scanty room and charge themselves with the entire burden of someone worse off than themselves.'

'On the whole', she claimed:

I think it more often happens than not that the tie between the old parents and the children is one of strong affection as well as of duty. One constantly finds on going into a cottage where the young wife is ill, or her children are ill, her mother managing the situation, the competent motherly old woman sitting by the fireside with one or more of the babies in her arms and seemingly steering the whole household.

[18] Lady Bell, *At the Works* (London 1907; repr. 1985).

Lady Bell described a society where family ties were close especially between mother and daughter, though different generations sharing a home occurred only in cases of extreme need.

THE CENSUS

The impressions of contemporaries about the family relationships of old people are reinforced by studies based on the decennial national censuses, which were carried out regularly from 1801. In the newly expanding textile town of Preston, Lancashire, between 1841 and 1861, the Poor Law was decidedly ungenerous.[19] There was a strong tendency for the generations to live together. Among poor migrants to a newly industrializing town where accommodation was scarce and costly, old people, especially women, could be helped and give help by caring for children whilst mothers worked in the textile mills. Only 17 per cent of widowers and 14 per cent of widows, aged 65 and above in Preston, had no known related person living in the same household.[20] Thirty-two per cent of those aged 65 or over lived with a married or widowed child, 36 per cent with unmarried children. About 67 per cent of those over 65 had at least one living child. Widowed old people were more likely than those whose partners were still alive to live with married children. Widowhood rather than old age itself led to the sharing of households. Almost all widowed people had no income or it was much reduced; some were infirm. Married or unmarried children might move back into the parental home when mother or father was widowed.[21]

In Preston and elsewhere, though not everywhere, three-generation households became more prevalent[22] during the nineteenth century. A common reason was economic need. Complex intergenerational relationships underlay the statistics. People in their sixties might still have teenage children living at home. Young couples often lived with parents early in marriage, before setting up their own household. In a district such as Preston where women could work more regularly and for better pay than in most parts of the country, the older generation could keep house and care for children. Over time the demands of space might require the younger family to move, but grandmaternal childcare could continue either from a separate household or by means of the older woman moving with the younger generation. At the end might come a period when the older person was wholly dependent, but this was by no means inevitable.

[19] M. Anderson, *Family Structure in Nineteenth-Century Lancashire* (Cambridge, 1971), 137–9.
[20] Ibid. 55.   [21] Ibid. 139.
[22] G. Fraser, 'The Household and Family Structure of Mid-Nineteenth Century Cardiff in Comparative Perspective', Ph.D. thesis (Cardiff, 1988). Alan Armstrong, *Stability and Change in an English County Town: A Social Study of York, 1801–51* (Cambridge, 1974). R. Wall, 'Regional and Temporal Variations in English Household Structure from 1650', in J. Hobcraft and P. Rees (eds.), *Regional and Demographic Development* (London, 1977), 89–116.

In Preston, even among the poorest, family support was far more important to the survival of older people than the exiguous poor relief system.[23]

Variations on the same story are told for other nineteenth-century communities. The Staffordshire Potteries was an older established industrial community by the 1840s than newly expanding Preston. It also provided secure work for women. The Poor Law played a minor role in the support of old people before as after the crusade against poor relief in the 1870s. The normal rate of out-relief in 1861 was only one shilling per week plus a loaf. However, Poor Law officials would assist families to care for old people, as would some charities, by providing relief in order to reinforce rather than substitute for family ties. Only 7 per cent of old people lived alone; 57 per cent lived with one or more children, either in their own household or those of an offspring, in similar shifting, reciprocal relationships to those in Preston. Few old people could not find a child or close relative to house them when they needed it.[24]

A similar picture emerges from a comparison of Bethnal Green in east London in 1851–71 with Wilmott and Young's famous study of the district in the 1950s. There were fewer three-generational households (5 per cent) than in Preston, but the need may have been less because accommodation was easier to find and relatives often lived in close proximity. Very few old people lived alone, compared with 25 per cent in the 1950s. A third of those over 60 lived with unmarried, slightly more with married, children, in the variety of arrangements found elsewhere.[25]

In all of these communities not only parents and offspring lived together, but grandparents shared homes with grandchildren who were orphaned or whose parents could not afford to keep them. In mid-nineteenth-century York, and surely not only there, older people adopted unrelated orphans, as they long had. Also, as in past generations, this may have been encouraged by Poor Law officials.[26] Older siblings, unrelated older people, or unrelated people of different generations shared households for mutual support.[27] Then as now,[28] those who had no close relatives available sought and often found substitutes. Marriage to a younger person, most often by an older man, continued to be a survival option.

People who were aged 50 or above in 1851 in the agricultural village of Colyton, Devon, over the following twenty years mostly shifted from being mainly carers for dependent children and grandchildren, through new, complex household arrangements as the widowed moved in with married children,

---

[23] Anderson, *Family Structure*, 142–3.

[24] Marguerite Dupree, *Family Structure in the Staffordshire Potteries, 1840–1880* (Oxford, 1995).

[25] Martin Clarke, 'Household and Family in Bethnal Green, 1851–71: The Effects of Social and Economic Change', Ph.D. thesis (Cambridge University, 1986). Fraser, 'Cardiff', describes a similar picture.   [26] See pp. 125–6.

[27] Rowntree, *Poverty: A Study of Town Life*, gives a number of examples.

[28] C. Jarvis, *Family and Friends in Old Age and the Implications for Informal Support: Evidence from the British Social Attitudes Survey of 1989*, Age Concern Institute of Gerontology, King's College (London, 1993), 20.

or married, unmarried, or widowed children joined parents. By the time they reached their seventies, almost two-thirds of parents were living with their children or, less frequently, with other relatives. An unmarried farmer brought in a nephew with his wife and children to live with him. Another married couple lived with a widowed relative, acting as housekeeper and farmhand. Nine people (17 per cent of those who survived into their seventies) had no family support. They were not necessarily neglected. One man had been born illegitimate and was partly deaf and dumb. In 1841 he was working as a manservant to a surgeon in Colyton. By 1851 his master had died but the master's son employed him in 'work about the garden etc.' In 1871 he was still living as an old man with his employer. In Colyton 'there can be no doubt that children and particularly daughters played a considerable part in caring for their elderly parents'. In Colyton, also, poor relief provided no more than residual back-up to family and other resources.[29]

Motives for all of these arrangements must have varied immensely, from affection, a sense of obligation or of pity, to economic calculation. But studies of these varied localities agree that relatives and to a lesser extent neighbours were essential for the survival of older, and very often also of younger, people.

ECONOMIC CHANGE AND FAMILY RELATIONSHIPS

The experience of Chilvers Coton near Nuneaton, Warwickshire, a small community dominated by cottage industry, between 1851 and 1901, suggests how economic change could influence family relationships. In 1851 most men worked in the coalmines and brickworks, while their wives, aged parents, and children wove silk ribbons at home. Fifty per cent of women over 70 and even 30 per cent in their eighties were employed, working at the less strenuous tasks such as bobbin-winding. At all ages almost as many women were in paid work as men.[30] Weaving declined and by 1901 only about 20 per cent of women of 65 were recorded as having any employment; among those aged 75 it had fallen to 10 per cent. Between 1851 and 1901 there was an increase from 20 to about 45 per cent of married and widowed older men and women living in their own homes with unmarried children. Work opportunities for young people were diminishing and marriage ages rose. However, these statistics may also mean that more ageing parents were keeping children at home, as their own work opportunities and incomes fell; or that more children were surviving to live with their parents as mortality rates fell. Probably all three changes were at work simultaneously.

---

[29] Jean Robin, 'Family Care of the Elderly in a 19th Century Devonshire Parish', *Ageing and Society*, 4/4 (1984), 505–516.

[30] Jill Quadagno, *Aging in Early Industrial Society* (Cambridge, 1982), 71.

Generally, adult sons and daughters did their best to look after ageing parents. Where older people lived with younger relatives the relationship was as often one of reciprocity as of dependency. In 1851, 18 per cent of people aged over 60[31] lived in three-generation households which they headed. In over two-thirds of such households the older generation was in paid work. Their childcare role was evidently minimal; their presence in the household had no significant influence upon whether or not a younger mother took paid work. In a typical household production unit, a 63-year-old coalminer and his 68-year-old wife, who worked as a silk winder, shared a home with their married daughter, who was a ribbon weaver and had an infant child; her husband worked as a labourer. The combined family income enabled all of them to survive. Half of the three-generation households containing children under 7 consisted of a parent and a single child, unmarried, separated, or widowed, plus grandchild. The economies of these households were often fragile, subsisting on the marginal labour of mother and daughter; for example, the household of 70-year-old ribbon-weaver Martha Capp, her 29-year-old unmarried daughter, also a ribbon weaver, and her 7-year-old granddaughter. Widowed men might also combine resources with offspring, most often a daughter. The decline of silk-weaving brought no substitute work for women and by 1901 there were almost no households consisting of older widowed women with single daughters and grandchildren.

Neither in 1851 nor in 1901 were there childless married couples living with parents. They apparently established independent households on marriage, but were often forced back into the parents' home when children were born and household costs rose. In his autobiography, the Coventry silk weaver Joseph Gutteridge described a period when he and his family were near starvation due to lack of work:

Notwithstanding the efforts made to conceal our poverty, it soon came to the knowledge of my wife's mother, who insisted upon our going to her house as soon as my wife could be safely removed and we were to stay until our circumstances brightened.[32]

But by 1901 there was a significant increase in the number of older men and women living in the households of their children and fewer taking children and other kin such as grandchildren into their own homes. This was presumably due to reduced opportunities for older people to be economically active enough to retain even nominal headship of a household. They were more dependent; with no clear role in an extended family household. Few mothers of young children were in paid employment and older people could contribute few earnings to the household. Between 1851 and 1901 the number of poor households taking in aged parents fell, the number of better-off households doing so rose.

---

[31] It is not always clear whether Quadagno is referring to over-60s or over-65s.   [32] Ibid. 85.

TABLE 15.1. *Occupation of head of household containing elderly relatives,*
Chilvers Coton, 1851–1901 (%)

Occupation of head	1851 (15)	1901 (19)
Prof. or manufacturer	0	19
White collar	0	31
Skilled trade	50	31
Farmer	14	0
Semi-skilled or unskilled	29	19
Weaver	7	0

Source: Quadagno, *Aging*, 88.

Table 15.1 describes the effects of the change in the economy of Chilvers Coton on household structure. The overall proportion of people over 60 living with relatives remained stable: 80 per cent in 1851, 84 per cent in 1901 but its social composition had changed. By 1901 more better-off families, and fewer poorer ones, shared their homes with ageing parents. Similarly in three Nottinghamshire villages between 1851 and 1881 old people did their best to remain independent until as late in life as possible, but with increasing difficulty as domestic framework knitting declined. Coalmining expanded, but that benefited some villages more than others and provided work for younger men and not for women or for older men. While framework knitting flourished women could run their own households until late in life. As it declined, they became more dependent and more likely to share households with relatives. Resources were pooled according to need and circumstances. As in Chilvers Coton, poor relief played a minor supplementary role in the survival of most poorer old people.[33]

'KINSHIP DOES NOT STOP AT THE FRONT DOOR'

Sharing a home is the form of family relationship which can be most readily assessed historically because it was systematically recorded in the censuses. As many of the above examples suggest, this does not mean that it was necessarily more important for everyday survival than relationships which are less easy to measure. As Michael Anderson puts it:

[33] Sonya O. Rose, 'The Varying Household Arrangements of the Elderly in Three English Villages: Nottinghamshire, 1851–1881', *Continuity and Change*, 3/1 (1988), 101–22. See also Elizabeth B. Wohniakowski, 'Family and Population Change in a Nineteenth Century English Village: Puddletown, 1851–71', Ph.D. thesis (Cornell, 1976).

kinship does not stop at the front door. There are few functions which can be performed by a co-residing kinsman which he cannot perform equally well if he instead lives next door or even up the street. Patterns of co-residence are easy to measure. Too much emphasis upon them however may lead to serious distortions in the analysis of family structure.[34]

In Preston, the Potteries, and Bethnal Green relatives made immense efforts to live close to each other, and older people received and gave a great deal of support whilst living in separate households.[35] Clarke concludes about nineteenth-century Bethnal Green:

the kinship system was still functioning at a fairly high level of efficiency despite the very low levels of co-residence and propinquity. The mere fact of sharing the same house or of living next door to one's relatives seems to have been largely incidental to the maintenance of kin-based links. There were certain expectations about the part to be paid by kin and, by and large, most people seemed to have acknowledged that this enjoined upon them certain obligations in respect of their own kin, although the scope for voluntaristic response still remained considerable.[36]

DUTIFUL DAUGHTERS

Such support was not confined to the poor. Many daughters in better-off families felt obliged to devote their lives to ageing parents. Even when the parents were well provided with servants, emotional as well as practical support from the daughter was expected. This was the experience of some prominent women. George Eliot was her father's housekeeper after the death of her mother and the marriage of her sister, from the ages of 17 to 30, between 1836 and 1849. She educated herself in her spare time and kept up a wide range of interests. Her published correspondence betrays no hint that caring for her 'dear father' was a burden, though letters between two of her friends in 1848 comment that she 'has the whole care and fatigue of nursing him night and day'. And, more revealingly, when he knew that he was dying that 'he takes opportunities now of saying kind things contrary to his wont. Poor girl it shows how rare they are by the gratitude with which she repeats the commonest expressions of kindness.'[37]

Harriet Martineau was recalled from her journalistic work in London to act as companion to her mother in Norwich in the 1830s. Charlotte Brontë resented the loneliness and frustration of her life in a remote village in the 1840s, caring for a cantankerous father, an anguish partly revealed in her novel *Shirley*. Rachel Macmillan was called from school when she was 18 to care for

[34] Anderson, *Family Structure*, 56–7.   [35] Ibid. 59–64. Dupree, *Potteries*, 100–45.
[36] Clarke, 'Bethnal Green', 212.
[37] Gordon S. Haight (ed.), *The George Eliot Letters*, i: *1836–1851* (Oxford, 1954), 272.

her sick grandmother. She did so willingly. It prevented her entering her career of social reform and labour politics for eleven years until 1888. It was, wrote the conservative feminist Frances Power Cobbe in 1881, the absolute obligation of daughters to care for their parents,[38] one expression of a broader sense of family obligation.

Less well-known was Sarah Acland, only daughter of Henry Wentworth Acland, first baronet, and Regius Professor of Medicine at Oxford. In 1878 her mother died and, still single, she became her father's dutiful daughter, housekeeper, and secretary—busy, unhappy, and treated with little affection by her father, for the following twenty-two years until his death when she was 60. The longevity of parents could make a crucial difference to the life of the daughter. By the time of his death Sarah felt old, in poor health, and that her life had no purpose. Her brothers gave her an allowance and, on the brink of her own old age, she found a new sense of purpose in philanthropic work.

Helen, daughter of William Ewart Gladstone, in 1882 became vice-principal of Newnham College Cambridge, while her younger sister Mary cared for the 'Grand Old People'. Mary was a capable manager with a passion for politics and enjoyed the task. Nevertheless Helen worried about whether she should stay so much away from home. In 1886 at the age of 30 Mary unexpectedly married and Helen, as the only unmarried daughter, inherited primary responsibility for their parents, despite the fact that they were extremely active and she had an absorbing occupation. She tried to respond unselfishly, but found this 'rather grim'. She made arrangements with Newnham 'for being a great deal at home'. She was then invited to become the first principal of Royal Holloway College. She agonized, circulating her friends to ask their views. Only Nora Sidgwick, her predecessor at Newnham, questioned the assumption that a single woman's primary obligation was to her parents. She refused the post as she later refused to become principal of Newnham, feeling obliged to make the sacrifice although she was far more effective and fulfilled at Newnham and did not enjoy political and social life. Helen Gladstone supported her father through the Home Rule crisis, the general elections of 1886–1892, and his final premiership, and both her parents through their last illnesses until her father died in 1898 and her mother in 1900. In 1901, aged 53, she became warden of the Women's University Settlement in Southwark and resumed her independent life.

Beatrice Webb, who cared for her father after his stroke in 1885 (when he was 68 and she 27), recorded in her diary both the pain of watching a parent fail and the constraints upon her own life. She had acted as the mistress of the household since her mother's death. Before her father's illness she was sanguine about this. Later she felt there was a problem of:

---

[38] Frances Power Cobbe, *The Duties of Women* (1881), quoted in Pat Jalland, *Women, Marriage and Politics, 1860–1914* (Oxford, 1986), 258.

how to reconcile the rival pulls on time and energy, on the one hand, of family affection backed up by the Victorian code of feminine domesticity and on the other . . .
an awakening desire for creative thought and literary expression.

She studied between five and eight a.m. leaving the rest of the day for domestic and social duties. By February 1886 she was almost suicidally depressed,
writing 'I struggle through each new day, waking with suicidal thoughts, trying to beat back Feeling into the narrow rut of Duty. Religion, Love and
Ambition have died.'[39] It was only with difficulty that she could escape her
responsibility for brief periods to continue her own pursuits:

two months here and resting and being the daughter in charge of the poor struggling dying father . . . it is horribly depressing and casts a gloom even over a happy
consciousness.   [27 Dec. 1891]

He died five days later. As Beatrice Webb and her eight sisters themselves
grew older they were important sources of emotional support for one another,
especially for those who had married unhappily or were widowed.[40] The three
husbands who outlived them remarried younger women.

'One spinster usually remained in each generation of the larger Victorian
families, suggesting that this was the consequence of parental pressure.'[41] Such
women are sometimes portrayed as sexually deprived and embittered. For the
great majority who did not go on to successful careers, their problem was at
least as much one of material deprivation and their greatest hardships came
late in life after the parent died, the greater the longer the period of caring. Their
lives convey how older people could control the lives of younger people, just as
they illustrate the devotion of the children and the strong customary obligation for daughters to provide care and companionship to ageing parents.

SERVANTS

As in earlier times an option for those who could afford it and had no family, or just preferred to live independently was to employ servants. A sample
of twenty-two census districts (urban and rural, north and south) between 1851
and 1911 revealed that servants were more likely to be employed in the households of widowed or single people than of two-generation nuclear families.
Servant-keeping was strongly influenced by family life-cycle and elderly spinsters, bachelors, and widowed people were frequent employers of servants.
For example in Hastings 16.8 per cent of all households were headed by
widowed people, but these were 22.6 per cent of servant-keeping households.

---

[39] Beatrice Webb, *My Apprenticeship* (Harmondsworth, 1938), xxix.
[40] B. Caine, *Destined to be Wives: The Sisters of Beatrice Webb* (Oxford, 1986), 192 ff.
[41] Jalland, *Women*, 253.

In poorer districts, the percentages were reversed, for example 15.5 and 13.3 in Coventry. The researchers commented:

> The role of many servants was not simply that of serving the 'classic' Victorian middle class family consisting of husband, wife and children. In many homes they must have undertaken numerous social and family-aid duties, caring for aged widows or one-parent families, who otherwise would have led a lonely or impossible life.[42]

OLD AGE AND 'INDEPENDENCE'

Describing the American experience in the nineteenth century Chudacoff and Hareven[43] stress 'the expectation of autonomy, both from adult children and from aging parents. While children were expected to marry and set up households, aging parents were also expected to maintain their independence by continuing to head their own households. This pull towards autonomy should not be misconstrued as an endorsement of solitary residence. Most people resided in family or surrogate family settings . . . these . . . norms imposed a double bind on older people and their children . . . in order to continue to maintain their autonomy in the face of exigencies caused by the loss of a spouse, older people had to rely on assistance from their children. Adult children on the other hand confronted the dilemma of having to help their parents just at the point when they were struggling to achieve autonomy. The timing of most transitions in and out of the household revolved around these interlocking—but often conflicting—expectations of autonomy both from the young and the old within the confines of nuclear residence.' This sums up also the English experience in the Victorian and Edwardian periods.[44]

THE IMPACT OF OLD-AGE PENSIONS: THE LOSS OF SONS IN THE GREAT WAR

Did the introduction of old-age pensions change this experience and 'crowd out' family support, as opponents warned and some still suggest? Evidence that, at least in the early years, pensions did not do so, emerged from the administration of First World War pensions. For the first time during the 'Great' War, the British state paid pensions to the dependants of men killed on active service. Initially they expected to pay pensions only to wives, but it soon became

---

[42] M. Ebury and B. Preston, ' Domestic Service in Late Victorian and Edwardian England, 1871–1914', *Geographical Papers* (University of Reading, 1980), 38.

[43] H. P. Chudacoff and T. Hareven, 'From the Empty Nest to Family Dissolution: Life Course Transitions into Old Age', *Journal of Family History* (Spring 1979), 69–83.

[44] See also Daniel Scott Smith, 'Life Course Norms and the Family Systems of Older Americans in 1900', *Journal of Family History* (Fall 1979), 285–98.

apparent that many servicemen had dependent parents and pensions were 'granted to parents . . . being incapable of self-support and in pecuniary need . . . the rate of pension was equal to the support given by the man prior to mobilization within the maximum of five shillings weekly (or ten shillings weekly if the parents had no other means)'. A gratuity only was granted to parents who were not incapacitated for work and judged not to be in need. This gratuity was the equivalent of one year's pay or one year's separation allowance if greater.

By 1917 it was apparent that these rules were causing hardship. The limit of the pension was raised to fifteen shillings and the gratuity was paid irrespective of incapacity for self-support or pecuniary need. The pension ceased to depend upon eligibility for separation allowance, provided that there had been bona fide dependence upon the serviceman. Pensions could also be paid to parents who had not been supported by a son before his enlistment, if he had been a student or an apprentice and unable to provide, on condition that the parent(s) were incapable of self-support, or if the father had died since the son's enlistment, leaving an impoverished widow. This arrangement was still insufficiently comprehensive and in September 1917 grants of up to fifteen shillings per week were allowed to 'all parents wholly or partly incapable of self-support through infirmity or age or in pecuniary need. The general idea of the scheme is to graduate the pension so that with any other income possessed by the parent the total means of support are raised a little above the point which is held to constitute need.' It was also decided that no pension to a parent should be less than three shillings and sixpence. Hence 'the parent of a soldier will never be allowed to fall into poverty through the disabling effects of age and infirmity'.[45]

Between 4 August 1914 and 31 March 1919, 221,692 pensions were paid to parents of servicemen, compared with 192,698 to widows. These figures exclude pensions to the widows and parents of officers.[46] The number of 'war-related' deaths of British males aged 16–60 between the beginning and end of the war was *c.*722,000.[47] These included many men whose families would not have been poor; army officers had higher casualty rates than men in the ranks. Wartime recruits to the services and consequently those at risk of death came disproportionately from the lower middle classes and above. Manual and casual workers were less likely to serve either because they worked in occupations essential for the war effort or were physically unfit.[48] Nevertheless very large numbers of working men served. The pension statistics suggest that a very high proportion of lower income men who served and died and had living parents were financial supporters of their parents, even after the introduction of the old-age pensions.

[45] *First Annual Report*, Ministry of Pensions, *Parliamentary Papers*, vol. xxvi (1919).
[46] *Second Annual Report*, Ministry of Pensions, *Parliamentary Papers*, vol. xxii (1920).
[47] Jay Winter, *The Great War and the British People* (Basingstoke, 1985), 68 ff.   [48] Ibid.

BETWEEN THE WARS

The largest social survey of the inter-war years was the New Survey of London, which tried in 1929–31 to replicate Booth's great survey of London in the 1890s in order to establish whether poverty had diminished. The New Survey investigated 26,915 working-class households. Almost one-third of people over 65 in the sample lived alone; almost 50 per cent of those over 80. In both age groups a majority were women. The change in household structure with increasing age was due to the move from the household of the last unmarried child and/or the death of the spouse. Fewer widows than in the nineteenth-century studies moved to the homes of offspring. Fewer than one-fifth of over-eighties lived in extended or multiple family units. About 32 per cent of all over 65 did live with children but the proportion fell with age, again in contrast with earlier periods.[49] This compares with 33 per cent of older people sharing households with children in Great Britain in 1961 and 15 per cent in 1981. These figures suggest a decisive shift in the propensity of the generations to share a household following the First World War. This is likely to have been due not to increasing neglect of older people by their relatives, but to the greater capacity of older people to retain an independent household, not necessarily in comfort, probably due to the increasing purchasing power of the pension.[50] The New Survey stressed the resistance of old people to living with married children; even some of those who did so ate separately from their children in order to preserve a semblance of independence.

The survey found that the main source of income for older men was employment, though this declined with advancing age, and for women, it was state benefits (mainly the pension). Few claimed to receive cash income from relatives, though more who were over than under age 75 did so, and more women than men. The amounts were small, the mean sum being less than one shilling per week. We do not know how much might have been transferred in goods or services.[51]

An important, regionalized, problem in the 1920s and 1930s was unemployment. There were some attempts to assess the effect of this upon the relations between generations. When Rowntree surveyed York for a second time in 1936,[52] he described a man of 74 and his 66-year-old wife, both old-age pensioners, living with a 15-year-old youth who had just started work at a factory and a 19-year-old male printer's assistant. No indication was given of

---

[49] See pp. 294–8.   [50] See pp. 327–30.

[51] H. Llewellyn-Smith, *New Survey of London Life and Labour* (London, 1930–5), 9 vols. D. Baines and P. Johnson, 'The Labour Force Participation and Economic Well-Being of Older men in London, 1929–31', *Working Papers in Economic History*, 37/97 (London School of Economics, 1997).

[52] What follows is drawn from B. Seebohm Rowntree, *Poverty and Progress: A Second Social Survey of York* (London, 1941), esp. 66–74.

their relationships. The investigator remarked: 'fairly clean and comfortable. Apparently no hardship.' A 65-year-old man and his 73-year-old wife were also pensioners living with a 38-year-old son who was a 'relief porter (temporary)'. It was remarked:

Front room re-let at 4*s*. 6*d*. per week. Son has been unemployed for five years and was only allowed 12*s*. 6*d*. per week transitional benefit. Would like a house with a smaller rent. In poverty.

Rowntree found that 14 per cent of all in poverty in York were 65 and above, compared with 29.6 per cent whose poverty was due to the unemployment of the chief wage-earner, and 32.8 per cent due to the inadequate wages of workers in regular employment.

Four hundred and forty-nine of the old people in the York survey were dependent entirely on their pensions. Of five hundred and sixty-one possessing other sources of income, twenty-two admitted to help from relatives, of an average of five to six shillings per week, while thirty-nine had some earnings. Two hundred and forty-nine old people received Public Assistance (the successor to poor relief after 1929). 'Wherever possible the [Public Assistance] Committee seeks to collect from relatives the amount granted in relief to old people and we came across a number of cases where the pensioners refrained from applying for Public Assistance because of this. They told the investigators that if their children would not voluntarily help them they would "rather starve than force them to do so by applying for out-relief".'

Sometimes pensioners pooled resources, though the result was still 'deficiency' in health and living standards. In a house with three bedrooms lived a widow of 78, her 73-year-old nephew, and a friend aged 89. All received the pension and the man had 2*s*. 9*d*. per week from his former employer: 'Deficiency 1*s*. 10*d*.' In another house lived:

Man aged seventy-two, wife fifty-nine and man's sister aged eighty-four. The man has ten shillings old age pension and fourteen shillings army pension. His sister who has just come to live here has 10*s*. old age pension. Deficiency 1*s*. 10*d*.

Another man of 69 and his 65-year-old wife lived with the wife's 44-year-old sister:

Income consists of two State old age pensions of ten shillings, a pension of ten shillings from the man's former employer and five shillings rent for a room let to an unemployed man. The wife's sister is unable to work and has no income. The house is very damp and is over-run with blackbeetles. . . . Deficiency four shillings per head.

A spinster of 59 was deaf and could not work:

Has father aged eighty living with her, who pays twenty shillings weekly out of his pension of twenty-four. Another spinster aged fifty-seven (a life-long friend) lives with her. She is in poor health but manages to earn a little by cleaning. She pays twelve shillings for her keep. Deficiency 2*s*. 11*d*. per head.

The proportion of the population of York aged 65 or over had risen from 4.65 per cent to 7.35 per cent since Rowntree's previous survey in 1899. Rowntree observed that in 1899 a person too old to work and with no other sources of income 'had as a rule to choose between two alternatives—either to live, often as an unwanted guest, with a married son or daughter, or to go into the work-house'. By 1936 such people could manage to live independently, though often in primary poverty, on their pensions, often supplemented by public assistance or from some other source including small sums of cash or services from relatives:

A few for instance keep a lodger, others earn a few pence or are paid in kind for rendering small services. To 'mind the baby' for a neighbour when the mother is out, or to wheel one in a pram on washing day and do any necessary errand, will probably mean a square meal or 'a mash of tea' and some coppers, as well as dis-carded garments, if the neighbour's husband is in good work.

The proportion of the population of York in primary poverty had fallen from 15.46 per cent in 1899 to 6.8 per cent in 1936 but old people were more prominent among them. In Class C, those living 'just above the minimum', 1,516 people in households whose head was 'too old to work' had total incomes of £1,125. 9s. 4d. Of this amount, £55. 18s. 7d. came from the earnings of the head of the household; £417. 7s. 3d. from 'payments for board and lodg-ings from supplementary earners'; £402. 5s. from state pensions; £14. 13s. from Public Assistance; £164. 16s. 1d. in pensions from employers; £5. 15s. 2d. in 'help from relatives'.

Though 31.1 per cent of the York working-class population were 'in poverty' , this was true of 47.5 per cent of those over 65; children under one year contributed 52.5 per cent and those aged 1 to 4 years 49.7 per cent. The severest poverty was most extensive among those aged 65 and over. The lowest proportion of poverty was among those aged 45 to 64 (20.7 per cent). It was still the case that larger numbers of young children than of old people experienced poverty. Rowntree estimated that about 1,700 pensioners lived with families better off than the strictly poor households under investigation, so that only about 33 per cent of all pensioners in York lived below the poverty line, compared with 52.5 per cent of all working-class children under the age of one, 47 per cent aged five years and under, and 31.5 per cent aged 10 years and under. Overall, Rowntree concluded, conditions had improved and fewer people were in the worst primary poverty than in 1899.

THE SECOND WORLD WAR

During the Second World War pensions were paid to the dependent parents of servicemen on terms which became more flexible than in the previous war, enabling 'the utmost weight to be given to any support to his parents which the dead son gave or might have given'.[53] The standard pension was twenty shillings for one parent, 27s. 6d. for two; in exceptional cases the maximum rates were 27s. 6d. and forty shillings. In this war many fewer such payments were made and more were paid to widows (97,902 by 31 March 1948) than to parents (53,897) in a war which was less lethal to servicemen than the last.[54] This further suggests that although a significant number of parents were dependent upon their sons, by 1939 the proportion was fewer than twenty years earlier; more old people could now achieve a degree of independence.

There is no evidence that the introduction of state pensions diminished family support for old people except in so far as it relieved some young people of the strain of stretching inadequate resources to keep a parent from the workhouse, and relieved some members of both generations of the stress of unwanted co-habitation. The pension may have facilitated more flexible, less emotionally stressed relations between generations.[55]

[53] *Twenty-Third Annual Report*, Ministry of Pensions (1 Sept. 1939–31 Mar. 1948).   [54] Ibid.
[55] For evidence of the contribution of families to the welfare of old people in other countries see: Christoph Conrad, 'Mixed Incomes for the Elderly Poor in Germany, 1880–1930', in Michael B. Katz and Christoph Sachsse (eds.), *The Mixed Economy of Social Welfare: Public/Private Relations in England, Germany and the US, 1870s–1930s* (Baden-Baden, 1996), 340–68. Elles Bulder, *The Social Economics of Old Age. Strategies to Maintain Income in Later Life in the Netherlands, 1880–1940* (Tinbergen Institute, 1993).

16

Pensions and Pensioners in War and Depression

The state pension, low and means-tested though it was, gave a regular and secure income to a higher proportion of old people than the poor relief system had ever done. It rescued some of them from painful and degrading labour, enabled more of them to keep independent households, and assisted families to support ageing relatives. It even stimulated saving among older people. What kind of lives did the new old-age pensioners live?

THE FIRST WORLD WAR

The first pensions were paid only five years before the outbreak of the First World War. The declaration of war was followed almost immediately by a rapid rise in prices, especially of essential foodstuffs, and, in many cities, of rents. This inflation hit especially hard those with low fixed incomes such as pensioners.[1] The cost of bacon, the only meat consumed by the poorest pensioners, rose by threepence to fourpence per pound in the first year of war. Some pensioners managed to re-enter the labour force as demand for labour rose after the first year of war. How many did so is unknown. Others benefited from the higher incomes of their families due to the unprecedented full employment of the war period; or, eventually, from separation allowances and pensions if they were supported by a son in the services.[2]

During the war civilian death-rates fell, due mainly to improved living standards. Among people of 65 and over they rose overall, especially in the first two years of war, having fallen between 1900 and 1914.[3] However, the death-rates of older people continued to fall in some poorer districts of London, such as Bethnal Green, Deptford, and Woolwich, though not in others, such as Stepney; and they rose, especially among women, in some more prosperous

---

[1] This was the conclusion of the *Report of the Committee Appointed by the Board of Trade to Investigate the Principal Causes which have led to the Increase of Prices of Commodities since the Beginning of the War*, Cd. 8398, *Parliamentary Papers* (1916), vol. xviii, para. 5.   [2] See pp. 302–3.
[3] J. M. Winter, *The Great War and the British People* (Basingstoke, 1985), 177 ff.; and 'Surviving the War: Life Expectation, Illness and Mortality Rates in Paris, London and Berlin, 1914–1919', in Jay Winter and J.-L. Robert (eds.), *Capital Cities at War: London, Paris, Berlin, 1914–1919* (Cambridge, 1997), 510–16.

districts, such as Paddington and Westminster. This may suggest that some at least of the poorest were sharing the general gain in working-class living standards, but that those with previously higher but fixed incomes from pensions, savings, or rent (a frequent source of income for better-off older people which was restricted by the introduction of rent controls in 1915), but lacking family assistance, were especially vulnerable to price rises. Also, old people in all classes were susceptible to the stress of bereavement or the absence of relatives at war. They were to suffer less than younger people from the post-war influenza epidemic, which was not evidently related to poverty.[4]

During the war, some old people transferred from the pension to poor relief, which in general increased in line with inflation as the pension did not. However, the total numbers of people above age 70 receiving outdoor relief fell from 8,900 in 1914 to 6,900 in 1919.[5] As some came onto poor relief, others left it. The indoor relief figures fell from 48,100 to 36,300, partly because some old people were decanted from institutions to make way for war casualties. The overall picture of the wartime living standards of old people is best interpreted as a modified version of that of the mass of the working-class population; for most people living standards improved, but those who did not share in the gains were relatively worse off. During the war fewer people than before were poor, but they were relatively poorer than before. The number of pensioners fell slightly from 948,443 in 1915 to 943,077 in March 1918, perhaps another indication that some old people shared the general improvement in living standards.

The government faced pressure to raise the pension to provide for inflation. Its first response, in April 1915, was a less costly concession: for existing pensioners only, earnings of up to thirty shillings a week were allowed without loss of pension, and support from family and friends was not to be assessed for the duration of the war. By January 1918 4,000 pensioners admitted to the relatively high earnings of thirty shillings. No concessions were made to new applicants for the pension, or to those just above the qualifying income limit, some of whom must have suffered serious hardship.

Pressure for further improvements was led by the Labour movement. This was part of a wider Labour campaign against the effects of inflation, which included demands for rent controls[6] and improved separation allowances and war pensions.[7] From July 1916 the pensioners' case was spearheaded by a new 'National Conference (of representatives of the National Free Church Council,

---

[4] Winter, *Great War*, 121. [5] K. Williams, *From Pauperism to Poverty* (London, 1981), 307.

[6] J. Melling, 'Clydeside Housing and the Evolution of State Rent Controls', in J. Melling (ed.), *Housing, Social Policy and the State* (London, 1980), 139–68.

[7] Gill Thomas, 'State Maintenance for Women during the First World War: The Case of Separation Allowances and Pensions', D.Phil. thesis (Sussex University, 1989). P. M. Williams (Thane), 'The Development of Old Age Pensions in the UK, 1878–1925', Ph.D. thesis (London School of Economics, 1970), 321–2. This thesis is much plundered by J. Macnicol, *The Politics of Retirement in Britain, 1878–1948* (Cambridge, 1998).

Friendly Societies, Trade Unions, Associated Federation of Councils etc.) on Old Age Pensions' (hereafter NCOAP). Its supporters included forty-seven members of parliament of all parties.[8] Under the slogan 'Do something and do it now' it campaigned for an increase in the pension of at least 2*s.* 6*d.* per week and the abolition of the means test.[9] Supporters also engaged in voluntary visiting and care of pensioners. Shortly afterwards the government announced an additional grant of up to 2*s.* 6*d.* per week to pensioners 'suffering special hardship from the high price of food and other economic conditions arising from the war'.[10] It was available only to those on maximum pension and pension committees were to establish 'special hardship' by reference to 'the general standard of living in the neighbourhood'.[11] By March 1917 511,263 pensioners, from a total of 947,780 were receiving the allowance.[12]

The concession did not silence the demand for a permanent increase in the pension, particularly since it was accompanied by the third increase since 1914 in levels of service dependants' allowance, which was an admission of the increased cost of living. Many but not all old people benefited from these enhanced allowances. The new coalition government led by Lloyd George, which ousted Asquith in December 1916, resisted. 'It would be almost impossible to take back when the war is over' stated the new, Conservative, Chancellor of the Exchequer, Andrew Bonar Law[13] to a deputation from the miners union. The NCOAP continued its campaign of demonstrations and deputations to ministers. In August 1917 the government conceded a general increase of 2*s.* 6*d.* for all receiving the maximum pension.[14] In March 1918 93.4 per cent of all pensioners received 7*s.* 6*d.* per week.[15] Nevertheless a pension which had been designed to be inadequate for subsistence in 1908 was still less adequate by 1918.

Pressure continued after the war for an overhaul of the level and the administration of pensions. The government again resisted, but events in 1918 enforced reconsideration, in particular the decision to abolish the Local Government Board (LGB) and replace it with a Ministry of Health. The main argument for abolishing the LGB was its close association with the Poor Law, which was felt to taint all of its now wide-ranging local government responsibilities.[16]

---

[8] Friendly Societies played a small role. Most were suffering financially from the abnormal lapse of younger members due to war service. Extended sickness benefit for older members was, however, less of a burden. Most societies had commuted the benefit for a permanent pension at age 70. Their funds benefited from high wartime interest rates. Williams, 'Old Age Pensions', 321 ff.

[9] Ibid. Andrew Blaikie, 'The Emerging Political Power of the Elderly in Britain, 1908–1948', *Ageing and Society*, 10/1 (1990), 22–3.　　　　[10] *Hansard* (5th ser.), House of Commons, vol. 75, col. 2266.

[11] Williams, 'Old Age Pensions', 325.

[12] *Hansard* (5th ser.), House of Commons, vol. 97, col. 762.

[13] PRO T. 1722/499 Feb. 1917.　　　　[14] Williams, 'Old Age Pensions', 328.

[15] Sir Arnold Wilson and G. S. Mackay, *Old Age Pensions: An Historical and Critical Study* (Oxford, 1941), 59.

[16] C. Bellamy, *Administering Central–Local Relations, 1871–1919: The Local Government Board in its Fiscal and Cultural Context* (Manchester, 1988).

In principle, the change provided an opportunity to overhaul the Poor Law itself. For this purpose a committee was set up by the Ministry of Reconstruction in 1917 under the Liberal MP Sir Donald Maclean to examine the whole range of local social services, including poor relief. The committee included the veterans of the 1909 Royal Commission, Beatrice Webb and Lord George Hamilton. They were determined this time to ensure the demise both of the Poor Law and the LGB. The former they hoped to dismantle, as both reports had recommended in 1909, by means of separation of its activities into specialized local services. Their recommendations were part of a wider urge at the time to rationalize public administration. They also wished to ensure that local authorities had a role of prevention and of care of those receiving any form of public aid. They hoped at last to dispose of 'less eligibility'.[17]

Lloyd George initially accepted the recommendations of this committee but when the Ministry of Health was established in 1919 the administration of the Poor Law and of pensions passed to it unchanged. Mrs Webb had failed again, largely due to resistance by the Guardians and the objections of other local authorities to taking over Poor Law functions. Such a long-established institution as the Poor Law was hard to break up.

THE RYLAND ADKINS COMMITTEE AND PENSIONERS
AFTER THE WAR

The government also had to confront the probable furore if they sought to withdraw the 'temporary' wartime increase in the pension. It responded by appointing a committee to investigate the problem. In February 1919 a Departmental Committee was announced, to be chaired by Sir Ryland Adkins, KC, to 'consider and report what alterations, if any, as regards rate of pension and qualification, should be made in the existing statutory scheme of old age pensions'.[18] The Committee included members of the relevant government departments, representatives of trade unions and Friendly Societies and of the NCOAP, MPs of all parties, and one female voluntary social worker. The Committee examined forty-five witnesses, over twenty-six sessions. It was one of the last parliamentary inquiries to print in full the evidence of witnesses; these often frank statements of a variety of views disappeared at the dawn of the era of mass democracy.[19] The witnesses were a cross-section of expert and committed opinion. The Committee investigated British occupational schemes[20] and state pensions in other countries, including

[17] Ministry of Reconstruction, Local Government Committee, *Report, Parliamentary Papers* (1917–18), vol. xviii, Cd. 8917. Williams, 'Old Age Pensions', 333–6.

[18] *Hansard* (5th ser.), House of Commons, vol. 110, col. 348.

[19] In 1918 the vote was extended to all men at age 21 and to most women aged 30 or above.

[20] See Ch. 12.

TABLE 16.1. *Deaths of pensioners from starvation, 1909–1918*

	Deaths from starvation over age 70	Deaths of pensioners
1909	119	3
1910	111	1
1911	100	11
1912	94	7
1913	63	8
1914	62	6
1915	40	9
1916	41	3
1917	66	6
1918	26	2

those of Australia and New Zealand, which were similar to, and pre-dated, the British.[21]

The Report provides a snapshot of the condition of pensioners in 1919. Representatives of pensions committees testified to the large numbers of people who had nothing to live on but their pensions. Treasury pensions officers insisted that such people were few. Witnesses, from the Assistant Secretary to the LGB to the representative of the most 'socialistic' pensions committee, presented a remarkable consensus that the pension should be raised to between ten shillings and one pound per week. The means test was also generally held to be irrelevant to present needs and it was argued that it required to be, at least, doubled, at most abolished. It was generally agreed that 'it is impossible to live on the pension alone'. The Assistant Secretary at the new Ministry of Health attempted to disprove allegations that pensioners actually starved to death by quoting the national statistics of death attributed to starvation, which were collected annually (see Table 16.1).[22] The Permanent Secretary at the Treasury, Sir John Bradbury, insisted that 'the underlying principle of the Old Age Pension Acts' was 'not to provide for the entire maintenance of the pensioner, but to supplement such provision as might otherwise be available to the point necessary to receive decent subsistence'.[23]

---

[21] They differed mainly in the racial groups they excluded. The New Zealand scheme excluded all 'aliens' and all 'Asiatics' even if they were British citizens by virtue of being born within the British Empire, but included Maori people. Australia excluded 'Asiatics' and 'aboriginal natives' but non-Asiatic 'coloureds' were acceptable if they met the birth and residence qualifications. Each pension scheme, including the British, expressed the racial fears of its nation.

[22] *Appendix to the Report of the Departmental Committee on Old Age Pensions, including Minutes of Evidence,* Cmd. 411 (1919) (hereafter Ryland Adkins Report), qn. 7339.   [23] Ibid., qn. 8092.

No one outside the Treasury defended the age limit of 70. Most argued that 65 was more just and realistic. Most of the disqualification clauses were criticized. The exclusion of 'aliens' and the wives of aliens from the pension had caused protest since the pension had come into effect.[24] After protest in 1911 widows and divorced ex-wives, but not wives, of 'aliens' were allowed to receive the pension. Protest continued on behalf of wives and of long-established immigrants themselves.[25]

There was frequent testimony to the efforts of adult children to support their parents and condemnation of excessive pressure put upon them by officials, such as the practice of assessing help in kind as 'means', for, as one eyewitness commented, 'they sometimes go short themselves to give help'.[26] The Committee concluded that a 'substantial number' of pensioners lived in severe poverty on little more than the pension. The most frequent supplement, still, was part-time work; women as cleaners or dressmakers, men as caretakers, nightwatchmen, or handymen. They commonly lived in squalid rented rooms or in lodging houses at four pence per night. Witnesses before the Committee believed that at the beginning of the war those who had always been very poor were not necessarily poorer on the pension. It was claimed that agricultural labourers: 'even in their married lives, have had to exist on 12*s.* and 13*s.* a week with their families, and 5*s.* or 6*s.* a week meant, up to recent years, practically what they had proportionally in their early days'; but that their relative position had deteriorated during the war.

Two pensioners were interviewed.[27] Mrs Caroline Thompson was a widow of 73. Her total income was 9*s.* 6*d.* per week, her pension plus two shillings from a Birmingham settlement house. Three shillings was spent on rent, 3*s.* 8*d.* on light, fuel, insurance, laundry. 2*s.* 10*d.* remained for food. The only meat she could afford was four ounces of bacon each week. She drank no fresh milk and a single tin of milk lasted a fortnight. Four ounces of butter, one loaf of bread, two ounces of tea and a little coffee formed the bulk of her weekly diet. She did not feel that she had enough to eat; sometimes she felt weak for lack of food. In winter she had a fire only every other day. She believed that when her husband was alive, before the war, they had lived in comparative comfort on eleven shillings per week. She had a son 'who used to allow me something up to his illness . . . if he had it he would be very, very good to me'.[28] Some friends passed on their used clothes to her and 'a bit of food', but no cash because 'they are not very well off'. She did her best to reciprocate:

[24] See p. 220.
[25] D. Feldman, *Englishmen and Jews: Social Relations and Political Culture, 1840–1914* (New Haven, 1994), 272. P. Thane, 'The British Imperial State and the Construction of National Identities', in B. Melman (ed.), *Borderlines: Gender and Identities in War and Peace, 1870–1930* (London and New York, 1998), 38–41.
[26] Ryland Adkins Report, qns. 4508, 4474–9, 2271 ff., 6154.
[27] They were selected by Mrs Cecile Matheson, a member of the Committee, through the Birmingham settlement with which she was connected.   [28] Ryland Adkins Report, qn. 5751.

'I try to make it up to them, but not what they give me'. About twice a week she did some tidying and washing up for them and 'a bit of sewing'. She could not manage anything heavier.[29]

Mrs Larton, also a widow, was 72. Her basic income was also 9s. 6d. a week. Some weeks she could earn eight or nine shillings caring for attempted suicides at a police station. She could not do this regularly because she was not strong and they were often violent. Rent cost four shillings and sixpence. She rented out a room to another woman for two shillings. Her son gave her what he could, but 'I cannot depend on it. You see he has very indifferent health.' She had no friends who could help her. A lady at the settlement helped her with occasional sewing work when her health was poor. She bought second-hand clothes and mended her own boots. In a good week she could afford a little fresh meat or corned beef, but when she was ill she lived mainly on milk. She felt undernourished and that her health suffered. She believed that she could afford better food and clothes on the same income before the war.[30]

This evidence was supported by a small sample of pensioners' budgets collected by Maud Pember Reeves of the Fabian Women's Group and Evelyn Lowe, who represented the Standing Joint Committee of Industrial Women's Organizations, which represented the large numbers of women in women's sections of the Labour Party,[31] the Women's Co-operative Guild,[32] and in trade unions, about half a million women in all. These organizations had long campaigned for improved pensions and Mrs Lowe's evidence was based upon a survey of the opinions of their members. This provided the most complete blueprint for reform placed before the Committee. They recommended abolition of the means test and a pensionable age of 60, because, women claimed, in many districts employment exchanges regarded women over 60 as unemployable. They believed that pensioners should be supervised and home helps provided as well as comfortable institutions for those unable to live independently. Lowe claimed that 'the majority of the pensioners are only able to get along because they are helped by relations. But the fact that they must be helped is not only hard on them but on their sons and daughters, who may have a hard struggle to support their own children. Where the pensioner has only one child it falls especially on that one individual.' Caring for an aged parent could cause overcrowding and difficulties for young children:

When it was five shillings the people who could offer hospitality but no money for the old people took them to an already crowded home . . . children had to share a small bedroom with the old people . . . unless proper accommodation can be provided

---

[29] Ryland Adkins Report, qns. 5737 ff.   [30] Ibid., qns. 5958–6151.

[31] Pat Thane, 'The Women of the British Labour Party and Feminism, 1906–45', in H. L. Smith (ed.), *British Feminism in the Twentieth Century* (Aldershot, 1990), 124–43.

[32] J. Gaffin and D. Thoms, *Caring and Sharing: The Centenary History of the Co-operative Women's Guild* (Manchester, 1983).

for old people living in a home with young people, it often has an extremely bad effect on the children and a very wearing effect on the mother of the young children.[33]

They have very kind landladies. The poor are extraordinarily good to one another. I know a number of them who could not exist but for the kindness of the women in whose houses they happen to be.[34]

None of the pensioners' budgets allowed for anything but necessities. A notable absence from all of them was clothing. Mrs Reeves believed that used clothes were a more frequent form of gift among the poor than food. Footwear was expensive and caused a particular problem. 'The fact is', said Mrs Lowe, 'that the majority have not boots at all which are watertight and have great difficulty in getting about in bad weather.'[35] Similarly, poor diets of old people were found to be typical in later surveys. The New Survey of London found in 1928–9 that less than half of the seven hundred and ninety old people interviewed had a hot meal every day and many complained of not getting enough to eat.[36] Surveys in the 1940s found similar conditions,[37] though the poverty of old people was not necessarily greater than among the young; malnutrition among children was identified as a major problem in the inter-war years.

It became clear to the Ryland Adkins Committee that the poorest pensioners would have been better off on poor relief, which rarely paid less than ten shillings per week and sometimes fifteen, often supplemented by services and in kind. But there was no sign that resistance to the Poor Law was diminishing; it remained a desperate last resort and old people opted for struggle and destitution on the pension rather than turn to the board of guardians. The trade unionist C. W. Bowerman, MP, confessed that he had been converted to universal pensions by his experience on a pension committee, stating that, 'Nothing is more painful to my mind than to have to sit and hear the Pensions Officer weigh up the value of this and that—food, lighting, rooms and so on.' His fellow trade unionist, G. H. Stuart Bunning, was asked whether pensions for the 'undeserving' on the same terms as the respectable 'would not offend the public conscience'. Bunning responded, as trade unionists long had:

I do not want to be offensive, but I think it is a little unfortunate that this question of hurting of public conscience always comes up when some demand is made on behalf of very poor people . . . in order to get rid of certain disabilities we have to include some people who in the ordinary way would not be entitled to consideration for pension.[38]

---

[33] Ryland Adkins Report, qn. 6278.   [34] Ibid., qn. 6275.

[35] Ibid., qn. 6280. Williams, 'Old Age Pensions', appendix A.

[36] H. Llewellyn-Smith (ed.), *New Survey of London*, iii. 208. British Library of Political and Economic Science, New Survey of London, 2/1, 3. 2/2, Original interviews: Miss Roscoe, Mr Stanley, Mrs Wheeler, Mr and Mrs Turner, Mrs Pincher; for dietary records see rough notebooks.

[36] Well surveyed in J. R. Fogerty, 'Growing Old in England, 1878–1949', Ph.D. thesis (Australian National University, Canberra, 1992), 85.   [38] Ryland Adkins Report, qns. 3158–76.

W. G. Martley of the COS was alone in favouring a contributory framework for future pensions:

The Society is still of opinion that voluntary insurance for old age and for other needs is a social factor of great value and makes for national stability. But they realize that until its possibilities take hold of the popular imagination public provision such as that made by the Old Age Pensions Act and National Insurance Acts are inevitable.[39]

Others argued that the national health insurance scheme had demonstrated the difficulty of including the poorest, especially women, in any such scheme.

The Committee heard strong evidence for amending almost every feature of the pensions system. The greatest obstacle to change was the Treasury. The Permanent Secretary's opinion was that the debts incurred by the war would require 'drastic curtailment of public expenditure'. The impending crisis was such that, he announced dramatically:

Every man in the community must necessarily be poorer, and have his standard of living reduced because of the war . . . I think it is quite impossible to restore people, like old age pensioners who are not part of the industrial machine, to as favourable a position as they occupied before the war . . . I would like to be understood that I would apply the principle much more drastically to the wealthy than the poor. I want to make economy principally at the expense of the wealthier classes. I want to prevent people riding in motor cars; I want to prevent people wearing expensive furs; I want to prevent people having unnecessary clothing and very soon the income tax will have that effect, I think.[40]

He was prepared to countenance a permanent increase in the pension to 8s., or preferably, 7s. 6d., with the prospect of a further rise to £1 when the economy recovered. He pointed out that prices were likely to fall after the war and in consequence the real value of the pension would rise. He acknowledged that it would be possible to link pension rates to a price index, 'but that kind of legislation is not, as a rule, looked on with favour, and I think rightly'.[41] The Treasury could not accept a universal pension: 'a pension of eight shillings a week is not a vested interest of the whole community . . . I cannot admit any inherent natural right in an aged person to receive maintenance at the expense of the community'. He rejected any significant extension of the non-contributory scheme, though he accepted that when the economy recovered, extensions such as lowering the age limit on a contributory basis might be acceptable.

This left the Committee little room for manoeuvre. Opinions among them differed, but no one was prepared to be quite as restrictive as Bradbury. In November 1919 the eighteen members produced two reports and five notes of reservation. The chairman and ten others reported with impeccable circumspection in all respects but one. They recommended a national pension

---

[39] Ryland Adkins Report. [40] Ibid., qn. 8122. [41] Ibid., qn. 8280.

rate of ten shillings, to be supplemented according to need by the Poor Law or its successor. They recognized that ten shillings barely compensated for price rises since 1914, but hoped that prices would soon fall. More radically, they concluded that they could recommend no way to administer a means test fairly and recognized that it was widely resented. They had been forced to conclude that 'only universal pensions will remove the very serious objections to the present system'. The better off should repay them through the tax system. If the estimated cost of £41m. proved unacceptable, they were prepared to accept the doubling of the means limit as a temporary measure.

The Committee could not realistically also recommend reducing the pensionable age, though they suggested further inquiry into the possible integration of pensions with national health insurance to provide a pension between ages 65 and 70. They believed that the evidence about the ages at which people ceased to be capable of regular work 'disclose[s] a state of things which cannot be left as it is. If National Insurance cannot be extended, the non-contributory pension scheme will have to be.' They also recommended abolishing the imprisonment disqualification and the unworkable 'failure to work' clause, and that 'aliens' should qualify for the pension after ten years' residence. Each of the ten signatories of the report, other than the chairman, dissented from some aspect of the recommendations. The three most radical members of the Committee recommended a universal pension of fifteen shillings at age 65. All of the civil servants and the two Unionist MPs signed a Minority report opposing universality and recommending doubling the means limit.

The new Chancellor of the Exchequer, Austen Chamberlain, was advised by his department to accept the Minority recommendations. His Private Secretary commented that the Committee had demonstrated that the standard of living of pensioners was 'so low that any further reduction is impossible and there is no doubt that they are suffering from hardship at present . . . it is almost impossible to suggest a cheaper alternative . . . this is a simple and logical scheme which merely restores pensions to something like their pre-war position . . . anything less . . . would fail to meet the objections of Friendly Societies and Trade Unions'.[42]

The 'selfish, malign lot' as Chamberlain described the new House of Commons[43] were intent upon stringent economy in public expenditure. Members of the Cabinet recognized, some of them reluctantly, that something must be done for pensioners.[44] In December they accepted the Minority recommendation, but with a lower means scale running from £26. 5s. to £47. 5s. A Bill was rushed through the Commons in the last few days of the

[42] PRO CAB 24/5/264 8 Nov. 1919.
[43] A. J. P. Taylor, *England 1914–45* (Oxford, 1965), 129.
[44] PRO T 172/1050; CAB 23/8, Cabinet Minutes, Dec. 8 1919. CAB 24/94/211, Memo Chamberlain to Cabinet, 26 Nov. 1919.

session, before opposition could mass.[45] It raised the pension to ten shillings; allowed a Poor Law supplement; female British subjects married to aliens were no longer disqualified, nor were those guilty of 'habitual failure to work', imprisonment, or conviction for drunkenness. The first three months' Friendly Society benefits in any one year were to be disregarded.

The Bill received just one hour's debate in an ill-attended House of Commons. Introducing it, Bonar Law commented: 'I am informed by the Ministry of Labour and it is reasonable to believe it, that, if we succeed in passing this Bill, it will have a quieting effect on the general unrest which exists in the country'. Labour members promised to keep up pressure for better pensions. The NCOAP kept up its campaign. In January 1921 its representatives addressed the crowd of 40,000 attending a football match between Newcastle United and Bradford City, who 'simultaneously and unanimously passed a resolution demanding the abolition of the means limit'.[46]

'ALL-IN' INSURANCE

A vigorous debate about the future of pensions followed which was an important preliminary to the Beveridge proposals of 1942. By 1921–2 there were 1,029,365 pensioners in the United Kingdom, of whom 93 per cent received the maximum rate; 70 per cent of pensioners were female. These figures remained roughly constant until 1925.[47] About 5 per cent received supplementary poor relief,[48] though many guardians refused to pay such supplements for fear of encouraging the gradual transfer of expenditure for pensions from the Exchequer to the local rates;[49] and many pensioners still refused to apply for poor relief. The number of pensioners was slightly increased by the Blind Persons Act, 1920, which granted pensions under the terms of the Old Age Pensions Acts to blind persons above the age of 50.[50]

Social politics from 1921 were dominated by economic depression and unemployment and the cuts in public expenditure which were the government's response. The first serious search for cuts, the Select Committee on National Expenditure of June 1921, chaired by Sir Eric Geddes—the 'Geddes axe' as it was known—could find no potential for savings on pensions, unless the government wished to reduce the rate of pension so soon after raising it.[51] The

---

[45] Blaikie, 'Political Power', overstates the role of the National Committee in bringing about the change.   [46] Ibid. 17–18.

[47] *Third Annual Report of the Ministry of Health, 1921–2, Parliamentary Papers* (1922), viii. 98. *Fourth Annual Report of the Ministry of Health, 1922–3,* 95.

[48] *First Annual Report of the Ministry of Health, 1919–20,* Cmd. 932, pt. III, p. 49.

[49] PRO PIN 1/2, *Report from the Ministry of Health on the Administration of Poor Relief,* 14th Jan. 1924.

[50] There were 10,702 in 1920–1; 9,107 in 1921–2; 12,355 in 1922–3. *Annual Reports of the Ministry of Health* (1921–3).

[51] *Interim Report, Select Committee on National Expenditure* (Dec. 1921), Cmd. 1581, 113.

report contained, however, a thoughtful appendix by Sir Alfred Watson, the government actuary, on the potential savings that might result from amalgamating the unemployment and health insurance systems. This was to grow into a campaign for the integration of all aspects of social security administration, including pensions, known as the campaign for 'all-in' insurance. It attracted both supporters of economy and progressive reformers such as the NCOAP, who now felt that this was the only realistic way forward.[52] The main effect of the campaign was to stimulate fresh thinking about social security and to give contributory pensions political and intellectual respectability for the first time in the century. Friendly Societies after ten years' experience of national insurance now favoured its extension, which they believed would extend their approved society work under the National Insurance Acts and increase their membership.

As unemployment worsened and unemployment relief expenditure rose, 'all-in' proposals became ever more popular. At first sight the concept appeared to provide the means to hold and even to extend necessary social provision whilst cutting costs. When Neville Chamberlain was appointed Minister of Health in February 1923 he found the idea appealing. Chamberlain was an efficient administrator who had inherited his father's interest in social questions. Like his father, Chamberlain was convinced of the moral as well as the financial superiority of contributory over non-contributory pensions. He was prevented from further immediate action by his promotion in August 1923 to the Chancellorship of the Exchequer.

Meanwhile 'all-in' proposals proliferated. Two years' deliberation by a group of Members of Parliament produced proposals for the payment, through a single administrative mechanism, in return for a single contribution, of sickness and unemployment benefits, an old-age pension at age 63, and pensions for widows and orphans. Pensions for widows and orphans were the subject of active campaigns especially by women's groups at this time.[53] Insurance reform was widely discussed in the press.[54] During the general election of December 1923 it was prominent in the manifestos of the Liberal and Conservative parties. The Labour manifesto promised, ambiguously: 'When Labour rules . . . generous provision for the aged people, the widowed mothers, the sick and disabled'.[55] Before the election was decided, the Conservative government established an interdepartmental committee to examine 'all-in' insurance, chaired by Sir John Anderson, Permanent Secretary at the Home Office.[56] It consisted of civil servants from all interested departments.

[52] Williams, 'Old Age Pensions', 383 ff.

[53] Thomas Broad, *All-In Insurance Scheme* (London, 1923). Pat Thane, 'Visions of Gender in the Making of the British Welfare State: The Case of Women in the British Labour Party, 1906–1945', in G. Bock and P. Thane (eds.) *Maternity and Gender Policies: Women and the Rise of the European Welfare States, 1880s–1950s* (London, 1991), 93–118.

[54] e.g. *Daily Chronicle*; *The Times*, Oct. 1923.   [55] *The Times*, 2 Dec. 1923.

[56] PRO T 161/220, file S 22430, 11, 13 Dec. 1923.

The election reduced the number of Conservative seats in the Commons; they were outnumbered by the combined strength of Liberals and Labour. In January 1924 they resigned, bringing Labour into government for the first time, as the second largest party but in the weak position of being heavily outnumbered by the Conservatives and Liberals in Parliament. The Anderson Committee continued its work. It was instructed to work speedily and on 9 January 1924 it presented an interim report to the Conservative government, in its last days in office. This report dealt only with old-age pensions. It rejected suggestions that the existing pension should become contributory, on the grounds that insurance 'depends upon employment' and the pension 'upon need . . . this is particularly true in the case of women. Approximately sixty-three per cent of the female population over seventy are in receipt of an old age pension whereas only about seven per cent of those between the ages of sixty and seventy contribute under the National Insurance scheme'.[57] The Committee stressed the probable political opposition to changing the basis of the existing scheme. The Report drew the obvious conclusion, as the Ryland Adkins Committee had done, that any improvement of the non-contributory scheme would increase the cost. It suggested an increase in the means limit, to encourage thrift earlier in life. It promised 'to examine the possibility of introducing a contributory pension for the sixty-five to seventy age group'.[58]

When Labour replaced the Conservatives in government, this report impressed Philip Snowden, the new Chancellor. He informed the Cabinet that 'an insistent demand has been raised in many quarters in recent years that . . . everyone should be entitled to ten shillings a week at the age of seventy'. But, though he had himself been among the most insistent and this had long been Labour policy, it was 'not my intention to discuss the merits of this suggestion, as its cost is, in present circumstances, prohibitive'. He was prepared to consider raising the means limit.[59] Criticism of the first Labour government for failing to keep its promises made before entering office is easy enough, if we ignore the fact that this was a weak, short-lived, minority government whose chances of getting any radical, expensive social measure through parliament were extremely slender.[60] Even so, Snowden's subsequent actions were less cautious. His first Budget earmarked £38,074,000 in the coming session for the reduction of food taxes (and hence food prices, raising the value of benefits), abolition of the 'thrift' qualification for the old-age pension and the introduction of widows' pensions.[61] Two months later he introduced legislation[62] which raised the means limit for the minimum pension to

[57] Committee on Insurance and Other Social Services, First Interim Report, Old Age Pensions, 8 Jan. 1924, PRO PIN 1/2, 5.　　　　　　[58] Williams, 'Old Age Pensions', 402–6.

[59] PRO CAB 24/165, Old Age Pensions, memorandum Snowden to Cabinet, 13 Mar. 1924.

[60] Macnicol, *Retirement*, does not resist the temptation, 193–9.

[61] *Hansard* (5th ser.), House of Commons, vol. 172 (1 May 1924), col. 1774.

[62] 15 & 15 Geo. V, c. 33 (1).

£88. 17*s*. 6*d*. Incomes of up to fifteen shillings per week would qualify for the maximum pension, provided that they were not earnings from employment. The full pension was paid if total income did not exceed £66. 5*s*. per year, of which only £25. 5*s*. could be earned income. Snowden urged that 'it would be wrong to do anything which might act as an encouragement to wage earning over seventy, in the present condition of unemployment'.[63] Labour MPs tried unsuccessfully to persuade him to go further.[64] This measure can be seen as 'shabby and parsimonious' backsliding by a party betraying all that it had previously stood for,[65] or as the first step in a cautious but credible policy by a minority government with aspirations to remain in office.

By the end of 1924 50,000 additional pensioners qualified under the new terms, bringing the total to 977,160, about 70 per cent of the over-seventy population.[66] The problem remained of the poverty of many pensioners without means to supplement the pension.

WILLIAM BEVERIDGE RETURNS TO SOCIAL SECURITY

Awareness that the Anderson committee was still deliberating encouraged further contributions to the 'all-in' debate. William Beveridge had been Director of the London School of Economics since 1919. In 1924 he published *Insurance for All and Everything* in which he returned to the arguments for social insurance which he had raised seventeen years earlier[67] and which he was to bring to fruition in 1942. The pamphlet was hurriedly produced, under the auspices of the Liberal Party, of which Beveridge was an active supporter. Beveridge was pleased by the general interest in social insurance, believing that 'it accords with popular sentiment against giving or getting something for nothing . . . it saves political parties from temptation to compete in easy promises of higher doles . . . it makes it possible without an objectionable device like the means limit to define the class of person to be insured'.[68] He argued that it enabled the state to provide for those in need in a manner most psychologically and morally desirable for claimants and for society, for 'the problem is not that of guaranteeing an income at all times to everyone regardless of his work or services. That way lies Communism.'[69]

Beveridge proposed to cut costs by simplifying social security administration into two sectors. Benefits which required investigation of eligibility—sickness, disability, maternity—should be administered under the national health

[63] PRO CAB 24/165 (above, n. 59).
[64] *Hansard* (5th ser.), House of Commons, vol. 176, col. 1253; PRO CAB 24/167, J. R. Clynes to J. R. MacDonald, 23 May 1924. Williams, 'Old Age Pensions', 411–12.
[65] As by Macnicol, *Retirement*, 195.
[66] *Hansard* (5th ser.), House of Commons, vol. 181, col. 810.   [67] See pp. 221–2.
[68] W. Beveridge, *Insurance for All and Everything* (London, 1924), 3.   [69] Ibid. 30.

insurance system. The unemployment insurance machinery would administer widows' and old-age pensions, for which eligibility was normally unambiguous. The existing pension scheme would gradually shift to a contributory basis to which all new entrants to insurance would become entitled. Beveridge did not recommend subsistence level benefits, lest they discourage thrift and filial responsibility. He emphasized that for all these schemes, so far as possible, 'the edges should fit, leaving no holes through which people can drop to destitution'.[70] He would, however, retain the Poor Law as a 'safety net' for the inevitable casualty who would still find holes to slip through.

Insurance for All and Everything has been seen as the genesis of Beveridge's 1942 report *Social Insurance and Allied Services*. It was, however, hastily composed and contained many loose ends. It did not propose subsistence level or universal benefits, as the report of 1942 was to do; in 1924 National Insurance was restricted to those earning £160 per year and below.[71] Beveridge's proposals were briefly adopted as official Liberal policy. They were scrutinized and criticized by the Anderson Committee for, among other things, ignoring the problem of including women and for optimism about the level of contribution which could deliver the proposed benefits.[72]

Other detailed and carefully thought-out publications followed on this theme.[73] Neville Chamberlain spent his enforced absence from administration chairing a number of Conservative Party committees on social questions, one of them on 'all-in insurance'. The minority Labour government could not last long and Chamberlain made clear that when the Conservatives returned to office he wished to return to the Ministry of Health rather than to the Chancellorship. The party committee prepared before the next election a proposal for the gradual phasing in of a contributory pension of twenty-five shillings per week from age 65.

The Anderson Committee delivered its second report in July 1924. It had now concluded that any further extension of non-contributory pensions was impossibly costly.[74] A contributory supplement to the over-seventy pensions for those who could afford it was also rejected because it would be seen, correctly, as an admission that the existing pension was inadequate. The Committee could therefore only recommend a contributory pension for the 65 to 70 age group, whose need they considered urgent. In addition to the natural infirmities of this age group, there was evidence from a Ministry of Labour survey that they were suffering disproportionately from unemployment.

[70] Beveridge, *Insurance*, 2.

[71] José Harris, *William Beveridge: A Biography*, 2nd edn. (Oxford, 1997), 338–40.

[72] Ibid. 340. Williams, 'Old Age Pensions', 416 n. 2.

[73] In particular Joseph Cohen, *Social Insurance Unified* (London, 1924), and Alban Gordon, *Social Insurance* (London, 1924), written originally as a Fabian Society pamphlet. Williams, 'Old Age Pensions', 413–20.

[74] Committee on Insurance and Other Social Services, Second Interim Report, Contributory Pensions; Pensions for Widows and Orphans and for Persons between 65 and 70, PRO PIN 1/3.

This investigation into the circumstances of 10,000 claimants for unemployment benefit showed that the percentages of 'unemployed age sixty or over who were considered to be verging on the unemployable' were: males, 17 per cent, females 30.8 per cent. The corresponding percentages for workers of all ages were 3.5 and 1.8.[75]

The Committee recommended that this supplement to the old-age pension and widows' and orphans' pensions could be administered through the health insurance mechanism in return for a single contribution. The new pensions should be paid at the same rate as the existing old-age pension, to avoid the protest that would result if they were higher.[76] A large part of the problem of uninsured women could be met by increasing the contribution of insured men sufficiently to cover a pension payable to their wives when both they and their husbands reached pensionable age.[77] Unmarried women, it was believed, would mainly be in employment and eligible to enter the insurance scheme.

THE INTRODUCTION OF CONTRIBUTORY PENSIONS

Snowden approved of the report, but the Labour government fell suddenly in October 1924. The 'red scare' election which followed returned the Conservatives with a secure majority. Neville Chamberlain returned eagerly to the Ministry of Health. A greater surprise was Baldwin's choice of Chancellor of the Exchequer: Winston Churchill, who in the recent election had stood as a Conservative for the first time after his long dalliance with the now split and weakened Liberal Party. Chamberlain immediately presented his department with a four-year, twenty-five-point plan, including the complete reform of the Poor Law, the overhaul of National Health Insurance, and introduction of contributory pensions for widows and the aged.[78] Twenty-one of his proposals were on the statute book in some form by the end of 1929. Within a fortnight of the election Chamberlain presented to the Cabinet an outline scheme of wholly contributory pensions based on the findings of the party committee.[79] The Cabinet accepted his proposals. They especially interested Winston Churchill, who had stepped straight into preparation of the 1925 Budget. A week later he called on Chamberlain, who recorded in his diary:

He was anxious to reduce taxation in order to relieve industry . . . but he would have to balance the benefits by doing something for the working class and for this he looked to pensions . . . it would have to be my Bill, but he would have to find the money and the question was would I start with him, would I enter partnership and plan with him, keeping everything secret.[80]

---

[75] Ibid. 18.   [76] Williams, 'Old Age Pensions', 423–4.   [77] Ibid. 424–7.
[78] K. Feiling, *The Life of Neville Chamberlain* (London, 1946), 218.   [79] Ibid.   [80] Ibid. 128.

Chamberlain's main concern was to see his proposals through, and collaboration with the Chancellor would limit the danger of Treasury opposition. He submitted readily to Churchill's minor blackmail. They agreed that a pensions bill would be prepared in time for the Budget speech.

In a third report, the Anderson Committee rejected the Conservative proposals because, among other problems, it was estimated that they required unrealistically high contributions; also the Committee argued that the proposed pension of twenty-five shillings would lead to demands to raise the non-contributory pension.[81] Chamberlain was convinced by these criticisms and set his department to produce a Bill based upon the Anderson Committee's previous recommendations. He was now convinced that it was impossible to break with the system established in 1908 without causing hardship and political resistance. Change had to be gradual.

The Bill and the Budget were prepared amid increasingly vocal demands, particularly from employers and in the press, for cuts in taxation and in public expenditure. The National Confederation of Employers informed the Minister of Health on the question of pensions:

Thrift and self-help have always been one of the greatest assets in the life of our country. It cannot be doubted that the whole tendency of this social service legislation in its development and administration has been towards the destruction of these natural assets . . . it is borne in upon employers that the independence and morale of the workers are being sapped by the provision that is being made. Work-dodging and dole-getting have become almost a profession.[82]

The draft Bill provided for the gradual shift of pensions finance to a wholly contributory basis by means of decennial increases in contributions, until 1956, by which time the scheme would be financed wholly by contributions, and available to all in need at age 70.[83] Contributors to national health insurance for at least five years would qualify for the pension at age 65. Dependent wives of insured men who were aged 65 or over would qualify at the same time as their husbands. Insured pensioners could draw the pension concurrently with wages from employment once the qualifying age was reached. Insured men and wives pensioned by virtue of marriage to an insured man would qualify automatically for the non-contributory pension at age 70, without further test, and might continue in paid work. All pensions would remain at ten shillings. Insured people who were already over 70 when the Act came into force qualified immediately for the full non-contributory pension. At age 65 contributions would cease as would eligibility for sickness or unemployment benefit. The

[81] Committee on Insurance and Other Social Services. Third Interim Report (9 Feb. 1925), 5–7, 12. Williams, 'Old Age Pensions', 432–3.
[82] PRO PIN 4/96, Widows and Old Age Pensions Contributory Pensions Bill, 1925. Bill papers. Memorandum on the social services. NCEO to Minister of Health, 4 March 1925. For further examples see Williams, 'Old Age Pensions', 435 n. 1.   [83] Ibid. 437–8.

contribution for the pension would be eightpence for a man, fourpence for a woman.[84] The scheme was to be under the control of the Ministry of Health and for the first time appeals would be made to a court of law rather than to the Ministry. Pensions would be paid through the Post Office. Non-contributory pensions for the non—insured would continue to be administered separately and by the same methods as before. Their numbers were expected to dwindle over time. The cost to the Exchequer of the new scheme (exclusive of the existing over-70 pension) was estimated at £3.7m. in 1928–8, rising to £11m. in 1931–2. Yet again, pensions legislation was driven above all by government determination to minimize costs.

Contributory pensions had a major place in Churchill's Budget speech. With characteristic military metaphor he proclaimed:

Now we can come forward, with our wagons and our field guns replenished, if not with ample, at any rate with an adequate supply of shot and shell . . . security for the wage-earner against exceptional misfortune, that is the first need.[85]

More interestingly, he urged that 'the old *laissez-faire, laissez-aller* ideas of mid-Victorian radicalism have been superseded'. He dismissed the 'idle' argument 'that the threat of adversity is a necessary factor in stimulating self-reliance'. He claimed that it had been active for years but had not left the poor with 'the strength or the means or the foresight or the habit of making provision'.[86] More determined intervention was necessary. Churchill's Budget of 1925 is best known for announcing the return to the Gold Standard. It also reduced direct taxation by £42m. As regards pensions, Churchill revealed that the Exchequer contribution was calculated to balance the estimated annual fall in the cost of war pensions over the coming decade. The net cost to the revenue would be nil. In reality the cost of war pensions was expected to fall rather faster than the rise in old-age pensions.[87] This explained the Treasury's ready acceptance of the scheme.

Some of Chamberlain's colleagues were annoyed at the amount of credit Churchill took for the scheme, but Chamberlain was more sanguine.[88] Generally it was well received, though the left-wing *Daily Herald* called it 'a heartless fraud on a helpless people'.[89] Labour in the Commons protested against the increased contributions amid the hardship of unemployment and against the

[84] The male rate was actuarially fixed at the level necessary to fund the pension of a 16-year-old entrant to the scheme. The female rate was fixed arbitrarily at half the male rate, due to the impossibility of fixing a 'fair' rate for the mass of women who would never qualify for pension by virtue of their own insurance but, who, it was felt, should make a contribution to the fund during their working lives. Cd. 5991, *Government Actuary's Report on the Financial Provisions of the 1925 Widows and Old Age Contributory Pensions Bill*, para. 5. Williams, 'Old Age Pensions', 439–41.

[85] *Hansard* (5th ser.), House of Commons, vol. 183, col. 71.   [86] Ibid., col. 72.

[87] Williams, 'Old Age Pensions', 444–5.

[88] Feiling, *Chamberlain*, 131. Williams, 'Old Age Pensions', 446.

[89] Quoted *Hansard* (5th ser.), House of Commons, vol. 184, col. 86. Williams, 'Old Age Pensions', 447–8.

danger that employers would pay pensioned men at rates which undercut younger workers, though whether employment of cheap older workers in place of fitter younger ones would appear to employers to make economic sense was an unanswered question. The new Member for Peckham Hugh Dalton (a future Chancellor of the Exchequer) complained of the meagre character of the scheme compared with the tax concessions to the wealthy and calculated that lesser tax-cuts would have made possible the funding of a more generous pension: 'The Chancellor functions for the . . . benefit [of wealthy taxpayers]. A gigantic penny slot machine, you put in your income tax and you pull out your war loan interest.'[90] Snowden attacked 'the worst rich man's Budget that was ever proposed' and went on to advocate an extended non-contributory pension which, he claimed, 'has always been the policy of Labour'.[91]

Radical Conservatives also attacked the Chancellor who 'has been laying too great a burden upon industry while he has been too tender to the millionaire and indulgent to the super tax payer . . . it is a good insurance scheme for the rich . . . they should pay up and avoid the danger of social revolution.'[92] Employers' representatives opposed the further 'burden on industry' of the contributions required of them. None the less, the Act passed with few amendments. One of these excluded 'aliens' in the British merchant service from the pension. The numbers of 'coloured' seamen in the British merchant navy had increased during the war when there was demand for their labour. They were treated indulgently whilst they were useful to the war effort. With the onset of unemployment there was strong pressure to restrict their social and civil rights as residents of the UK.[93]

The new pensions legislation increased the proportion of people over 70 who were eligible for the pension to 79 per cent. It was now the most comprehensive tax-financed benefit in Britain. On 1 January 1926 15,090,000 people entered pensions insurance.[94] On the same date 166,132 people aged 70 and over, regardless of their means, received the full pension by virtue of their previous national insurance contributions. Some of these were already receiving the pension at a lower rate. The contributory pension was paid to 539,000 people in the first full year, 1928–9; most of the recipients were male, though women were still the majority of the age group. On 1 January 1926 10,445,000 men were in insurable employment and 4,645,000 women. The first insurance pensions were paid to 360,000 men and 177,000 women aged between 65 and 70. This disparity continued: in 1938 524,493 men and 316,909 women received

[90] *Hansard* (5th ser.), House of Commons, vol. 184, col. 421.

[91] Ibid., vol. 183, cols. 171 ff.   [92] Ibid., col. 352.

[93] L. Tabili, 'The Construction of Racial Difference in Twentieth-Century Britain: The Special Restriction (Coloured Alien Seamen) Order, 1925', *Journal of British Studies*, 33/1 (Jan. 1994), 54–99. Thane, 'British Imperial State', 41–3. See also the account of the passing of the Act in D. Dilks, *Neville Chamberlain*, i: *1869–1929* (Cambridge, 1984), 378, 413, 420, 421, 426–35.

[94] i.e. all those already within the national health insurance scheme plus 30,000 voluntary contributors.

the pension. This was because the wives of insured men tended to be some years younger than their husbands; they qualified for the pension at age 65, provided that their husband was also aged at least 65. Like their husbands, they qualified automatically for the non-contributory pension at age 70. In 1938 the pension was paid to 593,639 insured men over age 70 and to 668,693 insured women and wives of insured men.[95]

The number of uninsured pensioners declined gradually from 1926. They continued to be subject to a means test and other disqualifications. The means limit was £88. 17s. 6d. compared with £160 for entry to the insurance system. The non-contributory pension took on second-class status, and the problem of severe poverty among these pensioners was unresolved. The NCOAP protested against this, but felt that it had no further reason for existence and dissolved itself.[96]

The crucial transition in the system of state pensions, the establishment of the framework on which the system was built for the remainder of the century, came not as is often suggested in the 1940s, but in the 1920s. The only wholly new principle embodied in the legislation of 1946 was universality. It is unlikely that Beveridge had any influence on the 1925 Act, but he strongly approved of the adoption of the contributory principle. He was dubious about the lowering of the pensionable age in view of his concern about the growing proportion of older people in Britain.[97] In consequence of this he believed that working life should be lengthened rather than shortened.[98]

'WHEN YOU GROW OLD, YOU ARE COLD': OLD PEOPLE AND THE DEPRESSION

The real value of the pension rose during the Depression of the 1920s. Retail food prices fell overall by 80 per cent between 1920 and 1923 and all retail prices fell by an average of 70 per cent,[99] though with local and regional differences. In 1924 the retail price index was 70 per cent above the 1914 level whereas the pension had risen by 100 per cent.[100] Nevertheless the life expectancy of people at age 65 rose by only 5 years over the whole first five decades of the twentieth century, a substantially smaller gain than that of all younger age groups, suggesting that the living standards of many older people were lagging behind.[101] In 1923, when prices were at their lowest point between 1920 and 1925, Bowley and Hogg, using Rowntree's stringent criteria, estimated that a married couple on maximum pensions still had

---

[95] Wilson and Mackay, *Old Age Pensions*, 141.
[96] Blaikie, 'Political Power', 26–7. Williams, 'Old Age Pensions', 450–2.
[97] See pp. 333–5, 343–4.   [98] Harris, *Beveridge*, 351.
[99] B. Mitchell and P. Deane, *Abstract of British Historical Statistics* (Cambridge, 1962), 478.
[100] Ibid. 478.   [101] Fogerty, 'Growing Old', 75.

2s. 2d. per week less than was needed to buy the 'necessaries of life'; the single pensioner was three shillings short.[102]

Fogerty points out that the estimates of the income needs of old people in this and other surveys were very largely based on guesswork. The many inter-war surveys of poverty provide, at best, an impressionistic account of the conditions of old people, who were peripheral to their central concern with the impact of unemployment on adults of working age and their children, a concern that was not unreasonable given the conditions of the time.[103] Rowntree assumed, on the basis of no clear evidence, that old women had only two-thirds the food needs of old men and that older adults had two-thirds the income needs of younger adults.[104] The New Survey of London noted in 1929 that the 'possible' very basic dietary which they constructed costing 4s. 4d. per week, 'for old people not at work', included no vegetables except potatoes, no fruit, and only skimmed milk; by comparison they allowed 7s. 1d. for 'an adult male in moderate work'.[105] Researchers overlooked the physical demands on women of the housework they continued to perform to late ages; also that and the food and heating expenses of elderly people were often greater than for younger people due to failing health, though this was recognized by some Poor Law medical officers in the nineteenth century and by most Public Assistance Committees in the twentieth. 'When you are old you are cold', one old woman commented in 1943. Poor Law and Public Assistance institutions also found that the old cost more not less than younger people to keep. Too often social researchers assumed that debility was the normal condition of older people and that they did not need more food than younger people. The extent to which debility was due to poverty and malnutrition was underestimated.[106] Hence the surveys served to perpetuate a widespread underestimate of the needs, and in consequence of the health potential of older people, most seriously when their studies influenced official benefit levels.

Stringent though its criteria were, the New Survey of London found the aged of east London in only slightly better condition than in 1899. They were generally adequately nourished in summer, but not in winter when the cost of fuel took a higher proportion of their incomes. Their clothes and household possessions generally were in poor condition. The survey estimated that a minimum of twelve shillings a week was required to live in east London, exclusive of rent. Rent averaged four to six shillings per week for a single room. The researchers discovered that 'none of the pensioners was grateful for the old age pension, all of them thinking it was due to them, and all of them

[102] A. Bowley and M. Hogg, *Has Poverty Diminished?* (London, 1925).

[103] Macnicol, *Retirement*, discusses these surveys in some detail, though he is perhaps excessively anxious to criticize them for insufficient concentration on the needs of old people. His study is weakly contextualized.   [104] B. Seebohm Rowntree, *The Human Needs of Labour* (London, 1918).

[105] Llewellyn-Smith, *New Survey*, iii. 73–7. Fogerty, 'Growing Old', 78–9.

[106] Fogerty, 'Growing Old', 84.

complained about the smallness of it'. The commonest complaint was that 'we can't live on it, we only exist'.[107]

Nationally, the numbers of people over 70 receiving 'domiciliary relief', as outdoor relief was now officially known (a figure which provides a reasonable indicator of the extent of serious destitution) rose from 8,600 in 1920 to 69,900 in 1928. The numbers receiving indoor relief, which were more sensitive to physical and/or mental incapacity than to absolute poverty, rose from 38,200 to 46,300. These statistics may mean several things: diminishing resistance to poor relief (which is not evident in the sources which investigated the feelings of old people about the poor relief system); rates of relief in many localities which were higher than the pension; a diminished capacity of families to assist due to unemployment; fewer supplementary jobs for old people for the same reason. Probably all had some influence. Rates of pension were still below average manual wages or even unemployment benefit. The latter fluctuated between twenty and twenty-five shillings (plus additional benefits for children) per week for a married couple between 1920 and 1925.

In the late 1930s a survey of the (ill) health of 'working class wives' included fifty-two aged 50 or above among the 1,250 women surveyed from many parts of Britain. The health of these older women was significantly worse than that of younger women. Decline was generally discernible after age 40. Of the older women, only nine were described as in 'apparently good' health, while thirty-nine were in 'very bad' health.[108] These included:

an unhappy elderly woman outside Derby . . . is very miserable; she has no leisure occupation and cannot read or write. She cannot go out much as her leg is too bad; she only goes to the shops once a week when well enough. She suffers from nerves, headaches (due to the worry of husband's unemployment)—general debility and shortness of breath, and a very bad ulcerated leg. Her leg has been bad for over twenty years; for two years she went three times a week to the Infirmary for treatment (ten miles distant) but had to stop two years ago owing to husband's unemployment; she said the lotion obtained at the Infirmary did much to ease the intolerable pain, but she cannot now afford the fares (1s.) or the lotion. The ulcers have now burst. She has had eight children; only one, a son of 23 now lives at home. He is a brass-glazer and a big man requiring adequate food. He gets it—the old people do not.

The report commented that these older women had not had the access to medical advice available to younger women. Nevertheless even younger women continued to put their own health, and food, needs after those of their husbands and children 'to such an appalling degree that one wonders how many of them will be able to enjoy the comparative rest which later life is bound to bring'. What the future might hold for them was represented by:

---

[107] Llewellyn-Smith, *New Survey*, ii: *Old Age Pensions*. British Library of Political and Economic Science.
[108] M. Spring-Rice, *Working Class Wives* (1939; repr. London, 1981), 209.

an elderly bed-ridden woman in a country village . . . She lives in a cottage by her-self but her married daughter who lives nearby spends a long time every day look-ing after her and is constantly in and out (an extra burden for the daughter who has six small children of her own and is the wife of an agricultural labourer earning 33s. a week). The old lady has rheumatoid arthritis and is very small and weak. The writer asked her whether she was able to enjoy her rest and the care her daughter now took of her, to which she replied: 'Oh my dear if I could have had a little of it twenty years ago, it would have saved a great deal of this' and she held out her hands, which as she put it are all 'housened up'.[109]

The women commented on doctors' lack of concern at the ill health of women in their forties and beyond.[110] The Report commented 'There is no need to attempt to prove that most of these women are under-nourished'.

Most of the inter-war social surveys made the error of assuming that food purchases were shared within the household according to nutritional need. Hence they overestimated the share going to women, children, old people, and other non-earners.[111] A Nuffield Foundation study found in 1947 that old people living in extended households readily acquiesced in receiving a smaller share than other family members, 'anxious not to be a nuisance', and put the needs of younger people first. None the less, the levels of nutrition of many poorer old people probably improved through the inter-war years. The social surveys highlighted areas of exceptional poverty, but many old people lived in districts where new industries and employment were expanding and enabling families better to assist aged relatives.[112] Improvements in other aspects of the living conditions of older people probably lagged behind those in diet. There was rarely suitable accommodation for them in the new housing estates of the inter-war years, and in any case rents for such housing were generally too high for those on very low incomes. Housework in the poor conditions which remained in older working-class housing, where old people were most likely to live, was heavy even for younger women.

WOMEN AND PENSIONS

There is little sign of protest by women against the fact that relatively few women gained a pension in their own right due to the introduction of con-tributory pensions. This is not because women were politically quiescent at this time. After gaining the vote women were active and effective on a wide range of issues.[113] They were perhaps mollified by the fact that wives of insured

---

[109] Spring–Rice, *Working Class Wives*, 80–2.   [110] Ibid. 45–6.

[111] Fogerty, 'Growing Old', 86.

[112] J. Stevenson and C. Cook, *Britain in the Depression: Society and Politics, 1929–39*, 2nd edn. (London, 1994).

[113] Cheryl Law, *Suffrage and Power: The Women's Movement, 1918–28* (London, 1997).

men were provided for, also by the grant of widows' pensions to a group of women long identified as the most needy, for which women's groups had been campaigning for some years. 725,000 widows received the pension in 1933. This was additional to the pensions paid to war widows under a separate scheme. The widows' pension was set at the same level as the old-age pension, ten shillings. Once granted, it was payable for life; the problem of an arbitrary pension age which did not relate to physical condition or to ability to be self-supporting was solved for some of the poorest women.

However, initially, widows qualified only if they had children under 14 at the time of the husband's death. Women, and men, protested that this discriminated unfairly against older widows, who were likely to have been out of the labour market for a considerable time, supporting husbands and children, and would find difficulty in supporting themselves. This was rectified in legislation introduced by the second Labour government in 1929. This extended entitlement to widows' pensions to all widows of insured men from the age of 55. Fifty-five was quite arbitrarily arrived at, primarily, as usual, 'fixed by expense'.[114] Employed unmarried women protested that widows could continue in paid work while receiving the pension and so competed unfairly for work.[115]

In 1937 the 'Black-coated Workers Act' enabled 'persons with small incomes, whether working on their own account or not' who were not in insurable employment, such as 'ministers of religion, shopkeepers, farmers, clerks, dressmakers and music teachers'[116] to become voluntary insurers under the Widows', Orphans' and Old Age Contributory Pensions Acts. The income limit for men was £400, for women £250. This new form of discrimination between the sexes, in the view of contemporary commentators, 'occasioned a good deal of controversy . . . It had however nothing to do with sex discrimination, and simply recognized facts. The scheme was intended to appeal mainly to married men whose income provided for at least two persons . . . and possibly more, including children, whereas a woman could insure for a single old age pension only. Not everyone accepted this view of the situation . . .'.[117] 759,683 applicants for the scheme were recorded by the end of December 1938.[118]

Labour made pensions a major issue in the later 1930s. In 1939 the Labour Party proposed a pension of £1 a week for a single person, thirty-five shillings for a couple, on condition of retirement. It was also proposed that from the age of 55 the wives of insured men should be eligible for pensions when their husbands reached pensionable age. Old people themselves were also becoming assertive proponents of their own interests. The National Association of Old Age Pensions Associations was formed in 1938 and,

---

[114] *Report of the Committee on Pensions for Unmarried Women*, Cmd. 3991 (1939).   [115] Ibid. 22.
[116] Wilson and Mackay, *Old Age Pensions*, 176.   [117] Ibid. 178.   [118] Ibid. 184.

through demonstrations, petitions to Ministers, and pressure upon Members of Parliament sought radical improvement in pensions.[119] Its influence is hard to assess though it may be that politicians were disturbed about the potential of the 'grey vote' were it to become effectively organized. It did not do so; old people had varied and divided interests and such organization has always been difficult. At the same time 'spinsters' were asserting the needs of older unmarried women.[120]

Neville Chamberlain, now Prime Minister, sought to resist these pressures, but felt that it was unavoidable to do something. The outcome was the Old Age and Widows' Pensions Act, 1940. This reduced the pensionable age to 60 for insured women and wives of insured male pensioners. The legislation increased women's contributions by threepence per week, raising the percentage of their benefits which was financed by contributions from 62 to 70, and hence compensating for the costs arising from previous schemes, about which the Treasury had become increasingly concerned. The outcome differed from the demands of the National Spinsters' Pensions Association but had it not been for their campaign, it is unlikely that the change would have come about. Uninsured unmarried women still had no access to a pension until age 70.

The Act of 1940 also provided for a needs-based supplementary pension to prevent pensioners needing any longer to seek poor relief. The supplement was lower for women than for men because the rates were based upon Rowntree's stringent estimate that old women needed only two-thirds of the food of old men. Also, the welfare of pensioners was transferred from the local authorities to the Unemployment Assistance Board, thus severing a further link with the Poor Law administration. Still in 1940 many old people lived in absolute, miserable poverty.

---

[119] Blaikie, 'Political Power'. Macnicol, *Retirement,* 319–22.   [120] See pp. 284–6.

17

The 'Menace' of an Ageing Population, the 1920s to 1950s

The British birth-rate started to fall from the later nineteenth century.[1] One outcome was a change in the age structure of the population and the beginning of a dramatic long-run increase in the proportion of older people. Old people became more numerous, in absolute and relative terms, over the twentieth century. Decline in the birth-rate was not accompanied by rising mortality among older age groups, indeed rather the reverse, hence British society was 'older' in the inter-war years than it had been since the mid-eighteenth century.[2] The percentage of the population of Great Britain composed of males over 65 and females over 60 was 6.2 in 1901, 9.6 in 1931, 12 in 1941, 13.5 in 1951, and the rise continued thereafter. Also the labour force was ageing. The percentage of the 15 to 65 age group (the bulk of people of working age) who were over age 40, had been 35 in the mid-nineteenth century and was 45 in 1947.[3] Britain was undergoing a decisive shift from a predominantly youthful age structure in the mid-nineteenth century to a predominantly older one. The fact of this shift and the realization that its economic and social implications were likely to be profound were gradually recognized and discussed.

KEYNES, BEVERIDGE, AND THE DECLINING BIRTH-RATE

Before the First World War, the discourse around the declining fertility rate paid little attention to ageing. There was by no means a consensus that the fertility decline was undesirable. It could plausibly be argued that high levels of poverty and underemployment suggested that the country was *over*populated. But proponents of all points of view sustained a lively debate involving prominent intellectuals and social reformers. This became more active after the First World War.

[1] M. Anderson, 'The Social Implications of Demographic Change', in F. M. L. Thompson (ed.), *The Cambridge Social History of Britain, 1750–1950*, ii (Cambridge, 1990), 1–70. S. Szreter, *Fertility, Class and Gender in Britain, 1860–1940* (Cambridge, 1996).
[2] R. Smith, 'The Structured Dependency of the Elderly as a Recent Development: Some Social Sceptical Historical Thoughts', *Ageing & Society* 4 (Cambridge, 1984), 409–28.
[3] John Ermisch, *The Political Economy of Demographic Change* (London, 1983), 12.

In 1923–4 the economist J. M. Keynes and Sir William Beveridge conducted a widely publicized discussion which found strong echoes in the (anti-Malthusian) left-wing weekly journal the *New Statesman*, and in the liberal political journal the *Nation* (which was owned by Keynes from April 1923). The editor of the *New Statesman* in September 1923 attacked Keynes's 'malthusian moonshine' on the grounds that it encouraged birth control propaganda. This, he argued, was 'One of the most dangerous movements that has ever threatened civilization' because it:

merely influences and always will mainly influence precisely those persons and classes which ought to be encouraged to bear children . . . the 'intellectual' class . . . it is probably the greatest factor that at present exists tending towards the deterioration of the white races.

Interestingly, he sought to distance himself from close association with eugenics:

We are not enamoured of 'eugenics' especially as a science as it is preached by the Eugenics Education Society, but every intelligent being must admit that there is such a thing as 'selection' and that the average quality of a race may rise or fall.[4]

Beveridge took a broadly anti-Malthusian position and advocated family allowances to stimulate the birth-rate. Keynes feared that the British, indeed the Western, economy was experiencing a fundamental long-run crisis which might be exacerbated if a reversal of the trend towards smaller populations unloosed the 'Malthus devil' and overpopulation undermined economic growth. Both Keynes and Beveridge, in fact, favoured 'rational' family planning and Beveridge in the last resort accepted the Malthusian analysis that population restraint was essential to avoid economic crisis,[5] but he shared, as Keynes apparently did not, the eugenist fear that birth control was mainly practised by the 'responsible' sections of society (in all classes), thus potentially damaging the quality of the 'national stock' in Britain; and that, internationally, the 'white' races were being differentially depleted with alarming potential effects. He wrote in 1924:

the questions now facing us are how far the fall will go; whether it will bring about a stationary white population after or long before the white man's world is full; how the varying incidence of restriction among different social classes and creeds will affect the Stock; how far the unequal adoption of birth control in different races will leave one race at the mercy of another's growing numbers or drive it to armaments or permanent aggression in self defence.[6]

---

[4] *New Statesman*, 22 Sept. 1923.

[5] José Harris, *William Beveridge: A Biography* (Oxford 1977), 341–2. D. Moggridge (ed.), *The Collected Writings of J. Maynard Keynes*, xix: *Activities (1922–9) Part 1* (London and Cambridge, 1981), 119–43.

[6] Sir William Beveridge, 'Population and Unemployment', in R. L. Smyth (ed.), *Essays in the Economics of Socialism and Capitalism: Selected Papers Read to Section F, the British Association for the Advancement of Science 1886–1932* (London, 1964), 270.

Fears both of national economic decline and of international war hung over the population debate in the inter-war years, giving it a different character from that of the pre-1914 period. Both Beveridge and Keynes were alert to the possible effects of ageing upon society, though neither gave it prominence at this stage.[7] Their central concern was with the broader effects of demographic change upon the economy and on international relations.

THE 'MENACE' OF UNDERPOPULATION

The debate intensified as the birth-rate continued to fall, reaching its lowest point in the early 1930s. In 1924 the statistician A. L. Bowley pointed out that if demographic trends continued on their current trajectories the population would reach a stationary state by 1971. He did not comment on the implications. Ten years later the projections of Grace Leybourne[8] and the still gloomier ones of Enid Charles[9] stimulated and further popularized the debate. These projections were in part a product of advances in statistical method as applied to demography and the emergence of demography as a distinctive field of study at this time. In particular the development of the concepts of net and gross reproduction rates enabled demographers to construct more sophisticated projections. Dramatic and widely publicized statistics intensified fears for the demographic future in scholarly, popular, and political circles.

Grace Leybourne was primarily a statistician who made little comment on the reasons for the trends she identified or on their social implications. Warning that 'an estimate' is not a prophecy',[10] she calculated that the total population of Britain would increase slowly for a few years and then decline. In 1941 it would reach about the level of 1931; by 1951 it would decline by about two million; by 1976 it would stand at 32,711,900. She assumed no significant changes in migration, some improvement in mortality, but the major anticipated change was the continuing fall in the birth-rate, since, she commented, 'it cannot be supposed that the practice of family limitation has yet nearly reached its limit';[11] in addition, the number of women in the childbearing age group was likely to fall. In consequence the population as a whole would become significantly older. Leybourne estimated that 17.5 per cent of the British population would be over 65 in 1976 compared with 7.2 per cent in 1931.

Enid Charles was a social biologist who was rather more interested in the social and ecological implications of the population change than in demographic

[7] Harris, *Beveridge*, 342. Moggridge, *Keynes*, 122.

[8] Grace D. Leybourne, 'An Estimate of the Future Population of Great Britain', *Sociological Review*, 26 (London, 1934), 130–8.

[9] Enid Charles, 'The Effect of Present Trends in Fertility and Mortality upon the Future Population of England and Wales and upon its Age Composition', *London and Cambridge Economic Service: Special Memorandum*, no. 40 (1935).

[10] Leybourne, 'Estimate'., 130.   [11] Ibid. 132.

projections in themselves. However, the projections she developed came to be more widely quoted than any others.[12] She also saw the spreading practice of family limitation as the key element in the change.[13] Her views of the future were embodied in her highly successful *The Twilight of Parenthood*, a biological study of the reduced population growth, published in 1934 and reissued in 1936, changed only in title to the more threatening *The Menace of Underpopulation*.

In 1935 Charles published three sets of projections based on the differing assumptions that (*a*) fertility and mortality would remain at the historic- ally low 1933 level, (*b*) the falling trend in both would continue at a constant rate, (*c*) fertility would rise again to the 1931 level. The last of these, the most optimistic projection (and, as it turned out the most accurate) she thought 'unlikely to be of more than theoretical interest'[14] and omitted it from future publications of her otherwise largely unrevised estimates. She placed more reliance upon the gloomiest assumption (*b*); accordingly, she estimated that the total population of Great Britain would remain stable until 1939, when it would begin to decline from about 40.5 million to 39.8 million in 1960, to 28.8 million in 1980, and a tiny 4.4 million in 2035. The number of over- sixties in the population would increase by 143 per cent by 1958, when they would form 18.6 per cent of the total. The rather more optimistic estimate (*a*) delayed the onset of decline until 1945; on this basis by 1980 the popula- tion would still number 34.6 million and in 2035 almost 20 million. Both Leybourne and Charles pointed out that the ageing of the population would perpetuate the female majority in the population if females continued to experience longer life expectancy than males.

THE AGEING OF BRITAIN

Much of the debate which followed, for the remainder of the 1930s, was alarmed and sometimes alarmist in tone. Expert opinion differed concerning the rel- ative desirability of approximately stable population size, slow growth, or rapid growth. There were very few supporters of decline and few favoured rapid growth.[15] Much of the discussion took place under the auspices of the Eugenics Society, largely in its journal the *Eugenics Review*. Indeed the debate may have played some part in the revival of the Society; its membership had flagged

---

[12] By, among others, D. V. Glass, 'The Population Problem and the Future', *Eugenics Review*, 26/1. (London, 1937), 39–47; and *The Struggle for Population* (London, 1936), 12. R. M. Titmuss, *Poverty and Population* (London, 1938). W. B. Reddaway, *The Economics of a Declining Population* (London, 1946), 31.
[13] Enid Charles, *The Twilight of Parenthood: A Biological Study of the Decline in Population Growth* (London, 1934), 2.
[14] Enid Charles, 'The Effects of Present Trends in Fertility and Mortality upon the Future Population of Great Britain and upon its Age Composition', in Lancelot Hogben (ed.), *Political Arithmetic: A Symposium of Population Studies* (London, 1938), 82.   [15] Glass, *Struggle*, 88.

in the 1920s, but it reached an all-time peak (768) in 1932–3.[16] Eugenics in the 1930s in Britain was not reducible to a single set of beliefs and the place of at least some of the tendencies within it in the intellectual history of progressive social reform is obscure but real. Charles herself was a determined opponent of eugenic theory. Her fears about the future were based on the effects of *total* population decline rather than on differentiation by class or levels of 'responsibility', which she dismissed as 'a temporary and exceptional phenomenon'.

For others, however, the Eugenics Society provided a natural forum for discussion of demographic issues. Since the quantity and quality—however defined—of the population lay at the core of its concerns, it was open to a variety of proposals as to how these should be maximized. Throughout the 1930s it sponsored research into the causes and effects of fertility decline. An important component of this debate, as it was carried on in the *Eugenics Review* and elsewhere, concerned the social and economic effects of an ageing society. Broadly there were two sides: on the one hand, those who believed that the effects would be harmful. One contributor to the *Review* wrote in 1937 that since human intelligence declined from around the age of 35, 'if a man has not done original work by the age of 40 he never will'.[17] Hence an ageing society would 'decline in intelligence and social competence' and necessarily become less innovative and less flexible at a time when the economy in particular had rarely needed flexibility and innovation more. Some, such as the economist H. D. Henderson, in a special issue of the *Sociological Review*, in 1937, which was given over to discussion of the problem of the declining birth-rate, were tempted to suggest that the ageing of western European societies from the beginning of the century was one of the causes of their economic difficulties, above all because it led to reduced demand. Keynes, on the other hand, was inclined to believe that there were links between high levels of unemployment and overpopulation, possibly indirectly; Western economies whose capacity for economic expansion had become problematic would, he feared, have difficulty in maintaining or improving the living standards of an expanding population. If no more, he asked, in 1937, in a lecture to the Eugenics Society, 'What is the use or purpose of all our strivings if they are to be neutralized or defeated by the mere growth of numbers?'[18]

Economists differed as to whether economies could satisfactorily adjust to the changing population structure. It was feared, variously, that investment would decline because older people were assumed to be spenders rather than savers; that the workforce would be less mobile, flexible, and productive; patterns of demand would shift 'from perambulators to bathchairs' and the range of goods demanded would narrow; promotion and advancement at work would

---

[16] G. R. Searle, 'Eugenics and Politics in Britain in the 1930s', *Annals of Science*, 36 (1979), 160.
[17] P. S. Bramwell, 'Falling Population and Positive Eugenics', *Eugenics Review*, 27/4 (1937), 274–5.
[18] Moggridge, *Keynes*, 121.

come relatively late in life causing frustration and disincentive to innovation. The relative immobility of older workers in depressed industries compared with younger workers and the reluctance of businessmen to site new and expanding industries in the old and ageing industrial centres was cited as evidence.[19]

The economist Roy Harrod shared most of these fears and was a strong advocate of family allowances as a means to increase fertility and to achieve a more balanced population structure. But the most persistent, prolific, and one of the most immoderate of the demographic pessimists was Richard Titmuss, then a young actuary in the insurance business and hence well aware of population trends. Later, as we will see, he became one of the foremost British academic experts on social security.[20] From 1938, when he published *Poverty and Population: A Factual Study of Contemporary Social Waste*, and through the years of the Second World War, he insisted upon the comprehensively harmful effects of the declining birth-rate and the ageing of the population, threatening what he described as 'national suicide'.[21] It would, he claimed at various times, lead to a 'decline in the mean intelligence quotient of the nation and a reduction in social competence'.[22] Class structure would become more rigid because the opportunities for mobility for younger people would be reduced. An older community would be more conservative because more interested in security and stability than in progress. The effects on the economy had, he believed, been disastrous. The need to care for the elderly would delay female marriage, hence further lowering the fertility rate as well as keeping women out of the paid labour force. Britain would also become militarily weaker. 'Can we', he asked in 1938,

maintain our present attitude to India while we decline in numbers and age . . . (and India's population expands)?[23] Can we in these circumstances retain our particular status in the world, our genius for colonization, our love of political freedom and our leadership of the British Commonwealth of nations . . . are we to bring to such a pathetic close, to such a mean inglorious end a history which with all its faults still shines with the lights of our gifts to mankind and still glows with the quite patient courage of the common people.[24]

Titmuss's views were widely disseminated and were summarized in a pamphlet issued to the armed forces in 1943.[25]

Others sought to inject some discipline and common sense into a discussion which was almost wholly conjectural. No one had any clear idea of the

---

[19] J. M. Keynes, 'Some Economic Consequences of a Declining Population', *Eugenics Review*, 27/2 (London, 1937), 13–17; Glass, 'Population Problem'; Glass, *Struggle*, 14–15; R. F. Harrod, 'Modern Population Trends', *Manchester School of Economic and Social Studies*, 10 (Manchester, 1939), 1–20; Titmuss, *Poverty*, 20 ff.

[20] See pp. 373–6.   [21] Titmuss, *Poverty*, xxi–xxiv.   [22] Ibid. 19–20.

[23] At this time India was demanding independence. Britain was engaged in protracted negotiations aimed at giving India a measure of independence within the Empire.

[24] Titmuss, *Poverty*, 53.   [25] R. M. Titmuss, *Problems of Population* (London, 1943).

actual effects of ageing on society; little evidence existed or was actively sought. The demographer David Glass, following the pessimism of his *The Struggle for Population* (1936), in an article 'The Population Problem and the Future' in 1937 made a strong case for the flexible potential of almost any given population structure; population could adjust to changing needs, education to the creation of an adaptable labour force. He wrote:

[An ageing population] may mean that fewer toys would be wanted; but on the other hand it may result in a greater demand for armchairs and slippers; and it may mean an increase in the amount spent on pensions, but also a decrease in the aggregate cost of education.[26]

New technology or changes in the organization of work might extend the work potential of older people. Indeed, Glass pointed out, their actual work capacity was quite unknown and uninvestigated and in any case could be expected to improve in the future with a steady general improvement in standards of health.[27] Glass rousingly dismissed what he called

those problems which arise largely from prejudice or unfounded fears . . . for example the anxiety that a fall in our numbers may result in a deterioration in our military position *vis a vis* the other powers. There is not a great deal of justification for this fear since, first . . . most of the countries of the western world are in a position very similar to our own; and secondly it ignores the possibility of attracting manpower from other countries by means of immigration facilities.[28]

Though he believed that a *decline* in population would be harmful, Glass was inclined to be sceptical that it would occur in the long run. He believed that a more or less stable population size and structure was attainable and desirable and that harmful effects could be avoided by careful planning of the economic system, perhaps including some social ownership of resources and of means of distribution. He was also sceptical that much could be done significantly to alter the trend in the birth-rate. One of his earliest publications was a study of population policies in a number of European countries, from which he concluded that efforts to increase fertility for example by offering family allowances or by making birth control devices easier and abortion harder to obtain, had nowhere been successful.[29]

   This debate in the 1930s should be placed in the context of the growing interest at the time in social and economic planning and its efficacy to redress the effects of impersonal economic and social forces, including those of demography. Glass believed that rather than expressing alarm it was more constructive to make the best of the probably unavoidable continuation of a low birth-rate. Keynes, in his Galton lecture to the Eugenics Society of 1937,

[26] Glass, 'Population Problem', 43.   [27] Glass, *Struggle*, 14–15.
[28] Glass, 'Population Problem', 44.
[29] Glass, *Struggle*. M. S. Quine, *Population Politics in Twentieth-Century Europe* (London, 1996), is a good review of population politics in France, Germany, and Italy in this period.

was inclined to believe that a static or declining population would lead to reduced investment and production, if only due to a loss of business confidence induced by the belief that a fall in the birth-rate was harmful. But he argued that this need not be so if people looked to the future with imagination. He pointed out that the decline in demand could be avoided by means of income redistribution, for which there was considerable scope; and government control of interest rates could help to regulate the relationships between consumption and saving and between changing patterns of demand and the timing and pattern of investment. Such recommendations could only be effective if the population size did not fall significantly and they implied a high degree of government planning and intervention. However, by this means it might be possible:

perhaps to get the best of both worlds and maintain the liberties and independence of our present system, whilst its more signal faults gradually suffer euthanasia as the diminishing importance of capital accumulation and the rewards attached to it fall into their proper position in the social scheme.[30]

The comments of Keynes and of Glass made a lesser public impact than those of the prophets of doom. Both sides had their own reasons for promoting the debate. Both the authors of the gloomy projections and the professional demographers who quoted them stressed that they *were* projections and not prophecies,[31] and that the range of unforeseeable influences, in particular upon future rates of fertility, was such that accurate demographic forecasting was impossible. They accepted that forecasting fifty or one hundred years ahead was of some technical, statistical interest but little more. But the non-specialist audience does not habitually take note of the caveats invariably associated with dramatic statistics, nor did the specialists, including the authors of the projections, make strenuous efforts to ensure that they did so. A vocal and alarmed response to predictions of doom was useful ammunition in a number of concurrent campaigns: for social and economic planning; for family allowances; for statisticians and demographers seeking advancement for their profession and improved demographic data with which to work. The latter was one of the aims of the Population Investigation Committee, which brought together most of the prominent demographers under the auspices of the Eugenics Society. Its purpose was to sponsor investigation of population trends. One of its campaigning successes was the Population Statistics Act, 1939, which for the first time required at registration of each birth information as to the age of the mother, the duration of the marriage, and the birth order of each child.[32]

[30] Keynes, 'Some Economic Consequences', 17.

[31] Glass, 'Population Problem'; R. R. Kuczynski, 'Future Trends in Population', *Eugenics Review*, 24/2 (London, 1937), 99–107. Glass, *Struggle*, 13. D. V. Glass and C. P. Blacker, *The Future of our Population* (London, 1937), 14–16.   [32] *Hansard* (5th ser.), vol. 329, cols. 1717 ff.

The more extreme manifestations of demographic pessimism, however, went beyond anything explicable as either pressure-group tactics or realistic fears arising from the unprecedented nature of the fertility decline. As was clear from at least the 1870s, concern about the total size and structure of the population, in Britain and elsewhere, touched off deep national unease. On some level, the size, physical quality, and youthfulness of the population were identified in the collective imagination with national pride and greatness. Titmuss vividly expressed some of these feelings. C. P. Blacker and David Glass also incorporated in their plea for improved demographic statistics the comment that:

All would agree that a decline to half its present size would make it very difficult for this country and other western powers to maintain their position and their present state of civilization. If the downward trend of the population were to become, as is threatened, a downward plunge, western culture and western ideals would go at the same time.[33]

In 1939 W. Reddaway, a Cambridge economist influenced by Keynes, published *The Economics of a Declining Population*,[34] an attempt at a balanced survey of the economic aspects of ageing which, unusually, apart from the work of Glass, who advised him, 'tried to preserve a sense of proportion and not to exaggerate the influence of the population factor'.[35] Reddaway aimed the book at both a popular and a specialized audience. He surveyed the pessimistic population projections and the assumptions on which they were based, and the possible effects of various projections upon employment and unemployment, National Insurance, public finance, and trade. He set out to separate the sense from the nonsense in discussion of the economic implications of the debate, which he felt had been less thoroughly explored than the demographic prophecies.

He confined his analysis to the 'comparatively near future', the thirty years or so immediately ahead, for which predictions were a little less hazy than for the more distant future. Over this period he believed that: 'the population will decline only slightly, the leading features being rather a great change in age composition and the absence of the customary increase in numbers . . . a changeover from an increasing to a stationary population'.[36] Reddaway's overriding view was that population change was by no means the greatest problem facing the British economy; it was not the determining factor for the future and any problems could be solved without tinkering with the birthrate. Provided, above all, that the major problem of the economy, the 'essentially manmade problem of general unemployment', could be overcome, 'the economic outlook must be regarded as at least potentially favourable. Provided that we can learn to take advantage of it, the new situation should enable us to raise our standard of living at least as rapidly as in the past.' This advantage

---

[33] Glass and Blacker, *Future*, 165.
[34] W. B. Reddaway, *The Economics of a Declining Population* (London, 1939).
[35] Ibid. 8.   [36] Ibid. 229.

could be achieved by employing the techniques of economic management advocated by Keynes which, by 1939, were becoming acceptable to government.

Reddaway pointed out that, although the age shift imposed some new costs on public finance, such as the costs of more old-age pensions, it reduced the costs of giving birth to, raising, and educating the very young. Successful attempts to increase fertility would raise the latter costs without reducing the absolute costs of providing for older people—issues which he felt had 'given rise to so much loose thinking and talking'. He believed that the economic problems would be more serious should the fertility rate fall below the levels of the late 1930s. Whether they would do so was hard to predict. Reddaway argued that such policy measures as family allowances, income tax relief for parents, improved maternity services, crèches, nursery schools, improved housing, and subsidized education might prevent further reductions in fertility whilst being desirable in themselves in increasing the incomes of families with children and improving the life chances of the children. More 'coercive' measures such as those practised in Italy and Germany,[37] such as marriage loans and taxes on bachelors might increase fertility, but 'whether a community which had to resort to such measures to secure its survival really deserves to survive is a question which as yet does not arise. For whatever may be the proper course in other fields, this is surely one in which a democracy should try voluntary methods first.'[38]

Reddaway eloquently expressed the centrality of the debate about the declining birth-rate to the ominous politics of the later 1930s. The publication of his book coincided with the return to war in 1939.

THE SECOND WORLD WAR

The impact of demographic pessimism was greater upon intellectuals than on official policy-makers. The war, of course, upset pre-war forecasts. Not only did it directly increase the death-rate, but in 1942 the birth-rate began to turn upwards again. It was some time, however, before this became clear. Pre-war assumptions about population trends continued to be influential for some years and the debate continued during the war years. The White Paper on *The Current Trend of Population*, published in 1942 but prepared in 1939, was a consciously balanced, official response to what it described as the 'rather sensational pre-war projections of population decline'. It commented, correctly:

it is hardly necessary to observe that no projection extending over so long a period (as a century) could be regarded as a forecast in the sense of its bearing any demonstrable probability value; on the contrary, in this particular matter it is not inconceivable that the portrayal of the possible extinction of the nation was deliberately intended to encourage forces necessary to prevent its materialization.

---

[37] Quine, *Population Politics*.   [38] Ibid. 245.

The White Paper broadly accepted that the pre-war trends were likely to continue and that by 1971 over 20 per cent of the population of Great Britain would be over 65. It emphasized, however, that this 'cannot be regarded as an unforeseen or undesirable feature of the population structure' since it was a result of medical and social improvements which were also enhancing the fitness of older people:

with lower mortality goes increased vitality, and with it an increase in the age up to which economic productivity can, if necessary, be maintained. The rate of mortality now experienced by persons of sixty-five years of age, for example, was reached as early as age sixty some forty years ago, and in another forty years, with the continued improvement in mortality anticipated in the future may well be delayed until age seventy; in any true comparison of the ratio of potential producers to dependants, allowance for this moving level of physical capacity would obviously go far to compensate for an apparently undesirable decline in the ratio derived from the use of a fixed age as the dividing point.[39]

The White Paper was followed by the establishment in 1944 of a Royal Commission on Population, to explore population trends in detail.

Roy Harrod thought the White Paper too optimistic and too complacent about the likely effects of demographic change. The prominent demographer R. R. Kuczynski firmly agreed. G. D. H. Cole, the Labour intellectual and Oxford social scientist, said that by the end of the war he had 'not met with any statistician who is prepared to defend it'.[40] Beveridge, in his Report on Social Insurance of 1942,[41] quoted the White Paper as a warning about the likely future cost of pensions and of services to the elderly, and against further encouragement of the trend towards retirement from work at earlier ages which had been emerging before the war and which would, he believed, tend to exacerbate such problems as there were. To maximize the number of producers and minimize the proportion of dependants, he believed that workers should be encouraged to remain in the workforce until as late ages as possible. He recommended, as an incentive, higher pensions in return for delayed retirement. Beveridge concluded:

There is no reason also to doubt the power of larger numbers of people to go on working with advantage to the community and happiness to themselves after reaching the minimum pensionable age of sixty-five for men or sixty for women . . . There is no statistical evidence that industrial development is making it harder for people to continue at work later in life than it used to be; such evidence as there is points in the opposite direction. The natural presumption with the increasing length of total life is that the length of the years during which working capacity lasts will also rise, as health improves, as by freedom from want in childhood and by freedom from want

---

[39] *The Current Trend of Population in Great Britain*, Cmd. 6358 (1942), 2–6.
[40] G. D. H. Cole, *The Intelligent Man's Guide to the Post-War World* (London, 1947), 433.
[41] See pp. 364–8.

and idleness in working years, the physique and the courage of the citizens are maintained. A people ageing in years need not be old in spirit and British youth will rise again.[42]

He recommended provision by the state of full subsistence pensions for all retired people.[43]

AFTER THE WAR

The debate on the declining birth-rate was muted during the war though, as we have seen, it was not silenced. It revived after the war and the government paid more attention to the question. This was largely due to the realization that the post-war world had not, as expected, brought a return to unemployment, but a labour shortage. The combination of the ageing of the labour force with the continuation of the trend towards retirement at earlier ages threatened to exacerbate the labour shortage and to reduce production levels. Intellectuals, rather than members of the government, expressed concern that the ageing of the workforce would hinder the necessary restructuring of important sectors of industry.

Although the fertility decline had been reversed it would take some time to impact on the labour market. The post-war debate on ageing took place in a different atmosphere from that of the 1930s: of victory, national pride, full employment, and optimism. Labour's National Insurance legislation of 1946 incorporated Beveridge's proposal of an additional one shilling per week pension for each six months of delayed retirement beyond the minimum pensionable age. It was not a great incentive and it ceased to operate at age 70, a proviso not proposed by Beveridge.

By 1947 the government's *Economic Survey* was emphasizing the problem of labour shortage and it appealed to older workers 'to contribute to the national task by staying on instead of retiring'.[44] Also in 1947 the Nuffield Foundation published the report of a committee chaired by Seebohm Rowntree which had been established in 1945 to examine the economic and social situation of the over-sixties. It was a thorough review of the limited state of knowledge of the subject. The committee repeated many of Beveridge's warnings, but emphasized how little was really known about the social and economic capabilities of older people. Most of the previous gloomy assumptions about the attributes of older people had been based upon guesswork, prejudice, or past experience, whereas it could be assumed that more recent and future generations of older people, having grown up with higher standards of living, including of health and education, than their predecessors, would remain active

---

[42] Sir William Beveridge, *Social Insurance and Allied Services*, Cmd. 6404 (1942), 99.
[43] See pp. 365–8.   [44] *Economic Survey for 1947*, Cmd. 7046 (London, 1947), 16.

until later ages; hence the effects of an ageing population should be less dire than was feared.[45]

Following this report the Foundation invested a great deal of money in the following decade and a half in developing research into social, medical, psychological, and economic aspects of ageing. During the 1950s research institutes in London, Cambridge, Bristol, and Liverpool carried out studies of the work experience and skills of older people, designed to discover whether an ageing workforce would indeed be so much less flexible and productive as was conventionally assumed. In general these studies reached optimistic conclusions about the productive capacities of older workers.[46]

Before these findings could become available, a largely ill-informed debate continued. In 1948 G. D. H. Cole contemplated 'the disagreeable prospect' of the ageing of society:

> the relatively old . . . may be, man for man and woman for woman, just as good workers as their juniors; but they will be definitely less adaptable to new jobs and it may be of great importance to us in view of rapidly changing techniques and products, to possess a highly adaptable labour force.[47]

Cole recognized that the problem required an urgent response, though he emphasized the difficulty of constructing a credible one. He believed that it was essential to reverse the decline in fertility, but difficult to suggest the means. He had little faith that family allowances could have this effect, though he believed that support for mothers, in the form of crèches and communal restaurants, would encourage them to have more children whilst being active in the paid labour market, which he also believed desirable and necessary for the economy. Cole was pessimistic that older people would be persuaded to delay retirement as pension provision improved, though he thought it worth while to seek to encourage this. More important, he argued, was to maximize the effectiveness of younger workers, for, with an ageing population 'it will be necessary to make the most of every young worker by training him or her for the highest type of work which is within his or her capacity'.[48]

---

[45] Nuffield Foundation, *Old People: Report of a Survey Committee on the Problems of Ageing and the Care of Old People*. (Oxford, 1947).

[46] These included at least sixteen publications by F. Le Gros Clark for the Nuffield Foundation. These include *Ageing in Industry* (with Agnes Dunn) (London, 1955). *Ageing Men in the Labour Force* (London, 1955). *Bus Workers* (London, 1957). *Women, Work and Age* (London, 1962). *Workers Nearing Retirement* (with Alastair Heron) (London, 1963). *Work, Age and Leisure* (London, 1966). Also I. M. Richardson, 'Age and Work: A Study of 489 Men in Heavy Industry', *British Journal of Industrial Medicine*, 10 (London, 1953), 269–84. R. M. Belbin, 'Difficulties of Older People in Industry', *Occupational Psychology*, 27 (London, 1953), 177–89; 'Older People and Heavy Work', *British Journal of Industrial Medicine*, 12 (London, 1955), 309–19. A. M. Shooter *et al.*, 'Some Field Data on the Training of Older People', *Occupational Psychology*, 30 (London, 1956), 204–15. Hilary M. Clay, 'A Study of Performance in Relation to Age at Two Printing Works', *Journal of Gerontology*, 11. (London, 1956), 417–24. R. A. Brown, 'Age and "Paced" Work', *Occupational Psychology*, 31 (London, 1957), 11–20. A. Welford, *Ageing and Human Skills* (Oxford, 1958). A. Heron and S. Chown, 'Semi-Skilled and Over 40', *Occupational Psychology*, 34 (London, 1960), 264–74.

[47] Cole, *Intelligent Man's Guide*, 434.   [48] Ibid. 446.

In 1948 the research organization Political and Economic Planning (PEP) produced the alarmist and strongly eugenist *Population Policy in Great Britain* on the implications of what it called 'the deterioration of the age structure'. It asserted that not only would the older labour force be less mobile and adaptable than in the past but

an elderly population was not likely to be either adventurous or vigorous in the social and political spheres . . . the frustration which would be felt by the young in a country where their elders could not only always outvote them but also put an effective damper on their initiative might well drive them to mass migration. By reducing still further the proportion of young people this might worsen the position beyond remedy.[49]

The solution offered by PEP was a gradual increase in the birth-rate, according to sound eugenic principles, largely by offering substantial family allowances. A book published in 1947 by the popular paperback Pelican imprint, *The Population of Britain* by Eva Hubback, an active feminist and a long-time campaigner for family allowances, was widely sold, and reinforced and popularized this message. The book was intended to provide a popular background to the impending publication of the report of the Royal Commission on Population. Hubback argued that the rise in the birth-rate was a temporary phenomenon and that the long-term trend towards the spread of the practice of birth control and falling fertility would reassert itself, due to the desire of all people for a higher standard of living and of women for greater freedom. She quoted a series of demographic projections of which the one she regarded as 'least hypothetical' put the total population of England and Wales at 39.5 million in 1969. (The actual total in 1971 was 48.7 million.) Hubback recognized that the impact of the falling birth-rate could be offset by migration, either from central or southern Europe or, less probably she believed, from Asia. She thought it unlikely that the latter would be welcome. Indeed she believed that 'immigration on a vast scale is a counsel of despair, as it is a sign that we have failed to maintain the vitality and spirit to keep our own community alive'.[50]

Against this background the report of the Royal Commission on Population was published in 1948. This also emphasized the current and probable future trend towards an ageing population, but in less alarmist terms. The Report pointed out that the trend was an outcome of reductions both in levels of mortality and in the excessive family sizes prevailing before the First World War, both of which were socially desirable; it emphasized that society was undergoing a major demographic shift with which all would have to come to terms.

The Royal Commission had established a committee of economists, which warned that an ageing labour force might lessen the flexibility of the economy because workers might become less mobile and adaptable at a time when the

[49]   PEP, *Population Policy in Great Britain* (London, 1948), 6.
[50]   Eva M. Hubback, *The Population of Britain* (Harmondsworth, 1947), 36 ff. and 246.

development of new skills and industries and the restructuring of old ones was necessary. On the other hand, they pointed out that older workers constituted a reservoir of essential skills; hence they recommended that in view of the current labour shortage the trend towards earlier retirement should be discouraged. The more so, they thought, since future generations of older people were likely to be fitter and more adaptable to later ages than the current generation. In order to maximize the future labour force and to minimize the burden of the dependent elderly upon the young, it would be desirable if the habit of retirement of people in their early to mid-sixties did not become firmly established. The committee argued that a flexible retirement age was preferable and that older people should be encouraged to think positively about their capacity to contribute to society.[51]

The Report of the Commission accepted that different age groups had broadly different characteristics. The 'experience, patience, wisdom and breadth of view' in which the old excelled over the 'energy, enterprise and enthusiasm' of the young, would not necessarily compensate for the danger of an ageing society becoming 'dangerously unprogressive, falling behind other communities not only in technical efficiency and economic welfare but in intellectual and artistic achievement as well'. The Commission was not sure how pessimistic it ought to be about the prospect. British society had, after all, been ageing throughout the twentieth century and its effects, in particular, on the inter-war economic depression, were difficult to assess. Probable future increases in the productivity of the workforce due to changing technology might offset any losses due to ageing; changing living standards should enable people to remain active to later ages and they should be encouraged to do so, since other potential sources of recruitment to the labour force—females and immigrants—were thought unlikely to provide substitutes, certainly in the short run, for experienced, especially skilled, men. The Commission concluded that more knowledge was needed about the effects of ageing on society, to facilitate planning; and that some increase in the birth-rate was desirable, if some means could be found to achieve it.[52]

In general, the manner in which ageing was discussed immediately after the war continued to present the prospect of an ageing society as a social and economic problem and took for granted a negative view of older people, their economic capability and social contributions. The Royal Commission, like the Nuffield Committee and Beveridge, tried, somewhat uncertainly, to modify this approach, hampered by lack of knowledge about the real effects of ageing on individuals or on society and the economy.

Government policy was contradictory. The 1946 pension scheme incorporated a financial incentive to defer retirement but it was small. It differed

---

[51] *Report of the Royal Commission on Population*, Cmd. 7695 (London, 1949), 115–16.
[52] Ibid. 21–57.

from the pre-war scheme and from those introduced elsewhere in Europe after the war in insisting upon almost total retirement as a condition of receiving the pension. In 1946 a strict, and low, limit of £2 per week was introduced for earnings permitted in addition to the pension. Pensions elsewhere in western Europe incorporated flexible combinations of variable rates of pension and part-time earnings, facilitating gradual rather than sudden and total retirement. Meanwhile, the Ministry of Labour from 1947 made increasing efforts to keep older people in the labour force. This was a minor but serious part of their effort to beat the labour shortage. Nationally, increasing numbers of men and women were retiring at the state pensionable ages in each year of the later 1940s.[53] On the basis that few people appeared to remain capable of sustained work past the age of 70, it was estimated that the labour force could be increased by about 6 per cent over the coming twenty-five years, if deferral of retirement could be encouraged.[54] To the Ministry this was a worthwhile saving, partly to compensate for the absence from the workforce of younger men still captive in the armed services, due to the continuation of compulsory military service, and because the percentage of older workers was highest in some of the most essential industries such as shipbuilding. It was also anxious to maximize the labour force of the future and hence to prevent earlier retirement becoming the norm.

In reality, in the later 1940s no one had any clear idea of the pattern of retirement, of the age structure of industry, or of the work potential of those staying on beyond 60 or 65. There had previously been no need or concern to collect such data. From 1948 to 1964 the Ministry monitored retirement and published (from 1951) annual statistics of retirement and of the age structure of major occupational groups.[55] It sought to persuade employers and workers of the attractions of later retirement and of its importance to the economy as a whole.

The Labour government's pensions policy seemed inconsistent with its labour policy. New and rapidly spreading occupational pension schemes in the public sector,[56] for example in the National Health Service, sanctioned and encouraged retirement at 60 or 65, at the same time that the Ministry of Labour was seeking to encourage delayed retirement. The reasons for these conflicts in government policy are not mysterious. The Labour Party and the trade union movement had been committed since before the First World War to policies of early retirement on adequate pensions as a just reward for a working lifetime. This commitment had been intensified by the experience of the inter-war years when the earlier retirement of older workers was seen, however mistakenly, as the means to release jobs for the young. In addition,

---

[53] See p. 386.

[54] *Report of the Committee on the Economic and Financial Problems of Old Age*, *Parliamentary Papers* (1955–6), xvii. 17.

[55] *Ministry of Labour Gazette* (London, 1948–64).   [56] See pp. 380–2.

the experience of the Poor Law and the 'dole' made Labour and its supporters hostile to pension arrangements incorporating means tests, such as
some of the more flexible European schemes. Trade unionists were also hostile
to pension schemes which enabled older workers to draw both wages and
pension, for fear that employers would take advantage of this subsidy to wages
to employ older people at below standard rates, thus undercutting the pay of
younger workers. It was claimed that this had occurred under the pre-war
pension scheme.

Nor were trade unionists convinced that full employment had come to stay,
and temporary and localized unemployment indeed continued throughout the
later 1940s and 1950s, hence they continued to favour early retirement with
adequate pensions. In the post-war years, they were indeed increasingly inclined
to accept and to bargain for occupational pensions as a means both of boost-
ing post-retirement incomes and of encouraging retirement. Previously, unions
had been hostile to occupational pensions, which they interpreted—often
correctly—as stratagems by employers for securing the loyalty of the workers
to the firm rather than to the unions.[57] Increasingly the unions came, rather,
to perceive occupational pensions as enhancing the job security of younger
workers. Hence union attitudes and practices worked in favour of earlier rather
than later retirement.[58] In 1951 the Labour government slightly modified the
earnings rules of the state pension scheme in order to encourage more
older people to remain in part-time employment, though this was as much
a response to the discovery of the large numbers being forced to supplement
their pensions with means-tested National Assistance benefits as to concern
about retirement patterns.

The trend towards larger numbers of workers retiring at the minimum
pensionable age was arrested rather than reversed in the later 1940s, only to
be resumed and to move with considerable speed from about 1956. However,
by this time concern about future population decline was diminishing. Richard
Titmuss, for one, had come to think, more calmly than in his younger days, that:

Viewed historically, it is difficult to understand why the gradual emergence in Britain
of a more balanced age structure should be regarded as a 'problem of ageing'. What
we have to our credit as humanists and good husbanders is a great reduction in premature death since the nineteenth century; as a result, we have derived many
benefits from our growing ability to survive through the working span of life. Much
of the inefficiency and waste of early death has been eliminated by an increase in the
expectation of life at birth of the working classes to a point that now approaches closer
to that achieved by more prosperous classes . . . I believe that the present alarm is
unjustified; that the demographic changes which are under way and are foreseeable
have been exaggerated and that unless saner views prevail harm may be done to the
public welfare.[59]

[57] See pp. 251–4.   [58] Trades Union Congress, *Annual Report* (London, 1957), 360.
[59] R. M. Titmuss, *Essays on the Welfare State* (London, 1958), 56.

He had come to believe, with good reason, that arguments about the financial burden of ageing had become part of the growing armoury of weapons deployed in the 1950s by enemies of the welfare state against its supposedly excessive costs. Titmuss now believed that the long-run shift from a younger to an older age structure 'does not appear to raise acute economic problems' though it would necessitate more careful economic planning than Britain had so far attempted.[60]

A POSITIVE VIEW OF OLD AGE

In the 1950s research sponsored by the Nuffield Foundation began at last to provide information about the effects of ageing upon individuals, from which could be compiled an assessment of the actual effects of ageing upon society and, especially, upon the economy. The data produced in London by the impressive series of industry-by-industry studies in industrial anthropology supervised by Frederick Le Gros Clark were supported by the findings of industrial psychologists, also funded by Nuffield, showing that men (women were rarely studied) could continue to work efficiently until at least their later sixties in a wide variety of occupations, including heavy manual labour, on condition that they could control the pace of their work. A study of miners in a Scottish pit demonstrated that men in their fifties and sixties could perform as well at handcutting coal as younger men; what caused them most strain was the walk through the mine to the coalface where the pace of the journey was set by younger, faster-moving men.[61] It was found that work efficiency deteriorated earlier in life (in the late forties or fifties) in those occupations in which pace was controlled by the machine or by management practices, such as piece-rates tied to the pace of work or bonuses linked to speed of production. Such practices were spreading through industry, but the research showed that they could be adapted in such ways as to sustain efficient working by older men. The research produced recommendations for the re-organization of work to suit the needs of the older worker.

Post-war studies also reached conclusions, which have been supported by more recent research,[62] that whatever older workers lost in terms of speed, adaptability, and capacity to learn new techniques (which was much less than was often asserted) was compensated in most occupations by skill, experience, and reliability. Most workers in youth and middle age were understretched and had reserves to call upon as they grew older and individuals varied as to which of their capacities deteriorated and at what rate. Workers in their sixties might be less productive than those at their peak, in their late thirties

---

[60] Titmuss, *Essays*, 56–74.   [61] Richardson, 'Age and Work', 279.
[62] N. Charness (ed.), *Ageing and Human Performance* (Chichester and New York, 1985).

or forties, but not less so than inexperienced workers in their twenties. Le Gros Clark in particular emphasized that where older people appeared to be conservative and inflexible it was often the product of socialization rather than the inevitable concomitant of ageing, of society's low expectations of older people, which they internalized, rather than of their actual potential.

By the end of the 1950s panic about the ageing of society was subsiding, but so also was public and political interest in old people. The panic lifted largely because the worst had not happened. The population had not dwindled, as had been forecast in the 1930s. The entry of many more women into the labour force and the unforeseen entry of migrant workers, especially from the Commonwealth, had compensated for the loss of older workers. The period of population panic had given rise to some new understandings of the effects of population ageing and of the capacities of older people. The surrounding discourse expressed conflicting positive and negative representations of older people. Most of this, however, was soon forgotten, only to be reinvented when fears of population ageing revived in the 1980s.

'I Don't Feel Old': The Reinvention of Old Age in the Welfare State

18

'A Remarkable Discovery of Secret Need': Pensioners in the 1940s

A negative view of the probable social impact of the increasing numbers of older people in Britain was perhaps understandable, in view of the poor health and living conditions of very many older people in the 1930s and 1940s. These conditions were made shockingly evident by the revelations following the introduction of Supplementary Assistance in 1940. The Old Age and Widows' Pensions Act, 1940, transferred responsibility for the welfare of old people from the local authorities (the successors to the Poor Law Boards) to the former Unemployment Assistance Board. This had been established in 1934 as the first official body empowered to undertake welfare work on a national scale. Since only 10 per cent of pensioners had previously applied for Poor Law Assistance, the government expected the cost of the new scheme to be relatively small, covering about 400,000 pensioners. In fact, 120,000 applications were received within the first four days of operations. By the time of the first payments, 1,275,000 applications had been filed. By 1941 the Assistance Board was supplementing one-third of all old-age pensions. These numbers were powerful testimony to the fear and hatred of the Poor Law which survived until its demise. *The Times* remarked on 'a remarkable discovery of secret need'; though the Conservative MP Lady Astor claimed, on no obvious evidence, that there were 'about four times as many people getting Assistance as needed it'.[1]

An immediate issue was that the household means test—one of the most thoroughly disliked features of Unemployment Assistance—was applied to the aged applicants for the supplement. In determining need, the resources of all members of the household were taken into account. This provoked a variety of problems, not least concerning the definition of a household. It was common enough at this time among working-class people for two households to share a house as independent units, perhaps exchanging some services. The number of such households increased during the war due to the effects of bombing and because the wives of absent servicemen moved in with their parents or parents-in-law. Many old people lived independently as lodgers in other people's houses. Officials found devious ways to assess the extent of

---

[1] Andrew Blaikie, 'The Emerging Political Power of the Elderly in Britain, 1908–1948', *Ageing and Society*, 10 1 (1990), 30.

interaction associated with such arrangements, arriving at mealtimes to try to catch pensioners sharing a meal with relatives or neighbours; or snooping for clothing not belonging to the pensioner.

After protest, in January 1941 the first of a series of Determination of Needs Bills was introduced into the Commons. This provided that where claimants resided with non-dependent wage-earning relatives no earnings of such relatives under twenty shillings per week would be taken into account. When claimants were dependent upon others, they should be allowed sufficient income to cover their own living expenses plus a contribution towards rent before other sources of income were taken into account. The amount of war savings to be disregarded was increased.[2] These changes enabled 200,000 more pensioners to receive the supplementary pension. It was pointed out in the House of Commons that the changes would especially assist low-earning children, often single daughters, on whom many old people depended. The Bill passed easily through parliament, though Labour continued to demand total abolition of the means test.[3] In the Determination of Needs Act, 1943, the new rules were extended to the administration of poor relief (Public Assistance) and the Blind Persons' Pensions. They did not affect the liability to maintain relatives living in a separate household. This resilient survivor of the Elizabethan Poor Law[4] could not be removed without a major revision of the Poor Law. This came in 1948 when the Poor Law was formally abolished after almost three hundred and fifty years.[5] The debate on the 1943 Determination of Needs Bill was notable for the number of MPs who took the opportunity to plead for higher old-age pensions, referring frequently to the Beveridge Report of the previous year.[6]

The obvious inference from the high take-up of supplementary pensions was that very many old people were in severe poverty but had been 'managing' on inadequate incomes rather than accept poor relief. This soon became starkly evident. An immediate problem encountered by the Assistance Board was that most local poor relief authorities in industrial areas had been supplementing the old-age pension on a larger scale than it was prepared to countenance. Pensioners who had benefited from this generosity were granted an 'Anomalies Allowance' so that their income did not fall due to the change-over. However, it also emerged that the larger, Labour-dominated, Scottish local authorities, including Glasgow, Edinburgh, and Aberdeen, had given pensioners not only an allowance which was five or six shillings above the Board's scale, but also included an annual grant of clothing. Under rarely used statutory provisions Edinburgh was giving more Exceptional Needs Grants to old people than the whole of England and Wales together. Under the new administration, old people began to find their claims for such grants refused.

---

[2] *Hansard* (1940–1), vol. 368, cols. 307 ff.   [3] Ibid., cols. 1543 ff.
[4] See pp. 141–5.   [5] *Hansard* (1943), vol. 389, cols. 1267 ff.
[6] Ibid., cols. 1272, 1295, 1306, 1318, 1319, among others.

Thousands appealed, creating consternation in the Assistance Board.[7] An experienced officer was dispatched to Scotland to investigate the clothing and household needs of supplementary pensioners. The standards at which needs were judged to be 'exceptional' were scarcely high. Based on a norm established in London, old people were believed to require: one dress or pair of trousers, one overcoat, one pair of shoes, two blankets, one pair of sheets (despite the difficulty of getting them washed and dried within one day, in the conditions in which many old people lived), one night-gown or pair of pyjamas, two sets of underclothing and two shirts for old men. A 'serviceable' garment was defined as one which would not fall apart within the next three months. The investigation found that half the pensioners visited did not reach even this miserable standard and several possessed almost none of the essential items. This was pitiful anywhere and particularly in the chilly climate of Edinburgh.

The Assistance Board set up a pilot survey in London, to begin to assess how widespread such conditions were. This confirmed that conditions in the south were as miserable as in Scotland. The interviews also revealed that about a third of the old people had further pressing, previously underestimated needs: unmet medical expenses, fares to the hospital or surgery for treatment, expenses for laundry or domestic help where the old person was too frail or ill to manage alone, the cost of special food or heating for those with health problems and special needs for nursing care, surgical appliances, spectacles, dentures, etc. In many cases old people had gone without food, or fallen into rent arrears, to meet such expenses from their pensions. A not uncommon case was an old lady who:

> at first professed to 'manage', then confessed to a serious shortage of clothing and bedclothes, and finally broke down, saying that she 'could not ask' . . . she had only what she stood up in . . . an old, thin skirt, a torn cardigan and no blouse—and slept under a single tattered blanket and meagre cotton coverlet.

The cardigan was pinned at the neck to hide the lack of a blouse, her apron and her 'scrupulous personal cleanliness' creating a misleading impression.[8] The report concluded that there was no need for a larger scale inquiry to establish whether old-age pensioners needs were being met. Clearly they were not.

Nevertheless such an inquiry, the Exceptional Needs Enquiry, took place later in 1942. In each Assistance Board district investigation was made of pensioners living alone or with only a spouse and with no resources beyond their pensions: about half a million pensioners in England, Wales, and Scotland; though it was protested that there were others outside the confines of the inquiry who were just as needy. In a number of cases the officials were criticized for

[7] PRO AST 7/441. AST 7/467.

[8] PRO AST 7/589, D. Ibberson, 'Special Investigation into the Condition of Supplementary Pensioners, 1942'; quoted J. R. Fogerty, 'Growing Old in England, 1878–1949', Ph.D. thesis (Australian National University, Canberra, 1992), 238.

the superficiality of their investigation, though some were encouraged in this by their superior officers, who believed that the standards of need laid down for old people were excessively generous because they were higher than many old people had enjoyed during their working lives. This may well have been true given the appalling poverty among younger people evident in parts of Britain before the war. Some officials were so reluctant to supply grants for sheets, warm underwear, night-gowns, and overcoats to pensioners, who they claimed had never previously enjoyed such luxuries, that the Board had finally to instruct that such items should be provided unless it was evident that the old person would not use them.

Despite the fact that the survey was less than thorough it disclosed over-whelming need. Over 70 per cent of those visited lacked some of the essential items and many required grants for such basic goods as saucepans and kettles. The average grant was three pounds; this did not include the 135,000 blankets which were issued from special stocks. The investigation uncovered a variety of needs. The availability of the grants stimulated applications from pensioners not covered by the survey because they were not receiving Supplementary Assistance, but who turned out to be in severe need. This resulted in payment of several thousand further grants.[9] Pensioners received grants of basic items with heart-rending gratitude. Pitifully, the Darlington District Officer noted of old women that:

whereas their need was for underclothing, what they longed for more than anything else was a new dress or a new coat . . . the fact that they must remain slightly shabby is a very great factor in the content or discontent of old people.[10]

Old men, similarly, hankered after a Sunday suit. Many pensioners received their first new clothes in decades. Some had such low expectations that they failed to apply for everything to which they were entitled. Too often their own clothes 'had little of the original material left, but were neat and tidy though a network of patches'. Some older, frailer pensioners were 'a mass of rags', sleeping under their clothes and 'old mats'. A Yorkshire Visiting Officer spoke of 'the uplift in pensioners'' manner and pride 'as a result of the inquiry and the help which followed'. Elsewhere some pensioners were said to have been enabled to visit relatives or to go to church, or even into town, for the first time in years because at last they felt that they could dress suitably and without shame.

The North-Eastern Regional Officer believed that the great majority of pensioners regarded this inquiry as 'the brightest event in their old age'. The discoveries shocked many Assistance officials. Many old people, especially in rural areas, had never had an income much higher than they received as supplementary pensioners. Many thousands had been unemployed for long before they became entitled to pensions and their possessions had been run down to minimal standards.

[9] PRO AST 7/599–608.   [10] PRO AST 7/604.

The government was dismayed at the resulting costs and sought an explanation. The Assistance Board mounted another survey, this time of new applicants for the pension. This revealed that almost half of these had previously been largely supported by relatives whose own incomes were so low that the Board was unable to take them into account in order to reject the application. A little under a quarter supplemented their pensions by remaining in employment, or by taking in boarders or lodgers, long after they should have given up for reasons of health. Almost another 25 per cent had been living on small savings which were almost exhausted. An investigator reported a situation in villages near Oxford which could have been discovered at any time over several centuries:

the administration of Public Assistance is still at its most stringent in some of the country districts, and the old people's memories go back to a still harsher regime . . . not only is it a public disgrace to be visited weekly by the Relieving Officer . . . but Relief has the visible character of charity from neighbours who are entitled to look down on the recipient. Some of the country people, indeed, said that they would 'rather die' than go to the Relieving Officer. Low rents, the kindliness of the church and neighbours, a bit of 'odd jobbing' and the occasional help of relatives who could ill afford it, had made it possible . . . to scrape along on, perhaps, their primary pension plus a Service Dependant's Pension . . . or even in rare cases, without any regular addition. No case was found . . . living independently on the bare primary pension without any help.[11]

Not that the Supplementary Pension banished poverty. The Nuffield College Reconstruction Survey reported in 1942:

There is practically unanimous agreement that the present amount of Old Age Pension, even with the Supplementary Pensions, is inadequate, and that old age pensioners find it very difficult to live on their pensions, unless they have other sources of income. It is particularly hard for single old people . . . Social workers in London point out that the cost of keeping old age pensioners who have been bombed out in Government Rest Homes is 30s. per week and ask 'If this figure is necessary when numbers of old people are being cared for jointly how can 19s. a week (Old Age Pension plus basic Supplementary Pension) possibly be regarded as adequate?'[12]

This basic sum could not cover clothing replacement or medical treatment and was usually not adequate to buy a nourishing diet suitable for frail old people or adequate fuel. Further allowances were needed for the mildest contingency. There was an additional allowance for 'advanced age'. A survey in 1941 showed that 30 per cent of pensioners were receiving discretionary supplements. But, still, in 1947 a Nuffield Foundation Survey found that many poor old people did not apply for the Supplementary Pension because they associated it with charity or thought that it compromised their independence.

[11] PRO AST 7/589.
[12] PRO CAB 87/80–1, Nuffield College Social Reconstruction Survey (NCSRS Memo. no. 2: Additional Pensions), 19 June 1942, 1 ff.

In 1945 a government social survey of over 12,000 households in England and Wales found that 71 per cent of people of pensionable age were receiving state pensions of some kind. Thirty-two per cent of these received Supplementary Pension—36 per cent of female pensioners, 27 per cent of men. Twenty per cent of all those of pensionable age were in paid employment; 39 per cent of men. Most of these also received pensions. The proportions possessing income from sources other than pensions decreased sharply with advancing age. Nevertheless, the survey discovered that 13 per cent of old people in the lowest income group were not receiving any pension. Some were men aged 60 to 65, or men and women who did not qualify for pension until age 70. Some, however, had not applied for pension or Public Assistance though they would have qualified, either through ignorance or on principle. Two per cent of the older people lived wholly on charity, including that of relatives, and others on small private savings. In addition to all of these, about 2 per cent lived in institutions, mainly Public Assistance institutions (the former workhouses) and were not entitled to pensions or supplementary pensions.[13] In 1951 the *Manchester Guardian* found that, 'thousands of old people for one reason or another still make the attempt [to manage without Supplementary Assistance]'.[14] An accumulation of surveys throughout the 1940s revealed the extent of malnutrition among old people which was the outcome of this situation.[15]

Nevertheless, commentators believed, probably correctly, that the new arrangements had lessened need in old age. It became clear how much worse conditions had been previously. The 1947 Committee established by the Nuffield Foundation, under the chairmanship of Seebohm Rowntree, to investigate the condition of older people, concluded, a little complacently in view of the evidence available, that:

as a result of the . . . Act of 1940, there is no longer acute poverty among the aged to anything like the extent that formerly existed, although there is still a measure of austerity.[16]

This 'austerity' was increasingly brought to public attention due to the growing numbers of professional social workers, often well-educated women, now employed by local authorities rather than by charities, with greater resources at their disposal than in the past and often less censorious in their attitude to poor people than some of their predecessors.

Another new feature was the emergence of organizations of and for pensioners. Old-age pensioners were establishing a collective identity. The Old Age Pensions Association was founded in Blackburn in October 1938, with

---

[13] Geoffrey Thomas, *The Employment of Older Persons: An Enquiry*, Central Office of Information Social Survey (London, 1947).

[14] 'No elderly need suffer hardship, but many do', *Manchester Guardian*, 16 Jan. 1951.

[15] Fogerty, 'Growing Old', ch. 7.

[16] Nuffield Foundation, *Old People: Report of a Survey Committee on the Problems of Ageing and the Care of Old People* (London, 1947), 7.

nine members. It claimed 3,500 by February 1940. The Scottish OAPA founded in February 1937 claimed 8,000 members by the start of 1941. These organizations became the National Federation of Old Age Pensioners Associations in 1942, claiming very large memberships. Their initial drive was for a doubling of the basic pension to one pound, paid at age 60, without means test.[17] They also protested about the invasion of privacy involved in the various official inquiries. They reported that some older people objected to visits from 'nosey women', though others enjoyed visits from the Assistance Board official as an opportunity for a friendly chat; but many old people felt that they had little choice but to 'accept the position and grumble'. Such organizations spoke up for pensioners and their problems, though they also helped to establish in the public consciousness a collective representation of 'old people' as needy old-age pensioners, which was accurate enough of some, but not of all older people.

Over the war years special grants came to be provided in a more routinized manner and the Assistance Board began to take an active role in establishing Home Help, Meals on Wheels, Friendly Visiting, and other support services either through voluntary agencies or local authorities. The war years saw an expansion of social services directed towards the needs of old people. Nevertheless a second Exceptional Needs Enquiry in 1947 produced results all too like the first and indicated that still too few old people knew of or applied for special needs grants.[18] Many of them found the bureaucracy too complex. Forms were filled with terrifying jargon and were difficult for fading eyesight in need of expensive spectacles. Some old people could not read, with or without spectacles. Old people denied grants rarely used the appeals procedures, unless assisted by a son or daughter. Some Assistance Board officers gave them little help or sympathy because they remained convinced of the existence of a category of 'low types' so long accustomed to squalor that they were unworthy of further help. In one rural district the Sanitary Inspector held that conditions in which an old woman's hand was being gnawed by rats as she lay asleep did not constitute a danger to health.[19]

However, it was found elsewhere that regular visits and assistance from support services gave apparently hopeless cases a sense of hope and greater interest in life so that they took greater care of themselves and their surroundings. Surveys of old people in mental hospitals showed that in some cases their condition was due to malnutrition and lack of social support and could be reversed, though tragic cases recurred of old people refusing help or institutional care and dying in neglect and squalor. Neighbours, sometimes themselves old,

---

[17] Blaikie, 'Political Power'; Blaikie and J. Macnicol, 'The Politics of Retirement, 1908–48' in Margot Jefferys (ed.), *Growing Old in the Twentieth Century* (London, 1989), 21–42, cover the same ground, mostly in identical words. The story is further repeated in Macnicol, *The Politics of Retirement in Britain, 1848–1948* (Cambridge, 1998), 319–22. For a fuller account see Henry J. Pratt, *Gray Agendas: Interest Groups and Public Pensions in Canada, Britain, and the United States* (Ann Arbor, 1993), 89 ff.

[18] PRO AST 7/925 'Supplementary Pensioners without Resources: Exceptional Needs Enquiry, 1947'. Fogerty, 'Growing Old', 247.   [19] Ibid. 250.

often gave devoted and extensive help, but not all old people were so lucky. A Nuffield College survey of 1944 found that support from neighbours was essentially unpredictable: one grumpy old woman 'apparently has half the street mobilized in her service'; another woman was left locked in her room for days between visits by a daughter living ten miles away. An 'old incapable man of eighty-three, wandered around the village half-dressed and was treated as a joke; only the Assistance Board officer troubled to arrange coal and food for his discharge from hospital'.[20]

One problem increasingly noted was the lack of suitable accommodation for old people, with or without supervision. Many thousands of older people lived in one or two rooms with no facilities but an open fire, while the great majority of the aged population lacked access to a bathroom and, in rural areas, to running water. So also did many younger people, but these were conditions with which it became still harder to cope with advancing age. The Assistance Board developed a policy long familiar under the Poor Law (and many of the Board's staff were former Poor Law officials) of seeking to encourage pensioners to take in lodgers when they were deemed to have space, in order to lessen their need for further assistance. Some local authorities opened registers of potential, often also elderly, tenants, and threatened to refuse to meet the cost of rent if the pensioner did not comply. Such enforced cohabitation and responsibility for a tenant, who was not necessarily compatible, could cause stress to sometimes frail old people.

An important discovery, or rediscovery, of the wartime surveys was the vital, supportive role of relatives. The 1942 Exceptional Needs Enquiry had excluded old people living with non-dependent relatives on the assumption that they would be in a superior condition to others. But more and more old people living in such circumstances applied for special needs grants. Most of them were found also to lack essential items of clothing, bedding, or household equipment. Offspring were castigated in official correspondence for shameful neglect of the elderly or for appropriating their clothing coupons for 'personal adornment'. Further investigation showed that the relatives were often only technically 'non-dependent', in that they received some other kind of state allowance. In some this was because they were physically or mentally disabled, or unemployed and in consequence placed financial, emotional, or sometimes physical strain upon the older person. Several very ill or frail old people were nursed by daughter-housekeepers who had little or no incomes of their own, and both generations were desperately poor. In most districts there were one or two old men with dependent children at home living in impoverished cirumstances. Cases of old people well cared for by their families were far from uncommon, but many families could afford very little. Some officials were disabused of their idealized notions of the caring capacities of families. One area officer for Newport stated that:

---

[20] PRO AST 7/737. NCSRS Draft memorandum, May 1944, 41. Fogerty, 'Growing Old', 253–4.

pensioners living in the same house with married children are *more often* in need than those living with strangers. They are often there on sufferance or deprive themselves to help the children [my emphasis].[21]

The Assistance Board received moving letters from married children who were trying to support their own children as well as their parents on quite inadequate resources.

Nevertheless, the official view remained that pensioners in close contact with relatives did not require regular visiting. It was assumed initially, without closer investigation of the family circumstances, that relatives could provide all the funds, domestic assistance, and nursing that was required. It was also assumed that older people, despite much evidence to the contrary, were always dependent upon younger relatives, if they shared a household. The reality of intergenerational reciprocity was more complex. The availability of supplementary pensions enabled some pensioners to relieve relatives of the strain of trying to support them, and they experienced a sense of relief and independence visible even to Assistance Board investigators.[22] The problems were eased by the gradual relaxation of pensions qualifications under the successive Determination of Needs Acts, but difficulties remained due to the Board's unwillingness to recognize the dependence upon old people for example of grandchildren or of other relatives; or to sanction payment for visits from the District Nurse to old people living with relatives, even where these—often an equally elderly husband or wife—were unequal to the task of nursing.

The Exceptional Needs and other inquiries of the 1940s made clear, above all, the extreme poverty of very many old people, and also the complex reciprocity of old people's relationships with others. Very many gave their clothing and even food coupons to children, grandchildren, and helpful neighbours in gratitude for services; or they would give meals or cash. They would endure striking privations rather than feel dependent upon those closest to them, an attitude which caused a perpetual headache for Board officials. It was conditioned by lifetimes of poverty in historically poor communities which survived on such reciprocity. As young adults they had themselves often struggled to help older relatives perhaps under pressure from the Poor Law and had themselves been helped by older people. One old Oxfordshire shepherd bitterly recalled having to pay one shilling a week out of his thirteen-shilling wages for his mother, who was on out-relief. Assistance Board Investigators remarked than many old people sincerely believed that the young had priority, saying 'Oh, the grandchildren must come first'. In particular they suffered because they refused to receive medical relief from the Assistance Board because their relatives would be liable for payment.

Against this background, the pension system was reconstructed after the war.

---

[21] PRO AST 7/608.   [22] PRO AST 7/596, 7/574. Fogerty, 'Growing Old', 256.

19

Pensions: From Beveridge to the Millennium

THE BEVERIDGE PLAN

Famously, the old-age pension was overhauled after the Second World War according to principles devised by William Beveridge during the war. The story of pensions policy since Beveridge published his White Paper *Social Insurance and Allied Services* in 1942 has been told too often to require repetition in detail. However, certain themes still deserve to be explored. First, we need to be clear about what Beveridge recommended concerning old people and the social security system, since it has been much mythologized.

When Beveridge was asked in 1941:

To undertake, with special reference to the inter-relation of the schemes, a survey of the existing national schemes of social insurance and allied services, including workmen's compensation, and to make recommendations,[1]

his opportunity had come to implement what he now called 'unified social security',[2] for the same reasons that had appealed to him when he entered the discussion of 'all-in insurance' in 1924.[3] The Report which resulted was his own work, assisted by advice from civil servants and a variety of experts.[4] As always, his proposals were rooted in clearly expressed and strongly held principles:

social security must be achieved by co-operation between the state and the individual. The State should offer security [in return for] for service and contribution. The State in organizing security should not stifle incentive, opportunity, responsibility; in establishing a national minimum it should leave room and encouragement for voluntary action by each individual to provide that minimum for himself and his family.[5]

The plan is not one for giving everybody something for nothing and without trouble, or something that will free the recipients for ever thereafter from personal responsibilities.

---

[1] *Social Insurance and Allied Services*, Report by Sir William Beveridge, Cmd. 6404 (1942), 2.
[2] Ibid. 15. [3] See pp. 321–3.
[4] The most judicious account of the making of this Report and the aftermath is José Harris, *William Beveridge: A Biography*, 2nd ed. (Oxford, 1997), 365–499. There is a detailed discussion in J. Macnicol, *The Politics of Retirement in Britain, 1878–1948* (Cambridge, 1998), 347–400, but his judgements should be approached with caution. See also Paul Addison, *The Road to 1945* (London, 1975), 168–70, 211–17.
[5] Cmd. 6404, 6–7.

The plan is one to secure income for subsistence on condition of service and contribution and in order to make and keep men fit for service . . . the plan leaves room and encouragement to all individuals to win for themselves something above the national minimum.[6]

It was the Edwardian progressive ideal of the national minimum yoked to the new vogue for planning, that the 'Plan for Social Security' (Beveridge's own term) sought to introduce: 'the minimum income needed for subsistence', not more. Even this, as the above quotation suggests, was strictly conditional on each individual accepting personal responsibility to give 'service' (i.e. work) and to pay contributions. The Report explicitly aimed 'to make and keep men fit for service' and expected individuals to provide for themselves 'something above the national minimum'. The Report resonates with the issues that had been central to the debate about pensions since it began in the 1870s. The pension should provide 'enough for subsistence even though the pensioner has no other resources whatever . . .', but no more. On the contrary, direct encouragement of voluntary insurance or saving 'to meet abnormal needs or to maintain standards of comfort above subsistence level is an essential part of the Plan'.[7] He was emphatic that 'The plan is not one for giving everybody something for nothing and without trouble, or something that will free recipients for ever from personal responsibilities'.

Central to the Report and to its popular appeal was Beveridge's expressed determination to achieve 'abolition of want after the war',[8] not to return to the conditions revealed by the social surveys of the 1920s and 1930s, which the Report summarized.[9] It was a means, Beveridge claimed, to spread more widely the prosperity which had increased since the beginning of the century, but in which those without a secure place in the labour market, especially older people, had shared least.[10] None of Beveridge's pensions proposals in 1942 were new, nor were they fully implemented. What was new was the extent of popular enthusiasm they aroused, at a grim stage of the war, which the politicians followed, with varying degrees of commitment.[11]

Beveridge proposed a universal flat-rate pension adequate to meet 'human needs', payable only on retirement. It was to be partially financed by flat-rate contributions and administratively fully integrated with other insurance benefits. Pension rates 'adequate for subsistence' were calculated in consultation with a sub-committee which included the veterans of poverty research, B. S. Rowntree and A. L. Bowley.[12] Their recommendations owed much to the stringent calculations of need employed by Rowntree in his second study of poverty in York, in 1936. Beveridge recognized that any pension proposed in wartime conditions would require adjustment in the inevitably changed

[6] Ibid. 170.   [7] Ibid. 92–3.   [8] Ibid. 8.   [9] Ibid. 166–7.   [10] Ibid. 166.
[11] Harris, *Beveridge*, 415–26. Nicolas Timmins, *The Five Giants: A Biography of the Welfare State* (London, 1995), 39–49. Macnicol, *Politics of Retirement*, 385–97.   [12] Cmd. 6404, 77.

conditions after the war. He was concerned to establish principles on which an 'adequate' pension could be based.[13]

Unlike others, such as Rowntree,[14] Beveridge assumed that 'the subsistence needs of retired pensioners are in some ways less and in other respects more than the needs of persons of working age'.[15] He pointed out that 'the food requirements of old people are placed by all authorities at substantially less than those of persons of working age. In calories they need about seventy-five per cent of what is needed by working age adults.' However, he recognized that the cost of suitable food for older people might be greater 'because of their failing mastication and digestion'. He proposed that their food needs be costed at 85 per cent of those of younger people, though old women were assumed to require only 5s. 6d. per week, men 6s. Beveridge also assumed that the clothing requirements of old people were only two-thirds of those of younger people, but that their requirements for fuel and lighting were higher, and their 'margin', for items of expenditure other than the absolute essentials of food, clothing, rent, fuel, and light, was the same: 1s. 6d. per week for one person. At 1938 prices this yielded a pension of 17s. 10d. for a single man, 17s. 4d. for a women, and 29s. 8d. for a married couple. For all its stringency, this was well above the actual, 10s., pension level in 1938.[16]

The pensionable ages were to be unchanged, but as an incentive to work to later ages, more generous pensions should be paid in return for deferred retirement. This was an outcome of Beveridge's long-established and real concern about the effects of the ageing of the population.[17] He insisted that the purpose of a subsistence pension was to relieve 'want' among those who could not work for a living, rather than to encourage the retirement of those who could. He anticipated a buoyant labour market after the war and was in any case sceptical that retirement of older workers freed equivalent numbers of jobs for the young. He perhaps expected, reasonably enough, that very few who were still capable of working for a reasonable wage would be tempted to retire in favour of a pension which would certainly be of lower amount than their wages from employment. More important, however, were his fears that as the population aged, the pool of younger workers would contract, to the detriment of the economy; and also his conviction that work in itself was good:

Early retirement of men on pension is not wanted or useful as a cure for unemployment. On the contrary there should be as few idle mouths as possible at any age after childhood is passed . . . adequate pensions with a flexible age will increase happiness and wealth in many ways.[18]

---

[13] Cmd. 6404, 87 ff.   [14] See pp. 328–30.   [15] Cmd. 6404, 87.   [16] Ibid. 87–8.
[17] See pp. 335–6, 343–4. Macnicol, *Politics of Retirement*, 357, 367, interprets the use by Beveridge and his advisers, such as W. B. Reddaway, of the language of fear of the effects of the ageing of the population as largely cynical and designed to justify a low rate of pension. This is to underrate the long-standing concern of Beveridge, Reddaway, and others with this issue, and the genuineness of this concern, however wrong-headed it might seem with hindsight. See Ch. 16.   [18] Cmd. 6404, 59.

Beveridge practised what he preached. He was aged 63 when he wrote the Report and remained active in public life until his late seventies.[19] In keeping with his belief in the importance of paid work, his Plan suggested removal of the right of widows of working age without dependent children to work for pay while drawing the pension, and proposed the introduction of training benefits when necessary to assist them to re-enter the labour market.

Beveridge was persuaded by Keynes to propose a gradual transition to full subsistence pensions over twenty years. Meanwhile those in need would continue to receive means-tested supplements. Reluctantly, Beveridge agreed; he strongly opposed means-testing, but recognized the heavy cost of full pensions to the post-war economy.[20] Of the key principles he advocated for a revised social insurance system: universal benefits and contributions he had always advocated as administratively more cost-efficient than means-testing and free of the anomalies and deterrence inseparable from such rationing devices; though at least as important was his equally long-held vision of universal insurance as a force capable of promoting social cohesion, since it embraced the whole working population.[21] The proposal for a flat-rate benefit arose from his belief that social security should provide no more than basic subsistence. A flat-rate contribution was not the inevitable corollary. Beveridge favoured it for social rather than actuarial reasons. As he put it: 'Contribution means that in their capacity as possible recipients of benefit the poorer man and the richer man are treated alike'. He did not propose, as became common in social insurance systems elsewhere in post-war western Europe, to build a redistributive element into the contributory system, by fixing the contributions of the higher-paid at high levels relative to benefits, and those of the lower-paid at relatively lower levels. The outcome of the Beveridge proposals was that contributions were regressive, taking a higher proportion of the incomes of lower than of higher earners. However, contributions were not expected to match the cost of benefits. This was partly because poorer workers could not afford the full cost. Also Beveridge aimed to build in redistribution by other means. In part this was the role of the employers' contributions, but also:

Taxation means that the richer man because of his capacity to pay, pays more for the general purposes of the community. These general purposes may, and in practice they must, include bearing a part of the cost of social security.[22]

A permanent contribution to the pension from direct taxation was part of the Plan. Few manual workers paid income tax at this time.

What Beveridge proposed was more generous than the state pension had ever been. Yet even when fully implemented it would provide only a basic subsistence income, at the same level for all. It was designed to relieve poverty rather than, like the pensions systems emerging in most other west European

---

[19] Harris, *Beveridge*, 452 ff.   [20] Ibid. 410.
[21] Ibid. 338–40. See p. 222.   [22] Cmd 6404, 108.

countries, to provide in old age an income related to income during working life, to stabilize income over the life cycle, preventing a catastrophic decline when paid work ceased.

The Labour Party and trade union movement welcomed the Beveridge proposals with especial enthusiasm, some even claiming as 'socialism' this quintessential piece of liberalism. This was understandable since it delivered what they had been proposing for fifty years: a universal, flat-rate pension at subsistence level. Nevertheless, it is perhaps surprising that more Labour supporters did not have higher expectations by the 1940s and were not more critical of the minimal, residual character and the regressive contribution system proposed by Beveridge, and were not more interested in alternatives such as income-related contributions and benefits. Discussion of pensions in Britain was dominated, still, by the drive to escape from the Poor Law; thinking about social security remained shackled to this centuries-old institution even when its end was at last in sight. Hennock's comments on the pensions debate in the 1880s are apposite for the 1940s:

The major developments in social policy in twentieth century Britain have been prompted by a revulsion against the Poor Law and a determination to provide services free from its associations. In this way the Poor Law has exercised a profound and pervasive influence over the history of social policy in Britain, shaping the new developments by the force of negation and denial.[23]

The welcome given to Beveridge's proposals in the 1940s was that of a still largely impoverished working class, with memories of still greater, recent, misery and with low expectations of how far their living standards might rise. It was also the welcome of an essentially liberal society, indeed of an essentially liberal Labour Party, which asked for little more than minimal social security from the state and supported the principle that this should be supplemented by private effort. Perhaps also 'ordinary people' were realistic that this was the best they were likely to get and better than anything that had gone before. Nevertheless, the atmosphere of public euphoria which surrounded the Beveridge proposals, and which he encouraged, in a period of war when all news and public debate were carefully managed by government, stifled serious debate about alternative approaches to social security, indeed bred a profound complacency about the British pension system, with unfortunate long-term consequences.[24]

---

[23] E. P. Hennock, *British Social Reform and German Precedents: The Case of Social Insurance, 1880–1914* (Oxford, 1987), 111.

[24] José Harris, 'Political Ideas and the Debate on State Welfare, 1940–5', in H. L. Smith, *War and Social Change* (Manchester, 1986), 250; Harriet Jones, 'The Conservative Party and the Welfare State, 1942–1955', Ph.D. thesis (University of London, 1992), 89.

Conservative Party opinion was far less welcoming. Many Conservatives regarded Beveridge's proposals as genuinely undesirable. They believed in targetting benefits on those in need, rather than 'wasting' them on those who were not, and they were nervous of the range of provisions he proposed. There was strong and consistent Conservative opposition to universal social insurance during the war and after. Conservatives were, however, 'bewildered' by the overwhelming popular support for Beveridge[25] and felt inhibited from public criticism of it. A minority of progressive Conservatives—later to form the Tory Reform Group—argued for compromise, partly for fear of the political consequences of opposing the Beveridge Plan.[26]

The wartime coalition government responded clumsily, largely because leading Conservative members shared the hostility to the report of the party rank and file. In the Cabinet the Chancellor of the Exchequer acidly opposed universality. The civil service committee established to cost the Beveridge Report doubted the practicability of funding a universal level of adequate provision which could apply realistically throughout the country.[27] A Conservative Party committee on the report strongly opposed universalism. It agreed with the need for a better co-ordinated insurance scheme and a comprehensive health service, but feared that the cost of the proposals as a whole would retard economic reconstruction by diverting funds from industrial investment. It argued that the scheme put rights before duties; incorporated insufficient incentives to work; feared that it would become increasingly redistributive and that contributors would be paid too small a percentage of benefits.[28] Such unpopular views were not strongly expressed in public but were deeply felt and survived to influence later Conservative policy.

THE LABOUR GOVERNMENT, 1945–1951

The grudging Conservative response to Beveridge was one reason why they lost the election of 1945 decisively to Labour, which for the first time formed a government with a large majority. Social security reform was one of the priorities of the new government. The National Insurance Act, 1946, introduced pensions for those already within the National Insurance scheme initially at a slightly higher level than Beveridge had proposed, in response to Labour back-bench pressure. Labour appears to have believed that they had set the pension at current subsistence level, but this had been incorrectly measured using misleading indices produced by both the wartime and the Labour governments. By the time the scheme came into effect in 1948, benefit rates were significantly below a rate adequate for subsistence.[29] The desire of

---

[25] Jones, 'Conservative Party', 68–9. [26] Ibid. 80. [27] Ibid. 71–2.
[28] Ibid. 76–7. [29] Timmins, *Five Giants*, 136.

the Minister of Pensions and National Insurance, James Griffiths, to link the pension rate to the index of prices or wages was rejected by civil servants.[30] Newcomers to the state scheme (higher income earners previously excluded from National Insurance) became eligible for the pension after ten years' contributions. It made political sense for Labour to buy middle-class support for the scheme in this way,[31] and also many middle-class people needed the pension because they lacked the security of a guaranteed income in old age, or the means to acquire one, but this concession stored up an inadequately funded upsurge in expenditure for 1958. In most other respects, including the introduction, for the first time in the state pension system, of compulsory retirement (with a small increment built in for deferral of retirement), Beveridge's pension scheme was adopted. The level of pensions was limited, once again, by Treasury resistance to the cost. A Labour government anxious to prioritize economic recovery even over welfare expansion responded to such constraints more willingly than is always recognized.[32] In 1951 it cut Exchequer subsidies to the National Insurance fund, as one of a range of cuts in welfare expenditure in response to economic difficulties due at least in part to British involvement in the Korean War.[33] Arguably, Beveridge was unrealistic to believe that an adequate flat-rate universal pension, even at the minimal level he envisaged, was achievable within British political culture. The chances were particularly poor in an economy in serious need of investment and reconstruction after the war, and with an ageing population. Beveridge's convictions, and those of the bulk of the Labour movement, were born of an admirable desire to banish the poverty and indignity the poor had long known. But Beveridge's simple, sweeping, attractive proposals could not realistically solve the problems. As early as 1946 James Griffiths was contemplating the advantages of linking contributions to income as a means to increase benefits.[34] Beveridge, however, believed that his proposals could only be fully effective in eliminating Want if supported by a range of measures, including minimum-wage legislation, subsistence-level family allowances, rationalization of the labour market, industrial training, strict price control, statutory limitation of free collective bargaining, public ownership of land and essential services, and, if necessary, the phasing out of private ownership of most of the means of production. Here again, even if theoretically correct he was politically unrealistic.

[30] Timmins, *Five Giants*, 136.

[31] Peter Baldwin, *The Politics of Social Solidarity: Class Bases of the European Welfare States, 1875–1975* (Cambridge, 1990), 116–34.

[32] In particular by Corelli Barnett, *The Audit of War* (London, 1986), and *The Lost Victory* (London, 1995). Barnett has been convincingly criticized by José Harris, 'Enterprise and the Welfare State: A Comparative Perspective', in A. O'Day and T. Gourvish (eds.), *Britain Since 1945* (London, 1991), 39–58. Jim Tomlinson, 'Corelli Barnett's History: The Case of Marshall Aid', *Twentieth Century British History*, 8/2 (1997), 222–38; and 'Welfare and the Economy: The Economic Impact of the Welfare State, 1945–51', *Twentieth Century British History*, 6 (1995), 194–219.   [33] Baldwin, *Class Bases*, 232.

[34] Ibid. 232. *Hansard* (30 May 1946), col. 1456.

Labour's unwillingness or inability to implement most of these corollaries of his Plan help to explain its extremely limited effects.[35]

The post-war pension system did not succeed in rescuing poor old people from means-testing. Even in its first year of existence, 1948, 495,000 old-age and widowed pensioners and 143,000 others above pensionable age received the means-tested National Assistance supplement, which now replaced Public Assistance. Post-war inflation eroded the value of the pensions. Between 1946 and 1957 prices of basic commodities rose by more than 50 per cent. By law National Assistance benefits were regularly adjusted in line with inflation, National Insurance benefits were subject to review only at five-year intervals. By 1951 the numbers of older people receiving National Assistance had risen to 969,000.[36] There was never an adequate universal pension scheme which liberated the poorest from means-testing. In 1948 the pension equalled 19.1 per cent of average male manual earnings; by 1955 it had fallen to 18.4; it then climbed gradually back to the 1948 level.[37] Substantial numbers of old people could not live on the pension without further supplement. As their continuing hardship became apparent, the Labour government responded in June 1950 by raising National Assistance rates but not by increasing the pension. This was praised by the Conservatives as moving in the right direction, towards targetted pensions.

CONSERVATIVE GOVERNMENTS, 1951–1964

Labour was proposing also to raise National Insurance pensions when it lost the election of 1951.[38] The Conservatives maintained their wartime hostility to universalism and their preference for targetted benefits. Ian Macleod, reputedly one of the more socially progressive Conservatives, wrote in 1949: 'Increasingly [the social services] are being used not for the relief of destitution or misfortune or ill-health, but as a means to redistribute wealth and as a means to realise in the end a Communist society'. He further commented that:

The Conservative Party does not regard the true function of the social services to be either the provision of an average standard or the redistribution of wealth. It approves the historic function of the social services as the relief of the unfortunate from misfortune, of the sick from ill-health, of the needy from distress.[39]

The Conservatives in government showed little public interest in pensions. There was strong party pressure to cut public expenditure and to reorient

[35] Harris, *Beveridge*, 450.
[36] R. Lowe, *The Welfare State in Britain since 1945* (London, 1993), 144.
[37] P. Johnson and J. Falkingham, 'Is there a Future for the Beveridge Pension Scheme?', in S. Baldwin and J. Falkingham (eds.), *Social Security and Social Change: New Challenges to the Beveridge Model* (London, 1994), 257.
[38] Jones, 'Conservative Party', 219.   [39] Ibid. 180.

social policy around accepted Conservative goals, in particular to withdraw services from all who were not believed to need them. But there were constraints upon the speed with which this path could be trodden. Their Commons majority was small and they could not afford to alienate lower-middle-class voters who were clear beneficiaries of Labour's 'welfare state'.[40] Also a significant proportion of Conservative voters were pensioners on fixed incomes. These people were suffering due to inflation, but were reluctant to apply for means-tested National Assistance. The Conservatives raised National Insurance pensions, and contributions, in their first budget, partly because they were also cutting food subsidies which would further raise prices of essential items.[41]

The Cabinet was concerned about the growing cost of pensions in the light of the continuing apprehension about the ageing of the population.[42] It considered raising the pensionable age and increasing contributions, but dared not risk the political repercussions, though the Conservatives advocated voluntary deferment of retirement.[43] The Minister of Pensions and National Insurance, Osbert Peake, expressed regret at the abolition in 1948 of the household means test and, at last, of the 'liable relatives' clause:[44]

there was no longer any legal liability on children to maintain parents; the only remaining legal liability for maintenance was between husband and wife . . . all these measures had tended to destroy any sense of family responsibility. People had been encouraged to seek national assistance and this was wrong. It had become too easy and pleasant to draw national assistance . . .[45]

These concerns led to the establishment of the—hardly neutrally titled—Phillips Committee on the Economic and Financial Problems of Provision for Old Age in 1953. It was composed mainly of Conservatives and reported in the following year. It took a gloomy view of likely trends in sickness and death-rates at later ages and recommended raising the retirement age. This was supported by the Treasury, but still feared by the politicians as an electoral liability. Instead pensions were raised before the election of 1955. This was financed by raising the flat-rate contribution above the level actuarially required, which especially penalized the lower-paid. Successive Conservative Budgets gradually shifted more of the cost of insurance benefits from the Exchequer to contributions, in part to cover the cost of the entry of the previously uninsured into entitlement to benefits in 1958. The redistributive mechanism proposed by Beveridge was eroded.

Some see the post-war years as a period of 'consensus' in which Conservatives and Labour shared essentially similar economic and social policies. To the limited extent that this was so, it was due not to ideological convergence but to electoral constraints which prevented the Conservatives from making the

---

[40] Jones, 'Conservative Party', 194.   [41] Ibid. 217.   [42] See pp. 348–51.
[43] Jones, 'Conservative Party', 218–19.   [44] See pp. 141–2.
[45] Jones, 'Conservative Party', 219.

kind of radical changes in social policy that became possible in the different economic and social climate of the 1980s.[46] They did not introduce the improvements in state pensions that could reasonably have been expected had Labour remained in government in the 1950s.

LABOUR AND NATIONAL SUPERANNUATION

By the later 1950s Beveridge himself was campaigning vigorously for more adequate old-age pensions, pointing out how many in need would not apply for the means-tested supplement in addition to the unfortunately large numbers who did.[47] Another critic was Richard Titmuss, now the foremost academic expert on social security. He no longer expected the ageing of the population to be so rapid or the consequences so dire as he once had[48] and regretted that excessive gloom about population trends had caused excessive restraint in pensions policy. He pointed out that sickness rates in the population at large had been lower and death-rates of pensioners higher than had been assumed when National Insurance contributions had been calculated after the war; hence contribution income could sustain higher benefit rates.[49] Titmuss was highly critical of the increased reliance of pensions funding on the regressive flat-rate contribution at a time when the income tax system was becoming more progressive. The limited weekly contribution the lowest paid could afford held down pensions for everyone. He also pointed out that, for all the government protest about the high cost (£45m. a year) of pensions, there was no mention that at least £100m. tax income was annually foregone in tax allowances for buyers of private pensions.[50] The very growth of the private sector,[51] Titmuss feared, was creating 'two nations in old age and greater inequality in living standards after work than in work'. The fact that better-paid workers, including many trade unionists especially in the public sector, benefited from occupational and other private pensions reduced their incentive to demand improved state pensions.

Titmuss was increasingly convinced that the Beveridge flat-rate principle was a brake on the development of an adequate state pension system—'the very opposite of social justice, a poll tax which hurts the poorest most and it also directly restricts the size of the old age pension'[52]—and that improvement was urgent, for old people now seemed to be the group in greatest poverty in the full-employment 'welfare state'. From 1955 Titmuss was adviser to a Labour Party committee on pensions whom he persuaded that since the Treasury opposed the financing of pensions through general taxation—and

[46] Ibid. 387–90.   [47] Harris, *Beveridge*, 463.   [48] See p. 338.
[49] R. Titmuss, 'Pension Systems and Population Change', in R. M. Titmuss, *Essays on the Welfare State* (London, 1958), 56–74.   [50] Ibid. 69.
[51] See pp. 381–2.   [52] The Labour Party, *National Superannuation* (London, 1957), 8–9.

taxpayers themselves would resist tax increases—the only alternative was a system of earnings-related contributions with a redistributive element which could provide the necessary resources for improvements without burdening the lower-paid.

Titmuss's proposals were embodied in a Labour Party publication, *National Superannuation*, in 1957. This was an official statement of party policy, the product of a party committee chaired by R. H. S. Crossman and advised by Titmuss and his colleagues at the London School of Economics.[53] The proposals aimed to guarantee to the 'average wage earner' a pension equivalent to half-pay at age 65, by adding an income-related pension scheme to the basic National Insurance pension. Labour was making the transition from perceiving the pension as relief of poverty to the pension as income replacement, extending to state pensioners the advantages occupational schemes gave to better-paid workers. *National Superannuation* stated:

We believe that an adequate pension . . . means the right to go on living in the same neighbourhood, to enjoy the same hobbies and to be able to afford to mix with the same circle of friends.

To this end, the better-paid would pay a higher contribution than was actuarially necessary, the lower-paid a lower one.

Labour saw social security policy as complementary rather than as an alternative to the drive for economic growth. *National Superannuation* warned:

We would emphasize that the much more generous provision for old age which we propose will demand both self-restraint and hard work from the rest of the community. If the old are to spend more, the rest of us will have that much less to spend—unless we make up the loss by increased production . . . Collectively we must be ready to see national consumption held back and the necessary savings built up in our new National Pensions Fund. These savings must be used wisely for capital investment.

Titmuss like Beveridge did not consider pensions in isolation from the wider economy. He had become increasingly concerned at the investment power which was building up in the growing private pension funds and wanted the state to acquire equivalent power. This, the pamphlet stated, would assist economic growth and enable the country 'to pay the constantly increasing bill for old age pensions over the next 25 years'. Abolition of the retirement rule was also recommended, for 'we now realize that the interest of the national economy requires old people to postpone their retirement for as long as possible. With more people living longer and remaining in good health until a later age the retirement rule does not look such obvious good sense as it appeared in 1942.'[54]

Women workers should have the same pensions rights as men and the same obligations. Married women would not be allowed to opt out as they could

[53] The Labour Party, *National Superannuation*, 4.   [54] Ibid. 8.

under the existing scheme. Since by the 1950s increasing numbers of women were returning to paid work after a period of childrearing, they would benefit from the additional pension related to their years of earning and contribution. Though the proposals recognized women's changed working patterns and gradual changes in their status, they still assumed (accurately enough in 1957) that most women married and remained married, so that their main income after retirement would be the husband's pension followed by widows' pension.[55] There was no reference to the effects upon pension rights of divorce or separation. The flat-rate National Insurance pension of £3 would be payable only to those who had paid full contributions. Paying it to all of pensionable age was considered, but:

This would however mean giving pensions to married women who choose never to go out to work. As a result the joint income of a married couple might in some circumstances be higher in old age than in working life. There has therefore to be some test of work and we suggest that 40 years of work should qualify for the maximum of £3. This would benefit the married woman by allowing ten years at home without reduction of her basic pension.[56]

Women who did not enter insurable employment would be eligible for the dependants' pension. Women who paid the additional contributions would not be eligible for full National Superannuation pensions until age 65, though they might receive the lower basic pension from age 60 onwards, and:

We hope that in time it would be possible for women to draw pension at the same age as men. If they are to share equal rights with men in the proposed scheme and accept equal obligations, then it is desirable that they should defer their right to a pension to the same age as in many other countries.[57]

The proposals assumed a fifteen-year transition to equal pensionable ages.

The National Superannuation scheme did not imply simple perpetuation into old age of the inequalities of working life. This was a frequent criticism of the proposals within the Labour Party, though it is hard to see that the 1946 legislation did, or was intended to do, otherwise. There would be a ceiling of contributions and benefits (in the latter case £75 a year) and a benefit floor below which no pensioner would be allowed to fall, for:

one of our socialist aims is to reduce the gross inequalities of existing society and national superannuation would play an important part in achieving this end.

To protect pensioners against inflation, pension rates should be linked to average earnings and to a cost-of-living index. The exact balance of funding between contributions and the Exchequer was left to be decided by the government,

[55] Ibid. 43–5.
[56] Ibid. 62; but only if she started work at age 15 and worked without a break until age 65.
[57] Ibid. 75 n.

though it was assumed that the scheme could not be wholly funded from contributions because the necessary rates would be 'intolerably high'. An annual Exchequer grant would be essential, especially to cover the increase in basic rate. Indeed a fully funded scheme would create a possibly embarrassing problem of investing a very large sum of contributions.[58] Members of occupational schemes which met approved standards would be allowed to opt out of National Superannuation.

National Superannuation was approved by the Labour Party conference of 1957. Beveridge criticized the plan in the House of Lords, in which he sat as a Liberal, on unswerving liberal grounds, as:

Not a serious contribution . . . state provision should be at a basic level above which private insurance operated . . . the individual should share some responsibility for himself and not be spoon-fed by the welfare state.[59]

There was opposition in the Labour Party and the TUC to any move away from the principles of flat-rate universality, which had completed their curious transition from liberal proposal to becoming a touchstone of 'socialist' social policy despite their gross inadequacy and regressive character.[60] There was, however, growing trade union pressure for income-related pensions of the kind available to white-collar workers and increasingly to manual workers in the public sector.[61]

The Swedish Social Democratic government at around the same time and for similar reasons shifted from the Beveridge-style flat-rate system it had introduced after the war—in conscious imitation of Beveridge—to an income-related system. This also was a response to trade union demands for earnings-related pensions comparable to the occupational pensions available to white-collar workers.[62] Labour, however, was not in government in Britain.

PENSIONS POLICY, 1959–1989

The Conservatives were sufficiently alarmed to develop counter-proposals. They criticized National Superannuation on actuarial grounds and as 'back-door nationalization' since the investment of a large public pension fund would greatly increase potential government control of business. They produced instead, in 1959, a minimalist, non-redistributive graduated scheme which excluded the lowest paid and minimized the Exchequer contribution by calculating the income-related contribution in such a way that it contributed to paying off the deficit in the insurance fund. This new pension was payable on a very

---

[58] The Labour Party, *National Superannuation*, 85–9. [59] *Hansard*, House of Lords, 4 Dec. 1959.
[60] Baldwin, *Class Bases*, 233. [61] See pp. 380–2.
[62] Margaret S. Gordon, *Social Security Policies in Industrial Countries: A Comparative Analysis* (Cambridge, 1988), 47–9.

narrow band of earnings (£9–£15 a week) and was not index linked. The Chancellor stressed the 'irretrievable financial deficits' looming for the National Insurance scheme,[63] whilst granting the largest increase since the war to the flat-rate pension, just as 500,000 better-off people qualified for the pension for the first time, and one year before a general election, which the Conservatives won. The Chancellor described the scheme as a 'bargain', Labour as a 'swindle'.[64] In line with previous Conservative policy the new scheme encouraged the private sector by allowing contracting out on favourable terms.[65]

Labour returned to government in 1964. Inexperienced Ministers with a very small majority, dealing with a legacy from their predecessors of serious economic difficulties, abandoned the carefully worked-out pre-election pension strategy:

That we should switch as early as possible from flat-rate to earnings-related contributions and in this way pile up enormous sums in the pension fund which we could use to dynamize the existing flat-rate pension.[66]

Instead Labour responded to party pressure for an immediate substantial increase in the flat-rate pension to 12s. 6d. a week, which necessitated an increase in contributions. As Crossman rightly commented:

The net result is the worst of all worlds as we can't raise the flat-rate contributions any higher without imposing an intolerable burden on the lower-paid worker. Even worse, the income guarantee which we had pledged ourselves to introduce would now be at an absurdly low level as a result of the money we had wasted on the huge initial increase in the flat-rate pension.[67]

Labour won a secure majority in 1966, but serious financial problems persisted. Also the ten-year-old National Superannuation scheme required updating. Nor did pensions appear to be regarded with particular seriousness by the Labour leadership. It was January 1970 before Crossman, now Secretary of State for Social Services, was able to place a Bill before parliament. Labour lost the election of 1970 before the Bill had completed it passage.

Labour returned to office in 1974 as a minority government facing the prospect of another election. Almost immediately, they repeated the mistake of a decade earlier, giving a large cash increase to the flat-rate pension. This was, in part, an element in their 'social contract' with the trade unions following a period of industrial strife. The Trades Union Congress, urged on especially by Jack Jones, General Secretary of the Transport and General Workers Union (and still in the 1990s, as a pensioner, fighting publicly for improved pensions), urged a pension of £10 a week for a single person,

[63] Speech to the Office Management Association, reported in *Financial Times*, 30 June 1960.
[64] Timmins, *Five Giants*, 195.   [65] Baldwin, *Class Bases*, 239–40.
[66] Richard Crossman, *The Diaries of a Cabinet Minister*, i: *Minister of Housing, 1964–6* (London, 1975), 276.
[67] Ibid. 276–7.

£16 for a married couple. This was conceded; and, importantly, pensions were linked for the first time to average earnings and to the cost of living.

Barbara Castle, now the Minister in charge of social security, moved to implement a version of the (now dead) Richard Crossman's pensions proposals, though again the increase in the flat-rate pension had narrowed the room for manoeuvre. Also, there were greater obstacles to overcome than a decade earlier, in particular the much larger number of occupational pension schemes, and of interests vested in them, carefully nurtured by the Conservatives. What emerged in 1975 was a modest compromise. A flat-rate pension ensured for the poorest an improved minimum. Above this level earnings-related benefits tapered off on a scale that produced a degree of downward redistribution. Benefits were calculated from the best years of income. Contributions were somewhat more heavily loaded onto employers than workers. The scheme was named the State Earnings Related Pension (SERPS). Contracting out of the state scheme was so formulated that statutory superannuation did not directly compete with occupational schemes, which were guaranteed against inflation.[68] Once again the cost to the Exchequer was increased as a result of payment of the new pensions sooner than was actuarially justified, at a reduced rate from 1978, with the expectation that they would reach the full rate in 1998.[69] The system was highly complex.

When the Conservatives returned to office in 1979, led by Mrs Thatcher, they sought to modify Labour's pension scheme. The flat-rate pension's short-lived link with earnings was broken in 1980, when it was at a post-war peak of 19.8 per cent of average male earnings. It stood at 16 per cent in 1990.[70] In 1986 the government substantially modified SERPS but did not follow urgings from within the party to scrap it. Its complexities made it a useful vehicle for tax increases in the shape of increased contributions. Under the new provisions, from 2000 benefits were to be reduced from 25 per cent to 20 per cent of maximum pensionable earnings, the entitlement basis changed to average lifetime earnings from the best twenty years, and the costs approximately halved. This was in line with Conservative preference for a minimal pension and was accompanied by further encouragement of private sector schemes. The standards required for contracted -out schemes were reduced and incentive payments were introduced for contracting out.

By the 1990s the substantial number of older people with no income but their state pension still lived seriously below the living standards of most of the population, though increasing numbers of unemployed people were crashing to join them.[71] From the 1960s to 1990 the numbers of pensioners receiving a means-tested supplement was remarkably stable at around

---

[68] Baldwin, *Class Bases*, 144–6.
[69] Paul Johnson and Jane Falkingham, *Ageing and Economic Welfare* (London, 1992), 140–1.
[70] Ibid. 143.
[71] John Hills, *Joseph Rowntree Foundation Inquiry into Income and Wealth*, 2 vols (York, 1995).

1.7 million.[72] The proliferation of old-age pressure groups after the war (Age Concern, Help the Aged, Centre for Policy on Ageing, etc.) did nothing to reverse the problem, effective though they may have been in other respects.[73]

The fiftieth anniversary of the Beveridge Report in 1992 provided an opportunity for commentators to compare the situation in the 1990s unfavourably with that following the Second World War.[74] The calls of the early 1990s, from Labour and Conservatives, for the substantial overhaul of the welfare state generally assumed that the post-war social security system had initially been good, but was failing under pressure of social change, in particular changes in gender roles and in patterns of marriage, divorce, and work,[75] though Beveridge was criticized for ignoring the specific needs of women even in the 1940s.[76] There was little appreciation that the post-war pension system had been inadequate for the needs of very many pensioners from the beginning. Indeed, one of the curiosities of British history in the second half of the twentieth century is the remarkably low level of public awareness of the relatively low standard of British state pension provision.

Despite the sustained rhetoric since 1945, mainly from the Conservative Party and its supporters, about the high costs of social security, 'British expenditures on social security have been appreciably lower in relation to GDP than those of most continental west European countries throughout the post-war period', though they were higher than those of the US and comparable with other Commonwealth countries and Ireland. From the 1960s to the end of the millennium, the value of British state pensions in relation to average male earnings was lowest or next to lowest (vying for bottom place with Denmark) of all OECD countries. In 1979 the basic pension equalled 42 per cent of average net income, in 1990 32 per cent. The standard advocated by the European Union in the 1990s was 50 per cent.[77] The leading Conservative Michael Portillo prophesied, before his unexpected defeat in a firmly middle-class constituency in the 1997 election, that the basic pension 'is going to be worth a nugatory amount in the coming century'. Poverty surveys in the 1990s once more showed high concentrations of poverty among old people, especially among the very old (aged 75 and above), who were dependent upon state pensions.[78]

The Labour government which came to power with a large majority in 1997 took a course strikingly similar to that set out by Beveridge in 1942, seeking

[72] Johnson and Falkingham, *Ageing*, 54.

[73] Henry J. Pratt, *Gray Agendas: Interest Groups and Public Pensions in Canada, Britain, and the United States* (Ann Arbor, 1993), 117–46.

[74] Sally Baldwin and Jane Falkingham, *Social Security and Social Change: New Challenges to the Beveridge Model* (London, 1994).

[75] From the side of Labour see *Social Justice: Strategies for National Renewal*, a Report of the Commission on Social Justice (London, 1994).

[76] Baldwin and Falkingham, *Social Security*.

[77] A. B. Atkinson, *Incomes and the Welfare State* (Cambridge, 1995), 305–23.

[78] Hills, *Joseph Rowntree Foundation Inquiry into Income and Wealth*.

to establish a basic, subsistence, guaranteed state pension for all, which income earners were obliged to supplement with a sound occupational or private pension, managed ideally by the type of non-profit-making institution of which Beveridge profoundly approved. Friendly Societies looked set for an unexpected revival at the end of the millennium.

'PRIVATE' PENSIONS SINCE THE SECOND WORLD WAR

Much of the story of state pensions can be better understood in the context of developments in occupational and other private sector pensions. Public sector employment grew fast during and after the Second World War, due partly to the growth of activity of central and local government, and to the post-war nationalization of important sectors, especially railways, mines, the health service. By 1950 25 per cent of the labour force was in the public sector. Unions and workers in the newly nationalized occupations negotiated to emulate the best pensions already available in that sector, after some tough and protracted bargaining, in the face of some resistance from the Labour governments of 1945–51. The government's and the unions' preference was for a high-quality state scheme.[79] Since the government failed to deliver this, the unions became increasingly willing to support occupational schemes. The unions themselves were strong and confident again, their bargaining power enhanced by full employment and labour shortage, but their own welfare benefit funds had been much weakened by the Depression and the war and in 1946 they and the Friendly Societies lost their role in administering national insurance. They accepted this with equanimity. They still did not push for an earnings-related scheme. They were perhaps optimistic about the level of the flat-rate pension; and perhaps feared that an earnings-related scheme would favour non-manual workers. But it must also have been important that the largest unions were concentrated in the public sector, more than ever, and had or could negotiate earnings-related occupational schemes. They had correspondingly less need to demand equivalent state schemes.

Unions in the railways and mining sought successfully to bring all workers' pension schemes up to the best practice of existing schemes in those occupations; and in the health service, much of which had previously been in the voluntary sector with poor or non-existent pension provision, to raise pensions to local government standards. This especially benefited manual workers in the public sector, only one-fifth of whom had had pension rights before nationalization. Importantly also, in 1948 occupational pensions became wholly transferable between occupations within the public sector, so that employees changing jobs within the public sector did not lose their pension rights. In the private sector this was rare.

[79] A. Russell, *The Growth of Occupational Welfare in Britain* (Aldershot, 1991), 128–9.

After the war, employers used pensions less as an instrument of industrial relations than before and expansion in the private sector was mainly driven by tax incentives. Hence, again, manual workers believed that they had less reason than in the past to be suspicious of occupational schemes. There are signs also that they increasingly resented the fact that non-manual workers had access to occupational pensions when they did not; and in the unprecedented full employment of the post-war period they felt better able than before to pay contributions.[80] By the 1970s the unions were increasingly looking at the higher standards available to workers elsewhere in Europe and believed that they were less likely to receive these from the state than through occupational schemes. At a more fundamental level, there was still a widely shared belief that this was a field in which the state *should* intervene only minimally, with individuals and mutual aid organizations making provision above the minimum. This view was shared by many employers and, as we have seen, by employees.

Private sector schemes also expanded with the further growth of large-scale bureaucratized organizations in a period of labour shortage and full employment. The government surveyed the occupational pension sector in 1956. By this time there were 37,000 such schemes covering one in three workers. It was rare for large companies not to provide a pension scheme, but companies which did so still admitted to them only just under half of their male employees, generally the better paid, and only about 25 per cent of female employees. Some large private sector schemes, such as that of ICI, were gradually extended to include manual workers.

The post-war Labour government took little overt interest in occupational pensions, other than seeking unsuccessfully to discourage them in the public sector. Their hostility derived not only from ideological preference for state provision. Existing private sector schemes conflicted with their labour market policy by hindering labour mobility, by encouraging retirement at 60 or 65 when it was government policy to encourage older workers to stay in the workforce, and by discouraging hiring of older workers.[81] These weaknesses could have been overcome by legislation had the government given serious thought to the role of occupational pensions in the economy, but of that there was little sign. At the same time rising rates and coverage of direct taxation during and after the war increased the tax advantages for individuals and employers of participating in occupational schemes. In 1947 the government tried, imperfectly, to restrict such advantages.[82] Tax law in relation to pensions had become very muddled and this together with the proliferation of

---

[80] Ibid. 130–1.

[81] S. Harper and P. Thane, 'The Consolidation of "Old Age" as a Phase of Life', in M. Jefferys (ed.), *Growing Old in the Twentieth Century* (London, 1989), 43–61.

[82] L. Hannah, *Inventing Retirement: The Development of Occupational Pensions in Britain* (Cambridge, 1986), 44–5.

schemes necessitated some review. This was done in the Finance Act of 1956.[83] Conservative Party actions both directly and indirectly gave an exceptional boost to private pensions.

The Finance Act, 1956, and its successor in 1970, also a Conservative measure, gave significant tax advantages to employers and employees in pension funds operated by insurance companies. These were so dramatic that in the 1970s pension funds accounted for one-third of personal savings in the British economy, significantly higher than in the US. This appears to have been mainly a response to tax incentives.[84] The finance legislation did, however, impose standards and controls on the private sector schemes. Generally tax relief was offered only to schemes which fitted within the traditions of existing public sector schemes and good private sector schemes: typically this meant paying pensions of no more than two- thirds of final salary or lump sums of no more than one and a half times final salary: 'This maintained standards but of a conservative kind and left little room for innovation.'[85]

On the other hand, Labour's *National Superannuation* proposals of 1957 were designed to curb the increasing power of occupational pension funds and to replace them with a state scheme. At this stage occupational pensions covered only about one-third of the British workforce and, as Hannah comments, this 'probably represented the last practical moment at which a state earnings related pension scheme could have wiped out the bulk of demand for private provision in Britain'.[86] When the scheme was announced shares in insurance companies dropped sharply. Private employers and insurance companies argued against it publicly, insisting that the role of the state should be no more than to provide a basic pension. The greatest weakness of occupational pensions, they conceded, could be overcome by introducing transferability. Privately, they proposed to Conservative ministers legislation to compel all employees to join occupational pension schemes.

The Conservative government did not yet think compulsory membership of occupational schemes possible, not least because of the difficulty of including casual and part-time workers and employees of small firms, a high proportion of whom were female. They recognized that there was a certain demand for a state earnings-related scheme among those excluded from existing occupational schemes. The Conservative response to this in the National Insurance Act, 1959, was sufficient to defuse support for the more comprehensive Labour proposal and to allow occupational pensions a clear field for development without further controls, such as statutory transferability. Insurance companies stepped up their sales efforts. Employers now had an additional incentive to introduce occupational schemes since if they did not they were required to contribute to state pensions. In the following decade, pensions coverage spread to cover almost half the workforce. In 1970 78 per cent of

---

[83] Hannah, *Retirement*, 44–5.   [84] Ibid. 50–1.   [85] Ibid. 51.   [86] Ibid. 56.

non-manual male full-time workers belonged to private pension schemes; the figure for manual workers was 50 per cent and for unskilled manual workers, 38 per cent.[87]

The Labour Social Security Act, 1975, was a compromise with a much strengthened private sector, in particular in allowing schemes of adequate quality to contract out on reasonable terms. It retained the regulatory Occupational Pensions Board set up in 1973 by the Conservatives. The 1975 Act put pressure on occupational pension schemes to raise their standards to meet the opting out requirements. Opposition was muted at this time because the oil crisis and the collapse in the value of investments was pushing many pension funds into crisis. Barbara Castle wooed the pension companies probably more vigorously than was necessary or desirable, by encouraging further contracting and effectively guaranteeing contracted-out schemes against collapse and against failure to provide the inflation proofing which was now required.[88]

In the 1960s and 1970s company mergers brought pensions to firms where they had not existed before. Large numbers of specialized advisers emerged, dedicated to hastening the spread of schemes. In the 1960s the merchant banks moved into the field. Occupational pensions improved in quality and quantity in the 1960s and 1970s, without compulsion. Nevertheless growth slowed after the later 1960s and stabilized at a lower level than, for example, in the Netherlands, where there was a more clearly structured partnership between state and occupational schemes. The British 'system', being evidently unplanned, was not optimally benefiting either public or private sector, or the consumer. In the Netherlands, the state provided only a flat-rate pension but occupational pensions were of a high standard and wholly transferable. In Britain, by 1979, coverage was almost complete in the civil service, armed forces, and nationalized industries, and had reached 90 per cent in local government and the health service for full-time male and female employees; very many women, however, worked part-time and were excluded. In the private sector, only 50 per cent of men and 25 per cent of full-time women workers were covered, and the numbers fell in the 1970s. Many small firms probably continued to make ex gratia payments to retired workers, though the numbers were probably declining. It remained normal for manual workers and staff to belong to separate schemes.[89]

The patchwork of pension schemes was regulated by the Occupational Pensions Board, which also had the role of advising the Secretary of State generally on pension matters. Members of the Board were drawn from employers, trade unions, the lay public, and the actuarial profession. It survived into the 1980s as a regulatory body and as a useful channel of communication

[87] A. B. Atkinson, *The Economics of Inequality* (Oxford, 1975), 202.
[88] Hannah, *Retirement*, 62.   [89] Ibid. 65 ff.

between the public and private sectors. However, true to the spirit of the Thatcher governments, regulatory powers were diminished in the 1980s, and were reduced further in the early 1990s, with disastrous results. Unscrupulous employers, such as Robert Maxwell, misappropriated pension funds; unscrupulous financial institutions gave seriously misleading advice to private buyers of pensions. The process of privatization of the public sector in the 1980s and 1990s shifted many workers from favourable public sector arrangements into inferior pension regimes; as, from 1988, did tax incentives to reject often good occupational schemes in favour of inferior and inadequately regulated personal pensions. Such pensions were heavily subsidized from the National Insurance fund and tempted about two million people in the first year. The problems of recompensing many who were seriously deceived were unresolved by the time of the election of 1997 and for some time after, despite strenuous efforts by the Labour government elected in May 1997. Even for those who had not been victims of pensions mis-selling and who sought adequate protection in later life, the world of pensions in Britain was extraordinarily complicated and difficult to navigate with confidence. By the end of the millennium, many British people, in all classes, certainly had the worst of all pension worlds, yet few were aware of it, despite increasing government efforts to increase that awareness.

CONCLUSION

An overview of public and private pension provision in Britain from Beveridge to the end of the century highlights the low level of pensions available to most people in Britain throughout the second half of the twentieth century, relative to those of comparable countries; and the failure of the British strenuously to object to, or apparently quite to recognize, this situation. The British did not demonstrate or come out on strike against the erosion of pensions as did their peers in France and Germany in the 1990s. Low pension levels and popular acceptance of them have a common origin in the deep-rooted legacy of the Poor Law, and in an, associated, widely held commitment to an essentially liberal view of provision for social welfare: that the role of the state should be confined to providing the minimum that is desirable and acceptable, supplemented by private effort in various forms. This view was shared even by many who did not recognize its essential liberalism, such as 'socialists' who, even fifty years after its publication, praised the Beveridge Plan for the high standards it proposed for older people.

20

'Shocked into Idleness': The Emergence of Mass Retirement

How did the spread of pensions in post-war Britain affect the lives of older people? If there has been one period of especially dramatic change in the history of the lives of old people it is the mid-twentieth century. By the 1950s, for the first time in history, the overwhelming majority of people in Britain could expect to live from birth to their sixties and beyond as a result of falling death-rates at younger ages, especially in infancy, through the earlier part of the century. Even the poorest people could expect a secure, if not necessarily a generous, pension at a fixed, predictable, and early age. Most could expect a period of 'retirement' between the end of their working lives and the onset of serious physical dependency, if they indeed experienced this, since it was and is by no means universal. They could all expect secure access to health care, which, though often imperfect, was, especially for poorer women, better than anything available ever before. All of this amounted to an important cultural shift in experiences and expectations, in the ways in which people could imagine their life-courses.

It is also a period about which a great deal is known, because it generated more research about older people, as about other social groups, than ever before. This was partly because social research itself was expanding rapidly; partly because, as we have seen,[1] fears about the ageing of the population made old people a focus of concern for a variety of influential groups. Also, in the relative prosperity of the post-war, full-employment 'welfare state' old people appeared, for a while, to be the most conspicuous group still in poverty. Between the 1940s and the 1960s there were extensive studies of old people's economic circumstances, capacities for work, family and social networks, welfare and service provision, housing, diet, socio-medical conditions, and much else.

Much of this research was widely publicized. Its effects were ambiguous. It offered conflicting representations of older people. Many of the findings about employment, retirement, and family relationships, represented them positively, as active contributors to economy and society. But social research also often emphasized the poverty and isolation still experienced by older people in the 'welfare state'. It explored the lives of the poor and all too rarely those of the rich or the many middling strata in between. The intention, laudably,

---

[1] See Ch. 16.

was to rescue older people in need, but it also tended to objectify 'the elderly' (the most commonly used term) and to present them as a unified problematic category; like much social research of the period creating or reinforcing a stereotype, often embodying the very characteristics the researchers were most eager to dispel.[2] For some people old age was indeed miserable, but such representations disguised a variety of experiences: large and increasing numbers of older people were neither impoverished nor unhappy.

The discourses of the years following the Second World War completed the construction of 'old people', 'the elderly', or 'the old-age pensioner', the customary, interchangeable terms, as a distinct social category, defined by age and status in relation to the welfare system, rather than, as in the past, by physical condition and capacity to contribute to economic and social exchange.[3] But such representations did not go unchallenged. The emergence and the experiences of the 'old-age pensioner' have been discussed in previous chapters. This chapter examines how another important aspect of the experience of older people—retirement—was analysed and represented in these years.

THE GROWTH OF RETIREMENT

It was only gradually after the war that 'retirement' became the normal experience of most manual workers past a certain age. The facts about increased retirement from paid work at or around the state pensionable age are clear. According to the censuses, 73 per cent of men over age 65 were in paid work in 1881, 65 per cent in 1901, 48 per cent in 1931, 31 per cent in 1951, 23 per cent in 1961, 19 per cent in 1971, 13 per cent in 1980. The percentage of women over 60 recorded as being in paid employment fell from 13 to 5 between 1901 and 1951.[4] By 1991 it had risen to one in fourteen, most of them employed part-time and in service occupations, an outcome of the general increase in female employment in these sectors in the post-war years.[5] The bulk of older people in paid work were in their first five years past the state pensionable age.[6]

---

[2] For example, research on immigrants from the Commonwealth, see Chris Waters, ' "Dark Strangers" in our Midst: Discourses of Race and Nation in Britain, 1947–1963', *Journal of British Studies*, 36/2 (1997), 207–38.

[3] J. Macnicol and A. Blaikie, 'The Politics of Retirement, 1908–1948', 21–42, and Sarah Harper and Pat Thane, 'The Consolidation of "Old Age" as a Phase of Life, 1945–1965', 43–61, in Margot Jefferys (ed.), *Growing Old in the Twentieth Century* (London, 1989).

[4] For discussion of these statistics see Paul Johnson, 'The Employment and Retirement of Older Men in England and Wales, 1881–1981', *Economic History Review*, 47/1 (Feb. 1994), 115–17. A. Harrop, *The Employment Position of Older Women in Europe*, (Age Concern Institute of Gerontology, King's College (London, 1990), 23.

[5] J. Askham *et al.*, *Life after Sixty; A Profile of Britain's Older Population*, Age Concern Institute of Gerontology, King's College (London, 1992), 18.   [6] Ibid. 51–6.

The reasons for the change are elusive.[7] 'Retirement' has not had a stable meaning over the twentieth century. By 1951 most male manual workers (female patterns were different and will be discussed separately) 'retired' from full-time paid work into full-time worklessness. In earlier times, and still for many in the 1950s and 1960s, most men went through a gradual transition from full-time, through lighter and part-time and casual work to a 'retirement' that was often reluctant and impoverished, caused by physical decrepitude and often followed closely by death. They might record themselves officially as 'workers', expressing willingness to work, when the actual extent of their paid employment was limited or non-existent. In this sense census statistics at least up to 1951 are likely somewhat to overstate the levels of employment of older men.[8] The change after the Second World War to a general expectation of complete withdrawal from paid work at a certain age was an aspect of the wider shift to a 'modern' decasualized labour market, clearly demarcated between full-time paid work and full-time absence of it.[9] From the 1980s there was a further shift to widespread, sometimes reluctant, permanent exit from paid work into retirement at still earlier ages: 50 or even below.[10]

Among reasons for the post-war change lack of demand for labour can be ruled out. From at least 1947 the government actively encouraged older people to remain at work due to the labour shortage. Nor can the physical condition of older people explain it. Though higher survival rates to older ages may have led to the survival of more unfit people, it is reasonable to assume that rising living standards compensated sufficiently to ensure higher standards of fitness among older people in 1981 than in 1881.

Patterns of retirement differed among different groups of workers. Occupational pensions spread among white-collar workers in the inter-war years.[11] Generally, and increasingly, these specified a fixed retirement age. Later retirement remained more common in small firms and among the self-employed. Occupational pensions were associated with new management practices in large firms which favoured a fixed retirement age over previous arrangements which were flexible and discretionary but required sensitive management decisions about individual capacity for work.[12] This change came at a time when the white-collar lower middle class was itself expanding. They created a distinct and new retirement culture, focused on the bungalow in a coastal resort.

[7] See pp. 279–83.

[8] But not sufficiently to invalidate Johnson's general conclusion, despite Macnicol's attempts to dismiss them, J. Macnicol, *The Politics of Retirement in Britain, 1878–1948* (Cambridge, 1998), 22–8.

[9] Noel Whiteside and Robert Salais, 'Introduction: Political Economy and Modernization', in Whiteside and Salais, *Governance, Industry and Labour Markets in Britain and France: The Modernizing State in the Mid-Twentieth Century* (London, 1998), 1–22.

[10] M. Kohli *et al.*, *Time for Retirement: Comparative Studies of Early Exit from the Labour Force* (Cambridge, 1991).   [11] See pp. 250–4.

[12] L. Hannah, *Inventing Retirement: The Development of Occupational Pensions in Britain* (Cambridge, 1986), 134–6.

Occupational pensions spread to manual workers in the post-1945 period[13] but only slowly, and more slowly still to women in all occupations. Still, in 1971 only 13.6 per cent of pensioner income came from occupational pensions. The combination of somewhat improved state pensions, National Assistance, and perhaps more help from children who were enjoying the benefits of full employment,[14] may have enabled more older people to contemplate giving up work with a greater sense of security and optimism than at any previous time. For many of these people, this is merely to compare an intolerable with a bleak prospect, but it might have been preferable to the misery of dragging on in employment when no longer fit. The components of the poor older person's income package were shifting. The combination of state and family support may have enabled many at earlier ages than before to admit defeat in the struggle to support themselves by their own earnings.

But to what extent older workers in post-war Britain chose retirement or had it imposed upon them remains uncertain. Older men were unevenly distributed in industry. Men over 65 made up 3.3 per cent of the total manufacturing workforce, but were 4.1 per cent of workers in shipbuilding, 5.9 per cent in cotton spinning and cotton weaving, 10.9 per cent in lace textiles, 2 per cent in motor vehicle manufacture. They were concentrated in the older staple industries which most urgently needed restructuring in the post-war years, but where output and demand for labour was high. They were also relatively numerous in highly skilled manual occupations where labour shortage was acute. Hence their numbers and their position in the economy made the trend to retirement a particular issue for government policy.

THE LABOUR GOVERNMENT RESISTS RETIREMENT

Though it had been government policy to encourage retirement amid the unemployment of the inter-war years,[15] from the 1940s it was not. This was due first to fears about the economic effects of the ageing of the population, then to the labour shortage. The Labour government, however, was ambivalent. The needs generated by the labour shortage conflicted with the Party's and the trade unions' historical commitment to earlier retirement as the just reward for a hard-working life.[16] The Trades Union Congress (TUC) regularly debated the issue after the war and through the 1950s. It consistently resisted proposals for delayed retirement and higher pensionable ages.[17] Not least the trade unions did not feel confident that full employment had come to stay, or indeed that it had ever arrived in certain pockets of continuing insecure employment such as Clydeside and Merseyside. They were also

---

[13] See pp. 380–2.   [14] See pp. 369–72.   [15] See p. 321.   [16] See pp. 347–9.
[17] TUC, *Annual Reports* (1954), 444–6; (1955), 153.

concerned that the continued employment of older men would block the advancement of the young. Also, the spread of occupational pensions in the strongly unionized nationalized industries[18] encouraged retirement. In 1951 Labour modified the National Insurance scheme to encourage later retirement, by relaxing the earnings rule and modestly increasing the pension for those who deferred retirement, but not by a sufficient amount noticeably to affect retirement patterns.

The Conservative Party manifesto in the election of 1951 stated that 'the care and comfort of the elderly is a sacred trust . . . some of them prefer to remain in work and there must be encouragement for them to do so'. Following their success in the election they introduced a more flexible retirement policy for the civil service, the employment sector it could most readily control. The Ministry of Labour thereafter strove to encourage older workers to remain in the labour force. It raised the issue repeatedly with the National Joint Advisory Council, on which sat representatives of private employers, the TUC, and the nationalized industries. It issued pamphlets, held conferences, and funded research into maximizing the work capabilities of older people. In 1952 it appointed a National Advisory Committee on the Employment of Older Men and Women (the Watkinson Committee) to advise on how workers might be encouraged to delay retirement and on the best uses to be made of older workers. This Committee reported in 1953 and 1955. The Ministry meanwhile carried on a propaganda campaign, sending leaflets and speakers to trades councils, Chambers of Commerce, Rotary clubs, and individual firms about the importance of employing older workers. It offered the assistance of its industrial rehabilitation units to older workers. Material was inserted into radio programmes and the press; a film about the virtues of older workers was available for hire.[19]

The first report of the Watkinson Committee admitted that, despite isolated adjustments, no general or widespread changes had been achieved.[20] Employers in particular were unconvinced. The Committee strongly opposed a fixed retirement age and recommended that the test for engagement or retirement should be capacity, not age, and that all who could do so effectively should have the chance to continue in work if they wished. The second report was more optimistic about employers' responses, which the Committee attributed to the effects of acute labour shortages in some industrial areas.[21]

The Conservatives also appointed the Committee on the Economic and Financial Problems of the Provision for Old Age (Phillips Committee), part of a wider review of the costs of Labour's welfare legislation. This supplemented the argument from the point of view of the needs of the labour market,

[18] See pp. 380–2.
[19] First and Second Reports of the National Advisory Committee on *Employment of Older Men and Women*, Cmd. 8963 (1953); Cmd. 9628 (1955).
[20] Cmd. 8963 (1953).   [21] Cmd. 9628 (1955).

by emphasizing the costs of an ageing population, especially arising from pensions. It estimated in its report in 1954 that if the employment rates of older people did not increase, the proportion of 'dependent' older people in the population would rise from the current 12 per cent to almost one-third by 1979. They stressed, however, that the total dependency ratio (the proportion of people of working age in the population in relation to the whole) would not rise, due to the fall in the birth-rate. Others stoked the prevailing demographic fears by calculating, dubiously,[22] that pensioners were twice as costly to welfare services as children and three and a half times as costly as the active population.[23]

The Phillips Committee recommended a later age of retirement (68 for men, 63 for women) but was not optimistic about the likely outcome:

If there were no change in retirement habits over the next two years the elderly would constitute about six per cent of the labour force of about 24,000,000 persons and most of this six per cent would be in the age groups 65–69 and 60–64. (A major change in retirement habits would be required to turn this 6% into 7% and to add a bare 1% (or 240,000) to the numbers in work.)[24]

The trend towards earlier retirement among men was briefly arrested though not reversed in the mid-1950s.[25] Women, on the other hand, were more likely to be recorded as being in work beyond the state pensionable age than before the war, due to generally greater demand for their labour and also to more accurate official recording of their paid employment. From 1947 to 1956 about 60 per cent of men and just under 50 per cent of women who were in paid employment at the minimum retirement age remained in work, though for gradually diminishing periods of time. Manual were more likely than non-manual workers to stay on. In 1956 the numbers delaying retirement began to fall and a still faster sustained fall began in 1958–9. By 1962–3 about 45 per cent of men were staying beyond age 65, most for only one or two years.[26] The trend accelerated thereafter.

WHY RETIREMENT?

The shift to almost universal retirement at ages at which most people were still physically fit, indeed probably fitter than people of comparable ages at any previous time, marked a major cultural change. Especially for manual workers, the majority of the male population at this time, neither the level of pension nor government policy can wholly explain it.

---

[22] See pp. 482–3.

[23] B. E. Shenfield, *Social Policies for Old Age* (London, 1957), 11.

[24] *Report of the Committee on the Economic and Financial Problems of the Provision for Old Age*, Cmd. 9333 (1954), 50.

[25] *Ministry of Labour Gazette* (June 1963), 227.   [26] *Ministry of Labour Gazette* (June 1963), 227.

One reason was the disappearance of the work older workers had traditionally performed, as storekeepers, tea-ladies, sweepers-up, messengers,
watchmen, cloakroom attendants, and much else.[27] Rationalization, mechan-
ization, and other changes had gradually eliminated most of them. Modern
cleaning equipment needed strong, fit operatives; security increasingly
became too hazardous to be left to elderly watchmen; dispensing machines
replaced tea-ladies; modern communications systems replaced messengers.
Improved pensions may also have reduced the incentive to take such ill-paid
posts. How many of these posts disappeared entirely or changed their character can only be guessed but their numbers clearly dwindled, though they
did not wholly or suddenly vanish, especially from smaller businesses.[28]

The reasons why workers did or did not retire were equally puzzling to
contemporaries and they were increasingly investigated, first by the Ministry
of Pensions and National Insurance (MPNI), later by social researchers.
Interviews with workers before and after retirement indicated widespread hostility to compulsory retirement at a fixed age. Many workers believed that
they experienced compulsion from management to retire, directly or indirectly.
In most surveys around 50 per cent of (male) workers claimed that they wished
to retire from their normal full-time occupation at around the age of 65 due
to feelings of ill health or stress. The remainder did not. Even among those
who wished to retire, a high proportion expressed a preference to continue
working part-time in their accustomed occupation or a lighter one, because
they enjoyed work, needed the income, or simply could not imagine life without work.[29] A high proportion of men, however, already changed to less demanding work in the decade before retirement. A Ministry of Labour survey in
1950 indicated that almost one-fifth of men reaching the age of 65 had changed
jobs within the preceding five years. A few years later Le Gros Clark estimated that about 20 per cent transferred mainly to less skilled, less well-paid
jobs which did not make full use of their potential.[30]

The MPNI surveyed approximately 26,000 men and women who first drew
their pensions, or became eligible to do so, during the four weeks ending
11 October 1953. Sixty per cent chose to stay at work; half of them claimed
that this was for financial reasons. Of the 40 per cent who did retire, 25 per
cent were said to be suffering from long-term illness and a further 25 per cent
complained of some degree of ill health or strain on the job. Twenty-eight

---

[27] See pp. 89–95.　　[28] F. Le Gros Clark, *New Jobs for Old Workers* (London, 1955).

[29] Ministry of Pensions and National Insurance, *National Insurance Retirement Pensions: Reasons Given for Retiring or Continuing at Work* (1954). Acton Society Trust, *Retirement: A Study of Current Attitudes and Practices* (London, 1960). F. Le Gros Clark, *Pensioners in Search of a Job* (London, 1966). A. Heron and S. Chown, *Ageing and the Semi-Skilled: A Survey of Manufacturing Industry on Merseyside* (London, 1961). M. Pearson, 'The Transition from Work to Retirement', *Occupational Psychology*, 31 (1957), 80–8, 139–49.

[30] F. Le Gros Clark, *Age and the Working Lives of Men* (London, 1959), 37. See also A. Heron and C. Cunningham, 'The Experience of Younger and Older Men in a Work Reorganization', *Occupational Psychology*, 36 (1962), 10–16.

per cent had been compulsorily retired.[31] Smaller surveys supported this picture. A study of three hundred and twenty-three men aged 65 or over who attended the Rutherglen Health Centre for Older People in Rutherglen, in Scotland,[32] 75 per cent of whom were retired, found that roughly one-third had been compulsorily retired, one-third had retired due to ill health, and the remaining one-third voluntarily. A third of the latter, however, said that they had made the choice due to the severe physical or mental strain of their last job.[33]

The surveys indicate that poor health and the strain of work had a significant influence on the decision to retire, when that was within the control of the individual. But the responses to the surveys are far from easy to interpret. It is at least theoretically possible that ill health was the justification people thought publicly acceptable for a move which had complex motivations. Health cannot be the whole explanation since more people were retiring earlier than ever before, yet there is no evidence that the health of older people was deteriorating. Some may have experienced changes in the workplace which caused stress and related illnesses. Also workers may have been no longer willing, or no longer under acute financial pressure, to carry on working in conditions of severe ill health which would previously have been taken for granted. The precise relationship between ill health and retirement in this period remains uncertain.

Many workers felt that they had no choice and no control over their lives. A study of older male workers in Hull concluded that:

For the most part these men will tramp into old age as they have tramped through life, with their eyes on the ground immediately ahead of them.[34]

Altogether, research suggested that the Ministry of Labour was correct to believe that there was a reservoir of willing elderly workers that was underemployed and that much retirement was involuntary, but that the reservoir was not necessarily very large, nor were older workers likely to stay more than a few additional years in the workforce. The main reason given for *not* retiring was financial: the loss of income which would result.

Some employers responded to government persuasion to employ older workers. Most did not. The issue was of more immediate concern to older workers than to managers. Most of the latter were more concerned to compete for younger workers when labour was scarce and saw little long-run advantage in encouraging delayed retirement. Research showed that although

---

[31] MPNI, *Reasons Given for Retiring*.   [32] See pp. 445–7.
[33] W. F. Anderson and N. Cowan, 'Work and Retirement: The Influence on the Health of Older People', *Lancet*, 2 (1956), 1344. I. M. Richardson, 'Age and Work: A Study of 489 Men in Heavy Industry', *British Journal of Industrial Medicine*, 10 (1956), 269–84. F. Le Gros Clark, *Ageing on the Factory Floor* (London, 1957).
[34] A. B. Rose, *The Older Unemployed Man in Hull* (University College, Hull, Department of Social Studies, 1953), 16.

employers were prepared to agree in principle that fit older workers should remain in employment and acknowledged their reliability and the value of experience, when they had the choice most preferred to employ younger people and held rigidly stereotyped views of the low efficiency of older workers.[35]

A reason for the rise in retirement rates at the end of the 1950s appears to have been the response of employers to the temporary recession of 1958–9. The *Economist* criticized their short-sightedness in laying off older rather than younger workers. It pointed out that it was well established from British and American experience that older unemployed people had great difficulty in re-entering the labour force. Once laid off they were likely to be lost to the labour market, whereas younger workers would certainly return to work; such practices would exacerbate the labour shortage in the long run.[36] They were due not only to employer preferences, but to the preference of unions for negotiating redundancy with favourable pensions for older workers over redundancy on any terms for younger workers.

The accelerated trend to retirement at the state pensionable age at the end of the 1950s may also owe something to the fact that white-collar workers, who entered the National Insurance system for the first time in 1946, qualified for pensions in 1958. However, given the low level of state pensions and the fact that earlier retirement ages had been established for longer in the white-collar sector, the effect may have been small.

AGE AND THE WORKING LIVES OF MEN

Another possible contributory influence, similarly difficult to quantify, is the effect of changing technology and management practices. That such changes were inducing earlier retirement is suggested by research at the time into the work experience and capabilities of older people. Much of this was a direct outcome of the concern about the economic implications of an ageing workforce, and was funded by the Nuffield Foundation, the Ministry of Labour, or the Medical Research Council.

The Nuffield Foundation, following its report of 1947,[37] funded units for the study of ageing in industry in Cambridge, Bristol, and Liverpool and sponsored in London a series of industry-by-industry studies under the direction of the gifted, blind, anthropologist F. Le Gros Clark, which were carried out throughout the 1950s. It also established in 1947 the National Corporation for the Care of Old People (NCCOP). This was initially concerned mainly

---

[35] Acton Society Trust, *Retirement*, 53, 220–1, 366–7.

[36] Quoted in Le Gros Clark, *Age and the Working Lives of Men*, 7.

[37] Nuffield Foundation, *Old People: Report of a Survey Committee on the Problems of Ageing and the Care of Old People* (Oxford, 1947). See pp. 344–5, 350–1.

with housing and services for the aged poor but it turned increasingly to employment matters and to studying the attitudes of the community to retirement. It was a complementary body to the National Old People's Welfare Council (NOPWC), founded in 1940, chaired initially by the feminist Eleanor Rathbone and funded by the Nuffield Foundation from 1947.[38] Concern about the effects of the ageing of society encouraged the formation of such groups.

Clark studied mainly men at work in a variety of manual occupations including work in iron foundries and coalmines, electrical and several other branches of engineering, printing, motor vehicle manufacture, building, furniture-making, plate glass manufacture, paper-making, soap-making, bus driving and conducting, and the mass production of a variety of consumer goods.[39] He established, primarily, that workers stayed on longest in occupations in which they were self-employed or had a high degree of independent control of their working lives (e.g. shopkeepers); in those combining a high level of specialist skill with control over the timing and organization of work (e.g. hand composition in printing and some specialized sectors of engineering); and, more surprisingly, in heavy sectors of older industries such as shipbuilding, mining, and navvying. They were least likely to stay on in modern, tightly managed, fast-paced production-line industries such as motor manufacture. This also seems surprising since it might be thought that modern industry, being less physically demanding, would be easier on older workers. These differences were not due to the variable age of the industries themselves; that is, that newly established industries were likely to have younger workforces. Most of the studies allowed for this. Rather, certain types of work or work conditions were especially unsuited to older workers. From some time in their forties and certainly in their fifties many male and female workers complained of excessive strain if they were engaged in fast, continuous-paced work, where they had to keep up with the pace of the machine or with that of fitter workers. Modern management practices and forms of incentive payment could also impose strain. 'Group bonus' systems, which rewarded collective effort, led older men in Slough to leave the factory because they 'felt the pressure of disapproval from their younger mates' when they could not keep up the pace and held back the group.

The chief problems for older workers arose from the combination of pace and relentless continuity, especially since the pace of work on a production

----

[38] Nuffield Foundation, *Annual Report* (1949). Nesta Roberts, *Our Future Selves* (A history of the NOPWC) (London, 1970).

[39] The resulting publications (place of publication London, in all cases) included: by F. Le Gros Clark: *The Working Fitness of Older Men* (1954); *New Jobs for Old Workers* (1955); *Ageing Men in the Labour Force* (1955); *The Employment Problems of Elderly Men* (1956); *Ageing on the Factory Floor* (1957); *Bus Workers* (1957); *The Importance for Ageing Men of Some Continuity in Work Habits* (1958); *Age and the Working Lives of Men* (1959); *Growing Old in a Mechanized World* (1961); *Women, Work and Age* (1962); *The Years Still Unexplored* (1964); *Work, Age and Leisure* (1966); *Pensioners in Search of a Job* (1968); (with Agnes Dunn): *Later Working Life in the Building Industry* (1954); *Ageing in Industry* (1955); *New Jobs for Old Workers* (1955); (with Alastair Heron): *Workers Nearing Retirement* (1963).

line was fixed in relation to the measured capabilities of younger workers. Workers could cope for longest when they were able to work and rest at a rhythm which they could control.[40] There was a distinct tendency for men in their fifties to abandon fast-paced work for heavy labouring jobs. Contrary to expectations, they could cope physically with the heavy labour because it generally allowed time for rest pauses when they felt the need, they were not working at an externally imposed pace.

The work of industrial psychologists supported the findings of sociologists and anthropologists. Investigations both in the laboratory and on the shop floor concluded that most workers could continue at most jobs at a high level of efficiency until at least their later sixties, provided that they retained some control over the pace of work. This was partly because the capabilities of most workers were understretched for most of their working lives. Hence in later life they had reserves to call upon which could be combined with the advantages of skill and experience.[41] Several of the studies were critical of the waste of labour power that resulted from the mismatch between the pace of work and the capabilities of a large and growing sector of the workforce. Employers would not adjust the pace of work to the needs of older workers because in general the expanding sectors of newer industries, where modern techniques of management and production were most prevalent, were able to attract younger labour by paying higher wages. Older men moved on to jobs which did not use their capabilities to the full, though some moved to similar jobs with smaller firms. Indeed the techniques which most disadvantaged them were spreading fast through industry with the encouragement of the Ministry of Labour, which assumed that this was the inevitable and desirable way forward for the British economy.[42] This was discouraging for those convinced that employment of older workers would be a permanent feature of the British labour market. Once again the policies of different sections of government were in conflict.

The research group funded by the Nuffield Foundation in Cambridge, led by Welford, set out to identify the types of work best suited to older workers, and methods of retraining those whose skills became outmoded. Their main conclusions were that, whilst there were major changes in mental and physical

---

[40] Richardson, 'Age and Work'.

[41] R. M. Belbin, 'Difficulties of Older People in Industry', *Occupational Psychology*, 27 (1953), 177–90; 'Older People and Heavy Work', *British Journal of Industrial Medicine*, 12 (1955), 309–19. R. A. Brown, 'Age and "Paced" Work', *Occupational Psychology*, 31 (1957), 11–20; H. M. Clay, 'A Study of Performance in Relation to Age at Two Printing Works', *Journal of Gerontology*, 11 (1956), 417–24; A. Heron and S. Chown, 'Semi-Skilled and Over 40', *Occupational Psychology*, 34 (1960); H. F. King, 'An Attempt to Use Production Data in the Study of Age and Performance', *Journal of Gerontology*, 11 (1956), 410–16; A. W. M. Shooter *et al.*, 'Some Field Data on the Training of Older People', *Occupational Psychology*, 30 (1956), 204–15; D. Speakman, 'Bibliography of Research on Changes in Working Capacity with Age', Ministry of Labour and National Service (London, 1957); A. T. Welford, *Skill and Age* (Oxford, 1951).

[42] Le Gros Clark, *Mechanized World*.

capacity with age, most of these could be overcome, to varying degrees, by altering the work environment. It was found, for example, that the slowing of performance in later years did not generally arise from loss of physical speed, but from slowness in perception and in decision-making. This might be off-set by increased accuracy. Simplification of tasks could reduce the problem of the increasing difficulty in dealing with complexity which occurred with age.[43] They discovered that learning ability need not diminish with age to the degree normally assumed, if memory in particular was kept in practice.[44] Welford and Le Gros Clark emphasized the importance of training workers from early in life for flexible adaptation to changing skill requirements.

The Ministry disseminated many of these findings to employers with little evident effect.[45] Few admitted to having read anything published by the Ministry or any other source about the work capabilities of older people.[46] Only 10 per cent of Sheffield cutlery executives had read any publication on the sub-ject by the early 1960s, despite the fact that 18 per cent of employees in the industry were over 65 compared with a national average of 3.5.[47] By contrast in Hull in 1953 79 per cent of a sample of unemployed older men knew 'that the country was asking people to stay on at work after retirement age'.[48] Surveys of employers' reactions revealed the extent of negative attitudes to older work-ers. The forties were seen as the age of transition from young to old, though the greater reliability of older workers was generally acknowledged. A survey of just under one thousand firms in the 1950s[49] found that even among employ-ers of skilled workers, one-third were doubtful about the worth of employing those over 45; 6 per cent explicitly considered them 'too old'. A survey of Merseyside managers and employers in 1961 found that three-quarters indic-ated that there was no upper age limit for promotion, but that the average age of promotion to foreman was 40, with just over 25 per cent achieving it after 45, 10 per cent after 50. Among the reasons given were 'preference for younger men', 'lack of availability or adaptability', or 'a man is not worthy of promotion if he has not gained it before a specified age'.[50] The researchers concluded that:

Most people in industry regard the word 'older' as implying 'over fifty years of age' and many managers and supervisors admit that they have encountered problems with men 'who are in their forties and fifties'.[51]

---

[43] Welford, *Skill and Age*; and 'Extending the Employment of Older People', *British Medical Journal* (1953), 1193–7.

[44] A. T. Welford, 'Industrial Work for Older People: Some British Studies', *Gerontologist* (Mar. 1966), 4–9.

[45] H. M. Clay, *The Older Worker and His Job*, DSIR (London, 1960).

[46] Industrial Welfare Society, *The Employment of Elderly Workers* (London, 1951).

[47] C. Fleming, 'The Age Factor in the Sheffield Cutlery Industry', *Via Humana*, 6/4 (1963), 177–212. For similar finding from Liverpool see Heron and Chown, 'Semi-Skilled'.   [48] Rose, *Hull*, 14.

[49] Industrial Welfare Society, *Elderly Workers*.   [50] Heron and Chown, 'Semi-Skilled', 268–9.

[51] Ibid. 268.

WOMEN, WORK, AND AGE

Clark made the only known study of the working lives and retirement of older women. He pointed out that an important change in the labour market in post-war Britain was due to the dwindling number of unmarried women in the population and the increasing numbers of married women returning to work in their forties and fifties. He believed that the latter group had particular characteristics to which employers had been slow to adjust. Their choice of paid work was generally related to their domestic commitments. Hence they often preferred part-time work, or they changed jobs frequently and worked episodically 'as an occasional means to support the family income'.[52] They worked in a limited range of mainly low-paid, low-skilled jobs.[53]

Clark found that statistics of female retirement were difficult to compile and that the reasons which women gave for retirement were different from those of men. Older women returning to the labour force often had no fixed expectation of when they might retire:

The disposition of women is to resume work in middle life and to continue in it for an indefinite period. What the actual duration of that period shall be cannot be determined by any known principle.[54]

Women who worked episodically did not always make a conscious decision to 'retire'; rather the occasion to return to work disappeared. It was often claimed that women retired at earlier ages than men due to poorer health. Clark thought there was some substance in this, and it matched medical evidence of the poorer health of older women.[55] But he also suspected that the more complex commitments of women led them to give up paid work when they were less debilitated than men:

Women at such times have usually to weigh their total daily commitments against what they feel themselves capable of managing in the course of a day. They have to do this unsentimentally; and any awareness of a slight increase in malaise has to be soberly scrutinized. I am doubtful whether men would normally weigh up any domestic commitments they may have in the same detached and calculating manner.[56]

And women did not 'retire' from unpaid domestic work until very late ages.[57] Nevertheless women stayed on longer in some occupations than in others (Table 20.1).

Women gave up paid work at earlier ages in clerical work and in the modern light industries which operated the fast-process systems which caused difficulties for all older workers. Like men, they stayed to the latest ages in occupations where they could regulate the pace of work:

---

[52] Le Gros Clark, *Women*, 34–5, 84.   [53] Ibid. 107.   [54] Ibid. 106.
[55] See p. 441.   [56] Le Gros Clark, *Women*, 100.   [57] See pp. 283–6.

TABLE 20.1. *Employment of older women, 1951 (%)*

Occupational categories	45–54	55–59	60–64	65–69
Clerical and commercial employees, farm employees, workers in textiles, clothing, ceramics, and footwear; laundry workers, warehousewomen, etc.	38.8	32.5	26.9	22.8
Domestic kitchen and catering workers, caretakers, charwomen	26.8	34.9	38.5	42.0
Employers and managers; women working 'on their own account'	12.1	13.4	18.2	24.1
Totals occupied.	1,191,394	371,819	181,150	92,975

Source: F. Le Gros Clark, *Women, Work and Age*, 84.

a good number of elderly women probably retain their place at work simply by moderating their efforts; and this they can do only in very specialized conditions of employment.[58]

Clark optimistically believed that older married women would gradually force both employers and partners to adjust to their preferred work patterns:

It is not so unimaginable as it once was that men should share more or less equally with women in running the home and family . . . the most likely outcome of the present trends is that the mature woman will be bargaining with her man that he shall take his own share of childminding and in the affairs of the household. This would also amount in the end to a domestic revolution; and it could lead to one or two incidental gains . . . more significant for the man could be the greater readiness his growing or grown family would show for identifying him with their image of 'home' . . . the gain would be the most appreciable when the time came for him to retire from outside employment.[59]

THE 'SHOCK' OF RETIREMENT

Another set of studies emphasized the effect upon the individual (usually male) of enforced and sudden retirement. The belief that retirement led directly to ill health, even death, had been out of favour during the inter-war depression, but was resurrected after the war,[60] supported by the medical profession. Le Gros Clark noted the 'growing medical evidence we now have that satisfying occupations help to prolong the physical and mental health of elderly men'.[61] 'The literature is overwhelming', stated Anderson and Cowan, 'in its indica-

[58] Le Gros Clark, *Women*, 84.   [59] Ibid. 107.
[60] A. Emerson, 'The First Year of Retirement', *Occupational Psychology*, 34 (1959), 197–208.
[61] Le Gros Clark, *Factory Floor*, 167.

tions that retirement is detrimental to the health of older men.'[62] Shenfield revealed that:

In general the weight of medical opinion is that sudden demise of mental and bodily functions, previously regularly exercised, such as may happen through retirement is likely to cause atrophy and degeneration which are harmful to the health of older persons.[63]

There was, however, little evidence underpinning these assertions. Anderson and Cowan and Welford did discover better health and a higher degree of satisfaction among men over 65 who were in paid work than among the retired.[64] The high death-rate in the year following retirement was often quoted to prove the lethal effects of retirement.[65] However, as Shenfield pointed out: 'It is just as likely that mental and physical morbidity leads to prompt retirement as that retirement leads to mental and physical deterioration'.[66] Absence of clear evidence did not prevent the belief in the harmful effects of retirement being widely accepted; it was said to contribute to high rates of suicide,[67] sleep disorders,[68] acceleration of senility and physical disabilities.[69] Official publications reinforced such assumptions. A Ministry of Health report in 1954 purported to describe the fate of a 65-year-old retired clerk, as a warning to others:

After six weeks of this existence (retirement), life began to pall. He became unsettled, restless and irritable. He really had nothing to do and he longed to be back at work. He was repeatedly asked to take up some form of hobby, which he readily promised to do but his restlessness prevented him from seriously attempting it and a laissez-faire attitude resulted. He felt he was too old to attempt anything new. Eventually getting up in the morning became an effort, and in a short time all his interest in everything flagged. The peace of death came to him soon.[70]

Such descriptions can have encouraged no one to look forward to retirement.

Peter Townsend's study of old people in east London also in 1954 told a similarly dismal story in sociological rather than medical terms. He described retirement as one of 'the social problems of old age': 'the chief theme is that retirement is a tragic event for many men, which has great repercussions on most aspects of their lives, not least their individual happiness and their security in home and family'.[71] Of the sixty-four old men he interviewed, thirty-nine had retired at ages between 48 and 80, mostly involuntarily, often following

---

[62] W. F. Anderson and N. Cowan, 'A Consultative Health Centre for Older People: The Rutherglen Experiment', *Lancet*, 2 (1955), 239.

[63] Shenfield, *Social Policies*, 59.

[64] Anderson and Cowan, 'Rutherglen'. Welford, 'Industrial Work'.

[65] Shenfield, *Social Policies*, 83.   [66] Ibid.

[67] World Health Organization, *Mental Health Problems of Ageing and the Aged*, Technical Support Series (Geneva, 1959).   [68] Anderson and Cowan, 'Work and Retirement'.

[69] J. H. Sheldon, *The Social Medicine of Old Age* (Oxford, 1948).

[70] Ministry of Pensions and Natural Insurance, *Natural Insurance Retirement Pensions: Reasons Given for Retiring or Continuing at Work* (1954), 7.

[71] P. Townsend, *The Family Life of Old People* (London, 1957), 137.

ill health. Like other investigators he found the reasons for retirement complex and unclear. He ascribed their dread of retirement, and misery when it came, primarily to loss of status and independence: male identity was bound up with work, without work they felt useless. He perhaps stressed less than he might the fact that they also dreaded the fall in income, mostly by over a half, some by as much as two-thirds. This caused social as well as material loss. In the pub an old man could no longer afford to buy drinks for others as well as receive them; he felt dependent even in his leisure time. It is not obvious, and was certainly not proven, that in British culture a retired toolmaker or accountant or anything else is *ipso facto* accorded less status than an active worker; but an individual who is always the receiver, never the giver, who cannot reciprocate in a culture in which mutual exchange is an important feature of its social cohesion, is likely to experience diminished status.[72]

Women also suffered from loss of income on retirement from paid work, but even if they were unmarried or had no children, they experienced less change and loss of fulfilment when they gave up paid work. Their domestic tasks remained. They were more likely to feel, and to be, useful to and needed by others, very often to their depressed retired husbands. If they had children their relations with them were closer than their husbands'.[73] They could be givers as well as receivers to a wide range of family and friends.

Townsend's solution to the 'problem' of retired men, which was widely shared by socially concerned and generally better-off people, was to keep them at productive work, if necessary rather artificially in subsidized workshops, of the sort established in Finsbury, London, in 1951. This provided work for four hours each weekday for one hundred and ten people, three-quarters of them in fact female, at low-paid outwork for commercial firms:

assembling electric iron elements and special bottles, sorting and packing medical dressings and animal wool. They also make articles for direct sale—aprons, night-dresses, coat-hanger coverings. Each person is paid a flat-rate of 10s. per week.

Other London boroughs adopted similar schemes. Townsend suggested extending them to provide outwork (long condemned as the classic, exploited lowest depth of the London labour market) to old people in their own homes: for 'many bed-ridden and housebound old people have nimble minds and hands that would welcome an occupation. The development of outworking for them may be one of the rewarding innovations of the future.'[74] Such solutions may have been the only imaginable options for men who had known little in their adult lives but work and had never learned to enjoy family life, or for sociologists fixated on the notion that occupation rather than income conferred status and dignity; but a higher pension and medical and social

---

[72] Avner Offer, 'Between the Gift and the Market: The Economy of Regard', *Economic History Review*, 50/3 (Aug. 1997), 450–76.
[73] See Ch. 21.　　[74] Townsend, *Family Life*, 152.

work support might have been more merciful and, arguably, as effective at relieving stress. Social problems which had previously been defined in terms of poverty, in the 1950s and 1960s were increasingly, and sometimes more dubiously, defined in sociological and psychological terms.

One effect of all of this official and academic gloom was to increase old people's own fears of retirement.[75] This was further encouraged by a variety of agencies and by the press. The *Nursing Times*[76] and the *Nursing Mirror*[77] stressed the importance of work 'in preserving mental alertness and bodily health'. The radical Conservative journal *Crossbow* stated the dubious proposition that:

Boredom, loneliness and the feeling that one has become a useless burden upon others, these factors, *far more than poverty*, constitute the tragedy of old age. They can, and they frequently do, hasten the onset of senility and death [my emphasis].[78]

The Conservatives probably underestimated the depressive effects of severe poverty. From another political perspective, in 1964, the Socialist Medical Association declared:

Old age is imposed by society, if retirement is involuntary, bringing a sense of uselessness. Infirmity then develops more quickly and, in fact, forced retirement is a definite threat to health.

In 1953 the British National Conference on Social Work took up the theme and old people's welfare committees acted to find work for older people. In 1951 the Employment Fellowship, formerly the Winter Distress League,[79] formed the Finsbury Workshops in co-operation with Finsbury Borough Council.[80] Perhaps fifty similar workshops were established around Britain. NOPWC reported in 1963 that about nineteen employment agencies were being run by old people's welfare committees, to prevent older people 'being thrown on a human scrap heap where their physical and mental health suffered and some became prematurely incapable of leading independent lives'.[81] It also encouraged employers to open workshops to enable older workers to continue part-time. They reported that about five hundred people were employed in this way in 1961.[82]

Employers, once more, were not very responsive. They were more enthusiastic about the theme which emerged in the 1960s of preventing the 'tragedy' of the transition to retirement by preparing employees for it in advance. This was especially promoted by NOPWC from 1961, supported by both the Industrial Welfare Society and the Institute of Directors, which in 1962 established a Retirement Advisory Bureau. By 1965 at least twenty major national and international companies had established pre-retirement schemes and

---

[75] Emerson, 'First Year', 206. Le Gros Clark, *Workers Nearing Retirement*. B. Groombridge, *Education and Retirement* (London, 1960). Townsend, *Family Life*.   [76] *Nursing Times*, Aug. 1957.
[77] *Nursing Mirror*, Dec. 1957.   [78] *Crossbow* (1961), 25.
[79] The Employment Fellowship, *Workrooms for the Elderly* (London, 1958).   [80] Ibid. 1.
[81] National Old People's Welfare Committee, *Employment and Workshops for the Elderly* (London, 1963).
[82] Ibid.

seventeen pre-retirement associations were running courses for business firms and the general public throughout the country. These aimed to extend the range of interests of older people, mainly men, so that they could develop positive identities when retired 'as bowls club secretary or church sidesman or local snooker champion. Another is to have an interest like fishing or growing prize chrysanthemums which is more absorbing than is sometimes implied by the word "hobby".'[83] A spokesman for Unilever stated in 1960:

In the olden days retirement was considered to be synonymous with the first step through the cemetery gate; nowadays it means giving up the whole or part of one's life occupation, and replacing what is lost by other less absorbing interests. In other words, retirement should be the entry into a period of continued usefulness.[84]

Such schemes were generally directed at all employees, manual, white-collar, and managerial, although the proportion of each group attending and their responses are unclear.

An unexpected cultural change was in progress which especially changed the lives of working-class men, through which researchers and social reformers tried earnestly, awkwardly, and often uncomprehendingly to assist them. Manual workers were perceived as being 'shocked into idleness'[85] as more privileged men were not:

Even today the self-employed and members of the professions seldom stop in that abrupt fashion. The watchmaker, the cabinet-maker, pursue their absorbing craft until hand and eye tire. The higher civil servant may leave Whitehall at sixty, but it is usually to a busy five years acting as chairman of commissions and assisting investigations of one kind and another. The elderly lawyer decides he will come into the office on four days a week only; the older doctor leaves more of the running round to his juniors while he makes the best of his perfected skill in less exhausting ways. Businessmen, unless they are unfortunate enough to have sunk into the manic state of 'living for their work', turn to public affairs. These are various kinds of adjustment, not to traumatic change but to the organic developments of one's life.'[86]

Whereas working men were expected suddenly and traumatically to stop. In fact, however, we know little about the later lives of older professionals and business-people.

And, as always, class differences were not so simple. In the 1970s:

Former Midland carworkers and Jarrow shipbuilders seemed worn out and despairingly lost, cut off from former workmates. They wept on their last day at work. 'I felt terrible.' 'It seemed as though you were suddenly cut off from life.' They lay in bed in the morning 'puzzled about how to fill me time in'. Yet in a former Durham pit village, although all had either been made redundant or been forced out of work by

[83] Roberts, *Future Selves*, 99.

[84] L. Hubbard, 'The Preparation for Retirement Committee', *Society of Housing Managers Quarterly Journal*, 5 (1962), 5.

[85] Roberts, *Future Selves*, 94.   [86] Ibid.

ill-health, a group of miners was so sustained by the community network of neigh-bours and relatives that giving up work seemed a positive blessing. 'When a person's been underground for so many years its a new lease of life.' 'It's just a grand feeling.'[87]

Family and community as well as class influenced the experience of retire-ment. This was equally true of older people in south London a decade later.[88]

Psychological research, pointing out the inadequacy and imprecision of most previous studies, concluded that many of the problems of retirement came during the first 'transitional' year and were later resolved; and that most of the one hundred and twenty-five 65-year-old men studied by one researcher did not experience any problems of adjustment.[89] Rather, the minority of gen-uinely sad cases which came to the attention of professionals was represented as the norm. Townsend concluded that 'in time, they were more likely to re-concile themselves to the reality of being old age pensioners and were more likely to join old people's clubs'.[90] Indeed by the 1970s retirement ceased to be so widely regarded as a social problem, though not because older people embraced old people's clubs as their route to 'reality' in later life, many of them indeed rejected them as old-age ghettos.[91] And still many older men, though fewer older women, experienced retirement as empty and depressing though more found the process of adjustment easier to a situation for which they, unlike many of the retired of the two previous decades, had had time to prepare.[92] By the 1990s, by contrast, there was an almost eerie public silence about the effects of retirement which increasing numbers of people were ex-periencing at ever earlier ages.

For the first generation of manual workers to experience retirement en masse in the 1940s and 1950s, it was a sudden shock for which they were quite unpre-pared; for later generations it was an expected phase of life for which more of them were better prepared, though it was still harder for many male man-ual workers than for better-off men and for women.

In the 1960s the government gave up trying to stem the tide of retirement. Concern about old age went out of fashion in the youth decade of the 'swing-ing sixties', largely because the worst predictions had not been fulfilled. The birth-rate remained above pre-war levels, though another sustained fall began in the later 1960s. The post-war 'baby boomers' began to enter the labour market from the end of the 1950s. Compulsory National Service came to an end in 1960 releasing more younger workers. Female labour, especially older women, had come forward in quantities unforeseeable in the 1940s. Even more unforeseen, even unwanted by some, Commonwealth immigration reached significant levels in the 1950s, encouraged by employers short of labour.

[87] P. Thompson, C. Itzin, M. Abendstern, *I Don't Feel Old: Understanding the Experience of Later Life* (Oxford, 1990), 10, quoting C. Phillipson, 'The Experience of Retirement: A Sociological Study', Ph.D. thesis (University of Durham, 1978), 135, 272–3.
[88] Thompson, *Old*, 139–45.   [89] Emerson, 'First Year'.   [90] Ibid. 147.
[91] See pp. 462–3.   [92] Thompson, *Old*, 139–46.

Furthermore, a belief that 'automation' would soon render vast areas of labour redundant took hold.[93] This was premature, but it was reinforced by the content of Labour's successful election campaign of 1964 with its theme that the way forward for British industry was a high-tech revolution.[94] Under the new government the Ministry of Labour stopped publishing analyses of retirement and of the age structure of industry. Research into the work capacities of older people declined. They even lost their ambiguous status as the poorest social group, as child poverty was rediscovered as a major problem in the mid-1960s.[95] Alarm about the ageing of society died away, only to revive in the 1980s with all this history forgotten.

CONCLUSION

Retirement from paid work at or very close to the state pensionable age became a cultural norm for working-class men in Britain in the twenty-five years following 1945; women and men of other social classes did not experience such sudden change. Much less clear are the reasons. Leslie Hannah has described retirement as 'a luxury good' and argues that the main reason for its spread has been 'the increased capacity to finance retirement and the reduced dependence of the old on income from employment'.[96] For the decades immediately following the Second World War this interpretation is appealing. As we have seen, through the centuries preceding industrialization retirement was an option only available to those who could afford to live without income from paid work. From the later nineteenth century to the 1920s, the reduction in the numbers of older men who could find work was driven primarily by the fall in agricultural employment; then in the Depression of the inter-war years by the effects of unemployment for manual workers combined with the spread of occupational pensions for the smaller numbers of male white-collar workers. After 1945 the more rapid spread of retirement through a wider range of sectors of the economy coincided with the improvement in the level of state pensions, ungenerous though they remained, together with increased access to occupational pensions for, mainly, skilled workers, and a possibly increased potential for family support in a period of full employment and improved living standards for working people. In such a situation it is reasonable to suppose that many workers did choose retirement, even at relatively low pension levels, to struggling on in work, or felt that a period of leisure was preferable even to work that was not such a struggle.

---

[93] e.g. Leon Bagrit, *The Age of Automation: The BBC Reith Lectures* (London, 1965).

[94] D. Butler and A. King, *The British General Election of 1964* (London, 1965), 60 ff.

[95] B. Abel-Smith and P. Townsend, *The Poor and the Poorest* (London, 1965).

[96] Hannah, *Inventing Retirement*, 124. For a similar analysis see Carole Haber and Brian Gratton, *Old Age and the Search for Security: An American Social History* (Bloomington, Ind., 1994).

Yet, much direct evidence from retired men in the 1940s and 1950s suggests that they retired reluctantly and/or unhappily. Some may not have expected unhappiness and emptiness to follow retirement. Other clearly retired unwillingly. There is evidence for the post-war period that technological change and change in management techniques, such as, on the one hand, the growth of fast-paced, production-line manufacture, on the other, management incentives to produce by traditional methods but at a faster pace, disadvantaged older workers. Such changes were evident in the 1930s, but on a smaller scale; our knowledge of their impact in the post-war decades is all the greater due to the expansion of the social research and the interest of researchers in such matters. Post-war research also showed that adjustments to work and management procedures could increase the productivity of older workers. Also many of the light or part-time jobs to which older men had gradually moved were eroded faster in the post-war years than before as a result of a combination of technological and social change and management decisions. Many male workers expressed a preference for a gradual transition from the habitual employment of their adult years, via part-time work, to retirement, but the availability of this option dwindled. Over time, male workers seem to have found it easier to accept the transition from full-time work to full-time retirement. For the first generation, in the late 1940s and 1950s, it was a new, unexpected, unplanned-for experience; also it was often retirement into poverty. It is difficult, in view of the biases of much research of the time, to distinguish between the psychological and material deprivation felt by retired men. For the retired people of the 1960s and 1970s it was an expectation for which they could plan, and more of them would have accumulated sufficient resources with which to make it a comfortable experience.

Retirement, then, spread due to shifting combinations of individual choice with the effects of change in technology and in management practices. Its effects varied among individuals, among occupations, and over time. An explanation which does not fit the evidence privileges demand for the labour of older workers decisively over other explanations, the 'political economy' argument that the relentless onward march of technological change progressively de-skilled and marginalized older workers, pushing them out of the labour force, to languish, at best, as a 'reserve army of labour', to be summoned at times of acute labour shortage.[97] Retirement spread fastest during the first period of full employment, indeed of labour shortage, in modern Britain, between 1945 and the 1960s, when demand to mobilize rather than to confine to barracks the 'reserve army' should have been at its peak, had it ever existed. Governments in the 1940s and 1950s tried to encourage the employment of older workers in the cause of economic recovery and growth, and to disseminate

[97] J. Macnicol, *Politics of Retirement*, 9–12. C. Phillipson, *Capitalism and the Construction of Old Age* (London, 1982).

to employers the growing evidence of the efficiency of older workers. Many employers were reluctant to accept the evidence or the pressure. They were propelled by images of older workers and their capacities so negative that it is difficult to believe that they perceived them as suitable recruits even to a reserve army. A combination of demand and supply-side explanations of the post-war spread of retirement is more satisfactory than wholesale reliance upon a single explanation.

The spread of retirement has been described as one of several changes in the twentieth century which have increasingly defined old people as a distinct social group defined by marginalization and dependency. This dependency is said to have been 'structured' very largely by socially imposed retirement and pension schemes.[98] This is greatly to romanticize the social inclusion, dignity and status associated with the low-paid and often demeaning work previously carried on by people past what became in the twentieth century the recognized age of retirement. In many cases their dignity must have been enhanced by the opportunity to abandon servile and exhausting labour even for a low pension. Receipt of a state pension and participation in a ritual—retirement—once accessible only to the better-off may indeed have increased their sense of inclusion in civil society.[99] But for many older people, especially old men, it was the form rather than the fact of dependency and marginalization that changed in the twentieth century; they exchanged marginalized labour for the social exclusion signified by their inability to buy a round in a pub.

The 'structured dependency' approach also generalizes excessively about what 'old people' signifies in different periods. The spread of retirement from paid work from the later 1940s affected mainly male manual workers and had a much lesser impact upon working-class women or men or women of other classes. For many of the first generation of working-class males to experience mass retirement the shock was painful, for many of these in later generations it was 'viewed as a new phase of life, a time for older people to pursue what they want to do, and a time of freedom and independence'.[100] In the later decades of the twentieth century the increasing numbers of people retiring in their fifties meant that retirement became a less certain signifier of old age.

[98] Macnicol, *Politics of Retirement*, Phillipson, *Capitalism*, and, among others P. Townsend, 'The Structured Dependency of the Elderly: A Creation of Social Policy in the Twentieth Century', *Ageing and Society*, 1 (1981), 5–28. For critiques see: Richard Smith, 'The Structured Dependence of the Elderly as a Recent Development: Some Sceptical Historical Thoughts', *Ageing and Society*, 4 (1984), 409–28. Paul Johnson, 'The Structured Dependency of the Elderly: A Critical Note', Jefferys, *Growing Old*, 62–72.

[99] M. Kohli, 'Retirement and the Moral Economy: An Historical Interpretation of the German Case', *Journal of Aging Studies*, 1/2 (1987), 125–44, argues that some such process occurred in Germany.

[100] C. Phillipson, M. Bernard, J. Phillips, and J. Ogg, 'The Family and Community Life of Older People: Networks and Social Support in Three Urban Areas', ESRC Population and Household Change Programme, *Research Results*, 9 (1998); and 'The Family and Community Life of Older People: Household Composition and Social Networks in Three Urban Areas', *Ageing and Society*, 18/3 (1998), 259–90.

21

The Family Lives of Old People

A persistent theme in Western culture over many centuries, as we have seen, has been the conviction that younger people in each generation, more than in 'the past', neglect their older relatives, even their parents, both emotionally and materially. This belief has survived tenaciously, despite equally persistent assertions to the contrary. Before the twentieth century evidence either way is scanty and anecdotal. The uneven survival of historical sources makes it easier over long time periods to study the structure of households, who lives with whom, than to understand relationships within families, who may, or may not, share a household.[1] Only after the Second World War were there systematic studies of the relationships between old people and their families which clarify the role of intergenerational family relationships within English culture, in the twentieth century. This was partly an outcome of the expansion and somewhat increased rigour of social research at this time. Awareness that close relationships existed between the generations, even when they did not share a household, that they were important in a variety of ways both for the older and the younger people, initially emerged unexpectedly from surveys with other concerns. The surprise expressed by researchers indicates how widespread was the belief that old people were often and increasingly isolated and helpless. The conviction that this was so was well established in medical and social work discourse, not surprisingly since health and social workers were more likely to encounter older people in difficulties than those who were not. A different picture began to emerge when researchers looked at 'normal' old people in their homes and communities rather than focusing on those in contact with professionals. These researches provide a vivid picture of the lives of many older people, from varied social backgrounds, in the second half of the twentieth century.

The increasing marginalization of older people had also become a taken-for-granted and powerful assumption of mid-twentieth-century sociological theory, promoted in particular by Talcott Parsons's influential assertion that the increased geographical mobility of younger people in modern society left old people isolated.[2] This was not derived from empirical findings and, when investigated, turned out not to be so, even in the USA, where the belief was born.[3] Of more lasting influence, and empirically equally dubious, is the assumption of economic theory that most voluntaristic transfers, including those

[1] See Chs. 7, 15.   [2] Talcott Parsons, *The Social System* (New York, 1950).   [3] See p. 433.

between generations, are abandoned in 'the great transformation' from pre-commercial to modern economies, being irrational, inefficient behaviour for naturally profit-maximizing, self-interested humankind, which is unconcerned about the welfare of others.[4]

OLD AGE IN WOLVERHAMPTON

The first widely noticed British survey to stumble upon the importance of old people's family networks and the variety of exchanges within them was not primarily sociological but medical, conducted by J. H. Sheldon in 1945–7 for the Nuffield Foundation. This was one of the cluster of investigations into aspects of ageing established by the Foundation after the Second World War.[5] Sheldon, Director of Medicine at the Royal Hospital, Wolverhampton, investigated the health of a representative sample of old people (583 in all: 186 men and 397 women) living in their own homes in Wolverhampton.[6] It was a pioneering attempt to assess the health of 'normal' old people in order to expand the currently limited understanding of 'normal' ageing. Sheldon soon discovered the 'surprising fact' that:

contact with old people in their homes immediately brings to light the fact that the family is of fundamental importance. This is best seen by the extent to which old people who are ostensibly living alone . . . are in actual fact by no means living alone, but are in close and regular contact with their children.[7]

In over 20 per cent of the sample:

the old people had relatives living so close that the limitations imposed by architecture were resolved by family affection—in times of ease each household more or less going its own way, in times of stress functioning together as one unit.[8]

Contact between generations took a variety of forms. Sheldon described, among others:

A man aged 72—a widower—lives by himself. A married daughter lives some fifty yards away with an entrance through the garden. Subject does his own housework, but the daughter does his shopping and brings him a hot meal every day, while he goes to the daughter on Sundays. Subject is very lonely, but prefers this arrangement. It preserves his independence and prevents him having to spend the whole day in a house full of small children.

A widow aged 70 lives by herself. She habitually spends the day with a married daughter living in the same street and helps to look after the grandchildren, which she greatly

---

[4] A. Offer, 'Between the Gift and the Market: The Economy of Regard', *Economic History Review*, 50/3 (Aug. 1997), 450–76.

[5] See pp. 344–5.   [6] See pp. 440–3.

[7] J. H. Sheldon, *The Social Medicine of Old Age* (Oxford, 1948), 140.   [8] Ibid. 152.

enjoys and at which she is very useful. She only uses her own home for bed and break-fast. In case of illness, of either the subject or the daughter, each would look after the other.

Fifty-three per cent of widowers and 51 per cent of widows in the sample lived alone but with children close by. Sheldon judged that for 40 per cent of the sample their 'happiness and domestic efficiency was dependent on the access-ibility of their children or other relatives . . . each family is independent in health and co-operative in illness'. 'It is clear that the decision of a widowed subject to live alone is dependent, in half the cases, on the fact that relatives—usually children—are living close at hand.'[9]

Living 'near' was defined by Sheldon as 'a distance within which a hot meal could be carried from one house to another without needing re-heating, 'or not more than five minutes walking distance'. He found that many meals were carried to and from the houses of older people, or daughters regularly cooked at and/or cleaned the parental home.[10] Thirty per cent of the sample had relatives living 'near' on this definition. Many more had children living beyond this narrow range with whom they were in constant contact. For example:

A woman aged 64 is very lonely, living by herself after the recent death of her hus-band. She has 4 sons who come regularly to see her and a granddaughter aged 16 comes regularly to sleep. Subject wishes to continue living by herself and says the granddaughter's company makes all the difference.[11]

In nine cases married daughters 'had to make regular journeys of consider-able extent in order to assist their parents to run their houses'. All of these had tried to move closer but had been unsuccessful due to the shortage of housing following the war. Sheldon concluded that 'the whole question of the part played in the economy of old people's households by their children liv-ing in other houses is one of great importance and merits a full-dress study', and that health and welfare policy should in future take it into account.[12]

A number of older people had no close relatives, living near or far. Sheldon found that:

Where there are no family ties, these tend to be replaced by friendships formed earl-ier in life—as when two women of the same occupation such as nursing or teaching set up home together when they retire.

And that in the mid-twentieth as in earlier centuries old people held on to their independence for as long as they were able:

The majority of old people are responsible for their own domestic care and they con-sistently make every effort to maintain this state of affairs, so that the percentage of women doing their own housework unaided remains at a steady figure up to the period 75–9 years of age . . . more old people are looking after themselves than are dependent

---

[9] Ibid. 154.   [10] Ibid. 150.   [11] Ibid. 156.   [12] Ibid. 156.

on others (but) those in the older groups inevitably become increasingly dependent on the younger generation, especially the daughter.

Sheldon was convinced that: 'There is little doubt that up to the age of 75 at least, women give the community more than they take in the matter of domestic responsibility'.[13] When unmarried children lived with parents, forms of reciprocity varied: 'another common mode of existence is that of the daughter in employment who is looked after by her parents during the week, but does the housework over the weekend'.[14] The stress on reciprocity and the contribution of old people to the care of others, in place of the stereotype of the passive dependency of the aged, was to become another major theme of post-war research.

Sheldon estimated that about 7 per cent of old people were struggling to maintain independence when they were physically incapable of it. But his main conclusion was that it was misleading to treat households as discrete units:

It should again be emphasized that to regard old people in their homes as a series of individual experiences is to miss the point of their mode of life in the community. The family is clearly the unit in the majority of instances.[15]

Only a few old people 'withdraw into a solitary existence'.[16] And

while a considerable number of old people may ostensibly be living alone and would be so classified in the census, their children may be living sufficiently close for the two families to function as one where necessary, so that the phrase 'living alone' is not a true description of the state of affairs.

The old people in Sheldon's sample lived in a variety of arrangements. Widowhood might prompt a move to live with married children, usually a daughter, though more commonly and at earlier ages for widowers than for widows. Widows had a greater variety of opportunities for independent living, such as taking in boarders or sharing a household with another woman. Fourteen of them kept shops, six single-handed. These women 'were all of vigorous mentality—one women of 80 ran a small mixed shop entirely alone, in addition to looking after herself and said it was the contact with people in the shop that kept her alive'.[17]

Sheldon was eager to convey the positive picture of normal old age which emerged so surprisingly to him from the survey, in contrast with the image of old age he had acquired in his twenty years' experience in medical practice. In consequence he may have underestimated the tensions in family relationships. Nevertheless he usefully challenged firmly established stereotypes and pointed to a world of intergenerational reciprocity which was real, whatever its—surely immensely varied—emotional content. He commented that:

---

[13] Sheldon, *Social Medicine*, 141.   [14] Ibid. 159.   [15] Ibid. 142.
[16] Ibid. 148.   [17] Ibid. 150.

Old age undoubtedly places great strains on the younger generation, but that is only part of the picture, and it is well to remember the debt owed by the community to the domestic work done by the older woman.[18]

Eight of the sample (1.67 per cent) were cared for by younger relatives, usually daughters, who had given up paid work to look after them. This was often possible only because other siblings worked to provide the family income, but 'she then undergoes a particular hardship by becoming dependent on others for pocket money'.[19] Alternatively, when the household could not afford to lose her income:

a daughter may by having to remain at work, become almost a slave—at work all day, and doing the housework or nursing that may be required in the early mornings and evenings. No less than 43 per cent of the younger generation concerned in the care of old people were in employment and there were instances of severe hardship in this group.[20]

Married daughters might carry no less strain:

A woman aged 62 who was a member of the sample, is a tower of physical strength, keeping home for her husband and daughter and does everything including the washing and mangling. She also has the care of an aged mother (aged 89) who is bedridden after a fall downstairs. She has looked after her for 24 years and for the last eight years has had no break. She says she is dying to have a fortnight by the sea with her husband, but the domestic ties make this totally impossible.[21]

On the other hand, ten old women were bringing up grandchildren, often also in considerable hardship.

Sheldon was surprised by the number of men—35 per cent of the sample —who 'assisted' with housework:

the usual feature is for the man to make the morning cup of tea, light the fire and do the washing up. He frequently makes himself responsible for the heavy work in the house—such as scrubbing and cleaning, getting the coal in etc. The shopping is usually done by the woman, if her health is sufficiently good, but several men were encountered who made a speciality of shopping, doing it for several households. The cooking is done by the women in most cases but not all—some of the men being particularly skilled and enjoying it . . . Almost every division of labour was found, but except where the woman was physically incapable the man was virtually never trusted to make the beds.[22]

FAMILY AND KINSHIP IN EAST LONDON

Peter Willmott and Michael Young's sociological study of Bethnal Green in east London in the mid-1950s made a wider impact than Sheldon's and played

[18] Ibid. 157.   [19] Ibid. 160.   [20] Ibid.   [21] Ibid. 25.   [22] Ibid. 158.

an important role in establishing, at least in academic circles, awareness that active family networks were still important in modern societies; though like Sheldon they made this discovery by accident, in a study primarily focused on housing policy. This revealed that a high proportion of adults lived close to their parents, though daughters lived closer than sons. A significant proportion lived with parents for a time after marriage, more often daughters and more often youngest than older daughters. As in Wolverhampton, most older people asserted that living independently of close relatives, but close at hand, was the ideal relationship.

Willmott and Young described, often in tones of surprise, a world of closely interconnected family reciprocity. For example, Mr and Mrs Banton took over Mrs Banton's grandfather's private tenancy when he went into a home, when her mother 'had a word' with the rent collector. The old man had been looked after by a relative living near by until her house was 'cleared' by the council and she was moved to an estate outside London. Mrs Banton's mother lived near by and Mrs Banton went round several times a day to see her and to fetch her shopping. Her mother was less active than when she was younger but could still look after the grandchildren when the need arose.[23] Mothers could find their children homes in the neighbourhood through their knowledge of local movements, but with increasing Council control of the property market such arrangements were becoming more difficult.

Willmott and Young commented:

These accounts put a new light on the ordinary idea of the household. People live together—they are considered to be in the same household. But what if they spend a good part of the day and eat (or at least drink tea) regularly in someone else's household? The households are then to some extent merged . . . the daily lives of many women are not confined to the places where they sleep; they are spread over two or more households, in each of which they regularly spend part of their time.[24]

They described a community in which links between the generations were strong, though two adult generations rarely lived in the same household, except sometimes for short periods following marriage or at the very end of the older people's lives. Families centred upon 'Mum'. There was constant exchange of visits and services which official social services sometimes complemented but did not replace. Mothers helped out when children were born, cared for children while their mothers worked. There were often close relationships between grandchildren and grandparents.

In the 1950s many people moved from overcrowding and poor housing in inner-city Bethnal Green to suburban council housing estates. The central purpose of Willmott and Young's study was to investigate whether such moves destabilized family relationships. They surveyed Bethnal Greeners' moves

[23] M. Young and P. Willmott, *Family and Kinship in East London* (Harmondsworth, 1957), 37–8.
[24] Ibid. 47.

to 'Greenleigh', less than twenty miles away on a direct underground line. Some of the migrants brought their relatives to join them. One man explained how his mother had moved after them. His 13-year-old daughter went to see her twice a week; 'she clears the place and runs errands. All the children go round there and help. And I help with the gardening and I decorated her house. My father came down too and my brother Tom has moved to Greenleigh as well.'[25] Immediately following their move, most migrants saw less of relatives and less help was exchanged, for example in sickness and child-birth, due to distance and cost of travel. But over time more relatives moved to be together and increasingly telephones were installed in order to keep in touch. Families adjusted to changed circumstances.

Willmott and Young were surprised to find the extended family alive and well in inner London. In their rather stilted study they treated this as a sur-vival from the hard times of the past, destined for extinction as prosperity brought into being what they believed was the modern norm of the nuclear household headed by companionate parents, as predicted by sociological theory. Nevertheless their interpretation of family life in Bethnal Green was positive, even nostalgic and perhaps romanticized. They accepted their subjects' accounts very much at face value, presenting Bethnal Green as a model urban village in which there was remarkably little strife, in contrast to the conflicts vividly evident in accounts of Bethnal Green in earlier[26] and later[27] decades.

THE FAMILY LIVES OF OLD PEOPLE

Old people and their families were not the main concern of Willmott and Young's study though they emerged prominently in it. They were central to a companion study by Peter Townsend, also carried out in the mid-1950s. This was funded by the Nuffield Foundation and designed to establish whether Sheldon's and other comparable[28] findings about the family relation-ships of old people could be replicated elsewhere.[29] Townsend also found that old people in Bethnal Green often chose to live alone after widowhood. They wanted to be independent, to remain in their homes for as long as they could. They expressed fears—as old people long had—of the conflict that might arise if they lived with younger people. As various old people told him: 'It's nice to be near, but not too near.' 'You need a private place.' 'It's right to be

---

[25] Ibid. 125.

[26] Ellen Ross, *Love and Toil: Motherhood in Outcast London* (Oxford, 1993). Raphael Samuel, *East-End Underworld: Chapters in the Life of Arthur Harding* (London, 1981); Anna Davin, *Growing Up Poor: Home, School and Street in London, 1870–1914* (London, 1996).

[27] Jocelyn Cornwell, *Hard-Earned Lives* (London, 1984).

[28] National Council of Social Service, *Over Seventy* (London, 1954); G. F. Adams and G. A. Cheeseman, *Old People in Northern Ireland* (London, 1951).

[29] P. Townsend, *The Family Life of Old People* (London, 1957).

independent.' They had good reason to prefer independence. The report of the committee chaired by Rowntree for the Nuffield Foundation suggested in 1947 that old people dependent upon others were sometimes inadequately fed; resources were not necessarily equally distributed within households.[30]

Townsend found that sometimes two generations shared a house, but kept separate households, though the women might spend a lot of time together during the day. As the older generation aged, the households might increasingly merge. As in Wolverhampton, most old couples and singles living alone received help from and gave help to relatives. Townsend, like Sheldon, stressed the reciprocity between generations in contrast to the stereotype of old people as dependent objects of care. Among many examples he found:

Mrs Hopkins, a widow in her early sixties, lived alone in a new council flat. She did most of her own shopping, cooking, cleaning and washing, although she had some help with the errands from one of her daughters in law, a grandson and one of her two sons, all of whom lived in an adjoining borough. In the day she looked after a grandson aged six, and at midday her son came for a meal and so did her other son's wife. She charged them 2s. each for the meal. 'I wouldn't trouble to cook for myself. That's why I like them coming.' She spent her weekends with one or other of her sons.[31]

A woman and her married daughters living near by were able to organize domestic work and care of the children in such a way that each of them was able to maintain a part-time job. The grandmother went off to work as an office cleaner at 6 in the morning, returning home at 10 a.m. She then had the care of the grandchildren while two married daughters went out to work, one as a waitress, one as a part-time newspaper wrapper. The daughters did her shopping on their way home from work.[32] Such relationships were complex. Townsend noted that:

part of the strength of family relationships comes from individuals receiving and returning services. Some old people can no longer reciprocate the services performed for them and this seems to make them less willing to accept help and their relatives sometimes less willing to give it. Among infirm people it was noticeable that a few getting least help were not in a position to give anything in exchange.[33]

Townsend, like Sheldon and Willmott and Young, concluded that:

It was wrong to consider the domestic affairs of the elderly in terms of the bricks and mortar of a structurally separate home as much for those living alone as for those living with relatives of two or three generations.[34]

He found that financial transfers were most common where the generations shared a household, but 'many old people had financial help from children

[30] Nuffield Foundation, *Old People: Report of a Survey Committee on the Problems of Ageing and the Care of Old People* (Oxford, 1947), 30.   [31] Ibid. 45.

[32] Ibid. 150.   [33] Ibid. 56.   [34] Ibid. 46.

living elsewhere and the day-to-day provision of meals and care of grand-children led to many exchanges of money and goods in kind'. Sixty-one per cent of Townsend's sample of old people depended upon or were assisted by regular contributions from relatives. If regular help in kind was included, the proportion rose to 75 per cent. Financial transactions were of three main kinds: money paid by children or other relatives for their board in the household; cash or gifts from relatives living elsewhere, usually children; payments in money or kind for services performed by old people, such as provision of meals for married children or care of grandchildren. The value of the cash trans-actions were generally small and must have been much less than the real value of services exchanged. Many old people treated such transactions as a mat-ter of course. 'It would be their duty, just like we did for our parents', one person put it. She and her husband received between ten shillings and a pound a week from their children, and emphasized that this would increase if needed. Gifts were usually small—between two shillings and sixpence and ten shillings—irregular and given for a specific purpose: they might pay for costly necessities, like boots, or luxuries like holidays. Sons were more likely than daughters to give money. They often had easier access to ready cash, though this may also suggest a less close relationship with parents.[35] Those who received nothing generally had no close relatives or the relatives were themselves too poor to assist.[36] Such transactions could be difficult to identify, partly because they were such a taken-for-granted feature of family relationships:

A widow at first said she had no help from her children. 'I'd sooner go without than ask. They shouldn' t need to be asked should they?' A son lived outside London and a daughter in the next street. It turned out she had just spent a month at her son's home, at his expense, and apart from staying with him from time to time in the year he had helped her buy clothing and linen recently. It also turned out her daughter's husband had artificial legs and lived for frequent spells on sickness benefit[37]

and so could not help her.

Reciprocity within the families of older people was more complex than Townsend was able to scutinize, but he concluded that 'principles by which household budgets of elderly people are normally collected and evaluated may require re-examination'.[38] They could indeed be complex. One widow

lived with her two married daughters and had a housekeeping allowance from one of them, while the eldest contributed to the rent . . . The youngest daughter's allowance was roughly £4 for herself, her husband and child, and in addition she paid her mother between 10s. and £1 for looking after the child. Sometimes the widow had a meal with her eldest daughter. A nephew was given a bed in the house four nights of the week and the nephew's mother paid 10s. in addition to the sum he paid for meals. Two married sons living nearby gave the widow a few shillings each week and she

---

[35] Offer, 'Economy of Regard', 454.   [36] Townsend, *Family Life*, 64–6.
[37] Ibid. 66.   [38] Ibid. 67.

had meals in their homes at week-ends. She quoted instances of one or the other in the family paying for an oil-stove, a dress and club subscriptions.[39]

Such transactions were important in the economics of many old people—though how important for how many remained unclear. The system of means-testing for state benefits was an incentive for old people to be reticent about them, as the Poor Law had long been. The extent of poverty in retirement, even after the introduction of old-age pensions, which Townsend also documented,[40] meant that the need for support from relatives was real. Many old people still lived 'lives of expedients', patching together a variety of resources, as they had over centuries. When wives received gifts they would not necessarily tell their husbands, just as they were themselves mostly ignorant of their husbands' earnings when at work.[41] But when the man retired generally the wife controlled the pension and doled out his pocket-money.

The family relationships which Townsend described were similar to those uncovered by Willmott and Young. Again Mum was the central figure and grandmothers, especially, often had close relationships with grandchildren and were closely involved in their upbringing. Sometimes grandchildren would stay with them whole or part-time, for company, for assistance, or to relieve pressure on the parental family. One small boy told Townsend: 'I've got two homes. I live with my Nan and go upstairs to my Mummy to sleep.' Many of the older people were in their late fifties or sixties when their youngest child reached marriageable age; most children lived with their parents until marriage. Following marriage, relationships with children varied. Daughters who married men of higher social status tended to see less of their parents; though sons who rose in status saw as much of their parents as other sons. Very few of the old people in Bethnal Green lost contact with all of their children.

Fifty-eight per cent of Townsend's sample (of 203 people, two-thirds of them women) were members of three-generation families and saw relatives of the other generations every day or almost every day. More distant relatives provided a support system which might be called upon in emergencies, as were neighbours; though unless neighbours happened also to be relatives they were less important than relatives in old people's lives. Very few old people were isolated. Those who described themselves as lonely Townsend believed were likely to be 'desolated' due to the loss of a loved close relative, rather than isolated.[42] Some had no living relatives or had lost touch with them. Townsend examined the recent records of a local geriatric hospital and of east Londoners who had died in LCC Homes and concluded that:

Old people who make claims on the institutional and domiciliary services of the state seem to form a very unrepresentative group. More live alone, are unmarried, childless or have sons not daughters or are separated from the daughters they have.[43]

---

[39] Townsend, *Family Life*, 67.   [40] Ibid. 154 ff.   [41] Ibid. 222.   [42] Ibid. 182.
[43] This was confirmed by his later study of old people in institutions, *The Last Refuge* (London, 1964).

The Bethnal Green survey suggested that between 5 and 10 per cent of the sample would have required institutional care but for help from relatives or friends. Other older people lived with less struggle with a lesser degree of support from others. Six per cent had their cleaning done by local authority home helps, 43 per cent by relatives and friends. Much the same was true of other services. Townsend concluded that social services should take account of the regularity and importance of family reciprocity, and support family networks rather than, as they did, treat them as a reason to refuse services. Services could not substitute for the family and generally neither older people nor their relatives wanted them to, but they could complement family support and reduce the strain of interdependence for both generations. Townsend found little 'hard evidence of neglect on the part of old people's children' despite the fears about this that were still frequently publicly expressed. He commented:

Doctors, social workers and others who express such fears may sometimes forget that they are in danger of generalizing from an extremely untypical sub-section of the population or from a few extreme examples known personally . . . and the fact that these fears have been expressed by one generation after another inclines one to be sceptical.[44]

Townsend traced the relationships and tensions within families,[45] with greater subtlety than Willmott and Young. He did not believe that he was observing family forms which were declining archaisms in the modern world, but saw families as flexible institutions adaptive to a variety of environments. Townsend's more detailed, warmer and more empathetic, study was more alert to the nuances and conflicts of family life and the complex motivation of exchange among relatives than those of Willmott and Young. He concluded that still 'the three generation extended family . . . provides the normal environment for old people. No other ties were so important to them.'[46]

What had changed by the mid-twentieth century, compared with the centuries before, was that more old people lived alone and fewer lived as boarders in the homes of non-relatives. With greater prosperity, more could maintain their own households. The proportions living with married children had increased compared with pre-nineteenth-century estimates,[47] due above all to the higher proportion of people living to old age, with surviving children. Fewer older people had unmarried children living at home. Women now completed their families at earlier ages and parents in their sixties were less likely to have children still in their teens. Average ages at marriage had fallen and a higher proportion of the population married than fifty years before, so that fewer unmarried children remained with their parents. In compensation, relationships with married children had become increasingly important for the rising numbers of older people.

[44] Townsend, *Family Life*, 202.   [45] e.g. ibid. 220–8.
[46] Ibid. 228.   [47] See pp. 122–3.

FAMILY AND CLASS IN A LONDON SUBURB

Sheldon had interviewed a cross-class sample of old people in Wolverhampton. The Bethnal Green samples were exclusively working class. Willmott and Young believed that the path of change towards more 'modern' family relationships, with greater emotional distance between generations, might be more evident in a middle-class environment. In order to explore this proposition, in 1959 they embarked on a study of 'Family and Class in a London Suburb', in Woodford, to the north-east of London. Again they were surprised by what they found.

In Woodford, compared with Bethnal Green, parents and adult children more rarely lived in the same borough and fewer still within five minutes' walk. Many younger people had moved away from their parents' neighbourhood to better homes or jobs. Older people took this for granted. Yet, still, 30 per cent of younger married people had seen their mothers in the twenty-four hours before their interviews (compared with 43 per cent in Bethnal Green); 33 per cent within the previous week (31 per cent in Bethnal Green); 37 per cent had not seen her for longer than one week (26 per cent in Bethnal Green). Contact between the generations was not negligible, but in view of the distances between their homes, there was less casual 'dropping in' in Woodford than in Bethnal Green.

The proportion of unmarried children living with pensioner parents in Woodford was almost identical to that in Bethnal Green. Twenty-three per cent of married children shared a dwelling with parents (21 per cent in Bethnal Green), 17 per cent lived within five minutes (32 per cent), 22 per cent within the same borough (11 per cent). Younger people in Woodford were more likely to possess cars and/or could more easily afford public transport. Close proximity was less intimately related to regular contact than for the poorer people of Bethnal Green. Willmott and Young were 'surprised' that the similarities between the two boroughs were more notable than the differences.

They found that although many older people in Woodford lived far away from *most* of their children they were likely to live close to at least *one* of them, and the likelihood that this was so increased with age, consequent on removal by one or other generation. The similarities between the boroughs were greater the higher the ages of the older generation. As they aged, parents were visited more and were more likely to share a home with married children, often following widowhood or illness. It was harder than in Bethnal Green for the two generations to find homes close by, due not least to the income and class gap. Often the older people moved from elsewhere to live with children and the unfamiliarity of the neighbourhood could cause problems. In consequence, Willmott and Young saw many of these old people as relatively deprived compared with Bethnal Greeners, despite the relative prosperity of their surroundings. Some families did, however, function much like those of Bethnal Green:

Mr Randall, a retired surveyor, also belongs to an extended family. His day as he described it himself in his diary, is very much mixed up with his daughter's. He visits her home constantly. 'Bicycled up to my daughter Joan. I usually go to lunch with her when my sister is at work. She was in the middle of cooking dinner so I went to the baker's for bread and two tins of food for the cat. Up the Green I ran into my friend Arthur and had a chat. Said cheerio and went back to my daughter. She was still getting dinner ready and as there was no-one to talk to I went into the lounge and strummed on the piano.'

He had lunch with his daughter, son-in-law, and grandson, then listened to a recording of Chopin with his grandson.[48]

Willmott and Young found that still in Woodford 'among the older parents it is the minority who do not belong to some kind of continuing family group, whether in the one house or spread over several'.[49] They discovered that:

In ill-health, infirmity or widowhood the aged people are, by and large, cared for by their children. Asked what use she made of various social services, Mrs Broadbent said, 'It's unnecessary when you've got children isn't it?' Kinship may mean less in the suburb at other stages in life, but in old age, when the need arises, the family is once more the main source of support. The old felt they could call on their children, the children that they should respond, 'When they've brought you up', said Mr Burgess 'you feel you've got a certain amount of moral obligation to them.' This sense of filial duty was as strong in one district as another.[50]

What about older people without children? The researchers discovered from a special analysis of the 1951 census returns, that only a minority (21 per cent) of these lived alone. Fifty-three per cent shared a household with relatives, 26 per cent with friends. Twenty-five unmarried people lived with siblings: one household of two sisters and a brother, all never-married, had lived together all their lives. Other single people lived with nieces, cousins, friends. Six lived alone, but had good contact with others. Willmott and Young commented:

In fact one of the striking things in Woodford as in the East End is how single people generally make up for the absence of other relationships by seeing more of their brothers and sisters.[51]

Only one single person and three childless, widowed people in the sample had no relatives or friends. On Townsend's rough and ready definition of 'isolation'—three or fewer contacts in a day—11 per cent of older people in Woodford were isolated compared with 10 per cent in Bethnal Green. Widowhood and infirmity could cause isolation and depression anywhere.

There were differences between Woodford and Bethnal Green. Retired middle-class men in Woodford had more common interests with their wives and closer contact with their children than the working-class men in Bethnal

---

[48] M. Young and P. Willmott, *Family and Class in a London Suburb* (London, 1960), 48–9.
[49] Ibid. 49.   [50] Ibid. 50.   [51] Ibid. 53.

Green. Older people gave less help to younger people than in Bethnal Green, but they received as much.[52] There were close links between mothers and daughters, but mother was less dominating in Woodford.

Willmot and Young concluded:

Most people are not solitary. Old people without children are on the whole no more isolated or neglected than those with them. The main reason is that the family, as adaptable in the suburbs as in the city, is efficient at providing substitutes for the missing parts. . . .

Almost everybody succeeds, somehow or other, in surrounding himself with a family or its atmosphere . . . why people need a family of some kind, especially in later life is obvious. What is less obvious is why the relatives who are thus sought after should respond. Often, of course, the arrangement is of mutual benefit—the spinster sisters or friends both need each other. Where this is not so, the relatives . . . seem to feel a sense of obligation, perhaps weaker than that of children to their parents, but at least akin to it. Mr Loder's niece, with whom he lives, confides 'He's an awful nuisance sometimes, but I can't turn him out can I? After all he's father's brother and there's no-one else he could go to.'[53]

But the Woodford study did not dissuade Willmott and Young of their conviction that reciprocity, beyond the nuclear core of the family, was bound for the dustbin of history.[54] Further research did not bear out their pessimism.

THE NATIONAL PICTURE

Research on old people and their families continued to pour out. In 1959 Peter Townsend published a review of thirty-three surveys of old age in Great Britain conducted between 1945 and 1958. These included his own, but not those of Sheldon, Wilmott and Young, and others which were not primarily social surveys of old people.[55] The surveys were scattered through the British Isles and were mainly though not exclusively urban. They were of variable scope and methodological quality, but they agreed strikingly on two things: the strength of family ties and the 'isolation and deplorable condition of a small minority who do not seem to be contacted by any welfare services'.[56] Townsend concluded:

The fact is that the large majority of people in Great Britain lead a reasonably secure life within their families . . . most old people have children living nearby even when they live alone e.g. seventy-four per cent of those in a Nottinghamshire town,

---

[52] Young and Willmott, *Family and Class*, 71.   [53] Ibid. 58.

[54] This argument was further developed in M. Young and P. Willmott, *The Symmetrical Family: A Study of Work and Leisure in the London Region* (London, 1973), which pays remarkably little attention to family relationships beyond the nuclear core.

[55] P. Townsend, 'Surveys of Old Age in Great Britain, 1945–1958', *Bulletin of the World Health Organization*, 21 (Geneva, 1959), 583–91.   [56] Ibid. 586.

eighty-seven per cent of those with children in Andover; eighty-five per cent of retired men in Aberdeen had a child in the city; eighty-nine per cent in a rural district in Anglesey had at least one child in the same dwelling or parish. The contacts are generally close.[57]

Only 8 per cent of a Liverpool sample had no 'regular' contact with family; 92 per cent in two districts of Nottinghamshire were regularly visited daily or weekly by relatives. These and subsequent surveys indicated that perhaps two-thirds of older people had a reasonable degree of security within their families, receiving help with their everyday chores when needed, as well as in emergencies. Half the remainder were likely to impose a severe strain upon their families; the other half were isolated.[58]

Between 1961 and 1964 a series of comparable cross-national surveys of people over 65 were carried out in the USA, Britain, and Denmark.[59] The British national survey, conducted by Townsend and Dorothy Wedderburn, interviewed 4,000 older people, alongside smaller studies of old people in institutions and of those living alone. It found, yet again, that old people preferred to live in their own homes and could long continue to do so, given adequate support for themselves and their families; but that publicly funded support services, such as home helps, district nurses, mobile chiropodists, were still inadequate. Townsend and Wedderburn concluded that 'the relationship between the family and the welfare state is much more subtle than has been implied'.[60] They were not alternatives, as current sociological orthodoxy suggested, but complemented one another. Services provided what families could not, such as specialist medical care, and assisted families to care for dependent older people. The survey also confirmed the reciprocal nature of transfers and how often help was transferred downwards as well as upwards through the generations.

They found that income from the state, in the form of pensions and/or National Assistance, was now the most important source of income of most old people. Only 2 per cent revealed financial help from relatives.[61] Much more help was in kind: 'gifts of food, clothing and help with holidays, outings and so on . . . This survey has confirmed that such help is extensive'. Sixty per cent of old women and one-third of couples living alone were receiving help of this kind which was worth 'upwards of two or three shillings a week' (the single person's retirement pension at this time was £2 a week). Assistance when the generations lived together was harder to calculate.[62]

In a complementary study, Jeremy Tunstall studied 538 older people, living alone in four areas: suburban Harrow, in London, the medium-sized southern

[57] Ibid. 586–7.

[58] Ibid. 587. C. Rosser and C. C. Harris, *The Family and Social Change* (London, 1965).

[59] P. Townsend and D. Wedderburn, *The Aged in the Welfare State* (London, 1965), 6. Ethel Shanas, P. Townsend, D. Wedderburn, H. Friis, M. Paul, J. Stehoalwer, *Old People in Three Societies* (London and New York, 1968).

[60] Townsend and Wedderburn, *The Aged*, 34.   [61] Ibid. 97.   [62] Ibid. 102.

town of Northampton; Oldham, a northern town of equivalent size; and rural south Norfolk. The book opened with a gloomy reinforcement of popular stereotypes:

Old people are eight times more likely to live alone than are people aged under 65. About 1,300,000 people aged 65 and over in Britain today live alone. A larger number, about 1,600,000, in reply to a question will say they are lonely (a quarter of these being 'often' lonely). About a million old people in Britain are socially isolated.[63]

Tunstall also pointed out that about 5,000,000 older people were not isolated.

In describing old people who were largely isolated, Tunstall perhaps gave too little weight to the effects both of poverty and of individual personality in limiting the social contacts of older people. One man whose work in the cotton industry had been his life had been made to retire at age 76, when his employers discovered his real age. He would have liked to continue going to the working men's club, but 'where-ever you go, you need the money . . . I'd be made welcome; people would buy me drinks. How would you feel about that if you couldn't buy them back?' He had a daughter living across the road with whom he spent one evening a week, and his son and grandchildren visited him every Saturday morning. They were willing to shop for him, but he feared they would spend too much money. The interview conveys the effects of poverty, as much as retirement or of isolation in themselves, on his social relationships, and the loss of status he experienced when unable to reciprocate. He also revealed a bad-tempered tone—perhaps the result of his new hardship, perhaps a longer-established barrier between himself and others—which itself might have distanced him from close contacts, including with his children, who none the less continued to see him frequently.[64] By contrast, an outgoing and better-off woman, a retired college lecturer, who had no contact with relatives, had recently moved to a village where she knew no one, but had already made friends and had wide interests.[65]

None the less, Tunstall's study was more psychologically aware than others. He speculated as to how far isolation in later life was connected with personality patterns established in earlier years; and how much with specific crises of later life due to retirement, bereavement, or disability. As he put it: 'old age is for each person who reaches it a new experience . . . ageing people have to learn the social role of the old person'; how they performed that role was influenced by their life histories.[66] Old age, he argued, should be studied in the context of the individual life cycle, for 'patterns of ageing stretch far back into the individual's past', influenced by whether they had siblings or children, by their occupations, income, and intellectual resources;[67] rather than in terms of currently fashionable generalized theories such as that of

---

[63] J. Tunstall, *Old and Alone* (London, 1966), 1.　　[64] Ibid. 26–7.
[65] Ibid. 36.　　[66] Ibid. 233.　　[67] Ibid. 268.

'disengagement'. Like Sheldon almost twenty years before,[68] Tunstall complained that the pattern of 'normal' social development in old age was still
not defined, not least because individual experiences were very variable, more
so probably than those of other phases of the life-course.[69]

The 'overwhelming majority' of old people in Tunstall's sample said they
preferred to live alone, though Tunstall wondered how often this was putting
a brave face on a situation over which they had little control.[70] Nevertheless,
he concluded that 'the popular preference, given reasonable health, is to maintain regular contact with children, siblings or others, without imposing upon
them or becoming too dependent upon them. Other things being equal, many
(or even most) widowed or single old people prefer to live alone while maintaining close ties with relatives outside the household. However, other things
often are not equal . . .'.[71] An older person might face a choice between living with a daughter or rarely seeing her because of distance; ill health might
bring incapacity.

In Britain in the 1960s, Tunstall concluded, 'there is no automatic respect
paid to old people, but the most respected and powerful people in our society are often quite elderly'.[72] He found no clear social class differences in relations between the generations:

On the present evidence pictures of the working class as either callously neglecting
all its elderly parents or cosily integrating them into three-generation households are
equally without foundation.[73]

He found the highest proportion of old people living alone in inner London,
the lowest in the London suburbs, a pattern replicated in other conurbations.
'Extreme isolation' was greatest in rural south Norfolk, which contained
25 per cent of old people in the sample but 50 per cent of all isolates. The
sample was too small to provide an explanation but, he commented, 'the
evidence points away from any comfortable conclusions about the true sociability of rural life'.[74] 'The popular idea of old people being more alone in
urban centres than in rural areas is without foundation'.[75] Loneliness did not
only afflict those who lived alone. Twenty-seven per cent of the 'often lonely'
were married and lived with their partners, though often in a state of conflict
or with one partner in poor health. Women who lived alone were less likely
to describe themselves as 'lonely' than men.

Like other researchers Tunstall called for social services to support families, noting that a number of local authorities would not provide a home help
if the old person had a daughter in the local authority area. He argued that
social services should make an effort to discover what old people wanted and
provide choices. For example,

[68] See pp. 408–11.   [69] Tunstall, *Alone*, 240.   [70] Ibid. 55.   [71] Ibid. 56–7.
[72] Ibid. 256.   [73] Ibid. 53.   [74] Ibid. 83.
[75] Ibid. 108. Nuffield Foundation, *Old People*, 53.

an old woman whose arthritis prevents her from cooking should be able to choose between having mobile meals delivered or having her home help cook them or being transported to a club or Centre to eat the meals there, or a combination of the three.[76]

Clubs could help overcome isolation, but those specifically for old people were slightly less attractive to his sample than clubs and associations unrestricted by age.[77]

Later studies reinforced all of these findings. A study in the early 1970s of retirement to the seaside[78] found exceptionally large numbers of older people living in seaside resorts. In 1971 people of pensionable age made up 45 per cent of the population of Bexhill, 39 per cent in Clacton, and 33 per cent in Eastbourne (all southern seaside resorts) compared with a national percentage of 16.[79] Those who retired to the seaside came disproportionately from the higher social classes, mostly moved as couples and were more likely than average to have no surviving children. Those with children lived at a greater distance from them than in other studies, for example retirees to the Sussex coast often had children in London, whence they had migrated. However, they still saw them regularly and there were strong reasons to suppose that many old people returned to live near their children as they aged, in particular following widowhood; or sometimes children moved to them. The pattern was similar to that of Woodford. Some older people appeared to be experiencing in retirement a period of happy independence of family ties before greater dependence upon them became unavoidable.[80]

Elizabeth Roberts's oral history of women and their families in three Lancashire towns between 1940 and 1970 confirmed the findings of contemporary studies of southern communities. Despite changes affecting families over the post-war period, more striking was continuity with the findings of Roberts's earlier study of the same towns from 1890 to 1940:[81] 'It is always important to remember that much help from kin was not only dependent upon relations living in the same house, much assistance being rendered by members of the family living nearby'.[82] For example, when Mrs Brayshaw was growing up in the 1950s and 1960s:

We had relatives living next door, my mother's cousin and her husband. My grandmother and her sister lived next door but one. When I was a small child I remember having two breakfasts most days. I used to have one at home then shuffle off next door.

The combined efforts of this family enabled the grandmother to stay in her own home. She moved in with her daughter only in the last year of her life.[83]

[76] Tunstall, *Alone*, 296.   [77] Ibid. 297.   [78] V. Karn, *Retiring to the Seaside* (London, 1977).
[79] Ibid. 14.   [80] Ibid. 75.
[81] Elizabeth Roberts, *A Woman's Place: An Oral History of Working-Class Women, 1890–1940* (Oxford, 1984).
[82] Elizabeth Roberts, *Women and Families: An Oral History, 1940–1970* (Oxford, 1995), 175.
[83] Ibid. 191.

In the late 1950s Mrs Kennedy's mother became unable to look after herself. Her daughter had no room in her small house, so she went to live with
her son in the next street.

So when they went to work, she used to come round to me all day and then go back
to them when she had had her tea. That was for about eighteen months before she
died. She was no trouble at all. The boys used to play with her and if I wanted to
go to the shops she would look after them for me.[84]

In 1970 Mrs Owen had lived in the same house since 1940. Her mother and
an aunt still lived near by, her daughter and family across the road. She and
her daughter spent much of the day together when Mrs Owen was not visiting her own mother, whom she saw on most days: 'I always used to say I
was going home.' Her mother-in-law, who had become blind, lived near by
and was more likely to visit the Owens than was Mrs Owen's mother.

There had been some decline in co-residence over time, but that this 'does
not necessarily imply any lowering of standards of care for relatives nor a loos-
ening of the bonds of kinship'. But the emotional relationships involved were
not simple:

Some respondents expressed irritation with and even resentment of relatives, but these
feelings did not necessarily lead to abandonment of long-established norms regard-
ing obligations to help kin.[85]

The motives expressed were a mixture of love, duty, affection, obligation, and
self-interest, such as the hope of inheriting property. More often, care for old
people was simply taken for granted: 'Relatives were cared for because it
was assumed that that was what one did'. Ties with neighbours seemed to
be weakening, but not those with kin. 'Blood is thicker than water' remained
an important axiom. Sometimes a sense of obligation was reinforced by fear
of gossip and social disapproval if relatives were thought to be neglected.[86]
Grandmothers were not invariably loving partners in the family network of
reciprocity. One woman recalled how her parents lived for most of their marriage with her father's tyrannical mother who dominated him and would not
allow them to leave, despite his wife's unhappiness. The older woman refused
to look after her granddaughter 'because she said it was my mother's place
to stay at home and do the cooking and cleaning and not to go out to work'.[87]
Other grandmothers were too busy with their own lives to have time to care
for grandchildren.[88]

Another woman was living in a bedsitter with her husband and new baby
in 1948 when her mother's cousin offered her a house at a low rent if she
would care for the relative's blind mother. This arrangement lasted sixteen
years. The old woman was very difficult. The house had only two bedrooms
and soon another child was born. The younger people felt that they could

[84] Ibid.   [85] Ibid. 175.   [86] Ibid. 180.   [87] Ibid. 181.   [88] Ibid. 188.

not put the old woman in a residential home, because the house belonged to her daughter, nor could they leave and abandon her: 'I wouldn't have done that. You see we had been brought up to look after one another'.[89] Roberts concluded:

Clearly those in our study did not give help to just anyone claiming kinship . . . the most usual help was given up and down a straight genealogical line of grandparents, parents and children. While it is clear that respondents were aware of rules and obligations governing their relations with kin, it is much less apparent that they consciously assessed the various considerations . . . as with their forebears, respondents appeared to possess norms which had been internalized . . . (and) generally acted towards kin because 'it was the thing to do'.[90]

Only a small minority had few contacts with relatives due to personal conflict or migration.

Roberts, like Willmott and Young and Townsend, studied settled and secure if not necessarily prosperous neighbourhoods. Coates and Silburn's study of the very poor 'slum' district of St Ann's in Nottingham in the mid-1960s found that much lower proportions of people had relatives near by. Everyone who could afford to moved away. When they studied a more comfortable Nottingham council estate the pattern was similar to that in Bethnal Green.[91]

INTERPRETING FAMILY RELATIONSHIPS

In the 1960s a group of anthropologists, led by Raymond Firth, studied 'Families and their Relatives' in two middle-class districts of north London. They produced a more subtle analysis of intergenerational relationships within families than most of the sociologists had achieved, but also stressed the importance of reciprocity and the strong sense of obligation of younger to older generations. They found that the 'standard view', an 'ideal norm', was that families 'ought to stick together', but that such sentiments were stronger for immediate than for more distant relatives. The sense of responsibility for 'elderly relatives' was especially firmly expressed:

It has various constituents, ranging from actual monetary help or advice on financial problems, to performance of small manual services, visiting, entertainment and the provision of a place to live . . .[92] Undoubtedly to many people one of the most important obligations is that of visiting, of 'seeing something' of the relative. Most people have a kind of 'model' of social existence. There is a tacit assumption that it is necessary to maintain some social relationships in order to keep going as a fully

---

[89] Roberts, *Women and Families*, 185.   [90] Ibid. 197.

[91] K. Coates and R. Silburn, *Poverty: The Forgotten Englishmen* (Harmondsworth, 1970).

[92] Raymond Firth, Jane Hybert, Anthony Forge, *Families and their Relatives: Kinship in a Middle-Class Sector of London* (London, 1969), 102–3.

functioning personality . . . The notion here is that a person exists through his own activities primarily while he remains able-bodied, but that he sometimes continues to be socially effective as he grows older increasingly through the efforts that others make on his behalf.[93]

Mrs Maskell expressed especially clearly, 'the general norms of obligation to kin' and the tensions involved in responding to them. She told the researchers:

I was brought up very strongly by my mother that everyone should be independent and able to look after themselves. But I've changed my views on the subject . . . Just looking at people, and how nasty it was to look at people who had no-one in particular to look after them in any way . . . Relatives shouldn't do anything unless they want to . . . but if a situation arises then they should cope with it to some degree . . . Unless they like them (their kin) I feel they have only duties towards them, in times of trouble I think. And then I think they have very strong duties towards them because it is very unpleasant and very difficult, in times of difficulty, to get outsiders to cope at all.[94]

Others more clearly expressed these obligations to older relatives as unpleasurable though inescapable burdens, in particular when parents had themselves been unsupportive in the past.[95] One woman said she believed that people had a duty to look after their mothers and that this was the strongest kinship obligation. She herself had never felt any obligation towards her father, who was a 'strange man' and 'never there'. She believed that 'fathers who had fulfilled their obligations to their children ought to be looked after when they got old, but not otherwise'. The researchers found that:

Another type of response is the development of a sense of guilt in response to inadequate fulfilment of obligation (or of what is regarded as inadequate). One woman expressed a strong sense of obligation towards older relatives, but worried that she found her mother-in-law 'dull and trying' (a view confirmed by the field worker who met her) with no common interests. Her husband also found his mother 'slow and conventional and generally rather uninteresting'. Yet despite all this, he saw his mother every week as he knew how much it meant to her; and his wife also saw her frequently. But clearly the wife felt that she could do more, and that she had to justify why she was not doing it. Her husband and her friends said that if one did not get on with relatives one should not visit because neither side would enjoy it. She agreed 'but I do feel that if my mother-in-law needed anything I would do it . . . what people do for relatives is very dependent on their circumstances anyway . . . I suppose you *might* feel that because they're relatives you should keep on seeing them, but I find it very tedious to have to see people when there's nothing in common with them'.[96]

Others resented the fact that they carried out their obligations to older relatives whereas other family members did not.

For 85 per cent of the sample, 'relations between these parents and their sons or daughters were good or reasonably equitable'. For the remainder,

---

[93] Ibid. 105–6.   [94] Ibid. 106.   [95] Ibid. 109.   [96] Ibid. 109–11.

'relations were described as bad, or non-existent; or there was dislike by the married son or daughter for the parent without this necessarily being reciprocated or even understood'.[97] The study concluded with a subtle reconstruction of the emotional content of the relationships the researchers had uncovered:

A central point of all this is that instead of dealing with conventional stereotypes of 'mother-love', 'Mum', 'father -figures' or whatever, our evidence shows a set of highly complex patterns of relationship between married adults and their parents. Fathers and mothers are people formerly in the domestic circle for whom on the whole there is a very great deal of affection, admiration and respect, and willingness to commit much time and energy in gratifying their wishes. At the same time, while it is recognized that they have a prior right to make demands, such demands may be resented, even while being fulfilled . . . some demands may be regarded as excessive, as blackmail, employing as instruments those emotional ties which are felt to be properly a free, not enforced, tribute to affection and gratitude. Yet very rarely is there sufficient explosion of resentment to lead to complete breakdown of social relationship between married son or daughter and parent. The upshot is often a kind of elaborate strategy of relations, in which there is much manipulation of personal wants and resources against the background of admitted social obligation.[98]

FAMILY AND KINSHIP IN THE 1980S AND 1990S

A government-sponsored national survey of 'the elderly at home' in 1976 reinforced the picture of generally supportive family networks, however complex or confused their emotional content.[99] There were, however, fewer surveys of kinship in the 1970s. They revived in the 1980s in the context of revived concern about the ageing of the population. Thompson, Itzin, and Abendstern found in south London:

That patterns of family care have not changed over the past fifty years. Both then and now many children look after their elderly parents and today, as in the past, the work which this care involves falls largely to women.[100]

Families allowed older people to enter residential homes only when they needed care beyond the capacity of the family to provide. Even when a father who had long ago deserted his wife and daughters turned up expecting his daughters to care for him at the end of his life, 'bitter and reluctant, they nevertheless took him on and he lived with them—one after the other—until he died'.[101] Older people also explained to the researchers that they had expected the last living parent or parent-in-law to live with them for the last few years of their lives, even if this meant sharing a bedroom with the older person or giving up the front parlour to them for their bedroom.

---

[97] Firth, Hybert, Forge, *Families and their Relatives*, 400.
[98] Ibid. 406–7.   [99] A. Hunt, *The Elderly at Home* (London, 1978).
[100] Paul Thompson, Catherine Itzin, Michele Abendstern, *I Don' t Feel Old* (Oxford, 1990), 208.
[101] Ibid. 209.

But in south London, as elsewhere, the older people were more often 'fit and active—offering support to their children and grandchildren rather than the other way around'.[102] They had close relationships with children, but moved to live with them with the greatest reluctance, however willing their children to give them a home. One woman said, echoing other old women through the centuries:

Charles wants me to go, he's had a room built for me. Our Norman has had a room built for me, but I'm not giving my little home up and that's what upsets them. They think I shouldn't be on my own now. But I'm not giving up my home for nobody.[103]

A study in Sheffield in the mid-1980s addressed the increasing fears that the growing numbers of middle-aged women in the paid workforce would rob old people of their accustomed carers. Such apprehensions overlooked how throughout history, as we have seen, women had combined the care of older people with both paid work and the heavier domestic work, larger families, greater poverty, and less convenient homes of previous centuries. The Sheffield study revealed the lengths to which married women went to care for elderly relatives and to keep them in the community, despite the demands of their immediate families and of paid work, as they always had.[104] It stressed also something probably understated in other studies, but long recognized by older people themselves, that 'family care can be among the very best and the very worst experiences that human beings can devise for one another ... within families it is possible for people to experience the most damaging and emotionally destructive relationships'.[105]

By 1989 another researcher could comment:

It is now generally accepted that most care, help and support in old age comes from informal sources. An image of the family as an available and responsible source of support has gradually replaced an earlier stereotype of the fragmented modern family in industrial societies as unavailable and unconcerned with the plight of its older generations.[106]

By this time it was equally widely recognized that old people gave as well as received help;[107] and that when families needed support from social services because an elderly relative had become burdensome, it was unlikely to be forthcoming. Still, for many local authorities the availability of family care was a reason to withhold services.

---

[102] Ibid. 210.   [103] Ibid.

[104] Hazel Qureshi and Alan Walker, 'Caring for Elderly People: The Family and the State', in C. Phillipson and A. Walker, *Ageing and Social Policy: A Critical Assessment* (Aldershot, 1986), 109–27. See also Roberts, *Women*, 176.   [105] Qureshi and Walker, 117.

[106] G. Claire Wenger, 'Support Networks in Old Age: Constructing a Typology', in Margot Jefferys (ed.), *Growing Old in the Twentieth Century* (London, 1989), 166. See also Wenger, *The Supportive Network: Coping with Old Age* (London, 1984).   [107] Wenger, 'Support Networks', 167–8.

Middle-class family networks were more widely dispersed than working-class ones, but also less constrained by distance due to readier access to transport and telephones. Older middle-class people also turned more readily to friends for support.[108] Working-class people were slower to seek help outside the family. A comparison made in 1990 of samples of old people in central Liverpool (where they were mainly working class) and in rural North Wales (where a high proportion were middle class, and had often moved there on retirement) found that a high proportion of the Liverpudlians had lived for at least thirty years in their neighbourhood and had strong family and other local ties. In North Wales the mainly Welsh-speaking, mainly working-class, long-settled inhabitants were closer in pattern to the Liverpool sample than to the middle-class incomers. This challenged the continuing image of the city as less supportive than the countryside, and of Liverpool in particular as an area of social disruption.[109]

The inadequacy of support services for families led in the 1980s to a literature of concern about 'carers', generally portrayed as single women whose lives were seriously constrained by looking after aged parents. The problem was real, as it had long been, for a minority of women.[110] Such representations, however, had the unintended consequence of reinforcing the sterotype of 'old people' as objects of care and of fuelling alarm about the inevitability of a period of serious dependency at the end of life.[111] Out of understandable concern for seriously disadvantaged and under-supported carers, it risked understating the extent to which 'caring' could be pleasing and fulfilling.[112] It also underestimated the amount of 'caring' performed by men, especially for their spouses. An analysis drawn from the General Household Survey (GHS) of Britain in 1985 found that about one adult in seven (about six million people) provided unpaid care. One in five households contained a carer; 1.4 million, 3 per cent of the population, devoted at least twenty hours a week to caring.[113] Two per cent of female and 2 per cent of male adults cared for someone sick, handicapped, or aged in their household. Ten per cent of women and 7 per cent of men gave 'some regular service or help' to a sick, handicapped, or older relative, friend, or neighbour who did not live with them. 'Service' could

[108] P. d'Abbs, *Social Support Networks: A Critical Review of Models and Findings* (Institute of Family Studies Monograph, 1; Melbourne), D. I. Warren, *Helping Networks: How People Cope with Problems in the Urban Community* (Bloomington, Ind., 1981).

[109] G. Claire Wenger, 'A Comparison of Urban with Rural Support Networks: Liverpool and North Wales', *Ageing and Society*, 15 1 (1995), 59–82.

[110] J. Lewis and B. Meredith, *Daughters Who Care: Daughters Caring for Mothers at Home* (London, 1988.) J. Finch and D. Groves (eds.), *A Labour of Love: Women, Work and Caring* (London, 1983).

[111] S. Arber and J. Ginn, *Gender and Later Life* (London, 1991), 130.

[112] Martin Rein and Harold Salzman, 'Social Integration, Participation and Exchange in Five Industrial Countries', in Scott A. Bass (ed.), *Older and Active* (New Haven and London, 1995), 237–62.

[113] Offer, 'Economy of Regard', 462; H. Green, *Informal Carers*, General Household Survey, 1985, series GN5, no. 15, supplement A (1988).

include gardening or shopping. It was provided mainly for spouses, parents, or, to a lesser extent, parents-in-law. Half of all caring was for a parent or, less frequently, a parent-in-law. Co-resident care averaged fifty-three hours a week, non-resident care nine hours, mainly because older people living with younger relatives were generally more infirm and in need of care. Gender differences in the provision of care were negligible.[114]

Not all carers were 'young'. People over 65 provided 35 per cent of caring for others above that age—a conservative estimate since the GHS excluded from its survey 'normal' domestic activities performed by women (only) for others.[115] By the 1990s more people were living to be very old, into their eighties, and also becoming dependent, if at all, at later ages. In consequence their children might themselves be past retirement when the older generation needed support, all the more probably in view of the declining age of retirement. About 20 per cent of all people over 60 were caring for people who were older still.

It continued to be clear that old people 'do not give up their independence easily: with few exceptions they are reluctant subjects in caring and dependency . . . elderly people desire, often more than anything else, the preservation of their independence'.[116] Indeed there was evidence that many old people preferred state services, when they were adequate and responsive, and even preferred residential care, when it was comfortable and supportive, to feeling that they burdened their children; though they would opt for it only when they were incapable of living in their own homes.[117] Reciprocity was more important in family than in professional care. When old people could no longer give to family members as well as receiving they resisted dependence upon them.[118]

Fears continued in the 1990s that the further increase in the numbers of married women in paid work, together with changing household patterns, would, at last, destroy family cohesion and reciprocity. The British Social Attitudes survey showed a fall between the mid-1980s and the mid-1990s in the frequency with which married women in full-time work visited their mothers. But still almost 50 per cent of those who did not share a household with their mothers visited her at least once a week. It was not clear whether frequency of contact increased with the increasing age and disability of the mother, as earlier surveys had shown. There was every sign that, as they had always done, women maintained their supportive role as well as their paid work, often at considerable physical and emotional cost to themselves and still with exiguous support from social services. This was as true of women who

[114] Arber and Ginn, *Gender*, 131–4.   [115] Ibid. 135.

[116] H. Qureshi and A. Walker, *The Caring Relationship* (London, 1989), 18–19. Arber and Ginn, *Gender*, 18–19.

[117] A. Sixsmith, 'Independence and Home in Later Life', in C. Phillipson, M. Bernard, P. Strang (eds.), *Dependency and Interdependency in Old Age* (London, 1986), 338–47.

[118] J. Finch, *Family Obligations and Social Change* (Cambridge, 1989). Arber and Ginn, *Gender*, 140–3.

expressed support for feminist goals of equal opportunities in the workplace as of those who did not.[119] Still, about 60 per cent of older people lived within one hour's journey of at least one close relative, one-quarter to one-third within fifteen minutes, and contact was frequent.

If not women's paid work, then divorce and the increasing flexibility of partnership and household arrangements were widely expected to diminish the family contacts of older people. Not, of course, that loss of a spouse was an historically new experience; as we have seen, throughout history widowhood had frequently broken up marriages in middle life. Complex step-families often resulted from remarriage, or widows and their children survived in mutually supportive relationships with elderly parents. Research indicated that divorce also could strengthen intergenerational family ties, as lateral ties with partners weakened. After divorce or separation people, especially women, often moved closer to parents, for mutual support. Remarriage and the formation of step-relationships could increase rather than diminish family resources.[120]

The changing ethnic population of much of the British Isles and the different cultural expectations of the family relationships of various immigrant groups and their descendants complicates analysis of change in the late twentieth century. By the 1990s Britain, especially in the cities, was a profoundly different, more multicultural, society than it had ever been. The largely white working-class Bethnal Green of the 1950s,[121] had become in the 1990s Tower Hamlets with a substantial population of residents of Bangladeshi and other overseas origins. Wolverhampton was a 'white' town when Sheldon investigated it in the 1940s. By the 1990s it had a substantial population of Caribbean and Asian origin; and Woodford was home to many relatively affluent British Asians. Family support and reciprocity was at least as strong in these cultural groups of immigrant origin, though sometimes in forms different from British tradition, for example expectations about sharing homes with elders differed.

Cross-national studies, time and again, in the late twentieth century found that family reciprocity was the norm in developed and less developed countries, showed little sign of vanishing as a correlate of economic development, though its form might change, and was everywhere a major component of the care of old people.[122] In advanced countries younger people rarely supported elders with cash, certainly they gave vastly less than they received, but

[119] Joanna Bornat, Brian Dimmock, and Sheila Peace, 'The Impact of Family Change on Older People: The Case of Stepfamilies', *Research Results*, no. 2, ESRC Population and Household Change Research Programme (Oxford, 1998).

[120] R. Flowerdew, Richard Davies, and Jennifer Mason, 'Migration, Kinship and Household Change', *Research Results*, no. 12, ESRC Population and Household Change Findings; K. W. Wachter, 'Kinship Resources for the Elderly', *Philosophical Transactions of the Royal Society*, 352, 1363 (1997), *Ageing: Science, Medicine and Society*, 1811–19.

[121] About 8 per cent of the population had been composed of descendants of East European Jewish migrants. Young and Willmott, *Family and Kinship*, 13.

[122] Offer, 'Economy of Regard', 461–2. World Bank, *Averting the Old Age Crisis* (Oxford, 1984), 49.

they reciprocated equally massively in the form of care.[123] In a sample of developed countries, including USA, Japan, West Germany, Sweden, more old people were living alone than in the past, but close contact with relatives was not diminishing. In Sweden at least it was increasing as the technology of communication improved.[124] Increased prosperity and modern technology enabled family relationships to adapt to changed circumstances; the deep-freeze and microwave oven made it easier to provide meals for a dependent older person; motor vehicles, air transport, telephones, e-mail eased regular contact and response to emergencies over long distances. The fact of contact between the generations had changed little over time, though the content of relationships may have changed, and the time devoted to them on the part of both younger and the older people, not necessarily in predictable ways: older people also led fuller lives than in previous generations and often had less need of contact with their families. Such changes do not fit easily into a narrative of family decline.

The researchers were impressed by 'the pervasiveness of family integration everywhere. Children not only maintain communication with their aged parents . . . but provide [them] with concrete care and services. These services are regular and important for the survival of older people.'[125] They found no strong relationship between the level of formal welfare services and informal family services. Contrary to what had long been suggested by critics of state welfare, a strong welfare state did not 'crowd out' family care. Levels of family support were higher in West Germany, where welfare services were strong, than in the USA where they were weaker. The USA and Britain, with different state welfare traditions, had similar levels of family support.[126] In Britain official policy continued, as it had since the 1950s, and indeed through the whole history of the Poor Law, to assume that formal services were ancillary and complementary to those of the family; and it continued to provide them very unevenly. In the mid-1980s it was estimated that unpaid family services were saving the national social services budget about £24b. a year at a time when the cost of local authority personal social services was about £3.4b.[127] Based on local authority pay rates (£7 per hour in 1989) the market value of caring provided by unpaid carers was £39.1b. in 1992, or about 7.5 per cent of National Income. Eighty-three per cent of this was spent on caring for older people. In total this was almost four times as much as joint public and private expenditure for long-term care and about as much as total expenditure on the National Health Service.[128] Family support for older people was not a negligible feature of the British welfare state in the late twentieth century.

---

[123] Offer, 'Economy of Regard', 462; World Bank, *Averting*, table 2.3, p. 63.
[124] Rein and Salzman, 'Social Integration', 237–62.   [125] Ibid.   [126] Ibid.
[127] P. Johnson and J. Falkingham, *Ageing and Economic Welfare* (London, 1992).
[128] Offer, 'Economy of Regard', 462.

CONCLUSION

This chapter has surveyed just some of the mass of evidence which showed with striking consistency between 1945 and the end of the millennium that families extremely rarely provided substantially for the material support of older people; with the coming of universal pensions they did not need to. They did provide a very great deal of material support when it was needed, most often in the form of services and this support was vital to the well-being of very many old people, indeed it was often the only buffer between them and a residential institution. At least as important were continuing high levels of emotional support and companionship.[129]

But most older people needed little or no more physical or material assistance than did younger people, often less; still less did they need 'care'. The family relationships of old people have never been only about 'welfare', and the flow of support has never been only one way. Very many of them gave at least as much as they received to their families and communities. Their roles in family life form an important theme in the cultural history of older people, in a variety of ways. A central theme of research on family relationships in the twentieth century has been the importance for older people, as in earlier centuries, of maintaining an independent home and control of their own lives for as long as possible. By the end of the twentieth century, more led active, varied lives than fifty years earlier and families were less central to their lives. The nature of family relationships changed over time. But certainly as striking as change was continuity in the importance of family relationships in the social worlds of old and young people, contrary to widespread rhetoric about their diminishing importance.

Family ties are always multifaceted and they could constrain older as well as younger people. Younger relatives' stereotypes of the capacities of older people might cast them in dependent roles, restraining independence and adventurousness. Nevertheless, even at the latest ages some older people were independent and adventurous, though unavoidably some were frail. It is unnecessary to romanticize relations between the generations to acknowledge that for most people they remained close and that giving support, though not necessarily love, or even liking, to older relatives when it was needed was customary in the late twentieth century, part of the taken-for-granted way of life, which most people assumed was age-old custom. With good reason; relations between older people and their relatives in Britain in the distant past are elusive, but there is convincing evidence that they were close and that family

[129] A recent study which stresses the continuing importance of family in the lives of older people throughout the second half of the 20th cent., despite important social and economic changes is C. Phillipson, M. Bernard, J. Phillips, and J. Ogg, 'The Family and Community Life of Older People: Household Composition and Social Networks in Three Urban Areas', *Ageing and Society*, 18/3 (1998), 259–90.

support had long been an important element in the economy of survival (emotional and material) of old people. It is improbable that researchers in the late twentieth century were detecting something quite new in British culture, since this was a period when more older people were physically fitter and better off and hence had a greater capacity to live independently of family than in earlier times. More probably they were detecting the continued centrality of reciprocity to human relationships even in the most 'developed' societies, and the continuing importance of non-monetary, non-market transfers in such societies.[130] Ancient complementary structures of public and private welfare survived into the welfare state, facilitated rather than destroyed by greater prosperity and ease of communications, integral to the structures and functions of state welfare institutions rather than attenuated remnants of a bygone age.

[130] Ibid.

22

Inventing Geriatric Medicine

One response to the growing proportion of older people in twentieth-century societies has been greater attention to their health. Interest in the (ill) health of older people has a very long history,[1] but it was always a marginal and un-fashionable enterprise among medical specialists, and by the early twentieth century both medical understanding of older people and capacity to cure their ailments remained severely limited as, indeed, did the capacities of most medical specialisms.

It was in the USA around the time of the First World War that the specialism was named 'geriatrics' by Ignatz Nascher (1863–1945). Nascher was concerned above all to redress the neglect of older patients by the medical profession, who, he correctly believed, generally thought them uninteresting and unworthy of the effort of treatment. This view was slow to change, if indeed it ever has. The practice of geriatric medicine spread slowly in the USA, Germany, USSR, Britain, and elsewhere in the middle years of the twentieth century. Diagnosis and treatment of conditions especially affecting old people improved, for example for heart conditions, hypertension, and some cancers though generally as an outcome of concern about their effects on younger people.[2]

Conventionally the development of modern geriatrics in Britain is traced to 1935 when the West Middlesex County Hospital, in London, of which Dr Marjorie Warren was deputy medical superintendent, took over a former Poor Law infirmary. This was an outcome of the Local Government Act of 1929 which transferred Poor Law institutions into the control of local authorities in the hope of improving conditions in these institutions. Both district hospitals, such as the West Middlesex, and voluntary teaching hospitals generally specialized in acute medicine, treating the more 'interesting' and supposedly more curable patient; the chronically, supposedly incurably, ill, very many of them aged, were relegated to Poor Law infirmaries unless they could afford better. Doctors in training had no contact with such patients. A rationing system, providing inferior medical care for most older patients, was firmly in place.

Following the 1929 Act, for the first time at the West Middlesex highly trained staff were exposed to conditions in the chronic wards. Warren was appalled

---

[1] See pp. 37–8, 35–41, 59–62.

[2] Pat Thane, 'Geriatrics', in W. F. Bynum and Roy Porter (eds.), *Companion Encyclopaedia of the History of Medicine*, 2 vols. (London, 1993), 1092–1118. Pat Thane, 'Old Age', in R. Cooter and J. Pickstone (eds.) (forthcoming).

to find that she was responsible for about seven hundred mostly bedbound old people, in large, dismal wards. They were kept clean and fed but given little further care or hope of recovery, whatever the cause of their condition. Doctors largely ignored them. Nurses on these wards had inferior training to those on surgical and medical wards. Marjorie Warren described the outcome:

Only those who have had charge of such patients can know anything of their misery and degradation. Having lost all hope of recovery, with the knowledge that independence has gone and with a feeling of helplessness and frustration, the patient rapidly loses morale and self-respect and develops a pathetic or peevish, irritable, sullen, morose and aggressive temperament . . . Lack of interest in the surroundings, confinement to bed, and a tendency to incontinence soon produce pressure sores . . . and an inevitable loss of muscle tone make for a completely bedridden state. Soon the well-known disuse atrophy of the lower limbs, with postural deformities, stiffness of joints, and contractures completes the unhappy picture of human forms who are not only heavy nursing cases in the ward and a drag on society but also are no pleasure for themselves and a source of acute distress to their friends. Still, alas in this miserable state, dull, apathetic, helpless, and hopeless, life lingers on sometimes for years, while those round them whisper arguments in favour of euthanasia.[3]

Warren had the wards painted in attractive colours, with improved lighting, individual lockers, day rooms and activities, so that there was an incentive for patients to get out of bed. She introduced serious diagnosis of the patients' conditions in place of the previous, largely silent, because taken-for-granted, assumption that, whatever the precipitating cause of hospitalization, older people were close to death; that illness was an unavoidable correlate of ageing and it was hardly worth seeking to improve or cure their conditions. Warren discovered that cure, or at least considerable improvement, was possible but often more difficult than in younger people. Older people were more likely to suffer from multiple conditions and it was even more difficult than in younger people to disentangle the physical, mental, and social components of their problems. Some did not improve because they were depressed and lonely, with little to look forward to if they left the institution. Warren promoted physiotherapy and other forms of rehabilitation, inventing exercises to encourage movement in the previously bedridden. A high proportion of the patients were stroke victims whose paralysis was assumed to be irreversible. Doctors had been trained to confine them to bed to avoid the danger of another stroke. After rehabilitation two hundred of the initial patients were able to leave hospital to live with their families or in residential homes, after Warren interviewed family and friends to ensure that they would be released into suitable environments. A further one hundred and fifty patients were transferred to psychiatric wards.

[3] M. Warren, 'Care of the Chronic Aged Sick', *Lancet* (8 June 1948), 841–2.

Warren's innovative work came about partly due to institutional change following the 1929 Act. But the situation she encountered of so many bed-bound old people was also new. Until the inter-war years few older people, especially among the poorest, had long survived acute illness. They died relatively quickly from infection or pneumonia. Improved conditions in work-house hospitals since the First World War, especially improved standards of nursing and more effective treatment of infection, resulted in more older people surviving strokes and other acute episodes, but no one then knew what to do with them other than to leave them in bed. The introduction of sulphonamide drugs from the mid-1930s held out the prospect that still more would survive acute infection. Warren was tackling a new and extensive problem. She castigated her medical colleagues for overlooking a situation of great human and 'great economic importance'.[4]

Others in Britain in the 1930s were increasingly concerned with the health of old people, notably in Glasgow. Glasgow public health clinics, which had no equivalent in England, had an active role of ensuring that old people in need had speedy access to care, including referral to hospital, though conditions after referral were variable. Also in Glasgow, the closer association between teaching hospitals and old Poor Law hospitals after 1929 revealed to appalled consultants conditions at least as bad as those discovered by Warren.[5] In London, Trevor Howell, a general practitioner in Chelsea, encountering older patients, became puzzled as to how much ill health and of what kinds to expect among them, but could find no answers in the medical texts. He tackled the problem by comparing the condition of his patients with that of men in the nearby Chelsea Hospital for ex-servicemen. These Chelsea pensioners underwent medical examination before entering the 'hospital', which was in fact a residential home, usually at later ages, and were generally active and independent. They provided a possible measure of 'normal' fitness in old age. Howell's research was in progress at the opening of the Second World War.

THE SECOND WORLD WAR

At the beginning of the war, the Emergency Medical Service was established to co-ordinate health institutions, public and private, nationwide under official

---

[4] M. Warren, 'Care of the Chronic Sick: A Case for Treating Chronic Sick in Blocks in a General Hospital', *British Medical Journal*, 2 (25 Dec. 1943), 822; 'Geriatrics: A Medical, Social and Economic Problem' *Practitioner*, 157 (1946), 384–90; 'The Evolution of Geriatric Care', *Geriatrics*, 3 (1948), 42–50.

[5] Professor Sir Ferguson Anderson, interviewed by Pat Thane. Transcript in possession of the Wellcome Unit for the History of Medicine, University of Glasgow. Also interviewed by Professor Margot Jefferys, copy with National Life History Collection, National Sound Archive of the British Library. Sir Ferguson Anderson, 'Geriatrics', in G. McLachlan (ed.), *Improving the Common Weal: Aspects of Scottish Health Services 1900–98* (Edinburgh, 1985), 373–7.

control to ensure efficient provision for the victims of the expected bombing and other casualties. On the outbreak of war 140,000 patients, mostly aged and chronic sick, were discharged from hospital within just two days, some to unsuitable private homes, others to distant public assistance institutions, to make room for the expected war casualties. Others who needed hospital treatment were removed from waiting lists. The majority of the beds thus freed remained empty for at least the following nine months and, throughout the war, the need for hospital beds never matched the initial estimates.[6] Nevertheless, this prioritization of what the Ministry of Health called 'potential effectives' over old people continued throughout the war and still in 1946 older people often could not secure necessary medical treatment and care.[7] Mortality rose, particularly among older people in institutions. A few were fortunate, where the upheaval drew the attention of sympathetic doctors to the problems of older people. For example, L. Z. Cosin was Medical Superintendent at Orsett Lodge Hospital in Essex, previously a Poor Law hospital, when a number of old people were transferred from London to join the long-stay patients already in the hospital. Cosin encountered conditions similar to those experienced by Warren and was equally shocked. Patients were seldom visited by doctors and their medical notes often did not include a diagnosis, other than the reason for admission which might have taken place many years previously. He used exercise and massage to help the bedridden to walk.[8]

Few yet benefited from such work. In 1942 the National Council of Social Service reported that 'it is felt generally that many pensioners go without medical assistance or do not ask for it soon enough'.[9] Old people, and many younger ones, often had expectations of their health as low as those of the professionals. An official investigation of the condition of a sample of pensioners receiving Public Assistance in 1944 rated 39 per cent of them as in 'good health'. Some of these were described as follows:

Has rheumatoid arthritis and is almost helpless.
Had a stroke six years ago and another eighteen months back. She is very frail.
Owing to septic foot has been forced to give up work. Daughter and hospital cannot do anything for him.
Failing eyesight caused by sugar diabetes. Daily injections and special diet.
Had to give up work owing to bronchitis and myocardial degeneration.
Much crippled by rheumatism (hospital treatment).
Suffering from anaemia and a cancer growth.[10]

---

[6] B. Abel-Smith, *The Hospitals 1800–1948* (London, 1964), 424–30.

[7] J. Fogerty, 'Growing Old in England, 1878–1948', Ph.D. thesis (Australian National University, Canberra, 1992), 153.

[8] Cosin, interviewed by Margot Jefferys, in National Sound Archive. M. Jefferys, 'Lionel Cosin (1910–1994): A Pioneer Geriatrician who Thrived on Controversy', *Generations Review*, 4/3 (Sept. 1994), 2–4. [9] Fogerty, 'Growing Old', 148.

[10] Ibid. 157–9.

To be classified as in 'poor' health required the pensioner to be bedridden.

The chief providers of medical care for older working-class people under the National Insurance system were overworked 'panel' doctors. One London doctor was reported to be dealing with thirty to forty cases an hour, another with sixty. A third had spent two hours in his surgery, in the first dealing with twenty-five panel patients, in the second with six private cases.[11] Those who were not covered by National Insurance, including most women, were entitled only to still hastier treatment under the Poor Law, unless they could afford to pay for a doctor. Those who could not, might buy patent or herbal medicines or, frequently, neglect serious problems.

That the needs of older people took lower priority than those of the young was taken for granted. Even the Beveridge Report of 1942, the blueprint for the post-war Welfare State, asserted: 'It is *dangerous* to be in any way lavish to old age until adequate provision has been assured for all other vital needs, such as the prevention of disease and the adequate nutrition of the young' (my emphasis).[12]

SHELDON AND THE INVESTIGATION OF 'NORMAL' AGEING

At this time almost all of the limited number of studies of the (ill) health of older people were of those already receiving medical treatment. Almost nothing was known of the 'normal' health potential of older people; to what degree and in what ways, if at all, old age was unavoidably associated with ill health, or whether certain conditions were specific to, or more prevalent in, old age. Nor was there any clear picture of how much ill health among older (or indeed younger) people went undetected and unreported. There were indications that the extent was great. Doctors who examined 1,001 pensioners living in Glasgow tenements in 1946 could find only twenty-nine without ailments. Almost half were suffering from more than one condition. Two hundred and ninety-five had cardiovascular, and one hundred and eighty-one had pulmonary, diseases; only four hundred and eight were thought fit enough to care for themselves.[13]

J. H. Sheldon's survey in 1945–7 of a representative sample of older people in Wolverhampton[14] was funded by the Nuffield Foundation to survey the health of old people living in their own homes. Wolverhampton was a town of average size, with a mixed economy. In a sensitive and thoughtful survey, by the standard of the time, Sheldon was impressed by the generally good health and level of activity of the old people he surveyed in contrast with those he had encountered during twenty years of medical practice. He commented, 'One of the dominant impressions formed during the survey was of their almost

---

[11] Fogerty, 'Growing Old', 156–7.
[12] Cmd 6404, *Social Insurance and Allied Services* (1942), 92.
[13] Fogerty, 'Growing Old', 170.   [14] See pp. 408–11.

incredible determination and "guts".'[15] In the light of his previous experience, however, his expectations were low. He classified the health of 24.5 per cent of the sample as 'normal plus', 46.2 per cent as 'normal', and 29.3 per cent as 'subnormal'. This classification was, as he admitted, impressionistic, based on interview, observation, and discussion with the GP and/or sometimes family and friends of the old person, but not on physical examination. 'Normal' was defined as 'led for the most part an active life, with retention of their faculties and without undue emotional disturbance'.[16]

Sheldon found to his surprise that only 2.5 per cent of the sample were confined to bed, 8.5 per cent to their houses, 22.5 per cent to the immediate neighbourhood. The numbers who were confined increased with age, and were few before age 70. Many had little contact with doctors. He concluded that old age in the ordinary sense of the words began to show itself 'in most cases at about the age of seventy and thereafter becomes increasingly frequent'.[17] Before age seventy, ailments seemed much the same as in the remainder of the adult population. Thereafter what Sheldon described as 'specific problems of old age' emerged: 'weakness, vertigo, spondylitis, difficulty with traffic and loss of confidence', a list which suggests the blend of psychological, social, and medical conditions which characterized the experience of old age and also medical discourse about it.

Sheldon met some impressive old people:

A woman of eighty has reared six children as a widow, earning her own living at the same time. She now looks after her son, who is a permanent invalid and does all the housework, the cooking and the shopping.

And:

A man of 95 began life as a flying-trapeze artist and later worked as a boilermaker for fifty years. He is now the centre of a large and devoted family—and has seventy five living descendants. He lives at home and does not go out much, but does all the repairs in the house and stood up by preference throughout the interview.[18]

He found that women exhibited poorer health than men although they lived longer. They were more likely than men to be housebound or restricted in mobility due to rheumatism, bladder, and foot ailments, but they had 'a more tenacious hold on life'. They were often suffering the legacy of childbirth in poor conditions, but they were less likely than men to be confined to bed with minor ailments, and they were more lively and vigorous. Sheldon concluded that this was because women did not 'retire' but carried on with housework, rarely thinking of giving up before their late seventies.

Of the total sample (of 583 old people) one hundred and twenty-one had received no medical attention for three years or more, seven had never seen

---

[15] J. H. Sheldon, *The Social Medicine of Old Age* (Oxford, 1948), 188.
[16] Ibid. 117.   [17] Ibid.   [18] Ibid. 35.

a doctor in their lives, another seven not for more than thirty years. This might have meant either that they had suffered no illness, or that real problems went unattended. Sheldon took the optimistic view and judged their appearance healthy. This might have been correct; his expectations were limited by his past experience of encountering unfit old people in his medical practice. An important finding was that very many were seriously disabled or disadvantaged not by major illnesses but by problems which were, in principle, minor and curable: bad feet, defective vision and hearing, borderline incontinence. Too many had poor eyesight but did not have spectacles of their own due to cost. Sheldon decided that 'the most important cause is ignorance of the individual nature of spectacles—no less than ten per cent obtain them in haphazard ways—as by a gift or after the decease of a relative'. Or they were bought cheaply in chain stores, without adequate testing or awareness about how the eyes might change over time. One person explained: 'The glasses are all right; it's my eyes that have gone weak—I've got too old for glasses'.[19] Sheldon found that 'A very large proportion of old people are in the habit of using spectacles which at the best are almost useless and at the worst harmful.'[20] One woman of 70 used her late father's glasses, which were prescribed for him at hospital twenty years before. 'She says she "can hardly see through them", but "has to manage".' Hearing aids were rare and the quality available to poor people was low. Only fourteen of the sample had a full set of teeth, but Sheldon pointed out that 'the individuals now in the sample had passed in middle life through a phase of medical opinion in which the wholesale extraction of teeth was advised . . . the figures therefore do not in themselves give a true indication of the natural state of the teeth in old age'.[21] Lack of teeth did not appear to correlate with poor health as precisely as prevailing medical opinion believed.

Only twenty of the sample seemed undernourished and Sheldon judged that this was mainly because they had difficulty in shopping. The mental health of the old people was generally good, so far as it could be judged from interviews, and certainly much better than he had experienced among old people in institutions. Sheldon concluded that when old people seemed depressed or apathetic it was generally due to loneliness, economic anxieties, poor health, or limited mobility; again, it was potentially curable.[22]

Sheldon was well aware of the limitations of his study and was convinced of the need for further work to establish what was 'normal' in old age, just as the new specialty of paediatrics had established what was normal for each stage of childhood. He concluded that so little was known about the distinctive characteristics of old people that it was 'premature' to speak of a specialty of geriatrics. He emerged convinced of the importance of enabling people to live in their accustomed homes for as long as possible, for

---

[19] Sheldon, *Social Medicine*, 85.   [20] Ibid. 76.   [21] Ibid. 53.   [22] Ibid. 122.

'rehabilitation, which is so valuable and necessary in the treatment of many hospital patients, is not so necessary for old people living at home, for they subject themselves to a continuous process of what one can only call "auto-rehabilitation" '.[23]

THE NATIONAL HEALTH SERVICE

Sheldon's survey was published in 1948, on the eve of the inauguration of the National Health Service (NHS). At that time, the chronic sick, most of them old people, occupied some 70,000 hospital beds. There were great variations in their periods of stay in hospital. In Birmingham the mean duration of stay for female chronic patients was thirty-seven months. The national average was two hundred and sixty days. At Orsett Lodge Cosin had it down to fifty-two days. He had devised a system of 'progressive patient care' which focused upon rehabilitation and preparation for functioning outside the hospital almost immediately acute treatment was complete. Old people who could not manage after discharge could be readmitted. Some criticized this system as efficient rather than patient-friendly but, not surprisingly, it appealed to some senior figures in the Health Service. In 1950 Cosin became consultant geriatrician at the Cowley Rd Hospital, Oxford, where he continued to innovate, becoming a respected figure in the growing, international world of geriatrics.[24]

In 1947 Warren, Howell, Cosin, and Lord Amulree (an administrative medical officer at the Ministry of Health, who was shortly to take up a consultant post in geriatric medicine at University College Hospital, London) were among the leaders in forming what became the British Geriatrics Society. This worked to promote improved medical services for old people, and research and training of medical professionals to care for them. Its members gave advice to the Ministry and were also members of the committee which produced for the British Medical Association (BMA) in 1948 a report on 'The Care and Treatment of the Elderly and Infirm'. This pointed out that those over 60 were not an undifferentiated mass, but varied greatly in their condition and needs. It summarized the dismal state of their treatment at the time, the likely costs for the health service of the growing numbers of old people, and recommended the establishment of co-ordinated medical services based in general hospitals, with comprehensive assessment and rehabilitation facilities and linkages with other medical and community services. It asserted that 'the care of the chronic sick requires complete and revolutionary change', designed among other things to ensure that 'no patient shall be regarded as irremediable while still capable of further improvement'.[25] Those who did require long-stay care should have a friendly and homely environment, in small units with access to outdoors and entertainment, close to friends and relatives.

---

[23] Ibid. 190.   [24] Cosin: Jefferys interview.

[25] T. Howell, *Our Advancing Years: An Essay on the Modern Problems of Old Age* (London, 1976), 138.

When the NHS came into being, it offered no clear guidelines for the treatment of older people. There was continuing controversy as to whether geriatrics should exist as a specialism and uncertainty about the boundaries between the social and medical problems of older people and how they interacted. Professor A. P. Thomson of Birmingham University medical school protested in 1949 that there was nothing distinctive about ill health in old age and that all age groups should be considered solely in terms of their illness. This view was widely shared, including by Lord Amulree, who favoured the establishment of geriatric units to ensure that the needs of older people were not neglected, but not geriatrics as a specialism. He established a geriatric unit at University College Hospital in London. He retained a part-time post at the Ministry of Health, visited progressive geriatric centres in Britain and elsewhere in Europe, and encouraged improved practice under the NHS.

GERIATRICS IN SCOTLAND

There was less dispute in Scotland, where geriatrics was more readily accepted and clinical posts sooner established. This was partly because it was already established in one important centre, Glasgow. Also there was less resistance in the Royal Society of Physicians of Edinburgh than in England. Because of the lesser separation between teaching and local authority hospitals, Scottish medical students were more likely to encounter geriatric patients. In 1960, despite resistance from English members, the Scots formed a separate branch of the British Geriatics Society on the grounds that they worked in different conditions, under different legislation from doctors in England and Wales.

The further development of geriatrics in Scotland owed much to the work of W. Ferguson Anderson, who had trained in Glasgow before the war and had encountered the appalling conditions of old people in old Poor Law institutions. He returned to work in Glasgow in 1952 as Consultant Physician and Advisor on Diseases of Old Age and Chronic Sickness, after some years working in Wales. He found that conditions had worsened with the coming of the NHS. The public health clinics had been closed. More hospitals had become acute hospitals and were reluctant to take old people. It was assumed that the chronically ill would be cared for at home by the GP and would be admitted to hospital only if acutely ill. But even then, claimed Anderson, 'they would have to wait because they were all for younger preference. If you'd one empty bed and you had a (seriously ill case) of 28 and a stroke of 75, nature demanded that you look at the one of 28.' Anderson fiercely resisted this 'natural' assumption and was reinforced by a visit to Marjorie Warren in 1952. He observed her work for about a month. He thought her 'a wonderful woman . . . she had thrilled me by showing me that the diagnosis of old people was difficult because there was a list of diseases nearly always, not one. And you had to disentangle the physical, mental and social components of these ill-nesses and this was what she was adept at . . . she wasn't well regarded in her own hospital because they hadn't the insight to see what a brilliant woman this was'.[26]

Anderson was convinced that the only way to protect older people and ensure that they got treatment, was to give them special entry to a unit of their own so they did not have to compete for beds with the young, 'because if they stood in line with the young they would never get in . . . the elderly deserved a bit of justice too . . . there was always going to be a young person with an acute illness in a city like Glasgow where beds were short . . . if geriatrics hadn't been invented it would have had to have been invented because they would never have got into hospital. They would just have to die at home.'[27] Still, he claimed as late as 1958, that the Glasgow teaching hospitals had 'a rigidly enforced if never officially recognized ban on the admission of patients over the age of sixty-five'.[28] This was Anderson's main reason for establishing hospital geriatric units in each of the five hospital districts in Scotland.

This led to competition among GPs to get 'their' old people into the few beds in the unit. Anderson started a system of 'home assessments' in order to select patients, an idea borrowed from E. B. Brook of St Helier Hospital, Carshalton, another independent innovator in geriatrics working in an old Poor Law hospital, whom Anderson also visited. Anderson was trying to estab-lish in Glasgow the best practice devised elsewhere. Home assessment required the consultant to visit the patient at home to assess his or her con-dition and the kind of support available on release from hospital. Anderson and his colleagues carried out hundreds of such visits in the often horrific conditions of the city with the worst housing in north-western Europe. Anderson was initially quite uncertain whether the medical conditions of old age were distinctive, and if so, in what respects. Convinced, like Sheldon, of the importance of studying 'normal' old people at home as well as those in medical care, he worked closely with Nairn Cowan, who established the famous Rutherglen Centre for Older People in 1953. GPs in the densely crowded dis-trict of Rutherglen in Glasgow were asked to refer to the Centre people aged 55 and over with minor complaints who would not normally visit a special-ist. Anderson, Cowan, and others gave thorough physical examinations, car-rying out no more than five in a morning, and taking detailed case histories. They discovered, above all, how much investigation was needed to establish the medical needs of older people: 'the symptoms are much more insidious . . . the older people tend to have more than one thing wrong with them, so one gets interwoven with the other'.[29] They found, as Marjorie Warren had

---

[26] Anderson: Jefferys interview.   [27] Ibid.

[28] 'Foresthall Hospital Glasgow, 1958–1964', Extracts from the Memoirs of Bernard Isaacs, Apr. 1994. In possession of archive of Greater Glasgow Health Board, University of Glasgow.

[29] Anderson: Jeffreys interview.

done, that bed-rest, the commonest recommendation for old people, was especially inappropriate, for joints stiffened and limbs weakened faster than among younger people. Older people quickly got bedsores and internal problems as a result.[30] Anderson encouraged younger doctors to attend the clinics to enable them to build up knowledge of 'the clinical picture of an active healthy, elderly person'. Otherwise from their hospital work 'they may have the impression that all old people are ill or depressed. They may also treat physiological changes accompanying ageing as if they were pathological.'[31] Like Sheldon, Anderson was impressed by how many older people were healthy. He became convinced that 'chronological age is almost meaningless and many individuals are extremely fit until over ninety'.[32]

Anderson and Cowan published a string of research papers defining the characteristics of old age and forms of treatment,[33] emphasizing the interaction of the medical and the social and the importance of treating apparently mundane conditions such as bad feet in order to improve the lives of older people and reduce their demands on medical services. Anderson gave the example of a woman who was bedridden, apparently deaf and thought to be suffering from mild dementia. Once her severe corns were treated, the impacted wax removed from her ears, and her severe constipation dealt with she was active again.[34] He was convinced that much illness and disability in old age was remediable and that active life could be prolonged, but that it required close collaboration of medical doctors with other professionals such as social workers and chiropodists. Anderson concluded that certain principles should guide geriatric medicine:

Older people are happier and healthier in their own homes if they are fit enough to be there and so desire.
They are ill not due to advancing age but due to illness.
They have an altered physiology which may render the presentation of disease atypical.
Pathology when it occurs is commonly multiple.
Older people have an immense potential for recovery.
Their altered physiology might lead to impaired hearing, diminishing sensations of pain and perception of temperature.
There were real physiological differences in old people. The two greatest changes were loss of elasticity in skin, bone, arteries, lungs, brain and loss of reserve function in heart, liver, lungs, kidneys, brain.

[30] In the 1960s the problem of 'normal ageing' also preoccupied the major, rival, Institutes of Gerontology in Kiev and Baltimore. Sir Ferguson Anderson, 'An Historical Overview of Geriatric Medicine', in M. J. Pathy (ed.), *Principles and Practice of Geriatric Medicine* (London, 1985), 7–13.

[31] W. F. Anderson, 'Life's Equities after 65', *Transactions and Studies of the College of Physicians of Philadelphia*, 5th ser. 6/4 (1984), 263–73.   [32] Ibid. 266.

[33] Between the early 1950s and mid-1970s Anderson authored one book, co-edited two, was single author of 23 contributions to books and 69 articles, co-authored eight articles with Cowan, and co-authored a number of others all on aspects of geriatrics. List of publications provided by Sir Ferguson Anderson.

[34] W. Ferguson Anderson and Bernard Isaacs (eds.), *Current Achievements in Geriatrics* (London, 1964), 2–4.

Presenting symptoms altered making accurate diagnosis difficult.
It was necessary to assess the home environment.[35]

It was also important to examine the apparently healthy in order to catch
disease in its early stages. Regular check-ups were more important in the old
than the young and middle-aged. Depression might be present as insomnia
or constipation. Multiple diseases might lead doctors to prescribe too many
harmfully interacting drugs and to compound the harm by prescribing them
for too long. These were new insights, shared with other geriatricians. They
still formed the fundamentals of British geriatrics in the 1990s.[36] Still, in the
early 1960s, Anderson was concerned that it was not yet possible to reach an
accurate and complete diagnosis of cerebro-vascular disease and that numerous neurological disorders of older people were still undefined. Still too many
not very elderly patients were 'labelled on very flimsy clinical evidence'.
Apparently minor symptoms which could warn of the possibility of a stroke
were often overlooked.

Anderson achieved important advances in Glasgow. They were much
needed. The problems to be overcome were still immense. Their extent was
vividly described by one of Anderson's young assistants, Bernard Isaacs, later
also an eminent geriatrician, as he described his first encounter with the chronic
wards of what had once been a Poor Law hospital in Glasgow, in 1958.

I stood in the day room of Ward C8 in utter disbelief at the sight. I was overwhelmed
with horror, numbed with sorrow. Tears rose to my eyes. I had not expected to see
a cheerful picture here, but the mass of misery and degradation which greeted me
lay far beyond expectation, outside the realm of my previous experience, at a level
of irresponsibility, disorganization, neglect and humiliation I had not dreamed existed
in a democratic egalitarian society.

The dayroom was not a large room, perhaps six metres square. Its main item of
furniture was a great grimy black stove, which stood in the centre of the room. It
emitted very little heat, but evil smelling wisps of smoke escaped from cracks and
seams in its structure, blackened the walls and ceiling and set the inhabitants of the
room coughing and spluttering.

Bunched around this stove, sitting on rickety wooden kitchen chairs were some
thirty or forty old men of terrifying appearance . . . Their countenances expressed a
kind of dying rage, a wrath that had been replaced by despair, now become lifeless,
unmoving, as though carved out of cold, grey stone.

The bunch of crouched, unmoving bodies, silent apart from the occasional wrack-
ing cough or the switch of spittle into the stove . . . were dressed in what answered
for blue jackets and blue trousers . . . The clothes had suffered from the ravages of
ageing as bitterly as had the old men whose feeble bodies they now covered; or,
more correctly left uncovered. The jackets were shrunken, crumpled, shapeless, devoid
of all buttons, thickly stained with dried soup, saliva, caked tobacco. The trousers,

---

[35] Anderson, 'Historical Overview', 8–9.
[36] B. Isaacs, *The Challenge of Geriatric Medicine* (Oxford, 1992).

unsupported by belt or braces, devoid of all fly buttons, remained in position only by virtue of a chance fit between the circumference of the garment and that of the wearer's waist. This piece of good fortune was rare. In most cases the trousers had shrunk even more than the patient. With difficulty they covered the upper half of the wearer's legs, in monstrous imitation of Bermuda shorts; but they abandoned all effort to conceal his abdomen and his genitals were exposed for all to see. The more slender patients wore trousers which were many sizes too large and which fell to the floor if they attempted to stand.

The blue jacket and trousers were virtually all that the patients wore. There were no vests, no shirts, no ties, no underpants, no pullovers and cardigans.

Thus 'dressed' the old men queued out of doors in all weathers for their unappetizing meals. The remainder of their experience in the institution was equally degrading. The women, who were in separate wards, fared no better, though they did not have to stand outdoors before their meals. The condition of the bedbound was worst of all:

Most were appallingly malnourished and emaciated. Many lay in urine and faeces, waiting to be cleaned up. Pressure sores were numerous, many of them deep and gangrenous.

He found that the General Hospitals still routinely refused to admit old people, though GPs could persuade them to take their better-off older patients:

General practitioners who worked in the middle class suburbs of the city enjoyed an alternative means of having their patients accepted by the wards of the voluntary hospitals. This route was via the private golf courses which surrounded the city. There the practitioners, especially those who had done their house jobs in the Teaching Hospitals, developed friendships with the leading hospital consultants, played a round of golf, enjoyed a glass of whisky in the clubhouse, invited them to see a patient privately.[37]

Isaacs's fellow medical practitioners were convinced that the problems of geriatrics were caused by neglect by families, 'feather-bedded' by the welfare state. Home visits taught him a more complex reality. He found that old people who were neglected and ill-treated had often ill-treated their children:

I learned that nice young people become nice old people; while nasty young people become nasty old people. And it became apparent that many of the old people whom I was called out to see had been nasty young people. They had grown up in the worst slums in Europe, a brutal world of poverty, squalor, drunkenness, overcrowding, prostitution, violence, incest. Many had preserved their decency and their morality in these appalling circumstances; but many others had been dragged down by the prevailing mores of their society, and had been incapable of providing their families with the love and stability which I had known. The result was that when the parents reached old age, the children did not feel the reciprocal bond expected of them.[38]

---

[37] 'Extracts from the Memoirs of Bernard Isaacs', prepared 1994, MS Greater Glasgow Health Board Archives, University of Glasgow.   [38] Ibid. 52.

Nevertheless, many old people in Glasgow lived contentedly with adult children: 'In between the extremes was a range of interpersonal reactions which reflected a lifetime of relationships.'[39] As a consultant from 1961 to 1964 he was, with difficulty, able to make some improvements, for example in the clothing of the old men, but the conditions remained appalling. Around the same time Peter Townsend found similar misery in Old People's Homes in England, the 'last refuges', also often former workhouses.[40]

In 1963 Ferguson Anderson was still pleading with Glasgow University for adequate funding for geriatric research to alleviate these tragic conditions:

The aim of such research is not to make the endeavour of prolonging life but to try to conquer the long, eventually bedridden state of many, particularly female, elderly people. Such patients by slow degrees sink to a state of mere existence, without brain, and occupying a great army of wonderful nurses of varying knowledge but of unfailing kindness and humanity. I am convinced that this array of long-term patients could be substantially reduced and the period of active intelligent life prolonged.[41]

All too little had changed.

BRITISH GERIATRICS UNDER THE NATIONAL HEALTH SERVICE

In 1953–4 the Ministry of Health surveyed services for older people and the chronically ill throughout Britain. It found that in a few places hospital turnover had increased and waiting lists had been reduced, but they were few. This occurred where there were specialist geriatric units staffed with remedial therapists as well as medical house officers to ensure prompt assessment and initiation of both acute and rehabilitative care; where patients were directly referred by GPs rather than after admission for acute illness; when entry to hospital was preceded by a home assessment; where the service was managed by a full-time geriatric consultant. Such places were few. Improvement was slow where geriatric care was controlled by those uncommitted to it. Provision was often best where an individual took the initiative, such as Warren, Anderson, or Cosin. A study by Richard Titmuss and Brian Abel-Smith for the Guillebaud Committee of 1956 concluded that 'by and large the older age groups were currently receiving a lower standard of service than the main body of consumers and that there were substantial areas of unmet need among the elderly'.[42]

In Britain in 1962–3 around 900,000 old people were bedridden or unable to walk unaided outside their place of residence; 140,000 were in institutions,

---

[39] Ibid.   [40] P. Townsend, *The Last Refuge* (London, 1964).

[41] W. F. Anderson, 'Memorandum on the Need for a Research Unit in Geriatric Medicine', Glasgow University Archives, Files of the Principal, 1963.

[42] Ministry of Health, *Report of the Committee of Enquiry into the Cost of the National Health Service* (Guillebaud Report), Cmd. 9663 (1956), 40.

750,000 in private households. There were still high rates of unreported ill-ness. Doctors continued to attribute symptoms to ageing rather than to dis-ease, leaving many treatable conditions undiagnosed (as they continued to do in the 1990s).[43] Old people complained that their GPs never examined them. Most doctors still assumed that past age 70 most people had only inactive lives ahead. There were few signs that younger doctors were more sympa-thetic than their older colleagues; if anything the reverse was true.

This is not surprising when we examine the textbooks available to them. The widely used *Our Advancing Years: An Essay on the Modern Problems of Old Age*: by Trevor Howell, first published in 1953 and going through a number of subsequent editions, declared:

Of course the basic fact is that old people consume more of our national wealth then they produce . . . in fact from the economic point of view most old people are parasites.[44]

Whilst encouraging improved prevention, rehabilitation, and care, Howell commented on the need to be aware of old people's 'lack of response to logical reasoning, the mental processes of later life are so strongly coloured by past experience, by suspicion, by previous modes of thought and by subconscious dread of the future, that rational trains of thought are almost impossible . . . old people are naturally suspicious'. Howell's *Old Age: Some Practical Points in Geriatrics*, first published in 1944, reaching its third edition in 1973, again gen-eralized pessimistically about 'old people':

the aged do not readily make new contacts . . . they dwell more and more in the past . . . the process of learning if not impossible in old age . . . is extremely laborious and most fatiguing to the mind.

Though he stressed, 'we must never forget that the aged are human beings like ourselves, not a race of creatures apart.'[45]

A similar incapacity to be as positive about old age as the evidence seemed to warrant characterized other texts. *Social and Medical Problems of the Elderly*, edited by Kenneth Hazell, first published in 1960, in its fourth edition by 1976, insisted upon the need for a positive and active image of old age, whilst taking for granted that different age groups could not comfortably mix socially; that older men disliked the company of older women; that neither was sexually attractive. It emphasized the loneliness and poverty of old age and described 'the care of the elderly, covering over seven million people', as 'a major social problem'.[46] Other influential textbooks promoted similar negative images of old people. This may explain why it was found in the USA in the 1960s and 1970s that medical students became *less* sympathetic to geriatric patients in the course of their training. The development of

---

[43] Morag Farquhar and Ann Bowling, 'Older People and their GPs', *Generations Review*, 1/1 (Dec. 1991), 7–9.   [44] Howell, *Our Advancing Years* (1976 edn.), 13.

[45] T. Howell, *Old Age: Some Practical Points in Geriatrics* (London, 1944, 3rd edn., 1973), 1–4.

[46] K. Hazell, *Social and Medical Problems of the Elderly* (London, 1960; 4th edn., 1976), 15, 311.

geriatrics as a specialism may have had ambiguous effects. It enhanced the care of older patients, but it encouraged some doctors to take even less interest in them, consigning them to the specialist care of geriatricians alone.

Initially, psychological theory was no more positive. Cumming and Henry's influential *Growing Old: The Process of Disengagement* (1961) erected into a general theory the observation that many older people withdrew from social engagement. This, the study concluded, was the normal and necessary process of adjustment to ageing. But it came to be questioned whether 'disengagement' was not rather a response to rejection by younger people, and whether it indeed characterized a high proportion of 'normal' older people. In the 1990s it was challenged by the more optimistic 'activity theory' that 'the majority of older persons maintain fairly constant amounts of activity or social participation, the amount depending more upon past life style and socio-economic forces than upon age itself'.[47]

Similarly, later textbooks in geriatric medicine, such as those of Bernard Isaacs, were more unambiguously positive, insisting that:

- The word 'geriatric' is not a noun and does not describe a person. Hospitals do not treat 'geriatrics' any more than schools teach 'paediatrics'.
- When we talk of 'the elderly' we generalize. When we talk of 'elderly people' we particularize.
- There are three stages of life after retirement . . . in the Bronze Age the body is fit and the mind is whole. The world and its sunshine are explored and enjoyed. In the Iron Age the body is fettered but the mind is free. In the Stone Age both body and spirit are rock.
- The characteristic feature of old people is diversity. There is no homogeneous mass called 'the elderly'.[48]

In the 1970s Ferguson Anderson divided old age into two phases, before and after the age of 75. By 1984, he revised this upward to seventy-nine.[49] Those in the younger phase, he believed, 'should be regarded as a resource and use found for their skills, knowledge and experience, if they desire them. The aged in contrast in many instances need assistance of various kinds.'[50] Sheldon, almost forty years earlier had placed the boundary at age 70. The contrast represented real change in the capacities of successive cohorts of older people, which probably owed more to socio-economic than to medical change.

Anderson established himself internationally as a leading geriatrician, though he is strikingly absent from the English geriatricians' surveys of the origins of 'British' geriatrics. He became the first Professor of Geriatrics in Britain at Glasgow in 1964 and was knighted in 1974. He was able to build status for geriatrics in Scotland more readily than was possible in England.[51]

[47] R. Havinghurst 'Successful Aging' in R. H. Williams, C. Tibbits, and W. Donahue (eds) *Process of Aging*, vol. 1 (Chicago), 311–15.
[48] Isaacs, *The Challenge*, 5–7.   [49] Anderson, 'Life's Equities'.
[50] Anderson, 'Historical Overview', 7.   [51] Anderson, Jefferys interview.

But still he had difficulty. Even in Glasgow 'there was a prejudice against those who worked with old folk as second-rate'. He felt that he got away with it because he had such an outstanding record, with so many fellowships and prizes that he could not easily be dismissed.[52] By 1965 a substantial amount of geriatric training was obligatory for Glasgow medical students.[53] Only in 1976 did a BMA working party, chaired by Ferguson Anderson, urge such training in all medical schools, as the World Health Organization, in a report also chaired by Anderson, had done two years earlier.[54]

Acute care improved with the increase in expenditure on hospital services under Conservative and Labour governments in the 1960s. District General Hospitals, in principle, replaced the old division between acute and chronic hospitals in England and Wales. These provided the full range of services for populations of 100,000 to 150,000; geriatric services were specifically to be included. The Department of Health and Social Security encouraged the appointment of geriatric consultants. The number of posts grew and by the 1970s there were hospital-based geriatric units in all health districts in England and Wales, though often still in outdated buildings and understaffed.[55]

COMMUNITY CARE

One cause which united the Scottish and English geriatricians and NHS administrators throughout the years from 1945 was the desirability of keeping older people at home for as long as possible. This can be interpreted as a desire for cheaper services and as placing the burden of care on the family, especially on women, rather than the state. This was not the intention of the geriatricians, or of the social researchers, who recognized that families did a great deal for older people and needed support for this work, from district nurses, health visitors, deliveries of hot meals, home helps, and social services, all of which were slow to be made available even for older people living alone. Professionals were convinced that the surest guarantee of a fit and active old age was to retain independence for as long as possible—echoing folk wisdom through the ages. They emphasized that old people were not necessarily a burden on their relatives and friends, but were active contributors to their families and communities, except for a minority of unfortunate cases or for a short period of decline before death.

[52] Anderson, Jefferys interview.

[53] W. F. Anderson, 'Education in Geriatric Medicine', *Annals of the Academy of Medicine of Singapore* (1986), 148.

[54] British Medical Association Board of Science and Education, *Report of the Working Party on Services for the Elderly* (London, 1976). W. F. Anderson, Chairman, *Planning and Organization of Geriatric Services*, World Health Organization Technical Report, series no. 548 (1974).

[55] W. H. Barker, *Adding Years to Life* (Baltimore, 1987), 20–32.

The need for support in the community for those with and without sup-portive relatives was made clear by a survey in 1951 of thirty-nine old people admitted to a Liverpool hospital suffering from malnutrition. Not illness or inability to manage were responsible for their condition, but poverty, isola-tion, poor living conditions, and inadequate cooking facilities. At least fifteen of thirty-one patients were trying to survive only on the inadequate Old Age Pension. All but three were anaemic due to lack of protein; nineteen had scurvy, all but two cases because they could not afford fresh fruit and vegetables. Another had false dementia due to Vitamin B deficiency. A number suffered from incon-tinence which cleared up when they were given adequate food. A very few, not included in the survey, were suffering from 'extreme starvation' and died within a few days of admission. Half of the patients were discharged to the same unsatisfactory diets and living conditions that had caused their admis-sion, with no official attempt to help them.[56] Similar problems were discovered in Edinburgh and London.[57]

Improved community care services for old people became part of the elec-toral armoury of both Labour and Conservative parties from the mid-1950s, supported by official reports in the 1950s.[58] Action lagged behind the rhetoric, underpinned by largely unspoken scepticism about whether the costs of pre-vention, rehabilitation, community support, and treatment of old people would extend their active lives to a worthwhile extent in national cost-benefit terms. No one knew, but uninformed prejudice ruled. Certainly domiciliary services affecting children, such as health-visiting, grew more rapidly after 1948 than those specifically for older people, such as chiropody, which was not available free on the NHS. There were explicit assertions that helping old people too much would encourage filial irresponsibility. A survey of services published in 1976 concluded:

If the elderly person is living with relatives, especially children, the service is with-held on the assumption that the family will provide needed care. In other situations it would seem that even when family members cannot or will not provide care, the service is refused on the basis that they should do so. In practice, then, some author-ities are still guided by the principle of family responsibility as enunciated in 43rd Elizabeth.[59]

This was still the case in the 1990s.

[56] H. Fuld and K. V. Robinson, 'Malnutrition in the Elderly', *Lancet* (24 Oct. 1953), 860–4. Fogerty, 'Growing Old', 172.

[57] J. Williamson, I. H. Stoke *et al.*, 'Old People at Home: Their Unreported Needs', *Lancet* (23 May 1964), 1117. Royal College of Physicians of Edinburgh, *The Care of the Elderly in Scotland* (Edinburgh, 1963).

[58] *Report of the Committee of Enquiry into the Cost of the National Health Service* (Guillebaud Report), Cmd. 9663 (1956). *Report of the Committee on the Economic and Financial Problems of the Provision for Old Age* (Phillips Report), Cmd. 9333 (1951).

[59] R. Moroney, *The Family and the State: Considerations for Social Policy*, quoted R. Means and R. Smith, *The Development of Welfare Services for Elderly People* (London, 1985), 294.

MEDICAL KNOWLEDGE

The medical needs of older people were best provided for when they were shared with younger people. Free spectacles, dentures, and dental care were available as never before on the NHS after 1948; chiropody was not. From 1951 charges were gradually introduced and increased for the new services. Still in the 1960s, as a result of charges and lack of information to poorer older people about access to services, there were old people with poor eyesight but no spectacles, or wearing those fitted for someone else. Few with hearing problems had hearing aids; many needed but still did not receive chiropody treatment.[60]

Yet medical research made breakthroughs of especial value to older people, most notably the use of cardiac pacemakers from the 1960s, kidney dialysis from the late 1960s, coronary artery surgery from the 1970s, cataract, hip, and organ replacement surgery. Except for the birth-control pill, all of the major breakthroughs in medical technology from the 1950s to the 1990s had their most widespread impact on people past their fifties, and the further past their fifties the greater the impact. The growth after the Second World War of various forms of state subsidy for health services in many countries gradually made these advances widely available. However, from the 1970s the effects of economic recession in many countries, combined with increased demand due to increased awareness among old people of the treatments available and belief in their right to receive them, together with the potential growth in demand due to the growing numbers of older people, again raised publicly, at least in Britain, the question of age-based rationing of treatment. Whether rationing indeed became more prevalent at this time or had never been abandoned, remained, as it had always been, a secret of the medical profession. Greater publicity for incidents of rationing which came to light may have been an expression of greater assertiveness on the part of older people and their friends and relatives, promoted by mass media less deferential to professional groups than in the past.

Despite fears about the growing costs of increasingly high-tech medicine, reductions in some causes of death in older age groups—above all a drop in cardiovascular disorders from the late 1960s—owed hardly anything to medical advance, but rather to improved exercise and diet. Hypertension has been shown to respond to low-cost techniques and sometimes very ancient therapies, such as yoga, which induce relaxation and control over mind and body. At the other extreme were developments in medical technology to a point at which people could be kept technically 'alive' but hardly meaningfully functioning apparently indefinitely. In the 1990s these posed medicine with one of its greatest ethical dilemmas. The improvements in mortality rates from

---

[60] J. Tunstall, *Old and Alone* (London, 1966), 272–6.

some of the killer diseases at later ages—such as heart disease and strokes—were highly variable among similarly developed countries. Britain performed poorly in most of them and there were major regional variations within Britain—Scotland had a notably poor record in the mid-1990s as earlier.[61] This suggested scope for further improvement in Britain and elsewhere.

Awareness grew of the interaction of physical and mental illness with the environment: that poverty, bereavement, lack of status, and disability can lead to depression, which in Britain was known to afflict between 10 and 30 per cent of the older population in the 1990s. Yet counselling for older people was not readily available. Both outpatient and institutional services for older people with psychiatric or neurological disorders, though less appalling than before the Second World War, remained in most countries markedly inferior to other health care services.

In 1994 the Medical Research Council (MRC) pointed out trenchantly how persistently older people had been excluded from research, screening programmes, and treatment for medical conditions, for example breast and cervical cancer screening, admission to coronary care units, clinical trials for cancer therapy, coronary bypass surgery, hypertensive and thrombotic therapies—the very conditions most likely to afflict them. As the MRC put it: 'Many opportunities have been foregone to obtain baseline health status data and to improve or maintain the health of older people by their unfortunate exclusion from these studies'.[62] In consequence people died or were disabled at earlier ages than need have occurred and there was a serious deficiency of knowledge about how medical conditions and the effects of drug and other therapies might differ between older and younger patients, though the likelihood of major differences was strong. The MRC attributed these deficiencies largely to the fact that:

There is a view, unsubstantiated by research, which is pervasive among health and social service professionals and the population at large, including older people themselves, that elderly people benefit less from medical and surgical interventions than do younger age ones. This may in turn contribute to an attitude that older people are less deserving than younger people because they may be viewed in some respects as having less to offer society.[63]

The MRC queried whether:

the use of chronological age as a proxy for biological fitness, and the use of advanced age as the sole criterion for deciding whether or not a patient should receive a given healthcare intervention are appropriate . . . Using age rather than physiological

---

[61] K.-T. Khaw, 'Epidemiological Aspects of Ageing', *Philosophical Transactions of the Royal Society: Biological Sciences, Ageing: Science, Medicine and Society*, 352/1363 (29 Dec. 1997), 1829–1836.

[62] Medical Research Council, *The Health of the UK's Elderly People*, MRC Topic Review (London, 1994), 13.

[63] Ibid. 37.

status to determine the care given to an individual appears not to be based on solid foundations.[64]

In consequence, it was unknown whether the ageing of the population was associated with increased levels of illness, as was popularly believed, or whether the process of the onset of illness in old age was being delayed to later ages. The report pointed out that:

> It is a matter of profound concern that it is currently not possible to determine whether the health status of the older population has improved, deteriorated or remained the same during the past decades of mortality decline.[65]

The MRC urged the importance of change in all of these aspects of the conventional medical approach to older people for the purpose of extending understanding of the health and ill health, in order to maximize the fitness, and minimize the costs to society and the economy, especially the costs of health care, of an ageing population.

The outcome at the end of the twentieth century was the simultaneous emergence of the largest proportion of fit older people ever known and the largest number of chronically ill elderly people ever known. Older people might recover from acute medical problems which would have killed them in the past only to succumb to sometimes complex sets of chronic non-lethal disorders (such as Alzheimer's disease) for some of which relatively little could yet be done other than keeping them alive with diminishing functional capacity.

An irony of modern medicine is that the least valued medical specialism takes up most of general practitioners' time and fills most hospital beds (though only 2.5 per cent of old people were in hospital at any one time) at the end of the millennium, and funding is relatively sparse for research into the unglamorous conditions which fill them. Bernard Isaacs wrote in 1992, 'Geriatric medicine is the treatment of underprivileged patients by underprivileged doctors in underprivileged buildings'.[66] Some still argued against the existence of geriatrics as a specialism on the grounds that it singled out older patients for marginalization; but there remained the danger which had brought geriatrics into existence: that without it they might be wholly neglected.

CONCLUSION

The emergence of geriatric medicine over the twentieth century has been accompanied by a debate, which is still unresolved, as to whether it should exist. Some medical specialists argue that the medical needs of older people are not different from those of other age groups, others deny this; the MRC has trenchantly pointed out that so scanty is the research available in this field

---

[64] Medical Research Council, 39–40.   [65] Ibid. 23–6.   [66] Isaacs, *Challenge*, 3.

that it is impossible to know. Geriatricians such as Sir Ferguson Anderson and Bernard Isaacs argued that, whatever the facts about the medical needs of older people, it was essential to provide separate centres of care for them if they were not to continue persistently to be neglected in favour of younger people.

Clearly, as the MRC recognized in 1994, the medical treatment of older people was influenced at least as much by deeply rooted and widely held cultural assumptions about the capacities and social roles of older people as by clinical judgement; assumptions often shared by older people themselves. Some social scientists have argued that this low evaluation of older people in society is in part a product of the emergence of geriatrics itself, which they describe as the 'medicalization of old age', which together with other changes of the twentieth century such as the introduction of pensions and the spread of retirement they believe have increasingly defined old people as a separate and also an increasingly marginalized social group.[67] Such processes of change *may* have increased the salience of the cultural definition of old age as a separate stage of life, though such judgements may underestimate the awareness in previous centuries of the distinctiveness of old age. Whether the growth of geriatric medicine has contributed to the increasing marginalization of old people is even more questionable. It emerged very largely as a means to protect older people from the exclusion from medical care and treatment they had long experienced and was often accompanied by attempts by geriatricians to improve the lives of older people and to enhance the value accorded to them in British culture. That these have not been wholly successful—or wholly unsuccessful from the point of view of improved care and treatment—is not evidence that older people are more marginalized in the late twentieth century than 'before'. The contrary is more probable.

---

[67] Among others, P. Townsend, 'The Structured Dependency of the Elderly: A Creation of Social Policy in the Twentieth Century', *Ageing and Society*, 1 (1981). Alan Walker, 'Dependency and Old Age', *Social Policy and Administration*, 16 (1982). J. Macnicol, *The Politics of Retirement in Britain, 1878–1948* (Cambridge, 1998), 7–15.

23

'You're as Old as you Feel': Images and Self-Images of Older People at the end of the Millennium

It is commonly claimed in late twentieth-century Britain that in 'the past' old people were more respected and culturally less marginalized than in the present; that the modern world especially values youth, and far more than in 'the past', old people are stereotyped as decrepit, dependent burdens; that old women are regarded more negatively than old men; and that in other, distant, countries they do things differently and better and show more respect for elders.

But, as we have seen, in earlier centuries there was no single, benign, representation or set of conventional experiences of older men or women, but rather a variety of images, corresponding, though not always exactly, to the variety of human experience at later ages.[1] Changed perceptions of old age, from whatever source, were rarely simple responses to changes in experience. Representations of older people in the past have varied over time, not always in the direction of deterioration. At any one time there have been conflicting and competing discourses and representations of old women and old men. This is so in the present and expresses the varied subjective experiences of being old.[2]

Anthropological studies of older people 'elsewhere' suggest that even in Asian societies where older people are routinely given shelter, care, and ritualized expressions of respect, as in Western societies, they are accorded genuinely high status and respect when they can enforce it by command of material or cultural power or have won it through evident wisdom or past or present services to the community.[3] A study of ageing in less developed countries in the 1990s comments:

[1] See Chs. 2, 3, 4, 13.

[2] P. Thompson, C. Itzin, M. Abendstern, *I Don't Feel Old: Understanding the Experience of Later Life* (Oxford, 1990). Alice T. Day, *Remarkable Survivors: Insights into Successful Aging among Women* (Washington, 1991).

[3] P. A. Amos and S. Harrell (eds.), *Other Ways of Growing Old. Anthropological Perspectives* (Stanford, Calif., 1981). C. L. Fry *et al.*, *Aging in Culture and Society* (New York, 1980). Nancy Foner, *Ages in Conflict: A Cross-Cultural Perspective on Inequality between Old and Young* (London, 1984).

ageing is much more graceful if you have accumulated knowledge and economic resources (financial and otherwise) or have access to a pool of resources provided by the community. Being old is also related to the society's evaluation or perception of one's contribution and of one's role. The rich and the powerful usually age 'later' than the poor, in part because of the control that they keep over the assets of their community and society.

Gender aspects of the notion of 'old' are closely related to the economic power of women and the society's perception of their social role. In general control over economic resources and the organization of power within the household and in the society at large would have a strong bearing over the attribution of old to an individual. The British Queen (who turned 70 in 1996) is rarely referred to as an 'old woman'![4]

Nor indeed was her exact contemporary, Margaret Thatcher, until she lost her political power.

'Old people' are not and have never been a single, simple category. They are divided by gender, class, income, race, by multiple individual characteristics, and also by age; people in their sixties may—or may not—be very different from those in their nineties.[5] Nor are cultural assumptions about them simple. Sociological and psychological studies suggest—at least for Australia where the most thorough studies were carried out—that there is no dominant stereotype and that popular images of old people are mixed, but not predominantly negative unless negativity is suggested to the subject by the interviewer. Individuals thought in terms of their personal knowledge of individual old people rather than of old people as a group. They were not more negative about old women than about old men.[6] Most people in most societies are and long have been accorded little status or respect at any stage in their lives; it is not clear that they fare worse in this respect in later life.

In late twentieth-century Britain media representations of older people similarly convey mixed messages, despite widely held, unproven, assumptions to the contrary.[7] One study of television found that:

There was no dominant emphasis on passivity or dependency. If anything there was a tendency to present a selective view of old age and play down the possible connections between old age, disability, ill-health and death . . . old people were represented as largely active, competent, fit and independent.

[4] M. Messkoub, 'Crisis of Ageing in Less Developed Countries: A Crisis for Whom? Some Conceptual and Policy Issues', Leeds University Business School Paper E97/01 (Feb. 1997), 5–6.

[5] C. Conrad, 'Old Age in the Modern and Post-Modern Western World', in T. R. Cole, D. Van Tassell, R. Kastenbaum (eds.), *Handbook of Ageing and the Humanities* (New York, 1992); Jean Pierre Bois, *Des vieux de Montaigne aux premières retraites* (Paris, 1989).

[6] V. Braithewaite, D. Gibson, J. Holman, 'Age Stereotyping: Are we Over-Simplifying the Phenomenon?', *International Journal of Aging and Human Development*, 22/4 (1986), 315–25. Braithewaite, 'Old Age Stereotypes: Reconciling Contradictions', *Journal of Gerontology*, 414/3 (1986), 353–60; and 'The Ageing Experience: Loss Threat or Challenge?', in P. Heaven (ed.), *Lifespan Development* (Sydney, 1992), 268–300.

[7] G. Fennell, C. Phillipson, H. Evers, *The Sociology of Old Age* (Milton Keynes, 1988). J. Bornat et al., *A Manifesto for Old Age* (London, 1985).

Such representations were perhaps conscious attempts to redress negative images.[8] Where negative representations were evident, for example in soap operas, they expressed not passive vulnerability, but active, even aggressive, interference, complaint, dissatisfaction on the part of old people.

Nevertheless a dominant negative stereotype is widely believed to exist by both older and younger people, beliefs which may express either direct experience or fear of impending marginalization. We have seen that such fears are not without foundation, for example in the negative representations of older people evident in discourses about work, retirement, pensions, and the medical treatment of older people in twentieth-century Britain. But it is not clear that these negative views were more intensely held in the twentieth century than before and nowhere did they go unchallenged. Both medical and social research also stressed the positive potential of older people. Over the twentieth century 'old age' appeared to become a more rigidly fixed category, defined by ages of qualification for retirement and for receipt of a pension. Yet within fifty years, by the end of the century, these boundaries were destabilized as, for many, the age of retirement slipped downwards, into the fifties, at the same time as more people, often the same people, remained physically fit to later ages than before. Clear, uncontested definitions of 'old age' remained elusive.

The relatively greater affluence of old people at all social levels, the availability of a new and wider range of consumer goods, plus the effects of medical and technological change, profoundly influenced the experience and representation of old age in the twentieth century. New technologies created new and widely disseminated sources of imagery of older people, as of everything else, in magazines, advertisements, films, television. Individuals could manipulate their own images with the use of a growing range of items of make-up, hair-dyes, cosmetic surgery, together with increasingly widespread attention in the later part of the century to the very long-established age-retardants of diet and exercise. All of these techniques were most easily available to the most affluent, but more of them were accessible to more people as the century progressed. The use of cosmetics was acceptable at an earlier date for women, conspicuous adornment having been unacceptable for men since the early nineteenth century, though increasingly in the later twentieth century it became acceptable for younger men and increasingly, if discreetly, practised by some older men.

Disguising the visible signs of age by some older women was condemned by some in the later twentieth century as obeisance to a cult of youth, encouraged by the mass media, as an unrealistic and demeaning refusal to accept the realities of ageing and to 'grow old gracefully' and 'naturally', as it was

---

[8] G. Rodwell *et al.*, 'Images of Old Age on British Television', *Generations Review*, 2/3. (Sept. 1992), British Society of Gerontology.

thought that women had once done. As we have seen, 'natural' ageing, unassisted by adornment or medical intervention, in pre-industrial England could be far from 'graceful'. The assumption that at a certain age women should cease practices such as the use of make-up and hair-dyes that had been a part of their everyday experience since youth, or should cease to dress in jeans at a certain age, smacked of another kind of stereotyping, the survival of an age-old belief that older people, especially women, should present themselves 'fittingly', adopting a dress code suited to their years. In 1754 Lady Jane Coke wrote disapprovingly of current fashion trends at court:

One thing is new, which is that there is not such a thing as a decent old woman left, everybody curls their hair, shows their neck and wears pink, but your humble servant, people who have covered their heads for 40 years now leave off their caps and think it becomes them.[9]

It was unclear in the twentieth century as in the eighteenth who had the right to decree what was a fitting appearance for people at all ages from the sixties to past one hundred, and that it was 'unnatural' to grow old 'disgracefully' as some women and men preferred. In all ages older people rebelled against such social prescriptions. And perhaps codes of appearance were becoming more flexible at the end of the twentieth century and more older people were willing, and could afford, to rebel against social prescription and to create their own identities.

Medical advances, such as hip replacements and heart bypass surgery improved the quality of life of many older people, despite the extraordinary lack of research into the causes and effects in older people of some of the diseases most likely to afflict them, in particular cancer and heart disease.[10] It became possible to recover from previously crippling conditions of later life. Also the last days and months of some old people were made miserable by the capacity of modern medical technology to sustain life past the point at which it was worth living.

The menopause was more extensively discussed as a medical problem in the twentieth century, as indeed were very many conditions in the century in which scientific medicine made unprecedented advances. Remedies, such as Hormone Replacement Therapy, were introduced to counter the ill-effects of menopause. However, it remained quite unclear whether the menopause caused women more discomfort than in earlier centuries and, if so, to what proportion of women and why. It was less obviously than in previous centuries a visible marker of the onset of old age for women, in view of the proliferation of means to disguise it.[11]

---

[9] Quoted in Anne Buck, *Dress in Eighteenth Century England* (New York, 1979), 340.
[10] See pp. 455–6.
[11] Lynne Botelho, 'Old Age and Menopause in Rural Women in Seventeenth Century Suffolk' in L. Botelho and P. Thane (eds.) *Women and Ageing in British Society since 1500* (London, 2000).

In the later twentieth century surviving representations and self-representations of the old age of rich and poor, men and women, were as conflicting as in previous centuries and by no means overwhelmingly negative. The dialogue glimpsed in the the diaries of Beatrice Webb and William Gladstone[12] between the self-image of these older people and their perceptions of the images of old held by others is expressed in the later twentieth century by less publicly prominent people. It is best summed up in the title given by Paul Thompson, Catherine Itzin, and Michele Abendstern to the book they based upon interviews with older people in south London in the 1980s—*I Don't Feel Old*.[13] Time and again the people they met contrasted how they felt as 'old people' with popular stereotypes and with their own expectations. One woman described how:

I could never imagine getting old. I still can't although I'm old . . . I still don't realize I've got to 73 because I don't feel 73. I don't feel what I imagine 73 to be like—you know?[14]

A retired butler, aged 86 and his 57-year-old son expressed a range of generational experiences of ageing. The older man said, 'I've never felt my age.' His son replied, 'I don't think of you as being old.' The older man thought that age depended upon being physically active and on attitude: 'one person might be old at 60 and another won't be old till he's 80, or 90 perhaps.' The son responded: 'your father would have felt old when he got to 60. I can remember him with a big beard and being very tottery'. The son himself had expected to feel old at 50, but still felt young.[15]

The ageing Londoners believed that they were popularly represented as being different from other age groups. That was not how they felt—often to their surprise. Most of their lives were characterized by 'variety, vitality, diversity, activity, energy, interest'.[16]

They seemed to have no problem with their actual age or condition but with the label 'old' and the stereotypes and prejudice that went with it—this was what they resisted and denied.[17]

However, few of them could see anything positive about growing old and many did think certain forms of dress and activities inappropriate at older ages. 'Consciously or unconsciously some had adapted their attitudes and behaviours to conform to stereotyped images.'[18] Yet all but one of the people interviewed did not prefer the company of people of their own age and had friends of all ages. They refused to join old people's clubs, objecting to the ghettoization

---

[12] See pp. 263–5, 266–9.   [13] Thompson, Itzin, Abendstern, *Old*.   [14] Ibid. 121.
[15] Ibid. 107.   [16] Ibid. 121.   [17] Ibid.   [18] Ibid. 123–4.

of older people and the assumption that age alone rather than shared interests was a reason for association. They presented 'a very strong and clear message about the actual experience of ageing . . . that [it] is nothing like as bad as it is represented or imagined'. Many of the older people admitted to 'slowing down' but not to the transformation they had expected. Most had stopped heavy work or active sports, but most younger people do not engage in such activities and would have no reason to complain, as one 70-year-old did, that he could no longer run ten miles.[19] These responses could be interpreted, knowingly, as denial of old age in a society which values youth, but they emerge more strongly as expressions of lived experience and as denials of popular assumptions about the experience of living at older ages.

Most of the older people in south London agreed that not chronological age but physical fitness determined whether people were 'old'. A 60-year-old woman said:

I would say that old age begins when you begin to feel really old. You know there must be a time in your life when you say to yourself, 'Well I'm not able to do that any more'. I would say that is when you are getting old . . . I don't think it really goes by the calendar at all. I think it goes by itself, your own attitude to life.

A 71-year-old man said that he still felt 21 and could see no reason why he should not feel the same in ten years' time. He said:

People are never old, it's only when they look upon themselves as being old. It's an attitude of mind all the time, I think. You do realize you're getting old when the stairs get steeper and the miles get longer, but I can climb up a ladder and paint the roof . . . It's got to stop somewhere, but I can't see it.[20]

For most of these older people, 'old people' were other people, whom they stereotyped as 'complaining' and 'moaning'.[21] Class differences in attitude were not striking and differences were greater within than between age cohorts. Unhappiness and loneliness were more often due to widowhood and loss of friends than to old age in itself. The researchers concluded that:

It is a myth that old age is typically a time of passivity. The truth is closer to the opposite: since later life is a time of sharp change, it demands a special responsiveness and imaginative adaptability.[22]

'MASS OBSERVATION' OF OLD AGE

In 1992 Mass Observation invited its regular panel of respondents to write about their observations of 'Growing Older'. Mass Observation was formed in 1937 as a forum for the anthropological study of everyday life in Britain.

---

[19] Ibid. 127–8.   [20] Ibid. 130.   [21] Ibid. 100 ff.   [22] Ibid. 245.

It went into decline after the Second World War, but was reborn in 1981, amassing observations now by inviting a regular panel of about 2,500 people to respond in writing to twice-yearly 'directives' on a variety of topics. Mass Observers were not representative of the British population in any strict sense. They were literate, as were the great majority of the late twentieth-century British population. They were substantially middle class, though many were lower middle class and some were manual workers. They often made great efforts to gather the views of others in order to present a wider view than their personal one. Two-thirds of the panel were female, half came from southern England.[23] None appeared to be either very wealthy or to have serious financial difficulties. Overwhelmingly they were white. They can be said to come from backgrounds comparable with those of a very high proportion of the British population at the end of the twentieth century. Mass Observation provides an unusual opportunity to read the opinions, expressed at length, in their own words, of people whose views are rarely made public.

A dominant theme of the responses was the relativity of the process of ageing. A 65-year-old retired local government officer, living in Sussex, summed up a widespread feeling that: 'its this habit of wanting to treat all people of a certain age group in the same way that seems wrong, whatever that age group is. People are no longer allowed to be individuals.'[24] A retired library assistant from Rotherham (Yorkshire) commented:

Now that I am 67 I must consider myself to be 'elderly'. General outlook and attitude seem to be the deciding factor in placing people in age categories. The old saying 'you're as old as you feel' has some truth in it and we all know people who are old at 40 and some who are much older but have an interest in life and an awareness of all about them, who give an impression of comparative youthfulness in spite of the lines and wrinkles.[25]

A 67-year-old housewife from Kent wrote:

These days you aren't classed as old until you are 80. I don't feel old, with fashions very flexible you can look fashionable up to any age. My mother is 95 and she wears very fashionable clothes.[26]

A 59-year-old retired radiographer also felt 'quite put out when the media describe anyone under 80 as "old". My 100 year old mother has only just agreed to being called "old".'[27] The 'flexibility' of modern fashion, the disappearance of age-related dress codes was often mentioned as central to the blurring of age boundaries that was widely perceived.[28]

A 74-year-old retired barmaid from Harrogate (Yorkshire) wrote:

[23] D. Sheridan, B. Street, D. Bloome, *Writing Ourselves: Mass Observation and Literary Practice* (Cresskill, NJ 1999), app. B (iii). The Mass Observation Archive is housed at the University of Sussex.   [24] Mass Observation, 'Growing Older', Directive, file C. 2091.   [25] B. 60.   [26] B. 1665.   [27] B. 2154. On old age starting at 80 see also B. 2611, C. 1786; C. 2142, C. 1878, aged 72, chose 85.   [28] B. 2258.

Titles of age, young, middle age etc. really don't mean much, do they? I know young people of 25 who are 90 in their head and 90 year olds who are young and outgoing. I decide how to age people by their behaviour . . . I think a lot of age is in your own head . . . unless you are unfortunate enough to have ill-health, even then keeping your mind lively helps.[29]

Such relativism cannot simply be ascribed to self-deception among old women, seeking to deny the unpleasant reality of ageing, for it was shared by younger people. A shop supervisor from Plymouth (Devon), who was approaching the age of 40 discussed in some detail the varieties of ageing she saw among women around her:

I remember my mother saying 'I may be a wrinkled 57 on the outside, but I'm 17 inside', when I caught her playing hopscotch out on the pavement with my daughter. I'm beginning to understand what she meant. . . . some people are born 'middle aged' while some old folk sparkle, are open-minded and have a zest for life.

I find it very difficult to estimate people's ages. Indeed age doesn't seem a very important consideration in view of improved housing, nutrition and medicine . . . with extended life expectancy, I believe you can be considered young until the late 40s, then be at a peak until 55–66 years (perhaps retirement age is one of life's landmarks) then enjoy a further rewarding and active phase (perhaps this is middle age) until the physical deterioration which eventually comes with advancing years forces you to slow down into 'old age', which can still be a rewarding experience if you have your faculties and a decent standard of living. Of course, there are many factors other than chronological age which determine whether you are perceived to be young, middle-aged or old. Good health . . . social and economic status . . . doing a job one enjoys.

As a volunteer worker for social services, I have supported women I've regarded as being a generation older than myself and suddenly realized that they are ten years younger than me. They have a poor self-image, are worn down by marital and financial problems, are in poor shape physically . . .

On the other hand as a member of a keep-fit association, I am often amazed when fellow-members reveal their ages. Women in their 70s with trim, supple bodies glow with vitality and enthusiasm for life and look twenty years younger.

She compared her parents, mother aged 67, father 70, with her mother-in-law aged 68. Her parents:

dress well and keep abreast of change. Mum is interested in trends in fashion and make-up and adapts them to suit her—they are active, alert and open-minded. They feel they are valued members of society who have 'earned' their retirement . . . [though] everything takes a bit longer now and there are a few twinges.

On the other hand my mother-in-law's whole life has been tied up in the domestic issues of her family. She has no hobbies or special interests, doesn't have strong views

[29] B. 736. See also B. 1224, B. 1281, B. 1521, B. 1665, B. 2134, B. 1386, B. 2197, B. 2258, B. 2605, B. 2670, C. 1624, C. 1405, C. 1713, C. 1786, C. 1878, C. 1883, C. 2053, C. 2079, C. 2091, C. 2295, C. 2142.

on anything and just potters through life. She's perfectly content and a lovely lady but I can't believe she's only a year older than my mother. Her hair turned white years ago. She never wears make-up or colourful, adventurous clothes and has a very diffident manner. To an outsider she must look an 'old lady' whereas my mother is still attractive and a force to be reckoned with![30]

Another woman who was not yet old by any definition, a 47-year-old civil servant in Kent commented:

Old is definitely not for oneself. My mother says 'These old people' . . . not including herself at 80, but she means doddery, decrepit, won't do for themselves, some of them are younger than her.[31]

A 63-year-old sales assistant, also from Kent, offered her own 'ages of men' and women, adopting a trope that was centuries old:[32]

at 60 Retirement becomes imminent and needs thought
at 70 enjoy what you have, throw caution to the wind
at 80 impart your knowledge of life to others
at 90 sit back and enjoy everything.

Similarly, a 44-year-old receptionist described the 'ages of woman', in more pessimistic terms:

By 50 the grey hairs might be showing slightly and there might be menopausal problems, but notwithstanding she is still living life to the full. By 60 she might be slowing down, but can still keep up looking after the grandchildren and taking exercise. By 70 and 80 though there is a big difference, with not being as active and having a lined face.[33]

The respondents were divided as to whether women aged faster than men, though most emphasized the negative impact of retirement on men and the benefit to women of the continuity in their working lives at later ages and of the acceptability of the use of cosmetics for women. But the receptionist quoted above thought that 'women show their age more than men no matter how careful you are'. The Rotherham respondent thought:

It appears that women are more resilient and are tougher than men in some ways, but I should think they age at about the same rate although old men look more decrepit then old women particularly if they have no-one to care for them.[34]

Another retired library assistant, age 69, from London, wrote:

men dislike old age more than women because of loss of physical strength. Some women seem to *look* old and so act as frail etc. Men seem to be more vocal over aches and pains.[35]

---

[30] B. 1215.   [31] C. 1990.

[32] The Directive invited respondents to 'try setting out your thoughts on a man or woman of 20, 30, 40, 50, 60, 70, 80, 90'.

[33] C. 1715.   [34] B. 60, see also B. 2170.   [35] B. 86.

The widow from Winchester believed:

Men would seem to stay younger until they retire when often they settle down to old age, whereas women have a slow decline. . . . Women look younger and stay younger because they take more pride in their appearance. They enjoy looking nice, buying clothes, using cosmetics, having their hair done, all this makes for ageing for women to be superficially slower than men.[36]

The Kent housewife wrote that 'a woman doesn't seem to age as quickly as a man as she can always find something to do and go out shopping therefore speaks to other people'.[37] A retired social worker commented that 'in my experience men deteriorate *mentally* more than women'.[38] A 39-year-old voluntary social worker in 'an award winning day centre for the so-called elderly' observed:

There are some cases where men seem to age rapidly on retirement and seem to feel their lives are over, whilst women if they survive the transition from mother to 'mother-whose-children-have left home' often seem to gain a new lease of life.

But 'one cannot generalize'.[39]

Relatively few mentioned the menopause in this connection[40] and those who did so had mixed views. A 58-year-old clerk in London wrote:

Women are worse affected by ageing, because often they think when they lose their physical attractiveness they are done for. I don't think men care about that quite so much. Then too there is the age barrier of the menopause for women, some women think that once past that, they are indeed 'past it' and there is no equivalent barrier for men, nothing so sudden and drastic.[41]

A 61-year-old retired civil servant in Middlesex was more optimistic about the lives of older women: 'Hopefully they will sail through menopause, perhaps with medical help and feel in better health than they have had for years'.[42] A 64-year-old secretary/administrator from Hove (Sussex) 'had a very nasty "change of life", but was rescued by HRT, which is *the* greatest invention since cut bread'.[43] The lack of reference to it suggests that many women experienced menopause in a less negative fashion than commentators have suggested.

A stronger theme, and another that was age-old, was the need and capacity of older people for independence. Inability to sustain independent living emerged as the most important marker of the onset of old age, for women and men. A 60-year-old midwife from Grimsby (Lincolnshire) stated that

---

[36] B. 2646, see also B. 2671.   [37] B. 1424, see also C. 1878, C. 2142.
[38] C. 1405.   [39] B. 2197, C. 2079.
[40] Other surveys showed that, contrary to stereotype, most women experienced little difficulty with menopause and did not view its effects on their lives negatively. J. Harrison 'Women and Ageing: Experience and Implications', *Ageing and Society*, 3/2 (1983), 209–35. Sara Arber and Jay Ginn, *Gender and Later Life* (London, 1991), 46–7.   [41] B. 1665, see also B. 1553, B. 2066, B. 1386.
[42] B. 2605.   [43] B. 2671.

' "old" is when you can no longer do what you want'.[44] The retired library assistant from Yorkshire confessed:

Now we come to my fear. I would hate to think that I could not continue to live an independent life in my own home. Having to rely on other people must be dreadful, but how much worse if one is in a Home.[45]

A widow from Winchester (Hampshire) wrote:

I regard anyone under 40 as young. From 45–65 as middle aged. Elderly under 75 and old as 75 plus. *But* although I am aged 78 I do not think of myself as old but elderly. Perhaps because I am fairly independent and can look after myself.[46]

Another woman was willing:

to give up my own home if disabled, not otherwise. I would *not* expect any of my family to care for me in their own homes.[47]

The retired civil servant from Middlesex wrote:

I would rather stay in my own home when I am widowed, with my family not too far away or perhaps move to a sheltered flat, or even a home, dependent on my state of mind. I would never to make [*sic*] my family feel guilty if they could not care for me. I would not expect them to.[48]

Several respondents expressed fears that when they ceased to live independently they would be stereotyped and patronized. The writer from Rotherham described how an 'old lady' in a residential home:

was infuriated by the patronizing tone adopted by many of the staff when talking to old people, as though they were half-witted or, at any rate, small children. I used to notice this on my book trolley round on geriatric wards.[49]

   Conventional stereotypes were seen as undeservedly constraining the lives of older people.[50] A 66-year-old retired social worker living in rural Wales commented:

The need to look young [for men and women] is much more to do with careers and getting jobs. And this is, I think, the crucial point about ageing, how it gets in the way when job hunting or seeking promotion, and in other aspects of social life. Ageism is not seen as a problem like racism or sexism yet it is as damaging and as widespread.[51]

A writer and counsellor living in London expressed her response to conventional stereotypes:

Yesterday I was 60. There—I have come out and said it. How does it feel? Well a whole lot better than I thought. Never, but never have I so dreaded a birthday. But why should this be such a milestone? We are indoctrinated, that's why. I got my travel

[44] B. 2605.   [45] See also C. 602, C. 1990, C. 1990.   [46] B. 2645.
[47] B. 1553 see also C. 1624.   [48] B. 2605.   [49] B. 60.
[50] C. 2078.   [51] B. 1553.

pass this morning and hoped I would not bump into anyone I knew at the office. So I am a Senior Citizen and an old age pensioner? This is ludicrous because I feel 25 going on 18. The years I suppose have been kind to me but no-one stays the same. Still I know my personality is as eccentric and adventurous as it ever was . . . is it my imagination or are people stepping outside the age categories as it becomes increasingly difficult to tell how old they are . . . even if they almost kill themselves with aerobics etc. ultimately it is what is in the mind that is going to make the difference . . . I know a very chic lady, not thin, looks about 65 or so, who has just had her 80th . . . good personality, sharp, attractive . . . Another local lady died before Christmas at 89 years . . . again, good personality and she kept her own house to the end . . . But I cannot say I would wish to be another age or that there was a favourite time. NOW! that's it. Never have I been so happy, secure, had a job I love with such satisfying hobbies and interests.[52]

This optimistic woman had a good marriage to a younger man, following an earlier disastrous marriage. The ageing of their husbands influenced the outlook of many women on their own ageing. A 67-year-old retired clerk wrote:

I feel considerably older than I did even five years ago, probably because I have a husband who has Parkinson's disease and I am unable to leave him to himself for more than a week . . . I am not enjoying getting old and I don't believe if everyone was honest they would not agree with me.[53]

Individual personality and other aspects of their environment affected outlooks on ageing. A female information assistant from the Isle of Wight, aged only 54, wrote:

I have lived too long. I am not decrepit but I no longer think the world such a wonderful place. I live in an insular community where progress is slow.

The writers had divided views about whether older people were respected in British society, a question to which they were asked to respond. In general they took a relativistic view. The Harrogate barmaid wrote: 'Respect, what on earth is that? Lots of people today have no respect for themselves, never mind old people.'[54] The 58-year-old London clerk wrote:

No. I don't think we respect elderly people. I think the general feeling is 'They've had their life, why don't they just die and make room for younger people'. Respect in this country at this time seems to be tied very much to money and earning capacity. We respect rich people, and a rich old person is respected for his wealth, not his age.[55]

A 52-year-old Shropshire school secretary reflected:

I am beginning to be aware of a lack of respect for age and experience . . . haven't all older people felt that the younger generation have little respect for them. I doubt today's younger people are any different to previous generations.[56]

[52] B. 1120.   [53] A. 1223.   [54] B. 736.   [55] B. 1665, B. 2258.   [56] B. 1386.

The retired social worker in Wales felt that she had 'lost status by retiring, no-one asks my opinion any more'.[57] On the other hand, an 'almost 65'-year-old housewife from Lancashire thought:

Yes, I think most people respect the elderly. In fact some elderly don't respect the younger ones today.[58]

Others were unwilling to generalize.[59] A 48-year-old carer commented:

No, I don't think as a society we respect older people en masse, but I certainly respect my older friends in Oldham.[60]

A part-Chinese civil servant, aged 47, commented:

We were brought up to respect our grandparents and that attitude continues in this family (the Chinese influence) but this means that grandparents are remote. They get their own way and people running round after them but they are not their grand-children's friends.[61]

Several writers discussed the changing experience of old people over the century by making comparisons between their own ageing and that of their parents and grandparents. A retired social worker from south London recalled:

my grandparents did not *do* very much outside their homes whereas my elderly and old friends attend day classes (university extra-mural) and visit family and friends in this country and abroad.[62]

Or they recalled memories of their own attitudes earlier in life. A 44-year-old receptionist from Preston (Lancashire) wrote:

When I was 20 or 30 then 50 seemed quite old to me. In the 1980s 50s can be seen as attractive, interesting, experienced and valuable. This wasn't the case in the 1960s when I was in my teens as the Twiggy thin-as-rake-look was in and everything seemed to revolve around teenagers . . . I don't think of 60 year olds as doddery any more but only as middle aged.[63]

Most of the above observations came from women, appropriately, since women were more likely than men to experience old age. The views of men, however, were similar. A retired male civil servant from Surrey expressed per-ceptively some of the gains and losses of ageing:

I expect like myself most people like to think of themselves as young. Some don't of course. My next door neighbour who's five years older than me has been saying for as long as I can remember 'You wait till you're my age'. I think he's been fairly ancient all his life.

At 70 a lot of people may think, in biblical terms, that they're living on borrowed time and going into decline—but most of the 70 year olds I know are active, physic-ally and mentally, and think, as I do, that life has lots to offer.

---

[57] B. 1533, see also B. 1521, C. 1786.   [58] B. 1661.   [59] B. 2611.
[60] C. 2078, see also C. 2091.   [61] C. 1990.   [62] C. 1405.   [63] C. 1713, C. 2142.

I'm aware that my senses now aren't as acute and I think that my hearing, sight and sexual awareness are all diminished.

He expected further decline by the age of 80. He added:

It would be nice to think that you became wiser and had a greater understanding of the world around you as you get older. I suppose this is true to a certain extent, but the social and technical changes are so marked that you find as you get older that you lose touch with what is happening around you.

As far as I am concerned the main gain of being older is that I don't have to go to work and don't have to suffer that Monday morning feeling. I can please myself to a large extent as to what I do with my time. And when you think that from the age of five to the age of retirement you have to stick to a rigid timetable conditioned by school and work, it's a great improvement. Although I enjoyed a great deal of what I did. I've enjoyed what I've done since a lot more.

It would be nice to say that in old age younger people showed the sort of respect and deference that we were required to do when I was young . . . but they don't— they tend to push you off the pavement. That's generalizing again because I have many young friends who treat you as an equal and I like that.

It isn't all blue skies and sunshine of course. I've lost eight good friends in the last ten years; but I've had time to develop in ways that weren't possible before retirement . . . I can give more and need more time in fact, to keep my garden neat and productive. I've had time to discover my family history—and to explore the countryside—and to take up long distance walking and marathons (I completed the London marathon when I was 71 and have done many harder cross-country runs). More recently I've discovered that I can sing quite well and have taken part in musicals with the local operatic society.

I deplore not being able to remember anything and not being able to see or hear properly—and having my hair turn white; but I've been immensely lucky with my health . . . And I'm very afraid of being the sort of bore that some of my neighbours have become in old age. One thing I'm not afraid of now is being different to other people and that is one of the good things about growing old.

His grandparents

led very sedentary lives—never did anything active and had very little money: they were exactly how I thought of old people in fact and I should have been amazed if they had not been like that.

I don't think that much respect is felt by young people for old people and the reverse is probably true as well. Old age has never really been respected in our society, as far as I'm aware, and I'm thinking of what I've read in, for example, Kilvert's and Woodforde's diaries and Pepys' diary: old people were never respected ipso facto . . . Today I get the impression that in general old people are given rather more respect—though perhaps not as much as in my grandparents and parents' time when young people were more disciplined and family bonds were much closer. Old people have more channels today than ever before for airing their views and having their requirements made known.[64]

[64] G. 2134.

A working-class man, a 60-year-old retired, divorced, toolmaker felt that

Apart from my ubiquitous short sight and deafness, I do not feel any older than 30–40. 60 is middle age to me. Age categories anyway are only convenient labels that mean little to me. I was at:

20 stupid, athletic, raunchy, cocky and hedonist,
30 stupid, athletic, raunchy,
40 thoughtful, fit, reflective,
50 thoughtful, reflective, fit, attentive, scholarly, misogynist,
60 thoughtful, fit, reflective, disillusioned, scholarly, attentive, cynical, misogynist,

So age does not unduly worry me—I seem to be improving . . . have been an impulsive autodidact after being a youthful pratt.

Compulsory retirement on a works occupational pension suits me. No responsibilities, ties, beady eyed gaffers, strident spouse. Can do what I want within (financial) reason. Quite contented if lonely at times.

The elderly *are* respected but do not always appreciate it. Think world owes them a living.

CONCLUSIONS

It is sometimes argued that there has been an increased emphasis on youth and beauty in twentieth-century consumer society which has led to increased age discrimination. In reality, popular attitudes to old age are as varied as ever. In no time or place is it evident that old age, especially very old age, is especially valued in itself, independently of the attributes of specific old people. Nor that in 'the past' or in 'other cultures', old, as distinct from middle aged, people, in general were repositories of knowledge and skill in contrast to their obsolescence in fast-moving modern cultures, though individuals, in specific circumstances may have been so. In all times a general dread of the unknowable personal future of the later years of life induces a bias towards pessimism and negative representations of old age, but in all times there has been an ongoing dialogue between differing conceptions of what it is to be old, in which most people engage to varying degrees. The subjective and objective experiences of being old are immensely varied. The variety of representations and self-representations suggest above all that there is and has been no single 'natural' way to grow old, whether 'gracefully' or otherwise.

Conclusion

24

Into the Twenty-First Century:
An Ageing Society—Burden or Benefit?

Throughout the world in the later twentieth century populations are ageing. The process will continue, and probably accelerate, in the next millennium. It is far advanced in most developed countries and is visible and projected to advance further and faster in less developed countries, where an assumed 'crisis' of low fertility and ageing populations is overtaking the long-established concern with high fertility and youthful populations.[1] Internationally the change is due to historically unprecedented trends of long-run decline in birth-rates combined with declining death-rates.[2] (See Table 24.1.)

In the recent past the process has moved fastest in the most rapidly developing countries. Seven per cent of the population of Japan was aged over 65 in 1970, 14 per cent in 1996. This doubling of the proportion of older people which took twenty-six years in Japan, took forty-five years in Britain (to 1975), one hundred and fifteen years in France, eighty-five years in Sweden, and seventy-five years in the United States (see Table 24.2). Countries as different as China and Venezuela are predicted to undergo still more rapid transitions.[3]

As in Britain and France, when this long-run shift was first noted in the 1930s,[4] the most common international response has been alarm and pessimism, as expressed in the title of the World Bank's review of the situation: *Averting the Old Age Crisis* (1994).[5] A common reaction to the success of the campaigns to reduce mortality and to control fertility, the realization of the dreams of many people over many centuries for longer, healthier lives, is not pleasure but gloom and despondency. How justified is this response? Now, as in the 1930s, much of the alarm is rooted in pessimistic assertion rather than in

[1] K. Tout, *Ageing in Developing Countries* (Oxford, 1989). K. Sen, *Ageing* (London, 1995). M. Messkoub, 'Crisis of Ageing in Less Developed Countries: A Crisis for Whom? Some Conceptual and Policy Issues', Leeds University Business School Discussion Paper, E97/01 (Feb. 1997).

[2] For a discussion of these issues see Lincoln H. Day, *The Future of Low Birthrate Populations* (London, 1992).

[3] World Bank, *Averting the Old Age Crisis: Policies to Project the Old and Promote Growth* (Oxford, 1994).

[4] See Ch. 16. A. Sauvy, *General Theory of Population*, trans. C. Campos (New York, 1969), and 'Social and Economic Consequences of Ageing of Western Populations', *Population Studies*, 2/1 (June 1948), 115–24. P. Bourdelais, 'The Ageing of the Population: Relevant Question or Obsolete Notion?', in Paul Johnson and Pat Thane (eds.), *Old Age from Antiquity to Post-Modernity* (London, 1998), 110–31.

[5] See also OECD, *Ageing Populations: The Social Policy Implications* (Paris, 1988).

TABLE 24.1. *Percentage distribution of population by age group: selected countries, 1960, 1990, 2020, 2050*

Country	Estimates						Projections					
	1960			1990			2020			2050		
	0–15	15–60	60+	0–15	15–60	60+	0–15	15–60	60+	0–15	15–60	60+
Mid. Income												
Angola	41.8	53.4	4.8	47.1	48.1	4.8	42.6	52.8	4.6	26.3	65.2	8.5
Algeria	43.7	50.4	5.9	41.9	52.6	5.5	25.3	65.9	8.8	20	59.2	20.8
Argentina	30.8	60.4	8.8	30.6	56.5	12.9	23.2	60.7	16.1	19.7	56.8	23.5
Bolivia	42.8	51.7	5.5	41.2	53	5.8	31.1	60.8	8.1	21.8	61.8	16.4
Botswana	47.4	47.8	4.8	45	51.4	3.6	32.8	60.2	7	22.6	61.6	15.8
Brazil	43.6	51.6	4.8	34.4	58.4	7.2	23.4	63	13.6	19.4	57	23.6
Chile	39	53.5	7.5	30.1	60.9	9	23	61.5	15.5	19.9	56.9	23.2
El Salvador	45.5	50.2	4.3	43.5	50.7	5.8	29.7	63.1	7.2	21.2	60.9	17.9
Iran	44.8	48.9	6.3	45	49.4	5.6	31.6	61	7.4	21.6	60.9	17.5
Malaysia	45.3	49.4	5.3	38.2	56	5.8	27.7	61.5	10.8	19.8	59.1	21.1
Mexico	45	48.3	6.7	38.1	56.1	5.8	24.1	64.6	11.3	19.6	57	23.4
Peru	43.3	51.1	5.6	37.8	56.3	5.9	25.7	63.3	11	19.9	58.2	21.9
Philippines	44.7	50.4	4.9	39.7	55.2	5.1	26.8	63.7	9.5	20.6	66.1	13.3
Poland	33.4	57.2	9.4	24.8	60.3	14.9	20.4	58.5	21.1	19.4	55.4	25.2
Rep. of Korea	41.9	52.8	5.3	25.9	66.4	7.7	19.2	62.8	18	18.5	55.3	26.2
Russia	30	60.7	9.3	23	61	16	17.2	59.9	22.9	17.9	52.4	29.7
South Africa	40.9	53	6.1	38.3	55.2	6.5	29.9	61	9.1	22	61.3	16.7
Syria	44.4	49.8	5.8	48.1	47.5	4.4	36.8	58.3	4.9	23.4	63.4	13.2
Thailand	44.7	50.8	4.5	31.8	61.5	6.7	22.2	63.9	13.9	19.4	55.8	24.8
Turkey	41.3	52.2	6.5	34.7	58.2	7.1	23.5	64.5	12	19.5	58.6	21.9
High Income												
Australia	30.1	57.7	12.2	21.9	62.6	15.5	19.7	62.1	18.2	18.3	53.5	28.2
France	26.4	56.8	16.8	20.3	60.6	19.1	17.2	56.7	26.1	17.6	52.1	30.3
Germany	21.2	61.5	17.3	16.1	63.5	20.4	12.9	58.8	28.3	14.2	48.6	37.2
Italy	24.8	61.6	13.6	16.7	63.1	20.2	12.1	57.6	30.3	13.1	46.6	40.3
Japan	30.2	60.9	8.9	18.4	64.2	17.4	14.2	54.8	31	15.7	48.5	35.8
Sweden	22	60.7	17.3	18	59.2	22.8	18.1	55.4	26.5	18	54.1	27.9
UK	23.2	59.9	16.9	19	60.3	20.7	17.8	58.2	24	18.1	53.5	28.4
US	31.1	55.7	13.2	21.7	61.5	16.8	19.8	57.7	22.5	18.8	54.7	26.5

TABLE 24.2. *Time taken to double population aged over 60* (selected countries)

	Years taken to double over-60 population from 9% to 18%	Date at which 18% of population are aged over 60
France	140	1976
Italy	100	1982
Sweden	86	1962
United States	73	2008
Hungary	59	1979
United Kingdom	45	1965
China	34	2026
Japan	31	1992
Egypt	30	2049
Venezuela	22	2035
Singapore	21	2013

Sources: World Bank, *Averting the Old Age Crisis*, 26; United Nations, *World Prospects, 1992* (New York, 1993), quoted in P. Lloyd-Sharlock and Paul Johnson eds., *Ageing and Society. Global Comparisons* (London, 1996), 8.

substance. We still know remarkably little about the effects of changing age structure upon economies and societies. This chapter seeks to sort out what we do know and what we do not about the actual and likely future effects of the ageing of contemporary Britain.

Certain facts about the present and recent past are clear. Following the rapid rise in the proportion of people over 65 in the British population between the 1920s and the 1970s, a plateau was reached at about 15 per cent. The proportion is unlikely to rise again before c.2020, when the post-war 'baby-boomers', who have themselves had relatively low fertility, enter their sixties. This rise after 2020 could be offset by a rise in the birth-rate or, in a world which we are told is characterized by increasing international mobility and 'globalization', by an influx of migrants of younger ages (see Fig. 1).

However, within this stable proportion of over sixty-fives into the twenty-first century, the proportion of the very old, aged 75 and above, will continue to increase (see Table 24.3). In the late twentieth century the over-eighties are the most rapidly growing age group. Also women continue to outlive men and hence to predominate in older age groups, though there are signs of a slight narrowing of this gender gap (see Table 24.4).

Another feature of the lives of older people is their increasing propensity to live alone. This was true of 13 per cent of people over 60 in 1951, 36 per cent in 1985. It is also increasingly characteristic of younger age groups (see Table 24.5).

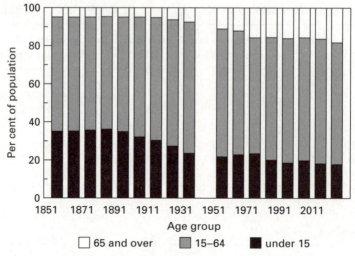

Sources: Censuses of England and Wales and Mid-1985-based population projections for local Authority areas in England, London: Office of Population Censuses and Surveys, Monitor PP3, 88/1.

Fɪɢ. 1. The age structure of the population of England and Wales, 1851–2021

Tᴀʙʟᴇ 24.3. *The very old as a percentage of elderly people in the United Kingdom, 1901–2025*

	All elderly people* (millions)	Elderly people* under 75 (millions)	The very old—75 and over (millions)	Percentage of all elderly people who are very old
1901[a][†]	2.4	1.9	0.5	21
1951[a]	6.9	5.1	1.8	26
1981[a]	10.0	6.8	3.2	32
1989[b]	10.5	6.5	3.9	37
1991[c]	10.5	6.5	4.0	38
2001[c]	10.7	6.3	4.4	41
2011[c]	11.7	7.1	4.5	38
2025[c]	13.6	8.2	5.4	40

Note: Due to rounding, not all details add to totals.

* Males over 65, females over 60.

† UK as then constituted.

[a] Figures derived from CSO, *Social Trends*, no. 13 (1983), table 1.2, p. 12.

[b] Estimated figures derived from OPCS, *Population Trends*, 62 (Winter, 1990), 43.

[c] Projected figures from OPCS, *Population Projections, 1989–2059* (1989-based) (OPCS, series PP2, no. 17; HMSO, 1991).

TABLE 24.4. *Expectation of life at birth for those born 1841–1991, United Kingdom*

Year of birth	Males	Females	Year of birth	Males	Females
1841	39	42	1921	61	68
1851	40	43	1931	66	72
1861	42	45	1941	69.6	75.4
1871	44	49	1951	72.7	78.3
1881	47	52	1961	73.6	79.1
1891	48	54	1971	74.6	79.7
1901	51	58	1981	75.5	80.4
1911	56	63	1991	76.0	80.8

Source: OPCS (1991), table 2, p. 5.

TABLE 24.5. *Proportion of older men and women reported as living alone, England and Wales, 1684–1985*

	Males	Females	All
1684–1769	6	14	10
1891	10	16	13
1901	7	13	10
1911	8	9	9
1921	10	18	14
1951	8	16	13
1962*	11	30	22
1980*	14	38	28
1985	20	47	36

Note: Cell counts as in Table 24.4.

* Refers to those over 60 years of age.

Sources: J. Falkingham and C. Gordon, Fifty Years on: The Income and Household Composition of the Elderly in London and Britain', in B. Bytheway and J. Johnson (eds.), *Welfare and the Ageing Experience* (London, 1990), 148–71, table 12.4, p. 157, and 1985 General Household Survey datafiles.

Some draw gloomy conclusions from all of these statistics. It is suggested, as it was in the 1930s,[6] that a population in which older age groups are growing whilst younger ones are shrinking must impose ever-growing costs of pensions and medical and other forms of care upon the shrinking population of working age. The fact that the numbers of *very* old people are growing especially fast is expected further to increase this 'burden', the more so because most of them are women who are relatively poorer than men in old age due

[6] See Ch. 17.

to the lesser opportunities of many of them to amass assets in their earlier years. The growing numbers of older people living alone is taken to signify increasing neglect by relatives and hence to impose further costs to be borne by the community. Some expect an older society to be culturally and politically conservative and economically less adventurous and innovative. How realistic are these gloomy predictions?

OLD AND ALONE?

We have already[7] surveyed the persuasive evidence that old people who live alone are rarely neglected and isolated. They receive a great deal of support from family and friends and they give much in return. Very many older people live alone by choice, preferring independence to dependence in the homes of relatives. Those without close relatives make greater use of public services than those with, which further suggests the importance of family support for those who have relatives. Contrary to a popular view that older people will have fewer family contacts in future due to falling family size and increased rates of divorce, the reality may be quite different.[8] An important demographic change over the twentieth century is that fewer families contain large numbers of children; an equally important change is that fewer women have had *no* children and children are more likely to live into adulthood, indeed into old age than at the beginning of the century and at all previous times. And a higher proportion of people form long-term partnerships than was normal at the beginning of the twentieth century. The very old of the 1980s and 1990s, born before the First World War, are more likely to have had no children than subsequent cohorts. Twenty-four per cent of women reaching retirement age in the early 1970s had no living children; this was true of only 15 per cent of those reaching the same age in the early 1990s. The proportion of older women with only one living child also fell from 24 to 15 per cent. In the later 1990s fertility continued to fall and future cohorts of older people may, again, have few children, but this is uncertain.

It is often assumed that increasing divorce will diminish family resources, but the signs are at least as strong that they may increase them. Family ties are not necessarily destroyed by divorce; and most divorced people form new partnerships and acquire new family relationships. The weakening of lateral links, with partners of the same generation, through separation and divorce can strengthen intergenerational links between parents and children. Divorced children often move to live with or close to parents for mutual support.[9]

[7] See Ch. 21.   [8] See pp. 431–2.

[9] R. Flowerdew, Richard Davies, and Jennifer Mason, 'Migration, Kinship and Household Change', *Research Results*, no. 12, ESRC Population and Household Change Programme (Oxford, 1998). S. McCrae (ed.), *Changing Britain: Families and Households in the 1990s* (Oxford, 1999). K. Wachter, 'Kinship Resources for the Elderly', *Philosophical Transactions of the Royal Society of London*, ser. B: 352 (1997), 1811–18.

It is also feared that the increased numbers of middle-aged women in the paid workforce will be less able to care for ageing parents. There is no clear evidence that this is so.[10] Such assertions underestimate the extent to which women in middle life have throughout history combined demanding domestic labour with paid work and a variety of caring roles; the change in the late twentieth century may be one of form rather than of degree. Also as the age of onset of real dependency is tending to rise, so in consequence is that of the 'children' of dependent old people, with the result that increasingly they also are past the age of regular paid work.[11] Caring for a dependent elder may not be an enticing prospect for people who are themselves ageing and retired, but few old people are severely dependent for a very long period and many older and younger people rather than being burdened with the responsibility of care give it willingly, though for a minority it is indeed a hard and distressing task.[12]

THE COSTS OF OLD AGE

The direct costs to public expenditure attributable to people aged 65 and over were estimated at £8.4 m. for health care and £2.8m. for personal social services (England and Wales) in 1989–90; £23.8m. for state pensions (Great Britain) in 1990–1. By far the greatest cost is that of pensions. The distribution of costs and the total pensions cost is likely to remain stable until *c.*2020, since the total population of pensionable age is expected to be stable, unless there is a significant rise in state pensions expenditure, or a significant shift in priorities for welfare spending, of which there was little sign in the late 1990s in the political statements of either of the main political parties. It should be remembered that both in absolute and in international comparative terms the levels of British state pensions at the end of the twentieth century are low and 'cannot guarantee an adequate minimum standard of income in old age'.[13]

After 2020 levels of pensions expenditure will be determined by political decisions rather than driven by demographic change. Political choices can be, and are being, made about the extent to which the cost of pensions falls upon the individual, through inducements to saving, or upon public expenditure.[14] The increases in pensions expenditure in the 1960s and 1970s owed less to demography than to political decisions to increase levels of pension and the range of people eligible for them. Since that time, levels of expenditure on

[10] See pp. 431–2.   [11] Scott A. Bass (ed.), *Older and Active* (New Haven and London, 1995), 100.
[12] Ibid. A. Offer, 'Between the Gift and the Market: The Economy of Regard', *Economic History Review*, 50 (1997), 450–76.
[13] A. B. Atkinson, 'State Pensions for Today and Tomorrow', David Hobman Annual Lecture Age Concern Institute of Gerontology, King's College London (1994); also see p. 384.
[14] For discussion of the options see P. Johnson and J. Falkingham, *Ageing and Economic Welfare* (London, 1992), 133 ff.

pensions and services for older people have not moved in line with their pro-portionate numbers. Successive governments have responded to the ageing of the population by cutting back per capita expenditure on older people; this is one cause of the well-documented growth in inequality in income and health in later twentieth-century Britain. On past experience, the cost of age-ing to the public purse cannot be estimated simply by extrapolating present expenditure into the future.

WHO IS 'DEPENDENT'?

In other respects, the assumption that the growing proportion of older people will automatically load a heavy new burden of 'dependency' upon a shrink-ing population in paid work is more questionable than it might intuitively appear. The size of the population of conventional working age is, in any case, not predicted to diminish until *c*.2020, on the assumption that the demographic trends of the 1990s remain unchanged. Social scientists have conventionally calculated a 'dependency ratio' of paid workers in relation to the remainder of the population, assuming that those aged 16 to 65 are mostly engaged in productive work and that those younger and older are not. Any increase in the numbers and costs of dependent older people is being offset to some degree by the falling numbers and costs of dependent young people as fertility rates fall. When these are taken together, strictly age-related dependency is seen to have been remarkably stable over this century (see Fig. 2).

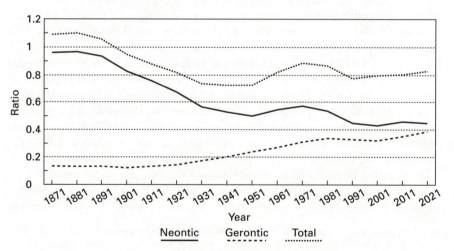

Note: Women aged 60 and over, men aged 65 and over.

Sources: Census Volumes 1871–81; OPCS *National Population Projections, 1987–2027*, series PP2, no. 16 (London, 1987).

Fig. 2. Dependency ratios, Great Britain, 1871–2021

But are the costs of younger and older people equal? In the 1980s and 1990s the *public* costs of support for those under 15 were roughly half of those for the over-sixty-fives.[15] To public costs should be added private costs such as those for child care and private education; and the opportunity costs to parents, mainly mothers, of income foregone whilst caring for young people. These are considerably greater than the equivalent private costs of caring for older people: all children require total support from someone for a substantial period of their lives—a period which lengthened over the twentieth century; few old people do so and very few indeed for a period equivalent to the normal length of child dependency. In Britain the estimated cost of earnings foregone for an average woman with three children was £202,000 in 1990 prices—about 46 per cent of her potential lifetime earnings. To this should be added about £50,000 for direct costs of childrearing.[16] Such costs should not be overlooked—though they generally are—in calculating the relative costs to the community of older and younger people. In addition, as we shall see below, older people make positive inputs into the economy as producers and consumers to an immensely greater degree than could be possible for very young people.

A further difficulty with the conventional usage of the concept of dependency in this context is that the numbers of people in paid work between ages 16 and 65 have risen in the recent past due to the increasing numbers of women in the paid labour force. Simultaneously they have been reduced due to increased participation of people over age 18 in higher education and to high levels of unemployment among adults of all ages. The age structure of the population is by no means the only or the major determinant of the 'dependency ratio'. Labour market trends are more important.[17] Lower rates of unemployment could go far to offset the effects of the ageing of the population, as could increased rates of immigration of younger people. The concept of dependency should be used with great caution in this context.

THE COSTS OF MEDICAL CARE

None the less, it seems reasonable to assume that the growing numbers of very old people will increase the numbers of physically dependent people, with a resultant increase in costs, especially arising from their need for care due to ill health. It seems natural to believe that those who die in their eighties or nineties must experience a longer period of illness and dependency before death than those who die at earlier ages. In 1988/90 per capita UK public expenditure on hospital and community and family health services was:

---

[15] *Johnson and Falkingham, Ageing,* 135.

[16] H. Joshi, 'The Cash Opportunity Costs of Childbearing: An Approach to Estimation Using British Data', *Population Studies,* 44 (1990), 41–60; and 'The Cost of Caring', in C. Glendinning and J. Miller (eds.), *Women and Poverty in Britain in the 1990s* (London, 1992), 110–12. Offer, 'Economy of Regard', 460. [17] Johnson and Falkingham, *Ageing,* 45.

aged 14–44   £187
aged 45–64   £306
aged 65–74   £730
aged 75–84   £1,409
aged 85+   £2,407.

People over 75 occupied 50 per cent of all hospital beds in the 1980s.[18]

However, there is also evidence that the older the age attained without becoming disabled and dependent, the shorter the period of dependency before death. Evidence from the USA suggests that the prevalence of disability at later ages has been falling while average lifespan has been increasing; and that this has come about not because of improvements in medical care but because successive age cohorts of older people are remaining healthier to later ages.[19] What is true of specific age groups at one point in time may not hold good for the same age groups at other times. The relatively low cost of health care for younger compared with older people in recent years is partly due to the fact that younger people are dependent, ill, and hospitalized much *less* than the same age groups in the past.[20] Health standards have risen in society at large. Younger age cohorts are growing up fitter, with a greater sense of personal responsibility for their health and greater concern about exercise and diet. As they age they may, in consequence, require less medical care. Different age cohorts have different life experiences which may affect their later lives in unforeseen ways. People who were over 80 in the mid-1990s were born during or before the First World War, perhaps in severe poverty. They are survivors of birth cohorts depleted by high death-rates at all ages from infancy. Only at the end of the twentieth century are almost complete birth cohorts surviving into old age, beneficiaries of improved environmental and health care conditions through their lifetimes. They may, in consequence, be more rather than less vulnerable to ill health at later ages, since those who lived into old age in previous generations were survivors, the physically more vulnerable having failed to survive the hazards of earlier life; but this cannot reliably be predicted.[21]

Those who have their eightieth birthdays in 2020 will have grown up with the greater prosperity, improved health services and health awareness of the post-war period. But some of them, and members of younger age cohorts, will have experienced the effects of unemployment and increasing poverty in the 1980s and 1990s, though these may not be the survivors to the oldest ages.[22]

[18] A. Tinker, *Elderly People in Modern Society* (London, 1992), 94.

[19] J. Grimley Evans, 'Implications for Health Services', in Royal Society/ British Academy, *Ageing: Science, Medicine and Society* (1997), 1892. K. G. Manton, L. Corder, E. Stallard, 'Chronic Disability Trends in Elderly United States Populations, 1892–1994', *Proceedings of the National Academy of Sciences, USA*, 94/6 (1997), 2593–8.

[20] N. Bosanquet, *A Future for Old Age* (London, 1978).   [21] Day, *The Future*, 32 ff.

[22] K. Moser, A. Fox, and D. Jones, 'Unemployment and Mortality in the OPCS Longitudinal Study', *Lancet*, 2 (1984), 1324–8; M. Whitehead, *The Health Divide: Inequalities in Health in the 1980s* (London, 1987). R. Wilkinson, *Unhealthy Societies: The Affliction of Inequality* (London, 1997).

By contrast, others of the same cohort have experienced great prosperity—which is not necessarily good for health. Furthermore, we cannot easily assess the long-term effects of environmental degeneration in the late twentieth century. Future health experience in old age, or at any age, is hard to predict.

Yet even in the 1980s and 1990s most people dying at age 80 or above did not experience a prolonged period of expensive ill health. One of the few surveys of the oldest old (people over 90) concluded that 'the picture is not at all one of unremitting gloom. Extreme old age should not be equated—on present findings—with overwhelming levels of morbidity or extreme dependence.'[23] Even at these late ages there was marked variety of physical and mental condition. Most people had some problems; few were forced into dependency by them.

Predictions about the future health conditions of older people differ widely, from those who believe that life expectancy is already close to its optimum[24] to those who think that it can be further extended,[25] to those who admit that with present knowledge the future cannot be predicted;[26] from those who think that people are both living longer and will remain fitter until later ages, to those who believe that longer life is not necessarily matched by prolonged health, due in part to the intractability at present of diseases which mainly afflict the very old, such as Alzheimer's.[27]

Potential human longevity is unknown. In most developed countries in the 1990s men have a mean life expectancy of 70 to 75, women of 75 to 80, and the mean has been rising for both sexes. Increasing numbers of people are living past 85, to 100 and a few even beyond. Japan at the end of the millennium has the highest life expectancy in the world and the largest numbers of people living past 100. In 1960 there were 144 Japanese centenarians; in 1997, 8,500, most of them female and living in the south of Japan. In England and Wales an average of seventy-four people a year reached their

[23] M. Bury and A. Holme, 'Longevity and the Quality of Life: A Study of People Aged Ninety and Over in England', in M. Bury and J. Macnicol (eds.), *Aspects of Ageing: Essays on Social Policy and Old Age*, Department of Social Policy and Social Science, Royal Holloway College (London, 1990), 145.

[24] J. F. Fries, 'Ageing, Natural Death and the Compression of Morbidity', *New England Journal of Medicine*, 303 (1980), 130–5.

[25] S. J. Olshansky, 'On Forecasting Mortality', *Milbank Memorial Fund Quarterly*, 66/3 (1988), 482–530.   [26] David W. E. Smith, *Human Longevity* (Oxford, 1993).

[27] Among others, K. Manton, 'Changing Concepts of Mortality and Morbidity in the Population' *Milbank Memorial Fund Quarterly*, 60 (1982), 183–244; E. L. Schneider and J. A. Brody, 'Ageing, Natural Death, and the Compression of Morbidity: Another View', *New England Journal of Medicine*, 309 (1983), 854–6; J. A. Brody, 'Prospects for an Ageing Population', *Nature* (1985), 315; E. Grundy, 'Mortality and Morbidity among the Old', *British Medical Journal*, 288 (1984), 663–4, and 'Age-Related Change in Later Life', in M. Murphy and J. Hobcraft (eds.), *Population Research in Britain* (London, 1991), 133–56. Day, *The Future*, 50 ff. On the historical debate about whether trends in mortality and morbidity match or diverge see J. Riley, *Sickness, Recovery and Death: A History and Forecast of Ill Health* (London, 1989); R. Woods and N. Williams, 'Must the Gap Widen before it can be Narrowed? Long-Term Trends in Social Class Mortality Differentials', *Continuity and Change*, 10 (1995), 105–37.

century in 1911–20; in 1997 3,000 people reached their hundredth birthday.[28] One hundred and twenty is the maximum age that currently seems to be attainable. Some argue that this is the genetically determined human maximum, which past generations were prevented by environmental conditions from achieving, but that improvements in health and living standards will make it increasingly attainable. Since the relevant gene has not been identified this remains speculative. We do not know whether in the future people will live longer or in what condition they will spend their last phase of life. More diseases are in principle conquerable and there are signs, though as yet not conclusive evidence, that people are remaining healthier to later ages and are not experiencing a longer period of dependency before death, rather that onset of physiological old age is being postponed. It can hardly be postponed indefinitely. People must eventually die, and of something. Yet the causes of death of the oldest old are more often uncertain than those of the merely very old. Most people in their late seventies and eighties die, like the younger old, of cancers, heart disease, cerebro-vascular disease. The causes of death of the very old are more obscure. Very little is known about why some people die at 70, others at 80, 90, or 100.[29] Those who live to the oldest ages at present seem to be less vulnerable than the younger old to certain diseases especially characteristic of old age such as Alzheimer's.[30] Very late age remains a mysterious territory.[31]

If the future health conditions of the oldest old are uncertain, that of the mass of older people is no less so, in the present as well as the future. The Medical Research Council pointed out in 1994, in the course of a lengthy plea for more research on health and illness in old age:

Current data sources do not provide adequate information on the real health status of the elderly population nor of the changing health status over time. As a result the controversy over whether the increase in longevity achieved during the present century has been accompanied by increases in the length of disability and dependence remains to be resolved.[32]

We do know that in the 1990s the amount and length of medical treatment received rose from age 50 and was higher among women than men. Why this was so and to what extent it was remediable is obscured by the 'unfortunate exclusion of older people from major epidemiological studies . . . the present data sources are not adequate for monitoring the health of older people'.[33] 'It is a matter of profound concern that it is currently not possible

---

[28] J. W. Vaupel, 'The Remarkable Improvements in Survival at Older Ages', in *Ageing, Science, Medicine*, 1799–1804.
[29] Ibid.   [30] Smith, *Human Longevity*.
[31] Which a current French study of all French centenarians will begin to explore.
[32] Medical Research Council, *The Health of the UK's Elderly People* (London, 1994), 23.
[33] Ibid. 25.

to determine whether the health status of the older population has improved, deteriorated or remained the same during the past decades of mortality decline.'[34] 'The balance of evidence at the present time would appear to show that most of the years of life gained are without major disability although there would appear to be a minor increase in the total period of disability (including less serious disability)'; but the evidence was slight.[35]

Studies of the influence of socio-economic conditions on health and on the use of health services excluded old people, on the extraordinary assumption that such factors were of lesser significance in later life. Only in the 1990s have older people been included in any studies of lifestyle determinants of health. At least as seriously, older people were excluded from health care:

There is a widespread tendency amongst health care professionals, purchasers and providers of care to use age as a criterion for the exclusion of older people from certain types of health care . . . There is a view, unsubstantiated by research, which is pervasive among health and social service professionals and the population at large, including older people themselves, that elderly people benefit less from medical and surgical interventions than do younger age ones. This may in turn contribute to an attitude that older people are less deserving than younger people because they may be viewed in some respects as having less to offer society.[36]

In accordance with Department of Health guidelines women over 65 were excluded from regular invitations for screening for breast or cervical cancer, despite trials which showed these to be beneficial up at least to the age of 74.[37] Also the MRC commented;

Less overt inequalities stem from the policies to exclude older age groups from admission to specialist coronary care units, or from access to thrombotic therapy or referral to specialist care in diabetes until a crisis supervenes.[38]

The extent of such rationing was unknown in 1994 (or in 1999) because it had not been researched.

Older people were also excluded from clinical trials including for cancer therapy, coronary bypass surgery, hypertensive and thrombotic therapies—the conditions most likely to afflict them. 'The consequence', stated the MRC, 'is ill-informed health care decisions.'[39] Where older people were included in trials of treatment for thrombosis, hypertension, and depression they were found to benefit at least as much and sometimes more than younger people.[40] They were excluded from preventive programmes because:

There is widespread fear that preventive action may, by lengthening survival, subject individuals to risks of worse disability and suffering. This concept however has no theoretical foundation.[41]

---

[34] Ibid. 26.   [35] Ibid.   [36] Ibid. 37.   [37] Ibid. 38.
[38] Ibid.   [39] Ibid. 45.   [40] Ibid.   [41] Ibid. 50.

On the contrary, there was growing knowledge of:

The significant role that exercise has in the maintenance of physical and mental health and functional ability at all ages . . . (there are) strong correlations between physical and mental health and functional ability at all ages . . . between physical fitness and the retardation of cognitive change in old age.[42]

The MRC feared that welfare services often assumed and reinforced passivity among older people rather than encouraging activity. Also, the need for psychotherapy for the emotional burdens of old age, such as bereavement, was still not taken as seriously as for younger people.

The MRC recommended that:

Unless there are strong scientific grounds, clinical trials of prevention or treatment of diseases which are likely to affect older people should have no upper age limit on recruitment.[43]

It concluded that:

One of the fundamental issues that needs to be considered is whether the use of chronological age as a proxy for biological fitness and the use of advanced age as the sole criterion for deciding whether or not a patient should receive a given health care intervention are appropriate . . . a change in the philosophy for rationing care must now take place.[44]

Though, on average, older people responded less well to treatment than younger people, little was known about the effect of age on the outcome of treatment largely due, again, to the exclusion of older people from research studies:

However, at no age—'young' or 'old' . . . and it must be recognized that such a distinction in this context is arbitrary—will such impairments affect all individuals equally . . . like younger individuals but perhaps to a greater degree, older people are a heterogeneous group and should be considered as such . . . stereotyping overlooks important heterogeneity in age . . . using age rather than physiological status to determine the care given to an individual appears not to be based on solid foundations . . . In some areas, for example, intensive care, it has been demonstrated that if sufficient is known about an individual's physiological status, age contributes very little further to the prediction of outcome.[45]

The MRC said nothing about gender differences in ill health. Though women outlive men, they continue to do so in poorer health. Medical researchers sometimes treat this as genetic in origin, though researchers need to take account of the greater poverty and associated poorer nutrition of many older women and the likely impact of these conditions on health.

Certain conditions differentially afflict the very old and certainly cause long-term dependency, notably Alzheimer's disease, whose causes and future patterns are unknown. In the mid-1990s about 20 per cent of all people over 80

---

[42] Medical Research Council, 52.　　[43] Ibid. 38.　　[44] Ibid. 39.　　[45] Ibid. 39–40.

were victims of Alzheimer's. But it is quite unknown whether this will be the pattern for future age cohorts, or whether a cure will be discovered.

On present evidence we cannot easily predict the health status of future generations of old people and cannot safely assume that they will replicate those of past cohorts. The present was unpredictable fifty years ago and the next fifty years is equally mysterious now.

THE ECONOMIC CONTRIBUTION OF OLDER PEOPLE

Whatever their state of health, it is too readily assumed in statistical analyses and in popular discourse that all of those past retirement age are more or less automatically dependent burdens on the economy rather than contributors to it. It is obviously absurd to assume that a 66-year-old retired millionaire is more dependent in an economic sense than a 64-year-old employed roadsweeper,[46] yet this is precisely the type of assumption that statistical calculations of strictly age-related dependency invite us to make.

Indeed the assumption that men over 65 and women over 60 are necessarily more 'dependent' than younger people is diverging increasingly from reality. On the one hand, more people are retiring from paid work in their fifties.[47] On the other, increasing numbers of retired people are physically fitter and have greater power as consumers than in the past. The total number of employees covered by occupational pensions was 11.4m. in 1975, slightly lower at 10.7m. in 1991. The numbers with private personal pensions rose from 600,000 in 1974 to 15.2m. in 1991 and 19.9m. in 1995,[48] largely as a result of the encouragement given by Conservative governments to personal rather than occupational pensions. In 1985 only 47 per cent of household heads aged over 65 were house-owners (itself a great increase on previous decades). In the same year 65 per cent of household heads aged 30 to 60 were house-owners. In future, increasing numbers of people will enter old age in possession of a considerable capital asset which can be traded down to release income or used as loan security.

But early retirement may mean that many run down their assets from earlier ages than in the past, whilst facing a longer period with limited incomes and assets before death. And, although some of the most affluent members of society are above the official pensionable age, so are many of the poorest. Inequalities among the aged are greater than between the aged and other age

---

[46] P. Johnson, 'The Structured Dependency of the Elderly', in Margot Jefferys (ed.), *Growing Old in the Twentieth Century* (London, 1989), 66.

[47] M. Kohli *et al.*, *Time for Retirement: Comparative Studies of Early Exit from the Labour Force* (Cambridge, 1991).

[48] Martin Evans, 'Social Security: Dismantling the Pyramids?', in H. Glennerster and J. Hills (eds.), *The State of Welfare: The Economics of Social Spending*, 2nd edn. (Oxford, 1998), 283–4.

groups. In income as in health, older age groups contain the best and the worst off, and in both cases the oldest women fare worst.[49] Mean income levels of older people at the end of the century are lower than is probable in future, and simple projections into the future from the current situation have little value.

It is often claimed that the ageing of society will bring shifts in patterns of spending and saving which will be economically harmful. The one-time commonplace of economic theory that older people are dissavers has not survived scrutiny; indeed they may save more than younger groups, not least because of the uncertain length of life ahead of them.[50] Age in itself has little effect upon consumer demand once account is taken of differences in income and household composition.[51] The ageing of the population is likely to bring about some shifts in demand but they are not necessarily easy to predict or necessarily economically disadvantageous. There may be less demand for schools, but perhaps the buildings will be used for lifelong education; older households may want smaller housing units, but so will the many single people in younger age groups—or with greater affluence not all single person households will prefer small dwellings. We may need fewer pushchairs but more wheelchairs. The future is elusive.

Old people who are not poor contribute significantly to the economy as consumers and as savers. Rich and poor old people provide a wide variety of services and other forms of labour, paid and unpaid. The great majority of older people are fit and active, are in their sixties and seventies, and are not in paid employment.[52] In 1991 only 5 per cent of people aged 65 or above were officially included in the labour force (i.e. were employed, self-employed, or actively seeking work). However, this average masks differences between age groups and between men and women. In 1988 15 per cent of men aged 60 to 65 were in paid employment and 7 per cent of women; between ages 70 and 74, 7 per cent of men and 4 per cent of women were in paid work. Among those over 80 the percentages were 3 and zero per cent respectively.[53] It is reasonable to assume that all such official statistics underestimate the productive activities of older people. There are no estimates of the numbers who continue to apply their skills, for example as accountants or carpenters, on a part-time and informal basis.

A large number of older people provide a wide range of formal and informal voluntary services. In 1981 42 per cent of people over 65 gave regular help to other elderly people, most often a close relative; 11 per cent helped

---

[49] Joseph Rowntree Foundation, *Inquiry into Income and Wealth* vols. i/ii (York, 1993). R. Hancock and P. Weir, *More Ways than Means: A Guide to Pensioners' Incomes in Great Britain during the 1980s*, Age Concern Institute of Gerontology, King's College (London, 1994).

[50] Johnson and Falkingham, *Ageing*, 172–4. Day, *The Future*, 91 ff.

[51] Johnson and Falkingham, *Ageing*, 153.   [52] See p. 386.

[53] J. Askham *et al.*, *Life After Sixty: A Profile of Britain's Older Population*, Age Concern Institute of Gerontology, King's College (London, 1992), 52–4.

neighbours.[54] A large US survey in 1991 revealed that 26 per cent of Americans aged over 65 were giving help to relatives, friends, or neighbours, 15 per cent of them for twenty hours or more each week. Up to the age of 85 about 28 per cent engaged in a median four hours per week of work for a voluntary agency. Substantial financial and non-financial support (from giving advice and emotional support to childminding) was given to children, grandchildren, and great-grandchildren.[55] Between 1968 and 1985 in Britain 22 per cent of local authority councillors were aged over 65; this age group made up 14 per cent of the population.[56] Large but uncertain numbers were engaged in voluntary work.

Most older people are women who continue long past the conventional retirement ages to perform the conventional unpaid but essential tasks which are almost universal among women of all ages: domestic and other services for themselves and others, some younger, some older, some the same age. They support and help to keep efficient people active in the paid labour force and provide services which would otherwise fall to the health and social services. Elderly men provide such services to a greater degree than is normally assumed, mainly though not entirely for their spouses.[57] In the US, also, the extent and type of care given differed between men and women far less than is often assumed.[58] Just as the unpaid inputs into the economy arising from the domestic tasks of women are being factored into some national accounting systems, attention should also be given to those of all older people if we are to obtain an accurate picture of their role in the economy and of the extent to which they are a net 'burden' upon it.

The potential of older people as direct producers may be greater still. The conventional age of retirement was fixed at a time when fewer people remained fit to later ages. Even in the 1940s and 1950s,[59] and still more strongly since, there has been clear evidence that a high proportion of people in their sixties and seventies are physically capable of remaining longer than they currently do in the paid labour market, if, of course they wish to do so, as many claim that they do. They can continue to work effectively at their accustomed or preferred occupation even when this is physically heavy or makes significant intellectual demands. At many tasks workers in their sixties and seventies can out-perform those in their twenties, though not those at their peak in their thirties and early forties. Losses in speed and agility are compensated by greater experience, concentration, and motivation. Mental and physical deterioration of course occurs with age, but its speed and effects are popularly exaggerated. Practice keeps most skills active, such as memory, flexibility, and decision-making. Most workers are understretched for much of their working lives and

---

[54] *Social Trends*, vol. 14 (Central Statistical Office, London, 1984), tables 11.4 and 11.6.
[55] Offer, 'Economy of Regard'; Bass, *Older*.   [56] Tinker, *Elderly*, 221.
[57] S. Arber and Jay Ginn, *Gender and Later Life* (London, 1991), 129–57.
[58] Bass, *Older*, 112 ff.   [59] See pp. 393–8.

have spare capacity as well as experience on which to draw at later ages. Older people may take longer to retrain for new tasks than younger, but not to a degree than makes retraining not worth while.

Few people decline in all spheres of competence at once and they decline in a variety of ways. Mental functioning and range of capabilities at any age is related at least as much to expectation and habit as to age and physical condition. Problems are most likely to arise for older workers where work is at a fast, continuous pace, suited to younger workers and over which the older worker has no control. Where these problems are absent there appears to be little that a reasonably fit older person cannot do as efficiently as a high proportion of younger workers.[60] In recent decades production-line manufacturing has declined and been replaced by service occupations which are less closely monitored and should be better suited to the needs of older workers. Average physical and mental performance declines with age but the variance within the age group does not alter with age. While on average 60-year-olds will exhibit slower mental and physical reactions than 40-year-olds, a substantial proportion of 60-year-olds will have reaction times at least as good as the average among 40-year-olds. Many of the tasks at which older people perform less well in laboratory experiments—such as remembering and recognizing word sequences—have little relevance to work situations, and their relatively poor performance may be a function less of age than of poor motivation for pointless tasks. With practice older people can improve performance at mental and physical activities to the levels of much younger people.[61]

Where employers have employed older people they have found them highly employable, with less absenteeism and mobility and requiring less supervision than younger people.[62] The spread of early retirement in the later twentieth century has had more to do with cutting the costs of employing higher paid workers than with the lesser competence of older people. There are signs at the end of the century that some employers are regretting the loss of the accumulated experience of early retired older workers and are reversing their policies. The common belief that technological change drives older people out of employment has never fitted easily with empirical reality and fits especially ill the situation of the late twentieth century in which technological change in some occupations is so rapid that the skills of people at any age may become redundant. Strictly in terms of work capacity and the likely return on training there is at least as much to be said for retraining a 50-year old as a 30-year-old.[63]

The ageing of societies will affect economies at all levels of development. But these changes are too complex to be easily predictable for, 'our understanding of the processes of economic growth and innovation is really too

---

[60] M. J. Stones and A. Kozma, 'Physical Performance', in N. Charness (ed.), *Ageing and Human Performance* (Chichester and New York, 1985), 210–31.

[61] A Welford, 'Changes in Performance with Age: An Overview', in Charness, *Human Performance*, 36.

[62] Johnson and Falkingham, *Ageing*, 182.   [63] Ibid.

primitive to permit confident long-run economic assessments to be made'.[64] Probably the greatest disability affecting older people in the labour market is the mistaken belief of employers and others, including older people themselves, that competence at most tasks declines seriously with age. This is capable of change. Sex discrimination in the labour market has diminished, if imperfectly, in the recent past, and age discrimination may do so also in future, especially if employers come to recognize the positive advantages of employing older people. The labour market changed in unforeseeable ways over the twentieth century and can continue to do so. At the end of the century retirement ages were being raised or abolished in a number of developed countries (Sweden, Japan, Australia, USA). It is unnecessary to demand that armies of 70-year-olds should march out to work to support those older still, and certainly many will not wish to do so, but we need to shift out of the mode of thinking that assumes that somewhere in their sixties most people become dependent, incapable burdens, to realize that most of them have at least as much to offer as much younger people, and seek ways to use their capacities positively.

We should—and can—conceive of older people as a resource, not as a burden. Their capacities and needs at any point in time are not fixed but are malleable in response to policy and environmental change and to their own needs and wishes. Certainly the capacities of most of them are underestimated, including often by themselves. There is no convincing evidence that older people are inherently more conservative, culturally or politically, than the young.[65] Older people, in the late twentieth century, make fewer demands on natural resources, create less waste, and require services such as public transport, small-scale and accessible shopping, and local parks and recreation.[66] They are model citizens of the 'sustainable' society to which many people increasingly aspire—but this too may change over time.

The future is unpredictable. This does not mean that we should give up the attempt to plan for a future in which there will probably permanently be a higher proportion of old people than at any past time, but we should ensure that plans are based upon evidence of real experience, not on assertion driven by panic. The generations do not have to compete for resources in the future, but can share them equitably.[67] At no time is it adequate simply to extrapolate from current costs and patterns of use to the future. It is necessary to examine the different experiences, expectations, and needs of different age cohorts. We need to work with a more complex and realistic picture of who older people are and of their roles in society and the economy than the simple, depressing, inaccurate, image of burdensome dependency.

[64] Ibid. 175–6.   [65] Day, *The Future*, 95 ff.   [66] Ibid.
[67] D. Thomson, *Selfish Generations?* (Oxford, 1991). Johnson and Falkingham, *Ageing*, 177–88.

Bibliography

ARCHIVAL SOURCES

Professor Sir Ferguson Anderson, interviewed by Pat Thane. Transcript in Wellcome Unit for the History of Medicine, University of Glasgow.

Professor Sir Ferguson Anderson, interviewed by Margot Jefferys. National Life History Collection, National Sound Archive, the British Library.

W. F. Anderson, 'Memorandum on the Need for a Research Unit in Geriatric Medicine', Glasgow University Archives, Files of the Principal.

H. H. Asquith Papers, the Bodleian Library.

Arthur J. Balfour Papers, the British Library.

William J. Braithewaite Papers, the British Library of Political and Economic Science.

John Burns Papers, the British Library.

Joseph Chamberlain Papers, University of Birmingham Library.

Charleston Papers, University of Sussex Library.

Lionel Cosin, interviewed by Margot Jefferys. National Sound Archive, the British Library.

Mass Observation, University of Sussex Library.

Memoirs of Bernard Isaacs, Greater Glasgow Health Board Archives, University of Glasgow.

Passfield Papers, the British Library of Political and Economic Science.

PUBLIC RECORD OFFICE

For details of documents consulted *see* Reference Notes.

PARLIAMENTARY PAPERS

Factories Enquiry Commission, *First Report of the Central Board*, vol. xx (1833).

Report from His Majesty's Commissioners for Inquiry into the Administration and Practical Operation of the Poor Laws, vol. xxvii (1834).

Report from the Select Committee of the House of Lords on the Poor Law Amendment Act, vol. xxviii (1837–8).

Report by Mr Tufnell on the State of the Poor in the Township of Rochdale, vol. xxxv (1842).

Children's Employment Commission, vol. 14 (1843).

First Report from the Select Committee on Poor Relief, vol. iv (1862).

Final Report from the Select Committee on National Provident Insurance, vol. xi (1887).

Report of the Royal Commission on the Aged Poor, vol. xiv (1895).

Report of the Committee on Old Age Pensions, vol. xlv (1898).

Report from the Select Committee on the Cottage Homes Bill, vol. ix (1899).

Report of the Select Committee on the Aged Deserving Poor, vol. viii (1899).

Report of the Departmental Committee on the Financial Aspects of the Proposals made by the Select Committee of the House of Commons of 1899 about the Aged Deserving Poor, vol. x (1900).

Circular of 4 Aug. 1900, 30th Annual Report of LGB, 1901.

Report of the Royal Commission on Superannuation in the Civil Service, vol. xxxiii (1903).

Circular from the LGB to Friendly Societies, Mar. 1908, vol. lxxxviii (1908).

Royal Commission on the Poor Laws. Reports, 1909 Cd. 4499, vol. xxxvii, *Minutes of Evidence*, 1910 Cd. 5066, vol. 48; Cd. 5068, vol. 49.

37th Annual Report of the Local Government Board for Ireland (31 Mar. 1909), Cd. 4810.

38th Annual Report of the Local Government Board for Ireland (1910), Cd. 5319.

Old Age Pensions and Irish Pauperism (1913), Cd. 7015.

43rd Annual Report of the Local Government Board for England and Wales (1913–14).

Report of the Committee Appointed by the Board of Trade to Investigate the Principal Causes which have Led to the Increase of Prices of Commodities since the Beginning of the War, vol. xviii (1916), Cd. 8398.

Report, Ministry of Reconstruction, Local Government Committee, vol. xviii (1917–18).

Report of the Departmental Committee on Old Age Pensions, including Minutes of Evidence (1919), Cmd. 411.

First Annual Report, Ministry of Pensions, vol. xxvi (1919).

First Annual Report, Ministry of Health, vol. viii (1919–20).

Second Annual Report, Ministry of Pensions, vol. xxii (1920).

Third Annual Report of the Ministry of Health, vol. viii (1921–2).

Interim Report, Select Committee on National Expenditure (Dec. 1921), Cmd. 1581.

Fourth Annual Report, Ministry of Health, vol. viii (1922–3).

Report of the Committee on Pensions for Unmarried Women (1939), Cmd. 5991.

Social Insurance and Allied Services (1942), Cmd. 6404.

The Current Trend of Population in Great Britain, Cmd. 6358 (1942).

Economic Survey for 1947, Cmd. 7046 (1947).

Twenty-Third Annual Report, Ministry of Pensions (1 Sept. 1939–31 Mar. 1948).

Report of the Royal Commission on Population, Cmd. 7695 (1949).

Report of the Committee on the Economic and Financial Problems of the Provision for Old Age (Phillips Report) (1951), Cmd. 9333.

First Report of the National Advisory Committee on the Employment of Older Men and Women (1953), Cmd. 8963.

Second Report of the National Advisory Committee on Employment of Older Men and Women (1955), Cmd. 9628.

Ministry of Health, *Report of the Committee of Enquiry into the Cost of the National Health Service* (Guillebaud Report) (1956), Cmd. 9663.

Report of the Committee on the Economic and Financial Problems of Old Age, vol. xvii (1955–6).

The Civil Service, vol. i: *Report of the Committee 1966–8*, vol. xviii (1967–8).

NEWSPAPERS AND PERIODICALS

Charity Organization Review
Crossbow
Daily Chronicle
Daily News
Financial Times
Grand United Magazine
Manchester Guardian

Ministry of Labour Gazette
Morning Post
New Statesman
Nursing Mirror
Nursing Times
The Times

THESES AND DISSERTATIONS

BARKER-READ, MARY, 'The Treatment of the Aged Poor in Five Selected West Kent Parishes from Settlement to Speenhamland, 1662–1797', Ph.D. thesis (Open University, 1988).

BOTELHO, LYNN, 'Provision for the Elderly in Two Early Modern Suffolk Communities', Ph.D. thesis (Cambridge University, 1996).

CLARKE, MARTIN, 'Household and Family in Bethnal Green, 1851–71: The Effects of Social and Economic Change', Ph.D. thesis (Cambridge University, 1986).

FOGERTY, J. R., 'Growing Old in England, 1878–1949', Ph.D. thesis (Australian National University, Canberra, 1992).

FRASER, G., 'The Household and Family Structure of Mid-Nineteenth Century Cardiff in Comparative Perspective', Ph.D. thesis (Cardiff, 1988).

FUKASAWA, KAZUKO, 'Voluntary Provision for Old Age by Trade Unions in Britain before the Coming of the Welfare State', Ph.D. thesis (University of London, 1996).

GRITT, A. J., ' "I ham old, broken down and ready to die": Approaches to the Poor, Experiences of Poverty and the Life-Cycle in South-West Lancashire during the Eighteenth and Early Nineteenth Centuries', BA diss. (University of Central Lancashire, 1995).

GROVES, DULCIE M., 'Women and Occupational Pensions, 1870–1983: An Exploratory Study', Ph.D. thesis (University of London, 1986).

JONES, HARRIET, 'The Conservative Party and the Welfare State, 1942–1955', Ph.D. thesis (University of London, 1992).

JONES, MARGARET, 'The Old Age Pensions Act, 1908: A Break with the Poor Law?', MA diss. (University of Huddersfield, 1996).

KING, STEPHEN, 'The Nature and Causes of Demographic Change in an Industrializing Township: Calverley, 1681–1820', Ph.D. thesis (University of Liverpool, 1993).

MAWSON, P., 'Poor Law Administration in South Shields, 1830–1930', MA thesis (Newcastle University, 1971).

PARKIN, TIM G., 'Age and the Aged in Roman Society', D.Phil. thesis (University of Oxford, 1992).

PHILLIPSON, C., 'The Experience of Retirement: A Sociological Study', Ph.D. thesis (University of Durham, 1978).

SCHEN, C., 'Charity in London, 1500–1620: From the "Wealth of Souls" to the "Most Need" ', Ph.D. thesis (Brandeis University, 1995).

SHARPE, PAMELA, 'Gender-Specific Demographic Adjustment to Changing Economic Circumstances: Colyton, 1538–1837', Ph.D. thesis (University of Cambridge, 1988).

SOKOLL, THOMAS, 'Household and Family among the Poor: The Case of Two Essex Communities in the Late 18th and Early 19th Centuries', Ph.D. thesis (University of Cambridge, 1988).

THOMAS, GILL, 'State Maintenance for Women during the First World War: The Case of Separation Allowances and Pensions', D.Phil. thesis (University of Sussex, 1989).

THOMSON, D., 'Provision for the Elderly in England, 1830–1908', Ph.D. thesis (University of Cambridge, 1981).

WILLIAMS (THANE), PATRICIA M., 'The Development of Old Age Pensions in the UK, 1878–1925', Ph.D. thesis (London School of Economics, 1970).

WOHNIAKOWSKI, ELIZABETH B., 'Family and Population Change in a Nineteenth Century English Village: Puddletown, 1851–71', Ph.D. thesis (Cornell University, 1976).

BOOKS AND ARTICLES

ABEL-SMITH, B., *The Hospitals 1800–1948* (London, 1964).

—— and TOWNSEND, P., *The Poor and the Poorest* (London, 1965).

ACTON SOCIETY TRUST, *Retirement: A Study of Current Attitudes and Practices* (London, 1960).

ADAMS, G. F., and CHEESEMAN, G. A., *Old People in Northern Ireland* (London, 1951).

ADDISON, PAUL, *The Road to 1945* (London, 1975).

—— *Churchill on the Home Front 1900–1955* (London, 1993).

AMOS, P., and HARRELL, S. (eds.), *Other Ways of Growing Old: Anthropological Perspectives* (Stanford, Calif., 1981).

ANDERSON, M., *Family Structure in Nineteenth-Century Lancashire* (Cambridge, 1971).

—— 'The Social Implications of Demographic Change', in F. M. L. Thompson (ed.), *The Cambridge Social History of Britain, 1750–1850*, ii (Cambridge, 1990), 1–70.

ANDERSON, W. F., Chairman, *Planning and Organization of Geriatric Services*, World Health Organization Technical Report, ser. no. 548 (1974).

—— 'Life's Equities after 65', *Transactions and Studies of the College of Physicians of Philadelphia*, 5th ser. 6/4 (1984), 263–73.

—— 'Geriatrics', in G. McLachlan (ed.), *Improving the Common Weal: Aspects of Scottish Health Services 1900–1984* (Edinburgh, 1985), 369–81.

—— 'An Historical Overview of Geriatric Medicine', in M. J. Pathy (ed.), *Principles and Practice of Geriatric Medicine* (London, 1985), 7–13.

—— 'Education in Geriatric Medicine', *Annals of the Academy of Medicine of Singapore* (1986), 146–50.

—— and COWAN, N., 'A Consultative Health Centre for Older People: The Rutherglen Experiment', *Lancet*, 2 (1955), 239.

—— —— 'Work and Retirement: the Influence on the Health of Older People', *Lancet*, 2 (1956), 1344–6.

—— and ISAACS, BERNARD (eds.), *Current Achievements in Geriatrics* (London, 1964).

ARBER, SARA, and GINN, JAY, *Gender and Later Life: A Sociological Analysis of Resources and Constraints* (London, 1991).

ARCHER, IAN, *The Pursuit of Stability: Social Relations in Elizabethan London* (Cambridge, 1991).

ARCHER, ROWENA E., 'Rich Old Women: The Problem of Late Medieval Dowagers', in Tony Pollard (ed.), *Property and Politics: Essays in Later Medieval English History* (Gloucester, 1984), 15–35.

ARISTOTLE, *The Art of Rhetoric*, trans. H. C. Lawson-Tancred (Harmondsworth, 1991).

ARKELL, T., 'The Incidence of Poverty in England in the Later Seventeenth Century', *Social History*, 12/1 (1987), 23–47.

ARMSTRONG, ALAN, *Stability and Change in an English County Town: A Social Study of York, 1801–51* (Cambridge, 1974).

ASKHAM, J., et al., *Life After Sixty: A Profile of Britain's Older Population*, Age Concern Institute of Gerontology, King's College London (London, 1992).

ATKINSON, A. B., *The Economics of Inequality* (Oxford, 1975).

—— 'State Pensions for Today and To-morrow', David Hobman Annual Lecture, Age Concern Institute of Gerontology, King's College London (London, 1994).

—— *Incomes and the Welfare State* (Cambridge, 1995).

BAGRIT, LEON, *The Age of Automation: The BBC Reith Lectures* (London, 1965).

BAINES, DUDLEY, and JOHNSON, PAUL, 'The Labour Force Participation and Economic Well-Being of Older Men in London, 1929–31', *Working Papers in Economic History*, 37/97 (London School of Economics, 1997).

BALDWIN, PETER, *The Politics of Social Solidarity: Class Bases of the European Welfare States, 1875–1975* (Cambridge, 1990).

BALDWIN, SALLY, and FALKINGHAM, JANE, *Social Security and Social Change: New Challenges to the Beveridge Model* (London, 1994).

BARKER, W. H., *Adding Years to Life* (Baltimore, 1987).

BARNES, G., *From Workshop to War Cabinet* (London, 1924).

BARNETT, CORELLI, *The Audit of War* (London, 1986).

—— *The Lost Victory* (London, 1995).

BARRON, CAROLINE, and BILL, CHRISTOPHER (eds.), *The Church in Pre-Reformation Society: Essays in Honour of F. R. H. Du Boulay* (Woodbridge, 1985).

BASS, SCOTT, A. (ed.), *Older and Active* (New Haven and London, 1995).

BEAUVOIR, SIMONE DE, *Old Age*, trans. Patrick O'Brian (Harmondsworth, 1977).

BEDELL, J., 'Memory and Proof of Age in England, 1272–1327', *Past and Present*, 162 (1999), 3–27.

BEIER, A. L., 'Poor Relief in Warwickshire, 1630–60', *Past and Present*, 35 (1966), 77–100.

BELBIN, R. M., 'Difficulties of Older People in Industry', *Occupational Psychology*, 27 (1953), 177–89.

—— 'Older People and Heavy Work', *British Journal of Industrial Medicine*, 12 (1955), 309–19.

BELL, LADY, *At the Works* (1907; London, 1985).

BELLAMY, C., *Administering Central–Local Relations, 1871–1919: The Local Government Board in its Fiscal and Cultural Context* (Manchester, 1988).

BENNETT, JUDITH M., 'Conviviality and Charity in Medieval and Early Modern England', *Past and Present*, 134 (1992), 19–41.

BERESFORD, J. (ed.), *James Woodforde: The Diary of a Country Parson, 1758–1802* (Oxford, 1978).

BERMAN, L., and SOBKOWSKA-ASHCROFT, I., *Images and Impressions of Old Age in the Great Works of Western Literature (700 BC–1900 AD): An Analytical Compendium* (Lewiston, NY, 1987).

BEVERIDGE, WILLIAM, *Insurance for All and Everything* (London, 1924).

BIRRELL, A., *Things Past Redress* (London, 1937).

BLACK, CLEMENTINA, *Married Women's Work* (1915; repr. London, 1983).

BLACKLEY, M. J. J., *Thrift and National Insurance* (London, 1906).

BLACKLEY, W. L., 'National Provident Insurance', *Nineteenth Century* (Nov. 1878), 834–7.

BLAIKIE, ANDREW, 'The Emerging Political Power of the Elderly in Britain, 1908–1948', *Ageing and Society*, 10/1 (1990), 17–39.

BOIS, JEAN PIERRE, *Des vieux de Montaigne aux premières retraites* (Paris, 1989).

BONFIELD, L., 'Was there a "Third Age" in the Pre-Industrial English Past? Some Evidence from the Law', in J. Eekelaar and D. Pearl (eds.), *An Ageing World: Dilemmas and Challenges for Law and Social Policy* (Oxford, 1989), 37–53.

—— and POOS, L. R., 'The Development of the Deathbed Transfer in Medieval English Manor Courts', *Cambridge Law Journal*, 47 (1988), 403–27.

BOOTH, C., *Life and Labour of the People*, 3 vols. (London, 1889).

—— 'The Enumeration and Classification of Paupers and State Pensions for the Poor', *Journal of the Royal Statistical Society*, 54/4 (Dec. 1891), 600–41.

—— *Pauperism—a Picture and Endowment of Old Age, an Argument* (London, 1892).

—— *The Aged Poor in England and Wales* (1894; repr. New York, 1980).

—— *Life and Labour of the People of London*, 17 vols. (London, 1903).

BORNAT, JOANNA, et al., *A Manifesto for Old Age* (London, 1985).

—— DIMMOCK, BRIAN, and PEACE, SHEILA, 'The Impact of Family Change on Older People: The Case of Stepfamilies', *Research Results*, no. 2, ESRC Population and Household Change Programme (Oxford, 1998).

BOSANQUET, H., *The Poor Law Report of 1909* (London, 1909).

BOSANQUET, N., *A Future for Old Age* (London, 1978).

BOSWELL, J., *Life of Samuel Johnson*, 6 vols. (Oxford, 1964).

Boswell's Life of Johnson, 6 vols., ed. G. Birkbeck Hill (Oxford, 1934).

BOTELHO, LYNN, ' "The Old Woman's Wish": Widows by the Family Fire? Widows' Old Age Provisions in Rural England, 1500–1700', in R. Wall (ed.), *The History of the Family* (forthcoming).

—— and THANE, PAT (eds.), *Women and Ageing in British Society since 1500* (London, 2000).

BOTT, E. (ed.), *A Collection of Decisions of the Court of King's Bench Upon the Poor Laws Down to the Present Time* (London, 1773).

BOULTON, JEREMY, *Neighbourhood and Society: A London Suburb in the Seventeenth Century* (Cambridge, 1987).

—— 'London Widowhood Revisited: The Decline of Female Remarriage in the 17th and Early 18th Century', *Continuity and Change*, 5/3 (1990), 323–55.

BOWLEY, A., and HOGG, M., *Has Poverty Diminished?* (London, 1925).

BOYER, GEORGE R., *An Economic History of the English Poor Law, 1750–1850* (Cambridge, 1990).

BRAITHEWAITE, V., 'Old Age Stereotypes: Reconciling Contradictions', *Journal of Gerontology*, 41/3 (1986), 353–60.

—— 'The Ageing Experience: Loss Threat or Challenge?', in P. Heaven (ed.), *Lifespan Development* (Sydney, 1992), 265–301.

—— GIBSON, D., and HOLMAN, J., 'Age Stereotyping: Are We Over-Simplifying the Phenomenon?', *International Journal of Aging and Human Development*, 22/4 (1986), 315–25.

BRAMWELL, P. S., 'Falling Population and Positive Eugenics', *Eugenics Review*, 27/4 (1937), 273–5.

BREWER, JOHN, *The Sinews of Power: War, Money and the English State 1688–1783* (London, 1989).

BRIGDEN, SUSAN, 'Religion and Social Obligation in Early 16th Century London', *Past and Present*, 103 (1984), 67–112.

BRITISH MEDICAL ASSOCIATION BOARD OF SCIENCE AND EDUCATION, *Report of the Working Party on Services for the Elderly* (London, 1976).

BROAD, THOMAS, *All-In Insurance Scheme* (London, 1923).

BRODSKY, V., 'Widows in Late Elizabethan London: Remarriage, Economic Opportunity and Family Orientation', in L. Bonfield, R. M. Smith, and K. Wrightson (eds.), *The World We Have Gained: Histories of Population and Social Structure* (Oxford, 1986), 122–54.

BROWN, R. A., 'Age and "Paced" Work', *Occupational Psychology*, 31 (1957), 11–20.

BUCK, ANNE, *Dress in Eighteenth Century England* (New York, 1979).

BULDER, ELLES, *The Social Economics of Old Age: Strategies to Maintain Income in Later Life in the Netherlands, 1880–1940* (Tinbergen, 1993).

BULLOUGH, V., and CAMPBELL, C., 'Female Longevity and Diet in the Middle Ages', *Speculum*, 55 (1980), 317–55.

BUNBURY, SIR HENRY N. (ed.), *Lloyd George's Ambulance Wagon: Being the Memoirs of William J. Braithewaite, 1911–1912* (London, 1957).

BURN, A. R., '*Hic Breve Vivitur*: A Study in the Expectation of Life in the Roman Empire', *Past and Present*, 4 (1953), 3–31.

BURNETT, JOHN, *Useful Toil: Autobiographies of Working People from the 1820s to the 1920s* (London, 1974).

BURY, M., and HOLME, A., 'Longevity and the Quality of Life: A Study of People Aged Ninety and Over in England', in M. Bury and J. Macnicol (eds.), *Aspects of Ageing: Essays on Social Policy and Old Age*, Department of Social Policy and Social Science, Royal Holloway College (London, 1990), 129–52.

BUTLER, D., and KING, A., *The British General Election of 1964* (London, 1965).

BYTHEWAY, B., and JOHNSON, J. (eds.), *Welfare and the Ageing Experience* (London, 1990).

CAINE, BARBARA, *Destined to be Wives: The Sisters of Beatrice Webb* (Oxford, 1986).

CARLTON, CHARLES, 'The Widow's Tale: Male Myths and Female Reality in 16th and 17th Century England', *Albion*, 20 (1978), 118–29.

CHAMBERLAIN, AUSTEN, *Politics from Inside* (London, 1936).

CHAPMAN, S. J., and HALLSWORTH, H. M., *Unemployment: The Results of an Investigation made in Lancashire* (Manchester, 1909).

CHARLES, ENID, *The Twilight of Parenthood: A Biological Study of the Decline in Population Growth* (London, 1934).

—— 'The Effect of Present Trends in Fertility and Mortality upon the Future Population of England and Wales and upon its Age Composition', *London and Cambridge Economic Service: Special Memorandum*, no. 40 (1935).

—— 'The Effects of Present Trends in Fertility and Mortality upon the Future Population of Great Britain and upon its Age Composition', in Lancelot Hogben (ed.), *Political Arithmetic: A Symposium of Population Studies* (London, 1938), 3–20.

CHARNESS, N. (ed.), *Ageing and Human Performance* (Chichester and New York, 1985).

CHUDACOFF, H. P., and HAREVEN, T., 'From the Empty Nest to Family Dissolution: Life Course Transitions into Old Age', *Journal of Family History*, 4 (1979), 69–83.

CHURCHILL, RANDOLPH S., *Winston S. Churchill, Young Statesman, 1901–14* (London, 1967).

CICERO, *Selected Works*, trans. M. Grant (Harmondsworth, 1960).

CLARK, ELAINE, 'Some Aspects of Social Security in Medieval England', *Journal of Family History*, 7/4 (1982), 307–20.

CLARK, PETER, *The English Alehouse: A Social History, 1200–1830* (London, 1983).

CLAY, HILARY M., 'A Study of Performance in Relation to Age at Two Printing Works', *Journal of Gerontology*, 11 (1956), 417–24.

—— *The Older Worker and his Job* (London, 1960).

COFFMAN, GEORGE R., 'Old Age from Horace to Chaucer: Some Literary Affinities and Adventures of an Idea', *Speculum*, 9 (1934), 249–77.

COHEN, JOSEPH, *Social Insurance Unified* (London, 1924).

COLE, G. D. H., *The Intelligent Man's Guide to the Post-War World* (London, 1947).

COLE, THOMAS R., *The Journey of Life: A Cultural History of Aging in America* (Cambridge, 1992).

COMMISSION ON SOCIAL JUSTICE, *Social Justice: Strategies for National Renewal* (London, 1994).

CONRAD, CHRISTOPH, 'Old Age in the Modern and Post-Modern Western World', in T. R. Cole, D. Van Tassell, R. Kastenbaum (eds.), *Handbook of Ageing and the Humanities* (New York, 1992), 62–95.

—— 'Mixed Incomes for the Elderly Poor in Germany, 1880–1930', in Michael B. Katz and Christoph Sachsse (eds.), *The Mixed Economy of Social Welfare: Public/Private Relations in England, Germany and the US, 1870s–1930s* (Baden-Baden, 1996), 340–67.

CORNWELL, JOCELYN, *Hard-Earned Lives* (London, 1984).

CROSSMAN, RICHARD, *The Diaries of a Cabinet Minister*, i: *Minister of Housing, 1964–6* (London, 1975).

CROWTHER, M. A., *The Workhouse System, 1834–1929* (London, 1981).

DAUNTON, M., *House and Home in the Victorian City: Working-Class Housing, 1850–1914* (London, 1983).

—— (ed.), *Charity, Self-Interest and Welfare in the English Past* (London, 1996).

DAVIN, ANNA, *Growing Up Poor: Home, School and Street in London, 1870–1914* (London, 1996).

DAWSON, W. H., *Social Insurance in Germany, 1883–1911: Its History, Operation and Results and a Comparison with the National Insurance Act, 1911* (London, 1912).

DAY, ALICE T., *Remarkable Survivors: Insights into Successful Aging among Women* (Washington, 1991).

DAY, LINCOLN, *The Future of Low Birthrate Populations* (London, 1992).

DIGBY, ANNE, *Pauper Palaces* (London, 1978).

DILKS, D., *Neville Chamberlain*, i: *1869–1929* (Cambridge, 1984).

DOBBIE, B. M. W., 'An Attempt to Estimate the True Rate of Maternal Mortality, 16th–18th Centuries', *Medical History*, 26/1 (1982), 79–90.

DOROTKA BAGUELL, P. VON, and SOPER, P. S., *Perceptions of Aging in Literature: A Cross-Cultural Study* (Westport, Conn., 1989).

DOVE, MARY, *The Perfect Age of Man's Life* (Cambridge, 1986).

DRAKE, M., 'The Census, 1801–1891', in E. A. Wrigley (ed.), *Nineteenth-Century Society* (Cambridge, 1972), 7–33.

DUNKLEY, P., *The Crisis of the Old Poor Law in England, 1795–1834: An Interpretive Essay* (New York, 1982).

DUPREE, MARGUERITE, *Family Structure in the Staffordshire Potteries, 1840–1880* (Oxford, 1995).

DYER, C., *Standards of Living in the Later Middle Ages* (Cambridge, 1989).

EBURY, M., and PRESTON, B., 'Domestic Service in Late Victorian and Edwardian England, 1871–1914', *Geographical Papers* (1980).

EDEN, SIR FREDERICK MORTON, *The State of the Poor*, 3 vols. (London, 1797).

ELLIS, K., *The Post Office in the Eighteenth Century* (Durham, 1958).

EMERSON, A., 'The First Year of Retirement', *Occupational Psychology*, 34 (1959), 197–208.

EMMISON, F. G., 'Poor-Relief Accounts of Two Rural Parishes in Bedfordshire, 1563–98', *Economic History Review*, 3 (1931), 102–16.

—— 'The Care of the Poor in Elizabethan Essex', *Essex Review*, 62–3 (1953), 7–28.

THE EMPLOYMENT FELLOWSHIP, *Workrooms for the Elderly* (London, 1958).

ERMISCH, JOHN, *The Political Economy of Demographic Change* (London, 1983).

EVANS, J. G., 'Implications for Health Services', in *Philosophical Transactions of the Royal Society of London, Biological Sciences*, 352, 1363 (1997), *Ageing: Science, Medicine and Society*, 1887–93.

EVANS, MARTIN, 'Social Security: Dismantling the Pyramids?', in H. GLENNERSTER and J. HILLS (eds.), *The State of Welfare: The Economics of Social Spending*, 2nd edn. (Oxford, 1998), 257–307.

FALKNER, T. M., and DE LUCE, J., *Old Age in Greek and Latin Literature* (Albany, NY, 1989).

FARQUHAR, MORAG, and BOWLING, ANN, 'Older People and their GPs', *Generations Review*, 1/1 (1991), 7–9.

FEILING, K., *The Life of Neville Chamberlain* (London, 1946).

FELDMAN, D., *Englishmen and Jews: Social Relations and Political Culture, 1840–1914* (New Haven, 1994).

FENNELL, G., PHILLIPSON, C., and EVERS, H., *The Sociology of Old Age* (Milton Keynes, 1988).

FINCH, J., *Family Obligations and Social Change* (Cambridge, 1989).

—— and GROVES, D. (eds.), *A Labour of Love: Women, Work and Caring* (London, 1983).

FINLEY, MOSES, 'The Elderly in Classical Antiquity', *Ageing and Society*, 4/4 (1984), 391–408.

FIRTH, RAYMOND, HYBERT, JANE, and FORGE, ANTHONY, *Families and their Relatives: Kinship in a Middle-Class Sector of London* (London, 1969).

FISSELL, MARY, ' "The sick and drooping poor" in Eighteenth-Century Bristol and its Region', *Social History of Medicine*, 2/1 (1989), 35–58.

FITZGERALD, R., *British Labour Management and Industrial Welfare, 1846–1939* (London, 1988).

FLEMING, C., 'The Age Factor in the Sheffield Cutlery Industry', *Via Humana*, 6/4 (1963), 177–212.

FONER, NANCY, *Ages in Conflict: A Cross-Cultural Perspective on Inequality between Old and Young* (London, 1984).

FRASER, P., *Joseph Chamberlain* (London, 1966).

FRIES, J. F., 'Ageing, Natural Death and the Compression of Morbidity', *New England Journal of Medicine*, 303 (1980), 130–5.

FRY, C. L. *et al.*, *Aging in Culture and Society* (New York, 1980).

FULD, H., and ROBINSON, K. V., 'Malnutrition in the Elderly', *Lancet* (24 Oct. 1953), 860–4.

GAFFIN, J., and THOMS, D., *Caring and Sharing: The Centenary History of the Co-operative Women's Guild* (Manchester, 1983).

GARLAND, R., *The Greek Way of Life: From Conception to Old Age* (London, 1990).

GAUNT, DAVID, 'The Property and Kin Relationships of Retired Families in Northern and Central Europe', in R. Wall, J. Robin, and P. Laslett (eds.), *Family Forms in Historic Europe* (Cambridge, 1983), 249–80.

GILBERT, B. B., *The Evolution of National Insurance in Great Britain* (London, 1966).

GLASS, D. V., *The Struggle for Population* (London, 1936).

—— 'The Population Problem and the Future', *Eugenics Review*, 26/1 (1937), 39–47.

—— and BLACKER, C. P., *The Future of our Population* (London, 1937).

GOLDBERG, P. J. P., 'Mortality and Economic Change in the Diocese of York, 1390–1514', *Northern History*, 24 (1988), 38–55.

GOODICH, M. E., *From Birth to Death: The Human Life Cycle in Medieval Thought, 1250–1350* (Lanham, Md., 1989).

GOODY, J., THIRSK, J., and THOMPSON, E. P. (eds.), *Family and Inheritance: Rural Society in Western Europe, 1200–1800* (Cambridge, 1976).

GORDON, ALBAN, *Social Insurance* (London, 1924).

GORDON, MARGARET S., *Social Security Policies in Industrial Countries: A Comparative Analysis* (Cambridge, 1988).

GORSKY, MARTIN, 'The Growth and Distribution of English Friendly Societies in the Early Nineteenth Century', *Economic History Review*, 51/3 (1998), 489–511.

GOSDEN, P. H. J. H., *The Friendly Societies in England, 1815–1875* (Manchester, 1961).

—— *Self-Help: Voluntary Associations in Great Britain* (London, 1973).

GOUGH, R., *History of Myddle* (London, 1993).

GROOMBRIDGE, B., *Education and Retirement* (London, 1960).

GRUMAN, G. R., 'The Rise and Fall of Prolongevity Hygiene', *Bulletin of the History of Medicine*, 35 (1961), 221–9.

—— 'A History of Ideas about the Prolongation of Life', *Transactions of the American Philosophical Society*, 56/9 (1966), 1–97.

GRUNDY, E., 'Mortality and Morbidity among the Old', *British Medical Journal*, 288 (1984), 663–4.

—— 'Age-Related Change in Later Life', in M. Murphy and J. Hobcraft (eds.), *Population Research in Britain* (London, 1991), 133–56.

HABER, CAROLE, and GRATTON, BRIAN, *Old Age and the Search for Security: An American Social History* (Bloomington, Ind., 1994).

HAIGHT, GORDON S. (ed.), *The George Eliot Letters*, 2 vols. (Oxford, 1954).

HAJNAL, J., 'European Marriage Patterns in Perspective', in D. V. Glass and D. Eversley (eds.), *Population in History* (London, 1965), 101–43.

—— 'Two Kinds of Pre-Industrial Household Formation System', *Population and Development Review*, 8 (1982), 449–94.

HANAWALT, BARBARA, 'Keepers of the Lights: Late Medieval English Guilds', *Journal of Medieval and Renaissance Studies*, 14/1 (1984), 21–37.

—— *The Ties that Bind: Peasant Families in Medieval England* (Oxford, 1986).

—— and McREE, B. R., 'The Guilds of *Homo Prudens* in Late Medieval England', *Continuity and Change*, 7/2 (1992), 163–79.

HANCOCK, R., and WEIR, P., *More Ways than Means: A Guide to Pensioners' Incomes in Great Britain During the 1980s*, Age Concern Institute of Gerontology, King's College London (London, 1994).

HANNAH, LESLIE, *Inventing Retirement: The Development of Occupational Pensions in Britain* (Cambridge, 1986).

HERLAN, R., 'Poor Relief in London during the English Revolution', *Journal of British Studies*, 18 (1979), 30–49.

HARPER, RICHARD A., 'A Note on Corrodies in the 14th Century', *Albion*, 15 (1983), 95–101.

HARRIS, FRANCES, *The Life of Sarah, Duchess of Marlborough* (Oxford, 1991).

HARRIS, JOSÉ, *Unemployment and Politics: A Study in English Social Policy, 1886–1914* (Oxford, 1972).

—— 'Political Ideas and the Debate on State Welfare, 1940–5', in H. L. Smith, *War and Social Change* (Manchester, 1986), 233–63.

—— 'Enterprise and the Welfare State: A Comparative Perspective', in A. O'Day and T. Gourvish (eds.), *Britain Since 1945* (London, 1991), 39–58.

—— *Private Lives, Public Spirit: A Social History of Britain, 1870–1914* (Oxford, 1993).

—— *William Beveridge: A Biography*, 2nd edn. (Oxford, 1997).

HARRISON, J., 'Women and Ageing: Experience and Implications', *Ageing and Society*, 3/2 (1983), 209–35.

HARROD, R. F., 'Modern Population Trends', *Manchester School of Economic and Social Studies*, 10 (Manchester, 1939), 1–20.

HARROP, A., *The Employment Position of Older Women in Europe*, Age Concern Institute of Gerontology, King's College London (London, 1990).

HARVEY, BARBARA, *Living and Dying in England, 1100–1540: The Monastic Experience* (Oxford, 1993).

HATCHER, J., 'Mortality in the Fifteenth Century: Some New Evidence', *Economic History Review*, 2nd ser. 39/1 (1982), 19–36.

—— *Plague, Population and the English Economy, 1348–1530* (London, 1994).

HAY, J. R., 'Employers and Social Policy in Britain: The Evolution of Welfare Legislation, 1905–14', *Social History*, 4 (1977), 435–56.

HAZELL, K., *Social and Medical Problems of the Elderly*, 4th edn. (1960; London, 1976).

HEAL, FELICITY, *Hospitality in Early Modern England* (Oxford, 1990).

HELD, THOMAS, 'Rural Retirement Arrangements in 17th and 18th Century Austria: A Cross-Community Analysis', *Journal of Family History*, 7/3 (1982), 227–50.

HENNOCK, E. P., 'The Measurement of Urban Poverty: From the Metropolis to the Nation, 1880–1920', *Economic History Review*, 40 (1987), 208–27.

—— *British Social Reform and German Precedents: The Case of Social Insurance, 1880–1914* (Oxford, 1987).

HERLIHY, D., 'Life Expectancies for Women in Medieval Society', in R. T. Morwedge (ed.), *The Role of Women in the Middle Ages* (London, 1975), 1–22.

HERON, A., and CHOWN, S., 'Semi-Skilled and Over 40', *Occupational Psychology*, 34 (1960), 264–74.

—— *Ageing and the Semi-Skilled: A Survey of Manufacturing Industry on Merseyside* (London, 1961).

—— and C. CUNNINGHAM, 'The Experience of Younger and Older Men in a Work Reorganization', *Occupational Psychology*, 36 (1962), 10–16.

HIGGS, E., 'The Tabulation of Occupations in the Nineteenth-Century Census with Special Reference to Domestic Servants', *Local Population Studies*, 28 (1982), 58–66.

HILL, WILLIAM THOMSON, *Octavia Hill* (London, 1958).

HILLS, JOHN, *Joseph Rowntree Foundation Inquiry into Income and Wealth*, 2 vols. (York, 1995).

HILTON, R. H., *A Medieval Society: The West Midlands at the End of the 13th Century* (London, 1966).

HITCHCOCK, T., KING, P., and SHARPE, P. (eds.), *Chronicling Poverty: The Voices and Strategies of the English Poor, 1640–1840* (Basingstoke, 1997).

HOLLIS, PATRICIA, *Ladies Elect: Women in English Local Government 1865–1914* (Oxford, 1987).

HOPKINS, K., 'On the Probable Age Structure of the Roman Population', *Population Studies*, 20 (1966–7), 245–64.

HORDEN, P., 'A Discipline of Relevance: The Historiography of the Later Medieval Hospital', *Social History of Medicine*, 1/3 (1988), 371–2.

HORRELL, SARAH, and HUMPHRIES, JANE, ' "Old Questions, New Data and Alternative Perspectives": Families' Living Standards in the Industrial Revolution', *Journal of Economic History*, 52/2 (1992).

HOULBROOKE, R., *The English Family, 1450–1700* (London, 1984).

HOWELL, T., *Old Age: Some Practical Points in Geriatrics*, 3rd edn. (1944; London, 1973).

—— *Our Advancing Years: An Essay on the Modern Problems of Old Age* (1953; London, 1976).

HUBBACK, EVA M., *The Population of Britain* (Harmondsworth, 1947).

HUFTON, OLWEN, *The Poor of Eighteenth-Century France, 1750–1799* (Oxford, 1974).

—— *The Prospect Before Her: A History of Women in Western Europe, 1500–1800* (London, 1995).

HUME, DAVID, *Enquiry Concerning Human Understanding* (London, 1748).

HUMPHREYS, NOEL A., 'Old Age Pensions in the UK', *Journal of the Royal Statistical Society*, 74 (Dec. 1910), 71–3.

HUMPHRIES, JANE, 'Enclosures, Common Rights and Women: The Proletarianization of Families in Late 18th Century and Early 19th Century Britain', *Journal of Economic History*, 50/1 (1990), 17–42.

HUNT, A., *The Elderly at Home* (London, 1978).

HUNT, E. H., 'Paupers and Pensioners, Past and Present', *Ageing and Society*, 9 (1989), 408–22.

INDUSTRIAL WELFARE SOCIETY, *The Employment of Elderly Workers* (London, 1951).

ISAACS, BERNARD, *The Challenge of Geriatric Medicine* (Oxford, 1992).

JALLAND, PAT, *Women, Marriage and Politics, 1860–1914* (Oxford, 1986).

JARVIS, C., *Family and Friends in Old Age and the Implications for Informal Support: Evidence from the British Social Attitudes Survey of 1989*, Age Concern Institute of Gerontology, King's College London (London, 1993).

JEFFERYS, MARGOT (ed.), *Growing Old in the Twentieth Century* (London, 1989).

—— 'Lionel Cosin (1910–1994): A Pioneer Geriatrician who Thrived on Controversy', *Generations Review*, 4/3 (1994), 2–4.

JOHANSSON, S. R., 'Sex and Death in Victorian England', in M. Vicinus (ed.), *Suffer and Be Still* (Bloomington, Ind., 1971), 163–81.

—— 'Excess Female Mortality: Constructing Survival during Development in Meiji Japan and Victorian England', in A. Digby and J. Stewart (eds.), *Gender, Health and Welfare* (London, 1996), 32–66.

JOHNSON, PAUL, *Saving and Spending: The Working-Class Economy in Britain 1870–1939* (Oxford, 1985).

—— 'The Employment and Retirement of Older Men in England and Wales, 1881–1981', *Economic History Review*, 47/1 (1994), 106–28.

—— and FALKINGHAM, JANE, *Ageing and Economic Welfare* (London, 1992).

—— —— 'Is there a Future for the Beveridge Pension Scheme?', in S. Baldwin and J. Falkingham (eds.), *Social Security and Social Change: New Challenges to the Beveridge Model* (Hemel Hempstead, 1994), 255–70.

—— and THANE, PAT (eds.), *Old Age from Antiquity to Post-Modernity* (London, 1998).

JOSEPH ROWNTREE FOUNDATION, *Inquiry into Income and Wealth*, 2 vols. (York, 1993).

JOSHI, H., 'The Cash Opportunity Costs of Childbearing: An Approach to Estimation Using British Data', *Population Studies*, 44 (1990), 41–60.

—— 'The Cost of Caring', in C. Glendinning and J. Miller (eds.), *Women and Poverty in Britain in the 1990s* (London, 1992), 112–33.

KARN, V., *Retiring to the Seaside* (London, 1977).

KEELEY, EDWARD, J., 'Anglo-Norman Policy: The Public Welfare', *Albion*, 104 (1978).

KENNEDY, LIAM, 'Farm Succession in Modern Ireland: Elements of a Theory of Inheritance', *Economic History Review*, 2nd ser. 44 (1991), 477–99.

KERMODE, JENNIFER I., 'Urban Decline? The Flight from Office in Late Medieval York', *Economic History Review*, 2nd ser. 35/2 (1982), 179–98.

KERSHAW, IAN, *Bolton Priory: The Economy of a Northern Monastery, 1286–1325* (Oxford, 1973).

KEYNES, J. M., 'Some Economic Consequences of a Declining Population', *Eugenics Review*, 27/2 (1937), 13–17.

KHAW, K.-T., 'Epidemiological Aspects of Ageing', *Philosophical Transactions of the Royal Society of London*, ser. B: *Biological Sciences*, 352/1363 (1997), 1829–36.

KING, H. F., 'An Attempt to Use Production Data in the Study of Age and Performance', *Journal of Gerontology*, 11 (1956), 410–16.

KING, P., 'Customary Rights and Women's Earnings: The Importance of Gleaning to the Rural Labouring Poor, 1750–1850', *Economic History Review*, 44/3 (1991), 461–76.

KING, STEPHEN, 'Reconstructing Lives and Social Structures in Britain: The Poor, the Poor Law and Welfare in Calverley, 1650–1820', *Social History*, 22/3 (1997), 318–38.

—— *Poverty and Welfare, 1700–1870* (Manchester, 2000).

KOHLI, M., 'Retirement and the Moral Economy: An Historical Interpretation of the German Case', *Journal of Aging Studies*, 1/2 (1987), 125–44.

—— et al., *Time for Retirement: Comparative Studies of Early Exit from the Labour Force* (Cambridge, 1991).

KUCZYNSKI, R. R., 'Future Trends in Population', *Eugenics Review*, 24/2 (1937), 99–107.

THE LABOUR PARTY, *National Superannuation* (London, 1957).

LASLETT, PETER, *The World We Have Lost* (London, 1965).

—— *Family Life and Illicit Love in Earlier Generations* (Cambridge, 1977).

—— *The World We Have Lost—Further Explored* (London, 1983).

—— 'Family, Kinship and Collectivity as Systems of Support in Pre-Industrial Europe: A Consideration of the "Nuclear-Hardship" Hypothesis', *Continuity and Change*, 3 (1988), 153–76.

—— *A Fresh Map of Life: The Emergence of the Third Age* (London, 1989).

—— and WALL, R. (eds.), *Household and Family in Past Time* (Cambridge, 1972).

LAW, CHERYL, *Suffrage and Power: The Women's Movement, 1918–28* (London, 1997).

LE GROS CLARK, F., *The Working Fitness of Older Men* (London, 1954).

—— *Ageing Men in the Labour Force* (London, 1955).

—— *New Jobs for Old Workers* (London, 1955).

—— *The Employment Problems of Elderly Men* (London, 1956).

—— *Ageing on the Factory Floor* (London, 1957).

—— *Bus Workers* (London, 1957).

—— *The Importance for Ageing Men of Some Continuity in Work Habits* (London, 1958).

—— *Age and the Working Lives of Men* (London, 1959).

—— *Growing Old in a Mechanized World* (London, 1961).

—— *Women, Work and Age* (London, 1962).

—— *The Years Still Unexplored* (London, 1964).

—— *Pensioners in Search of a Job* (London, 1966).

—— *Work, Age and Leisure* (London, 1966).

—— and DUNN, AGNES, *Later Working Life in the Building Industry* (London, 1954).

—— —— *Ageing in Industry* (London, 1955).

—— and HERON, ALASTAIR, *Workers Nearing Retirement* (London, 1963).

LEES, LYNN HOLLEN, *The Solidarities of Strangers: The English Poor Laws and the People, 1700–1948* (Cambridge, 1998).

LEIBOWITZ, J. O., 'Early Accounts in Geriatric Pathology (Leonards, Harvey, Keill)', *Koruth*, 7 (1980), ccliv–cclvi.

LEWIS, J., and MEREDITH, B., *Daughters Who Care: Daughters Caring for Mothers at Home* (London, 1988).

LEYBOURNE, GRACE D., 'An Estimate of the Future Population of Great Britain', *Sociological Review*, 26 (1934), 130–8.

LIDDINGTON, JILL, *The Life and Times of a Respectable Rebel: Selina Cooper, 1864–1946* (London, 1984).

LLEWELLYN-SMITH, H., *New Survey of London Life and Labour*, 9 vols. (London, 1930–5).

LOANE, MARGARET, *The Common Growth* (London, 1911).

LOCH, C. S., *The Charity Organization Society* (London, 1961).

LOWE, R., *The Welfare State in Britain since 1945* (London, 1993).

McBRIAR, A., *An Edwardian Mixed Doubles: The Bosanquets versus the Webbs, a Study in British Social Policy 1890–1929* (Oxford, 1987).

McCRAE, S. (ed.), *Changing Britain: Families and Households in the 1990s* (Oxford, 1999).

MACFARLANE, ALAN, *The Origins of English Individualism* (Oxford, 1978).

—— *Marriage and Love in England* (Oxford, 1986).

McINTOSH, MARJORIE, 'Local Responses to the Poor in Late Medieval and Tudor England', *Continuity and Change*, 3 (1988), 209–45.

—— *A Community Transformed: The Manor and Liberty of Havering* (Cambridge, 1991).

McKEE, P., and KAUPPINEN, H., *Art of Aging: A Celebration of Old Age in Western Art* (New York, 1987).

MACKENZIE, NORMAN and JEANNE (eds.), *The Diary of Beatrice Webb*, 4 vols. (London, 1982–5).

MACNICOL, JOHN, *The Politics of Retirement in Britain, 1878–1948* (Cambridge, 1998).

McREE, BARRY, 'Charity and Guild Solidarity in Late Medieval England', *Journal of British Studies*, 32 (1993), 195–225.

MANDLER, P., 'The Making of the New Poor Law *Redivivus*', *Past and Present*, 117 (1987), 131–57.

MANTON, K., 'Changing Concepts of Mortality and Morbidity in the Population', *Milbank Memorial Fund Quarterly*, 60 (1982), 183–244.

—— CORDER, L., and STALLARD, E., 'Chronic Disability Trends in Elderly United States Populations, 1892–1994', *Proceedings of the National Academy of Sciences of the United States of America*, 94/6 (1997), 2593–8.

MARSH, JAN, *Pre-Raphaelite Sisterhood* (London, 1985).

MARSHALL, D., *Poor Law in the Eighteenth Century* (London, 1928).

MARSHALL, J. D. (ed.), *The Autobiography of William Stout of Lancaster, 1665–1752* (Manchester, 1967).

—— *The Old Poor Law, 1795–1834*, 2nd edn. (London, 1985).

MATTHEW, H. C. G., *The Gladstone Diaries*, xii: *1887–1891* (Oxford, 1991).

—— *Gladston 1875–1898* (Oxford, 1995).

MAYHEW, HENRY, *London Labour and the London Poor* (1861–2; New York and London, 1968).

MEANS, R., and SMITH, R., *The Development of Welfare Services for Elderly People* (London, 1985).

MEDICAL RESEARCH COUNCIL, *The Health of the UK's Elderly People*, MRC Topic Review (London, 1994).

MESSKOUB, M., 'Crisis of Ageing in Less Developed Countries: A Crisis for Whom? Some Conceptual and Policy Issues', Leeds University Business School Paper, E97/01 (Feb. 1997), 5–6.

MIDWINTER, E., *Social Administration in Lancashire 1830–1860* (Manchester, 1969).

MINISTRY OF PENSIONS AND NATIONAL INSURANCE, *National Insurance Retirement Pensions: Reasons Given for Retiring or Continuing at Work* (London, 1954).

MINOIS, GEORGES, *History of Old Age: From Antiquity to the Renaissance*, trans. Sarah Hanbury-Tenison (Oxford, 1989).

MITCHELL, B., and DEANE, P., *Abstract of British Historical Statistics* (Cambridge, 1962).

MITTERAUER, M., and SIEDER, R., *The European Family* (Oxford, 1982).

MOFFREY, R. W., *A Century of Oddfellowship* (Manchester, 1910).

MOGGRIDGE, D. (ed.), *The Collected Writings of J. Maynard Keynes*, xix: *Activities (1922–9)*, part 1 (London and Cambridge, 1981).

MONTAIGNE, MICHEL DE, *Essays*, trans. J. M. Cohen (Harmondsworth, 1958).

MORGAN, DAVID H., 'The Place of Harvesters in Nineteenth-Century Village Life', in R. Samuel (ed.), *Village Life and Labour* (London, 1975), 27–72.

MOSER, K., FOX, A., and JONES, D., 'Unemployment and Mortality in the OPCS Longitudinal Study', *Lancet*, 2 (1984), 1324–8.

NASH, LAURA, 'Greek Origins of Generational Thought', *Daedalus* (Fall 1978), 1–21.

NATIONAL COMMITTEE OF ORGANIZED LABOUR, *Ninth Annual Report and Balance Sheet* (London, 1908).

NATIONAL COUNCIL OF SOCIAL SERVICE, *Over Seventy* (London, 1954).

NATIONAL OLD PEOPLE'S WELFARE COMMITTEE, *Employment and Workshops for the Elderly* (London, 1963).

NUFFIELD FOUNDATION, *Old People: Report of a Survey Committee on the Problems of Ageing and the Care of Old People* (Oxford, 1947).

OAKLEY, ANN, *Sex, Gender and Society* (London, 1972).

OECD, *Ageing Populations: The Social Policy Implications* (Paris, 1988).

OFFER, A., 'Between the Gift and the Market: The Economy of Regard', *Economic History Review*, 50/3 (1997), 450–76.

OLSHANSKY, S. J., 'On Forecasting Mortality', *Milbank Memorial Fund Quarterly*, 66/3 (1988), 482–530.

The Oxford Dictionary of English Proverbs, 3rd edn., rev. F. P. Wilson (Oxford, 1970).

OXLEY, G. W., 'The Permanent Poor in South Lancashire under the Old Poor Law', in J. R. Harris (ed.), *Liverpool and Merseyside* (London, 1969).

PAINE, THOMAS, *The Rights of Man*, ed. Henry Collins (Harmondsworth, 1969).

PARKIN, TIM G., *Demography and Roman Society* (Baltimore, 1992).

PARKINSON, R. (ed.), *The Autobiography of Henry Newcombe MA* (Manchester, 1852).

—— (ed.), *The Life of Adam Martindale* (Manchester, 1895).

PARSONS, TALCOTT, *The Social System* (New York, 1950).

PEARSON, P., 'The Transition from Work to Retirement', *Occupational Psychology*, 31 (1957), 80–8, 139–49.

PEDEN, GEORGE, *The Treasury and British Public Policy, 1900–59* (Oxford, 2000).

PELLING, MARGARET, 'Healing the Sick Poor: Social Policy and Disability in Norwich, 1550–1640', *Medical History*, 29 (1985), 115–37.

—— 'Thoroughly Resented? Older Women and the Medical Role in Early Modern London', in L. Hunter and S. Hutton (eds.), *Women, Science and Medicine, 1500–1700: Mothers and Sisters of the Royal Society* (Stroud, 1997), 63–88.

—— *The Common Lot* (London, 1998).

—— and SMITH, R. M. (eds.), *Life, Death and the Elderly: Historical Perspectives* (London, 1991).

PEP, *Population Policy in Great Britain* (London, 1948).

PHILLIPS, G. A., and WHITESIDE, N., *Casual Labour: The Unemployment Question in the Port Transport Industry, 1880–1970* (Oxford, 1985).

PHILLIPSON, C., *Capitalism and the Construction of Old Age* (London, 1982).

—— BERNARD, M., PHILLIPS, J., and OGG, J., 'The Family and Community Life of Older People: Household Composition and Social Networks in Three Urban Areas', *Ageing and Society*, 18/3 (1998), 259–90.

—— —— —— —— 'The Family and Community Life of Older People: Networks and Social Support in Three Urban Areas', *Research Results*, no. 9, ESRC Population and Household Change Programme (Oxford, 1998).

PHYTHIAN-ADAMS, C., *Desolation of a City: Coventry and the Urban Crisis of the Late Middle Ages* (Cambridge, 1979).

THE PILGRIM TRUST, *Men Without Work* (Cambridge, 1938).

PLATO, *The Laws*, trans. T. J. Saunders (Harmondsworth, 1970).

—— *The Republic*, trans. Desmond Lee, 2nd rev. edn. (London, 1987).

PLOMER, WILLIAM (ed.), *Selections from the Diary of Rev. Francis Kilvert* (Harmondsworth, 1969).

PRATT, HENRY J., *Gray Agendas: Interest Groups and Public Pensions in Canada, Britain, and the United States* (Ann Arbor, 1993).

PULLEN, B., 'Support and Redeem: Charity and Poor Relief in Italian Cities from the 14th to the 17th Century', *Continuity and Change*, 3/2 (1988), 177–208.

QUADAGNO, JILL, *Aging in Early Industrial Society: Work, Family and Social Policy in 19th Century England* (Cambridge, 1982).

QUINE, M. S., *Population Politics in Twentieth-Century Europe* (London, 1996).

QURESHI, HAZEL, and WALKER, ALAN, 'Caring for Elderly People: The Family and the State', in C. Phillipson and A. Walker, *Ageing and Social Policy: A Critical Assessment* (Aldershot, 1986), 109–27.

—— *The Caring Relationship* (London, 1989).

RANSOM, R., and SUTCH, R., 'The Impact of Ageing on the Employment of Men in American Working-Class Communities at the End of the Nineteenth Century', in D. Kertzner and Peter Laslett (eds.), *Ageing in the Past: Demography, Society and Old Age* (Berkeley, 1995), 301–27.

RAPHAEL, MARIOS, *Pensions and Public Servants: A Study of the Origins of the British System* (Paris, 1964).

RAWCLIFFE, C., 'The Hospitals of Late Medieval London', *Medical History*, 27 (1984), 1–21.

RAZI, ZVI, *Life, Marriage and Death in a Medieval Parish: Economy, Society and Demography in Halesowen, 1270–1400* (Cambridge, 1980).

RAZI, ZVI, 'Family, Land and the Village Community in Later Medieval England', *Past and Present*, 93 (1981), 3–36.

—— 'The Myth of the Immutable English Family', *Past and Present*, 140 (1993), 3–44.

REAY, BARRY, *Microhistories: Demography, Society and Culture in Rural England, 1800–1939* (Cambridge, 1996).

REDDAWAY, W. B., *The Economics of a Declining Population* (London, 1939).

REIN, MARTIN, and SALZMAN, HAROLD, 'Social Integration, Participation and Exchange in Five Industrial Countries', in Scott A. Bass (ed.), *Older and Active* (New Haven and London, 1995), 237–62.

Report of the Proceedings at a Public Presentation Made to Mr Frederick Rogers at Browning Hall on Nov. 5th 1909 (privately printed, 1909).

RHODES, G., *Public Sector Pensions* (London, 1965).

RICHARDSON, BESSIE ELLEN, *Old Age Among the Ancient Greeks* (Baltimore, 1933).

RICHARDSON, I. M., 'Age and Work: A Study of 489 Men in Heavy Industry', *British Journal of Industrial Medicine*, 10 (1953), 269–84.

RIDDLE, S., 'Age, Obsolescence and Unemployment: Older Men in the British Industrial System, 1930–39; a Research Note', *Ageing and Society*, 4/4 (1984), 517–24.

RILEY, J., *Sickness, Recovery and Death: A History and Forecast of Ill Health* (London, 1989).

ROBERTS, ELIZABETH, *A Woman's Place: An Oral History of Working-Class Women, 1890–1940* (Oxford, 1984).

—— *Women and Families: An Oral History, 1940–1970* (Oxford, 1995).

ROBERTS, NESTA, *Our Future Selves* (London, 1970).

ROBIN, JEAN, 'Family Care of the Elderly in a 19th Century Devonshire Parish', *Ageing and Society*, 4/4 (1984), 505–16.

RODWELL, G. *et al.*, 'Images of Old Age on British Television', *Generations Review*, 2/3 (1992), 6–8.

ROEBUCK, JANE, and SLAUGHTER, JANE, 'Ladies and Pensioners: Stereotypes and Public Policy Affecting Old Women in England, 1880–1940', *Journal of Social History*, 13/1 (1979), 105–14.

ROGERS, FREDERICK, *Labour, Life and Literature* (London, 1913).

ROSE, A. B., *The Older Unemployed Man in Hull* (University College Hull, Department of Social Studies, 1953).

ROSE, SONYA, 'The Varying Household Arrangements of the Elderly in Three English Villages: Nottinghamshire, 1852–1881', *Continuity and Change*, 3/1 (1988), 101–22.

ROSENTHAL, JOEL, *Old Age in Late Medieval England* (Philadelphia, 1996).

ROSS, ELLEN, *Love and Toil: Motherhood in Outcast London* (Oxford, 1993).

ROSSER, C., and HARRIS, C. C., *The Family and Social Change* (London, 1965).

ROSSER, GERVASE, 'Communities of Parish and Guild in the Late Middle Ages', in S. J. Wright (ed.), *Parish, Church and People: Local Studies in Lay Religion, 1350–1750* (London, 1988), 29–55.

ROWNTREE, B. SEEBOHM, *Poverty: A Study of Town Life*, 2nd edn. (London, 1902).

—— *The Human Needs of Labour* (London, 1918).

—— *Poverty and Progress: A Second Social Survey of York* (London, 1941).

—— and KENDALL, MAY, *How the Labourer Lives: A Study of the Rural Labour Problem* (London, 1912).

ROYAL COLLEGE OF PHYSICIANS OF EDINBURGH, *The Care of the Elderly in Scotland* (Edinburgh, 1963).

RUBIN, M., *Charity and Community in Medieval Cambridge, 1200–1500* (Cambridge, 1987).

RUGGLES, S., *Prolonged Connections: The Rise of the Extended Family in Nineteenth-Century England and America* (Madison, 1987).

RUSHTON, P., 'Lunatics and Idiots: Mental Disability, the Community and the Poor Law in North-East England, 1600–1800', *Medical History*, 32 (1988), 34–50.

RUSSELL, A. K., *Liberal Landslide: The General Election of 1906* (Newton Abbot, 1973).

RUSSELL, ALICE, *The Growth of Occupational Welfare in Britain* (Aldershot, 1991).

SAMUEL, RAPHAEL, *East-End Underworld: Chapters in the Life of Arthur Harding* (London, 1981).

SAUVY, A., 'Social and Economic Consequences of Ageing of Western Populations', *Population Studies*, 2/1 (June 1948), 115–24.

—— *General Theory of Population*, trans. C. Campos (New York, 1969).

SCHNEIDER, E. L., and BRODY, J. A., 'Ageing, Natural Death, and the Compression of Morbidity: Another View', *New England Journal of Medicine*, 309 (1983), 854–6.

SEARLE, EVELYN, 'Seigneurial Control of Women's Marriage: The Antecedents and Function of *Merchet* in England', *Past and Present*, 82 (1979), 3–43.

SEARLE, G. R., 'Eugenics and Politics in Britain in the 1930s', *Annals of Science*, 36 (1979), 150–72.

SEARS, E., *Ages of Man: Medieval Interpretations of the Life-Cycle* (Princeton, 1986).

SEN, K., *Ageing* (London, 1995).

SENECA, *Letters from a Stoic*, trans. R. Campbell (Harmondsworth, 1969).

SHAHAR, SHULAMITH, *Growing Old in the Middle Ages* (London, 1997).

SHANAS, ETHEL, TOWNSEND, P., WEDDERBURN, D., FRIIS, H., PAUL, M., STEHOALWER, J., *Old People in Three Societies* (London and New York, 1968).

SHARPE, P., 'Literally Spinsters: A New Interpretation of Local Eonomy and Demography in Colyton in the 17th and 18th Centuries', *Economic History Review*, 44/1 (1991), 46–65.

SHEEHAN, M. M. (ed.), *Aging and the Aged in Medieval Europe* (Toronto, 1990).

SHELDON, J. H., *The Social Medicine of Old Age* (Oxford, 1948).

SHENFIELD, B. E., *Social Policies for Old Age* (London, 1957).

SHERIDAN, D., STREET, B., and BLOOME, D., *Writing Ourselves: Mass Observation and Literary Practice* (Cresskill, NJ, 1999).

SHOOTER, A. W. M., *et al.*, 'Some Field Data on the Training of Older People', *Occupational Psychology*, 30 (1956), 204–15.

SIMEY, T. S. and M., *Charles Booth* (Oxford, 1960).

SIXSMITH, A., 'Independence and Home in Later Life', in C. PHILLIPSON, M. BERNARD, and P. STRANG (eds.), *Dependency and Interdependency in Old Age* (London, 1986), 338–47.

SLACK, PAUL, 'Vagrants and Vagrancy in England, 1598–1664', *Economic History Review*, 27/3 (1974), 360–79.

—— (ed.), *Poverty in Early Stuart Salisbury* (Devizes, 1975).

—— *Poverty and Policy in Tudor and Stuart England* (London, 1988).

—— *The English Poor Law, 1531–1782* (Cambridge, 1990).

SMITH, ADAM, *The Wealth of Nations*, 3 vols., 3rd edn. (London, 1784).

SMITH, DANIEL SCOTT, 'Life Course Norms and the Family Systems of Older Americans in 1900', *Journal of Family History*, 4 (1979), 285–98.

SMITH, DAVID W. E., *Human Longevity* (Oxford, 1993).

SMITH, J., 'The Computer Simulation of Kin Sets and Kin Counts', in J. Bongaarts, T. Birch, and K. J. Wachter (eds.), *Family Demography, Methods and their Applications* (Oxford, 1987), 249–66.

SMITH, R. M., 'The Structured Dependency of the Elderly: A Twentieth-Century Creation?', *Society for the Social History of Medicine Bulletin*, 34 (1984), 35–41.

—— 'The Structured Dependence of the Elderly as a Recent Development: Some Sceptical Historical Thoughts', *Ageing and Society*, 4 (1984), 409–28.

—— (ed.), *Land, Kinship and Life Cycle* (Cambridge, 1984).

SMITH, STEVEN R., 'Growing Old in Early Stuart England', *Albion*, 8/2 (1976), 125–41.

SNELL, J. G., 'Maintenance Agreements for the Elderly: Canada 1900–50', *Journal of the Canadian Historical Association*, NS 3 (1992), 197–216.

SNELL, K. D. M., *Annals of the Labouring Poor: Social Change and Agrarian England, 1660–1900* (Cambridge, 1985).

SOKOLL, THOMAS, *Household and Family among the Poor: The Case of Two Essex Communities in the Late 18th and Early 19th Centuries* (Bochum, 1993).

SOLAR, PETER M., 'Poor Relief and English Economic Development before the Industrial Revolution', *Economic History Review*, 48/1 (1995), 1–22.

SPEAKMAN, D., 'Bibliography of Research on Changes in Working Capacity with Age', Ministry of Labour and National Service (London, 1957).

SPENDER, J. A., *The State and Pensions in Old Age*, 2nd edn. (London, 1894).

SPRING-RICE, M., *Working Class Wives* (1939; repr. London, 1981).

SPUFFORD, MARGARET, *Contrasting Communities: English Villagers in the Sixteenth and Seventeenth Centuries* (Cambridge, 1974).

STEELE, RICHARD, *Discourse Concerning Old Age* (1688).

STEER, J., *Parish Law: Being a Digest of the Law* (London, 1830).

STEVENSON, J., and COOK, C., *Britain in the Depression: Society and Politics, 1929–39*, 2nd edn. (London, 1994).

STONE, LAWRENCE, *The Family, Sex and Marriage in England, 1500–1800* (London, 1977).

—— 'Walking over Grandma', *New York Review of Books*, 24, no. 8, May 1977.

SUPPLE, B., 'Legislation and Virtue: An Essay on Working-Class Self-Help and the State in the Early Nineteenth Century', in N. McKendrick (ed.), *Historical Perspectives: Studies in English Thought and Society in Honour of J. H. Plumb* (London, 1974), 211–54.

SWIFT, JONATHAN, *Gulliver's Travels* (Harmondsworth, 1967).

SZRETER, SIMON, *Fertility, Class and Gender in Britain, 1860–1940* (Cambridge, 1996).

TABILI, LAURA, 'The Construction of Racial Difference in Twentieth-Century Britain: The Special Restriction (Coloured Alien Seamen) Order, 1925', *Journal of British Studies*, 33/1 (1994), 54–99.

TAWNEY, R. H., and POWER, EILEEN, *Tudor Economic Documents*, vols. ii and iii (London, 1924).

TAYLOR, A. J. P., *England 1914–45* (Oxford, 1965).

TAYLOR, INA, *Victorian Sisters* (London, 1987).

TAYLOR, J. S., 'The Impact of Pauper Settlement, 1691–1834', *Past and Present*, 73 (1976), 42–74.

—— *Poverty, Migration and Settlement in the Industrial Revolution: Sojourners' Narratives* (San Francisco, 1989).

THANE, PAT, 'Contributory vs Non-Contributory Old Age Pensions, 1878–1908', in Pat Thane (ed.), *Origins of British Social Policy* (London, 1978), 84–106.

—— 'Women and the Poor Law in Victorian and Edwardian Britain', *History Workshop*, 6 (1978), 29–51.

—— 'Government and Society in England and Wales, 1750–1914', in F. M. L. Thompson (ed.), *The Cambridge Social History of Britain 1750–1950*, iii (Cambridge, 1990), 1–62.

—— 'The Women of the British Labour Party and Feminism, 1906–45', in H. L. Smith (ed.), *British Feminism in the Twentieth Century* (Aldershot, 1990), 124–43.

—— 'Visions of Gender in the Making of the British Welfare State: The Case of Women in the British Labour Party, 1906–1945', in Gisela Bock and Pat Thane (eds.), *Maternity and Gender Policies: Women and the Rise of the European Welfare States, 1880s–1950s* (London, 1991), 93–118.

—— 'Geriatrics', in W. F. Bynum and Roy Porter (eds.), *Companion Encyclopaedia of the History of Medicine*, 2 vols. (London, 1993), 1092–1118.

—— 'Women in the British Labour Party and the Construction of State Welfare, 1906–39', in S. Koven and S. Michel (eds.), *Mothers of a New World: Maternalist Politics and the Origins of Welfare States* (London and New York, 1993), 343–77.

—— *The Foundations of the Welfare State*, 2nd edn. (London, 1996).

—— 'The British Imperial State and the Construction of National Identities', in B. Melman (ed.), *Borderlines: Gender and Identities in War and Peace, 1870–1930* (London, 1998), 29–46.

—— 'Old Age', in R. Cooter and J. Pickstone (eds.) (forthcoming).

THIRKELL, ANGELA, *Three Houses* (Oxford, 1932).

THOMAS, GEOFFREY, *The Employment of Older Persons: An Enquiry*, Central Office of Information Social Survey (London, 1947).

THOMAS, KEITH, *Religion and the Decline of Magic* (Harmondsworth, 1973).

—— 'Age and Authority in Early Modern England', *Proceedings of the British Academy*, 62 (1976), 205–48.

THOMPSON, FLORA, *Lark Rise* (Oxford, 1939).

THOMPSON, PAUL, ITZIN, CATHERINE, and ABENDSTERN, MICHELE, *I Don't Feel Old: Understanding the Experience of Later Life* (Oxford, 1990).

THOMS, W., *Longevity in Man: Its Facts and Fiction* (London, 1873).

THOMSON, D., 'The Decline of Social Security: Falling State Support for the Elderly since Early Victorian Times', *Ageing and Society*, 4 (1984), 451–82.

—— *Selfish Generations?* (Oxford, 1991).

TIERNEY, B., 'The Decretists and the "Deserving Poor"', *Comparative Studies in Society and History*, 1 (1958–9), 360–73.

—— *Medieval Poor Law: A Sketch of Canonical Theory and its Application to England* (Berkeley and Los Angeles, 1959).

TIMMINS, NICOLAS, *The Five Giants: A Biography of the Welfare State* (London, 1995).

TINKER, A., *Elderly People in Modern Society* (London, 1992).

TITMUSS, R. M., *Poverty and Population* (London, 1938).

—— *Problems of Population* (London, 1943).

—— *Essays on the Welfare State* (London, 1958).

TODD, BARBARA, 'The Re-marrying Widow: A Stereotype Reconsidered', in Mary Prior (ed.), *Women in English Society, 1500–1800* (London, 1985), 54–92.

TOMLINSON, JIM, 'Welfare and the Economy: the Economic Impact of the Welfare State, 1945–51', *Twentieth Century British History*, 6 (1995), 194–219.

TOMLINSON, JIM, 'Corelli Barnett's History: The Case of Marshall Aid', *Twentieth Century British History*, 8/2 (1997), 222–38.

TOUT, K., *Ageing in Developing Countries* (Oxford, 1989).

TOWNSEND, P., *The Family Life of Old People* (London, 1957).

—— 'Surveys of Old Age in Great Britain, 1945–1958', *Bulletin of the World Health Organization*, 21 (1959), 583–91.

—— *The Last Refuge* (London, 1964).

—— 'The Structured Dependency of the Elderly: A Creation of Social Policy in the Twentieth Century', *Ageing and Society*, 1 (1981), 5–28.

—— and WEDDERBURN, D., *The Aged in the Welfare State* (London, 1965).

TREBLE, J. H., 'The Attitudes of Friendly Societies towards the Movement in Great Britain for State Pensions, 1878–1908', *International Review of Social History*, 15/2 (1970), 266–99.

TROYANSKY, DAVID G., *Old Age in the Old Regime: Image and Experience in Eighteenth-Century France* (Ithaca, NY, and London, 1989).

TUNSTALL, J., *Old and Alone* (London, 1966).

VAUPEL, J. W., 'The Remarkable Improvements in Survival at Older Ages', in *Philosophical Transactions of the Royal Society of London*, ser. B: *Biological Sciences*, 352/1363 (1997), *Ageing: Science, Medicine and Society*, 1799–1804.

VICINUS, M., and NEEGAARD, B. (eds.), *Ever Yours Florence Nightingale: Selected Letters* (London, 1989).

VON DOROTKA BAGUELL, P., and SOPER, P. S., *Perceptions of Aging in Literature: A Cross-Cultural Study* (Westport, Conn., 1989).

WACHTER, K., 'Kinship Resources for the Elderly', *Philosophical Transactions of the Royal Society of London*, ser. B: *Biological Sciences*, 352/1363 (1997), *Ageing: Science, Medicine and Society*, 1811–18.

WALKER, ALAN, 'Dependency and Old Age', *Social Policy and Administration*, 16/2 (1982), 115–35.

—— (ed.), *The New Generational Contract: Intergenerational Relations, Old Age and Welfare* (London, 1996).

WALL, R., 'Regional and Temporal Variations in English Household Structure from 1650', in J. Hobcraft and P. Rees (eds.), *Regional and Demographic Development* (London, 1977), 89–116.

WARD, JENNIFER C., *English Noblewomen in the Later Middle Ages* (London, 1992).

WARREN, D. I., *Helping Networks: How People Cope with Problems in the Urban Community* (Bloomington, Ind., 1981).

WARREN, M., 'Geriatrics: A Medical, Social and Economic Problem', *Practitioner*, 157 (1946), 384–90.

—— 'Care of the Chronic Aged Sick', *Lancet* (8 June 1948), 841–2.

—— 'The Evolution of Geriatric Care', *Geriatrics*, 3 (1948), 42–50.

WATERS, CHRIS, ' "Dark Strangers" in our Midst: Discourses of Race and Nation in Britain, 1947–1963', *Journal of British Studies*, 36/2 (1997), 207–38.

WEBB, BEATRICE, *My Apprenticeship* (Harmondsworth, 1938).

WEBB, BEATRICE and SIDNEY, *English Poor Law Policy* (London, 1910).

—— *Soviet Communism: A New Civilization?* (London, 1935).

—— *English Local Government*, 11 vols. (London, 1963).

WEBSTER, C., *The Great Instauration* (London, 1976).

WELFORD, A. T., *Skill and Age* (Oxford, 1951).

—— 'Extending the Employment of Older People', *British Medical Journal* (1953), 1193–7.

—— *Ageing and Human Skills* (Oxford, 1958).

—— 'Industrial Work for Older People: Some British Studies', *Gerontologist*, 1 (Mar. 1966), 4–9.

WENGER, G. CLAIRE, *The Supportive Network: Coping with Old Age* (London, 1984).

—— 'A Comparison of Urban with Rural Support Networks: Liverpool and North Wales', *Ageing and Society*, 15/1 (1995), 59–82.

WESTLAKE, H. F., *The Parishes of Medieval England* (London, 1919).

WHITEHEAD, M., *The Health Divide: Inequalities in Health in the 1980s* (London, 1987).

WHITESIDE, NOEL, *Bad Times: Unemployment in British Social and Political History* (London, 1991).

—— 'Social Welfare and Industrial Relations, 1914–1939', in C. Wrigley (ed.), *A History of British Industrial Relations, 1914–1939*, 2nd edn. (London, 1993), 211–42.

—— and SALAIS, ROBERT, 'Introduction: Political Economy and Modernization', in Noel Whiteside and Robert Salais, *Governance, Industry and Labour Markets in Britain and France: The Modernizing State in the Mid-Twentieth Century* (London, 1998), 1–22.

WHITMORE, C. A., 'Is the Unionist Party Committed to Old Age Pensions?', *National Review*, 33 (July 1899), 709–19.

WILKINSON, R., *Unhealthy Societies: The Affliction of Inequality* (London, 1997).

WILLIAMS, K., *From Pauperism to Poverty* (London, 1981).

WILLIAMSON, J., STOKE, I. H., *et al.*, 'Old People at Home: Their Unreported Needs', *Lancet* (23 May 1964), 1115–17.

WILSON, SIR ARNOLD, and MACKAY, G. S., *Old Age Pensions: An Historical and Critical Study* (Oxford, 1941).

WINTER, J. M., *The Great War and the British People* (Basingstoke, 1985).

—— 'Surviving the War: Life Expectation, Illness and Mortality Rates in Paris, London and Berlin, 1914–1919', in Jay Winter and J.-L. Robert (eds.), *Capital Cities at War: London, Paris, Berlin, 1914–1919* (Cambridge, 1997), 510–16.

WOOD-LEGH, K. W., *Perpetual Chantries in Britain* (Cambridge, 1965).

WOODS, R., and WILLIAMS, N., 'Must the Gap Widen before it can be Narrowed? Long-Term Trends in Social Class Mortality Differentials', *Continuity and Change*, 10/1 (1995), 105–37.

WORLD BANK, *Averting the Old Age Crisis: Policies to Project the Old and Promote Growth* (Oxford, 1994).

WORLD HEALTH ORGANIZATION, *Mental Health Problems of Ageing and the Aged*, Technical Support Series (Geneva, 1959).

WRIGHTSON, K., and LEVINE, D., *Poverty and Piety in an English Village: Terling 1525–1700* (Cambridge, 1979).

WRIGLEY, E. A., 'Fertility Strategy for the Individual and the Group', in C. Tilly (ed.), *Historical Studies in Changing Fertility* (Princeton, 1979), 135–54.

—— and SCHOFIELD, R. S., *The Population History of England 1541–1871: A Reconstruction* (Cambridge, 1989).

—— DAVIES, R. S., OEPPEN, J. E., and SCHOFIELD, R. S., *English Population History from Family Reconstitution, 1580–1837* (Cambridge, 1997).

YAHNKE, R. E., and EASTMAN, R. M., *Aging in Literature: A Reader's Guide* (Chicago and London, 1990).

YOUNG, M., and WILLMOTT, P., *Family and Kinship in East London* (Harmondsworth, 1957).

———— *Family and Class in a London Suburb* (London, 1960).

———— *The Symmetrical Family: A Study of Work and Leisure in the London Region* (London, 1973).

Index